The Principle of Non-Refoulement under the ECHR and the UN Convention against Torture and Other Cruel, Inhuman or Degrading Treatment or Punishment

International Studies in Human Rights

VOLUME 115

The titles published in this series are listed at *brill.com/ishr*

The Principle of Non-Refoulement under the ECHR and the UN Convention against Torture and Other Cruel, Inhuman or Degrading Treatment or Punishment

By

Eman Hamdan

BRILL

NIJHOFF

LEIDEN | BOSTON

Library of Congress Cataloging-in-Publication Data

Names: Hamdan, Eman, author.
Title: The principle of non-refoulement under the ECHR and the UN Convention Against Torture and Other Cruel, Inhuman or Degrading Treatment or Punishment / By Eman Hamdan.
Description: Leiden ; Boston : Brill Nijhoff, 2016. | Based on author's
   thesis (doctoral - University of Geneve, 2015). | Includes bibliographical
   references and index.
Identifiers: LCCN 2016017852 (print) | LCCN 2016018121 (ebook) | ISBN
   9789004319387 (hardback : alk. paper) | ISBN 9789004319394 (E-book)
Subjects: LCSH: Refoulement. | Convention for the Protection of Human Rights
   and Fundamental Freedoms (1950 November 5) | Convention against Torture
   and Other Cruel, Inhuman, or Degrading Treatment or Punishment (1984
   December 10)
Classification: LCC KZ6530 .H355 2016 (print) | LCC KZ6530 (ebook) | DDC
   342.08/2--dc23
LC record available at https://lccn.loc.gov/2016017852

Want or need Open Access? Brill Open offers you the choice to make your research freely accessible online in exchange for a publication charge. Review your various options on brill.com/brill-open.

Typeface for the Latin, Greek, and Cyrillic scripts: "Brill". See and download: brill.com/brill-typeface.

ISSN 0924-4751
ISBN 978-90-04-31938-7 (hardback)
ISBN 978-90-04-31939-4 (e-book)

This book is printed on acid-free paper and produced in a sustainable manner.

Printed by Printforce, the Netherlands

Contents

Acknowledgements

This book is mainly based on my doctoral thesis, which was defended at the University of Geneva, Switzerland, on 30 April 2015. Many people have supported me over the past few years, some of whom I would like to thank individually.

First and foremost, I would like to express my gratitude to my supervisor, Professor Maya Hertig Randall, for all her continuous support, guidance, encouragement and friendship over the past seven years. One simply could not wish for a better supervisor.

I am grateful to the University of Geneva for providing me the possibility to make my research. Many thanks to my Ph-D examiners, Professors Michel Hottelier, Robert Roth, Barbara Wilson, for their useful comments to the original manuscript. Thanks are due, too, to Professor Christine Chappuis, Dean of the Faculty of Law of the University of Geneva.

I also would like to express my sincere thanks to my publisher, Brill Nijhoff Publishers, especially Lindy Melman and Bea Timmer, for taking interest in my manuscript and for being patient and co-operative until the end.

My deepest thanks to my parents, Yahya and Heyam, and my brothers, Waleed and Bassel, for their faithful support and encouragement over all these years of studies.

Special gratitude goes to my husband Abdulmaola, who encourages, supports and loves me through all the way; and to our twins Rose and Noor, who were born during my doctoral program and have been the source of my motivation.

Finally, my interest in the refugee issues dates back to 2008 when Syria was ranked as the second major refugee-hosting country. At the time I am writing this acknowledgements Syria is the largest source country of refugees. Therefore, this book is dedicated to my country, Syria; with hope soon it will be safe for all Syrians again.

List of Abbreviations

CAT	Convention against Torture and Other Cruel, Inhuman or Degrading Treatment or Punishment
CE	Council of Europe
CIDTP	Cruel, Inhuman or Degrading Treatment or Punishment
ComAT	Committee against Torture
CPT	European Committee for the Prevention of Torture and Inhuman or Degrading Treatment or Punishment
CSR	Geneva Convention Relating to the Status of Refugees
DAS	Diplomatic Assurances
EC	European Council
ECHR	European Convention on Human Rights and Fundamental Freedoms
EComHR	European Commission of Human Rights
ECtHR	European Court of Human Rights
EU	European Union
GC	Grand Chamber of the European Court of Human Rights
HRC	Human Rights Committee
ICCPR	International Covenant on Civil and Political Rights
ICJ	International Court of Justice
ICTFY	International Criminal Tribunal for the Former Yugoslavia
IDP	Internally displaced person
ILC	International Law Commission
MOUS	Memorandums of understanding
NGOS	Non-Governmental Organisations
OPCAT	Optional Protocol to the CAT
RoP	Committee against Torture's Rules of Procedure
SAR	International Convention on Maritime Search and Rescue
SOLAS	International Convention for the Safety of Life at Sea
UDHR	Universal Declaration of Human Rights
UK	United Kingdom
UKAIT	British Asylum and Immigration Tribunal
UN	United Nations
UNGA	United Nations General Assembly
UNHCR	United Nations High Commissioner for Refugees
UNSC	United Nations Security Council
VCLT	Vienna Convention on the Law of Treaties
US	United States of America

Introduction

I   Setting of the Problem

The principle of Non-Refoulement, in general terms, protects individuals from being forcibly removed to a country where they risk facing ill-treatment. While it is the right of a State to control the entry and residence of foreigners in its territory, a State is obligated to refrain from removing a person to another State where he runs a risk of being ill-treated upon return.

In recent years, there has been a great increase in the number of immigrants and international protection seekers in some States. By end-2013, 51.2 million individuals were forcibly displaced worldwide due to conflict, persecution, generalized violence, or human rights violations.[1] Europe received 398,234 asylum claims in 2013, a 32% increase compared to 2012 (300,632). With 109,580 asylum claims, Germany received the largest number of individual applications, followed by France (60,095), Sweden (54,259), Turkey (44,807), United Kingdom (UK) (29,190), Italy (27,832) and Switzerland (19,440).[2] In order to face the increasing flow of immigrants and international protection seekers, States of destination have adopted measures that aim to control the entry of foreigners to their territories, such as the interception of vessels suspected of carrying irregular migrants or protection seekers before they enter the State's territorial water, the imposition of visa requirements combined with carrier sanctions for bringing passengers with suspect documentation, the creation of international zones at airports, the deployment of immigration control officials at overseas embarkation points to advise and assist the local authorities in identifying false documents and the posting of airline liaison officers at main international airports in order to prevent the embarkation of improperly documented persons or assist airline personnel to identify them. In application of such measures, 128,902 persons were denied entry at the EU's external borders in 2013: 50,054 for not having valid visa or residence permit, 26,588 for not having appropriate documentation justifying the stay, 9,001 for not having valid travel documents, 2,647 for using forged travel documents, 1,560 for using a forged visa or residence permit, and 3,077 for being considered a threat for public policy, internal security, public health or the international relations

---

1   United Nations High Commissioner for Refugees, UNHCR, Global Trends 2013: War's Human Cost, 20 June 2014.

2   UNHCR, Asylum Trends 2013, Levels and Trends in Industrialized Countries, 21 March 2014.

of one or more EU Member States.[3] Against this background, immigrants and protection seekers increasingly try to cross borders illegally. In 2013, 107,365 persons were detected trying to cross the EU's external borders illegally; out of them 60,173 were detected at the sea borders.[4]

Given the fact that persons who face extraterritorial immigration control measures were citizens of States that have questionable human rights record (such as Eritrea, Afghanistan, Pakistan, Somalia, Russia, Syria, and Iran), the question then arises whether or not a State is obligated to respect its conventional obligations of Non-Refoulement while implementing such immigration control policies outside their borders.

The study of the principle of Non-Refoulement has also attracted a great deal of attention in recent years due to the increasing threat of international terrorism. The question arises whether it is acceptable to balance the risk of ill-treatment to an individual if removed and the threat he represents to the national security of the host State if not removed. After the 11 September 2001 attacks, and in the context of the so-called "war on terror", terrorist suspects were subjected to extra-judicial transfer to their country of nationality or to a third State for interrogation and detention, although there is a real risk of torture or ill-treatment. The practice is known as "extraordinary rendition". While extraordinary rendition operations are carried out by the United States (US), they cannot be accomplished without the collaboration, complicity or acquiescence of other governments by initially seizing a victim, turning a blind eye to his abduction by foreign agents on their national territories, allowing "rendition flights" to use their national airports, and hosting secret Central Intelligence Agency (CIA) detention facilities. Does the fight against terrorism justify the resort to use such extra-judicial transfer to torture? If responsibility for a violation of the principle of Non-Refoulement is engaged, is it only that of the US? Or are States who facilitate or cooperate in such operations also considered to violate their conventional obligations of Non-Refoulement?

Another practice increasingly resorted to in the context of "war on terror" is to seek diplomatic assurances against torture and cruel, inhuman or degrading treatment or punishment (DAs) from the proposed receiving State. The receiving State assures the sending State it will not subject the returnee to torture or cruel, inhuman or degrading treatment or punishment (CIDTP). The purpose of this practice is to facilitate the extradition of an individual,

---

3   European Agency for the Management of Operational Cooperation at the External Borders of the Member States of the European Union, FRONTEX, Annual Risk Analysis 2014, annex table 6.
4   Ibid., Annex table 1.

who is considered a threat to national security, to a country that is known for practicing torture. How can a State be trusted that does not respect its legal obligations under international multilateral treaties? Can such assurances, under certain conditions, ensure that the applicant would not be subjected to ill-treatment in the receiving State?

The multiple and recent challenges call for a systematic and in-depth analysis of the principle of Non-Refoulement, which will clarify to what extent new practices and policies are compatible with the State's obligations under this principle.

II   Purpose and Context of the Study

The principle of Non-Refoulement is a common feature of refugee law,[5] humanitarian law,[6] and human rights law.[7] This study focuses on the protection against refoulement under the ECHR and the CAT. Adopting a comparative approach, the study aims to examine the principle of Non-Refoulement from the perspective of the European Court of Human Rights (ECtHR) and the United Nations Committee against Torture (ComAT). Both of them are human rights treaty bodies, established to ensure observance of the engagements undertaken by States parties to the ECHR, and the CAT, respectively. While Article 3 CAT expressly prohibits the forcible removal of an individual to another country where he fears torture, the ECHR does not include any explicit prohibition of refoulement to ill-treatment. This prohibition has been developed through the case-law of the Strasbourg organs, i.e. the European Commission on Human Rights (EComHR) and later the ECtHR. Several Articles of this Convention, such as Article 2 (the right to life),[8] and Article 6 (the

---

5   Article 33, Geneva Convention Relating to the Status of Refugees, 1951 (CSR).

6   Article 45(4), Geneva Convention Relative to the Protection of Civilian Persons in Time of War, 1949.

7   Article 3, Convention against Torture and Other Cruel, Inhuman or Degrading Treatment or Punishment, 1984 (CAT); Article 3, European Convention on Human Rights, 1950 (ECHR); and Article 7, International Covenant on Civil and Political Rights, 1966 (ICCPR).

8   In many refoulement cases the applicants claimed that the removal would expose them to treatment contrary to Article 3 and would put their life in danger in violation of Article 2 ECHR. The ECtHR does not rule out that Article 2 prohibits expulsion if violation to the right to life is risked in the receiving State. However, the Court has often considered that the complaint under Article 2 is indissociable from the substance of the complaint under Article 3 and that it is more appropriate to examine both complaints together. See e.g., ECtHR, *Bader and Others v. Sweden*, Appl.No. 13284/04, 8 November 2005. Sometimes, after finding that the

right to a fair trial),[9] have been interpreted to include an implicit prohibition of refoulement.[10] In this context, the most developed Non-Refoulement case-law is based on an interpretation of Article 3 ECHR regarding the *prohibition of torture and inhuman or degrading treatment or punishment* (IDTP), which is the concern of this study.

The comparative approach in studying the prohibition against refoulement under Article 3 CAT and Article 3 ECHR is both of practical and theoretical significance. Practical significance lies in the fact that the protections against refoulement under these Articles are not identical. As February 2016, 47 States have ratified the ECHR,[11] so they automatically accept the jurisdiction of the ECtHR to review individual applications under Article 34 ECHR.[12] Out of 158 States parties to the CAT,[13] 66 States have declared that they recognise the competence of the ComAT to receive and consider individual complaints under Article 22 CAT.[14] All States parties to the ECHR are also parties to the CAT, but only 37 of these States have accepted the competence of the ComAT to

---

applicant's removal would be in violation of Article 3, the Court held it was not necessary to decide whether there would be a violation of Article 2. See e.g., ECtHR, *Al-Saadoon and Mufdhi* v. *the United Kingdom*, Appl.No. 61498/08, 2 March 2010, para. 145.

9   See e.g., *Othman (Abu Qatada)* v. *the UK* in which the ECtHR held that the applicant's deportation to Jordan would be in violation of Article 6 ECHR on account of the real risk of the admission of evidence at the applicant's retrial was obtained by torture of third persons. ECtHR, *Othman (Abu Qatada)* v. *the United Kingdom*, Appl.No. 8139/09, 17 January 2012.

10   For the application of Non-Refoulement principle under Articles other than Article 3 ECHR see, Cassese, A., Prohibition of Torture and Inhuman or Degrading Treatment or Punishment, in: St, R., MacDonald, J., Matscher, F. & Petzold, H., The European System for the Protection of Human Rights, Dordrecht: Martinus Nijhoff Publishers, 1993, 248–249, p. 225; Heijer, M.D., Whose Rights and Which Rights? The Continuing Story of *Non-Refoulement* under the European Convention on Human Rights, European Journal of Migration and Law, Vol. 10 no. 3: 2008, 277–314; Mole, N. & Meredith, C., Asylum and the European Convention on Human Rights, Strasbourg: Council of Europe, 2010, pp. 87–103.

11   ECHR, opening for signature on 4 November 1950 in Rome, entered into force 3 September 1953. See, <http://conventions.coe.int/Treaty/Commun/ChercheSig.asp?NT =005&CM=&DF=&CL=ENG>, last visit 26 February 2016.

12   Protocol No. 11 to the ECHR, restructuring the control machinery established thereby, entered into force on 1st November 1998, Article 34.

13   CAT, opening for signature on 10 December 1984 in New York, entered into force 26 June 1987. See, <https://treaties.un.org/Pages/ViewDetails.aspx?src=TREATY&mtdsg _no=IV-9&chapter=4&lang=en>, last visit 26 February 2016.

14   Report of the ComAT, UN. Doc. A/68/44, 2012–2013, annex III, p. 218.

receive and consider individual complaints.[15] Where a person faces a threat of refoulement by any of these States, he has to choose to bring his Non-Refoulement claim before the ComAT under Article 3 CAT or before the ECtHR under Article 3 ECHR. This study aims to provide a thorough examination of the principle of Non-Refoulement under these two Articles, in order to help practitioners to determine which of these human rights treaty bodies is more favorable for their specific Non-Refoulement case.

The theoretical significance follows from a hypothesis that there is a great level of interaction between the ECtHR and the ComAT in the field of the principle of Non-Refoulement. The study of the relationship between different human rights treaty bodies is important due to concerns of fragmentation of international law.[16] This study provides insight into the relationship between the ECtHR and the ComAT in the context of the principle of Non-Refoulement. To what extent is there convergence or divergence between the Non-Refoulement case-law of both bodies? How do they interact with each other in the context of Non-Refoulement? Do they explicitly refer to each other's case-law? If not, is there a silent dialogue between them? Differently, are they influenced by each other's Non-Refoulement case-law?

The composition of the ComAT reveals a high prevalence of members from European States. Out of 10 members, 3 are from European States, 3 are from Africa, while Asia and the Pacific, the Middle East and North Africa, North America, and Latin America have one member each.[17] Hence, a hypothesis is that there is a great level of convergence between the ECtHR's and ComAT's Non-Refoulement case-law.

As it is the case for other fundamental rights, the interpretation of the right to be protected of torture and ill-treatment plays a measure role in determining the scope and content of this right. Accordingly, the ECtHR's and the ComAT's interpretation of the principle of Non-Refoulement to torture or ill-treatment plays an important role in defining the dimensions of the right to be protected from refoulement to this treatment. This may encourage judicial

---

15   The States parties to the ECHR and the CAT that have not accepted the competence of the ComAT to receive and consider individual complaints are: Albania, Armenia, Estonia, Latvia, Lithuania, Romania, San Marino, Macedonia, Moldova, and the UK.

16   UNGA, Fragmentation of International Law: Difficulties Arising from the Diversification and Expansion of International Law, Report of the Study Group of the International Law Commission, UN. Doc. A/CN.4/L.682, 13 April 2006.

17   Truscan, I., Geneva Academy, The Independence Of UN Human Rights Treaty Body Members, Geneva Academy of International Humanitarian Law and Human Rights, December 2012, p. 22, available at: <http://www.geneva-academy.ch/docs/expert-meetings/ga_inbrief_web(1).pdf>, last visit 26 February 2016.

dialogue between these bodies through considering what the other body has concluded in adjudicating similar problems. In order to increase the persuasive authority of its own findings in a given case, a judicial body may explicitly or implicitly refer to similar findings by another body for a similar case. Such judicial dialogue helps to avoid contradiction between different judicial bodies' case-laws, which adversely affect the legitimacy of the judicial body's ruling and threaten the unity of the international legal order.[18]

However, as there is no hierarchy between the various judicial bodies in the field of human rights, this study makes the hypothesis that the ECtHR and the ComAT are reluctant to explicitly refer to each other's case-law in order to avoid the impression of hierarchy. In this context, the ECtHR, as a regional Court, is reluctant to explicitly cite the case-law of the ComAT, as a UN human rights treaty body. And the ComAT is reluctant to explicitly refer to the ECtHR's case-law to avoid the impression that it supports the European understanding of human rights. Accordingly, both the ECtHR and the ComAT are likely inclined to implicitly borrow from each other's Non-Refoulement case-law, without making explicit references.

III   Structure of the Book

The book is divided into five Chapters. *Chapter 1* examines the concept and scope of the principle of Non-Refoulement under Article 3 CAT and Article 3 ECHR in three sections. *Section I* addresses how Article 3 ECHR has been interpreted in the case-law of the Strasbourg organs to include an implied prohibition against refoulement to torture *and* IDTP. *Section II* discusses the absolute nature of the principle of Non-Refoulement under both Articles and whether the threat to national security and fight against terrorism may justify the derogation from this principle. *Section III* examines the personal and territorial scope of the application of the principle. It determines the persons who are protected from refoulement under these Articles: is it possible for the sending

---

18   For an overview of the judicial dialogue see, Allan, R., The European Court of Justice in Context: Forms and Patterns of Judicial Dialogue, European Journal of Legal Studies, Vol. 1 no. 2: 2007, 5–14; Law, D.S. & Chang, W.-C., The Limits of Global Judicial Dialogue, Washington Law Review, Vol. 86 no. 3: 2011, 523–577; Randall, M.H., Le dialogue entre le juge suisse et le juge européen, in: Bellanger, F. & Werra, J.d., Genève au confluent du droit interne et du droit international, Zürich: Schulthess: Mélanges offerts par la Faculté de droit de l'Université de Genève à la Société suisse des juristes à l'occasion du congrès 2012, 2012, 19–59.

State's nationals to benefit from this protection, or it is limited to foreigners? Does the person need to be recognized as a refugee? While it is clear that a State is obligated to respect its conventional obligation of Non-Refoulement within its national territory, it is not so clear where this obligation arises outside the State's own territory. This section also explores the places where the obligation of Non-Refoulement can arise for States parties to the ECHR and the CAT.

The purpose of *Chapter 2* is to consider the content of the principle of Non-Refoulement. *Section I* examines the treatment from which a person is protected by the prohibition against refoulement. Does the principle of Non-Refoulement require the possible future ill-treatment to emanate from acts of public officials in the receiving State, or does the protection also cover those who fear ill-treatment at the hands of non-State actors? What about the cases where a person faces a lawful sanction in the receiving State, such as the death penalty, detention or life imprisonment? Does the principle of Non-Refoulement apply where the person's removal would expose him to a risk of sanction that is unlawful in the sending State but lawful in the receiving State? *Section II* clarifies the prohibited conduct under the principle of Non-Refoulement. Does this principle prohibit only the formal transfers, such as extradition, return and expulsion, or does it also apply in cases of informal transfers, such as rendition? What about the immigration control policies and practices adopted in the course of the fight against terrorism. Is the State obligated to respect its conventional obligations of Non-Refoulement while considering visa applications or intercepting vessels on the high seas? Does a State's responsibility arise for refoulement because of the acts of carriers which prevent a traveller from boarding a flight in order to avoid sanctions imposed by a State of destination? Does a State violate the principle of Non-Refoulement by allowing "rendition flights" to use its national airports, or by hosting secret detention facilities?

Chapter 3 discusses the main individual complaints procedures in the context of the principle of Non-Refoulement. As irreparable harm may result from the removal in violation of the principle of Non-Refoulement, it is important to study the interim measures as a means to stay the applicant's removal pending the consideration of the merits of the Non-Refoulement application by the ComAT or the ECtHR. This is the topic of *Section I. Section II* addresses the criteria for admissibility of an individual application before the ECtHR and the ComAT. The application of the principle of Non-Refoulement depends on establishing the risk of ill-treatment, proof thus refers to a possible future event, which is not an easy task. The standard of proof required to apply the principle of Non-Refoulement under Article 3 CAT and Article 3 ECHR and the burden of proof are discussed in *Section III*.

Chapter 4 examines the ECtHR's and the ComAT's Non-Refoulement case-law in order to clarify the approaches adopted by each treaty body in assessment of whether the applicant's removal would expose him to a risk of future ill-treatment in the receiving State. The prospective nature of the risk affects all aspects of the treaty body's assessment in Non-Refoulement cases. As the treaty body has to assess the likelihood of future treatment, it is important to determine the material time for the risk assessment, which is the topic of *Section I*. *Section II* discusses what evidence, in the ECtHR's and the Co-mAT's views, may demonstrate that the applicant's removal would expose him to future ill-treatment in the receiving State. The factors and circumstances which, in the Court's and the Committee's views, may indicate that the applicant's removal would violate the principle of Non-Refoulement are examined in *Section III*. It may have been established that the applicant would be at a risk of ill-treatment in only a specific part of the receiving State but he can safely settle in another part. The proposed receiving State may have a national law that prohibits torture and ill-treatment, or this State may have provided assurances that the applicant would not be subjected to torture or ill-treatment upon removal. These factors and their effect on the ECtHR's and the ComAT's risk assessment in Non-Refoulement cases are addressed in *Section IV*.

Finally, *Chapter 5* contains a summary of the major conclusions of the previous Chapters, with special focus on the aspects of convergence and divergence between the ECtHR's and ComAT's Non-Refoulement case-law. This Chapter compares the protection against refoulement under Article 3 ECHR with that under Article 3 CAT in order to determine their effectiveness in practice and provides recommendations to improve the ECtHR's and the ComAT's Non-Refoulement case-law, for the purpose of ensuring more effective protection.

CHAPTER 1

The Principle of Non-Refoulement under the ECHR and the CAT

1 The Protection against Refoulement under the ECHR and the CAT

1.1 *Introduction*

For the purpose of this study, the principle of Non-Refoulement refers to the obligation of a State to refrain from forcibly removing an individual to another State where he might be ill-treated. There must be two States for the principle of Non-Refoulement to apply (the sending State and the receiving State). However, this principle does not determine the relationship between the sending and receiving States. Rather, it determines the relationship between the sending State and the individual being forcibly removed to the receiving State. This principle may only be applied if the removed individual is at real risk of ill-treatment in the receiving State.

Non-Refoulement cases should be distinguished from cases in which the manner of removal violates the sending State's obligation to refrain from ill-treatment, whether or not the removed individual is at risk of ill-treatment in the receiving State.[1] In contrast to cases concerned with the manner of removal, the risk of ill-treatment in the receiving State is an essential element in Non-Refoulement cases, even if the manner of removal does not, in itself, directly violate the sending State's obligation to refrain from ill-treatment.[2]

---

[1] See, e.g., *Mubilanzila Mayeka and Kaniki Mitunga v. Belgium* (2006), which concerned the deportation of the applicants to Congo. The Court noted that the second applicant, who was five years old, had to travel alone as the Belgian authorities had not assigned an adult to accompany her. The Belgian authorities merely informed the second applicant's uncle of her arrival without expressly requiring his presence at the airport. They further had not made any alternative arrangement for her arrival and she was ultimately taken into the home of a representative of the Congolese authorities after several hours' wait at the airport. The Court considered that, "the second applicant's deportation in such conditions was bound to cause her extreme anxiety and demonstrated such a total lack of humanity towards someone of her age and in her situation as an unaccompanied minor as to amount to inhuman treatment". ECtHR, *Mubilanzila Mayeka and Kaniki Mitunga v. Belgium*, Appl.No. 13178/03, 12 October 2006, paras. 67–69.

[2] Vermeulen, B.P., Chapter 7. Freedom from Torture and Other Inhuman or Degrading Treatment or Punishment (Article 3), in: Dijk, P.V., Hoof, F.V., Rijn, A.V. & Zwaak, L., Theory and

The first part of this section provides an overview of the prohibition of refoulement as envisaged in the CAT and case-law of the ECHR organs. The second part of this section focuses on the nature of the principle of Non-Refoulement under the CAT and the ECHR.

1.2   *CAT*

The CAT is an international convention adopted by the United Nations General Assembly (UNGA) in 1984.[3] The principal purpose of this Convention was to strengthen the already existing prohibition of torture in international law by adding a number of supportive measures.[4] During its drafting process, it was suggested to include a guarantee against refoulement in the CAT.[5] After long negotiations,[6] the obligation of Non-Refoulement in Article 3 was formulated as follows:

> No State Party shall expel, return ("refouler") or extradite a person to another State where there are substantial grounds for believing that he would be in danger of being subjected to torture.[7]

This was the first provision of an international human rights treaty that expressly prohibited the forcible removal or transfer of an individual who faces

---

Practice of the European Convention on Human Rights, Antwerp, Oxford: Intersentia, 4th Ed, 2006, 405–441, p. 428.

3   For a comprehensive analysis of the CAT see, Burgers, H. & Danelius, H., The United Nations Convention Against Torture. A Handbook on the Convention against Torture and Other Cruel, Inhuman or Degrading Treatment or Punishment, Dordrecht: Martinus Nijhoff Publishers, 1988; Nowak, M. & McArthur, E., The United Nations Convention against Torture. A Commentary, Oxford, New York: Oxford University Press, 2008.

4   The prohibition of torture was at the time already provided for in a number of international instruments; for instance, Article 5 UDHR48; Article 7 ICCPR66; 1975 Declaration on the Protection of all Persons from Being Subjected to Torture and Other CIDTP. Burgers, H. & Danelius, H., 1988, p. 1.

5   The guarantee against refoulement was suggested by the draft International Convention against Torture and other CIDTP which was submitted by the Swedish government. The Swedish draft mainly based on the 1975 Declaration on the Protection of all Persons from Being Subjected to Torture and Other CIDTP, however this Declaration did not provide for the obligation of Non-Refoulement. This suggestion was inspired by the emerging case-law of the EComHR relating to Article 3 ECHR. H. Burgers & H. Danelius, pp. 34–35. See in this Chapter, the prohibition of refoulement under the ECHR.

6   See, Ibid., pp. 31–110; Nowak, M. & McArthur, E., 2008, pp. 130–146.

7   CAT84, Article 3.

the risk of torture.[8] To a certain extent, the text of Article 3 CAT is based on Article 33 CSR, which provides that:

> No Contracting State shall expel or return ("refouler") a refugee in any manner whatsoever to the frontiers of territories where his life or free-dom would be threatened on account of his race, religion, nationality, membership of a particular social group or political opinion.[9]

As noted by the Special Rapporteur on Torture and Other CIDTP, the rationale behind the principle of Non-Refoulement is the following:

> ...it is the essential responsibility of States to prevent acts of torture and other forms of ill-treatment being committed, not only against per-sons within any territory under their own jurisdiction, as spelled out in article 2, paragraph 1, of the Convention, but also to prevent such acts by not bringing persons under the control of other States if there are substantial grounds for believing that they would be in danger of being subjected to torture.[10]

Since the aim of the CAT is to prevent torture, it is insufficient merely to inter-vene after torture, when the physical or moral integrity of a person has already been irremediably harmed. States are, therefore, bound to take all measures to prevent the infliction of torture.[11]

The ComAT rendered its first decision on the merits in a case based on Article 3 CAT in *Mutombo* v. *Switzerland* (1994). The Committee found substan-tial grounds for believing that the complainant would be in danger of being tortured upon expulsion to Zaire. The Committee concluded that expulsion

---

8   Mole, N. & Meredith, C., 2010, p. 19.

9   CSR51, Article 33(1). However, as we will see later in this study, there are several differ-ences between Article 3 CAT and Article 33 CSR with regard to the nature of the prohibi-tion contained in each of them, its territorial scope, personal scope and the conditions of application.

10   Report of the Special Rapporteur on Torture and other Cruel, Inhuman or Degrad-ing Treatment or Punishment, Theo van Boven, UN. Doc. A/59/324, 1 September 2004, para. 27.

11   See, the judgment of the International Criminal Tribunal for the Former Yugoslavia (ICTFY), *Prosecutor* v. *Furundzija*, IT-95-17/1-T, 10 December 1998, para. 148. See also, the Optional Protocol to the CAT (OPCAT) which reflected this understanding. OPCAT, adopted on 18 December 2002 at the fifty-seventh session of the UNGA by resolution A/RES/57/199, entered into force on 22 June 2006.

in the then prevailing circumstances would violate Article 3 CAT.[12] Since the *Mutombo* case, the overwhelming majority of individual communications submitted to the ComAT are based on Article 3 CAT. As of 22 October 2015, out of 276 complaints in which the ComAT rendered a decision on the merits,[13] 238 complaints were based on Article 3 CAT. The Committee found Article 3 was or would be violated in 71 of these complaints. Most of these Non-Refoulement complaints were directed against Switzerland (78 complaints; 18 violations), Sweden (63 complaints; 20 violations), and Canada (25 complaints; 7 violations). The majority of the communications were not directed against States practicing torture, but against sending States which are not generally known for using torture.[14] The Committee has stressed that it has no jurisdiction to establish or adjudicate the responsibility of the receiving State under the CAT, even if that State is a party to this Convention. For example, in *Seid Mortesa Aemei v. Switzerland* (1997), the individual was an active member of the People's Mojahedin of Iran. He was arrested several times by the Iranian authorities and allegedly tortured during interrogations. The Committee asserted that:

> ...it is by no means its responsibility to determine whether the author's rights as recognized by the Convention have been violated by Iran, the country to which he risks being expelled, regardless of whether or not this State is a party to the Convention. The question before the Committee is whether expulsion, return or extradition to the latter country would violate Switzerland's obligation, under article 3 of the Convention, not to expel or return an individual to a State where there are substantial grounds for believing that he would be in danger of being subjected to torture.[15]

1.3   *ECHR*

1.3.1   Introduction

The ECHR is an international convention that was adopted by the Council of Europe (CE) in 1950.[16] According to its preamble, it was adopted to take the

---

12   ComAT, *Mutombo v. Switzerland*, No. 13/1994, 27 April 1994, para. 9.4.

13   Report of the CoAT, UN. Doc. A/70/44, 2014–2015, para. 69.

14   Mostly, this is due to the fact that the individual complaints procedure under Article 22 CAT is optional, so it has been more readily accepted by States where torture is not usually used than by States with a record of systematic use of torture.

15   ComAT, *Seid Mortesa Aemei v. Switzerland*, No. 34/1995, 9 May 1997, para. 9.2.

16   For a comprehensive analysis of the ECHR see, P.V. Dijk, F.V. Hoof, A.V. Rijn & L. Zwaak, Theory and Practice of the European Convention on Human Rights, Intersentia, 2006;

first steps towards collective enforcement of certain rights set out in the Universal Declaration of Human Rights (UDHR).

Article 3 ECHR does not expressly provide for the principle of Non-Refoulement. The prohibition of refoulement under this Article has been developed through the case-law of the Strasbourg organs: the European Commission and later the European Court of Human Rights. Article 3 provides that:

> No one shall be subjected to torture or to inhuman or degrading treatment or punishment.[17]

In a series of decisions that began in 1962, the EComHR advanced a principle that a violation of Article 3 ECHR might arise when a person was to be returned to a country where he could face a gross deprivation of his human rights.[18] The case of *Soering* v. *The UK* (1989) provided the first opportunity for the ECtHR to address the applicability of Article 3 to refoulement cases.[19] In its later case-law, the Court has not elaborated the reasons that Article 3 ECHR applies to refoulement cases.[20]

I.3.2   The Seminal *Soering* Judgment

Jens Soering is a German national who grew up in the US. During his studies at the University of Virginia, he met his girlfriend, Elizabeth Haysom. Elizabeth's parents strongly objected to their relationship. In March 1986, Haysom's parents were stabbed to death with a knife. The young couple fled to the UK. When the couple was arrested in 1987, the US requested their extradition. Elizabeth did not challenge her extradition. She was surrendered to the US, tried and sentenced to two terms of 45 years in prison. Soering challenged his extradition before the ECtHR, on the basis of Article 3 ECHR. He maintained that prisoners in Virginia, the State to which he would be extradited, often awaited

---

White, R. & Ovey, C., Jacobs, White & Overy: The European Convention on Human Rights, Oxford: Oxford University Press, 5th Ed, 2010.

17   ECHR50, Article 3.

18   For a general analysis of the EComHR's case-law in this context see, Nance, D.S., The Individual Right to Asylum under Article 3 of the European Convention on Human Rights, Michigan Yearbook of International Legal Studies, Vol. 3: 1982, 477–495; Kellberg, L., The Case-Law of the European Commission on Human Rights on Art.3 of the ECHR, in: Cassese, A., The International Fight against Torture: La Lutte Internationale Contre La Torture, Baden-Baden: Nomos Verlagsgesellschaft, 1991, 97–129, p. 114.

19   ECtHR, *Soering* v. *the United Kingdom*, Appl.No. 14038/88, 7 July 1989.

20   Battjes, H., Landmarks: Soering's Legacy, Amsterdam Law Forum, Vol. 11 no. 1: 2008, 139–150, p. 140.

execution on death row for six to eight years. According to Soering, this constitutes inhuman and degrading treatment, and is contrary to Article 3 ECHR.

1.3.2.1 Arguments against the Applicability of Article 3 ECHR to Refoulement Cases

The ECtHR began by addressing the main arguments that the UK was entitled to extradite the applicant. First, the Court acknowledged that the Convention does not protect the mere right not to be extradited.[21] This position has been explained in the ECtHR' subsequent case-law, in which the Court emphasized that:

> [the] Contracting States have the right, as a matter of well-established international law and subject to their treaty obligations including Article 3, to control the entry, residence and expulsion of aliens.[22]

The ECtHR has repeatedly asserted that the Convention does not guarantee any right to enter, reside or remain in a State of which one is not a national.[23] It has also asserted that the right to political asylum is not contained in either the Convention or its Protocols.[24] The Court seems to have considered that the complaints about entry, residence and expulsion of foreigners are, in principle, inadmissible. However, their inadmissibility is not absolute.[25] In the *Soering* case, the Court added that:

---

21 The Court derived this conclusion from Article 5(1)(f) ECHR, which permits "the lawful [...] detention of a person against whom action is being taken with a view to [...] extradition". ECtHR, *Soering v. the United Kingdom*, para. 85.

22 See also, ECtHR, *Vilvarajah and Others v. the United Kingdom*, Appl.Nos. 13163/87, 13164/87, 13165/87, 13447/87 and 3448/87, 30 October 1991, para. 102; ECtHR, *Ryabikin v. Russia*, Appl. No. 8320/04, 19 June 2008; ECtHR, *Said v. The Netherlands*, Appl.No. 2345/02, 5 July 2005, para. 46. The right to control over the entry and residence of aliens has historically been considered to be inherent in the nature of the State sovereignty. Sinha, S.P., Asylum and International Law, The Hague: Martinus Nijhoff Publishers, 1971, p. 50.

23 ECtHR, *Bonger v. The Netherlands* (admissibility decision), Appl.No. 10154/04, 15 September 2005.

24 ECtHR, *Chahal v. the United Kingdom*, Appl.No. 22414/93, 15 November 1996, para. 73; ECtHR, *Ahmed v. Austria*, Appl.No. 25964/94, 17 December 1996, para. 38. Caflisch, L., The Contribution of the European Court of Human Rights to the Development of the International Law on Asylum, in: Chetail, V. & Debbas, V.G., Switzerland and International Protection of Refugee, Geneva: The Graduate Institute of International 2002, 207–217, p. 208.

...in so far as a measure of extradition has consequences adversely affecting the enjoyment of a Convention right, it may, assuming that the consequences are not too remote, attract the obligations of a Contracting State under the relevant Convention guarantee.[26]

Hence, the Court has followed the EComHR's approach that:

...the Contracting States have nevertheless accepted to restrict the free exercise of their powers under general international law, including the power to control the entry and exit of aliens, to the extent and within the limits of the obligations which they have assumed under the Convention.[27]

The Court moved on to address the second argument against the applicability of Article 3 to refoulement cases. The British government relied on the concept of jurisdiction, arguing that Article 3 should not be interpreted as imposing responsibility on a State party to the ECHR for acts that occur outside its jurisdiction.[28] The British government particularly stressed that extradition cannot trigger the sending State's responsibility for ill-treatment that the extradited person may suffer outside the State's jurisdiction. The Court made it clear that the pertinent issue under consideration in this case was whether Article 3 applies when removing a person causes him to suffer adverse consequences resulting from ill-treatment outside the sending State's jurisdiction, in the receiving State.[29] The Court noted that, according to the territorial limitation set out in Article 1 ECHR, a State party is obligated to "secure" rights and freedoms defined in Section I ECHR to all persons within its own "jurisdiction". The Convention does not apply to the actions of States not parties to it, nor does it require the States parties to impose the Convention standards on other States. The Court, therefore, observed that:

[Article 1 ECHR] cannot be read as justifying a general principle to the effect that, notwithstanding its extradition obligations, a Contracting State may not surrender an individual unless satisfied that the conditions

---

26   ECtHR, *Soering v. the United Kingdom*, para. 85.

27   EComHR, *X v. Austria and Yugoslavia*, Appl. No. 2143/64, Y.B.ECHR. 7, 1964, p. 328.

28   ECtHR, *Soering v. the United Kingdom*, para. 83.

29   Ibid., para. 85.

awaiting him in the country of destination are in full accord with each of the safeguards of the Convention.[30]

The Court added that the above considerations could not absolve a State party from responsibility under Article 3 for "all and any foreseeable consequences of extradition suffered outside its jurisdiction".[31] Although Article 1 ECHR imposes a territorial limitation on the State's obligations, the sending State may still have responsibility under Article 3 for adverse consequences of the removal suffered outside its jurisdiction. This conclusion is supported by the fact that the sending State's responsibility under the principle of Non-Refoulement results from the act of removal. A State violates the prohibition of refoulement when it removes a person, if there is a real risk of ill-treatment in the receiving State, whether or not the removed person is actually ill-treated in the receiving State. The ECtHR made this clear in *Iskandarov* v. *Russia* (2010). The applicant alleged that after his extradition by Russia to Tajikistan he was subjected to ill-treatment. The Russian government argued that it could not bear responsibility for any ill-treatment that the applicant might suffer in Tajikistan.[32] The Court rejected this argument and asserted that special features existed in this case that could and ought to have enabled the Russian authorities to foresee the applicant's ill-treatment in Tajikistan. The Court added that the impossibility of establishing the truth of the applicant's allegations of ill-treatment in Tajikistan did not affect its findings.[33]

1.3.2.2   *Application of Article 3 ECHR to Refoulement Cases*
As an international treaty, the ECHR should be interpreted in accordance with the rules of treaty interpretation expressed in the Vienna Convention on the Law of Treaties 1969 (VCLT).[34] However, as noted by van Dijk and van Hoof:

---

30   Ibid., para. 86.

31   Ibid., para. 86. The Court seems to be of the opinion that some of the Convention safeguards, including those contained in Article 3, are so important that the disrespect of them by another country precludes surrendering the person.

32   ECtHR, *Iskandarov* v. *Russia*, Appl.No. 17185/05, 23 September 2010, para. 118.

33   Ibid., paras. 131–132.

34   The ECtHR holds that it should be guided by Articles 31 to 33 VCLT. ECtHR, *Golder* v. *the United Kingdom*, Appl. No. 4451/70, 1975, p. 14. Article 31 VCLT provides that, "a treaty shall be interpreted in good faith in accordance with the ordinary meaning to be given to the terms of the treaty in their context and in the light of its object and purpose". Article 31 also provides that, for the purpose of interpretation, the context includes, in addition to the text of the treaty, any subsequent agreement or practice between the States parties and any applicable relevant rules of international law. Article 32 provides for some

The rules of the Vienna Convention do not provide clear-cut solutions to all problems of treaty interpretation. In fact, those rules themselves are not unequivocal. Depending on many factors of which the court's perception of its own role is perhaps the most important one, a court may be inclined towards an interpretation which is focused on the "ordinary meaning" of the treaty terms or, conversely, towards an "object and purpose" – orientated interpretation.[35]

In the light of the ECHR's character as a human rights treaty, the obligations contained in this Convention are objective.[36] This objective nature has had an impact on the methods of interpretation applicable to the Convention and accordingly has had an impact on the material scope of the treaty provisions.[37] Thus, alongside the Vienna Convention principles of interpretation, the Court has also developed principles of interpretation that reflect the special character of the Convention. In *Wemhoff* v. *Germany*, the Court stated that it is necessary to "seek the interpretation that is most appropriate in order to realise the aim and achieve the object of the treaty, not that which would restrict to the greatest possible degree the obligations undertaken by the Parties".[38]

The Court seems to have followed this approach in the *Soering* judgment, setting out a number of principles of interpretation that call for a broad reading of the Convention. The Court pointed out that interpretation of the ECHR must take into consideration that the Convention is "a treaty for the collective enforcement of human rights and fundamental freedoms".[39] In addition,

---

supplementary means of interpretation, including the recourse to the preparatory work of the treaty. Taking into consideration that the ECHR has been authenticated in two languages (English and French), in case of a comparison of these texts discloses a difference of the meaning which best reconciles the texts, having regard to the object and purpose of the treaty, shall be adopted. VCLT69, Articles. 31–33.

35   Dijk, P.v. & Hoof, G.J.H.v., Theory and Practice of the European Convention on Human Rights, The Hague: Kluwer Law International, 3rd Ed, 1998, p. 72.

36   EComHR, *Austria v. Italy*, Appl. No. 788/60, Y.B. ECHR. 4, 1961, p. 140.

37   Loucaides, L., The Rules of Interpretation of the European Convention on Human Rights, in: The European Convention on Human Rights, Collected Essays, Leiden: Martinus Nijhoff Publishers, 2007, 1–16; White, R. & Ovey, C., 2010, pp. 71–72.

38   ECtHR, *Wemhoff* v. *Germany*, Appl. No. 2122/64, 25 April 1968, para. 8.

39   In this regard, the Court cited the *Ireland v. The United Kingdom* judgment of 18 January 1978, Series A no. 25, p. 90. As noted by Lawson and Schermers, the intent behind this statement is to qualify the whole of the ECHR as *erga omnes* obligations, i.e. obligations are owed towards the community as whole. Lawson, R. & Schermers, H.G., Leading cases of the European Court of Human Rights, Nijmegen: Ars Aequi Libri, 2nd Ed, 1999, pp. 169–170.

"the object and purpose of the Convention [...] require that its provisions be interpreted and applied so as to make its safeguards practical and effective".[40] Interpretation must be made in accordance with "the general spirit of the Convention, an instrument designed to maintain and promote the ideals and values of a democratic society".[41] Hence, in addressing whether Article 3 contains a prohibition of refoulement, the Court follows a broad interpretation that respects the nature of the Convention and its object and purpose.

From this perspective, the Court has based its reasoning on the text of the ECHR itself, and concluded that the prohibition provided for in Article 3 has an absolute nature. Although the text of this Article does not explicitly provide for its absolute nature, this nature is highlighted by contrasting the text with that of other Articles of the Convention. In comparison to most of the substantive clauses of this Convention and its Protocols Nos. 1 and 4,[42] which allow for exceptions, Article 3 "makes no provision for exceptions and no derogation from it is permissible".[43] While Article 15(2) ECHR allows the State party to derogate from most of the Convention provisions in "time of war or other public emergency threatening the life of the nation", it prohibits derogation from selected groups of provisions, among them Article 3 ECHR.[44] The Court thus concluded that the absolute nature of the prohibition against torture and CIDTP under the "terms" of the ECHR demonstrates that Article 3 "enshrines one of the fundamental values of the democratic societies making up the Council of Europe".[45] This fundamental value also follows from the fact that this prohibition is found "in similar terms" in other international instruments and is recognised as "an internationally accepted standard".[46]

The ECtHR then turned to the main question in the *Soering* case:

> ...whether the extradition of a fugitive to another State where he would be subjected or be likely to be subjected to torture or to inhuman or

---

40   ECtHR, *Soering* v. *the United Kingdom*, para. 87.

41   Ibid., para. 87.

42   ECtHR, *Ireland* v. *the United Kingdom*, Appl.No. 5310/71, 18 January 1978, para. 163.

43   ECtHR, *Soering* v. *the United Kingdom*, para. 88; ECtHR, *Ireland* v. *the United Kingdom*, para. 163.

44   ECtHR, *Soering* v. *the United Kingdom*, para. 88. Article 15(2) provides that: "No derogation from Article 2, except in respect of deaths resulting from lawful acts of war, or from Articles 3, 4 (paragraph 1) and 7 shall be made under this provision".

45   Ibid., para. 88. See also, ECtHR, *H.L.R.* v. *France* (GC), Appl.No. 24573/94, 29 April 1997, para. 35.

46   ECtHR, *Soering* v. *the United Kingdom*, para. 88. The Court mentioned as example the ICCPR and the American Convention on Human Rights.

degrading treatment or punishment would itself engage the responsibility of a Contracting State under Article 3.[47]

First, the Court asserted that the CAT, as a specialised treaty,

> ...should spell out in detail a specific obligation attaching to the prohibition of torture does not mean that an essentially similar obligation is not already inherent in the general terms of Article 3 of the European Convention.[48]

The Court has considered that the obligation of Non-Refoulement may be inherent even in the absence of an express provision that provides for it.

The ECtHR has been aware that the absolute prohibition of torture and CIDTP under Article 3 ECHR would lose much of its force if a State party could expose a person to this treatment at the hands of others by removing him to a country where he is at risk.[49] Therefore, the Court noted that it would hardly be compatible with the values envisaged in the ECHR's Preamble,[50] if a State party knowingly surrendered a fugitive to another State when there were substantial grounds for believing that he might be subjected to torture, however hideous the crime he had allegedly committed. The Court added that while extradition under such circumstances is not explicitly referred to in the brief and general wording of Article 3, it would clearly be contrary to the spirit and intention of this Article. In contrast to Article 3 CAT, the Court considered that the inherent obligation of Non-Refoulement in Article 3 ECHR is not limited to the cases in which the fugitive would face a real risk of torture in the receiving State, but also extends to cases where there is a real risk of CIDTP.[51]

Finally, the Court concluded that:

> ...the decision by a Contracting State to extradite a fugitive may give rise to an issue under Article 3, and hence engage the responsibility of that State under the Convention, where substantial grounds have been shown

---

47   Ibid., para. 88.

48   Ibid., para. 88.

49   Mole, N., Problems Raised by Certain Aspects of the Present Situation of Refugees from the Standpoint of the European Convention on Human Rights, in: UNHCR, The European Convention on Human Rights and the Protection of Refugees, Asylum-Seekers and Displaced Persons, Geneva: UNHCR, 1996, Part 3, p. 9.

50   i.e. "common heritage of political traditions, ideals, freedom and the rule of law". ECHR50.

51   ECtHR, *Soering v. the United Kingdom*, para. 88.

for believing that the person concerned, if extradited, faces a real risk of being subjected to torture or to inhuman or degrading treatment or punishment in the requesting country.[52]

The rationale behind this interpretation is that the aim of the Convention is to offer an effective, and not just a formal, protection. The responsibility established under Article 3 ECHR in Non-Refoulement cases is thus that of the sending State party, because of its decision to remove an individual or, in general, because it has "taken action which has as a direct consequence the exposure of an individual to proscribed ill-treatment".[53] The Court has made it clear that although responsibility for this potential violation lies with the sending State, the human rights situation in the receiving State must be assessed against the standards of Article 3 in order to determine if the sending State has a responsibility. The Court has clearly reasserted:

> ...there is no question of adjudicating on or establishing the responsibility of the receiving country, whether under general international law, under the Convention or otherwise.[54]

Less than two years after the *Soering* judgment, the Court dealt with *Cruz Varas and Others* v. *Sweden* (1991). This was the first case that concerned the expulsion of refused asylum seekers. In this case, the Court observed that:

> Although the present case concerns expulsion as opposed to a decision to extradite, the Court considers that the above principle also applies to expulsion decisions and a fortiori to cases of actual expulsion.[55]

The implicit principle of Non-Refoulement under Article 3 ECHR has been firmly established in the following judgments of the ECtHR. The Court has repeatedly asserted, as settled case-law, that the expulsion or extradition of

---

52   Ibid., para. 91. After receiving assurances from the US that death penalty would not imposed, Soering was extradited, tried and sentenced to two life imprisonment. See, Lillich, R.B., The Soering Case, The American Journal of International Law, Vol. 85 no. 1: 1991, 128–149, p. 128.

53   ECtHR, *Soering* v. *the United Kingdom*, para. 91. See also, ECtHR, *Cruz Varas and Others* v. *Sweden*, Appl.No. 15576/89, 20 March 1991, paras. 69–70.

54   ECtHR, *Soering* v. *the United Kingdom*, para. 91; ECtHR, *Khaydarov* v. *Russia*, Appl.No. 21055/09, 20 May 2010, para. 97; ECtHR, *Gaforov* v. *Russia*, Appl.No. 25404/09, 21 October 2010, para. 111.

55   ECtHR, *Cruz Varas and Others* v. *Sweden*, para. 70.

a person by a State party may engage the responsibility of that State under Article 3, where substantial grounds have been established for believing that the person, if deported or extradited, would be at real risk of torture or CIDTP. In such a case, Article 3 implies an obligation not to deport or extradite this person to a country where he would face such a risk.[56]

While no statistics are available on the number of Non-Refoulement applications based on Article 3 ECHR that have been declared inadmissible by the ECtHR, there is a noticeable increase in the number of the refoulement cases dealt with on merits. This is due to the leading role the Court has played in this context, and reflects increasing reliance on the Court as a means for protection against refoulement to ill-treatment by refused asylum seekers. Increasing reliance on Article 3 in refoulement cases has helped the Court to develop its Non-Refoulement case-law. As of 28 February 2016, based on Article 3, the ECtHR had delivered judgments on the merits in 209 Non-Refoulement applications. Out of these, in 121 cases the Court found that removal of the applicant was or would be a violation of Article 3 ECHR. Most of these applications were directed against Russia (54 applications; 44 violations), Sweden (34 applications; 6 violations), the UK (19 applications; 9 violations), Italy (17 applications; 17 violations), France (15 applications; 10 violations), the Netherlands (12 applications; 3 violations), and Turkey (9 applications; 8 violations).

1.4   *Conclusion*

The aim of the principle of Non-Refoulement is to prevent the removal of a person in order to protect him from the real risk of ill-treatment awaiting him in the receiving State. While the CAT provides expressly for this principle in its Article 3, the ECHR does not. However, this principle has been derived from the absolute prohibition of torture and CIDTP under Article 3 ECHR by the EComHR, then confirmed and developed by the ECtHR through its case-law. Under both Conventions, the principle of Non-Refoulement is based on the rationale that the State is obligated to protect a person from proscribed ill-treatment. The State must not only refrain from subjecting him to ill-treatment, but it must also protect him from such treatment at the hands of another State. Consequently, the State is under an obligation to refrain from extraditing or expelling a person to another State where he faces the risk of such ill-treatment.

---

56   For expulsion cases see, e.g., ECtHR, *Ahmed* v. *Austria*, para. 39; ECtHR, *N.S.* v. *Denmark*, Appl. No. 58359/08, 20 January 2011, para. 69; ECtHR, *Al Hanchi* v. *Bosnia and Herzegovina*, Appl.No. 48205/09, 15 November 2011, para. 39. For extradition cases see, e.g., ECtHR, *Ismoilov and Others* v. *Russia*, Appl.No. 2947/06, 24 April 2008, para. 67; ECtHR, *Baysakov and Others* v. *Ukraine*, Appl.No. 54131/08, 18 February 2010, para. 48.

The essential element in applying the principle of Non-Refoulement is the existence of a real risk that the removed individual will be ill-treated in the receiving State. The application of the principle requires the assessment of the human rights situation in the receiving State; however, it does not include any judgment on the responsibility of this State. The principle of Non-Refoulement controls the relationship between the sending State and the person concerned, rather than between the sending State and the receiving State. Furthermore, the responsibility of the sending State under the principle of Non-Refoulement is not engaged due to the behaviour of the receiving State; its responsibility is based on its own act of removal, which led, or would lead to, the ill-treatment of the removed person in the receiving State.

II   The Nature of the Principle of Non-Refoulement

As we will find, the absolute nature of the principle of Non-Refoulement has been upheld on the basis of both Article 3 CAT and Article 3 ECHR. After the 11 September 2001 attacks in New York and Washington, and with the increasing threat of international terrorism, the principle of Non-Refoulement has come under greater threat. States have sought to undermine the principle by attacking its absolute nature. Several States have adopted policies that aim to circumvent the absolute prohibition of refoulement, such as seeking and accepting DAs from countries known to use torture, applying visa regulations, carrier sanctions, and safe third country policy.[57] Against this background, the question of the nature of the principle of Non-Refoulement has gained importance. The following subsections address this question under Article 3 CAT and Article 3 ECHR.

II.1   *CAT*
Although the CAT does not contain any provision that expressly provides for the absolute nature of the prohibition against refoulement contained in Article 3, its absolute nature is derived from the formulation of the Article itself. Article 3 is formulated in absolute terms, and does not leave any room to limit the prohibition of refoulement. Furthermore, Article 2(2) CAT provides that:

---

57   These topics are discussed below. See, applicability of the principle of Non-Refoulement to certain policies in Chapter 2 and diplomatic assurances in Chapter 4.

> No exceptional circumstances whatsoever, whether a state of war or a threat of war, internal political instability or any other public emergency, may be invoked as a justification of torture.[58]

Thus, the prohibition against torture under the CAT is absolute and non-derogable under any circumstances including any threat of terrorist activities, violent crimes, or armed conflicts.[59] The provision of Article 2(2) must be interpreted to include prohibition against refoulement under Article 3 CAT, since the aim of Article 3 is to prevent torture in the State to which a person may be returned.[60] As noted by Theo van Boven, the former Special Rapporteur on Torture, "the principle of Non-Refoulement is an inherent part of the overall absolute and imperative nature of the prohibition of torture and other forms of ill-treatment".[61]

The ComAT has repeatedly asserted that, "the test of Article 3 of the Convention is absolute".[62] The Committee has considered that the absolute nature of the protection accorded by Article 3 implies that no one can be removed by a State party, even if he poses a threat to its national security or has committed a crime, and irrespective of the seriousness of this crime.[63] The protection afforded by Article 3 is available even to an individual excluded from refugee status, and even when there is evidence that he has committed one of the crimes provided for under Article 1(F) CSR.[64] Moreover, the protection afforded by

---

58 CAT84, Article 2(2).

59 ComAT, General Comment No. 2, UN. Doc. CAT/C/GC/2/CRP.1/Rev.4, On the Implementation of Article 2 by States parties, 23 November 2007, para. 5.

60 ComAT, Consideration of the second periodic report of the United Kingdom of Great Britain and Northern Ireland and dependent territories, UN. Doc. CAT/C/SR.234, 22 November 1995, para. 38. See also, Nowak, M. & McArthur, E., 2008, p. 88.

61 Therefore, he recalled the ECtHR's position in *Chahal* v. *The United Kingdom* that the prohibition against ill-treatment under Article 3 ECHR is absolute in expulsion cases. Report of the Special Rapporteur on Torture and other Cruel, Inhuman or Degrading Treatment or Punishment, Theo van Boven, UN. Doc. A/59/324, para. 28.

62 ComAT, *Tapia Paez* v. *Sweden*, No. 39/1996, 28 April 1996, para. 14.5; ComAT, *Adel Tebourski* v. *France*, No. 300/2006, 1 May 2007, paras. 8.2–8.3; ComAT, Conclusions and recommendations on the fourth and fifth periodic reports of Canada, UN. Doc. CAT/C/CR/34/CAN, 7 July 2005, para. 5(a); ComAT, Conclusions and recommendations on the fourth periodic report of Italy, UN. Doc. A/62/44, para. 40, 7 May 2007, para. 12.

63 ComAT, *M.B.B.* v. *Sweden*, No. 104/1998, 5 May 1999, para. 6.4.

64 Article 1(F) CSR precludes a person from being granted refugee status, and consequently from the protection of the CSR, where there are serious reasons for considering that he has committed a crime against peace, a war crime, a crime against humanity, non-political

Article 3 CAT is wider than that provided for under Article 33(1) CSR. According to Article 33(2) CSR, it is not possible for a refugee to benefit from the protection against refoulement under the first paragraph of this Article if there are "reasonable grounds" for regarding him "as a danger to the security of the country in which he is", or if he, "having been convicted by a final judgment of a particularly serious crime, constitutes a danger to the community of that country".[65] But such a refugee may benefit from the protection afforded by Article 3 CAT by virtue of the absolute nature of the principle of Non-Refoulement under this Article.[66] Article 3 CAT protects terrorist suspects, as well as criminal offenders, from being returned to torture, regardless of the gravity of their crimes. In *M.B.B.* v. *Sweden* (1999), the Swedish authorities noted that the nature of activities carried out by the complainant in Iran (such as arbitrarily executing people) constituted crimes against humanity, and therefore, he was excluded from refugee status under Article 1(F) CSR. The ComAT recalled that, unlike the provisions of the CSR, Article 3 CAT applies whether or not the individual concerned has committed crimes, and without regard to the seriousness of those crimes.[67] In *V.X.N. and H.N.* v. *Sweden* (2000), the applicants were two Vietnamese nationals residing in Sweden, where they received refugee status. They had committed criminal offences, for which they served a five years prison sentence.[68] On the completion of their prison terms, the Swedish authorities ordered their repatriation for reasons of public order and security. The UNHCR advised the Swedish authorities that their expulsion did not violate Article 33(2) CSR, but the ComAT recalled the absolute character of the State's obligation of Non-Refoulement to torture under Article 3 CAT.[69]

The absolute nature of the prohibition of refoulement under Article 3 CAT caused the Committee to reject any attempt to balance the risk of torture if the person is removed against the danger he poses to the national security of the host State party if he is not removed. In *T.P.S.* v. *Canada* (2000), the Committee noted that one of the overriding factors behind the speedy deportation

---

         crime outside the country of refuge or has been guilty of acts contrary to the purpose and
         principles of the UN. CSR51, Article 1(F).

65   Ibid., Article 33(2).

66   UNHCR, Advisory Opinion on the Extraterritorial Application of Non-Refoulement
         Obligations under the 1951 Convention relating to the Status of Refugees and its 1967
         Protocol, 2007, para. 11; Schutter, O.D., International Human Rights Law. Cases, Materials,
         Commentary, Cambridge: Cambridge University Press, 2010, p. 263.

67   ComAT, *M.B.B.* v. *Sweden*, paras. 4.7 and 6.4. See also, ComAT, *Tapia Paez* v. *Sweden*,
         paras. 14.4 and 15; ComAT, *Adel Tebourski* v. *France*, paras. 8.2–8.3.

68   ComAT, *V.X.N. and H.N.* v. *Sweden*, Nos. 130/1999 and 131/1999, 15 May 2000, para. 5.6.

69   Ibid., paras. 5.9 and 13.7.

of the applicant was, as claimed by the State party, that his "continued presence in Canada represents a danger to the public". The ComAT was not convinced that extending his stay for a few more months would have been contrary to the public interest. Furthermore, the Committee referred to the ECtHR's decision in *Chapel* v. *The UK,* in which the Court maintained that scrutiny of the asylum claim "must be carried out without regard to what the person may have done to warrant expulsion or to any perceived threat to the national security of the expelling state".[70]

In the light of the increasing threat of terrorism, States have sought to undermine the prohibition of refoulement under Article 3 CAT by attacking its absolute nature. States have argued that to protect national security, the risk of torture to an individual if removed must be balanced against the threat he represents to national security if he remains. This approach was reflected in the decision of the Canadian Supreme Court in *Suresh* v. *Canada* (Minister of Citizenship and Immigration) (2002), which was adopted four months after the 11 September attacks.[71] *Suresh* v. *Canada* concerned a citizen from Sri Lanka, recognised as a refugee by the Canadian authorities in 1991. Based on allegations that he belonged to a Tamil terrorist group,[72] Canadian authorities detained Suresh in 1995. The Minister of Citizenship and Immigration ordered him to be deported on the grounds that he constituted a danger to the national security of Canada. Suresh challenged the deportation order in the Federal Court, arguing that he would face a risk of torture if he were expelled to Sri Lanka. The Federal Court, and thereafter the Court of Appeal, upheld the order. While the Supreme Court acknowledged that the prohibition of torture is absolute, it accepted that refoulement might be justified in "exceptional circumstances", as a consequence of the balancing test, if there is substantial risk to the national security of the sending State.[73] Although the *Suresh* decision was adopted by a national Court, its importance derived from the circumstances in which it was adopted and its impact on the absolute nature of the principle of Non-Refoulement under international Human Rights

---

70   ComAT, *T.P.S.* v. *Canada*, No. 99/1997, 16 May 2000, para. 15. 3.

71   Bourgon, S., The Impact of Terrorism on the Principle of 'Non-Refoulement' of Refugees: the Suresh Case before the Supreme Court of Canada, Journal of International Criminal Justice, Vol. 1 no. 1: 2003, 169–185, pp. 1–3.

72   He was accused of being a member in Liberation Tigers of Tamil Eelam (LTTE), an organisation engaged in terrorist activities in Sri Lanka, and involved in fundraising activities in Canada through World Tamil Movement in addition to working as coordinator for the Federation Association of Canadian Tamil.

73   The Supreme Court of Canada, *Suresh v. Canada* (Minister of Citizenship and Immigration), SCC 1, [2002] 1 S.C.R. 3, 2002, para. 78.

law. The ComAT expressed its concern with the failure of the Supreme Court of Canada in the *Suresh* case to recognize, at the level of national law, the absolute nature of the protection against refoulement under Article 3 CAT.[74] The Committee recommended the State party unconditionally to "respect the absolute nature of Article 3 in all circumstances and fully to incorporate the provision of article 3 into the State party's domestic law".[75]

Subsequent to the *Suresh* decision, in *Mostafa Dadar* v. *Canada* (2005),[76] the ComAT reasserted the absolute nature of the principle of Non-Refoulement under Article 3 in all circumstances. As noted by the Committee, although the Canadian authorities found that the applicant would be of limited interest to the Iranian authorities if he returned, they did not exclude an incorrect assessment and the possibility that the applicant might be tortured. According to the Canadian authorities, the finding that the applicant posed a danger to the Canadian citizens should prevail over the risk he would be tortured.[77] They concluded he should be expelled from Canada.[78] The ComAT recalled that the prohibition enshrined in Article 3 CAT is absolute.[79]

A State cannot rely on arguments about counter terrorism and protection of its national security to derogate from its obligation of Non-Refoulement. The ComAT has urged the State party to

> ...ensure that any measure to combat terrorism is in accordance with Security Council resolutions 1373 (2001) and 1566 (2004), which require that anti-terrorist measures be carried out with full respect for, *inter alia*, international human rights law, including the Convention and the absolute principle of Non-Refoulement.[80]

---

74   ComAT, Conclusions and recommendations on the fourth and fifth periodic reports of Canada, para. 4(a).

75   Ibid., para. 5(a).

76   ComAT, *Mostafa Dadar* v. *Canada*, No. 258/2004, 23 November 2005. Mr. Dadar, an Iranian national who was convicted in Canada of assault against his former wife, theft and aggravated assault upon his girlfriend. Ibid., para. 4.2.

77   ComAT, *Bachan Singh Sogi* v. *Canada*, No. 297/2006, 16 November 2007, para. 2.8.

78   The Minister of Citizenship and Immigration stated in the deportation order that: "I am guided by the principles expressed by the Supreme Court of Canada in the case of Suresh". ComAT, *Mostafa Dadar* v. *Canada*, para. 2.14.

79   Ibid., para. 8.8. See also, ComAT, *Bachan Singh Sogi* v. *Canada*, para. 2.8 and 10.2.

80   Report of the ComAT, UN. Doc. A/64/44, 2008–2009, p. 27. See also, ComAT, Concluding observations on the second periodic report of Yemen, UN. Doc. CAT/C/SR.952, 14 May 2010, para. 11; Concluding observations on the second periodic report of Jordan, Report of the ComAT, UN. Doc. A/65/44, 2009–2010, p. 105, para. 17. Fitzpatrick, J., Speaking Law

The Committee has reiterated that the Non-Refoulement principle under Article 3 CAT is absolute and the fight against terrorism does not absolve the State party from honoring its obligation to refrain from removing an individual to another State, where there are substantial grounds for believing that he would be in danger of being subjected to torture.[81] The fact that a person concerned is suspected of involvement in terrorist activities, or is believed to be preparing to carry out such activities, cannot justify refoulement to torture.[82]

II.2 ECHR

It is well established in ECtHR's case-law that the prohibition of ill-treatment provided for under Article 3 ECHR is absolute: the right not to be ill-treated is non-derogable, even in the most difficult circumstances, such as the fight against organised terrorism and crime.[83] Since the principle of Non-Refoulement has been derived from the absolute prohibition of torture and CIDTP, logically, a State cannot circumvent this prohibition by transferring a person to another State where he faces possible ill-treatment.[84] Arguably, the nature of the right of Non-Refoulement is derived from that of the right which may be violated after removal. Where this right is absolute, the right of Non-Refoulement is equally absolute, and is not subject to any derogation or limitations.[85] In *Chahal* v. *The UK* (1996), the ECtHR acknowledged this by extending

to Power: the War against Terrorism and Human Rights, European Journal of International Law, Vol. 14 no. 2: 2003, 241–264, p. 259; Bruin, R. & Wouters, K., Terrorism and the Non-derogability of Non-Refoulement, International Journal of Refugee Law, Vol. 15 no. 1: 2003, 5–29, pp. 7–8.

81   ComAT, *Nasirov* v. *Kazakhstan*, No. 475/2011, 14 May 2014, para. 11.6.

82   Vandova, V., Protection of Non-citizens against Removal under International Human Rights Law, in: Edwards, A. & Ferstman, C., Human Security and Non- Citizens, Law, Policy and International Affairs, Cambridge: Cambridge University Press, 2010, 495–523, p. 508.

83   ECtHR, *Aksoy* v. *Turkey* (admissibility decision), Appl.No. 21987/93, 18 December 1996, para. 62.

84   Droege, C., Transfers of Detainees: Legal Framework, Non-Refoulement and Contemporary Challenges, International Review of the Red Cross, Vol. 90 no. 871: 2008, 669–701, 678.

85   Frigo, M., Migration and International Human Rights Law, Geneva: International Commission of Jurists, 2011, p. 105. For instance, Article 8 ECHR imposes a duty on States to respect the "family life". This duty entails that a State cannot expel a person, if expulsion has adverse effects on his family life. The duty to respect family life is not absolute. Article 8(2) expressly provides for exceptions to this right for reasons of, such as, national security and public order. Thus, it is possible to expel a foreigner who has committed serious offences, even if this expulsion is contrary to his right to respect his family life. In such cases this right is balanced with the national security of the sending State.

the absoluteness of the prohibition under Article 3 ECHR to expulsion cases in which a State party wants to transfer a person to another State where he faces a risk of being ill-treated.[86]

The applicant in the *Chahal* case was an Indian national, a leading figure in the Sikh community.[87] He had been granted indefinite leave to remain in the UK. After he was suspected of terrorist activities inside the UK,[88] the Home Secretary decided Mr. Chahal should be deported on the ground that his continued existence in the UK was not conducive to the public good, for reasons of national security, including the fight against terrorism.[89] The British government argued that the guarantees afforded by Article 3 are not absolute when a State party proposes to remove a person from its territory. Instead, the threat posed to national security by the person is a factor to be weighed in the balance when the issues under Article 3 ECHR are considered.[90] This argument was rejected by the ECtHR, which reaffirmed that "Article 3 makes no provision for exceptions and no derogation from it is permissible".[91] The Court stated that:

> The prohibition provided by Article 3 against ill-treatment is equally absolute in expulsion cases. Thus, whenever substantial grounds have been shown for believing that an individual would face a real risk of being subjected to treatment contrary to Article 3 if removed to another State, the responsibility of the Contracting State to safeguard him or her against such treatment is engaged in the event of expulsion [...]. In these circumstances, the activities of the individual in question, however undesirable or dangerous, cannot be a material consideration.[92]

---

86   ECtHR, *Chahal* v. *the United Kingdom*, para, 80.

87   There were four applicants in this case, Karamjit Singh Chahal, his wife and their two children. While all the applicants claimed that the deportation of Mr. Chahal would violate the right to respect for family life under Article 8 ECHR, only the first applicant, Mr. Chahal, based on Article 3, by claiming that his deportation to India would constitute a violation of this Article.

88   Ibid., paras. 23–24.

89   Ibid., para. 75.

90   Ibid., para. 76.

91   Ibid., para. 79.

92   Ibid., para. 80. Almost six months later, it seems that the ComAT borrowed this language in *Tapia Paez* v. *Sweden* (1997), by stating that: "The nature of the activities in which the person concerned engaged cannot be a material consideration when making a determination under article 3 of the [CAT]". ComAT, *Tapia Paez* v. *Sweden*, paras. 14.5–15.

The ECtHR took into consideration the fact that the Non-Refoulement principle is necessary to protect the right to freedom from torture, which itself has a peremptory or *jus cogens* nature. Consequently, it considered the prohibition of ill-treatment under Article 3 as equally absolute in refoulement cases. The main consideration in determining if the State's responsibility under Article 3 is engaged is not national security interests of the sending State, but the possibility of ill-treatment of the applicant upon removal. Therefore, as asserted by the Court, there is no room for balancing the risk of ill-treatment against the reasons for expulsion.[93]

The Court acknowledged the absolute nature of the principle of Non-Refoulement under Article 3 ECHR for the first time in the *Chahal* case that concerned the extradition of a terrorist suspect. One month later, the Court reasserted this nature in a case that concerned the expulsion of a refugee after he was convicted of civilian crimes. The applicant had committed a series of offences, and therefore had been deprived of refugee status in Austria. The State party had ordered his deportation to Somalia,[94] but the ECtHR found that his deportation would breach Article 3 ECHR. The Court noted that the protection against refoulement afforded by Article 3 ECHR is wider than that provided by Article 33 CSR.[95] This conclusion has been reconfirmed in the subsequent expulsion cases.[96]

The absolute nature of Article 3 ECHR in Non-Refoulement cases might prevent criminals from being brought to justice in the receiving State if they seek protection under this Article. The ECtHR has been aware of this fact since the *Soering* case. The Court noted that as movement around the world becomes easier, and criminal activities are increasingly international in scope, it is in the interest of all nations to bring suspected offenders who flee abroad to justice.[97] The Court noted:

> ...the beneficial purpose of extradition in preventing fugitive offenders from evading justice cannot be ignored in determining the scope of application of the Convention and of Article 3 in particular.[98]

---

93 ECtHR, *Chahal* v. *the United Kingdom*, para. 81.

94 ECtHR, *Ahmed* v. *Austria*, paras. 12 and 16.

95 Ibid., para. 41. See also, ECtHR, *N.* v. *Finland*, Appl.No. 38885/02, 26 July 2005, para. 159. UNHCR, Advisory Opinion on the Extraterritorial Application of Non-Refoulement Obligations under the 1951 Convention relating to the Status of Refugees and its 1967 Protocol, para. 11.

96 ECtHR, *D.* v. *the United Kingdom*, Appl.No. 30240/96, 2 May 1997, para. 48.

97 ECtHR, *Soering* v. *the United Kingdom*, para. 89.

98 Ibid., para. 86.

Yet, the Court has made it clear that its remarks did not leave room for balancing the risk of ill-treatment of the applicant after removal against the State's reasons for his removal.[99] A State party cannot invoke the international community's interest in prosecuting suspected offenders to justify their removal to a State where they are at risk of torture or CIDTP.

The Court has taken this approach with regard to criminal offenders, regardless of the gravity of their crimes. For example, the applicant in *D. v. The UK* (1997) was from the island of St. Kitts. He was accused of trafficking drugs and sentenced to six years' imprisonment after he was found in possession of cocaine at Gatwick airport.[100] After three years, he was released and placed in immigration detention pending his removal. The Court noted the gravity of the offence the applicant committed, and acknowledged the problems confronting States parties in "their efforts to combat the harm caused to their societies through the supply of drugs from abroad".[101] The Court noted that in order to combat this scourge, severe sanctions might be applied to persons involved in drug trafficking, including expulsion of alien drug couriers. However, this does not affect the right of these persons to be protected against refoulement by virtue of the absolute character of Article 3 ECHR, irrespective of the nature and the gravity of their crimes.[102]

The Court has taken a similar position with regard to extraditing terrorist suspects. In *Chahal v. The UK* (1996), the Court stated that:

> ...[it] is well aware of the immense difficulties faced by States in modern times in protecting their communities from terrorist violence. However, even in these circumstances, the Convention prohibits in absolute terms torture or inhuman or degrading treatment or punishment, irrespective of the victim's conduct.[103]

Although it is legitimate for a State to be concerned and to take measures to protect its national security against terrorism, it cannot override the consideration on which the principle of Non-Refoulement is founded. Since no reason, including war or any other emergency situation, can justify derogation from the absolute prohibition against torture or other forms of ill-treatment, there

---

99   ECtHR, *Chahal* v. *the United Kingdom*, para. 81.

100   ECtHR, *D.* v. *the United Kingdom*, para. 7.

101   Ibid., para. 46.

102   Ibid., paras. 46 and 48.

103   ECtHR, *Chahal* v. *the United Kingdom*, para. 79; ECtHR, *Shamayev and 12 others* v. *Georgia and Russia*, Appl.No. 36378/02, 12 October 2005, para. 336.

is no reason that can justify a transfer that exposes a person to the risk of such ill-treatment.[104] It is well established in ECtHR's case-law that the principle of Non-Refoulement under Article 3 is absolute and must be respected regardless of the conduct of the person, however undesirable or dangerous.

As international terrorism increased, particularly after 11 September 2001, some European States have focused on the contribution of foreign nationals to the terrorist threat. Several governments have adopted deportation policies for foreigners suspected or convicted of terrorism. The absolute nature of the prohibition of refoulement has been attacked by some of the States parties to the ECHR. Their attack has developed in two different ways. First, they have adopted policies that aim to circumvent and weaken the absolute character of the prohibition of refoulement under Article 3 ECHR.[105] Second, several States parties intervened in refoulement cases as third parties, in accordance with Article 36(2) ECHR, attempting to urge the ECtHR to change its *Chahal* case-law.[106] This approach was evident in three major refoulement cases, *Ramzy* v. *The Netherlands* (2008), *A.* v. *The Netherlands* (2010), and *Saadi* v. *Italy* (2008). In these cases, the applicants were terrorist suspects considered a threat to the national security of the host State party, which had ordered their deportation. In their applications to the ECtHR, all these applicants argued that deportation to their countries of origin would expose them to a real risk of being subjected to treatment proscribed by Article 3.[107] The British government intervened alone in the *Saadi* case, and intervened together with the governments of Lithuania, Portugal, and Slovakia in the other two cases.[108] The intervening governments submitted the same written observations in these three cases.

---

104   Droege, C., 2008, p. 678; Frias, A.S.d., Counter-terrorism and human rights in the case law of the European Court of Human Rights, Strasbourg: Council of Europe, 2012, p. 87.

105   See below, Chapter 2, applicability of the principle of Non-Refoulement on certain policies and Chapter 4, diplomatic assurances.

106   This approach was mainly motivated by the 11 September 2001 attacks and was given further impetus by the train bombings in Madrid on 11 March 2004 and in London on 7 July 2005.

107   ECtHR, *Saadi* v. *Italy* (GC), Appl.No. 37201/06, 28 February 2008, para. 95; ECtHR, *Ramzy* v. *the Netherlands* (admissibility decision), Appl.No. 25424/05, 27 May 2008, para. 99; ECtHR, *A.* v. *The Netherlands*, Appl.No. 4900/06, 20 July 2010, para. 111.

108   In addition to these governments, several non-governmental organisations (NGOs) intervened in *Ramzy* v. *the Netherlands* (2008) and *A.* v. *the Netherlands* (2010). The intervening organisations focused on supporting the ECHR's case-law with regard to the absolute nature of the prohibition of refoulement under Article 3 ECHR. See, ECtHR, *Ramzy* v. *the Netherlands* (admissibility decision), paras. 131–140; ECtHR, *A.* v. *The Netherlands*, paras. 131–140.

The observations particularly argued against the absolute nature of the prohibition of refoulement as established in the *Chahal* case.[109]

The intervening governments noted that terrorism seriously endangers the right to life, which is the necessary precondition for enjoyment of all other fundamental rights.[110] This fact imposes an obligation on States parties to protect everyone within their jurisdiction from terrorism. The governments argued the rigidity of the approach adopted in *Chahal* made it too difficult for States to ensure national security because it prevented them from enforcing expulsion of those suspected of being foreign terrorists.[111] They complained that criminal prosecution of those individuals might not always be possible, because the individual concerned might not yet have committed any offence, or it might be difficult to establish his involvement in terrorism beyond reasonable doubt, especially since it is often impossible to use confidential intelligence information in criminal proceedings. Other measures, such as putting the suspect under surveillance or restricting his freedom of movement, provided only partial protection at best.[112] The intervening governments further attacked the essence of the principle of Non-Refoulement. While they accepted the absolute nature of the protection against torture and CIDTP afforded by Article 3 ECHR, they noted that in expulsion cases this treatment would be inflicted by the authorities of the receiving State, rather than by those of the sending State party. Since a State party was bound by an implied positive obligation to prevent treatment contrary to Article 3, a balancing test between the applicant's rights and the interests of the community was necessary.[113] The governments noted that several factors were relative in expulsion cases: States parties could only speculate on the degree of risk in the receiving State; prohibited treatment under Article 3 could range from torture (the most severe and serious form of ill-treatment) to degrading treatment; and, the nature of the threat presented by an

---

109   While the Italian government had declared at the hearing before the Court to agree in substance with the UK's arguments advanced in the *Saadi* case, the Dutch government acknowledged and announced that it had no desire to challenge the absolute nature of Article 3 ECHR in the *Ramzy* case. ECtHR, *Saadi* v. *Italy* (GC), para. 115; ECtHR, *Ramzy* v. *the Netherlands* (admissibility decision), para. 100.

110   ECtHR, *Saadi* v. *Italy* (GC), para. 119; ECtHR, *Ramzy* v. *the Netherlands* (admissibility decision), para. 127; ECtHR, *A.* v. *The Netherlands*, para. 127.

111   ECtHR, *Saadi* v. *Italy* (GC), para. 117; ECtHR, *Ramzy* v. *the Netherlands* (admissibility decision), para. 125; ECtHR, *A.* v. *The Netherlands*, para. 125.

112   ECtHR, *Saadi* v. *Italy* (GC), paras. 117–118; ECtHR, *Ramzy* v. *the Netherlands* (admissibility decision), para. 126; ECtHR, *A.* v. *The Netherlands*, para. 126.

113   ECtHR, *Saadi* v. *Italy* (GC), para. 120; ECtHR, *Ramzy* v. *the Netherlands* (admissibility decision), para. 128; ECtHR, *A.* v. *The Netherlands*, para. 128.

individual to the national security of the State party also varied significantly.[114] In light of these considerations, they maintained that the *Chahal* approach had to be "altered and clarified"; the possibility and the nature of the risk of ill-treatment a person faced in the receiving State had to be balanced against the degree and nature of the threat this person represented to the national security of the sending State.[115] Although the *Saadi* case was filed after the other two cases, it was the first to come to judgment. In February 2008, the Grand Chamber (GC) found that the decision to deport Saadi to Tunisia would breach Article 3 ECHR. The Chamber reached the same conclusion in *A. v. The Netherlands* on 20 July 2010.[116]

In the *Saadi* decision, the ECtHR (GC) addressed in detail the governments' arguments for a substantial change in the *Chahal* approach on Article 3 ECHR.[117] It reaffirmed the absolute nature of Article 3 in Non-Refoulement cases and again acknowledged the huge difficulties States currently face when they attempt to protect their community from terrorist activities.[118] The ECtHR observed that arguments similar to those made by the UK in this case were rejected in the *Chahal* judgment. Despite the increasing terrorist threat since *Chahal*, the conclusions it reached in the *Chahal*

---

114   ECtHR, *Saadi v. Italy* (GC), para. 121; ECtHR, *Ramzy v. the Netherlands* (admissibility decision), para. 129; ECtHR, *A. v. The Netherlands*, para. 129.

115   ECtHR, *Saadi v. Italy* (GC), para. 122; ECtHR, *Ramzy v. the Netherlands* (admissibility decision), para. 130; ECtHR, *A. v. The Netherlands*, para. 130.

116   ECtHR, *Saadi v. Italy* (GC), para. 149; ECtHR, *A. v. The Netherlands*, para. 151. Then, on 29 July 2010, the *Ramzy* case was struck out of the list because the applicant's whereabout was unknown. ECtHR, *Ramzy v. The Netherlands*, Appl.No. 25424/05, 29 July 2010, paras. 64–66.

117   The Court did not pay any attention to the right to life argument. This point was only addressed by Judge Myjer who stressed that this is true, but at the same time he noted that: "States are not allowed to combat international terrorism at all costs. They must not resort to methods which undermine the very values they seek to protect. And this applies the more to those 'absolute' rights from which no derogation may be made even in times of emergency". See, the Concurring Opinion of Judge Myjer, joined by judge Zagrebelsky. ECtHR, *Saadi v. Italy* (GC). In our opinion, the Court was right in ignoring this argument. In fact, it is nothing more than an attempt by governments to give human rights character to security issues in order to legally justify their conduct. However, the question here is not whether a State should do certain conduct to combat terrorism, but how far it is allowed to go in doing it. See also, Moeckli, D., Saadi v. Italy: The Rules of the Game Have Not Changed, Human Rights Law Review, Vol. 8 no. 3: 2008, 534–548, pp. 541–542.

118   ECtHR, *Saadi v. Italy* (GC), para. 137; ECtHR, *Chahal v. the United Kingdom*, para. 79; ECtHR, *Shamayev and 12 others v. Georgia and Russia*, para. 336.

judgment remained valid: the nature of Article 3 remained absolute.[119] The GC
rejected any distinction between treatment inflicted directly by a State party
and that might be inflicted by another State after an individual was expelled.
It reaffirmed that the protection against ill-treatment should not be weighed
against the interests of the community as a whole.[120] The GC made it clear that
assessment of "risk" and "dangerousness" must be independent of each other.
Either there is or there is not a risk if the person is sent back.[121] Despite the fact
that intervening governments strongly asserted the importance of considering
national security, the ECtHR (GC) was clear that an increase in the terrorist
threat does not justify, in any instance, any kind of balancing in the application
of Article 3 ECHR in refoulement cases.[122]

The *Saadi* judgment was a "landmark case". All subsequent judgments
in refoulement cases have reasserted the GC's approach to the various arguments against the absolute nature of the principle of Non-Refoulement.[123]
However, the Court has undermined the absolute nature of the principle of
Non-Refoulement under Article 3 by making a distinction between ill-treatment carried out by the State party in the domestic context, or by another State
in the refoulement context.[124]

II.3   *Conclusion*

The prohibition of refoulement is absolute under the ECHR and the CAT. No
derogation or limitation is permissible, either under Article 3 CAT, or under Article 3 ECHR, regardless of the conduct of the removed person. The
protection against refoulement under both Conventions is afforded to any
person under threat of being removed to another State, if he faces a risk of
ill-treatment. This includes criminal offenders as well as terrorist suspects.

---

119   ECtHR, *Saadi* v. *Italy* (GC), para. 141.

120   Ibid., para. 138; ECtHR, *Charahili* v. *Turkey*, Appl. No. 46605/07, 13 April 2010, para. 58.

121   ECtHR, *Saadi* v. *Italy* (GC), para. 139. See, Battjes, H., In Search of a Fair Balance: The Abso-
       lute Character of the Prohibition of *Refoulement* under Article 3 ECHR Reassessed, Leiden
       Journal of International Law, Vol. 22 no. 3: 2009, 583–621.

122   Smith, R., The Margin of Appreciation and Human Rights Protection in the „War on
       Terror": Have the Rules Changed before the European Court of Human Rights?, Essex
       Human Rights Review, Vol. 8 no. 1: 2011, 124–153, p. 151.

123   ECtHR, *Hamraoui* v. *Italy*, Appl.No. 16201/07, 24 Marsh 2009; ECtHR, *Dbouba* v. *Turkey*,
       Appl.No. 15916/09, 13 July 2010; ECtHR, *Auad* v. *Bulgaria*, Appl.No. 46390/10, 11 October
       2011, para. 101.

124   See below, Chapter 2, infliction of severe pain or suffering, physical or mental under the
       ECHR.

In spite of the strong attempts in recent years, by several States to justify the removal of terrorist suspects from their territories on the grounds of national security, neither the ComAT nor the ECtHR has accepted any derogation from the principle of Non-Refoulement. A State party to any of these Conventions is under an absolute obligation to respect the principle of Non-Refoulement as envisaged in the Convention concerned. Given this absolute obligation, we shall now consider the scope of application of the principle of Non-Refoulement.

III   The Scope of the Protection against Refoulement under the ECHR and the CAT

III.1   *Introduction*

For the purpose of this study, the scope of application of the principle of Non-Refoulement refers to the framework within which the State's obligation of Non-Refoulement exists. This section aims to determine the persons who may be protected by this principle, and where the obligation could arise. The intersection of the personal scope and the territorial and extraterritorial scope defines the perimeters within which a State exercises jurisdiction and consequently assumes obligations.[125]

Even if a State has jurisdiction according to either the ECHR or the CAT, this does not necessarily mean that this State is responsible for breaching the Convention. Although, jurisdiction and responsibility are intertwined, they are different concepts. The State's responsibility arises where that State breaches its international obligations. Those obligations arise only where that State has jurisdiction. Jurisdiction only relates to the applicability of human rights law, whereas responsibility defines whether the State concerned is

---

125   The word jurisdiction here refers to the jurisdiction of the States parties to the CAT and the ECHR, not to the jurisdiction of the ECtHR and the ComAT to deal with the matter. It indicates to the threshold criterion, which must be satisfied to consider that a State party is bound by the treaty obligations in the first place. However, the absence of a State's jurisdiction would automatically lead to a loss of the Convention body's jurisdiction ration materiae. O'Boyle, M., The European Convention on Human Rights and Extraterritorial Jurisdiction: A Comment on 'Life After Bankovic', in: Coomans, F. & Kamminga, M., Extraterritorial Application of Human Rights Treaties, Antwerp, Oxford: Intersentia, 2004, 125–139, p. 125.

liable for violating a certain human right.[126] Jurisdiction is a prerequisite for responsibility. Thus, the question of the State's responsibility would arise only if the ComAT or the ECtHR was satisfied first that the matters complained of were within the State party's jurisdiction.[127] Then, in order to determine if the State that has jurisdiction is responsible for violating the principle of Non-Refoulement, the conduct of the State concerned and the circumstances of the case under consideration must be considered in more detail.

In this section, we discuss the scope of the principle of Non-Refoulement as contained in Article 3 CAT and Article 3 ECHR. The first subsection contains an analysis of the personal scope. The second subsection examines the territorial scope.

III.2   *Personal Scope*

Under Article 1 ECHR, States parties are bound to secure to "everyone" within their jurisdiction the rights and freedoms provided for in Section I ECHR, including Article 3, of this Convention.[128] The word "everyone" in this Article indicates that the personal scope of the ECHR is not limited.[129] Article 3 ECHR also provides, in general terms, that "No one shall be subjected to torture [...]".[130] The protection against refoulement under this Article is thus guaranteed to all individuals, including those who are not nationals of any of the States parties,[131] stateless persons,[132] persons of unknown nationality,[133]

---

126   According to Articles 1 and 2 of the International Law Commission (ILC)'s Articles on State Responsibility, international responsibility of a State requires an "internationally wrongful act", i.e. there is a "conduct consisting of an action or omission: (a) Is attributable to the State under international law; and (b) Constitutes a breach of an international obligation of the State". UNGA, Resolution adopted by the General Assembly 56/83. Responsibility of States for internationally wrongful acts, UN. Doc. A/RES/56/83, 28 January 2002.

127   O'Boyle, M., 2004, p. 130.

128   ECHR50, Article 1.

129   Dijk, P.v. & Hoof, G.J.H.v., 1998, p. 13.

130   ECHR50, Article 3.

131   E.g. ECtHR, *R.J.* v. *France*, Appl.No. 10466/11, 19 September 2013, which concerned the expulsion of a national of Sri Lanka; ECtHR, *MO.M.* v. *France*, Appl.No. 18372/10, 18 April 2013, which concerned the expulsion of a Chadian national; ECtHR, *M.E.* v. *France*, Appl.No. 50094/10, 6 June 2013, which concerned the expulsion of an Egyptian national.

132   E.g. ECtHR, *Auad* v. *Bulgaria*, which concerned the expulsion of a stateless person of Palestinian origin to Lebanon. See also, EComHR, *Austria v. Italy*, p. 116.

133   E.g. ECtHR, *Aswat* v. *the United Kingdom*, Appl.No. 17299/12, 16 April 2013, which concerned the extradition of the applicant whose nationality was unknown to the US.

the nationals of the sending State itself,[134] or the nationals of the sending State who risk being removed after their citizenship is revoked.[135]

Under Article 3 CAT, States parties to the CAT are obligated to refrain from removing "a person" where there are substantial grounds for believing that he would be in danger of being subjected to torture. The personal scope of the protection against refoulement under the CAT is not subject to any limitation.[136] Any person who was faced with forcible removal may benefit from this protection, regardless of whether he was a foreigner, a national of the sending State,[137] or a national of this State before he was stripped of his nationality.[138]

---

134   In *Nsona* v. *The Netherlands* (1996), the ECtHR noted that the removal of "a non-national" may give rise to an issue under Article 3. ECtHR, *Nsona* v. *The Netherlands*, Appl.No. 23366/94, 28 November 1996, para. 92(b). However, the Court's subsequent Non-Refoulement case-law shows that Article 3 applies to nationals and non-nationals. E.g. ECtHR, *Garabayev* v. *Russia*, Appl.No 38411/02, 7 June 2007, which concerned the extradition of a Russian national from Russia to Turkmenistan; ECtHR, *Harkins and Edwards* v. *the United Kingdom*, Appl.No. 9146/07 and 32650/07, 17 January 2012, in which one of the applicants was a British national who faced a risk of being extradited from the UK to the US.

135   E.g. ECtHR, *Al Husin* v. *Bosnia and Herzegovina*, Appl.No. 3727/08, 7 February 2012, in which the applicant was a Syrian national who fought alongside Bosnian Muslims during the War in Bosnia and Herzegovina (BH) as a member of El Mujahedin, Muslim foreigners. After the end of the war, he applied for BH citizenship and continued to live there. As a consequence of the 11 September attacks, the applicant, as many of the foreign mujahedin, lost his BH citizenship and became an unlawful resident in BH. Later, he was considered a threat to national security and ordered to deport. Mole, N. & Meredith, C., 2010, p. 24.

136   The commentary to CAT stated that: "... article 3 of the present Convention applies to any person, who for whatever reason, is in danger of being subjected to torture if handed over to another country". Burgers, H. & Danelius, H., 1988, p. 125.

137   E.g. ComAT, *Boily* v. *Canada*, No. 327/2007, 14 November 2011, which concerned the extradition of a Canadian national to Mexico. See also, the discussion of the initial report of Kenya, where the ComAT expressed, with reference to Article 3, its concern about the returns and renditions of individuals, nationals and non-nationals, to Somalia, Ethiopia and Guantánamo Bay on the basis of national security and actions to fight terrorism. Conclusions and recommendations on the initial report of Kenya, Report of the ComAT, UN. Doc. A/64/44, UN. Doc. A/64/44, p. 42, para. 17.

138   E.g. ComAT, *Adel Tebourski* v. *France*, para. 2.2, in which the Committee applied Article 3 to the deportation of the applicant who was stripped of his French nationality and ordered to deport on the grounds of the State security and public safety. During the consideration of the periodic report of Jordan, the ComAT expressed its concern at the reported withdrawal of nationality from more than 2,700 Jordanians of Palestinian origin between 2004 and 2008. The Committee noted that this withdrawal was conducted in a

Protection of the principle of Non-Refoulement under both these Conventions is wider than that provided for in Article 33 CSR.[139] Protection under Article 33 CSR is afforded only to "a refugee", as defined in Article 1(A)(2) of the same Convention: a person who has left the country of his nationality or habitual residence and is unable or unwilling to return, owing to a well-founded fear of persecution for reasons of race, religion, nationality, membership of a particular social group or political opinion.[140] It is impossible for a person inside his country of origin to benefit from the protection of Article 33 CSR. Even a person who fulfils the criteria contained in Article 1(A)(2) CSR can be deprived of the protection of the CSR under Article 1(F).

The principle of Non-Refoulement applies to a person regardless of his legal status in the State party concerned.[141] Both the ComAT and the ECtHR have applied the prohibition of refoulement to refused asylum seekers,[142] those deprived of the protection of CSR under its Article 1(F),[143] recognized refugees or asylum seekers registered with UNHCR,[144] trafficking victims,[145] persons

---

random and arbitrary manner, without a clear basis in law, thereby putting them at risk of expulsion without the guarantees pursuant to Article 3 CAT. ComAT, Consideration of second periodic report of Jordan, UN. Doc. CAT/C/JOR/CO/2, 25 May 201025 May 201, para. 24.

139   ComAT, Consideration of the second periodic report of Venezuela, UN. Doc. CAT/C/SR.538, 21 November 2002, para. 43; ECtHR, *Saadi* v. *Italy* (GC), para. 138.

140   CSR51, Article 1(A)(2). However, the protection is not limited to formally recognised refugees, but it also covers asylum seekers who fulfill the criteria contained in Article 1(A)(2) but have not been formally recognised yet as refugees. For further information on this point, see Goodwin-Gill, G.S. & McAdam, J., The Refugee in International Law, Oxford: Oxford University Press, 2007, p. 232; Coleman, N., European Readmission Policy: Third Country Interests and Refugee Rights, Leiden: Martinus Nijhoff Publishers, 2009, p. 236.

141   ComAT, *M.B.B.* v. *Sweden*, para. 6.4.

142   ECtHR, *Jabari* v. *Turkey*, Appl.No. 40035/98, 11 July 2000; ECtHR, *Khaydarov* v. *Russia*; ComAT, *Avedes Hamayak Korban* v. *Sweden*, No. 88/1997, 16 November 1998; ComAT, *S.V. et al.* v. *Canada*, No. 49/1996, 15 May 2001.

143   ECtHR, *Paez* v. *Sweden* (admissibility decision), Appl.No. 29482/95, 30 October 1997; ComAT, *M. A.* v. *Canada* (admissibility decision), No. 22/1995, 14 December 1994, para. 3.

144   ComAT, Concluding observations on the initial report of Syria, UN. Doc. CAT/C/SYR/CO/, 25 May 2010, para. 18.

145   ComAT has considered the trafficking victims are a particularly vulnerable group, which should be covered by the protection afforded by Article 3. ComAT, Consideration of the initial periodic report of El Salvador, UN. Doc. CAT/C/SR.422, 15 December 2000, para. 31. For the applicability of Article 3 ECHR on the trafficking victims see, Seaman, A., Permanent Residency for Human Trafficking Victims in Europe: The Potential Use of Article 3 of the European Convention as a Means of Protection, Columbia Journal of Transnational Law, Vol. 48 no. 2: 2010, 287–320.

without a residence permit,[146] and those who have visitor's status,[147] or a residence permit pending the decision of the Court or the Committee;[148] regardless of whether they entered the State party concerned legally or illegally.[149]

In terms of personal scope, neither the CAT nor the ECHR has imposed any limitation on the principle of Non-Refoulement. It applies to foreigners, whether nationals of another State or stateless persons, as well as nationals of the sending State. It should be noted here the Constitutions of almost all States prohibit the expulsion of citizens of the State concerned and protect their right to enter their own State.[150] Article 12(4) ICCPR prohibits the arbitrary denial of the right to enter one's own country.[151] The Human Rights Committee (HRC) "considers that there are few, if any, circumstances in which deprivation of the right to enter one's country could be reasonable".[152]

III.3   *Territorial Scope*

According to Article 29 VCLT, a treaty is binding upon each State party in respect of its entire territory unless a different intention appears from the treaty or is otherwise established.[153] Under this provision, a State party to a treaty must, in principle, respect the obligations imposed by this treaty on the whole of its territory, with the possibility of restricting the application of

---

146   ECtHR, *N. v. Sweden*, Appl.No. 23505/09, 20 July 2010; ComAT, Consideration of second periodic report of Senegal, UN. Doc. CAT/C/SR.247, 29 May 1996, para. 15; ComAT, *A.D. v. The Netherlands*, No. 96/1997, 12 November 1999, para. 7.3.

147   ComAT, *J.A.M.O. et al. v. Canada*, No. 293/2006, 9 May 2008, para. 9.3; ComAT, *Prashanthan Chelliah v. Australia* (admissibility decision), Application no. 211/2002, 3 May 2005, para. 2.2.

148   The Court considered that granting the applicant a residence permit pending the decision of the Court did not amount to resolution of the matter, even if as a result of this permit the applicant was not liable to expulsion at that time, ECtHR, *Salah Sheekh v. The Netherlands*, Appl.No. 1948/04, 11 January 2007, para. 117.

149   The ECtHR applied Article 3 to the applicants who had illegally entered the sending State such as in, ECtHR, *Chahal v. the United Kingdom*. See also, ComAT, *Elif Pelit v. Azerbaijan*, No. 281/2005, 1 May 2007, in which the ComAT applied Article 3 to the extradition of the applicant, who had entered Azerbaijan illegally.

150   According to Article 3 of the Protocol No. 4 ECHR, "1. No one shall be expelled, by means either of an individual or of a collective measure, from the territory of the State of which he is a national. 2. No one shall be deprived of the right to enter the territory of the State of which he is a national". Protocol No. 4 to the ECHR, entered into force on 2nd May 1968.

151   ICCPR66, Article 12(4).

152   HRC, General Comment No. 27, Freedom of movement (Article 12), U.N. Doc CCPR/C/21/Rev.1/Add.9 (1999), 2 November 1999, para. 21.

153   VCLT69, Article 29.

the treaty to parts of its territory. But this Article does not deal with the question of the extraterritorial application of the treaties.[154] Taking into account Article 29, the territorial and extraterritorial scope of the State's obligation of Non-Refoulement under both the CAT and the ECHR must therefore be determined by reference to their own provisions.

As mentioned above, Article 1 ECHR provides that the Convention is applicable to everyone "within the jurisdiction of the Contracting States". This general provision determines the scope of application of the Convention inside and outside the State's territory. The CAT does not contain such a general provision; instead, it includes several jurisdiction clauses, like those in Articles 2(1), 7(1), 11, 12, 13, 16 and 22(1), which generally confine the obligations assumed by the States parties under these Articles to "any territory under its jurisdiction".

Although the question of territorial and extraterritorial scope of both the CAT and the ECHR have been examined by their treaty bodies in several cases, none of them relate specifically to the principle of Non-Refoulement.[155] This question was not addressed in relation to the application of a certain treaty Article, but in relation to the general application of the Convention concerned. Thus, the jurisprudence of both the ECtHR and the ComAT in this regard is relevant for the application of the principle of Non-Refoulement.[156] In the following subsections, we discuss the territorial and extraterritorial application of this principle first for Article 3 ECHR, and then for Article 3 CAT.

III.3.1   ECHR

According to Article 1 ECHR, a State party is bound to secure to everyone within its "jurisdiction" the rights and freedoms set forth in Section I of this Convention. Thus, jurisdiction under Article 1 is deemed a "threshold

---

154   The extraterritorial application means that at the moment of the alleged violation of the individual's human rights, he is not physically located in the territory of the State party concerned. Milanovic, M., Extraterritorial Application of Human Rights Treaties, Law, Principles, and Policy, Oxford: Oxford University Press, 2011, pp. 8–11.

155   It is possible to apply other rules of international law to the extraterritorial activities, such as international humanitarian law in the case of armed conflicts or customary international law of human rights. However, the application of the ECHR and the CAT has an added value, because of their implementation mechanisms, according to which States may be held responsible for violations of their obligations.

156   Klug, A. & Howe, T., The Concept of State Jurisdiction and the Applicability of the Non-Refoulement Principle to Extraterritorial Interception Measures, in: Ryan, B. & Mitsilegas, V., Extraterritorial Immigration Control: Legal Challenges, Leiden: Martinus Nijhoff Publishers, 2010, 69–101, pp. 75–76.

criterion".[157] Wherever a State party exercises jurisdiction, it is under an obligation to secure the enjoyment of the Convention rights, including the right to be protected against refoulement, to everyone within its jurisdiction. The interpretation of the meaning of "jurisdiction" under Article 1 ECHR, particularly when it is exercised outside the national territory, is an unsettled and controversial question.[158] Through their case-law, the Strasbourg organs have developed general principles relevant to jurisdiction under Article 1 ECHR, outlined by the ECtHR in *Al-Skeini and Others* v. *The UK* (2011).[159] This section defines where a State party's obligation of Non-Refoulement under Article 3 ECHR is established, whether inside or outside the State's territory, in light of the general principles of jurisdiction under Article 1 ECHR.

III.3.1.1   *Jurisdiction Inside the State's Territory*
The ECtHR has repeatedly asserted that the notion of jurisdiction within the meaning of Article 1 ECHR must be considered as reflecting the position under public international law.[160] This notion of jurisdiction is "primarily" or "essentially" territorial.[161] Hence, the Court presumes that a State party

---

157   ECtHR, *Al-Skeini and Others* v. *the United Kingdom*, Appl. No. 55721/07, 7 July 2011, para. 130.

158   For a comprehensive analysis of the Strasbourg organs' case-law on this question see, e.g., Pedersen, M.P., Territorial Jurisdiction in Article 1 of the European Convention on Human Rights, Nordic Journal of International Law, Vol. 73 no. 3: 2004, 279–305; Costa, K.D., The extraterritorial application of selected human rights treaties, Leiden: Martinus Nijhoff Publishers, 2012, pp. 93–254.

159   ECtHR, *Al-Skeini and Others* v. *the United Kingdom*, paras. 130–142.

160   The Court's approach has been criticized widely on the basis of the difference between the meaning of jurisdiction in each of the general international law and the human rights law. While the jurisdiction in the general international law refers to the State's right to regulate the conduct of persons and the consequences of their actions under its domestic law, in the human rights treaties it denotes a certain kind of power a State exercises over a territory and its inhabitants. The two concepts may relate but they cannot possibly be the same. Milanovic, M., From Compromise to Principle: Clarifying the Concept of State Jurisdiction in Human Rights Treaties, Human Rights Law Review, Vol. 8 no. 3: 2008, 411–448, p. 429; Pedersen, M.P., 2004, p. 305; Bhuta, N.C., Conflicting International Obligations and the Risk of Torture and Unfair Trial, Journal of International Criminal Justice, Vol. 7 no. 5: 2009, 1133–1147, p. 1139.

161   To reach this conclusion the Court based on the "ordinary meaning" of the term "within their jurisdiction" in the light of the States' practice and the travaux préparatoires of the ECHR. ECtHR, *Soering* v. *the United Kingdom*, para. 86; ECtHR, *Bankovic et al* v. *Belgium and 16 other Contracting States* (admissibility decision), Appl.No. 52207/99, 12 December 2001, paras. 59–66.

normally exercises jurisdiction throughout its territory.[162] A State party is therefore obliged to secure the right to be protected against refoulement for all persons present within its own territory.

This raises the question whether the physical presence of a person within a State's territory is sufficient to consider him within its jurisdiction, and thus protected against refoulement, or whether he must have legally entered and stayed within this territory. The Court dealt with this question in *D.* v. *The UK* (1997). On 21 January 1993, the applicant in this case arrived at Gatwick Airport and sought leave to enter the UK for two weeks as a visitor. This request was refused because he had been found at the airport terminal to be in possession of cocaine. He was prosecuted, accused of trafficking drugs, and sentenced six years' imprisonment. He was released after three years, and placed in immigration detention pending his deportation. Since the applicant was in an advanced stage of AIDS, he requested he be granted leave to remain in the UK on the grounds that his removal to St. Kitts would deprive him of the medical treatment he was receiving in the UK, and thus shorten his life expectancy. The Chief immigration officer refused his request, on the grounds that a person, such as the applicant, who had been denied leave to enter but was physically in the UK pending his removal, did not fall within the State's jurisdiction. The Court of Appeal upheld the Chief immigration officer's position.[163] But the ECtHR mentioned that the principle of Non-Refoulement is applicable to a person threatened with removal,

> ...regardless of whether or not he ever entered the United Kingdom in the technical sense [...] it is to be noted that he has been physically present there and thus within the jurisdiction of the respondent State within the meaning of Article 1 of the Convention since 21 January 1993. It is for the respondent State therefore to secure to the applicant the rights guaranteed under Article 3.[164]

The physical presence of the person within the State's territory, regardless of the legality of his entrance or existence, is sufficient to consider him within its jurisdiction. The host State is, therefore, under an obligation to protect him against refoulement.[165] The question here is if it is possible for a State party to

---

162   ECtHR, *Al-Skeini and Others* v. *the United Kingdom*, para. 131.

163   ECtHR, *D.* v. *the United Kingdom*, paras. 6–7, 11–12 and 25.

164   Ibid., para. 48.

165   Blake, N., Developments in the Case Law of the European Court of Human Rights, in: Bogusz, B., Cholewinski, R., Cygan, A. & Szyszczak, E., Irregular Migration and Human

exclude a certain part of its territory from its jurisdiction for the purpose of the ECHR, and if this State can remove persons existing within this part, regardless of its obligation of Non-Refoulement under Article 3 ECHR.[166]

Although it is possible, under Article 57 ECHR, for States parties to make reservations in respect of any particular provision of the Convention, to the extent that any law then in force in their territory is not in conformity with the provision, reservations of a general character are not permitted under this Article.[167] A reservation is considered to be of a general character "if it does not refer to a specific provision of the Convention or if it is worded in such a way that its scope cannot be defined".[168] Furthermore, Article 19(c) VCLT prohibits reservations that are incompatible with the object and purpose of the Convention.[169] Since the obligation envisaged in Article 1 ECHR is of fundamental importance for the enjoyment of the rights and freedoms provided for in the Convention,[170] any restriction to this obligation through making a reservation is incompatible with the object and purpose of the Convention and must therefore be considered inadmissible.[171] Thus, it is not possible for a State party to the ECHR to limit, in general, the territorial scope of the Convention inside its territory through a reservation made under Article 57 ECHR.[172] Any

---

Rights: Theoretical, European and International Perspectives, Leiden: Martinus Nijhoff Publishers, 2004, 431–451, p. 433.

166   Such as, by creating transit or international zones at airports. See below, Chapter 2, transit zones.

167   ECHR50, Article 57(1).

168   EComHR, *Temeltasch* v. *Switzerland*, Appl.No. 9116/80, EComHR Dec & Rep. 31, 5 May 1982, para. 84.

169   Under Article 19 VCLT, it is possible for a State, when signing, ratifying, accepting, approving or acceding to a treaty, to make a reservation unless: (a) the reservation is prohibited by the treaty; (b) the treaty provides that only specified reservations, which do not include the reservation in question, may be made; or (c) in cases not failing under subparagraphs (a) and (b), the reservation is incompatible with the object and purpose of the treaty. VCLT69, Article 19.

170   All Articles contained in Section 1 ECHR describe rights of individuals and do not, in terms, impose any obligations on States. The Role of Article 1 ECHR is to transform those rights into obligations for States parties to the ECHR.

171   Flinterman, C., Chapter 38. Reservations (Article 57), in: Dijk, P.V., Hoof, F.V., Rijn, A.V. & Zwaak, L., Theory and Practice of the European Convention on Human Rights, Antwerp, Oxford: Intersentia, 4th Ed, 2006, 1101–1114, p. 1110.

172   In this context, the ECtHR noted that if "the applicability of the Convention could be selectively restricted to only parts of the territory of certain States parties, thus rendering the notion of effective human rights protection underpinning the entire Convention meaningless while, at the same time, allowing discrimination between the States parties,

reservation that has the effect of excluding a part of the State's territory from
its jurisdiction is invalid because it is incompatible with the object and purpose of the Convention. No State party has made any reservation or declaration regarding the application of Article 3 ECHR within all or part of its territory. Article 3 "enshrines one of the fundamental values of the democratic
societies making up the Council of Europe",[173] and its absolute nature under
the ECHR makes any reservation to this Article incompatible with the object
and purpose of the ECHR and thus invalid.

Sometimes, States find it difficult to secure compliance with the Convention,
including the principle of Non-Refoulement, in certain parts of their territory,
for example, when another State intercepts the boats of protection seekers
within its own territorial water, when the military forces of another State occupies part of its territory, or when a separatist movement exists in this part. The
question here is if a State party continues to have jurisdiction over this part of
its territory, and therefore remains under an obligation to respect the principle
of Non-Refoulement within it. Although the ECtHR has presumed that a State
party normally exercises jurisdiction throughout its territory, it has accepted
that this presumption may be rebutted in exceptional circumstances, when a
State party faces difficulties in securing compliance with the Convention in a
specific part of its territory.[174] The Court has distinguished between two cases.
In the first case, a part of the State's territory does not have separatist aspira-
tions and no other State exercises effective control there. In this case, the State
party continues to have jurisdiction over all its territory, including this part,
and is thus under an obligation to protect all persons present within any part
of its territory against refoulement.[175] In the second case, the State is prevented
from exercising *de facto* control over a part of its territory because, for example,
it is under military occupation by the armed forces of another State, which exercises effective control over this part. In this case, the Court has asserted that
a State party does not cease to have jurisdiction over that part. But at the same
time, the Court has accepted the possibility that such factual situations reduce
the extent of the State party's jurisdiction under Article 1. In the sense that,
the Court must consider the State party's undertakings under this Article only
in light of the State's positive obligations to prevent human rights violations

---

that is to say between those which accepted the application of the Convention over the
whole of their territory and those which did not". ECtHR, *Assanidze* v. *Georgia*, Appl.No.
71503/01, 8 April 2004, paras. 140 and 142.

173   ECtHR, *Soering* v. *the United Kingdom*, para. 88; ECtHR, *H.L.R.* v. *France* (GC), para. 35.

174   ECtHR, *Ilascu and Others* v. *Moldova and Russia*, Appl.No. 48787/99, 8 July 2004, para. 312.

175   ECtHR, *Assanidze* v. *Georgia*, paras. 140 and 146.

within its own territory, even when such violations are committed by another State.[176] The Court has considered the State party's positive obligations related both to the measures needed to re-establish its control over the concerned part of its territory, as an expression of its jurisdiction, and to the measures to ensure respect for the applicants' rights.[177] If a person is deported inside a State party's territory by the agents of another State, the State party must seek, with all the legal and diplomatic means available to it vis-à-vis the foreign State and international organisations, to guarantee respect for the principle of Non-Refoulement. It is the task of the Court to verify that the measures actually taken were appropriate and sufficient in the case under consideration. In case of total failure to act, the Court's task is to determine to what extent a minimum effort was nevertheless possible, and whether it should have been made.[178]

III.3.1.2   *Jurisdiction Outside the State's Territory*

While the ECtHR has considered the notion of jurisdiction within the meaning of Article 1 ECHR to be essentially territorial, it has accepted that acts of a State party performed or which have effects outside its territory can constitute an exercise of jurisdiction only in exceptional cases.[179] The Court has asserted that the question of the existence of exceptional circumstances, which justify a finding that the State was exercising jurisdiction extraterritorially, must be determined with reference to the facts of each case.[180] The Court has distinguished between two grounds for extraterritorial jurisdiction: in the first, the State, through its agents, exercises control and authority over an individual outside its own territory; in the second, the State exercises effective control over an area outside its national territory.[181]

---

176 According to the Court, a State party to the ECHR has a positive obligation under Article 1 of the Convention to take the diplomatic, economic, judicial, or other measures that it is in its power to take and are in accordance with international law to secure to the applicants the rights guaranteed by the Convention. ECtHR, *Ilascu and Others* v. *Moldova and Russia*, para. 331; ECtHR, *Ivanţoc and Others* v. *Moldova and Russia*, Appl. No. 23687/05, 15 November 2011, para. 105; Wouters, K. & Heijer, M.D., The Marine I Case: a Comment, International Journal of Refugee Law, Vol. 22 no. 1: 2010, 1–19, p. 11.
177 ECtHR, *Ivanţoc and Others* v. *Moldova and Russia*, para. 106.
178 ECtHR, *Ilascu and Others* v. *Moldova and Russia*, paras. 312–313, 332–334.
179 ECtHR, *Bankovic et al* v. *Belgium and 16 other Contracting States* (admissibility decision), para. 67; ECtHR, *Al-Skeini and Others* v. *the United Kingdom*, para. 131.
180 Ibid., para. 132.
181 See, Ibid. This distinction is consistent with the understanding that the term "jurisdiction" in the extraterritorial context is generally understood as the relation between the State concerned, on the one hand, and either the foreign territory where its conduct

It should be noted that the principle of Non-Refoulement is usually referred to as a form of practicing jurisdiction extraterritorially, since the aim of this principle is to protect a person from being ill-treated within the territory of another State.[182] We argue that, although the application of the principle of Non-Refoulement includes extraterritorial elements like the assessment of the risk of ill-treatment in the receiving State, the sending State cannot be considered to be practicing jurisdiction extraterritorially in all cases for many reasons. The person concerned usually is within the territory of the sending State party and his removal decision is taken on the territory of this State.[183] Furthermore, under this principle, the sending State's responsibility is not engaged for any act of ill-treatment committed by the authorities of the receiving State,[184] but for its decision to transfer a person to such a State, despite of the risk he will be subjected to ill-treatment there. Where the person concerned is outside the sending State's territory, such as within a foreign territory occupied by this State, or on the boats of protection seekers intercepted by its coast guard on the high seas, he can be considered within the extraterritorial jurisdiction of this State based on one of the two grounds for this jurisdiction, control or authority over persons and effective control over a foreign area, which we discuss in the following two subsections.[185]

III.3.1.2.a   Control or Authority over Individuals

In its established case-law, the ECtHR has accepted that, as an exception to the essentially territorial notion of jurisdiction, acts of the State party performed outside its territory or producing effects there can constitute extraterritorial

---

took place or the individual affected by this conduct. Wilde, R., Compliance with Human Rights Norms Extraterritorially: 'Human Rights Imperialism'?, in: Chazournes, L. & Kohen, M., International Law and the Quest for its Implementation/Le droit international et la quête de sa mise en oeuvre, Boston, Leiden: Brill, Martinus Nijhoff Publishers, 2010, 319–350, p. 324.

182   ECtHR, *Loizidou* v. *Turkey*, Appl.No. 15318/89 (Preliminary Objections), 23 March 1995, para. 62; ECtHR, *Bankovic et al* v. *Belgium and 16 other Contracting States* (admissibility decision), para. 68.

183   See, Ibid., para. 68.

184   ECtHR, *Soering* v. *the United Kingdom*, paras. 86–91; ECtHR, *Klein* v. *Russia*, Appl.No. 24268/08, 1 April 2010, para. 44.

185   Nowak, M., Obligations of States to Prevent and Prohibit Torture in an Extraterritorial Perspective, in: Gibney, M. & Skogly, S., Universal Human Rights and Extraterritorial Obligations, Philadelphia: University of Pennsylvania Press, 2010, 12–29, p. 19.

exercise of jurisdiction in the meaning of Article 1 ECHR.[186] As noted by the Court, accountability of a State party in such situations stems from the fact that Article 1 cannot be interpreted in a way that allows State authorities to perpetrate violations of the Convention on the territory of another State, which it could not perpetrate on its own territory.[187] Thus, the State's agents working abroad not only remain within the State's jurisdiction under Article 1, but also bring any other persons within the jurisdiction of this State; to the extent they exercise control or authority over such persons.[188]

The ECtHR followed this exception for the first time in *Drozd and Janousek v. France and Spain* (1992),[189] by stating that:

> ...the term "jurisdiction" is not limited to the national territory of the High Contracting Parties; their responsibility can be involved because of acts of their authorities producing effects outside their own territory.[190]

The Court has noted that the statement of this exception is very broad. To identify the dimensions of its application, it is necessary to examine the relevant case-law.[191] The Court has observed that this exception has been applied in three types of situations:

First, a State party exercises jurisdiction extraterritorially through the acts of its diplomatic and consular agents, who are present on foreign territory in accordance with provisions of international law. These acts may amount to an exercise of jurisdiction when these agents exercise authority and control over

---

186   ECtHR, *Drozd and Janousek v. France and Spain*, Appl.No. 12747/87, 26 June 1992, para. 91; ECtHR, *Bankovic et al v. Belgium and 16 other Contracting States* (admissibility decision), para. 67; ECtHR, *Ilascu and Others v. Moldova and Russian* (admissibility decision), Appl. No. 48787/99, 4 July 2001, para. 314; ECtHR, *Al-Skeini and Others v. the United Kingdom*, para. 133.

187   ECtHR, *Issa and others v. Turkey*, Appl.No. 31821/96, 16 November 2004, para. 71.

188   EComHR, *Stocké v. The Federal Republic of Germany*, Appl.No. 11755/85, Series. A Vol. 199, 12 October 1989, p.24, para. 166; ECHR, *Ocalan v. Turkey* (GC), Appl.No.6221/99, 12 May 2005, para. 88.

189   This exception was applied by the EComHR in several cases. See, e.g., EComHR, *X v. The Federal Republic of Germany*, Appl.No. 1611/62, Y.B. ECHR. 8, 25 September 1965, p. 158; EComHR, *Cyprus v. Turkey*, Appl.Nos. 6780/74 and 6950/75, EComHR Dec & Rep. 12, 26 May 1975, p. 125.

190   ECtHR, *Drozd and Janousek v. France and Spain*, para. 91. See also, ECtHR, *Bankovic et al v. Belgium and 16 other Contracting States* (admissibility decision), para. 69.

191   ECtHR, *Al-Skeini and Others v. the United Kingdom*, para. 133.

others.[192] In *W.M.* v. *Denmark* (1992), the EComHR extended the State party's jurisdiction extraterritorially to include persons under the authority of the State's diplomatic or consular agents. The applicant, a citizen of the German Democratic Republic, entered the Danish embassy in East Berlin to seek diplomatic asylum. But the Danish ambassador handed him over to the police of the host State. The Commission stated that:

> ...authorised agents of a State, including diplomatic or consular agents, bring other persons or property within the jurisdiction of that State to the extent that they exercise authority over such persons or property. In so far as they affect such persons or property by their acts or omissions, the responsibility of the State is engaged.[193]

The EComHR extended this exception to include, in addition to diplomatic or consular agents, all authorised agents of a State. Although a person who is under the authority of the State party's diplomatic or consular agents working abroad is outside the State's national territory, he is considered within its extraterritorial jurisdiction.[194] Therefore, the State concerned is under an obligation to protect him against refoulement.

Second, the ECtHR's case-law has demonstrated that, in certain circumstances, the use of force by a State's agents who operate outside its own territory may bring a person under the control of these agents into the State's jurisdiction. This exception has usually been applied where an individual is taken into the physical custody or factual control of a State's agents abroad.[195] The fact that a person is in the physical custody of State's agents working in a foreign soil strongly indicates that this person is within the extraterritorial jurisdiction of that State; therefore it is under an obligation not to refouler him to torture or CIDTP. The Court took this approach in *Ocalan* v. *Turkey* (2005). The applicant, a leader of the Kurdish Workers' Party (PKK), was arrested in Kenya by Kenyan officials and handed over to Turkish security officers inside an aircraft located at Nairobi airport. He was forcibly removed to Turkey where he was detained, subjected to an unfair trial and sentenced to death. The ECtHR found that:

---

192   ECtHR, *Bankovic et al* v. *Belgium and 16 other Contracting States* (admissibility decision), para. 73; ECtHR, *Al-Skeini and Others* v. *the United Kingdom*, para. 134.

193   EComHR, *W.M.* v. *Denmark*, Appl.No. 17392/90, 14 October 1992. See also, EComHR, *Cyprus* v. *Turkey*, p. 73; EComHR, *X* v. *The Federal Republic of Germany*, p. 158.

194   Milanovic, M., 2011, pp. 154–155.

195   ECtHR, *Al-Skeini and Others* v. *the United Kingdom*, para. 134.

It is common ground that, directly after being handed over to the Turkish officials by the Kenyan officials, the applicant was effectively under Turkish authority and therefore within the "jurisdiction" of that State for the purposes of Article 1 of the Convention, even though in this instance Turkey exercised its authority outside its territory.[196]

This conclusion indicates that the ECtHR has held the physical control over a person by a State's agents working abroad is sufficient to consider this person within the "jurisdiction" of the State concerned.[197] Furthermore, the decisive element for determining whether the Turkish agents exercised control over the applicant was the existence of physical control, regardless of its duration or the place in which such control or detention took place.[198] The same approach was taken by the Court in the refoulement case of *Al-Saadoon and Mufdhi v. The UK* (2010), which concerned the transfer of two Iraqi nationals from the British forces in Iraq to the Iraqi authorities. The Court held that the applicants fell within the extraterritorial jurisdiction of the UK since they were detained in British-controlled military prisons in Iraq, where the UK exercised total and exclusive control over the prisons and the detainees.[199]

The Court has also considered that the State party's jurisdiction extends extraterritorially where it exercises factual control over a ship and its crew by intercepting it. This was followed in the case of *Medvedyev and Others v. France* (2010), which concerned the interception of Cambodian vessel by the French authorities with the consent of the Cambodian authorities for suspicions of drug smuggling. Although the applicants (crew members) had never been transferred on board the French vessel, the GC found that they were within French jurisdiction by virtue of the full and exclusive control exercised by French agents over the ship and its crew from the time of its interception on the high seas.[200] The factual control over a ship and its crew was also the basis to find that Italy had jurisdiction over the applicants in *Xhavara and 12 Others v. Italy and Albania* (2001). This case concerned a collision between a ship of irregular migrants flying an Albanian flag, and an Italian coast guard vessel

---

196   ECHR, *Ocalan v. Turkey* (GC), para. 91.

197   Kunzli, A., Ocalan v. Turkey: Some Comments, Leiden Journal of International Law, Vol. 17 no. 1: 2004, 141–154, p. 145.

198   Klug, A. & Howe, T., 2010, p. 85. ECHR, *Ocalan v. Turkey* (GC), para. 91.

199   ECtHR, *Al-Saadoon and Mufdhi v. the United Kingdom* (admissibility decision), Appl.No. 61498/08, 30 June 2009.

200   ECtHR, *Medvedyev and Others v. France* (GC), Appl.No. 3394/03, 29 March 2010, paras. 65–67.

trying to stop the ship for inspection in accordance with an Italian-Albanian agreement that allowed the Italian fleet to board and search Albanian ships. The ship sank as a result of this collision and 58 persons died. The applicants, who had survived the incident, brought a complaint based on Article 2 ECHR against Italy and Albania. The Court found that Italy, as the flag State of the patrol vessel, was responsible for the human rights violations caused by its vessel to persons aboard the other vessel.[201] Accordingly, the principle of Non-Refoulement applies wherever the interception operations bring the intercepted persons under the full factual control of the intercepted State, such as by boarding their vessel, causing damage to the vessel, or by escorting the intercepted vessel to another location.

Despite of the fact that a State party in the above cases exercised control over the aircraft, buildings or ship in which the individuals were held, the Court made clear that the State's jurisdiction did not arise solely from this fact. The exercise of physical power and control over the person in question was decisive in such cases.[202] Thus, wherever a person is within the physical control of the agents of a State party working abroad, this person is considered within the State's jurisdiction in the meaning of Article 1 ECHR. It follows that the State is under an obligation to protect him against refoulement.

Third, the Court has recognised as an exception to the territorial notion of jurisdiction under Article 1 instances in which a State party, through the consent, invitation or acquiescence of the government of a foreign territory, exercises all or some of the public powers normally to be exercised by that government.[203] The acts of a State party carried out in another State, in accordance with custom, treaty or other agreement, fall within the extraterritorial jurisdiction of the State party, it is bound to respect the Convention rights and freedoms in carrying out these acts.[204] The jurisdiction of the State party extends outside its territory to the acts of the immigration control officers or airline liaison officers who are posted by the State to countries generating migrants, asylum or protection seekers in order to assist the officers who check the travel documents before boarding.

---

201   The application was declared inadmissible because domestic remedies had not been exhausted. ECtHR, *Umalatov and Others* v. *Russia*, Appl.No. 8345/05, 8 April 2010.

202   ECtHR, *Al-Skeini and Others* v. *the United Kingdom*.

203   ECtHR, *Bankovic et al* v. *Belgium and 16 other Contracting States* (admissibility decision), para. 71.

204   ECtHR, *Al-Skeini and Others* v. *the United Kingdom*, para. 134.

The ECtHR has left the door open for more exceptions on the ground of the authority or control over an individual exercised by the agents of a State party working abroad. The Court generally stated that:

> ...whenever the State through its agents exercises control and authority over an individual, and thus jurisdiction, the State is under an obligation under Article 1 to secure to that individual the rights and freedoms under Section 1 of the Convention that are relevant to the situation of that individual.[205]

Noticeably, the ECtHR made no distinction as to whether the State's agents act lawfully or unlawfully on foreign soil.[206] It has not distinguished between diplomatic and consular officers, border officials in customs-free zones, international peace-keeping or peace-enforcement troops and other State's agents who lawfully work in the foreign State, and those who might work there unlawfully, such as security agents kidnapping persons abroad and military forces occupying a foreign territory.[207] Arguably, in the Court's opinion, the nature of the relationship (legal or factual) between the State's agents working abroad and the alleged victim of the violation of the Convention rights and freedoms by those agents is irrelevant to establish whether those victims fall within the State's jurisdiction.[208] The decisive element is whether those victims are under the authority and control of the sending State through its agents.

III.3.1.2.b   Effective Control over Foreign Areas

In its settled case-law, the ECtHR has accepted, as another basis for exception to the territorial principle of jurisdiction under Article 1, that a State party has extraterritorial jurisdiction when, as a consequence of lawful or unlawful military action, it exercises effective control over an area outside its own national territory.[209] Where such effective control over a foreign area is proved,

---

205   Ibid., para. 137; ECtHR, *Hirsi Jamaa and Others* v. *Italy* (GC), Appl.No. 27765/09, 23 February 2012, para. 74.

206   ECtHR, *Bankovic et al* v. *Belgium and 16 other Contracting States* (admissibility decision), para. 59.

207   O'Boyle, M., 2004, p. 94; Nowak, M., Obligations of States to Prevent and Prohibit Torture in an Extraterritorial Perspective, 2010, p. 14.

208   A similar approach had been followed by the EComHR. See. King, H., The Extraterritorial Human Rights Obligations of States, Human Rights Law Review, Vol. 9 no. 4: 2009, 521–556, pp. 530–531.

209   ECtHR, *Loizidou* v. *Turkey*, para. 62; ECtHR, *Bankovic et al* v. *Belgium and 16 other Contracting States* (admissibility decision), para. 70.

this area is considered within the extraterritorial jurisdiction of the State party concerned, whether the State's authorities actually exercise control in a specific situation or not.[210] The State has an obligation under Article 1 ECHR to secure to all persons within this area the Convention rights and freedoms, including the right to be protected against refoulement.[211] The fact of exercising effective control over a foreign area creates the jurisdiction of the State party extraterritorially, whether this control is exercised directly through the State's own armed forces, or indirectly through a subordinate local administration.[212] The controlling State will be considered responsible for the policies and actions of the local authorities of the area under its control, and those persons who are affected by such policies and actions come under its jurisdiction for the purposes of Article 1 ECHR.[213] There is no need to determine whether the controlling State actually exercises detailed control over the authorities in this territory.[214]

According to this exception, the decisive element in determining whether a State has extraterritorial jurisdiction over a foreign area is the fact of exercising control over this area and the effectiveness of this control.[215] This raises the question of when a State is considered to have "effective control" over a foreign area outside its national territory. The ECtHR's case-law has not provided a clear criterion to determine the degree of control sufficient to serve as a basis for the State's extraterritorial jurisdiction. According to the Court, whether or not exceptional circumstances exist, which require and justify the finding that a State exercises jurisdiction extraterritorially in the case under consideration, must be determined with reference to particular facts of the case.[216] A State party's effective control over a foreign area is a matter of fact, determined in light of the circumstances of each case. The Court has observed that, in determining whether such effective control exists, it would primarily make reference

---

210   Lawson, R., Life After Bankovic: on the Extraterritorial Application of the European Convention on Human Rights, in: Coomans, F. & Kamminga, M., Extraterritorial Application of Human Rights Treaties, Antwerp, Oxford: Intersentia, 2004, 83–124, p. 98.

211   ECtHR, *Cyprus v. Turkey* (GC), Appl.No. 25781/94, 10 May 2001, paras, 76–77.

212   Ibid., paras. 76–77; ECtHR, *Loizidou v. Turkey*, para. 62; ECtHR, *Djavit An v. Turkey*, Appl.No. 20652/92, 20 February 2003, paras. 20–21; ECtHR, *Ilascu and Others v. Moldova and Russia*, para. 314; ECtHR, *Al-Skeini and Others v. the United Kingdom*, para. 138.

213   ECtHR, *Loizidou v. Turkey*, para. 56.

214   ECtHR, *Ilascu and Others v. Moldova and Russia*, para. 315.

215   Klug, A. & Howe, T., 2010, p. 79.

216   ECtHR, *Al-Skeini and Others v. the United Kingdom*, para. 139; ECtHR, *Hirsi Jamaa and Others v. Italy* (GC), para. 73.

to the strength of the State party's military presence in the area concerned.[217] This approach was taken in *Issa and others* v. *Turkey* (2004), which concerned allegations of ill-treatment and killing of six Iraqis by the Turkish army in Northern Iraq during a temporary military operation. The Court compared the level of Turkish control over Northern Iraq in this case, and that over Northern Cyprus, which was occupied by Turkey, in *Loizidou* v. *Turkey* (1996).[218] The Court noted that Turkey did not exercise effective overall control of entire area of Northern Iraq. Although the number of the troops in both cases was similar, in Northern Cyprus the troops were stationed throughout the whole of the occupied area and constantly patrolled through it, in addition to having check points on all main lines of communication between the northern and southern parts of the island.[219] Although the Turkish military operation in the *Issa* case was "temporary", between 19 March and 16 April 1995, the Court did not exclude the possibility that effective control over the area could be established as a result of such operation.[220] Thus, even if the State party's military forces exercise effective control over a foreign territory through a temporary operation, they are under an obligation to respect the right of Non-Refoulement to all persons within this territory.[221]

The Court's case-law indicates that the Convention may be applied extraterritorially, where a State party exercises full and exclusive control over a ship or aircraft registered in another State or buildings in a foreign territory.[222] In *Medvedyev and Others* v. *France* (2010), the ECtHR (GC) observed that, after the French Special Forces boarded the Cambodian ship, they were obliged to use their weapons to defend themselves. Subsequently, the French forces kept the

---

217   ECtHR, *Al-Skeini and Others* v. *the United Kingdom*, para. 139.

218   ECtHR, *Loizidou* v. *Turkey*, Appl.No. 15318/89, 18 December 1996.

219   ECtHR, *Issa and others* v. *Turkey*, para. 75.

220   Rozakis assumes that effective control means the capacity of a State to exercise power for a period of time allowing for the "effective" deployment of this power. In our opinion, the duration is not an essential element in determining the effectiveness of the control exercised by a State over a foreign territory. Although it could sometimes give some indications, the decisive element in determining the effectiveness of the control is the capacity of a State to exercise unhampered control over the foreign territory regardless to the duration of this control. See, Rozakis, C.L., The Territorial Scope of Human Rights Obligations: the Case of the European Convention on Human Rights, in: Commission, V., The Status of International Treaties on Human Rights, Strasbourg: Council of Europe, 2006, 55–73, p. 61.

221   See, Milanovic, M., 2011, pp. 136–141.

222   ECtHR, *Medvedyev and Others* v. *France* (GC), para. 67; ECtHR, *Al-Skeini and Others* v. *the United Kingdom*, para. 132 and 136.

crew members under their exclusive guard and confined them to their cabins during the journey to France where they were tried. The GC considered that France exercised full and exclusive control over the ship and its crew, at least *de facto*, from the time of its interception, in a continuous and uninterrupted manner until their trial. Therefore, the applicants were considered effectively within France's jurisdiction for the purposes of Article 1 ECHR.[223] The ECtHR has clearly not required the State's control over a foreign area to be lawful. Mere factual control is sufficient to consider that the State concerned has extraterritorial jurisdiction over that area.

After arresting the applicants in the Non-Refoulement case of *Al-Saadoon and Mufdhi* on 15 December 2003, they remained in one or another British detention facility until their transfer to the custody of the Iraqi authorities on 30 December 2008. The Court noticed that during the first months of their detention, the UK was an occupying power in Iraq and its detention facilities were established through exercising military force. The UK therefore exercised *de facto* control over the individuals detained in those facilities initially as a result of the use or threat of military force. Later, this *de facto* control over these premises became *de jure* control by providing for it in law.[224] Consequently, the Court stated that:

> ...given the total and exclusive *de facto*, and subsequently also *de jure*, control exercised by the United Kingdom authorities over the premises in question, the individuals detained there, including the applicants, were within the United Kingdom's jurisdiction.[225]

Noticeably, the Court has considered that a State party has jurisdiction where it exercises control, not over a territory or a wider geographical area, but over places and premises, such as embassies, military bases and detention places.[226] Since the Iraq occupation ended on 28 June 2004, when authority was transferred to the Iraqi Interim government and the Multi-national Forces – Iraq (MNF-I), which included British forces. The MNF-I remained there pursuant to requests by the Iraqi government and authorisations from the UN Security Council (UNSC),[227] it seems that the Court does not require the existence of occupation as such to consider the control practiced by a State party over a

---

223   ECtHR, *Medvedyev and Others* v. *France* (GC), paras. 66–67.

224   ECtHR, *Al-Saadoon and Mufdhi* v. *the United Kingdom* (admissibility decision), paras. 86–87.

225   Ibid., para. 88.

226   Milanovic, M., 2011, pp. 132–133 and 159.

227   ECtHR, *Al-Saadoon and Mufdhi* v. *the United Kingdom* (admissibility decision), para. 14.

foreign area to be effective. Thus, the extraterritorial exercise of jurisdiction of a State party includes cases in which a State, through effective control over a foreign area as a consequence of military occupation or through the consent, invitation or acquiescence of the government of that territory, exercises all or some of the public powers normally exercised by that government.[228] Effective control over a foreign area can be exercised by acceptance of the host State such as in the cases of military bases situated in the territories of other States.[229] This seems to appropriately characterize the situation of the multinational forces in Iraq after power was restored to the Interim Iraqi government, which requested in 2004 that multinational forces remain in Iraq.[230] Thus, as it was established in the case of *Al-Saadoon and Mufdhi,* a State party exercising effective control over such bases is under an obligation to protect the persons detained there against refoulement.

The Court has repeatedly asserted that a State party exercises extraterritorial jurisdiction in cases where it carries out activities on board craft and vessels registered in, or flying the flag of that State. In its conclusion, the Court has relied on customary international law and treaty provisions that recognise the State's extraterritorial jurisdiction in such situations.[231] This was the case in *Ocalan* v. *Turkey* (2005). Ocalan was arrested by the Turkish security forces inside an aircraft registered to Turkey.[232] This was also the case in *Hirsi Jamaa and Others* v. *Italy* (2012), which concerned the interception on the high seas, by Italian military ships, of three other vessels that carried a group of illegal migrants. The migrants were transferred onto the Italian ships and returned to Tripoli, Libya. Based on Article 3 ECHR, the applicants complained that they had been exposed to the risk of torture or inhuman or degrading treatment in Libya.[233] The Court observed that, under the international law of the sea, "a vessel sailing on the high seas is subject to the exclusive jurisdiction of the

---

228   ECtHR, *Bankovic et al* v. *Belgium and 16 other Contracting States* (admissibility decision), para. 71.

229   Gondek, M., Extraterritorial Application of the European Convention on Human Rights: Territorial Focus in the Age of Globalization?, Netherlands International Law Review, Vol. 52 no. 3: 2005, 349–387, p. 371.

230   UNSC, Resolution 1546, UN. Doc. S/RES/1546, 8 June 2004. Borelli, S., Casting Light on the Legal Black Hole: International Law and Detentions Abroad in the "War on Terror", International Review of the Red Cross, Vol. 87 no. 857: 2005, 39–68, p. 57.

231   ECtHR, *Bankovic et al* v. *Belgium and 16 other Contracting States* (admissibility decision), para. 73; ECtHR, *Medvedyev and Others* v. *France* (GC), para. 85; ECtHR, *Hirsi Jamaa and Others* v. *Italy* (GC), para. 75.

232   ECHR, *Ocalan* v. *Turkey* (GC), para. 91; ECtHR, *Al-Skeini and Others* v. *the United Kingdom*, para. 137.

233   ECtHR, *Hirsi Jamaa and Others* v. *Italy* (GC), paras. 9–14 and 83.

State of the flag it is flying". Based on this principle, the Court has considered the acts carried out on board vessels flying the State's flag as extraterritorial exercise of the State's jurisdiction, in the same way as registered aircraft.[234] The Court noted that the events were, in this case, carried out on the high seas, on board ships that flew the Italian flag, and whose crews were composed exclusively of Italian military personnel. The Court considered that, in the period between boarding the Italian ships and being delivered to the Libyan authorities, the applicants were under "the continuous and exclusive *de jure* and *de facto* control" of the Italian authorities.[235] The events that gave rise to the alleged violation fell within Italian jurisdiction, in the meaning of Article 1 ECHR.[236] The Court distinguished this case from *Medvedyev and Others* v. *France* (2010). In contrast to the *Hirsi Jamaa* case, the events in the *Medvedyev* case took place on board a vessel flying the flag of a third State, but its crew was under the control of French military personnel. Therefore, in the *Medvedyev* case, the Court examined the nature and scope of the actions carried out by the French forces in order to ascertain whether France exercised, at least *de facto*, full and exclusive control over the Cambodian ship and its crew in a continued and uninterrupted manner.[237]

The Court has made it clear that "effective control over a foreign territory" as a basis for extraterritorial jurisdiction does not replace the system provided for under Article 56 ECHR.[238] According to this Article, any State party at the time of its ratification, or at any time thereafter, may extend the application of the Convention to all or any of the territories for whose international relations it is responsible, by notification addressed to the Secretary General of the Council of Europe (Secretary-General of the CE).[239] The ECtHR stated that:

> The situations covered by the "effective control" principle are clearly separate and distinct from circumstances where a Contracting State has not, through a declaration under Article 56, extended the Convention or any of its Protocols to an overseas territory for whose international relations it is responsible.[240]

---

234   Ibid., para. 77.
235   Ibid., paras. 76 and 81.
236   Ibid., para. 82.
237   Ibid., para. 80.
238   ECtHR, *Al-Skeini and Others* v. *the United Kingdom*, para. 140.
239   ECHR50, Article 56. Dijk, P.v. & Hoof, G.J.H.v., 1998, pp. 7–8.
240   ECtHR, *Al-Skeini and Others* v. *the United Kingdom*, para. 140.

If a State party responsible for the international relations of a foreign territory does not make a declaration under Article 56 with regard to this territory, the State cannot be considered to have jurisdiction over it on the basis of exercising effective control.[241] And where a State makes the declaration, any person existing within such territory falls within its jurisdiction, in the meaning of Article 1 ECHR. Therefore, this State is obligated to secure the Convention rights and freedoms, including the right to be protected against refoulement, to all persons within this territory.

Finally, it should be noted here that the Court in the *Bankovic* case noted that:

> ...the Convention is a multi-lateral treaty operating [...] in an essentially regional context and notably in the legal space (*espace juridique*) of the Contracting States. [...] The Convention was not designed to be applied throughout the world, even in respect of the conduct of Contracting States.[242]

This provision could be interpreted as recognizing that exceptions to extraterritorial jurisdiction under the ECHR are applied only within the territories of the States parties to the Convention.[243] This interpretation can be criticized, because it is in conflict with the principle of the universality of human rights emphasised in the Preamble to the ECHR. Furthermore, later decisions of the ECtHR demonstrate that the Court does not believe that jurisdiction under Article 1 of the Convention never can exist outside the territory covered by the

---

241 In the refoulement case, *Yonghong v. Portugal* (1999), the applicant was Taiwanese national who was arrested in the territory of Macau when it was a Chinese territory under Portuguese administration. Based on Article 3 ECHR, he challenged his extradition to China. He argued that the Portugal's failure to make an Article 56 declaration with regard to Macau was not fatal to his claim since Portugal exercised extraterritorial jurisdiction under Article 1 in Macau. The ECtHR rejected this argument and asserted that the Convention cannot apply to acts of the State party in such territory unless a declaration was made under Article 56. ECtHR, *Yonghong v. Portugal*, Appl. No. 50887/99 Reports of Jud. & Dec. IX, 25 November 1999, p. 385.

242 ECtHR, *Bankovic et al v. Belgium and 16 other Contracting States* (admissibility decision), para. 80.

243 The UK House of Lords adopted this interpretation in the *Al Skeini* case with regard to the applicability of the ECHR in the area of Iraq controlled by the UK forces. House of Lords, Opinions of the Lords of Appeal Judgment in the Cause. Al Skeini and others v. Secretary of State for Defence, 2007 UKHL 26, 13 June 2007, paras. 71, 76–77, 91, 97, 109, 127.

CE Member States.[244] The Court's case-law has shown that the ECHR is applicable in territories outside the European legal space.[245]

III.3.2   CAT

III.3.2.1   *Jurisdiction Inside the State's Territory*

The CAT does not include a general jurisdiction provision or clause that determines the territorial scope of the Convention as whole. Instead, it contains several jurisdiction clauses in different Articles. Although Article 3 does not contain any jurisdiction clause to determine the territorial scope of the obligation of Non-Refoulement, Article 2(1) provides that:

> Each State Party shall take effective legislative, administrative, judicial or other measures to prevent acts of torture in any territory under its jurisdiction.[246]

According to the General Comment No. 2, the ComAT has held that the effective measures of prevention referred to in Article 2(1) include but are not limited to those measures contained in the subsequent Articles 3 to 16.[247] Thus, the jurisdiction clause provided for in Article 2(1) ("any territory under its jurisdiction") applies to the principle of Non-Refoulement contained in Article 3 CAT. Each State party to the CAT is therefore obliged to respect its obligation of Non-Refoulement within its territory, and any person inside this territory falls within the jurisdiction of the State concerned. The ComAT affirmed this in *Tebourski* v. *France* (2007) by stating "article 3 of the Convention offers absolute protection to anyone in the territory of a State party".[248] The protection against refoulement under Article 3 CAT is therefore afforded to any person inside the territory of the State party. The legal status of the person within the territory is irrelevant to the fact that he falls under the State's jurisdiction. A State party has jurisdiction over each person who is physically present inside its territory, regardless of the legality of his entrance or existence. The applicant in *Chahin*

---

244   ECtHR, *Al-Skeini and Others* v. *the United Kingdom*, para. 142.

245   The Court applied the Convention in Iraq, e.g. ECtHR, *Al-Saadoon and Mufdhi* v. *the United Kingdom* (admissibility decision); Kenya, e.g. ECHR, *Ocalan* v. *Turkey* (GC); Sudan ECtHR, *Ramirez Sanchez* v. *France*, Appl.No.59450/00, 4 July 2006; and in international water, e.g. ECtHR, *Hirsi Jamaa and Others* v. *Italy* (GC).

246   CAT84, Article 2(1).

247   ComAT, General Comment No. 2, paras. 16 and 19. See also Nowak, M., Obligations of States to Prevent and Prohibit Torture in an Extraterritorial Perspective, 2010, pp. 15–16.

248   ComAT, *Adel Tebourski* v. *France*, para. 8.3.

v. *Sweden* (2011) was considered within the State party's jurisdiction, despite the fact that he illegally resided in Sweden.[249] Although the applicant in *Elmi v. Australia* (1999) had arrived Australia without valid travel documents and his application for a protection visa was denied, he was considered within Australian jurisdiction.[250]

Although the CAT does not prohibit reservations to the Convention,[251] none of the States parties made any reservation on the applicability of Article 3 or the Convention to certain parts of its territory.[252] Such a reservation would be incompatible with the object and purpose of the CAT, which is the absolute prohibition of torture, and therefore it would be invalid under Article 19(c) VCLT.

III.3.2.2   *Jurisdiction Outside the State's Territory*

The jurisdiction clause in Article 2(1) CAT could be understood as imposing a territorial limitation on the applicability of Article 3 outside the State's territory. A State party does not exercise jurisdiction outside its national territory, even when it occupies a foreign territory, establishes military bases in another State, or on board the ships that fly its flag. Consequently, the State is not under an obligation to respect the principle of Non-Refoulement in such situations. The British government raised this argument during consideration of its fourth periodic report. The government maintained that those parts of the CAT that applied only in respect of territory under the jurisdiction of a State party could not apply in relation to the actions of its forces abroad.[253] By this argument, the British government excluded from its jurisdiction the refoulement acts committed by its forces working outside its own territory, such as in Iraq and Afghanistan. The ComAT expressed its concern at this position and observed that:

---

249   The applicant in this case returned to Sweden in 2003, despite a lifetime prohibition to re-enter the country after his deportation in 1997 for killing a man in Sweden. ComAT, *Chahin* v. *Sweden*, No. 310/2007, 30 May 2011, paras. 1.1–2.4.

250   ComAT, *Elmi* v. *Australia*, No. 120/1998, 14 May 1999, paras. 2.4 and 7.

251   VCLT69, Article 19. Although the CAT explicitly provides for the possibility to make reservations on Articles 20 and 30, it does not provide that these are the only reservations possible to be made on the Convention. CAT84, Articles 28.1 and 30.2.

252   See, Declarations and reservations on the CAT.

253   ComAT, Conclusions and recommendations on the fourth periodic report of the United Kingdom of Great Britain and Northern Ireland, UN. Doc. CAT/C/CR/33/3, 10 December 2004, para. 4(b).

...the Convention protections extend to all territories under the jurisdiction of a State party and considers that this principle includes all areas under the *de facto* effective control of the State party's authorities.[254]

The Committee's position was reaffirmed in its General Comment No. 2, when it noted that a State party's obligation to take effective measures under Article 2(1) CAT is not limited to its own territory but extends to "any territory under its jurisdiction". The Committee has recognised that:

> ..."any territory" includes all areas where the State Party exercises, directly or indirectly, in whole or in part, *de jure or de facto* effective control, in accordance with international law.[255]

Therefore, the ComAT asserted that the term "any territory" covers prohibited acts committed on a ship or aircraft registered by a State party, during military occupation or peacekeeping operations and in such places as embassies, military bases, detention facilities, or other areas over which a State party exercises "factual or effective control".[256] Consequently, the State party's obligations of Non-Refoulement under Article 3 CAT applies not only to its own territory (land and sea), but also to any other territories over which the civilian or military authorities of this State exercise jurisdiction through effective control, whether lawfully (such as aboard ships flying their flag, embassies and consulate or even secret prisons opened within the territory of another States with the consent of this State) or unlawfully (such as the case of military occupation of other State's territory).[257]

---

254 ComAT, Conclusions and recommendations on the fourth periodic report of the United Kingdom of Great Britain and Northern Ireland, para. 4(b). See, Milanovic, M., 2011, p. 127.

255 ComAT, General Comment No. 2, para. 16. ComAT, *Sonko* v. *Spain*, No. 368/2008, 25 November 2011, para. 10.5.

256 ComAT, General Comment No. 2, para. 16.

257 The position of the ComAT with regard to the extraterritorial applicability of the CAT, as international human rights treaty, to the situation of military occupation is in line with the approach has been followed by several international convention bodies and the International Court of Justice (ICJ). See, e.g., HRC, Report of the Human Rights Committee to the General Assembly/Fifty-third Session, UN. Doc. A/53/40, 15 September 1998, para. 306; HRC, Concluding observations on the report of Israel, Un.Doc. CCPR/CO/78/ISR, 21 August 2003, para. 11; ICJ, *Advisory opinion on the legal consequences of the construction of a wall in the occupied Palestinian territory*, 9 July 2004, paras. 109–111; ICJ, *Democratic Republic of the Congo v. Uganda*, 19 December 2005, para. 180.

The applicability of the prohibition of refoulement under Article 3 CAT, outside the national territory of the State, is supported by the text of the Article itself. The wording of this Article is mainly based on the text of Article 33 CSR, which prohibits "the expel or return ("refouler") of a refugee in any manner whatsoever...".[258] "Expel" literally means to "force (someone) to leave a place".[259] The word "return" means, "to bring, send, or put back to a former or proper place".[260] And the word "refouler" means, "to push back", "to turn back" and "to drive back".[261] The literal meanings of these words do not imply that the prohibited act must be carried out in a certain place. They have been interpreted as implying both territorial and extraterritorial application of the prohibition of refoulement, contained in Article 33 CSR. By analogy, based on the meaning of the same words, this interpretation must be applied to Article 3 CAT.[262]

In its second periodic report, the American government argued that Article 3 CAT does not apply to persons outside the US territory.[263] This position reflects the American goal that the detainees in the US detention centres, established outside its territory in the context of the so-called "war against terrorism", are exempt from its jurisdiction. These include the inmates of the detention facilities at Guantánamo Bay, as well as other persons who are under the control of US agents working all over the world, such as the victims of its extraordinary rendition program.[264] The ComAT found this position is regrettable, and asserted that:

> The State party should recognize and ensure that the provisions of the Convention expressed as applicable to "territory under the State party's jurisdiction" apply to, and are fully enjoyed by, all persons under the

---

258 CSR51, Article 33.

259 Oxford Dictionary, available at <http://oxforddictionaries.com>.

260 Merriam-Webster Online Dictionary, 2011, available at: <www.merriam-webster.com>.

261 Correard, M.H. & Grundy, V., The Concise Oxford-Hachette French Dictionary, Oxford: Oxford University Press, 4th Ed, 2007.

262 Wouters, K., International Legal Standards for the Protection from Refoulement, Leiden: Intersentia, 2009, pp. 50–51 and 436; UNHCR, Advisory Opinion on the Extraterritorial Application of Non-Refoulement Obligations under the 1951 Convention relating to the Status of Refugees and its 1967 Protocol, para. 27.

263 ComAT, Second periodic reports of the United States of America, UN. Doc. CAT/C/48/Add.3/Rev.1, 13 January 2006, para. 38. This position is in line with the US interpretation of human rights treaties to apply to persons living in the US territory, and not to any person with whom agents deal outside of its borders.

264 Nowak, M. & McArthur, E., 2008, p. 117.

effective control of its authorities, of whichever type, wherever located in the world.[265]

In this context, the ComAT called the British government to:

> ...publicly acknowledge that the Convention applies to all individuals who are subject to the State party's jurisdiction or control, including to its armed forces, military advisers and other public servants deployed on operations abroad.[266]

The ComAT has accepted that Article 3 CAT is applicable extraterritorially to persons under the effective control of the State's authorities acting on its behalf outside its national territory, whatever the type of those authorities. The State party's jurisdiction extends extraterritorially to cover all persons who are under the effective control of the State party's military forces, intelligence officers, diplomatic and consular agents, or any person or group of persons whose act is considered to be act of State under international law. It should be referred to Articles 8 and 9 of the ILC Articles on responsibility of States for internationally wrongful acts. According to these Articles, the conduct of a person or group of persons shall be considered as an act of State under international law if the person or group of persons is in fact acting on the instructions of, or under the direction or control of, that State in carrying out the conduct. This is also the case where the person or group of persons was in fact exercising elements of the governmental authority in the absence or default of the official authorities and in circumstances such as to call for the exercise of those elements of authority.[267] Therefore, the prohibition of refoulement under Article 3 CAT applies to the transfer of detainees from American detention centres abroad, such as in Iraq, Afghanistan, and secret prisons in Europe, as well as to persons subjected to extraordinary rendition. The Committee reasserted this position in its General Comment No. 2 by stating that:

---

265   ComAT, Concluding observations on the second periodic report of the United States of America, UN. Doc. CAT/C/USA/CO/2, 25 July 2006, para. 15. See also, United Nations Economic and Social Council, Report on the Situation of Detainees at Guantanamo Bay, UN. Doc. E/CN.4/2006/120, 27 February 2006, para. 11.

266   ComAT, Concluding observations on the fifth periodic report of the United Kingdom of Great Britain and Northern Ireland, UN. Doc. CAT/C/SR.1160 and 1161, 27 May 2013, para. 9.

267   UNGA, Resolution adopted by the General Assembly 56/83. Responsibility of States for internationally wrongful acts.

...the scope of "territory" under Article 2 must also include situations where a State Party exercises, directly or indirectly, *de facto or de jure* control over persons in detention.[268]

Where the authorities of a State party working abroad exercise effective control over a person, that person falls within its jurisdiction. However, the clause "persons in detention" in the General Comment may indicate that Article 3 applies only in case of physical custody or control over a person. Only persons within the physical control of State's agents working abroad are considered under the effective control of the State concerned and consequently within its extraterritorial jurisdiction. During the discussion of many periodic reports of several States parties who had military forces working abroad, the ComAT indicated that:

> With regard to the possible transfer of detainees within a State party's effective custody to the custody of any other State, the State party should ensure that it complies fully with article 3 of the Convention in all circumstances.[269]

In addition to cases in which persons are held in a detention centre or a prison abroad, physical control over a person can be exercised in other ways including halting or boarding a ship flying a foreign flag on the high seas or in foreign waters and controlling the persons on board. In the refoulement case of *J.H.A.* v. *Spain* (2007), the Committee observed that Spain maintained control over the rescued persons on board from the time the Spanish maritime rescued their vessel on the high seas, and throughout the identification and repatriation process.[270] The Court held that Spain was obligated to protect the rescued persons against refoulement, since they fell within its extraterritorial jurisdiction. Physical control over the applicants was the decisive element in determining that the State party exercised effective control over them. Limiting "effective control" over persons to cases where a State exercises physical control over persons excludes from the scope of extraterritorial jurisdiction of

---

268   ComAT, General Comment No. 2, para. 16. Milanovic, M., 2011, p. 179.

269   See, e.g., ComAT, Concluding observations on the fifth periodic report of Sweden, UN. Doc. CAT/C/SWE/CO/5, 4 June 2008, para. 14; ComAT, Conclusions and recommendations on the fifth periodic report of Denmark, Un. Doc. CAT/C/DNK/CO/5, 16 July 2007, para. 13; ComAT, Conclusions and recommendations on the fourth periodic report of the United Kingdom of Great Britain and Northern Ireland, para. 5(e).

270   ComAT, *J.H.A.* v. *Spain* (admissibility decision), No. 323/2007, 21 November 2008, para. 8.2.

a State party those cases where, although the State's authorities do not exercise physical control over a person abroad, their conduct directly affects a person's enjoyment of the right of Non-Refoulement protected in the CAT.

It is unclear why the ComAT used the misleading expression "persons in detention" in a General Comment on implementing Article 2 by States parties.[271] During consideration of several periodic reports the Committee has used broader expressions. In its concluding observations on the US second periodic report, the Committee used the expression "all persons under the effective control of its authorities".[272] Furthermore, during its discussion of the fifth periodic reports of both Denmark and Sweden, the ComAT stated that the obligation of Non-Refoulement under Article 3 CAT applies to a State party's military forces, wherever situated, where they exercise effective control, *de jure* or *de facto*, over an individual.[273] Therefore, it can be understood that even if a State's authorities do not exercise physical control over the person concerned, Article 3 CAT can apply extraterritorially when the conduct of the State's authorities, as a direct and foreseeable result, forces a person to go to another State where he is at risk of torture.

III.4   *Conclusion*

Neither the ECHR nor the CAT has imposed any limitation on the personal scope of the principle of Non-Refoulement as contained in Article 3 of each Convention. Every person, foreigner or national, within the State's jurisdiction has a right to be protected against refoulement. Both the ComAT and the ECtHR have considered it axiomatic that a State party has jurisdiction over its own territory. Consequently, States parties to both Conventions must respect their obligations under the principle of Non-Refoulement over the whole of their own territories. It is not possible for a State to exclude from its jurisdiction any part of its territory for the purpose of applying the principle of Non-Refoulement.

---

271   The Committee's position may be, to some extent, affected by the definition of torture under Article 1 CAT, which is interpreted to include an implied condition according to which the Convention is applied preliminary in a situation in which the victim has been deprived of his liberty or at least subjected to the factual control or power of the torturer. Burgers, H. & Danelius, H., 1988, pp. 120–121; Ingelse, C., The UN Committee Against Torture, An Assessment, The Hague: Kluwer Law International, 2001, p. 211.

272   ComAT, Concluding observations on the second periodic report of the United States of America, para. 15.

273   ComAT, Conclusions and recommendations on the fifth periodic report of Denmark, para. 13; ComAT, Concluding observations on the fifth periodic report of Sweden, para. 14.

Protection against refoulement is therefore afforded to every person physically present within the national territory of the State, regardless of his legal status within this territory.

This section demonstrated that jurisdiction has a wider scope than the State's national territory. It is well settled in the case-law of both the ECtHR and the ComAT that a State can exercise jurisdiction extraterritorially. Such extraterritorial jurisdiction arises either through exercise of effective control over a foreign territory, or over a person existing outside the State's own territory. Consequently, a State is under an obligation to respect the principle of Non-Refoulement in any territory over which it exercises effective control, whether lawfully (such as aboard ships flying its flag, embassies and consulate, military bases or detention facilities established by the consent of the host State) or unlawfully (such as the case of military occupation of other State's territory).

Where the State's authorities and those acting on its behalf exercise control or authority over a person in a territory of another State, this person falls within the extraterritorial jurisdiction of the State party concerned. Neither the ECtHR nor the ComAT has made any distinction between authorities or agents who lawfully or unlawfully operate on the foreign soil. Neither the Court nor the Committee has distinguished between diplomatic and consular officers, border officials in customs-free zones, international peace-keeping or peace-enforcement troops, or other State's agents who work lawfully in the foreign State, or those who maybe work there unlawfully, such as security agents who kidnap a person abroad, or military forces that illegally occupy foreign territory. The decisive element in this regard is whether those victims are under the State agent's effective control.

The Court and the Committee has clearly accepted that factual control exercised by the State's agents or authorities over a person is sufficient to find that he is subject to the extraterritorial jurisdiction of the State concerned. A person is considered within the jurisdiction of the State from the first moment he is subjected to its agents' physical control, regardless of where such control is practiced (in a formal detention centre, on board a ship flying a foreign flag, in the course of military operations in-field or in any other place). Even if such physical control or custody is exercised with the consent of the territorial State, the person is considered to be within the extraterritorial jurisdiction of the State party, and the State party can be considered responsible for violating his right of protection against refoulement. Moreover, a State's extraterritorial jurisdiction over a person in a foreign territory can be engaged, even in the absence of physical control, by virtue of a causal link between the conduct of its authorities or agents and the fact that a person is forced to go to another State contrary to the prohibition of refoulement. In other words, where the conduct of the State's agents or authorities directly and immediately forces a person to go to another State where he faces the proscribed ill-treatment, the person concerned is considered within the extraterritorial jurisdiction of the State party and it is deemed under an obligation to protect him against refoulement.

CHAPTER 2

The Content of the Principle of Non-Refoulement

I The Treatment from Which the Person is Protected

The principle of Non-Refoulement is intended to protect individuals from being subjected to certain forms of treatment in a receiving State. This section defines the forms of treatment from which a person is protected. While the principle of Non-Refoulement under Article 3 CAT applies only to torture,[1] Article 3 ECHR prohibits removal to torture and other CIDTP.[2] Protection against refoulement under Article 3 CAT is, in principle, narrower than the protection implied in Article 3 ECHR, since the CAT does not protect a person from removal to a State where there is a risk of CIDTP.[3] The treatment from which the person is protected under Article 3 CAT and Article 3 ECHR are separately addressed in the following subsections.

I.1 *CAT*

Although the CAT itself does not expressly make the link between Articles 1 and 3 of this Convention, the ComAT has continuously asserted that Article 3 will be read in relation to the definition of torture under Article 1 CAT.[4] According to Article 1 CAT the term "torture" in this Convention means:

---

1 Contrary to the obligations of Articles 10, 11, 12 and 13 CAT; Article 16 relating to prohibition against CIDTP does not include any indication to the States' obligation under Article 3 CAT. Burgers, H. & Danelius, H., 1988, pp. 70–71 and 74.

2 E.g., ECtHR, *Soering v. the United Kingdom*, para. 91; ECtHR, *Venkadjalasarma v. The Netherlands*, Appl.No. 58510/00, 17 February 2004, para. 61.

3 Weissbrodt, D. & Hortreiter, I., The Principle of Non-Refoulement: Article 3 of the Convention against Torture and Other Cruel, Inhuman or Degrading Treatment or Punishment in Comparison with the Non-Refoulement Provisions of other International Human Rights Treaties, Buffalo Human Rights Law Review, Vol. 5 no. 1: 1999, 1–74, p. 50; Duffy, A., Expulsion to Face Torture? Non-Refoulement in International Law, International Journal of Refugee Law, Vol. 20 no. 3: 2008, 373–390, p. 379.

4 The ComAT's General Comment No. 1 provides that: "Article 3 is confined in its application to cases where there are substantial grounds for believing that the author would be in danger of being subjected to torture as defined in article 1 of the Convention", ComAT, General Comment No. 1, UN. Doc. A/53/44, Annex IX, On the Implementation of Article 3 of the Convention in the Context of Article 22, 21 November 1997, para. 1. ComAT, *G.R.B. v. Sweden*, No. 83/1997, 15 May 1998, para. 6.5; ComAT, *H.M.H.I. v. Australia*, No. 177/2001, 1 May 2002, para. 6.4.

...any act by which severe pain or suffering, whether physical or mental, is intentionally inflicted on a person for such purposes as obtaining from him or third person information or a confession, punishing him for an act he or a third person has committed or is suspected of having committed, or intimidating or concerning him or a third person, or for any reason based on discrimination of any kind, when such pain or suffering is inflicted by or at the instigation of or with the consent or acquiescence of a public official or other person acting in an official capacity. It does not include pain or suffering arising only from, inherent in or incidental to lawful sanctions.[5]

This was the first definition of torture provided for in a convention.[6] Its wording was derived specifically from the UN Declaration against Torture (1975) and, at the same time, it is inspired by EComHR's case-law.[7] This definition binds States parties to the CAT. Because it is considered to represent customary international law, it binds even States that are not parties to the CAT.[8] The detailed definition of torture under Article 1 appears to restrict the ComAT's freedom to interpret the act from which a person is protected under Article 3 CAT. In almost all refoulement cases, the Committee has tried to avoid these restrictions, mentioning only that a complainant's removal in the circumstances of the case under consideration would be a violation of Article 3 CAT. The Committee has not carried out an extensive investigation to determine if all elements of the definition of torture are met, probably because it is difficult to determine how a person would be treated in the receiving State. The elements of this definition are discussed in the following subsections, with

---

5   CAT84, Article. 1(1). It was observed that this definition should be understood as "a description of torture for the purpose of understanding and implementation of the convention rather than a legal definition for direct application in criminal law and criminal procedure". Thus, Article 1 can be interpreted in a manner that broadens its scope. Burgers, H. & Danelius, H., 1988, p. 122.

6   Although many earlier international and regional instruments provided for a clear prohibition of torture, such as Article 5 UDHR48, Article 3 ECHR50, Article 7 ICCPR66, and Article 1 Inter-American Convention to Prevent and Punish Torture 1985, none of these instruments include any definition of torture. Burgers, H. & Danelius, H., 1988, p. 114.

7   This definition was based preliminary on the Opinion of the EComHR of 5 November 1969 in the *Greek* Case, its opinion of 25 January 1976 in *Ireland* v. *the UK* and the judgment of the ECtHR of 18 January 1978 in *Ireland* v. *the UK* (1978). Ibid., pp. 114–115.

8   According to the ICTFY, " there is now general acceptance of the main elements contained in the definition set out in article 1 of the Torture Convention". ICTFY, *prosecutor* v. *Furundzija*, case No. IT- 95- 17/1- T, 10 December 1998, paras. 160–161.

special focus on the way they are interpreted in the context of the principle of Non-Refoulement.

1.1.1   Act or Omission

According to Article 1(1) CAT, "torture" refers to "any act" by which severe pain or suffering is intentionally inflicted on a person. The argument that the definition of torture under Article 1 refers to acts, rather than omissions, and that certain omissions should be assimilated to an act (such as in the intentional failure to provide a prisoner with food or drink)[9] has been rejected on the ground excluding omissions from the scope of Article 1 would deviate from the object and purpose of the CAT: to regulate and prohibit all governmental conduct that inflicts severe pain or suffering, for the purposes stated in Article 1, whether the conduct is a positive act or an omission.[10] The decisive element in determining if such conduct constitutes torture is its purpose and effect. Since negative acts may inflict as much pain as positive acts, and achieve the same goals, excluding omissions from the scope of Article 1 is only a ploy on the part of States that wish to evade the provisions of the Convention.[11] Thus, omissions and positive acts may constitute torture as defined under Article 1 CAT.

The Committee refused to apply Article 3 when there was a risk that the complainant's state of health would deteriorate following removal.[12]

1.1.2   Infliction of Severe Pain or Suffering Physical or Mental

In order to qualify a conduct as "torture" within the meaning of Article 1 CAT, the said conduct must inflict pain or suffering of a certain level of severity. The minimum level of severity cannot be inferred from the *travaux préparatoires* of the CAT.[13] However, the way the provision of Article 1 is formulated suggests that only the victim can bear witness to the pain of torture and ascertain its intensity. Reliance solely on objective criterion that designates conduct as torture disregards the essential subjectivity of pain and suffering. The victim's

---

9   Burgers, H. & Danelius, H., 1988, p. 118.

10 Ingelse, C., 2001, p. 208; Miller, D.J., Holding States to their Convention Obligations: the United Nations Convention against Torture and the Need for Broad Interpretation of State Action, Georgetown Immigration Law Journal, no. 17: 2003, 299–323, p. 304.

11 Boulesbaa, A., The U.N. Convention on Torture and the Prospects for Enforcement, The Hague: Martinus Nijhoff Publishers, 1999, pp. 14–15.

12 ComAT, *G.R.B.* v. *Sweden*, para. 6.7; ComAT, *B.S.S.* v. *Canada*, No. 183/2001, 12 May 2004, para. 10.2.

13 Boulesbaa, A., Analysis and Proposals for the Rectification of the Ambiguities Inherent in Article 1 of the U.N. Convention on Torture, Florida International Law Journal, Vol. 5 no. 3: 1990, 293–326, p. 308.

experience should be taken into consideration when the determination is made. This is why the test of severity of pain under the CAT is subjective and depends on the circumstances of each case.[14]

Since protection against refoulement under Article 3 CAT applies only to torture, a distinction must be made between torture on the one hand, and other CIDTP on the other. Even though these terms are usually ordered hierarchically, based on the severity of the pain that results from the conduct, it is not easy to set clear boundaries between them. In the *Greek* case (1969), which was one of the main sources of inspiration for Article 1 CAT, the EComHR stated that:

> ...it is plain that there may be treatment to which all these descriptions apply, for all torture must be inhuman and degrading treatment, and inhuman treatment also degrading. The notion of inhuman treatment covers at least such treatment as deliberately causes severe suffering, mental or physical, which in particular situation is unjustifiable. The word "torture" is often used to describe inhuman treatment, which has purpose, such as the obtaining of information or confessions, or the infliction of punishment, and it is generally an aggravated form of inhuman treatment.[15]

Cruel and inhuman treatment, including torture, requires that severe pain or suffering be inflicted. The intensity of this pain or suffering is what distinguishes cruel and inhuman treatment and torture from merely degrading treatment.[16] The determination that a certain act of cruel or inhuman treatment amounts to torture depends on fulfilment of other elements of the definition of torture under Article 1 CAT, particularly the existence of intent, specific purpose, and the victim's helplessness.[17]

The CAT has not distinguished between physical or mental suffering and pain that results from the act. Pain does not need to be equivalent to that inflicted by serious physical injury (such as organ failure or impairment of

---

14   Ingelse, C., 2001, p. 209; Boulesbaa, A., 1999, p. 18.
15   Report the Commission of 5 November 1969, *The Greek Case*, Yearbook XXI, 1969, p. 186. Parry, J., Understanding Torture: Law, Violence, and Political Identity, Ann Arbor: The University of Michigan Press, 2010, pp. 47–49.
16   Report of the Special Rapporteur on torture and other cruel, inhuman or degrading treatment or punishment, M. Nowak, UN. Doc. A/HRC/13/39/Add.5, 5 February 2010, paras. 32 and 36.
17   Nowak, M. & McArthur, E., 2008, pp. 68–69; Lambert, H., Protection against Refoulement from Europe, Human Rights Law Comes to the Rescue, International and Comparative Quarterly, Vol. 48 no. 3: 1999, 515–544, p. 533.

bodily functions or even death) in order to be deemed "severe".[18] Pain or suffering can be solely mental, in absence of physical abuse.[19] In his 1986 report, the Special Rapporteur on Torture provided a detailed, albeit not exhaustive list of acts that inflict pain or suffering severe enough to constitute torture. Acts of physical torture includes beating, burns, electric shocks, suspension, exposure to excessive light or noise, sexual aggression, prolonged denial of rest or sleep, prolonged denial of food, and prolonged denial of medical assistance. Mental tortures includes total isolation and sensory deprivation, being kept in constant uncertainty in terms of space and time, threats to torture or kill relatives, total abandonment, and simulated executions.[20]

1.1.3 Intention and Purpose of the Act

To qualify a conduct as torture under Article 1 CAT, the infliction of severe pain or suffering must be intentional. Thus, torture as defined by the CAT does not include unintentional neglect or accidental infliction of severe pain or suffering.[21] The intention required here is general: the perpetrator must know that a certain conduct will cause severe pain or suffering, regardless of whether he intends this end or not.[22] The general intention may be established from the

---

18   Report of the Special Rapporteur on torture and other cruel, inhuman or degrading treatment or punishment, M. Nowak, UN. Doc. A/HRC/13/39/Add.5, para. 32.

19   Miller, D.J., 2003, p. 320. During the ratification of the CAT, the US expressed its "understanding" that mental pain or suffering refers to prolonged mental harm. In its concluding observations on the periodic report of the US, the ComAT stated that, "[the] State party should ensure that acts of psychological torture, prohibited by the Convention, are not limited to "prolonged mental harm" as set out in the State party's understandings lodged at the time of ratification of the Convention, but constitute a wider category of acts, which cause severe mental suffering, irrespective of their prolongation or its duration". ComAT, Concluding observations on the second periodic report of the United States of America, para. 13.

20   Report of the Special Rapporteur on torture and other cruel, inhuman or degrading treatment or punishment, P. Kooijmans, UN. Doc. E/CN.4/1986/15, 16 February 1986, para. 119.

21   Nowak, M., What Practices Constitute Torture?: US and UN Standards, Human Rights Quarterly, Vol. 28 no. 4: 2006, 809–841, p. 830. The infliction of severe pain or suffering resulting of unintentional neglect would give rise to an issue under Article 16 CAT, as a cruel, inhuman treatment. Ingelse, C., 2001, p. 209.

22   Wouters, K., 2009, p. 441. The US ratified the CAT with the "understanding" that "in order to constitute torture, an act must be specifically intended to inflict severe physical or mental pain or suffering". The US' reservations, declarations and understandings to the CAT, para. II.1.a. According to the US Defence Department, what is meant by the "specific intent" that the infliction of severe pain must be the defendant's precise objective. Thus, even if the defendant knows that severe pain will result from his action, but causing such

nature of the conduct.[23] For example, a State that failed to provide food and water to prisoners cannot escape responsibility by claiming that its neglect was unintentional. The State's responsibility depends on whether this omission is simple or gross neglect, according to a reasonable standard, based on the circumstances of each case.[24] Moreover, conduct that results in pain or suffering does not have to be systematic to qualify as torture; even an isolated act can constitute torture.[25]

Under Article 1 CAT, it is insufficient to qualify as torture a conduct that causes severe pain or suffering; the conduct must also have a particular goal. The purposes enumerated in Article 1 are as follows: extracting a confession; obtaining information from the victim or a third person; punishment; intimidating or coercing; and, discrimination.[26] The purposive element required in Article 1 CAT is the most decisive criterion in distinguishing torture from cruel or inhuman treatment,[27] so ill-treatment not inflicted for any of these purposes may still amount to cruel or inhuman treatment as prohibited under Article 16.[28] The words "such… as" in the text of Article 1 imply that this list is not an exhaustive, but only indicative.[29] It does not imply that any intentional

---

pain is not his object, his act is not considered torture under US law, although he did not act in good faith. Working Group Report on Detainee Interrogations in the Global War on Terrorism; Assessment of Legal, Historical, Policy, and Operational Considerations, Final Report, 4 April 2003, para. 3.1.1.1.a. For further discussion and criticism on this report see, Cassese, A., Are International Human Rights Treaties and Customary Rules on Torture Binding upon US Troops in Iraq?, Journal of International Criminal Justice, Vol. 2: 2004, 872–878. The ComAT recommended the American government to "enact a federal crime of torture in terms consistent with article 1 of the Convention and withdraw its reservations, interpretations and understandings relating to the Convention". The Committee implicitly held that the US' understanding is incompatible with the object and purpose of the CAT. Report of the ComAT, UN. Doc. A/55/44, 2 January 2000, the conclusions and recommendations of the Committee on the initial report of the United States of America, para. 180 (a).

23 ICTFY, *Prosecutor v. Kunarac, Kovac and Vukovic*, IT- 96–23 & IT- 96- 23/I- A, 12 June 2002, para. 153.
24 Boulesbaa, A., 1999, p. 20.
25 Burgers, H. & Danelius, H., 1988, p. 118.
26 Nowak, M., 2006 p. 831.
27 Report the Commission of 5 November 1969, *The Greek Case*, p. 186. See also Report of the Special Rapporteur on torture and other cruel, inhuman or degrading treatment or punishment, M. Nowak, UN. Doc. A/HRC/13/39/Add.5, para. 36.
28 Wendland, L., A Handbook on State Obligations under the UN Convention against Torture, Geneva: Association for the Prevention of Torture, 2002, p. 28.
29 Burgers, H. & Danelius, H., 1988, p. 118; Boulesbaa, A., 1999, p. 22.

act that causes severe pain or suffering constitutes torture. The words "such... as" imply that other purposes must be comparable with the purposes express- ly listed. The common element these purposes share is their connection with the interests or policies of a State and its bodies. The primary object of the CAT is to eliminate torture committed by or under the responsibility of public officials for purposes connected with their public functions.[30]

1.1.4   Identity of the Perpetrator of the Act

Article 1 CAT indicates that acts of torture must be "inflicted by or at the in- stigation of or with the consent or acquiescence of a public official or other person acting in an official capacity".[31] Thus, the definition of torture under the CAT includes only acts of torture for which the authorities could somehow be held responsible. According to the *travaux préparatoires* of the CAT, if pri- vate actors, without any involvement of State authorities, carry out torture, it is assumed and expected that the normal machinery of justice will address such a criminal act under the domestic legal system. The normal machinery of inves- tigation and prosecution might not operate normally when State authorities are involved in torture, and this is the problem that the CAT was intended to deal with.[32] Under the CAT, a State is considered responsible for acts of torture committed by its public officials, or persons acting in an official capacity. Once it is proved that the perpetrator of the act of torture was a public official, it is not acceptable for the higher officials to defend themselves with the claim that they do not approve nor have any knowledge of torture.[33]

The Committee has accepted that acts committed by non-State actors could, in certain circumstances, be considered comparable to a State's acts, for the purpose of defining torture under Article 1 CAT. In *Elmi* v. *Australia* (1999), the complainant was a Somali national who was under threat of being returned to Somalia, where he allegedly ran the risk of torture by the Hawiye clan, a powerful armed clan that controlled some parts of Somalia after the breakdown of the central government. The counsel referred to the ECtHR's judgment in *Ahmed* v. *Austria* (1996) in which the Court had found that de- portation to Somalia would breach Article 3 ECHR because it would expose

---

30   Burgers, H. & Danelius, H., 1988, pp. 118–119. It is not necessary for the purpose to be illegitimate. On the contrary, several purposes of the list, such as obtaining information or a confession, may be totally legitimate on condition that legitimate methods are used to achieve them. Ibid., p. 118.

31   CAT84, Article 1.

32   Burgers, H. & Danelius, H., 1988, p. 120.

33   Ingelse, C., 2001, p. 210; Miller, D.J., 2003, p. 305.

the applicant to ill-treatment by fighting clans. Without making an explicit reference to the ECtHR's judgment in the *Ahmed* case, the ComAT implicitly borrowed the Court's approach by refusing the respondent State's view that the acts of torture the complainant feared he would be subjected to in Somalia would not fall within the definition of torture as a perpetrator of the act was a non-State actor. The ComAT noted that Article 1 covers the acts of torture to which the complainant feared to be subjected in Somalia. The Committee added that:

> ...for a number of years Somalia has been without a central government, that the international community negotiates with the warring factions and that some of the factions operating in Mogadishu have set up qua-si-governmental institutions and are negotiating the establishment of a common administration. It follows then that, de facto, those factions exercise certain prerogatives that are comparable to those normally exercised by legitimate governments. Accordingly, the members of those factions can fall, for the purposes of the application of the Convention, within the phrase "public officials or other persons acting in an official capacity" contained in article 1.[34]

Accordingly, the Committee has refused to apply Article 3 where the risk of ill-treatment to the complainant in the receiving State might be inflicted by a non-governmental entity, "unless the non-governmental entity occupies and exercises quasi-governmental authority over the territory to which the complainant would be returned".[35] The essential element in determining if the acts of non-State actors fall within the scope of the CAT is whether or not those actors become a *de facto* government, in control of the territory to which the individual would be returned.[36]

Those who drafted the CAT intended that the clause "the consent or acquiescence of a public official" in Article 1 CAT be widely interpreted. When a public official commits the act of torture, the government is presumed to

34 ComAT, *Elmi v. Australia*, para. 6.5. In a subsequent case of *H.M.H.I.* v. *Australia* (2002), which also concerned removal to Somali, the ComAT dealt with very similar facts to those of the *Elmi* case. In contrast to its decision in the *Elmi* case, the ComAT referred that the circumstances in the *Elmi* case were exceptional as the State's authority was totally lacking and the non-governmental groups were exercising quasi-government authority. ComAT, *H.M.H.I.* v. *Australia*, para. 6.4.

35 ComAT, *S.S.* v. *The Netherlands*, No. 191/2001, 5 May 2003, para. 6.4; ComAT, *L.J.R.C.* v. *Sweden* (admissibility decision), No. 218/2002, 23 November 2004, para. 5.2.

36 Miller, D.J., 2003, p. 305.

acquiesce, unless the State can demonstrate that it has a policy against torture, has taken measures to counter torture, and has punished the official who committed torture. Since a State has a positive obligation to prevent torture within its own territory, a State is considered to "acquiesce" in torture inflicted by non-State actors when it is reported to the State's authorities, but they do not intervene to prevent it or to punish the torturers.[37] Thus, the involvement of State authorities can take different forms. It typically occurs directly through the conduct of torture by policemen, investigators or other public officials. The involvement of State authorities can also be indirect, as when authorities hire a torturer to help gather information, or even just accept or tolerate his actions.[38] The State's responsibility under the CAT is engaged for acts of torture that are committed with the explicit or implicit agreement of State officials, or where at least an official acting in the name of the State was able to intervene to prevent or to stop the acts of torture but he did not.[39]

It is well established in the ComAT's case-law that:

> ...the issue whether the State party has an obligation to refrain from expelling a person who might risk pain or suffering inflicted by a non-governmental entity, without the consent or acquiescence of the Government, falls outside the scope of article 3 of the Convention.[40]

---

37   Where the government is aware that non-State actors practice torture, but it is unable or unwilling to intervene to stop those activities, arguably the government has breached its responsibility to protect its nationals from torture. Rosati, K., The United Nations Convention against Torture: A self-Executing Treaty that Prevents the Removal of Persons Ineligible for Asylum and Withholding of Removal, Denver Journal of International Law and Policy, Vol. 26 no. 4: 1998, 533–590, p. 539; Miller, D.J., 2003, pp. 304 and 306. According to the US' understandings "the term 'acquiescence' requires that the public official, prior to the activity constituting torture, have awareness of such activity and thereafter breach his legal responsibility to intervene to prevent such activity". The US' courts went further by applying a restrictive interpretation requires to consider a State acquiesced in acts of torture by non-State actors not only "awareness" but "willful acceptance" of the activity of those actors. The protection of the CAT does not cover cases where a State is unwilling or unable to protect an individual against torture by non-State actors. This approach contradicts with the object and purpose of the CAT to absolutely prohibit torture. See, Vining, J.A., Providing Protection from Torture by "Unofficial" Actros, Brooklyn Law Review, Vol. 70 no. 1: 2004, 331–360.

38   Burgers, H. & Danelius, H., 1988, p. 120.

39   Report of the Special Rapporteur on torture and other cruel, inhuman or degrading treatment or punishment, M. Nowak, UN. Doc. A/HRC/13/39/Add.5, para. 39.

40   ComAT, *G.R.B.* v. *Sweden*, para. 6.5; ComAT, *M.P.S.* v. *Australia*, No. 138/1999, 30 April 2002, para. 7.4; ComAT, *A.A.R.* v. *Denmark*, No. 412/2010, 13 November 2012, para. 7.10.

In its General Comment No. 2 on Article 2 the Committee noted that:

> ...the failure of the State to exercise due diligence to intervene to stop, sanction and provide remedies to victims of torture facilitates and enables non-State actors to commit acts impermissible under the Convention with impunity, the State's indifference or inaction provides a form of encouragement and/or de facto permission.[41]

Hence, a State is not considered to acquiesce in torture inflicted by non-State actors when it exercises due diligence to intervene to stop this torture and punish the perpetrators. In such situation, the Committee seems to consider that a State fulfils its positive obligation to prevent acts of torture within its territory. The Committee referred to this paragraph of its General Comment No. 2 in *Njamba and Balikosa* v. *Sweden* (2010), which concerned the expulsion of a mother and her daughter to the Democratic Republic of the Congo (DRC), the country of their nationality. The complainants claimed that they would be victims of a violation of Article 3 if they were deported to their home country, where they faced a risk of being tortured.[42] The Committee found that the security of the complainants would be endangered upon return. It based this conclusion mainly on recent UN reports that indicated alarming levels of sexual violence against women, committed by armed men and civilians throughout the country and not only in areas of armed conflict.[43] The ComAT found that the conflict situation in the DRC made it impossible for the Committee to identify certain areas of the country which would be safe for the applicants in their current and evolving situation.[44] The main factor in the Committee's conclusion seems to be that there was no area in the country which would be safe for the complainants. The Committee did not examine whether or not the receiving State exercised due diligence to intervene to stop the sexual violence against women. The Committee may thus tend to interpret the positive obligations very broadly, rather as obligation of result instead of obligation of means, to avoid protection gaps when the risk stems from non-State actors.

In summary, a State party to the CAT is obligated, under Article 3 of this Convention, to refrain from expelling a person at risk of pain or suffering under

---

This approach was reasserted by the first General Comment of the Committee. ComAT, General Comment No. 1, para. 3.

41   ComAT, General Comment No. 2, para. 18.

42   ComAT, *Njamba and Balikosa* v. *Sweden*, No. 322/2007, 14 May 2010, para. 3.1.

43   Ibid., footnote. 12 and para. 9.5.

44   Ibid., para. 9.5.

the following three circumstances: when pain and suffering would be inflicted by a public officer; by a non-governmental entity that occupies and exercises quasi-governmental authority over the territory to which the complainant would be returned; or by a non-State actor in instances in which the receiving State fails to exercise due diligence to intervene to stop, sanction and provide remedies to the victims.

I.1.5   Lawful Sanctions

The last clause of Article 1(1) CAT provides for an important exception to the definition of torture in the scope of this Convention. Under this exception, the definition of torture "does not include pain or suffering arising only from, inherent in or incidental to lawful sanctions".[45] This clause was the most controversial element of the definition of torture when Article 1 was drafted,[46] and it is still a matter of debate today, since it might allow for a restrictive interpretation of the definition of torture. The Convention's purpose was to strengthen the already existing prohibition against torture in international law, and not to reform national systems of penal sanctions in the various States parties; otherwise, many States, particularly Islamic States, might have refused to be party to the CAT.[47]

Article 1 of each of the original Swedish draft for the Convention and the 1975 UN Declaration on the Protection of All persons from Being Subjected to Torture limited this exception to "the extent consistent with the Standard Minimum Rules for the Treatment of Prisoners".[48] This reference is omitted in the CAT. The objection was based primarily on the fact that the Convention as a binding instrument, could not refer in a definitional Article to non-legally binding Rules.[49] Moreover, there was no binding international instrument that

---

45   CAT84, Article 1(1).

46   Burgers, H. & Danelius, H., 1988, p. 121; Nowak, M. & McArthur, E., 2008, pp. 44–49.

47   Burgers, H. & Danelius, H., 1988, pp. 46–47, 103 and 121.

48   Ibid., pp. 41 and 121; Boulesbaa, A., 1999, p. 5. Article 31 of the Standard Minimum Rules for the Treatment of the Prisoners states that: "Corporal punishment, punishment by placing in a dark cell, and all cruel, inhuman or degrading punishments shall be completely prohibited as punishments for disciplinary offences". Standard Minimum Rules for the Treatment of Prisoners, adopted by the First United Nations Congress on the Prevention of Crime and the Treatment of Offenders, in 30 August 1955, and approved by the Economic and Social Council by its resolutions 663 C (XXIV) of 31 July 1957 and 2076 (LXII) of 13 May 1977.

49   Nowak, M. & McArthur, E., 2008, pp. 45–46. It was argued that, "the fact that the Standard Minimum Rules have no binding effect does not mean that they could not operate in binding manner through the Convention". Ingelse, C., 2001, p. 212.

strictly determined which penal sanctions are so severe as to be contrary to international law. The drafters of the CAT could not reach agreement on a reference to accepted international standards. The adopted text thus excludes pain and suffering that results from "lawful sanctions" and does not indicate the law (national, international or both) under which the legality of punishment is determined.[50]

While the Convention was drafted, some States sought to exclude the possibility that imposing existing punishments under national law would conflict with international law. In particular, several Islamic States sought assurances that the death penalty and certain forms of punishments based on Shari'a law were compatible with the Convention. They argued that the *travaux préparatoires* of the Convention indicated that assessment of the legality of the sanction depends on the national law.[51] But defining the legality of a sanction by relying only on national law is problematic. What is lawful in one legal system may be unlawful in another, and this approach could pave the way for the justification of the very torture that the Convention is intended to prohibit.[52] Such an exception would be open to misuse by States, since they could pass national laws to allow certain punishments that are normally regarded as torture. Relying only on national law to define the legality of a punishment would narrow the scope of the Convention and defeat its object and purpose in prohibiting torture.[53] This approach is contrary to the general rules of interpretation contained in Article 31 VCLT, which requires that a convention be interpreted "in good faith [...] and in the light of its object and purpose",[54] and with Article 27 VCLT, which prevents States parties to a treaty from invoking their national law to justify a breach of their international obligations under the treaty.[55]

Many arguments support the view that lawful refers to both national and international law. Article 1(2) CAT notes that Article 1 does not affect any international instrument or national legislation that contain provisions with

---

50   Burgers, H. & Danelius, H., 1988, pp. 46–47 and 121.

51   Ibid., p.121.

52   E.g., the amputation of the thief's hand is lawful in some Arab States that follow the Islamic Shari'a Law, but it is not lawful in others and the rest of the World. Boulesbaa, A., 1999, p. 31.

53   Burgers, H. & Danelius, H., 1988, p. 121. When ratifying the CAT, the US declared the understanding that, " 'sanctions' includes judicially-imposed sanctions and other enforcement actions authorized by United States law or by judicial interpretation of such law. Nonetheless, the United States understands that a State Party could not through its domestic sanctions defeat the object and purpose of the Convention to prohibit torture".

54   VCLT69, Article 31, para. 1.

55   Ibid., Article 27.

wider application. Article 16(2) CAT contains a similar provision, in respect of other CIDTP. Even if States parties rely on their national laws to determine the legality of a sanction, under these two Articles they are still obliged to comply with rules of international law, which provide for stronger protection.[56] States parties to the CAT must, for example, comply with Article 7 ICCPR, as interpreted by the HRC. They are obligated by general comments of the HRC on Article 7, which mention that the prohibition of torture also covered corporal punishment.[57]

The CAT was adopted to enhance the prohibition against torture that already existed. The preamble of the Convention refers particularly to the prohibition against torture, under Article 7 ICCPR. It is therefore hard to imagine that the CAT contains a provision that enables States parties to exclude a certain act of torture from the scope of the Convention by including it as a punishment under their national law.[58]

The legality of a sanction, for the purpose of application of the second clause of Article 1(1) CAT, should be defined in light of national and international laws.[59] The ComAT's decision in *A.S. v. Sweden* (2001) supports this conclusion. This case concerned the forcible return of a woman to Iran, where there was a real risk she would be subjected to torture, mainly because she had been sentenced to death by stoning for adultery. Although this punishment was regarded as lawful under Iranian national law, the Committee considered Sweden to be obligated to refrain from forcibly returning the woman to Iran, or to any other country where she ran a risk of being expelled or returned to Iran.[60]

---

56   Ingelse, C., 2001, p. 214.

57   HRC, General Comment No. 7, Torture or cruel, inhuman or degrading treatment or punishment (Article. 7), 30 May 1982, para. 2; HRC, General Comment No. 20, Replaces general comment 7 concerning prohibition of torture and cruel treatment or punishment (Article. 7), 3 October 1992, para. 5.

58   Ingelse, C., 2001, p. 214.

59   Weissbrodt, D. & Hortreiter, I., 1999, p. 11.

60   ComAT, *A.S. v. Sweden*, No. 149/1999, 24 November 2000, paras. 2.8, 8 and 9. During the consideration of periodic reports submitted by many States parties, the ComAT recommended the abolition of corporal punishment, which was permitted under national laws. The Committee thus made it clear that the legality of sanctions is defined under both national and international law. ComAT, Conclusions and recommendations on the initial periodic report of Yemen, UN. Doc. CAT/C/CR/31/4, 5 February 2004, para. E.7 (b); ComAT, Concluding observations on the second periodic report of Indonesia, UN. Doc. CAT/C/IDN/CO/2, 2 July 2008, para. 15.

The following subsections address the question of removal in cases where the applicant faces a risk of detention or the death penalty.

I.1.5.1 *Detention*

The ComAT has made it clear that the mere risk of arrest and investigation upon return does not constitute a breach of Article 3 CAT, if the complainant cannot show that he would be at risk of torture.[61] However, the Subcommittee on prevention of torture and other CIDTP has held that conditions of detention not only raise issues of CIDTP, but in some circumstances can also be a means of torture, if used in a manner that accords with the definition of torture under Article 1 CAT.[62] In *Josu Arkauz Arana v. France* (1999), the Committee noted that during its consideration of the periodic reports submitted by Spain, it had expressed concern about the complaints it had frequently received regarding acts of torture and ill-treatment. The Committee further observed that, despite legal guarantees as to the conditions under which the detention could be imposed, cases in which persons had been held incommunicado during prolonged detention, when the detainee could not receive the assistance of a lawyer of his choice, seemed to facilitate the practice of torture, since most of the complaints the Committee received concerned torture inflicted during such periods.[63]

During consideration of the initial periodic report of Mongolia, the ComAT was concerned with detention conditions in some facilities, including overcrowded cells with poor ventilation and heating, inadequate water supply, and the spread of infectious diseases, as well as ill-treatment, such as mixing convicted prisoners and pre-trial detainees, and guards who encourage prisoners to abuse certain detainees. The Committee further expressed its concern about the special isolation regime: solitary confinement for prisoners serving 30-year sentences. The Committee was particularly concerned by reports that death row prisoners were detained in isolation, kept handcuffed and shackled throughout their detention, and denied adequate food. The Committee noted that the UN Special Rapporteur on torture had described such conditions of

---

61   ComAT, *I.A.O.* v. *Sweden*, No. 65/1997, 6 May 1996, para. 14.5; ComAT, *S.S.H.* v. *Switzerland*, No. 254/2004, 15 November 2005, para. 6.8; ComAT, *Y.* v. *Switzerland*, No. 431/2010, 21 May 2013, para. 7.8.

62   Report of the ComAT, UN. Doc. A/66/44, 2010–2011, Fourth annual report of the Subcommittee on Prevention of Torture and Other Cruel, Inhuman or Degrading Treatment or Punishment, para. 107(d).

63   ComAT, *Josu Arkauz Arana v. France*, No. 63/1997, 9 November 1999, para. 11.4.

detention as constituting additional punishment that could only be qualified as torture, as defined in Article 1 CAT.[64]

While the mere risk of detention upon return does not in itself amount to torture, the condition of detention in some circumstances could constitute torture. Accordingly, the removal of a person to face such a risk would violate Article 3 CAT.

1.1.5.2   *Death Penalty*

The exception of pain or suffering that results exclusively from lawful sanctions and is inherent in such sanctions, or is caused thereby, raises the question of the applicability of Article 3 CAT where the complainant faces a risk of being subjected to the death penalty in the receiving State. During consideration of the periodic reports submitted by States parties, the ComAT has repeatedly recommended that States ensure that no person may be forcibly removed to any State where there is a serious risk of being subject to the death penalty, torture, or other CIDTP.[65] However, Article 3 CAT prohibits forcible removal to torture, and not to CIDTP; neither does it cover the death penalty. Although the ComAT has repeatedly called on States parties to abolish the death penalty,[66] it does not consider this sentence to be torture, or even a CIDTP.[67] Accordingly, the removal of a person to a State where he faces a risk of death penalty would not violate Article 3 CAT. However, the manner of execution could, in some circumstances, amount to torture. For example, in *A.S.* v. *Sweden* (2001), the Committee found that the removal of the complainant to her country of origin, Iran, would violate Article 3 largely because she was sentenced to death by stoning for adultery.[68]

---

64   ComAT, Consideration of the initial periodic report submitted by of Mongolia, Report of the ComAT, UN. Doc. A/66/44, para. 16.

65   ComAT, Concluding observations on the second periodic report of Zambia, UN. Doc. CAT/C/ZMB/CO/2, 26 May 2008, para. C. 6; ComAT, Consideration of first supplementary report of Canada, UN. Doc. CAT/C/SR.139, 20 July 1993, para. 27.

66   ComAT, Consideration of the second periodic report of Benin, UN.Doc. CAT/C/BEN/2, 16 November 2007, para. 19.

67   Report of the Special Rapporteur on torture and other cruel, inhuman or degrading treatment or punishment, M. Nowak, UN. Doc. A/HRC/10/44, 14 January 2009, paras. 44 and 47.

68   ComAT, *A.S.* v. *Sweden*, paras. 2.8, 8 and 9. During the consideration of periodic reports submitted by many States parties, the ComAT recommended the abolition of corporal punishment, which was permitted under national laws. The Committee thus made it clear that the legality of sanctions is defined under both national and international law. ComAT, Conclusions and recommendations on the initial periodic report of Saudi

I.2   *ECHR*

Article 3 ECHR, which has been interpreted as implicitly prohibiting refoulement, protects any person from being subjected to "torture or to inhuman or degrading treatment or punishment".[69] The ECHR contains no definition of any of these terms. One must therefore look at ECtHR's case-law to discern their meanings or, more precisely, to define the elements of ill-treatment from which a person is protected. The principle of Non-Refoulement requires that possible future treatment be assessed, but in most refoulement cases the Court does not specifically consider the nature of the treatment to which the applicant may be subjected. Whenever the Court has found that removal of the applicant would expose him to a real risk of being subjected to treatment contrary to Article 3 ECHR in the receiving State, it has normally refrained from considering if the possible treatment should be characterised as torture or CIDTP.[70] In the following subsections, we discuss the elements of treatment from which a person is protected under Article 3 ECHR in light of the ECtHR's Non-Refoulement case-law. We consider the nature of this treatment, whether an act or a mere omission is sufficient, the severity of pain, the identity of the perpetrator, and a possible exception based on lawful sanction.

I.2.1   Act or Omission

Through its Non-Refoulement case-law, the Court has repeatedly noted that Article 3 ECHR has been most commonly applied in contexts in which the risk that an individual will be subjected to any of the proscribed forms of ill-treatment in the receiving State emanates from intentional acts or omissions.[71] The Court has not made any distinction as to whether the future possible treatment in the receiving State is an intentional act or an omission. This approach is compatible with the Court's general approach of non-distinction between acts and omissions, with regard to the application of Article 3.[72] In this context, the Court has not excluded the possibility that:

Arabia, UN. Doc. CAT/C/CR/28/5, 12 June 2002, para. C.4 (b); ComAT, Concluding observations on the second periodic report of Yemen, para. 18.

69   ECHR50, Article 3.

70   ECtHR, *Chahal* v. *the United Kingdom*, para. 79–80; ECtHR, *Mamatkulov and Askarov* v. *Turkey* (GC), Appl.Nos. 46827/99 and 46951/99, 4 February 2005, para. 67.

71   E.g., ECtHR, *Bensaid* v. *the United Kingdom*, Appl.No. 44599/98, 6 February 2001, para. 34; ECtHR, *N.* v. *the United Kingdom* (GC), Appl.No. 26565/05, 27 May 2008, para. 43.

72   E.g. the Court has considered as a violation of Article 3 the failure of the authorities to provide adequate protection against domestic violence, ECtHR, *E.S. and Others* v. *Slovakia*, Appl.No.8227/04, 15 September 2009; ECtHR, *Opuz* v. *Turkey*, Appl.No.33401/02, 9 June 2009; the failure to conduct an effective investigation into credible allegations of

...the responsibility of the State under Article 3 might be engaged in respect of treatment where an applicant, who was wholly dependent on State support, found himself faced with official indifference in a situation of serious deprivation or want incompatible with human dignity.[73]

This approach was followed in *M.S.S.* v. *Belgium and Greece* (2011), where the ECHR (GC) considered Greece, through its inaction, to have forced an asylum seeker to live in conditions that reached a level of severity that fell within the scope of Article 3 ECHR.[74] In the Court's opinion, if the Greek authorities had examined the applicant's asylum request promptly, they could have substantially alleviated his suffering.[75] The Court further held that a State party that returns an asylum seeker to another State where he was at risk of being subjected to such situation would breach its obligation of Non-Refoulement under Article 3 ECHR.[76]

The ECtHR has expanded the application of the prohibition against refoulement under Article 3 ECHR to very exceptional cases, where a risk of ill-treatment results not from an intentional act or omission, but from a naturally occurring illness and the receiving State's insufficient resources to treat it.[77] The Court has held that the removal of a person in an advanced stage of a fatal, naturally occurring illness to a country where facilities for the treatment of that illness are inferior to those available in the State party, may raise an issue under Article 3. This is true only in very exceptional cases, where humanitarian grounds against the removal are compelling.[78] The Court has made it clear that although the circumstances that the applicant would face in the receiving State do not in themselves violate the standards of Article 3 ECHR, in these cases his removal would expose him to a real risk of death under most

---

ill-treatment, ECtHR, *Chember* v. *Russia*, Appl.No.7188/03, 3 July 2008; ECtHR, *Khashi-yev and Akayeva* v. *Russia*, Appl.Nos. 57942/00 and 57945/00, 24 February 2005. See also, the EComHR' approach in the *Greece* case (1969), in which the Commission held that: "the failure of the Government of Greece to provide food, water, heating in winter, proper washing facilities, clothing, medical and dental care to prisoners constitutes an 'act' of torture in violation of article 3 of the ECHR". Report the Commission of 5 November 1969, *The Greek Case*, p. 461.

73   ECtHR, *M.S.S.* v. *Belgium and Greece* (GC), Appl.No. 30696/09, 21 January 2011, para. 253.
74   Ibid., para. 263.
75   Ibid., para. 262.
76   Ibid., paras. 366–368.
77   ECtHR, *N.* v. *the United Kingdom* (GC), para. 43.
78   ECtHR, *D.* v. *the United Kingdom*, paras. 51–53; ECtHR, *N.* v. *the United Kingdom* (GC), para. 42.

distressing circumstances, and would therefore amounts to inhuman treatment.[79] The Court has followed the same approach in other very exceptional cases in which humanitarian grounds against removal are compelling, such as lack of sufficient resources to provide welfare provision in the receiving State. In *S.H.H.* v. *The UK* (2013), the applicant alleged that his removal to Afghanistan would expose him to a risk of ill-treatment because he was disabled.[80] The Court acknowledged that the applicant's disability could not be considered a "naturally" occurring illness, and that the applicant did not require medical treatment. Nevertheless, the Court considered it significant that:

> ...in both scenarios the future harm would emanate from a lack of sufficient resources to provide either medical treatment or welfare provision rather than the intentional acts or omissions of the authorities of the receiving State.[81]

Accordingly, the Court has held that the principles that apply where there is a real risk of expected ill-treatment due to a naturally occurring illness, should also apply to circumstances in which disability might create the risk of ill-treatment.[82]

1.2.2   Infliction of Severe Pain or Suffering Physical or Mental Harm

The Court has not made any distinction in refoulement cases between torture, on the one hand, and inhuman or degrading treatment or punishment, on the other. The Court has noted such a distinction is more easily drawn in the domestic context, where it is called upon to characterise or evaluate acts that have already taken place. In refoulement cases, where a prospective assessment is required, it is not always possible to determine if future possible ill-treatment will be severe enough to be qualified as torture.[83] The ECtHR

---

79   ECtHR, *D.* v. *the United Kingdom*, para. 53.

80   The applicant asserted that, because of his disability, he would be particularly vulnerable to violence and at increased risk of further injury or death in the ongoing, armed conflict in Afghanistan. He argued that, due to his lack of family support, he would face living conditions and discrimination in violation of Article 3. ECtHR, *S.H.H.* v. *the United Kingdom*, Appl.No. 60367/10, 29 January 2013, para. 80.

81   Ibid., para. 89.

82   Ibid., para. 89.

83   ECtHR, *Babar Ahmad and Others* v. *the United Kingdom*, Appl.Nos. 24027/07, 11949/08, 36742/08, 66911/09 and 67354/09, 10 April 2012, para. 170. The ECtHR referred that the ECHR is a living instrument, thus the present day conditions must be taken into account when interpreting this Convention. This means that certain acts which were classified in

has considered that it is necessary to assess conditions in the receiving State against the standards of Article 3 to determine whether the applicant will be at risk of being subjected to treatment contrary to the Article.[84] The Court has asserted:

> These standards imply that the ill-treatment the applicant alleges he will face if returned must attain a minimum level of severity if it is to fall within the scope of Article 3.[85]

Although it is irrelevant to the application of the principle of Non-Refoulement under Article 3 ECHR to define the borders between torture and other forms of ill-treatment, it is essential to define the minimum level of severity required to place a certain act within the scope of the Article. The Court has not adopted an abstract and absolute standard to distinguish harsh treatment from treatment prohibited under Article 3 ECHR.[86] The Court has considered that assessments of the minimum level of severity are relative.[87] In *Ireland* v. *The UK* (1978), the ECtHR stated that:

> As was emphasised by the Commission, ill-treatment must attain a minimum level of severity if it is to fall within the scope of Article 3. The assessment of this minimum is, in the nature of things, relative; it depends on all the circumstances of the case, such as the duration of the treatment, its physical or mental effects and, in some cases, the sex, age and state of health of the victim, etc.[88]

Accordingly, the test of severity of pain under Article 3 ECHR is subjective and depends on the circumstances of each case.

In Non-Refoulement cases, the Court has taken into consideration the approach adopted in the *Chahal* case, where it found no room to balance the risk of ill-treatment against the reasons for expulsion when determining if a State's responsibility under Article 3 was engaged.[89] In the *Saadi* case, the GC

---

earlier case-law as inhuman or degrading treatment as distinct from torture could be classified as torture in the future. ECtHR, *Selmouni* v. *France*, Appl.No. 25803/94, 28 July 1999, para. 101.

84   ECtHR, *Mamatkulov and Askarov* v. *Turkey* (GC), para. 67.

85   ECtHR, *Hilal* v. *the United Kingdom*, Appl.No. 145276/99, 6 March 2001, para. 60.

86   Vermeulen, B.P., 2006, p. 412.

87   ECtHR, *Hilal* v. *the United Kingdom*, para. 60.

88   ECtHR, *Ireland* v. *The United Kingdom*, 18 January 1978, Appl.No. 5310/71, para. 162.

89   ECtHR, *Chahal* v. *the United Kingdom*, para. 81.

made it clear that "risk" and "dangerousness" could only be assessed independently.[90] The Court found that the same approach must be followed when assessing the minimum level of severity for the purpose of Article 3. According to the Court, this assessment must be independent of the reasons for removal or extradition.[91] However, the Court has underlined that the absolute nature of the prohibition under Article 3 does not mean that risk of any form of ill-treatment in the receiving State will prevent the State party from removing the applicant. As the Court has repeatedly stated, the ECHR does not purport to be a means of requiring States parties to impose Convention standards on other States. In light of this, the Court has concluded that:

> ...treatment which might violate Article 3 because of an act or omission of a Contracting State might not attain the minimum level of severity which is required for there to be a violation of Article 3 in an expulsion or extradition case.[92]

For the purpose of determining if a certain treatment violates Article 3 ECHR and if the respondent State party is responsible for this treatment, the Court has distinguished whether the treatment in question is carried out by a State party in a domestic context, or by another State in an extra-territorial context. For example, the Court noted that while a State party's negligence in providing appropriate medical care within its jurisdiction has, on occasion, been found to violate Article 3, such violations have not been so readily established in an extra-territorial context. The Court also held that, in cases of ill-treatment of prisoners, some factors are considered decisive to conclude that Article 3 has been violated: imposing measures with the intention to break the applicant's resistance or will, to debase or humiliate him, the arbitrary punitive nature of the measure, and the length of time for which the measure was imposed. The Court observed that such factors depend closely upon the facts of the case under consideration. These facts will not be readily established prospectively in an expulsion or extradition context.[93] The Court noted that it has been very cautious in finding that removal from a State party would be contrary

---

90   ECtHR, *Saadi* v. *Italy* (GC), para. 138. See above, Chapter 1 the absolute nature of the prohibition of refoulement under Article 3 ECHR.

91   ECtHR, *Babar Ahmad and Others* v. *the United Kingdom*, paras. 172–176.

92   Ibid., para. 177.

93   ECtHR, *Harkins and Edwards* v. *the United Kingdom*, paras. 129–130; ECtHR, *Babar Ahmad and Others* v. *the United Kingdom*, paras. 177–178; ECtHR, *Yefimova* v. *Russia*, Appl. No. 39786/09, 19 February 2013, para. 211.

to Article 3, and that, since adopting the *Chahal* judgment, it has only rarely reached such a conclusion. The Court further added, in two cases concerning extradition to the US, that:

> Save for cases involving the death penalty, it has even more rarely found that there would be a violation of Article 3 if an applicant were to be removed to a State which had a long history of respect of democracy, human rights and the rule of law.[94]

This approach is open to criticism because it suggests that protection against refoulement under Article 3 depends on whether the receiving State is a party to this Convention. While Article 3 prohibits removal of a person to a real risk of certain ill-treatment in a receiving State that is party to the ECHR, it might not prohibit removal to the same ill-treatment to a receiving State which is not a party to the Convention. This approach is inconsistent with the absolute nature of the protection provided under Article 3 ECHR, for which no derogation is permissible under any circumstances. The Court, however, does derogate from this absoluteness by placing a certain conduct within the scope of the protection of Article 3 when a conduct is domestic, but placing it out of the scope of the protection of Article 3 in the refoulement context.[95]

The Court's remark that it has more rarely found that the removal of an applicant would be contrary to Article 3 if the receiving State had "a long history of respect of democracy, human rights and the rule of law"[96] is problematic, particularly because it was applied in cases of extradition to the US. The US has adopted widely criticised human rights policies in the last decade, such as indefinite detention in Guantànamo, extraordinary rendition, and secret prisons.

The Court has held that determining whether treatments reach the Article 3 threshold depends upon the facts of the case under consideration, which means that the risk of proscribed treatment cannot be easily established prospectively in a refoulement context. In taking this position, the Court has ignored the rationale behind the interpretation of Article 3 that implies the principle of Non-Refoulement. The Court has interpreted Article 3 to imply a

---

94   ECtHR, *Babar Ahmad and Others* v. *the United Kingdom*, para. 179; ECtHR, *Čalovskis* v. *Latvia*, Appl.No. 22205/13, 24 July 2014, para. 134.

95   Messineo, N.M.F., "Relatively Absolute? The Undermining of Article 3 ECHR in Ahmad v UK", The Modern Law Review, Vol. 76 no. 3: 2013, 589–619, pp. 600–603.

96   ECtHR, *Babar Ahmad and Others* v. *the United Kingdom*, para. 179.

prohibition of refoulement to prevent the incursion of irreparable harm and to render the safeguards under this Article practical and effective.[97]

Arguably, from its Non-Refoulement case-law, the Court's approach for the purpose of assessing if a certain treatment reaches the Article 3 threshold differs in accordance with the circumstances of the case under consideration. For example, in the *Soering* case, the Court stated that:

> ...having regard to the very long period of time spent on death row in such extreme conditions, with the ever present and mounting anguish of awaiting execution of the death penalty, and to the personal circumstances of the applicant, especially his age and mental state at the time of the offence, the applicant's extradition to the United States would expose him to a real risk of treatment going beyond the threshold set by Article 3.[98]

In *D. v. The UK* (1997), the Court took into account the very exceptional circumstances of the case: the applicant was in advanced stages of a terminal and incurable naturally occurring illness; and, there was no evidence that this person would be guaranteed required medical treatment or any form of moral or social support. Against those circumstances, the Court found that the applicant's removal would expose him to treatment contrary to Article 3.[99] On the contrary, in *N. v The UK* (2008), the facts that the applicant was not in advanced stage of the illness, his ability to obtain support and care from relatives who lived in the receiving State, and the existence of the required type of AIDS treatment in that State led the GC of the Court to conclude that it did not disclose the very exceptional circumstances it found in *D. v. The UK*.[100] The test of very exceptional circumstances thus applies where alleged future harm emanates not from the intentional acts or omission of public officers or non-State actors but from "a naturally occurring illness and the lack of sufficient resources to deal with it in the receiving country".[101] The Court has considered the test of very exceptional circumstances to also apply where dire humanitarian conditions in the receiving State were "solely or even predominantly

---

97   See above, Chapter 1, application of Article 3 ECHR to refoulement cases.

98   ECtHR, *Soering* v. *the United Kingdom*, para. 111.

99   ECtHR, *D.* v. *the United Kingdom*, paras. 51–52.

100   ECtHR, *N.* v. *the United Kingdom* (GC), para. 51. See also, ECtHR, *T.K.H.* v. *Sweden*, Appl.No. 1231/11, 19 December 2013, para. 51.

101   ECtHR, *Sufi and Elmi* v. *the United Kingdom*, Appl.Nos. 8319/07 and 11449/07, 28 June 2011, para. 281.

attributable to poverty or to the State's lack of resources to deal with a natu-rally occurring phenomenon, such as a drought".[102]

When the humanitarian crisis in the receiving State is predominantly at-tributed to direct and indirect actions of public officers or non-State actors in the receiving State, as was the situation in the *M.s.s.* v. *Belgium and Greece*, the Court has adopted a test

> ...which requires it to have regard to an applicant's ability to cater for his most basic needs, such as food, hygiene and shelter, his vulnerability to ill-treatment and the prospect of his situation improving within a reason-able time-frame.[103]

In *M.s.s.* v. *Belgium and Greece* (2011), the Court noted that Greek authorities did not have due regard for the applicant's vulnerability as an asylum seeker, and must be held responsible for inaction that led the applicant to live in the street for several months, with no resources or access to sanitary facilities, and without any means of providing for his essential needs. The Court considered such living conditions, combined with prolonged uncertainty on the outcome of his asylum application, to attain the level of severity required to fall within the scope of Article 3 ECHR.[104] However, the Court has held that in the absence of exceptionally compelling humanitarian grounds against removal, the mere fact that the applicant's material and social living conditions would be signifi-cantly reduced if he were to be removed from the State party is not sufficient to reach the Article 3 threshold.[105]

Finally, the Court has made no distinction between the mental and physical aspects of future severe pain or suffering.[106] As mentioned above, the anguish of awaiting execution of the death penalty was one of the factors that the

---

102 Ibid., para. 282; ECtHR, *M.s.s.* v. *Belgium and Greece* (GC), para. 254.

103 ECtHR, *Sufi and Elmi* v. *the United Kingdom*, paras. 283–291; ECtHR, *M.s.s.* v. *Belgium and Greece* (GC), para. 254.

104 Ibid., para. 263. The Court reached an opposite conclusion in ECtHR, *Sharifi* v. *Austria*, Appl.No. 60104/08, 5 December 2013; ECtHR, *Safaii* v. *Austria*, Appl.No. 44689/09, 7 May 2014. See also, ECtHR, *Mohammed Hussein* v. *the Netherlands and Italy* (admissibility deci-sion), Appl.No. 27725/10, 2 April 2013, para. 78. Nykanen, E., Fragmented State Power and Forced Migration: A Study on Non-State Actors in Refugee Law, Leiden, Boston: Martinus Nijhoff Publishers, 2012, pp. 257–259.

105 ECtHR, *Sufi and Elmi* v. *the United Kingdom*, pp. 281–292; ECtHR, *Mohammed Hussein* v. *the Netherlands and Italy* (admissibility decision), para. 71.

106 ECtHR, *Kochieva and others* v. *Sweden* (admissibility decision), Appl. No. 75203/12, 30 April 2013, para. 30.

Court took into account in the *Soering* case.[107] Pain or suffering can be solely mental, and do not need to be accompanied by physical abuse.[108] In the Non-Refoulement case of *Koktysh* v. *Ukraine* (2009), the ECtHR stated that it could not speculate on the possible outcome of the applicant's criminal case in the event of his extradition to Belarus, but added:

> However, the mere possibility of the imposition of capital punishment together with the prospect of an unfair trial, given the quashing of a final decision in the applicant's case, is sufficient in the Court's view to conclude that such situation generates for the applicant a sufficient anguish and mental suffering to fall within the ambit of Article 3 of the Convention.[109]

1.2.3   Identity of the Perpetrator of the Act

In its Non-Refoulement case-law, the ECtHR has considered that the responsibility of the sending State under Article 3 ECHR stems from State actions that have, as their direct consequence, exposure of the removed person to proscribed treatment in the receiving State.[110] The Court has repeated that removal by a State party may give rise to an issue under Article 3 ECHR where substantial grounds have been shown for believing that the applicant would face a real risk of treatment contrary to Article 3 in the receiving State.[111] The identity of the perpetrator of the treatment in the receiving State (the source of the proscribed treatment) is irrelevant in determining the responsibility of the sending State for the removal. The Court has clearly stated that the source of the risk does nothing to alter the level of protection guaranteed by Article 3 ECHR. Regardless of the source of the alleged risk, a State party to the ECHR must carry out a thorough and individualised examination of the situation of the applicant and suspend enforcement of his removal should the risk of ill-treatment be established.[112]

---

107   ECtHR, *Soering* v. *the United Kingdom*, para. 111. According to the EComHR, the mental torture means "the infliction of mental suffering through the creation of a state of anguish and stress by means other than bodily assault". Report the Commission of 5 November 1969, *The Greek Case*, p. 461.

108   ECtHR, *Al-Saadoon and Mufdhi* v. *the United Kingdom*, para. 144.

109   ECtHR, *Koktysh* v. *Ukraine*, Appl.No. 43707/07, 10 December 2009, para. 62.

110   ECtHR, *Soering* v. *the United Kingdom*, para. 91.

111   ECtHR, *Ahmed* v. *Austria*, para. 39; ECtHR, *Chahal* v. *the United Kingdom*, para. 74; ECtHR, *NA.* v. *The United Kingdom*, Appl.No. 25904/07, 17 July 2008, para. 109.

112   ECtHR, *Tarakhel* v. *Switzerland*, Appl.No. 29217/12, 4 November 2014, para. 104.

For the purpose of applying Article 3 to a refoulement case, the ECtHR does not require the perpetrator of the treatment to be a public official. The Court has stated that:

> ...the existence of the obligation not to expel is not dependent on wheth-er the risk of the treatment stems from factors which involve the respon-sibility, direct or indirect, of the authorities of the receiving country, and Article 3 may thus also apply in situations where the danger emanates from persons or groups of persons who are not public officials,[...]. What is relevant in this context is whether the applicant was able to obtain pro-tection against and seek redress for the acts perpetrated against him.[113]

The Court has therefore applied Article 3 to prevent refoulement, whether or not the risk of ill-treatment in the receiving State emanates from acts of pub-lic officials, or of non-State actors in cases where the authorities of this State could not or did not want to afford the applicant appropriate protection.[114] The ECtHR has considered that the obligation imposed on States parties under Article 1 ECHR, to secure to everyone within their jurisdiction the rights and freedoms defined in the Convention, taken together with Article 3, requires States to take measures to ensure that individuals within their jurisdiction are not subjected to any treatment contrary to Article 3, including such ill-treatment administered by private individuals.[115] Where it is established that a State takes reasonable measures to control the non-State actors, there is no violation to the State's positive obligation to prevent ill-treatment within its own territory. However, in Non-Refoulement cases, the Court has not given importance to whether or not the receiving State fulfied this positive obligation. There will be a violation of the principle of Non-Refoulement even if it is established that the receiving State has taken reasonable measures to prevent ill-treatment by non-State actors, but it failed to ensure protection for the applicant. The abso-lute nature of the right envisaged in Article 3 serves as the Court's justification for applying it in refoulement cases where non-State actors carry out future possible ill-treatment.[116] In such cases, the applicant must establish that, first,

---

113   ECtHR, *Salah Sheekh* v. *The Netherlands*, para. 147; ECtHR, *N.* v. *Finland*, para. 163.

114   ECtHR, *H.L.R.* v. *France* (GC), para. 32; ECtHR, *D.* v. *the United Kingdom*, para. 49; ECtHR, *N.* v. *the United Kingdom* (GC), para. 31.

115   ECtHR, *Mahmut Kaya* v. *Turkey*, Appl.No. 22535/93, 18 March 2000, para. 115; ECtHR, *M.C.* v. *Bulgaria*, Appl.No. 39272/98, 4 December 2003, para. 149.

116   ECtHR, *H.L.R.* v. *France* (GC), para. 40; ECtHR, *Salah Sheekh* v. *The Netherlands*, para. 137; ECtHR, *NA.* v. *The United Kingdom*, para. 110.

he would be at a real risk of being ill-treated by non-State actors in the receiving State; second, the authorities in this State are not able or not willing to obviate the risk by providing him appropriate protection. In this context, the Court has applied the principle of Non-Refoulement under Article 3 to the removal of persons who may face risk upon their return from non-State actors including, for example, family members,[117] criminals,[118] or armed groups.[119]

As described above, the ECtHR has expanded the principle of Non-Refoulement under Article 3 ECHR to apply to very exceptional circumstances where the risk of being ill-treated results from factors that cannot engage, either directly or indirectly, the responsibility of State authorities or non-State actors. The Court has followed this approach where the future harm would emanate from a lack of sufficient resources to provide either medical treatment or welfare provision,[120] or where the dire humanitarian crisis in the receiving State is solely or even predominantly due to poverty, or to the State's lack of resources to deal with a naturally occurring phenomenon, such as a drought.[121]

1.2.4   Lawful Sanctions

The ECHR does not include any clear exception that justifies the infliction of torture or IDTP for any reason. However, the ECtHR has noted that:

> In order for a punishment or treatment associated with it to be "inhuman" or "degrading", the suffering or humiliation involved must go beyond that

---

117 ECtHR, *D.N.M.* v. *Sweden*, Appl.No. 28379/11, 27 June 2013, para. 53 and ECtHR, *S.A.* v. *Sweden*, Appl.No. 66523/10, 27 June 2013, para. 51, in which the Court found that persons who are at risk of being subjected to honour-related crimes in Iraq might not receive effective protection from the authorities. See also, ECtHR, *N.* v. *Sweden*, para. 57.

118 ECtHR, *H.L.R.* v. *France* (GC), paras. 42–43, in which the Court accepted that the drug traffickers could be the source of the risk of ill-treatment in certain circumstances.

119 ECtHR, *Ahmed* v. *Austria*, paras. 44 and 47; ECtHR, *Salah Sheekh* v. *The Netherlands*, paras. 147 and 149. In these cases the Court considered that the expulsion of the applicants to Somalia would be in violation of Article 3 ECHR, although the source of future harm in both cases was a clan other than that to which the applicant was a member. The same can be said with regard to Christians, as a religious minority, in southern and central parts of Iraq. The Court noted that Christians in these parts of the country were targeted by organised extremist groups and the authorities there were generally unable to protect them and other religious minorities. ECtHR, *F.H.* v. *Sweden*, Appl.No. 32621/06, 20 January 2009 para. 97; ECtHR, *N.A.N.S.* v. *Sweden*, Appl.No. 68411/10, 27 June 2013, para. 32. See also, ECtHR, *Auad* v. *Bulgaria*, para. 98. Frigo, M., 2011, p. 100.

120 ECtHR, *D.* v. *the United Kingdom*, para. 49; ECtHR, *N.* v. *the United Kingdom* (GC), paras. 29 and 32; ECtHR, *Bensaid* v. *the United Kingdom*, para. 34.

121 ECtHR, *Sufi and Elmi* v. *the United Kingdom*, para. 282.

inevitable element of suffering or humiliation connected with a given form of legitimate treatment or punishment.[122]

The Court has held that the nature and context of the punishment, and the manner and method of its execution, should be also taken into account when it determines if a certain punishment violates Article 3.[123] The Court has accepted that removing an applicant to a State where he would face a real risk of receiving a "grossly disproportionate sentence" could violate Article 3 ECHR. However, the Convention does not purport to be a means to require States parties to impose Convention standards on other States. The Court has thus held that due regard must be given different sentencing practices among States, and that the length of sentences legitimately and reasonably differs from State to State, even for similar offences.[124] A sentence to which the applicant would be subject in the receiving State cannot be considered grossly disproportionate simply because it is more severe than the sentence that would be imposed in another State.[125] The Court has therefore decided that only in "very exceptional cases" can an applicant establish that the sentence he would face in a State not party to the ECHR would be grossly disproportionate, and thus contrary to Article 3.[126] The Court has required a high threshold of demonstration to show that the sentence the applicant would face in the receiving State is grossly disproportionate. In the following subsections, we discuss the applicability of Article 3 ECHR to cases of removal in which applicants face a real risk of life imprisonment, detention and death penalty.

I.2.4.1   Detention

In order for a punishment or treatment associated with it to be considered inhuman or degrading, the Court has required that the suffering or humiliation caused by this punishment go beyond the inevitable element of suffering or humiliation provoked by a given form of legitimate punishment. The ECtHR has noted that all measures that deprive a person of his liberty involve such an element. Article 3 therefore imposes a duty upon a State party to ensure that the conditions of detention are compatible with respect for the detainees' human dignity, that the method of execution of the measures does not

---

122   ECtHR, *Ramirez Sanchez* v. *France*, para. 119.

123   ECtHR, *Tyrer* v. *the United Kingdom*, Appl.No. 5856/72, 25 April 1978, para. 30.

124   ECtHR, *Harkins and Edwards* v. *the United Kingdom*, paras. 133–134; ECtHR, *Babar Ahmad and Others* v. *the United Kingdom*, para. 238.

125   ECtHR, *Čalovskis* v. *Latvia*, para. 141.

126   ECtHR, *Harkins and Edwards* v. *the United Kingdom*, paras. 133–134.

subject them to distress or hardship beyond the unavoidable level of suffering inherent in detention, and that their health and well-being are adequately secured.[127] For the purpose of assessing the conditions of detention, the Court has given consideration to the cumulative effects of these conditions, as well as to specific allegations submitted by the applicant. Consideration must be given for the length of the period during which a person is detained in those particular conditions.[128]

In several refoulement cases, the Court has dealt with the argument that removal of the applicant, who faces a risk of being detained in the receiving State, violates Article 3 ECHR because ill-treatment is present in the detention centres of that State. For the purpose of assessing whether conditions of detention in the receiving State reach the Article 3 threshold, the Court has accounted for their cumulative effects, as well as the applicant's specific allegations, and the duration of detention.[129] The Court held that extradition to Turkmenistan on criminal charges might constitute a violation of Article 3 ECHR. When it reached this conclusion, the Court took into account the following factors:

> ...credible and consistent reports from various reputable sources of widespread torture, beatings and use of force against criminal suspects by the Turkmen law-enforcement authorities; very poor conditions of detention; discrimination against persons of non-Turkmen ethnicity, which made them particularly vulnerable to abuses; the cumulative effect of the poor conditions of detention in view of the potential length of prison sentences; systematic refusal of the Turkmen authorities to allow any monitoring of the places of detention by international or non-government observers.[130]

The Court has held that detention of an ill person may raise Article 3 issues, and that lack of appropriate medical care in a detention centre may amount to treatment contrary to this Article. The Court has noted specifically that in

---

127   ECtHR, *Ramirez Sanchez v. France*, para. 119; ECtHR, *A. and Others v. the United Kingdom*, Appl.No.3455/05, 19 February 2009, para. 127; ECtHR, *Al-Saadoon and Mufdhi v. the United Kingdom*, para. 121; ECtHR, *Babar Ahmad and Others v. the United Kingdom*, para. 202.

128   ECtHR, *Ramirez Sanchez v. France*, para. 119.

129   ECtHR, *Garabayev v. Russia*, para. 75.

130   ECtHR, *Kolesnik v. Russia*, Appl.No. 26876/08, 17 June 2010, para. 68; ECtHR, *Soldatenko v. Ukraine*, Appl.No. 2440/07, 23 October 2008, para. 71. With regard to the conditions of detention in Uzbekistan see, ECtHR, *Muminov v. Russia*, Appl.No. 42502/06, 11 December 2008, para. 93; ECtHR, *Ismoilov and Others v. Russia*, para. 121.

assessing whether the detention conditions of a mentally ill person met the standards of Article 3 ECHR, his vulnerability and his inability, in some cases, to complain coherently or at all about how he is being affected by any particular treatment, needed to be taken into account. The Court has adopted three elements to consider when it assesses the compatibility of an applicant's health with his stay in detention: (a) the medical condition of the detainee; (b) the adequacy of the medical services available in detention; and, (c) the advisability of maintaining detention measures in view of the applicant's state of health.[131] In the refoulement case of *Aswat* v. *The UK* (2013), a person who suffered from an enduring mental disorder applied to avoid extradition to the US. The Court noted that the conditions in which he would be detained in the US, and the medical services that would be made available to him there, would determine if his extradition would breach Article 3. But, as the Court asserted, assessment of those conditions was hindered by its inability to determine with any certainty the detention facility or facilities in which the applicant would be placed, either before or after trial.[132] The Court noted that there was no guarantee that, if tried and convicted, the applicant would not be detained in ADX Florence, where he would be subjected to a "highly restrictive" regime with long periods of social isolation. In this context, the Court observed that while it had previously found that conditions in ADX Florence would not reach the Article 3 threshold for persons in good health or with less serious mental illness,[133] the applicant's situation in the *Aswat* case can be distinguished on account of the severity of the applicant's mental condition.[134]

1.2.4.2   Death Penalty

Protocol No.13 to the ECHR has abolished the death penalty in all circumstances.[135] In this subsection, we examine the qualification of the death penalty as inhuman and degrading punishment within the meaning of Article 3 ECHR.[136]

---

131   ECtHR, *Babar Ahmad and Others* v. *the United Kingdom*, para. 215; ECtHR, *Aswat* v. *the United Kingdom*, para. 50.

132   Ibid., paras. 51–52.

133   ECtHR, *Babar Ahmad and Others* v. *the United Kingdom*, paras. 222–223; ECtHR, *Čalovskis* v. *Latvia*, para. 138.

134   ECtHR, *Aswat* v. *the United Kingdom*, paras. 56–57. Compare with ECtHR, *Babar Ahmad and Others* v. *the United Kingdom*, para. 224.

135   Protocol No. 13 to the ECHR, concerning the abolition of the death penalty in all circumstances, entered into force on 1st July 2003.

136   Both Article 2 ECHR and Article 1 of Protocol No. 13 prohibit the refoulement of an individual to another State where substantial grounds have been shown for believing that

In *Soering* v. *The UK* (1989), the applicant argued that extraditing him to the US would violate Article 3 because it would expose him to a risk of "death row phenomenon".[137] The Court discussed whether the death penalty should be considered an inhuman and degrading punishment within the meaning of Article 3.[138] The Court noted that Article 2 ECHR, which provides for the right to life, does not prohibit the execution of a death penalty.[139] The subsequent practice of the States parties regarding the abolition of the death penalty could not be considered as an amendment to Article 2(1), because the adoption of Protocol No. 6 showed that States parties intended to follow the normal method of amending the Convention in order to introduce a new obligation to abolish capital punishment in time of peace.[140] Against these facts, the Court concluded that Article 3 could not be interpreted as generally prohibiting the death penalty, but the Court did not rule out the possibility that the circumstances relating to the execution of a death sentence could give rise to an issue under Article 3. The Court concluded that the applicant's extradition to the US would expose him to a real risk of treatment that exceeded the Article 3 threshold.[141]

In *Ocalan* v. *Turkey* (2005),[142] the ECtHR (GC) took into consideration the expansion of the legal prohibition of the death penalty and the increase of the number of States that had ratified Protocol No. 6. The Court concluded that Article 2(1) had been modified and "capital punishment in peacetime has come to be regarded as an unacceptable [...] form of punishment that is no longer permissible under Article 2".[143] However, the Court reasserted its case-law in the *Soering* case by noting that the circumstances of the imposition and execution of the death penalty, including the personal circumstances of the

---

he would face a real risk of being subjected to the death penalty. ECtHR, *Al-Saadoon and Mufdhi* v. *the United Kingdom*, para. 123.

137   ECtHR, *Soering* v. *the United Kingdom*, paras. 80–81.

138   This matter was raised by Amnesty International (AI) in their written comments submitted to the Court with regard to the *Soering* case. Ibid., para. 101.

139   Article 2 ECHR provides that: "1. Everyone's right to life shall be protected by law. No one shall be deprived of his life intentionally save in the execution of a sentence of a court following his conviction of a crime for which this penalty is provided by law".

140   Protocol No. 6 to the ECHR, concerning the Abolition of the Death Penalty, entered into force on 1st March 1985.

141   ECtHR, *Soering* v. *the United Kingdom*, paras. 103–104 and 111.

142   ECHR, *Ocalan* v. *Turkey* (GC). The application in this case did not relate to forcible return of the applicant. He argued that Articles 2 and 3 ECHR should be interpreted as no longer permitting capital punishment.

143   Ibid., para. 163.

condemned person and its disproportion to the gravity of the crime committed, could bring this treatment within the scope of Article 3. The ECtHR concluded that imposing the death penalty on a person after unfair trial when there was a real possibility that the sentence would be enforced would generate a significant degree of human anguish and fear, bringing this treatment within the scope of Article 3.[144] Hence, an Article 3 issue may arise if a State party deports a person who has suffered or risks suffering a flagrant denial of a fair trial in the receiving State, the outcome of which was or is likely to be the death penalty.[145]

The Court's judgment in *Al-Saadoon and Mufdhi* v. *The UK* (2010) has been the most important judgment in applying the principle of Non-Refoulement under Article 3 ECHR to a case of removal in the face of the risk of a death penalty. The applicants in this case were two Iraqi nationals arrested by soldiers from the UK contingent of the MNF in 2003. The British authorities held and investigated them for involvement in killing two British soldiers. After the end of the occupation of Iraq in June 2004, the death penalty was reintroduced into the Iraqi Penal Code for a number of offences, including murder. In 2005, the British authorities referred the applicants' cases to the Basra Criminal Court, which issued an order authorising their continued detention by British forces. In December 2008, upon request by the Iraq High Tribunal, the British authorities transferred the applicants to the custody of the Iraqi police. The ECtHR mentioned that Protocol No. 13, on the abolition of the death penalty in all circumstances, had been signed by all but two of the States parties, and had been ratified by all but three of the States that had signed it. This fact, coupled with the States consistent practice in observing the moratorium on the death penalty, led the Court to conclude that Article 2(1) was amended to abolish the death penalty in all circumstances:

> Against this background, the Court does not consider that the wording of the second sentence of Article 2–1 continues to act as a bar to its interpreting the words "inhuman or degrading treatment or punishment" in Article 3 as including the death penalty.[146]

The Court has held that the prohibition against refoulement implied in Article 3 ECHR includes removal of a person to a State where he would face a risk

---

144   Ibid., paras. 168–169.
145   ECtHR, *Jabari* v. *Turkey*; ECtHR, *Bader and Others* v. *Sweden*, para. 42; ECtHR, *Koktysh* v. *Ukraine*, para. 56.
146   ECtHR, *Al-Saadoon and Mufdhi* v. *the United Kingdom*, para. 120.

of being subjected to the death penalty.[147] Although the Court's conclusion in *Al-Saadoon and Mufdhi v. The UK* (2010) was confirmed in the subsequent case-law on refoulement,[148] the Court has never found a violation of Article 3 on the basis of this conclusion in any refoulement case. Taking into account that Protocol No. 13 abolishes the death penalty in all circumstances; this punishment is, unlike punishments such as mandatory life imprisonment, *per se* incompatible with the ECHR, whether or not it was imposed after unfair trial and despite the quality or kind of execution. In light of the absolute nature of the prohibition under Article 3, a State party cannot knowingly surrender a person to another State if there are substantial grounds for believing that he would be subjected to the death penalty, however grave the offence he allegedly committed. States parties must refrain from removing any person to a country where he would be at risk of being subjected to this form of inhuman or degrading treatment or punishment.

1.2.4.3   *Life Imprisonment*

It is well-established in the ECtHR's case-law that the imposition of a life imprisonment sentence on an adult does not in itself raise an issue under Article 3 ECHR, provided that it is not grossly disproportionate.[149] In its Non-Refoulement case-law, the ECtHR has had the opportunity to consider whether and when a life imprisonment sentence constitutes a grossly disproportionate sentence, and if it raises an issue under Article 3 ECHR. The Court has distinguished between three types of life sentences. The first is a life sentence with eligibility for release after serving a minimum period. The Court has held that in this case, no issue can arise under Article 3, since this sentence is clearly reducible.[150]

---

147   As the *Al-Saadoon and Mufdhi* case had been remitted for reinvestigation by the Iraqi authorities, the ECtHR referred that it could not be predicted, at the time of giving its judgment, the outcome of this retrial and whether or not the death penalty sentenced or executed. In all cases, as the Court noted, the action of the British authorities put the applicants in a case of well-founded fear of being executed by the Iraqi authorities, at least since May 2006, which gave rise to a significant degree of mental suffering constituted inhuman treatment in violation of Article 3. Ibid., para. 144.

148   ECtHR, *Kozhayev v. Russia*, Appl.No. 60045/10, 5 June 2012, para. 81; ECtHR, *Chentiev and Ibragimov v. Slovakia* (admissibility decision), Appl.Nos. 21022/08 and 51946/08, 14 September 2010.

149   ECtHR, *Trabelsi v. Belgium*, Appl.No. 140/10, 4 September 2014, para. 112.

150   ECtHR, *Harkins and Edwards v. the United Kingdom*, para. 136; ECtHR, *Babar Ahmad and Others v. the United Kingdom*, para. 240.

The second is a discretionary life sentence, without the possibility of parole. The Court has observed that this sentence is normally imposed for offences of the utmost severity, such as murder and manslaughter, which, if they do not attract a life sentence, will still attract a very long imprisonment sentence. The ECtHR has therefore held that any person convicted of such an offence must expect to serve long years in prison before he can realistically have any hope of release, regardless of whether he received a life sentence or a determinate sentence. The Court has found that when such a sentence is imposed by a court, after due consideration of all the mitigating and aggravating factors, the sentence does not raise an issue under Article 3 at the time it is imposed.[151] In this context, the Court has held that imposition of a discretionary sentence of life imprisonment without parole on a person convicted of terrorism offences, especially those carried out or inspired by Al-Qaeda,[152] or of a premeditated murder[153] after the trial court considered all relevant aggravating and mitigating factors, would not be grossly disproportionate with the offence.

The third type of life sentence is a sentence of mandatory life imprisonment without the possibility of parole. The Court has indicated that this sentence requires greater scrutiny than other forms of life sentence. The Court has noted that:

> The vice of any mandatory sentence is that it deprives the defendant of any possibility to put any mitigating factors or special circumstances before the sentencing court [...]. This is no truer than for a mandatory sentence of life imprisonment without the possibility of parole, a sentence which, in effect, condemns a defendant to spend the rest of his days in prison, irrespective of his level of culpability and irrespective of whether the sentencing court considers the sentence to be justified.[154]

However, according to the Court, these considerations do not mean that such a sentence is *per se* incompatible with the ECHR;[155] rather,

---

151   ECtHR, *Harkins and Edwards* v. *the United Kingdom*, para. 137.
152   ECtHR, *Babar Ahmad and Others* v. *the United Kingdom*, para. 243; ECtHR, *Aswat* v. *the United Kingdom*, para. 58.
153   ECtHR, *Harkins and Edwards* v. *the United Kingdom*, para. 141.
154   Ibid., para. 138; ECtHR, *Babar Ahmad and Others* v. *the United Kingdom*, para. 242.
155   The Court referred that the trend in Europe is clearly against such sentences. ECtHR, *Harkins and Edwards* v. *the United Kingdom*, para. 138.

... such a sentence is much more likely to be grossly disproportionate than any of the other types of life sentence, especially if it requires the sentencing court to disregard mitigating factors which are generally understood as indicating a significantly lower level of culpability on the part of the defendant, such as youth or severe mental health problems.[156]

In *Babar Ahmad and Others* v. *The UK* (2012), the fifth applicant faced multiple mandatory sentences of life imprisonment without the possibility of parole in the US after being charged with 269 murder charges. The Court did not find this sentence grossly disproportionate for such an offence, particularly since the applicant concerned did not establish that exceptional circumstances existed to significantly lower his level of culpability. The Court further asserted that even if the applicant, was convicted of these charges, and had discretion to adduce mitigating factors, it had difficulty conceiving any factor that would lead a sentencing court to impose a lesser sentence than life imprisonment without the possibility of parole.[157]

Through its case-law, the ECtHR has held that while the imposition of a life sentence, which is not grossly disproportionate, is not prohibited under Article 3 ECHR, the imposition of an irreducible life sentence may raise an issue under Article 3 ECHR.[158] Therefore, the Court has considered that, in the case of absence of any gross disproportionality at the moment of imposition of a discretionary or mandatory life sentence without the possibility of parole, an issue under Article 3 will arise when it can be shown:

(i) that the applicant's continued imprisonment can no longer be justified on any legitimate penological grounds (such as punishment, deterrence, public protection or rehabilitation); and (ii) [...] the sentence is irreducible *de facto* and *de jure*.[159]

The Court took the seriousness of the charges against the applicants in the case of *Babar Ahmad and Others* v. *The UK* (2012) into account when it decided that if the applicants were convicted and received discretionary or mandatory life sentences in the US, there might never be a point at which their continued imprisonment would no longer serve any purpose. Even if that point were

---

156   ECtHR, *Babar Ahmad and Others* v. *the United Kingdom*, para. 242.

157   Ibid., para. 244. See, ECtHR, *Harkins and Edwards* v. *the United Kingdom*, para. 139.

158   ECtHR, *Trabelsi* v. *Belgium*, para. 112.

159   ECtHR, *Harkins and Edwards* v. *the United Kingdom*, paras. 137–138; ECtHR, *Babar Ahmad and Others* v. *the United Kingdom*, para. 241.

reached, the Court noted, the applicants had not shown that the American authorities would refuse to allow them to resort to the mechanisms available for reducing their sentences. The Court concluded that the applicants did not establish that their extradition and sentencing would pose a real risk of treatment that reached the threshold of Article 3.[160]

The opposite decision was reached in *Trabelsi* v. *Belgium* (2014), which concerned the extradition of a Tunisian national from Belgium to the US where he was being prosecuted on charges relating to al-Qaeda-inspired acts of terrorism, for which, if he were convicted, he was liable to a discretionary life imprisonment sentence. First, the ECtHR held a discretionary life sentence would not be grossly disproportionate. Then, it moved on to consider if the possible life sentence is irreducible *de jure* or *de facto*. The Court inferred from the US legal provisions, referred to in the DAs provided by the US authorities, that even if the applicant received a life imprisonment, he had several options for having it reduced, including in case of his substantial cooperation with authorities in the investigation of his case and the prosecution of a third party, compelling humanitarian reasons, or Presidential pardon. However, the Court observed that these provisions did not provide for possible release on parole in the event of a life sentence, whether mandatory or discretionary.[161] The Court noted that although provisions of US legislation point to the existence of a "prospect of release",

> ...none of the procedures provided for amounts to a review mechanism requiring the national authorities to ascertain, on the basis of objective, pre-established criteria of which the prisoner had precise cognisance at the time of imposition of the life sentence, whether, while serving his sentence, the prisoner has changed and progressed to such an extent that continued detention can no longer be justified on legitimate penological grounds.[162]

---

160 Ibid., paras. 243–244. See also, ECtHR, *Harkins and Edwards* v. *the United Kingdom*, para. 140; ECtHR, *Rrapo* v. *Albania*, Appl.No. 58555/10, 25 September 2012, para. 91.

161 ECtHR, *Trabelsi* v. *Belgium*, para. 134.

162 Ibid., para. 137. The Court's judgment in this case was adopted in the light of the judgment of the ECtHR (GC) in *Vinter and Others* v. *the UK* (2013), in which the GC had found that life sentences without parole would violate Article 3 if, at the time of the imposition, there was no real prospect of release and no adequate mechanism to determine if there was still sufficient penological justification for continued detention of the person concerned. ECtHR, *Vinter and others v. the United Kingdom*, Appl.Nos. 66069/09, 130/10 and 3896/10, 9 July 2013.

Accordingly, the Court found that these provisions of us legislation did not fulfil the criteria which it has laid down for assessing the reducibility of a life sentence and its conformity with Article 3 ECHR.[163] The Court concluded that the applicant's extradition to the us amounted to a violation of Article 3 ECHR.[164]

In conclusion, the mere possibility of being subjected to a life imprisonment sentence, in the receiving State, is not sufficient in itself to give rise to an issue under Article 3 ECHR. Article 3 ECHR prohibits the removal of a person who faces, in the receiving State, a real risk of being subjected to a discretionary or mandatory life imprisonment sentence, without the possibility of parole, where this sentence is grossly disproportionate with the offence the removed person allegedly committed. However, even if such sentence were not grossly disproportionate with the offence, there would be a question of Non-Refoulement if a life imprisonment sentence the applicant would face in the receiving State were irreducible *de facto* and *de jure*. The ECtHR has held that the applicant has a "hope of release" at the time of imposition of a life imprisonment sentence where there is an adequate review mechanism requiring the authorities in the receiving State to determine, on the basis of objective, pre-established criteria of which the prisoner had precise knowledge at the time of imposition of this sentence, whether, while serving his sentence, he has progressed to such an extent that continued detention can no longer be justified on legitimate penological grounds.

1.3   *Conclusion*

This subsection has discussed the treatment from which a person is protected under the principle of Non-Refoulement, as provided for in Article 3 CAT and interpreted by the ECtHR under Article 3 ECHR. The main distinction between these two provisions, in this context, is that Article 3 CAT protects a person only from removal to torture as defined under Article 1 CAT; Article 3 ECHR prohibits removal to torture, as well as to CIDTP. Several differences follow from this distinction.

The definition of torture, within the meaning of Article 1 CAT, only includes conduct intentionally inflicted to achieve a purpose (extracting a confession, obtaining information from the victim or any other purpose connected with the public functions of the receiving State authorities, etc). But treatment

---

163   ECtHR, *Trabelsi* v. *Belgium*, para. 138.
164   Ibid., para. 139.

prohibited under Article 3 ECHR does not need to be inflicted intentionally, or for any specific purpose. Since torture is the most severe and serious form of ill-treatment, conduct must meet the minimum level of severity to qualify as torture. The threshold for meeting that minimum is higher for Article 1 CAT than for Article 3 ECHR, though this difference is not fundamental in Non-Refoulement cases because of the prospective nature of the assessment of the future ill-treatment.

Neither the ComAT nor the ECtHR has distinguished between intentional acts and acts of omission when they consider possible future treatment in the receiving State.

Both the ECtHR and the ComAT have applied the principle of Non-Refoulement where the ill-treatment in the receiving State emanates from acts of public officials or of non-State actors, where the authorities of this State do not want to afford the applicant appropriate protection. The divergence between the Committee's and the Court's case-law, in this context, appears where the ill-treatment in the receiving State emanates from acts of non-State actors where the authorities of this State are not able to obviate the risk by providing appropriate protection. The Court has found a violation of the principle of Non-Refoulement even if it is established that the receiving State has fulfilled its positive obligation to prevent ill-treatment within its national territory by taking reasonable measures to control the non-State actors but it does not manage to guarantee sufficient level of safety. In contrast to the Court, the Committee has given importance to the fact that the receiving State has fulfilled its positive obligation to prevent torture by non-State actors within its territory, by exercising due diligence to intervene to stop this torture and punish the perpetrator. The Committee has held that in this case it cannot be argued that the receiving State acquiesced in torture by non-State actors. This divergence is due to the fact that while Article 3 CAT applies only where there is a risk of torture inflicted, directly or indirectly, by the State authorities, Article 3 ECHR applies regardless of the source of the alleged risk.

However, this divergence between the Committee's and the Court's case-law may in reality not make a big difference for the following reasons:

a. The Committee has applied the principle of Non-Refoulement where the risk of torture would be inflicted by a non-governmental entity that occupies and exercises quasi-governmental authority over the territory to which the complainant would be returned.

b. To avoid protection gaps when the risk stems from private actors, it seems that the Committee has interpreted the State's positive obligations to prevent torture within its territory very broadly, rather as obligation of result instead of obligation of means.

In contrast to the ComAT, the ECtHR has expanded the application of the principle of Non-Refoulement under Article 3 ECHR to very exceptional cases where risk of ill-treatment results from factors that cannot engage, either directly or indirectly, the responsibility of State authorities or non-State actors. The Court has taken the same approach where future harm would emanate from a lack of sufficient health care resources or welfare provision, or where a dire humanitarian crisis in the receiving State is solely, or even predominantly, caused by poverty, or to the State's lack of resources to deal with naturally occurring phenomenon, such as a drought.

Finally, Article 1 CAT makes an important exception to the definition of torture under this Convention: it allows intentional infliction of severe pain or suffering that arises from, or is inherent in, or incidental to lawful sanction. The exact meaning of this exclusion clause is not clear. The ComAT seems to rely on national and international laws to define the legality of the sanction. Even if a certain sanction, such as detention or the death penalty, is not considered to be torture, the ComAT has accepted that the manner in which even legal sanctions are implemented may constitute a means of torture. Article 3 ECHR does not include any exception that justifies infliction of torture or IDTP for any reason. However, through its case-law, the ECtHR has held that suffering or humiliation must exceed the inevitable suffering or humiliation caused by a given form of legitimate punishment before a punishment is considered inhuman or degrading. The Court has considered that the nature and context of the punishment, and the manner of its execution, should be taken into account when it determines if a certain punishment violates Article 3 ECHR. Accordingly, a sending State party is obligated to ensure that the conditions of detention in the receiving State are compatible with respect for the detainees' human dignity, that the method of execution of the measures does not subject them to distress or hardship beyond the unavoidable level of suffering inherent in detention, and that their health and well-being are adequately secured.

Given its recent case-law, it has been argued that the Court should apply Article 3 ECHR to the removal of a person to a State where he faces a risk of life sentence without parole if, at the time the sentence is imposed, there was no real prospect of release or an appropriate mechanism to consider his release. Protocol No. 13 abolishes the death penalty in all circumstances, so this punishment is *per se* incompatible with the ECHR, whether or not it is imposed after unfair trial, and whether or not its execution is inhuman. In contrast to

the ComAT's case-law on refoulement, a State party to the ECHR cannot knowingly surrender a person to another State if there are substantial grounds for
believing that he would be in danger of being subjected to the death penalty,
however grave the offence allegedly committed.

The content of the treatment from which a person is protected under the
principle of Non-Refoulement is considerably wider under Article 3 ECHR
than under Article 3 CAT.

II   The Prohibited Conduct under the Principle of Non-Refoulement

II.1   *Form of the Prohibited Conduct*

According to Article 3 CAT, "no State Party shall expel, return ("refouler") or
extradite a person to another State".[165] This provision only refers to three ways
of handing a person over to another State: expulsion, return and extradition,[166]
but the Article is intended to cover all measures by which a person can be
physically transferred from one State to another, regardless of what the legal
setting in which this forcible removal takes place.[167] The Committee has held
that non-admission to a country may engage the responsibility of the State
party under Article 3 CAT, where the person's return would result in exposure
to torture.[168] Accordingly, the principle of Non-Refoulement under Article 3
CAT prohibits all forms of inter-State transfer of persons to torture, including

---

165   CAT84, Article. 3 (1).

166   The ComAT applies Article 3 CAT to extradition cases, e.g., ComAT, *Cecilia Rosana
      Nunez Chipana* v. *Venezuela*, No. 110/1998, 10 November 1998; ComAT, *L.J.R.* v. *Australia*,
      No. 316/2007, 26 November 2008, expulsion cases, e.g., ComAT, *Tahir Hussain Khan* v.
      Canada, No. 15/1994, 15 November 1994; ComAT, *K.T.* v. *Switzerland*, No. 118/1998, 19 No-
      vember 1999, and deportation cases, e.g., ComAT, *K.N.* v. *France* (admissibility decision),
      No. 93/1997, 18 November 1999; ComAT, *E. R. K. and Y. K.* v. *Sweden*, Nos. 270 & 271/2005, 2
      May 2007.

167   The wording of Article 3 CAT is mainly based on the text of Article 33 (1) CSR which pro-
      vides that: "No Contracting State shall expel or return ("refouler") a refugee in any man-
      ner whatsoever...". According to the UNHCR, this prohibition is applicable to any form
      of forcible removal, including deportation, expulsion, extradition, informal transfer or
      "renditions", and non-admission at the border. UNHCR, Advisory Opinion on the Extrater-
      ritorial Application of Non-Refoulement Obligations under the 1951 Convention relating
      to the Status of Refugees and its 1967 Protocol, para. 7.

168   Consideration of the initial report of Cameroon, Report of the ComAT, UN. Doc. A/47/44,
      26 June 1992, para. 255.

formal transfers, such as extradition, return and expulsion,[169] as well as informal transfers, such as rendition.[170]

It is well settled in the Court's case-law that expulsion, extradition, deportation, or any other measure of removing an alien may give rise to an issue under Article 3 ECHR when substantial grounds have been shown for believing that the person concerned would face a real risk of ill-treatment in the receiving State. In such circumstances, Article 3 implies an obligation not to remove the individual to that State.[171] As noted by the Court, the question of risk to a person in another State cannot depend on the legal basis for removal to that State. The Court's Non-Refoulement case-law demonstrated that, in practice, there may be little difference between extradition and other forms of removal. The Court observed that there may be cases in which the extradition request is withdrawn, but the State party to the ECHR decides to proceed with removal from its territory.[172] In other cases, a State party may decide to remove a person who faces criminal proceedings or who has been convicted in the receiving

---

169   The term "return" is usually used to describe the situations where a foreigner is removed from the territory of one State and transferred back to his country of origin. The term "extradition" refers to the formal surrender by one State to another of a person who is accused or convicted of an offence within the jurisdiction of the second State. The term "expulsion" refers to the removal of a foreigner from a country often on the basis that he is considered undesirable or a threat to the State. The term "deportation" refers to the removal from the State's territory of a person whose initial entry was illegal. Noll, G., Return of Persons to States of Origin and Third States, in: Aleinikoff, T.A. & Chetail, V., Migration and International Legal Norms, The Hague: T.M.C.ASSER PRESS, 2003, 61–74, p. 62; Bassiouni, M.C., International Extradition United States Law and Practice, Oxford: Oxford University Press, 5th Ed, 2007, p. 1.

170   The term "rendition" refers to the situations where a person is abducted and forcibly transferred to another State without any recourse to review procedures. This form of transfer has been used to avoid the formality of the extradition process or when there is not an extradition treaty. Nino, M., The Abu Omar case in Italy and the effects of CIA extraordinary renditions in Europe on law enforcement and intelligence activities, Revue internationale de droit pénal, Vol. 78 no. 1: 2007, 113–141, pp. 118–119.

171   ECtHR, *Soering* v. *the United Kingdom*, para. 91; ECtHR, *Cruz Varas and Others* v. *Sweden*, para. 70; ECtHR, *N.* v. *Finland*, para. 158.

172   ECtHR, *Muminov* v. *Russia*. See also, ECtHR, *Nizamov and others* v. *Russia*, Appl.Nos. 22636/13, 24034/13, 24334/13 and 24528/13, 7 May 2014, para. 37, in which the Russian authorities refused the applicants' extradition, considering that the offences they were charged with in the requesting State, Uzbekistan, were not punishable under the Russian criminal law. However, the Russian authorities decided to expel the applicants to Uzbekistan, being illegal aliens in Russia.

State in the absence of an extradition request.[173] Finally, there may be cases where an applicant fled a State because he was afraid a particular sentence, already imposed, would be implemented, and where he is to be returned to that State as a failed asylum seeker rather than under an extradition arrangement.[174] The Court has held that:

> it would not be appropriate for one test to be applied to each of these three cases but a different test to be applied to a case in which an extradition request is made and complied with.[175]

The prohibition of refoulement thus includes any measure taken by the sending State to remove the person concerned, regardless of the description of this measure: extradition, expulsion, deportation or return. Accordingly, the prohibition of refoulement under Article 3 ECHR covers cases of *de facto* refoulement, i.e., where a person fleeing from a real risk of ill-treatment by another State is forced to return to this risk as a direct and immediate result of measures taken by a State party.[176] The State party's responsibility for refoulement is engaged on the grounds that it has taken an action which has, as a direct consequence, risked exposing an individual to ill-treatment in another State. The decisive element is the role of the State's conduct as a "crucial link in the chain of events", regardless of the form of that conduct.[177] Therefore, conduct by a State that entails that risk is prohibited under Article 3 ECHR: States parties to the ECHR are obligated to avoid taking any measures that result in *de facto* refoulement.[178]

Neither the CAT nor the ECtHR's case-law has imposed any limits in relation to the place to which refoulement is prohibited. Article 3 CAT prohibits, in general terms, the return of a person to "another State" where he faces a risk of being subjected to torture. This prohibition thus extends to any State where he would be at risk, even if this State were not his country of origin or not a party to the CAT.[179] The ComAT's Non-Refoulement case-law supports this

---

173 ECtHR, *Saadi* v. *Italy* (GC).

174 ECtHR, *D. and Others* v. *Turkey*, Appl.No 24245/03, 22 June 2006.

175 ECtHR, *Babar Ahmad and Others* v. *the United Kingdom*, para. 168.

176 Wouters, K., 2009, p. 318.

177 ECtHR, *Soering* v. *the United Kingdom*, para. 91; ECtHR, *Cruz Varas and Others* v. *Sweden*, para. 76.

178 See, UNHCR, Human Rights and Refugee Protection Self-study, Module. 5 Vol. II, 15 December 2006, p. 60.

179 As noted by Burgers & Danelius, the undertaking under Article 3 CAT is especially important as to the transfer of a person to a State which is not a party to the CAT, since such a

conclusion. In *Avedes Hamayak Korban* v. *Sweden* (1998), the Committee found that Sweden was obligated to refrain from forcibly returning the applicant, an Iraqi national, to Jordan.[180] In the *Mutombo* case, the State of destination, Zaire, is not a party to the CAT, and this was a factor that led the Committee to conclude that expelling the complainant to Zaire would violate Article 3 CAT.[181] The ECtHR adopted the same approach in its Non-Refoulement case-law. In the *Soering* case, the Court considered that extraditing the applicant, a German national, to the US would give rise to a breach of Article 3 ECHR.[182] The destination in most refoulement cases have decided by the Court under Article 3 ECHR were States that were not parties to the Convention.[183] Article 3 of both the ECHR and the CAT protect an individual against refoulement, whether or not the State of destination is his country of origin, and whether or not it is a State party to the Convention.

Since expulsion, return and extradition require the movement of a person from the territory of one State to that of another,[184] some argue that the prohibition of refoulement does not apply to cases in which a person is transferred within the territory of the same State. The UK used this argument to assert that its transfer of detainees from the UK forces in Iraq and Afghanistan to local authorities was not prohibited under Article 3 CAT. The ComAT clearly recommended the State party to apply Article 3 to "transfers of a detainee within a State party's custody to the custody whether *de facto* or *de jure* of any other State".[185] The ComAT has had no opportunity to address a case that involved transfer within the territory of the same State, but it is clear that the Committee considers Article 3 CAT to apply when a person is transferred from the "effective control" of one State to the "effective control" of another State, even when he is

---

State may not have made any international legally binding undertaking to prevent torture in its territory. Burgers, H. & Danelius, H., 1988, p. 127.

180   ComAT, *Avedes Hamayak Korban* v. *Sweden*.

181   ComAT, *Mutombo* v. *Switzerland*, para. 9.6.

182   ECtHR, *Soering* v. *the United Kingdom*.

183   See, e.g., ECtHR, *Jabari* v. *Turkey*. The Court also applies Article 3 to cases of returning the applicant to a State party to the ECHR. ECtHR, *Shamayev and 12 others* v. *Georgia and Russia*.

184   Comments by the Government of the United Kingdom of Great Britain and Northern Ireland to the conclusions and recommendations of the Committee against Torture (CAT/C/CR/33/3), UN. Doc. CAT/C/GBR/CO/4/Add.1, 8 June 2006, paras. 14 and 17.

185   ComAT, Conclusions and recommendations on the fourth periodic report of the United Kingdom of Great Britain and Northern Ireland, para. 5(e). Nowak, M. & McArthur, E., 2008, p. 129.

transferred within the territory of the same State.[186] The wording of Article 3 CAT supports this position: it speaks of transfers to "another State", which implies that the focus is on the transfer from one authority to another and not on the territory in which the person is held. Similarly, the ComAT's decisions focus on transfer to a "State", and not to a "country" or "territory".[187]

In *Al-Saadoon and Mufdhi* v. *The UK* (2010), the ECtHR applied Article 3 ECHR to the transfer of the applicants (Iraqi nationals) from the UK forces working in Iraq to the Iraqi authorities.[188] The Court made it clear that the principle of Non-Refoulement under Article 3 ECHR does not only apply to cases in which the person concerned crosses the physical borders.

Under both the ECHR and the CAT, the principle of Non-Refoulement applies to the transfer of a person within the territory of the same State, even if this State were the State of his nationality.[189] In our view, this is the only interpretation compatible with the purpose and object of the principle of Non-Refoulement. Other interpretations open the possibility that States could circumvent their obligations under this principle by transferring a person to their embassies or military bases in another State, and then hand him over to the local authorities.

II.2 *Prohibition of Indirect Refoulement*

The principle of Non-Refoulement has been interpreted to prohibit not only direct refoulement to a State where the person concerned faces a risk of ill-treatment, but also indirect refoulement: the transfer of a person to a third State where he faces a risk of being transferred to his country of origin.

The ECtHR has determined that the principle of Non-Refoulement, as interpreted under Article 3 ECHR, prohibits direct and indirect removal of a person to a country where there is a risk he would be subjected to ill-treatment. In *T.I.* v. *The UK* (2000), the applicant was a Sri Lankan national who unsuccessfully sought asylum in Germany and then submitted a similar application in the UK. In application of the Dublin Convention, the British government ordered his transfer to Germany without examining the substance

---

186 Lauterpacht, S.E. & Bethlehem, D., The Scope and Content of the Principle of Non-Refoulement, Geneva: UNHCR, 20 June 2001, para. 63.

187 Gillard, E.C., "There's no Place Like Home: States' Obligations in Relation to Transfers of Persons", International Review of the Red Cross, Vol. 90 no. 871: 2008, 703–750, p. 713.

188 ECtHR, *Al-Saadoon and Mufdhi* v. *the United Kingdom*.

189 Contrary to the prohibition of refoulement under Article 33 CSR, which does not protect a person who exists inside the country of his nationality or habitual residence.

of his asylum claim.[190] The applicant argued before the ECtHR that the UK's conduct in ordering his removal to Germany, from where he will be summarily removed to Sri Lanka, would violate Article 3 ECHR. The Court asserted that, although the applicant was not threatened with any treatment contrary to Article 3 in Germany, his removal to that country was however one link in a possible chain of events which might result in his return to Sri Lanka where he would face the real risk of ill-treatment. The Court added that indirect removal to an intermediary country, which is also a State party, does not affect the UK's responsibility as sending State, to ensure that the applicant is not, exposed to treatment contrary to Article 3 ECHR as a result of its decision to expel him.[191] The obligation of Non-Refoulement under this Article prohibits removal of a protection seeker to a third State if that State might remove him to another State where there is a real risk of being subjected to the proscribed treatment. The Court has held that when a State party applies the Dublin Regulation, it must ensure that:

> ...the intermediary country's asylum procedure affords sufficient guaran-tees to avoid an asylum-seeker being removed, directly or indirectly, to his country of origin without any evaluation of the risks he faces from the standpoint of Article 3 of the Convention.[192]

Under Article 3 ECHR, risk assessment is a two-step process when a State party intends to remove a person to a country other than his country of origin. First, the Court must determine if there is a real risk the applicant will be subjected to proscribed ill-treatment in his country of origin. Second, the Court must determine if there is risk of a second transfer from the receiving State (the third country) to the applicant's country of origin. If this last risk exists, the Court must determine if the applicant's access to asylum proceedings is sufficient to allow examination of the merits of his claim in the third State.[193] The Court has made a distinction based on whether or not the intermediary country is a State party to the ECHR. In *T.I.* v. *The UK* (2000), the Court found no rea-son to believe that Germany would not honour its obligations under Article

---

190   ECtHR, *T.I.* v. *the United Kingdom* (admissibility decision), Appl.No. 43844/98, 7 March 2000, p. 4.

191   Ibid. See, ECtHR, *K.R.S.* v. *the United Kingdom* (admissibility decision), Appl.No. 32733/08, 2 December 2008; ECtHR, *Mohammed* v. *Austria*, Appl.No. 2283/12, 6 June 2013, para. 93.

192   ECtHR, *M.S.S.* v. *Belgium and Greece* (GC), para. 342. See also, ECtHR, *T.I.* v. *the United Kingdom* (admissibility decision); ECtHR, *Mohammed* v. *Austria*, para. 93.

193   ECtHR, *Mohammadi* v. *Austria*, Appl.No. 71932/12, 3 July 2014, paras. 71–73.

3 ECHR to protect the applicant from removal to Sri Lanka if he established substantial grounds for believing that he was at risk of ill-treatment in that country.[194] In another refoulement case, *K.R.S.* v. *The UK* (2008), the ECtHR upheld the "presumption" that Greece, the intermediary country, would abide by its obligations under EU Council directives on asylum procedures and qualification, and also gave weight to the possibility that the applicant could apply to the Court for an interim measure under Rule 39 of the Rules of Court, by virtue of Greece's obligations under the ECHR.[195] This presumption is based on the principle of mutual trust, according to which all States parties to the ECHR are assumed to comply with their obligations under it.[196] The applicant, therefore, must both provide an arguable claim and also rebut this presumption.[197] However, in the Court's view, this presumption is not irrebuttable.[198] In *M.S.S.* v. *Belgium and Greece* (2011),[199] the GC observed that many reports and materials had been added to the information available to it when it adopted the *K.R.S.* decision in 2008. All these reports noted the practical difficulties of applying the Dublin system in Greece, deficiencies of the asylum procedure, and the practice of direct or indirect refoulement on an individual or collective basis.[200] Against this background, the Court concluded that Belgium had violated Article 3 ECHR by expelling the applicant to Greece when "the Belgian

---

194   ECtHR, *T.I.* v. *the United Kingdom* (admissibility decision).

195   The Court referred to Council Directive 2005/85/EC on minimum standards on procedures in Member States for granting and withdrawing refugee status and Council Directive 2003/9/EC laying down minimum standards for the reception of asylum seekers. ECtHR, *K.R.S.* v. *the United Kingdom* (admissibility decision). See, ECtHR, *M.S.S.* v. *Belgium and Greece* (GC), para. 343; ECtHR, *Sharifi* v. *Austria*, para. 35; ECtHR, *Safaii* v. *Austria*, para. 47.

196   ECtHR, *M.S.S.* v. *Belgium and Greece* (GC), para. 150; ECtHR, *Ignaoua and others* v. *the United Kingdom* (admissibility decision), Appl.No. 46706/08, 18 March 2014, para. 55; Moreno-Lax, V., Dismantling the Dublin System: *M.S.S. v. Belgium and Greece*, European Journal of Migration and Law, Vol. 14 no. 1: 2012, 1–31, pp. 1–6.

197   Heijer, M.D., Reflections on Refoulement and Collective Expulsion in the Hirsi Case, International Journal of Refugee Law, Vol. 25 no. 2: 2013, 265–290, p. 15.

198   ECtHR, *Tarakhel* v. *Switzerland*, para. 103.

199   The applicant in this case was an Afghan national who had entered Europe seeking asylum through Greece, where his fingerprint was taken without claiming asylum. He travelled through France and made his asylum claim in Belgium. Pursuant to the Dublin Regulation, the Belgian authorities returned him to Greece, which exposed his to conditions of detention and living conditions that amounted to degrading treatment. ECtHR, *M.S.S.* v. *Belgium and Greece* (GC), para. 367.

200   Ibid., para. 347.

authorities knew or ought to have known that he had no guarantee that his asylum application would be seriously examined by the Greek authorities".[201]

The presumption adopted in the *K.R.S.* decision cannot be found where the intermediary country is not a State party to the ECHR. In *Hirsi Jamaa and Others* v. *Italy* (2012), the intermediary country was Libya. The ECtHR (GC) stated that:

> it is a matter for the State carrying out the return to ensure that the intermediary country offers sufficient guarantees to prevent the person concerned being removed to his country of origin without an assessment of the risks faced.[202]

The Court affirmed that prohibition on indirect refoulement under Article 3 "is all the more important when, as in the instant case, the intermediary country is not a State party to the Convention".[203] In examining if the applicants' transfer to Libya exposed them to the risk of arbitrary repatriation to Eritrea and Somalia, the ECtHR established first that the applicants could arguably claim that repatriating them to Eritrea and Somalia would breach Article 3. Then, the Court took into account the fact that Libya had not ratified the CSR, the absence of any form of asylum and protection procedure for refugees in Libya, the UNHCR' marginal role in Libya, and evidence of several earlier forced returns of asylum seekers and refugees to high-risk countries. Against this background, the Court concluded that Italy could not have reasonably expected Libya to offer sufficient guarantees against arbitrary repatriation.[204]

---

201   Ibid., para. 358. See also, ECtHR, *Sharifi and Others* v. *Italy and Greece*, Appl.No. 16643/09, 21 October 2014, paras. 232–234. Mallia, P., Case of M.S.S. v. Belgium and Greece: A Catalyst in the Re-thinking of the Dublin II Regulation, Refugee Survey Quarterly, Vol. 30 no. 3: 2011, 107–128, p. 123.

202   ECtHR, *Hirsi Jamaa and Others* v. *Italy* (GC), para. 147.

203   Ibid., para. 147.

204   Ibid., paras. 150–158. Heijer, M.D., 2013, p. 15; Moreno-Lax, V., Hirsi Jamaa and Others v. Italy or the Strasbourg Court versus Extraterritorial Migration Control?, Human Rights Law Review, Vol. 12 no. 3: 2012, 574–598, p. 585. In *Abdulkhakov* v. *Russia* (2012), the Court found it significant that the intermediary country, Tajikistan, was not a party to the ECHR and the applicant's transfer there removed him from the Convention's protection. Moreover, the Tajik authorities, when examining his case, would not be under an obligation to apply the Convention standards and to ascertain whether his removal to his country of origin, Uzbekistan, would be contrary to Article 3. Nor would he be able to apply to the

The ComAT has taken the same approach. According to General Comment No. 1 of the ComAT, the phrase "another State" in Article 3 CAT refers to the State to which the applicant is being removed, as well as to any other State to which he may subsequently be removed.[205] The Committee has thus found that the prohibition under Article 3 CAT is not limited to direct refoulement, but also covers indirect refoulement. This approach has been taken in several cases.[206] In *Korban* v. *Sweden* (1998), the complainant, an opponent of the Iraqi regime, arrived in Sweden from Jordan, (his wife's country of nationality). He was living in Sweden without permanent residence. After rejecting his application for a residence permit, the Swedish Immigration Board ordered his expulsion to Jordan without evaluating the risk that he would be deported from Jordan to Iraq. The Committee found that this risk could not be excluded, given the assessment made by different sources, including UNHCR, based on reports that indicated that some Iraqis were sent to Iraq against their will by Jordanian authorities, and that marriage to a Jordanian woman did not guarantee a residence permit in Jordan.[207] The Committee concluded that the State party must refrain from forcibly returning the complainant to Jordan, because of the risk he would subsequently be expelled to Iraq.[208] This is evidence of the Committee's position that a sending State party is obligated to consider if the third State's asylum procedures afford the removed asylum seeker sufficient guarantees to avoid his secondary removal, directly or indirectly, to his country of origin, contrary to Article 3 CAT.[209]

ECtHR for interim measure under Rule 39 of the Rules of Court. ECtHR, *Abdulkhakov* v. *Russia*, Appl.No. 14743/11, 2 October 2012, paras. 154–155.

205   ComAT, General Comment No. 1, para. 2. The UNHCR has adopted the same position. See, UNHCR, Advisory Opinion on the Extraterritorial Application of Non-Refoulement Obligations under the 1951 Convention relating to the Status of Refugees and its 1967 Protocol, para. 8.

206   ComAT, *Tahir Hussain Khan* v. *Canada*, para. 10; ComAT, *A.S.* v. *Sweden*, para. 9; ComAT, *A.F.* v. *Sweden*, No. 89/1997, 8 May 1998, para. 7; ComAT, *Orhan Ayas* v. *Sweden*, No. 97/1997, 12 November 1998, para. 7.

207   ComAT, *Avedes Hamayak Korban* v. *Sweden*, para. 6.5.

208   Ibid., para. 7.

209   ComAT, Concluding observations on the third periodic report of Liechtenstein, UN. Doc. A/65/44, para. 61, 5 May 2010, para. 15. The Committee expressed its concern at reports that not all persons that had applied for asylum in Liechtenstein had the opportunity to apply for asylum in the third State concerned (usually Switzerland and Austria), thus leaving them without sufficient safeguards against refoulement. The Committee recommend that the State party to ensure that those who are returned to "safe third countries" are guaranteed access to the asylum procedure in these States.

II.3   *Applicability of the Principle of Non-Refoulement to Certain Policies*
As we have found previously, both the ComAT and the ECtHR have prohibited
any measure taken by a State to remove a person regardless of its description.
This prohibition also includes indirect refoulement. Neither the ComAT nor
the ECtHR has imposed any limit on States to which refoulement is prohibited. The principle of Non-Refoulement under Article 3 CAT and Article 3 ECHR
applies without regard to the State of destination, whether or not it is a person's country of origin. This principle also applies to the transfer of a person
within the territory of the same State, even if this State were the State of his
nationality.

Against these findings, this section considers whether the principle of Non-
Refoulement applies to persons removed as a result of certain policies adopted
by States. Subsection (1) addresses the applicability of this principle to immigration control policies. Subsection (2) considers the applicability of this
principle to removal of a person by forces participating in multinational operations. And subsection (3) discusses the application of the prohibition against
refoulement to extraordinary rendition.

II.3.1   Immigration Control Policies (Interception Policies)
In order to reduce the increasing number of immigrants and asylum seekers,
States of destination for migratory movements (Western European countries,
the US, Australia and Canada) have sought, since the late 1980s, to tighten
their immigration policies and strengthen their border control mechanisms
by adopting non-arrival or interception policies.[210] There is no internationally
accepted definition of interception. UNHCR derived from the State practice
the following definition:

> ...interception is defined as encompassing all measures applied by a
> State, outside its national territory, in order to prevent, interrupt or stop
> the movement of persons without the required documentation cross-
> ing international borders by land, air or sea, and making their way to the
> country of prospective destination.[211]

---

210   Kjaerum, M., Human Rights for Immigrants and Immigrants for Human Rights, in: Guild,
        E., International Migration and Security: Opportunities and Challenges, London, New
        York: Taylor and Francis, 2006, 51–63, p. 54.
211   UNHCR, Interception of Asylum-Seekers and Refugee: The International Framework and
        Recommend- actions for a Comprehensive Approach, UN. Doc. EC/50/SC/CRP.17, 9 June
        2000, para. 10.

This definition includes all measures, whether taken on land or at sea, physical interception (such as the interception of vessels suspected of carrying irregular migrants or asylum-seekers, either within the territorial waters or on the high seas), and administrative measures (such as imposing visa requirements combined with carrier sanctions, creating international zones at airports, deploying immigration control officials at overseas embarkation points to advise and assist the local authorities in identifying false documents, and posting airline liaison officers at main international airports both in countries of departure and in transit countries with the intent of preventing embarkation of improperly documented persons or assist airline personnel in identifying them).[212] The practice of States is therefore not limited to the traditional form of denying admission to persons once they have arrived at or inside their territory or territorial waters. States have increasingly used extraterritorial mechanisms to prevent people from crossing their borders.[213] The purpose behind these extraterritorial mechanisms is apparently to enforce as many immigration control measures as possible outside State territory, where the presumption is that States lack jurisdiction.[214]

Although these policies officially aim to combat irregular migration and regulate migration flows, the fact that they do not distinguish between those who seek international protection and those who do not undermines the protection against refoulement.[215] These policies run counter to the principles of *pacta sunt servanda* and good faith under Articles 26 and 31 VCLT,[216] since they can lead to results incompatible with the purpose and object of both the ECHR and the CAT in prohibiting refoulement to ill-treatment.[217]

It is difficult to make a comprehensive list of all interception or non-arrival measures. New measures are continuously devised to control the increasing

---

212 Ibid., paras. 11–13.
213 Klug, A. & Howe, T., 2010, p. 69.
214 Ryan, B., Extraterritorial Immigration Control: What Role for Legal Guarantees?, in: Ryan, B. & Mitsilegas, V., Extraterritorial Immigration Control: Legal Challenges, Leiden: Martinus Nijhoff Publishers, 2010, 3–38, p. 4.
215 Lomba, S.D., The Right to Seek Refugee Status in the European Union, Antwerp: Intersentia, 2004, p. 112.
216 Under Article 26, "Every treaty in force is binding upon the parties to it and must be performed by them in good faith". Article 31 provides that: "[a] treaty shall be interpreted in good faith in accordance with the ordinary meaning to be given to the terms of the treaty in their context and in the light of its object and purpose". VCLT69.
217 Cruz, A., Carrier Sanctions in four European Community States: Incompatibilities Between International Civil Aviation and Human Rights Obligations, Journal of Refugee Studies, Vol. 4 no. 1: 1991, 63–81, p. 77.

number of migrants. In the following subsections, we address the applicability
of the principle of Non-Refoulement to some of the most common interception measures: visa requirements; carrier sanctions; transit zones; and interception and rescue at seas.

II.3.1.1   *Visa Requirements*

While it is a right of the nationals of a State to enter its territory,[218] non-
nationals are often required to obtain a visa to enter a foreign State and in
some cases to cross through the international transit areas of airports.[219] Visa
policies enable States to assess the situation of each person seeking entry into
their territory, and provide States with wide discretion in accepting or refusing
an applicant.[220]

Visa regulations vary from State to State. Some States impose visa requirements on all foreigners.[221] Most States impose these requirements on nationals
of particular States that generate migrants, asylum, or protection seekers.[222]
Visa requirements in many countries seem to track rising numbers of migrants
and protection seekers.[223]

There is a tension between a request for proper travel documents and a
visa on the one hand, and the principle of Non-Refoulement on the other. It
is unlikely that a person, who fears ill-treatment at the hands of his country's

---

218   UDHR48, Article 13 (2) provides that: "Everyone has the right to leave any country, includ-
        ing his own, and to return to his country".
219   E.g., Article 3 of the Visa Code adopted by the EC imposed airport transit visas on nation-
        als of twelve States (Afghanistan, Sri Lanka, Iran, Iraq, Ethiopia, Eritrea, Somalia, Nigeria,
        Ghana, Pakistan, Bangladesh and Congo). Furthermore, the airport transit visa require-
        ments can be imposed also on nationals of other countries in urgent cases of mass influx
        of illegal immigrants. EU Council: Regulation no. 810/2009 of the European Parliament
        and of the Council of 13 July 2009 establishing a Community Code on Visas. For more
        explanation about the Visa Code see, Peers, S., Legislative Update, EC Immigration and
        Asylum Law: The New Visa Code, European Journal of Migration and Law, Vol. 12 no. 1:
        2010, 105–131.
220   UNHCR, Interception of Asylum-Seekers and Refugee: The International Framework and
        Recommend- actions for a Comprehensive Approach, p. 8.
221   Australia requires visa from all foreigners.
222   Council Regulation (EC), No. 539/2001, listing the third countries whose nationals must
        be in possession of visas when crossing the external borders and those whose nationals
        are exempt from that requirement, 15 March 2001; For more details about the visa require-
        ments in the US, the UK and the EU see, Ryan, B., 2010, pp. 4–14.
223   For example, in 2015, Lebanon imposed visa requirements on Syrian nationals for the first
        time in the history between Lebanon and Syria, as a result of the increasing number of
        Syrian protection seekers.

authorities, will risk requesting travel documents from these same authorities or request a visa from a foreign embassy or consulate where the visa section is staffed by locals.[224] Even when a protection seeker takes a risk and applies for a visa, embassies and consulates rarely accept his application.[225] In some cases, the functions of the State may have broken down, and it may be impossible to obtain proper documents. Moreover, the absence of consulates in certain war-torn countries constitutes another practical obstacle for protection seekers to obtain visa. In order to solve this tension, States may totally abolish or temporary suspend visa requirements for asylum seekers producing countries.[226]

The extraterritorial jurisdiction of a State party to both the ECHR and CAT include activities of the State's diplomatic or consular agents abroad. Such agents remain under the State's jurisdiction, and also bring any person within the State's jurisdiction, to the extent those agents exercise the State's authority over him.[227] The protection seeker is under the authority of the State's agents as long as his application for entry visa is considered.

Any act or omission by the State's diplomatic or consular agents regarding a protection seeker's application for an entry visa bears on the applicant's rights. These acts or omissions may engage the responsibility of the State of destination under the principle of Non-Refoulement, if there is causal connection between rejection of an entry visa application by the State's agents, and a foreseeable risk the applicant will be tortured or ill-treated.[228] The diplomatic or consular agents of the State party must grant an applicant entry when rejection of an entry visa application will result, as an immediate and direct consequence, in the ill-treatment of the applicant, if no other protection is available to him.[229] For example, a protection seeker, who is at a real risk of

224   The question of the ability of the applicant to obtain a passport or visa without any difficulties is one of the circumstances which may be taken into consideration in the assessment of the risk in the State of destination. Feller, E., Carrier Sanctions and International Law, International Journal of Refugee Law, Vol. 1 no. 1: 1989, 48–66, p. 56.

225   Brouwer, A. & Kumin, J., Interception and Asylum: When Migration Control and Human Rights Collide, Refuge, Vol. 21 no. 4: 2003, 6–24, pp. 8–9.

226   Moreno-Lax, V., Europe in Crisis: Facilitating Access to Protection, (Discarding) Offshore Processing and Mapping Alternatives for the Way Forward, December 2015.

227   See above, Chapter 1, the scope of the protection of refoulement under the ECHR and the CAT.

228   Noll, G., Negotiating Asylum- The EU Acquis, Extraterritorial Protection and the Common Market of Deflection, The Hague: Martinus Nijhoff Publishers, 2000, p. 442.

229   Noll, G., Seeking Asylum at Embassies: A Right to Entry under International Law?, International Journal of Refugee Law, Vol. 17 no. 3: 2005, 542–573, p. 572; Hansen, T.,

being ill-treated, may resort to a foreign State's embassy in his country of origin, and request an entry visa. If this State is a party to the CAT and/or ECHR, it is obligated, under Article 3 of each of these Conventions, to grant the entry visa if rejecting his application may directly and immediately expose him to a risk of ill-treatment. However, if a protection seeker is in Somalia, for example, and he applies by electronic mail for an entry visa to a State party to any of these Conventions, basing his application on the claim that he suffers a risk of ill-treatment in his country of origin, the application State, when it refuses his request, has not exposed him to ill-treatment as a direct and immediate consequence of its actions.[230] An applicant in this situation is not subject to the effective control of the State he has applied to, and therefore this State does not have extraterritorial jurisdiction over him.

Granting an entry visa in such a situation is neither equivalent to granting protection under Article 3 CAT/ECHR,[231] nor to obliging the State party to admit that such person deserves their protection. The decision to grant this protection depends on the assessment of the circumstances of each case, as we discuss in detail later. If the Court determines that the applicant does not deserve the protection against refoulement under Article 3 CAT/ECHR, the State party may decide to remove him.[232] We do not argue here that it is generally illegal to apply visa requirements under Article 3 CAT/ECHR. What we do argue is that imposition of an entry visa application on all foreigners, including protection seekers, is contrary to the principle of Non-Refoulement as envisaged in this Article.[233]

The ECtHR's recent decision in *Al Ahmad* v. *Greece and Sweden* (2015) seems to follow this approach. The applicant in this case was a Syrian unaccompanied minor who fled Syria and arrived alone in Greece, in August 2014. Upon his arrival, the applicant was detained together with adults for three days and a deportation order was issued against him. This order was later suspended for six months. After his release, the applicant lived in parks without regular access to food and water, to healthcare and to any form of social or psychological support. On 23 December 2014, the applicant and his brother, who had

---

Access to Asylum, International Refugee Law and the Globalisation of Migration Control, Cambridge: Cambridge University Press, 2011, p. 134.

230   Wouters, K., 2009, p. 219; Hansen, T., 2011, p. 135.

231   Neither it corresponds with the diplomatic asylum, which under international law regulates relations between the sending and receiving States of a diplomatic representation. By contrast, the decision on entry visa application regulates the relation between the individual applicant and the State from which this visa is requested. Noll, G., 2005, p. 545.

232   Ibid., p. 565.

233   Noll, G., 2000, p. 443.

come from Sweden where he had refugee status, went to the Swedish embassy in Athens. In the embassy, the applicant submitted a request for international protection, a request for a visa on humanitarian grounds and a request for family reunification with his brother. The brothers refused to leave the embassy premises unless the embassy assumed the applicant's protection. The embassy gave the applicant two written notes in which they informed him that the asylum application could not be submitted to the Swedish embassy and that the embassy could not make a decision as to the request for family reunification, therefore this request had to be submitted to the Swedish authorities. Since this would take time, the embassy requested the brothers to leave the embassy premises and gave the applicant a "receipt of application", confirming that they had received his application for a residence permit on 23 December 2014. The brothers therefore left the embassy premises. In his application before the ECtHR, the applicant claimed, under Article 3, that Sweden had subjected him to ill-treatment because it refused him the right to seek asylum at the embassy and it turned him back to Greek jurisdiction on 23 December 2014. The ECtHR observed that although the Swedish embassy informed the applicant that it was not possible to lodge an application for asylum in Sweden at the embassy, it did accept his application for a residence permit on the ground of family re-unification, and transferred it to the Swedish Migration Board. The Court also noted that there was no indication that the applicant had been forced to leave the embassy premises. Moreover, since the applicant's adult brother accompanied him, there was no ground for the embassy personnel to believe that he was not taken care of by his brother while waiting for a reply to the request for residence permit. The Court concluded that the applicant's complaints relating to the Swedish embassy were manifestly ill-founded and must be declared inadmissible.[234] In our view, it is probable that the Court would have reached different conclusion if the Swedish embassy did not accept the applicant's application for a residence permit and forced him to leave the embassy premises and return to live in conditions that reached a level of severity that fell within the scope of Article 3 ECHR.

II.3.1.2   *Carrier Sanctions*
To enforce visa requirements, several States have imposed fines or other penalties on carriers (airline, train and shipping companies) that transport improperly documented passengers (without valid passport or visa) into their territory. The Carriers' sanctions policy complements visa policy. An absence

---

234   ECtHR, *Al Ahmad* v. *Greece and Sweden* (admissibility decision), Appl.No. 73398/14, 22 September 2015.

of pre-boarding checks could encourage persons who would not be granted a visa if they declared that they were seeking international protection, to travel to a State of destination and apply for protection upon entry.[235]

This practice is not new in the national legislations that govern the rules of entry. Carriers have long been held responsible for transporting, at their own expense, passengers without proper documents back to their country of departure.[236] Since the middle of the last century, most Western States gradually increased the responsibilities of carriers, making them liable for fines, as well as bearing the cost of detention and removal.[237] Influenced by this practice, the 1990 Convention implementing the Schengen Agreement of 17 June 1985, under its Article 26, obliged contracting States to incorporate in their national legislations provisions that impose sanctions on carriers, by air, sea or land, who brought a non-European national without proper documents to the external border of the Schengen area. They also imposed an obligation on the carriers to return such a passenger "to the Third State from which he was transported, to the Third State which issued the travel document on which he travelled or to any other Third State to which he is guaranteed entry".[238] In June 2001, this Article was supplemented by the Directive of the Council of the

---

235   Guiraudon, V., Chapter 5: Enlisting Third Parties in Border Control: a Comparative Study of its Causes and Consequences, in: Caparini, M. & Marenin, O., Borders and Security Governance: Managing Borders in a Globalised World, Geneva: Geneva Centre for the Democratic Control of Armed Forces, 2006, 79–98, p. 84.

236   E.g., the American Passenger Act 1902 imposed an obligation on steamship companies to re-transport, at their own cost, inadmissible passengers. Ibid., p. 82.

237   Such as the US Immigration and National Act 1952, the Australian Migration Act 1958, the Canadian Immigration Act 1976, and the Legal Status of Foreigners in Brazil 1980. European States started to adopt carriers' sanctions from the mid-1980s. German, Belgium and the UK in 1987, Denmark in 1989, Greece in 1991, France, Portugal and Italy in 1993 and the Netherlands in 1994. For details, see Feller, E., 1989, pp. 50–53; Cruz, A., Shifting Responsibility, Carriers' Liability in the Member States of the European Union and North America, Oakhill: Trentham Books, 1995, pp. 9–66. Although these legislations and laws vary from State to State, there are three elements shared among them. 1- imposing the duty of removing the passengers without proper documents on the carrier; 2- obliging the carrier to pay the cost of detaining the concerned passenger; 3- imposing fines or other penalties on the carrier for bringing such passenger. Feller, E., 1989, p. 51; Scholten, S., The Privatisation of Immigration Control through Carrier Sanctions, The Role of Private Transport Companies in Dutch and British Immigration Control, Boston, Leiden: Brill, Nijhoff, 2015.

238   Convention Implementing the Schengen Agreement of 14 June 1985, 19 June 1990, Article 26 (1)(a).

European Union, with the goal of effectively preventing illegal immigration by harmonizing the financial penalties imposed by member States on carriers who breach their obligations.[239] The practice of imposing sanctions on carriers has been strongly criticized on different grounds.[240] Here, we consider whether this approach is compatible with a State's obligations under Article 3 of both the ECHR and CAT.

To avoid sanctions, carriers take responsibility for checking travel documents before allowing passengers to board. Carriers now perform tasks traditionally entrusted to border control officers.[241] If a passenger is found to be travelling without proper documents and visas, airline representatives prevent him from boarding. Thus, the carrier agents who lack training or experience in asylum and international protection issues are often the first line of staff to handle protection requests on behalf of States.[242]

Some States post immigration control officers or airline liaison officers in countries of origin or important transit countries to assist the carrier agents who check travel documents.[243] States that have adopted this policy maintain

---

239   EC Directive 2001/51/EC of 28 June 2001 supplementing the provisions of Article 26 of the Convention implementing the Schengen Agreement of 14 June 1985. While both the Convention and the Directive provide that their application is without prejudice to the obligations resulting from the CSR51, as amended by the New York Protocol of 31 January 1967, there is not any explicit reference to their obligations under the ECHR or the CAT. Convention Implementing the Schengen Agreement of 14 June 1985, Article 26 (1) and (2); EC Directive 2001/51/EC of 28 June 2001 supplementing the provisions of Article 26 of the Convention implementing the Schengen Agreement of 14 June 1985, Preamble (3).

240   It has been argued that this practice is inconsistent with the CSR in several aspects. In addition to the possibility of being a violation of the principle of Non-Refoulement under Article 33, the carriers' sanctions constitute indirect penalties on refugees for their illegal entry, which is prohibited under Article 31. Cruz, A., 1991, p. 76. See also, Basaran, E., Evaluation of the "Carriers' Liability Regime as a Part of the EU Asylum Policy under Public International Law", USAK Yearbook of International Politics and Law, Vol. 2: 2009, 101–115, pp. 10–11.

241   Lomba, S.D., 2004, p. 112.

242   Whitney, K.M., Does the European Convention on Human Rights Protects Refugees from "Safe" Countries?, Georgia Journal of International and Comparative Law, Vol. 26: 1997, 375–408, p. 394; Lomba, S.D., 2004, p. 114.

243   Kjaerum, M., 2006, pp. 54–55. By the end of the 1990s, the UK, Canada, the US, Sweden and France employed immigration liaison officers at selected foreign airports. Australia, the Netherlands, and Norway sent immigration control officials abroad to advise and train airline staff at foreign airports to detect false or incomplete documentation. Gibney, M.J., Beyond the Bounds of Responsibility: Western States and Measures to Prevent the Arrival of Refugees, No. 22: January 2005, p. 8.

that their officers do not have extraterritorial authority. Their role is only to advise carrier staff, and help them identify false documents. These officers have no mandate to determine if improperly documented passengers need international protection.[244] Since it is difficult for at-risk applicants to obtain a visa and proper travel documents, it is likely that such rejected travellers include persons who fled from risk of torture or CIDTP, and who intend to request protection when they arrive in the State of destination. States that adopt this policy cannot legitimately claim that the conduct of carriers is at issue, rather than their own. The conduct of a person or a group of persons is attributed to a State under international law if that person or group of persons acts on the instructions of the State, or exercises elements of governmental authority in default of the official authorities.[245] Carrier officials are *de facto* officials of the State party.[246] Their conduct can be attributed to the State because they are acting under the State's instructions.[247] As the ECtHR asserts, States parties cannot relieve themselves of their responsibilities under the ECHR by delegating them to others.[248]

In the first Chapter, we demonstrated that a State's extraterritorial jurisdiction includes the acts of its immigration control officers, and this includes airline liaison officers who work at foreign airports. Where such officers prevent, directly or indirectly, a traveller from boarding a flight, they clearly control this

---

244 Brouwer, A. & Kumin, J., 2003, p. 10. In some cases, the posted immigration control officers intercept individuals with proper travel documents because of the expectation that they would apply for asylum upon their arrival to the State of destination. Ibid, p. 11.

245 UNGA, Resolution adopted by the General Assembly 56/83. Responsibility of States for internationally wrongful acts, Article 8.

246 Basaran, E., 2009, p. 112; Brouwer, E., Extraterritorial Migration Control and Human Rights: Preserving the responsibility of the EU and its Member States, in: Ryan, B. & Mitsilegas, V., Extraterritorial Immigration Control, Legal Challenges, Leiden: Martinus Nijhoff Publishers, 2010, 199–229, p. 219.

247 Nicholson, F., Implementation of the Immigration (Carriers' Liability) Act 1987: Privatising Immigration Functions at the Expense of International Obligations?, International and Comparative Law Quarterly, Vol. 46 no. 3: 1997, 586–634, p. 628. The State's responsibility may engage where the State concerned fails to take appropriate measures to protect the enjoyment of human rights for persons within its jurisdiction from harm committed by private persons or entities. Clapham, A., Non-State Actors, in: Moeckli, D., Shah, S. & Sivakumaran, S., International Human Rights Law, Oxford: Oxford University Press, 2nd Ed, 2010, 531–550, p. 535; Rodenhauser, T., Another Brick in the Wall: Carrier Sanctions and the Privatization of Immigration Control, International Journal of Refugee Law, Vol. 26 no. 2: 2014, 1–25, pp. 10–12.

248 ECtHR, *Van der Mussele* v. *Belgium*, Appl.No. 8919/80, (Series A, n. 70), 23 November 1983, para. 29.

person and their conduct falls within the extraterritorial jurisdiction of a State party, whether under the CAT or the ECHR. If preventing a person from travelling directly, foreseeably and immediately exposes the person concerned to ill-treatment, the State party is responsible for violating the principle of Non-Refoulement. The policy of imposing carrier sanctions undermines protections against refoulement provided for in both the CAT and the ECHR.[249]

II.3.1.3   *Transit Zones*

Transit or international zones include those through which passengers pass between landing at the port and a State's immigration control points where passengers receive approval to enter the territory of the State.[250] This concept has been broadly defined to also include hotels, hospitals and even sometimes a courtroom away from the airport.[251] States created such zones to justify their position on the basis that in order to enter the territory of a State, a foreigner must obtain authorization or approval of immigration or custom officials to do so. Passengers in international zones are not considered to be within the sovereign territory of the State, because they have not technically entered State territory.[252]

As previously noted, it is impossible for a State party to the ECHR to limit, in general, the territorial scope of the Convention inside its territory through a reservation made under Article 57 ECHR.[253] Along the same lines, territorial scope cannot be limited by the creation of international or transit zones at

---

249   See, EC, Recommendation 1163 (1991) on the Arrival of Asylum-Seekers at European Airports, available at: <http://www.refworld.org/cgi-bin/texis/vtx/rwmain?docid=3ae6b37f3c>, accessed on 22 April 2016, para. 10. Visa requirements and carrier sanctions policies have been criticized on the basis that they increase the criminalisation of migration and encouraging them to introduce and use false travel documents or to resort to services of smugglers. Brouwer, A. & Kumin, J., 2003, p. 8; Guiraudon, V., 2006, p. 15; Basaran, E., 2009, p. 110.

250   Etzwiler, N.G., The Treatment of Asylum Seekers at Ports of Entry and the Concept of "International Zones", in: Kjaerum, M., Hughes, J., Hansen, J. & Bodtcher, A., The Effects of Carrier Sanctions on the Asylum System, Copenhagen: Danish Refugee Council, 1991, 14–22, 14–22, p. 17.

251   Human Rights Watch, HRW, Lost in Transit, Insufficient Protection for Unaccompanied Migrant Children at Roissy Charles de Gaulle Airport, 2009, p. 8.

252   Etzwiler, N.G., 1991, p. 17; Mole, N. & Meredith, C., 2010, p. 113; HRW, Lost in Transit, Insufficient Protection for Unaccompanied Migrant Children at Roissy Charles de Gaulle Airport, p. 2.

253   See above, Chapter 1, the jurisdiction of the State party to the ECHR within its territory.

airports.[254] In *Amuur* v. *France* (1996),[255] the ECtHR mentioned clearly that holding the applicants in an international zone of Paris-Orly Airport made them subject to French law.[256] The Court added that: "despite its name, the international zone does not have extraterritorial status".[257]

Thus, the obligation of Non-Refoulement under Article 3 ECHR applies to transit zones. This conclusion is supported by the Court's position that the State is obligated to protect of refoulement persons physically present in its territory, even if they have not technically entered it.[258]

The ComAT has not addressed the question of applicability of Article 3 CAT to persons held in transit zones. In our opinion, its position should be similar to that of the ECtHR. Creating international or transit zones, as areas in which international legal obligations are non-applicable is inconsistent with international public law through which States exercise their authority and control over the whole of their territory.[259] These areas remain part of the State's territory under international public law because they are still subject to its authority

---

254   Establishment of international zones was a result of the growing feeling of certain States, late in 1980s and early in 1990s; that immigrants and asylum seekers contribute to state economic and sometimes security problems. For more information about the background of this policy and the States' practice in this regard see, Coley, W.J.G., The Evolution of International Zones: British Case Studies, International Human Rights and Refugee Law, 1996, 1–14, p. 3.

255   ECtHR, *Amuur* v. *France*, Appl.No. 19776/92, 25 June 1996. The applicants in this case were four Somali nationals, arrived from Syria at Paris-Orly Airport on March 9, 1992. They claimed that they had fled from Somalia because of the existence of danger on their lives there. The applicants were kept in the "transit zone" of the airport until March 29, when their applications for leave to enter were refused and they were sent back to Syria.

256   There are more than 70 transit zones in France and its overseas territories; the most important one is the transit zone in Roissy Charles de Gaulle Airport which is considered a main entry point into the Schengen zone. HRW, Lost in Transit, Insufficient Protection for Unaccompanied Migrant Children at Roissy Charles de Gaulle Airport, pp. 11–12.

257   ECtHR, *Amuur* v. *France*, para 52; Bello, J.H. & Kokott, J., Amuur v. France, American Journal of International Law, Vol. 91 no. 1: 1997, 147–152, p. 152. See also, ECtHR, *Shamsa* v. *Poland*, Appl.Nos. 45355/99 and 45357/99, 27 November 2003, para. 45; ECtHR, *Nolan and K.* v. *Russia*, Appl.No. 2512/04, 12 February 2009, para. 95. Although these cases relating to the right to liberty granted in Article 5(1) ECHR, the application of this Article to asylum seekers held in international zones at airports means that these zones are under the jurisdiction of the State party according to Article 1 ECHR.

258   ECtHR, *D.* v. *the United Kingdom*, para. 48. The EU Council has invited the governments of member States to ensure that the respect for the ECHR is guaranteed in the reception centers and transit areas at European airports. EC, Recommendation 1163 (1991) on the Arrival of Asylum-Seekers at European Airports, para. 11.

259   Wouters, K., 2009, p. 205; Klug, A. & Howe, T., 2010, p. 91.

and control. For instance, the State enforces criminal law, currency law, and immigration regulations within such areas.[260] Consequently, States may not, by adopting legal or administrative obstacles, hinder the right of persons who are physically present within their territories to be effectively protected from refoulement or prevent such persons from claiming this protection.[261]

II.3.1.4   Interception and Rescue at Sea

II.3.1.4.a   General Comments

Strengthening land border control by imposing visa requirements and carrier sanctions prompts international protection seekers to use alternative means of escape from the risk of ill-treatment. Such persons have increasingly re-lied upon alternatives like journeys by sea.[262] In order to limit the growing number of illegal immigrants, including protection seekers, States have tried to prevent their arrival on their shores by intercepting the vessels that carry them on the high seas. Sometimes they intercept them within the territorial water of other States. The most famous examples of such interception mea-sures at sea were the interception of boats of Haitians at the Caribbean Sea by the US Coast Guard,[263] the Australian Pacific,[264] and Malaysian Solutions;[265]

---

260   Etzwiler, N.G., 1991, p. 17.

261   Wouters, K., 2009, p. 323.

262   As a consequence of the revolutions in North African States (Tunisia, Libya and Egypt), an increasing number of asylum seekers have arrived on the Southern European coasts, particularly on the Italian coasts. From the beginning of 2011 until the end of the year, over 56,000 migrants arrived in Italy, compared to 4,400 throughout 2010. Nascimbene, B. & Pascale, A.D., The 'Arab Spring' and the Extraordinary Influx of People who Arrived in Italy from North Africa, European Journal of Migration and Law, Vol. 13 no. 4: 2011, 341–360; Frontex: JO Hermes – Situational Update, available at: <http://frontex.europa .eu/news/jo-hermes-situational-update-SKG07W>, last visit 3 February 2016.

263   About the US Caribbean Interception Program see, Legomsky, S.H., The USA and the Caribbean Interdiction Program, International Journal of Refugee Law, Vol. 18 no. 3–4: 2006, 677–695.

264   It is also called the Pacific Plan or Pacific Strategy. This policy was adopted after the inci-dent of Tampa (2001); a Norwegian ship rescued 433 asylum seekers from a sinking boat in international waters between Indonesia and Australia. Then, Australia refused the disembarkation of the rescued passengers. For more details about the Pacific Solution see, e.g., Magner, T., A less than ' Pacific' Solution for asylum seekers in Australia, Interna-tional Journal of Refugee Law, Vol. 16 no. 1: 2004, 53–90; Kneebone, S., The Pacific Plan: The Provision of 'Effective Protection'?, International Journal of Refugee Law, Vol. 18 no. 3–4: 2006, 696–721. The Australian government abandoned this policy in 2008.

265   The "Malaysian Solution" is an arrangement between the Australian and Malaysian gov-ernments was signed and announced on 25 July 2011. According to this arrangement, the

the Italian policy of intercepting migrants' boats on the high seas and returning them to Libya pursuant to a series of agreements concerning immigration
control concluded between Italy and Libya (the push-back policy);[266] and, the
interception measures by the navies of France, the UK, Greece, Italy, Malta,[267]
Spain and Portugal in the Adriatic and Mediterranean seas and around the
Canary Islands.[268] On the EU level, the European Agency for the Management
of Operational Cooperation at the External Borders of the Member States of
the European Union (FRONTEX) has played a leading role in the interception measures at sea.[269] In most of these interception operations, intercepted

---

Australian government would transfer up to 800 asylum seekers, including those who
were intercepted at sea in the course of trying to reach the Australian coast illegally, to
Malaysia in order to conduct the refugee status determination process. In return, Australia would accept 4000 UNHCR recognised refugees from Malaysia over four years. Lowes,
S., The Legality of Extraterritorial Processing of Asylum Claims: The Judgment of the High
Court of Australia in the 'Malaysian Solution' Case, Human Rights Law Review, Vol. 12 no.
1: 2012, 168–182, pp. 173–174.

266   In cooperation with the government of Libya, Italy initiated on 6 May 2009 so called
      "Push back-policy", by intercepting people on the high seas and returning them back to
      Libya. The returning of protection seekers' boats back to Libya has a special importance
      in the light of the fact that on the one hand the absence of an asylum system and the
      circumstances of the returned people in Libya. On the other hand, most of the migrants
      or protection seekers in Libya come from countries such as Sudan, Eritrea, Somalia, and
      the DRC, which raises concerns of indirect refoulement. For more information about the
      situation of migrations in Libya and the cooperation between Italy and Libya to counter
      illegal migration see, Klepp, S., A Contested Asylum System: the European Union Between
      Refugee Protection and Border Control in the Mediterranean Sea, European Journal of
      Migration and Law, Vol. 12 no. 1: 2010, 1–12; Pascale, A.d., Migration Control at Sea; The
      Italian Case, in: Ryan, B. & Mitsilegas, V., Extraterritorial Immigration Control: Legal
      Challenges, Leiden: Martinus Nijhoff Publishers, 2010, 281–310.

267   About intercepting protection seekers' boats by Malta and returning them back to Libya
      see, AI, Seeking safety, finding fear, refugees, asylum-seekers and migrants in Libya and
      Malta, December 2010.

268   Lutterbeck, D., Policing Migration in the Mediterranean, Mediterranean Politics, Vol. 11
      no. 1: 2006, 59–82, pp. 67–68. In some situations two or more States cooperate in carrying
      out the interception measures. This does not affect on the responsibility of each State.
      Heijer, M.D., European beyond its Borders: Refugee and Human Rights Protection
      in Extraterritorial Immigration Control, in: Ryan, B. & Mitsilegas, V., Extraterritorial
      Immigration Control, Legal Challenges, London, Boston: Martinus Nijhoff Publishers,
      2010, 169–198, p. 192.

269   FRONTEX was established by the EU Council Regulation no. 2007/2004 on 26 October
      2004. The purpose of this Agency is to assist Member States of the EU and to coordinate
      their actions with regard the application of the operational aspects of external border

persons have all been treated as if they were illegal migrants and were forced to return to their countries of origin. Passengers are not identified or individually assessed to determine if they are at risk of ill-treatment upon their return to receiving States; thus, these interception measures constitute a threat to the principle of Non-Refoulement.[270]

A State's interception activities at sea are based on a strictly territorial understanding of jurisdiction. States maintain that they do not violate their obligations under human rights conventions since they carry out these activities outside their territory.[271] Some States even assume that they have the right to withdraw their territorial jurisdiction, so even persons who are *de facto* present within their territory or territorial waters are deemed not to be *de jure* present.[272]

---

management including the returning of foreign nationals illegally present in the Member States. EU Council: no. 2007/2004, (26 October 2004).For more information about the FRONTEX operations at sea see, Moreno-Lax, V., Seeking Asylum in the Mediterranean: Against a Fragmentary Reading of EU Member States' Obligations Accruing at Sea, International Journal of Refugee Law, Vol. 23 no. 2: 2011, 174–220, pp. 181–182.

270   HRW, Pushed Back, Pushed Around Italy's Forced Return of Boat Migrants and Asylum Seekers, Libya's Mistreatment of Migrants and Asylum Seekers, 2009, pp. 7–10; Léonard, S., EU border security and migration into the European Union: FRONTEX and securitisation through practices, European Security, Vol. 19 no. 2: 2010, 231–254, p. 240.

271   E.g. Italian government has argued that it does not violate its human rights obligations by returning boat people to Libya because the interception measures are not done in Italian waters. AFP, Italy returns new wave of boat people to Libya, 19 May 2009. In *Sale* v. *Haitian Centers Council* (1993), the American government claimed that its practice of intercepting boats of Haitians in international waters and returning them to Haiti was not a violation of the CSR or international law generally. In a controversial decision, the US Supreme Court decided that neither the textual analysis nor the negotiating history of the CSR supported a position that Article 33 is applicable on the high seas. It accepted therefore that the American government's duty of Non-Refoulement under Article 33 applied only to refugees within the American territorial waters. The US Supreme Court, *Sale* v. *Haitian Centers Council*, 509 U.S. 155, 1993. For analysis of this judgment see, e.g., Neuman, G.L., Extraterritorial Violations of Human Rights by the United States, American University Journal of International Law and Policy, Vol. 9 no. 4: 1994, 213–242.

272   Hansen, T., The Refugee, the Sovereign and the Sea: European Union Interdiction Policies, in: Nissen, R. & Hansen, T., Sovereignty Games, Instrumentalizing State Sovereignty in Europe and Beyond, New York: Palgrave Macmillan, 2008, 171–195, p. 181. States adopting such policies justify their approach based on several arguments, such as the co-operation between States to prevent the smuggling of migrants by sea. See, e.g., Italy's justification for its "Push-back" Operations in UNHCR, Submission by the UNHCR in the case of *Hirsi and Others* v. *Italy* (Application no. 27765/09), available at: <http://www.unhcr.org/refworld/pdfid/4b97778d2.pdf>, March 2010, para. 2.1.

As noted in Chapter 1, each State exercises jurisdiction over the whole of its territory, which is not limited to land, but also includes territorial waters and the contiguous zone.[273] Interception measures taken by a costal State inside its territorial waters or contiguous zone are within its jurisdiction. Consequently, when States carry out such measures, they are obligated to respect their commitments under the Conventions to which they are party, including the principle of Non-Refoulement under Article 3 CAT and/or Article 3 ECHR. States cannot adopt administrative obstacles to deprive persons who are already *de facto* present within its territory from enjoying their rights. They cannot exclude part of their territorial waters from their jurisdiction in order to prevent the principle of Non-Refoulement from being implemented. For example, Australia's "Pacific Solution" excised the territories of Christmas Island, Ashmore and Cartier, and the Cocos Islands from Australian territory for the purpose of immigration.[274] This excision does not relieve Australia from the obligation, as a State party to the CAT, to refrain from forcibly returning individuals intercepted in those territories to another State where they would face a risk of torture contrary to Article 3 CAT.

The problem arises when such measures are taken on the high seas or within the territorial sea of another State.[275] A State exercises extraterritorial jurisdiction over vessels that fly its flag. Where an intercepted ship flies the flag of the intercepting State, or intercepted persons are transferred onto a vessel

---

273   "The sovereignty of costal State extends, beyond its land territory [...] to an adjacent belt of sea, described as the territorial sea". UNCLOS82, Article 2(1). According to Article 33 UNCLOS, a costal State may exercise, in a zone contiguous to its territorial sea, the control necessary to prevent infringement of its customs, fiscal, immigration or sanitary laws and regulations within its territory or territorial sea; and to punish infringement of the above laws and regulations committed within its territory or territorial sea. Ibid., Article 33. Thus, a costal State has a *de jure* jurisdiction over its contiguous zone. *De jure* jurisdiction is a strong evidence for *de facto* jurisdiction. Klug, A. & Howe, T., 2010, pp. 90, 92–94. According to the ECtHR's jurisprudence, the question of jurisdiction under Article 1 was not considered necessary to address in the case of costal State's act inside its territorial sea and contiguous zone. ECtHR, *Women on Waves and others* v. *Portugal*, Appl.No. 31276/05, 3 February 2009; ECtHR, *Mangouras* v. *Spain*, Appl.No. 12050/04, 28 September 2010. Mole, N. & Meredith, C., 2010, p. 110.

274   D.Fox, B., International Asylum and Boat People: The Tampa Affair and Australia's "Pacific Solution", Maryland Journal of International Law, Vol. 25 no. 1: 2010, 356–373, p. 358.

275   According to the UNCLOS, the high seas are open to all States, whether coastal or land-locked and no State may validly purport to subject any part of the high seas to its sovereignty. UNCLOS82, Articles. 87 and 89.

that flies the flag of the intercepting State,[276] this State exercises *de jure* and *de facto* jurisdiction over those intercepted persons. The intercepting State is thus obliged to respect their right of Non-Refoulement. A State also exercises jurisdiction extraterritorially where, through its agents, it has at least *de facto*, effective control over a ship that flies a foreign flag and/or its crew. Thus, where the intercepting State has effective control over the intercepted ship and/or its crew, the persons intercepted fall within the jurisdiction of the intercepting State and it is obligated to protect them against refoulement. The decision as to whether the intercepting State exercises effective control will depend on the circumstances of each case.

Under international maritime law, States are obligated to rescue persons in distress at sea. Almost all international maritime conventions impose this obligation, regardless of the status or number of the persons who need aid, or their mode of travel.[277] According to International Convention on Maritime Search and Rescue (SAR) and International Convention for the Safety of Life at Sea (SOLAS), States are obligated to "co-operate and co-ordinate" to ensure that shipmasters are permitted to deliver rescued passengers to a "place of safety".[278] This obligation raises two points of concern. The first relates to the meaning of the phrase, "place of safety". Under maritime law, this term refers to safety from the threat of shipwreck and drowning; under international human rights law it refers to safety from possible ill-treatment, including refoulement. Theoretically, a State that takes rescue measures is obligated to respect both these concepts of safety, particularly when rescued persons include protection

---

276 Such as in the case of the "push-back" operations by Italy. The intercepted boats were initially stopped on the high seas by Italian military vessels, and then returned directly to Libya after taking them on board the Italian vessels. Tondini, M., "Fishers of Men? The Interception of Migrants in the Mediterranean Sea and Their Forced Return to Libya", INEX Paper, Converging and conflicting ethical values in the internal/external security continuum in Europe, European Commission, 7th Framework Programme, 2010, p. 5 footnote. 13. As noted by the UNHCR "the Italian authorities were in full and effective control of the persons throughout the "push-back" operations until the formal hand-over to the Libyan authorities". UNHCR, Submission by the UNHCR in the case of *Hirsi and Others* v. *Italy* (Application no. 27765/09), para. 4.3.2.

277 Most important treaties concerned with the rescue obligation are the UNCLOS82; SAR79 and SOLAS74.

278 This obligation is provided for in the amendments to the SAR and SOLAS adopted by the International Maritime Organisation, entered into force 1 July 2006. See, Miltner, B., Human Security and Protection from *Refoulement* in the Maritime Context, in: Edwards, A. & Ferstman, C., Human Security and Non-Citizens, Law, Policy and International Affairs, Cambridge: Cambridge University Press, 2010, 195–224, p. 213.

seekers. Unfortunately, in some situations, it is difficult for a State or a shipmaster to reconcile these two concepts. For example, rescued passengers may need to be immediate disembarked for medical treatment.[279] The second point is that the activities described as "rescue" may, in fact, have as their preliminary aim the interception of illegal migrants, and may be designed to prevent them from reaching a State's territorial sea.[280] An intercepting State could argue that, when its vessel responds to persons in distress at sea, it is not engaged in interception.[281] The ComAT has not had the opportunity to address these two points of concern in the context of refoulement, but the ECtHR has dealt with them in the refoulement case of *Hirsi Jamaa and Others* v. *Italy* (2012), which will be discussed in more detail in the next section.[282]

The obligation of the intercepting State party to respect the intercepted person's right of Non-Refoulement under the CAT/ECHR arises even if

---

279   Wouters, K. & Heijer, M.D., 2010, pp. 6–7. In this context, efforts have been made to harmonise the search and rescue operations carried out by the member States of the EU participating in FRONTEX operations. Those efforts lead, in February 2014, to the adoption of draft regulation establishing rules for the surveillance of the external sea borders in the context of operational cooperation coordinated by FRONTEX. This draft regulation defines the "place of safety" as "a location where rescue operations are considered to terminate and where the survivors' safety of life is not threatened, where their basic human needs can be met and from which transportation arrangements can be made for the survivors' next destination or final destination, taking into account the protection of their fundamental rights in compliance with the principle of Non-Refoulement". However, in order to enter into force, the draft regulation still needs to be formally approved by the European Parliament and the Council. For the draft regulation see, EU Council: Proposal for a Regulation of the European Parliament and of the Council establishing rules for the surveillance of the external sea borders in the context of operational cooperation coordinated by the FRONTEX, (12 February 2014) 6269/14, Interinstitutional File: 2013/0106 (COD), Available at: <http://www.statewatch.org/news/2014/feb/eu-council-frontex-search-and-rescue-final-compromise-6269-14.pdf>. EU Council: New rules for the surveillance of the EU external sea borders, 6463/14, Presse 68, 20 February 2014.

280   Brouwer, A. & Kumin, J., 2003, p. 11; Moreno-Lax, V., 2012, p. 575.

281   UNHCR, Conclusion adopted by the Executive Committee on International Protection, Conclusion on Protection Safeguards in Interception Measures, 21 November 2008, p. 154.

282   In the refoulement case of *Hussun and others* v. *Italy* (2010), the applicants were intercepted or rescued at sea by Italian authorities and taken to the Italian island of Lampedusa. There applications to the ECtHR based, *inter alia*, on Article 3 ECHR. However, they were returned to Libya without having the opportunity to make applications of asylum. The case was struck out of the list because some of the applicants were expelled and the whereabouts of others was unknown. ECtHR, *Hussun and Others* v. *Italy*, Appl. Nos. 10171/05, 10601/05, 11593/05 and 17165/05, 19 January 2010; Mole, N. & Meredith, C., 2010, p. 113.

interception measures were carried out inside the territorial water of the intercepted person's own State.[283] Contrary to the protection against refoulement under Article 33 CSR, both Article 3 CAT and Article 3 ECHR protect the person against refoulement even if he is still inside the country of his nationality or habitual residence.

Finally, there is an argument that simply denying a ship entry into territorial waters is not the same as a breach of the principle of Non-Refoulement, since the latter requires that State action have the effect or result of returning the protection seekers to a place of ill-treatment.[284] A ship that is turned away may theoretically travel to any another coastal State in the world. However, a coastal State that simply denies the protection seekers' ship entry to its territorial waters breaches the principle of Non-Refoulement if there is sufficient proof that the passengers have no alternative than to return to a State where they face a risk of ill-treatment. Even if an action does not directly return a person to a place of ill-treatment, it would constitute indirect refoulement if it results in returning the person to a third State, from which he is forcibly returned to a place of ill-treatment.[285]

II.3.1.4.b   The Case-Law of the ComAT and ECtHR Relating to the Interception and Rescue at Sea

The ComAT addressed the question of applicability of the principle of Non-Refoulement in the context of interception and rescue at sea in *J.H.A. v. Spain* (2008).[286] On 31 January 2007, the Spanish maritime authority received a distress call from 'Marine 1', a vessel capsized in international waters with 369 immigrants of African and Asian origin on board. On 4 February, a Spanish maritime rescue tug reached the vessel and provided immediate relief to passengers by handing out water and food supplies. On the same day, Spain, Senegal and Mauritania began to negotiate the fate of Marine 1 and its crew. The Spanish and Mauritanian governments reached agreement on 12 February. Accordingly, the Spanish maritime rescue tug towed the ship to

---

283   Barnes, R., The International Law of the Sea and Migration Control, in: Ryan, B. & Mitsilegas, V., Extraterritorial Immigration Control, Legal Challenges, Leiden: Martinus Nijhoff Publishers, 2010, 103–150, p. 115.

284   Goodwin-Gill, G.S. & McAdam, J., 2007, p. 277.

285   Guilfoyle, D., Shipping Interdiction and the Law of the Sea, Cambridge: Cambridge University Press, 2009, p. 223; Heijer, M.D., 2010, p. 189.

286   The complainant in this case was J.H.A., a Spanish citizen and a member of non-governmental organisation. He was acting on behalf of P.K. et al., Indian citizens who were detained in Mauritania at the time of submission of the complaint. ComAT, *J.H.A. v. Spain* (admissibility decision), para. 1.1.

Nouadhibou, Mauritania, where Spanish national police proceeded to identify the immigrants who had landed. On 14 February, they finished identifying the immigrants. All but 23 of the immigrants requested asylum, or signed a voluntary repatriation agreement.[287] The remaining 23 immigrants, who claimed that they had fled from India because they feared persecution resulting from a conflict in Kashmir, remained in detention under Spanish control in Nouadhibou, housed in a former fish-processing plant.

Human rights organizations in Spain lodged several complaints about the conditions in which these remaining immigrants were held, including the complaint submitted to the ComAT. The complainant stated that, although the passengers were detained in Mauritania, they were effectively under Spanish control. He alleged that Spain assumed responsibility for them by rescuing them in international waters and Spain supervised them during the entire period of detention in Nouadhibou.[288] The complainant alleged that Article 3 CAT would be violated if Spain returned the alleged victims to India, where they would be subjected to torture or CIDTP as a result of the conflict in Kashmir.[289] The Committee noted that Spain exercised control over the alleged victims from the time of their rescue on the high seas, throughout the identification and repatriation process that took place in Mauritania; they were therefore subject to Spanish jurisdiction.[290]

Although this conclusion conforms with the earlier approach of the ComAT to the extraterritorial applicability of the CAT, this is the first time the Committee explicitly confirmed that States parties engaged in interception or rescue measures on the high seas are responsible under the CAT, and particularly under the principle of Non-Refoulement. The State party to the CAT must respect its obligation of Non-Refoulement under Article 3 CAT in the context of interception and rescue operations at sea. The obligations must be respected even if the interception or rescue measures are carried out in the territorial waters of another State. The ComAT has not had the opportunity to address this situation, in the context of the Non-Refoulement principle, under Article 3 CAT. However, in *Sonko* v. *Spain* (2011), which did not concern a Non-Refoulement complaint, the Committee found that victims were within

---

287   35 persons of African origin were readmitted by Guinea, 35 persons of Asian origin were transferred to the Canary Islands to initiate asylum application procedures. The 299 remaining persons were repatriated to India or Pakistan with the assistance of the International Organisation for Migration (IOM). Ibid., paras. 2.4–2.5.

288   Ibid., para. 2.9.

289   Ibid., para. 3.3.

290   Ibid., para. 8.2.

the jurisdiction of the respondent State party even though the interception measures were taken in the territorial waters of another State (Morocco). This case concerned a group of four Senegalese migrants who attempted swim to the Spanish enclave of Ceuta. They were intercepted by a vessel of the Spanish Civil Guard and pulled up alive, onto the vessel. After being brought near the Moroccan coast, they were forced to jump into the water. The Civil Guard officers had allegedly punctured their dinghies beforehand. The applicant was the only one who did not know how to swim. In spite of belated attempts by Spanish officers to take him ashore and revive him, he died shortly afterwards. The Committee observed that the Spanish Civil Guard officers had exercised control over the persons on board the vessel, and were therefore responsible for their safety.[291] The Committee found that Spain had violated Article 16 for ill-treatment, and violated Article 12 for not conducting a suitable investigation into the matter.[292]

With regard to the ECtHR's Non-Refoulement case-law relating to the interception and rescue at seas, the Court has noted that the States that form the external borders of the EU face considerable difficulties in coping with the growing influx of migrants and asylum seekers. The Court has not underestimated the burden and pressure placed on the EU border States, pressure that has increased with the present economic crisis.[293] The Court has been particularly aware of the difficulties that arise from migration by sea, which complicates control of the southern borders of the EU. However, the Court has asserted that, in the light of the absolute nature of the rights secured by Article 3 ECHR, this situation cannot absolve a State party of its obligations under this Article.[294]

The ECtHR had the opportunity to address the relation of the Italian push-back policy to the prohibition against refoulement in *Hirsi Jamaa and Others* v. *Italy* (2012).[295] On 6 May 2009, the Italian Revenue Police and the Coast Guard intercepted three vessels of migrants headed towards the Italian

---

291   ComAT, *Sonko* v. *Spain*, para. 10. 3.

292   Ibid., paras. 10.4–10.8.

293   ECtHR, *Hirsi Jamaa and Others* v. *Italy* (GC), para. 122; M.S.S. v. Belgium and Greece [GC], no. 30696/09, § 223, 21 January 2011.

294   Ibid., para. 122.

295   In *Hussun and others* v. *Italy* (2010), the applicants were intercepted or rescued at sea by Italian authorities and taken to the Italian island of Lampedusa. There applications to the ECtHR based, *inter alia*, on Article 3 ECHR. However, they were returned to Libya without having the opportunity to make applications of asylum. The case has been stuck out of the list because some of the applicants were expelled and the whereabouts of others were unknown. ECtHR, *Hussun and Others* v. *Italy*; Mole, N. & Meredith, C., 2010, p. 113.

coast and returned them to Libya. The interception took place on the high seas, in application of a bilateral anti-immigration cooperation agreement between Italy and Libya that entered into force on 4 February 2009. The intercepted migrants were transferred onto Italian military ships and directly returned to Libya. They were forcibly handed over to the Libyan authorities. The Italians did not identify the immigrants, or even inform them of their true destination.[296] The applicants claimed before the ECtHR that they had been exposed to the risk of torture or inhuman or degrading treatment in Libya, as well as the risk of return to their respective countries of origin, Eritrea and Somalia, where they faced a risk of similar ill-treatment.[297] The Italian government tried to circumvent its jurisdiction under the ECHR by describing the events in the case as a rescue operation designed to ensure the safety of human lives on the high seas. The government maintained that its obligation to rescue persons in distress under the United Nations Convention on the Law of the Sea did not create a link between Italy and those persons that established Italian jurisdiction.[298] The ECtHR rejected this argument and held that the events that gave rise to the alleged violation of Article 3 ECHR took place entirely on board ships that flew the Italian flag on the high sea, whose crews were composed exclusively of Italian military personnel. Thus, these events fell within the Italian jurisdiction.[299] The Court also noted that the rules of international law for the rescue of persons in distress at sea and those that prohibit the trafficking of persons both oblige States to fulfil their obligations under international refugee law, including the principle of Non-Refoulement. The Court concluded that the United Nations Convention on the Law of the Sea did not justify the action of returning the applicants to Libya.[300] The Court further stated that:

> Italy [could not] evade its responsibility [for refoulement] by relying on its obligations arising out of bilateral agreements with Libya. Even if it were to be assumed that those agreements made express provision for the return to Libya of migrants intercepted on the high seas, the Contracting States' responsibility continues even after their having entered into treaty

---

296   ECtHR, *Hirsi Jamaa and Others* v. *Italy* (GC), paras. 9–13 and 185.

297   Ibid., para. 83. Out of over two hundred intercepted migrants, the application lodged before the ECtHR by eleven Somali nationals and thirteen Eritrean nationals.

298   Ibid., para. 65.

299   Ibid., paras. 76–82.

300   Ibid., para. 134. This approach is completely in line with the Court's case-law that the applicability of other international legal obligations does not decrease the scope of application of the ECHR. ECtHR, *Soering* v. *the United Kingdom*, para. 86; ECtHR, *Bosphorus* v. *Ireland*, Appl.No. 45036/98, 30 June 2005, para. 135; Heijer, M.D., 2013, p. 8.

commitments subsequent to the entry into force of the Convention or its Protocols in respect of these.[301]

This position is compatible with the ECtHR's case-law that:

> Where States establish [...] international agreements to pursue co-operation in certain fields of activities, there may be implications for the protection of fundamental rights. It would be incompatible with the purpose and object of the Convention if Contracting States were thereby absolved from their responsibility under the Convention in relation to the field of activity covered by such [agreements].[302]

Along the same lines, member States of the EU that take part in joint interception operations cannot avoid responsibility for refoulement under Article 3 ECHR by transferring their powers to the FRONTEX.[303]

The ECtHR has determined that a State party must respect its obligation of Non-Refoulement under Article 3 ECHR while it carries out interception operations on the high seas. The Court's approach in the *Hirsi Jamaa* case is not limited to cases in which interception operations are carried out on the high seas, but also extends to situations in which a State party has effective control over an intercepted vessel and its crew, such as inside the another State's territorial water when that State has given consent.[304] Although the interception operations carried out by FRONTEX in the territorial waters of Mauritania and Senegal relied for their legal basis on bilateral agreements concluded by Spain with these States, consent granted by Senegal and Mauritania did not relieve Spain of its responsibilities under the principle of Non-Refoulement as developed under Article 3 ECHR.[305]

If the interception activities are carried out within the territorial waters of another State, the responsibility of the intercepting State does not exclude the host State's responsibility for its conduct. The State's obligation to respect

---

301   ECtHR, *Hirsi Jamaa and Others* v. *Italy* (GC), para. 129.

302   ECtHR, *T.I.* v. *the United Kingdom* (admissibility decision).

303   Papastavridis, E., 'Fortress Europe' and FRONTEX: Within or Without International Law?, Nordic Journal of International Law, Vol. 79 no. 1: 2010, 75–111, pp. 104–105; Moreno-Lax, V., 2011, p. 201. It should be mentioned here that, according to its Fundamental Rights Strategy, Frontex should "take into account the relevant ECtHR case-law in its activities"., FRONTEX Fundamental Rights Strategy, adopted on 31 March 2011, para. 6.

304   In this sense, see Wouters, K. & Heijer, M.D., 2010, p. 10; Moreno-Lax, V., 2012, p. 597; Kneebone, S., 2006, p. 713.

305   Moreno-Lax, V., 2011, p. 200.

human rights includes a positive obligation to prevent human rights violations within its territory, even when such violations are committed by another
State.[306] Thus, the host State will also be responsible for violating the principle
of Non-Refoulement if it participates in interception measures, or if it declines
to intervene to prevent the act of refoulement.[307]

II.3.2 Multinational Operations

The participation of several States in multinational forces that work overseas,
such as in Iraq, Afghanistan, the DRC and Sudan, has given rise to several com-
plex legal questions.[308] The question of the applicability of the principle of
Non-Refoulement on the transfer of detainees by multinational forces is of
special importance to this study. Such a transfer can be made either between
different contingents of the multinational forces, or from multinational forces to local authorities, where the transferred person may face a risk of being
tortured or ill-treated, or may face criminal proceedings leading to the imposition of the death penalty.[309] There is an argument that concerns about protection also arise in cases where detainees are released in certain areas where
they may face serious risk of ill-treatment from armed groups unconnected to
the State.[310] This subsection addresses the question of whether a State party

---

306   Wouters, K. & Heijer, M.D., 2010, p. 11. In *Ilascu and Others* v. *Moldova and Russia* (2004),
        the *de facto* jurisdiction of Russia did not replace the *de jure* jurisdiction of Moldova.
        ECtHR, *Ilascu and Others* v. *Moldova and Russia*, para. 333.

307   In *Mohammed Alzery* v. *Sweden* (2006), the applicant was subjected to extraordinary
        rendition by CIA on the territory of Sweden, the HRC held that: "at a minimum, a State
        party is responsible for acts of foreign officials exercising acts of sovereign authority on its
        territory, if such acts are performed with the consent or acquiescence of the State party".
        HRC, *Mohammed Alzery* v. *Sweden*, Communication No.1416/2005, 10 November 2006,
        para. 11.6. See also, Papastavridis, E., 2010, p. 107.

308   The term "multinational forces" refers to all forces working abroad such as peacekeeping,
        peace making or peace enforcement forces, whether working under the umbrella of the
        UN or a regional organisation such as the NATO. Katayanagi, M., Human Rights Functions
        of United Nations Peacekeeping Operations, The Hague: Martinus Nijhoff Publishers,
        2002, pp. 54–66.

309   According to the Afghan Independent Human Rights Commission, NATO countries
        handed over approximately 267 detainees to Afghan custody in 2009. Of those detainees,
        93 were turned over by the British forces, 163 by the Canadian forces, 10 by the Dutch
        forces, and 1 by Danish forces. HRW, Special Committee on the Canadian Mission in
        Afghanistan, Parliament of Canada, 5 May 2010, p. 4. For the transfer of detainees from
        ISAF States' custody to Afghan authorities, see also, AI, Afghanistan detainees transferred
        to torture: ISAF complicity?, ASA 11/011/2007, 13 November 2007.

310   Gillard, E.C., 2008, p. 704.

to the ECHR and/or the CAT remains bound by its conventional obligations, including the prohibition of refoulement, when its military forces participate in multinational operations overseas, or if they work under authorisation of the UN, or if they are placed at the disposal of the UN, a regional organisation, such as the North Atlantic Treaty Organization (NATO), or even another State. Does participation in the multinational forces absolve a State concerned from its Non-Refoulement obligation under the ECHR and the CAT?

Human rights law applies in wartime as well as in peacetime.[311] The prohibition of refoulement under both the ECHR and the CAT are non-derogable in any circumstances, even in wartime or public emergency situations. Both the ComAT and the ECtHR have held that a State remains bound by its obligations under the respective Convention even if it participates in multinational operations and transfers some of its powers to an international organisation.[312] While discussing the UK's fourth periodic report, the ComAT raised the following question:

> Has the State party informed its armed forces that the terms of the Convention, [...] are directly applicable to them when participating in peacekeeping or other military operations either alone or as part of an internationally authorised contingent?[313]

The Committee posits that when a State party to the CAT participates in the multinational forces, it remains bound by its obligations under the Convention.[314]

In the same context, the ECtHR has asserted that, although the ECHR does not prohibit States parties from transferring sovereign power to an international organisation in order to pursue cooperation in certain fields of activity, this does not absolve a State from its obligations under the Convention. The Court recognizes that absolving States parties completely from their conventional obligations in the areas covered by such a transfer is incompatible with

---

311   See, e.g., ICJ, *Advisory opinion on the legal consequences of the construction of a wall in the occupied Palestinian territory*, para. 106; HRC, General Comment No. 31, The Nature of the General Legal Obligation Imposed on States Parties to the Covenant, Adopted on 29 March 2004, UN. Doc. CCPR/C/21/Rev.1/Add.13, 26 May 2004, para. 11.

312   Droege, C., 2008, p. 685.

313   ComAT, Thirty-third session, list of Issues, the United Kingdom, UN. Doc. CAT/C/33/L/GBR, 15–26 November 2004, para. 24.

314   This conclusion is supported by the ComAT General Comment no. 2 which indicates that the phrase "any territory" in Articles 2, 5, 11, 12, 13 and 16 refers to prohibited acts committed, *inter alia*, during peacekeeping operations. ComAT, General Comment No. 2, para. 16.

the purpose and object of the ECHR, and would allow States to limit or exclude the guarantees of the Convention at will.[315]

States parties to the CAT/ECHR cannot absolve themselves from their conventional obligations by participating in multinational forces. Both Conventions impose an obligation of Non-Refoulement on States parties with regard to persons under the effective control of their military forces when those forces participate in multinational operations. The criterion for attributing a removal act either to the participating State or to the international organization is factual control over the act by the forces placed at the organization's disposal.[316] Where a State exercises factual control over transfer measures, the removal act is attributed to that State and that State is responsible when it transfers a person in violation of the principle of Non-Refoulement.

Thus, a simple authorization by the UNSC for States to carry out an operation will not usually be sufficient to attribute to the UN the acts of participating States' contingents. For example, even though UNSC resolution 1386 authorised the International Security Assistance Force (ISAF) in Afghanistan "to take all necessary measures to fulfil its mandate",[317] the decision to transfer lies exclusively with the participating States' contingents, and not with NATO

---

315   ECtHR, *Bosphorus* v. *Ireland*, paras. 152–154. States parties to the ECHR who participated in the multinational operations overseas, such as in Iraq or Afghanistan, maintained that the Convention does not apply on the conducts of their forces there, due to the ECHR's "espace juridique". As previously noted, the Court rejected this argument. Sitaropoulos, N., Refugees and the Principle of Non-Refoulement, United Kingdom: Dissertation, University of Essex, 1990, p. 122; Wilde, R., 2010.

316   According to the draft articles on Responsibility of International Organizations adopted by the ILC, the conduct of an organ of a State that is placed at the disposal of an international organization shall be considered under international law an act of the organization if the organization exercises effective control over that conduct. ILC, Report of the International Law Commission, Sixty-first session (4 May-5 June and 6 July- 7 August 2009), General Assembly, Official Records, Sixty-fourth session, Supplement No. 10 (A/64/10), Article 6. See also, Hirsch, M., The Responsibility of International Organizations toward Third Parties, Dordrecht: Martinus Nijhoff Publishers, 1995, pp. 64–67.

317   ISAF's was established under UNSC resolution 1386 to "assist the Afghan Interim Authority in the maintenance of security in Kabul and in surrounding areas". UNSC, Resolution 1386, UN. Doc. S/RES/1386, 20 December 2001, para. 1. The "necessary measures" referred to in this resolution include the power of detention. The authority of ISAF was expended to cover the whole of Afghanistan by UNSC resolution 1510. UNSC, Resolution 1510, UN. Doc. S/RES/1510 (2003), 13 October 2003. With regard to MNF-I, the UNSC resolution 1546 authorized the MNF-I "to take all necessary measures to contribute to the maintenance of security and stability" in Iraq, including "internment where this is necessary for imperative reasons of security".

or the UN.[318] The removal act is therefore attributed to the participating States and they can be considered responsible for transferring a person contrary to the principle of Non-Refoulement. Even States that participate in ISAF have accepted this conclusion. Several of those States concluded bilateral memorandums of understanding (MOUs) with the Afghan government to regulate the treatment of transferred detainees.[319]

The above claim is implicitly supported by the fact that neither the UK nor the ECtHR raised the attribution of transfer to the UN as a question in *Al- Saadoon and Mufdhi* v. *The UK* (2010). In this case, the ECtHR had the opportunity to address the application of the principle of Non-Refoulement under Article 3 ECHR to the States parties' military forces that participated in multinational forces overseas.[320] The British government argued that the UNSC, from the early stages of the occupation period, sought to uphold the sovereignty of Iraq and to establish the government of Iraq, by Iraq.[321] British forces were not entitled to arrest or detain Iraqi nationals on Iraq's territory, except as permitted by Iraq or authorised by a binding UNSC Resolution.[322] The British government maintained that UK forces in Iraq had no option other than to transfer applicants to Iraqi authorities, because the UN Mandate under UNSC Resolution No. 1790, which authorised the role of British forces in arrest, detention and imprisonment tasks in Iraq, would expire forthwith.[323] The government claimed that the UK's power to detain Iraqi nationals would be withdrawn in a matter of hours, and that the Iraqi authorities would then have had the right to physically remove the applicants from the British base.[324]

---

318   See statement by Colonel Stephen P. Noonan, who referred that although the Canadian forces were placed under operational control of NATO, the duties that were assigned to the Canadian Forces ISAF personnel in Afghanistan need to remain consistent with Canadian direction, so therefore they always held the ability to say no to military tasks. Federal Court of Canada, *Amnesty International Canada* v. *Canada (National Defence)*, 2007 FC 1147, 12 March 2008, para. 33.

319   Droege, C., 2008, p. 684.

320   Before the case of *Al- Saadoon and Mufdhi*, the Court addressed the application of other Articles of the Convention to such forces. See, ECtHR, *Bankovic et al* v. *Belgium and 16 other Contracting States* (admissibility decision), which concerned the application of Articles 2, 10 and 13; ECtHR, *Behrami and Behrami* v. *France and Saramati v. France, Germany and Norway* (Admissibility decision), Appl.Nos. 71412/01 and 78166/01, 2 May 2007, which concerned the application of Articles 5, 6 and 13.

321   It referred as example to the UNSCR 1483 of 22 May 2003.

322   ECtHR, *Al-Saadoon and Mufdhi* v. *the United Kingdom*, para. 111.

323   ECtHR, *Al-Saadoon and Mufdhi* v. *the United Kingdom* (admissibility decision), para. 87.

324   Ibid., paras. 75–81.

As previously mentioned, the ECtHR pointed out that the UK's authorities exercised control over the premises, and consequently the individuals detained there, including the applicants, who were within the UK's jurisdiction.[325] The Court decided that it was not material to the preliminary issue of jurisdiction whether the UK was under a legal obligation to transfer the applicants to Iraqi custody, or whether, if this obligation existed, it altered or replaced any obligation owed to the applicants under the ECHR.[326] The Court found that a State party is responsible under the Convention for all acts and omissions of its organs, even if these acts or omissions were a necessary consequence of complying with international legal obligations.[327]

The controversial *Behrami* case,[328] in which the Court considered that "the key question is whether the UNSC retained ultimate authority and control so that operational command only was delegated", is worth mention here.[329] While the Court accepted "the effectiveness or unity of NATO command in *operational* matters",[330] it observed that the establishment and presence of Kosovo Force (KFOR) in Kosovo was based on the UNSC resolution No. 1244, and noted that international military presence was exercising "lawfully delegated Chapter 7 powers of the UNSC". Furthermore, the leadership of the KFOR was required by the resolution to report to the UNSC, so the UNSC would be able to exercise its overall authority and control.[331] In this situation, the Court found that a one chain of command ran from the UNSC, which retained "ultimate authority and control", while KFOR was delegated only operational

---

325   Ibid., para. 88.

326   Ibid., para. 89.

327   ECtHR, *Al-Saadoon and Mufdhi* v. *the United Kingdom*, para. 128. The UK Divisional Court had earlier considered that the British forces had physical custody and control of the applicants and had it in their power to refuse to transfer them to the custody of the Iraq High Tribunal, even if to act in such a way would be contrary to the UK's international law obligations. ECtHR, *Al-Saadoon and Mufdhi* v. *the United Kingdom* (admissibility decision), para. 34.

328   ECtHR, *Behrami and Behrami* v. *France and Saramati* v. *France, Germany and Norway* (Admissibility decision). In this case, the applicants argued that France violated Article 2 ECHR because the French KFOR troops in Kosovo had failed to mark or defuse a number of undetonated cluster bombs which caused seriously injury to one of the applicants and the death of a member of his family. In the *Saramati* case, the applicant alleged that his detention by KFOR between July 2001 and January 2002 constitutes violation of Articles 5, 6 and 13 ECHR.

329   Ibid., para. 133.

330   Ibid., para. 139.

331   Ibid., para. 134.

command.[332] Accordingly, the Court concluded that the act under complaint was "attributable" to the UN.[333] This analysis was strongly criticised on the grounds that attribution of the conduct of KFOR to the UNSC cannot be convincingly established by examining the legality of the delegation of its Chapter 7 powers under resolution 1244.[334] One author noted that, while the UNSC might have retained such "ultimate authority and control" over KFOR as was necessary to render the delegation of its powers lawful under the UN Charter, the question that should have been addressed by the ECtHR is whether or not the UNSC exercised "effective control" over KFOR sufficient to attribute KFOR's conduct to the UN, in accordance with the law of international responsibility.[335] As the ILC mentioned when implementing the criterion of "effective control", "operational" control would seem more important than "ultimate" control, because the latter hardly involves a role in the act complained of.[336]

The ComAT has not had the opportunity to address an individual application that concerns the applicability of Article 3 CAT to the transfer of detainees in the course of multinational operations. This question has been addressed during discussion of the periodic reports of the States parties that participated in ISAF and MNF-I.[337] The ComAT expressed concern at the argument raised by the UK, that the principle of Non-Refoulement under Article 3 CAT does not apply to the transfer of detainees from its forces in Iraq and Afghanistan to the local authorities because the element of transfer to another State is absent.[338] The Committee recommended the State party to apply Article 3 to "transfers of a detainee within a State party's custody to the custody whether *de facto* or

---

332 Ibid., para. 135.

333 Ibid., para. 141.

334 Sari, A., Autonomy, Attribution and Accountability: Reflections on the Behrami Case, in: Collins, R. & White, N.D., International Organisations and the Idea of Autonomy, London: Routledge, 2010, 257–277.

335 Sari, A., Jurisdiction and International Responsibility in Peace Support Operations: the Behrami and Saramati cases, Human Rights Law Review, Vol. 8 no. 1: 2008, 151–170, p. 164.

336 ILC, Report of the International Law Commission, Sixty-first session (4 May-5 June and 6 July–7 August 2009), p. 67.

337 ComAT, Thirty-third session, list of Issues, the United Kingdom, para. 25; ComAT, Concluding observations on the second periodic report of the United States of America, para. 20; ComAT, Consideration of the fifth periodic report of Norway, UN. Doc. CAT/C/SR.791, 12 November 2007, para. 19; ComAT, Consideration of fifth periodic report of Denmark, UN. Doc. CAT/C/SR.757, 2 May 2007, para. 31.

338 Comments by the Government of the United Kingdom of Great Britain and Northern Ireland to the conclusions and recommendations of the Committee against Torture (CAT/C/CR/33/3), paras. 14 and 17.

de jure of any other State".[339] This approach was reaffirmed in discussion of the fifth periodic reports from Sweden and Norway. States parties maintained that transfer by their forces participating in ISAF, of any Afghan national to the Afghan authorities, was carried out under a MoU that obliges the Afghan government to treat all transferred persons in accordance with international law.[340] The Committee noted that States parties were still under the obligation of Non-Refoulement under Article 3 CAT, and should ensure that they fully comply with these obligations in all cases.[341]

The ComAT also addressed the question of applicability of Article 3 CAT to the transfer of persons between different contingents of the multinational forces. In a report submitted to the Committee during the discussion of the fifth periodic report from Denmark, AI mentioned that, in 2002, 31 Afghan men had been transferred from Danish to US custody in Afghanistan; they were reportedly subsequently ill-treated.[342] The Danish government argued that these men had been detained under the US command and control, and that Danish forces were structurally fully integrated with American forces.[343] After recalling its consistent view that Article 3 applies extraterritorially where a State's military forces exercise effective control over an individual, the ComAT stated

339   ComAT, Conclusions and recommendations on the fourth periodic report of the United Kingdom of Great Britain and Northern Ireland, para. 5(e). See also, ComAT, Concluding observations on the fifth periodic report of the United Kingdom of Great Britain and Northern Ireland, para. 9.

340   ComAT, Consideration of the fifth periodic report of Norway, UN. Doc. CAT/C/SR.794, 13 November 2007, para. 16; ComAT, Concluding observations on the fifth periodic report of Sweden, para. 14. Several States participating in the multinational forces, such as in Iraq and Afghanistan, concluded MOUs with the host State addressing the issue of detainee transfers. See Chapter 5. Gillard, E.C., 2008, p. 715; AI, Afghanistan detainees transferred to torture: ISAF complicity?.

341   ComAT, Conclusions and recommendations on the fifth periodic report of Norway, UN. Doc. CAT/C/NOR/CO/5, 5 February 2008, para. 7; ComAT, Concluding observations on the fifth periodic report of Sweden, para. 14.

342   AI, Denmark: A Briefing for the Committee against Torture, EUR 18/001/2007, April 2007, p. 9.

343   Danish Ministry of Defence, Report on the factual and legal questions in relation to the Danish forces' detention and transfer of persons in Afghanistan in the first half of 2002, 13 December 2006, p. 12; referred to in Rehabilitation and Research Centre for Torture Victims, Alternative report to the list of issues (CAT/C/DNK/Q/5/rev.1) dated 19 February 2007 to be considered by the UNCAT during the examination of the 5th periodic report of Denmark, April 2007, footnote. 54.

that: "this remains so even if the State party's forces are subject to operational command of another State".[344]

A State that participates in multinational forces must therefore assess whether the transfer of a person to the US' forces would expose him to a risk of torture. To make this assessment, the sending State must consider that the US refuses extraterritorial application of the CAT; thus, the CAT does not protect persons transferred to the US forces.[345] Since Article 3 CAT prohibits indirect refoulement, a State that participates in multinational forces must not transfer detainees from its contingent's effective control to that of another State's contingent where the detainee faces a risk of second transfer to a third State, contrary to the principle of Non-Refoulement.[346]

II.3.3   Extraordinary Rendition

II.3.3.1   *General Background*

The term rendition has usually been used to describe the extra-judicial transfer of a criminal suspect from a State unable or unwilling to prosecute him, to another State where he would face criminal trial.[347] This method of bringing a suspect back to the US to stand criminal trial was used by the US government long before the 11 September 2001 attacks took place.[348] After these attacks, and in the context of the so-called "war on terror", the US government initiated the practice of "extraordinary rendition", designed to transfer terrorist suspects to foreign countries where they face a risk of extended detention without trial, and a high possibility of torture.[349] By adopting this practice,

---

344   ComAT, Conclusions and recommendations on the fifth periodic report of Denmark, para. 13.

345   Rehabilitation and Research Centre for Torture Victims, Alternative report to the list of issues (CAT/C/DNK/Q/5/rev.1) dated 19 February 2007 to be considered by the UNCAT during the examination of the 5th periodic report of Denmark, p. 24.

346   Droege, C., 2008, p. 677.

347   EU Council: Parliamentary Assembly, Alleged secret detentions and unlawful inter-state transfers of detainees involving Council of Europe member states (Marty first report), Doc. 10957, 12 June 2006, para. 26; Boon, K.E., Huq, A. & Lovelace, D.C., Terrorism, Commentary on Security Documents, Extraordinary Rendition, Oxford: Oxford University Press, 2010, p. viii.

348   Nadelmann, E.A., The Evolution of United States Involvement in the International Rendition of Fugitive Criminals, New York University Journal of International Law and Politics, Vol. 25 no. 4: 1993, 813–886, p. 857–858.

349   On 17 September 2001, just six days after the attacks, the US president, George W. Bush, signed a presidential finding authorizing the CIA to disrupt terrorist activities and capture, detain, and interrogate Al-Qaeda leaders. Johnston, D., At a Secret Interrogation, Dispute Flared Over Tactics, The New York Times, 10 September 2006; Lavers, T., Extraordinary

the US government has avoided inquiries about the circumstances of a terrorist suspect's capture and transfer back to the US. Most of the victims of the extraordinary rendition program were not formally charged with any crime in the US.[350] Individuals were either seized directly by the CIA agents in a foreign State, or arrested by the local authorities of a foreign State and then handed over to the CIA. While high value terrorist suspects are typically kept in US custody in secret detention facilities located outside US territory, but operated by the CIA,[351] other suspects are extra-judicially transferred to their country of nationality, or to a third State for interrogation and detention; they often face a real risk of torture and ill-treatment. The person being transferred does not face a criminal charge, and is not subject to prosecution by a judicial body.[352]

Although the practice of extraordinary rendition is mostly, though not exclusively, carried out by the US, it cannot be accomplished without the collaboration, complicity or acquiescence of other governments. States have reportedly facilitated extraordinary rendition by providing intelligence, initially seizing a suspect, or turning a blind eye to the abduction of a victim by foreign agents on their national territories. States have allowed "rendition flights" to use their national airports, and hosted secret CIA detention facilities.[353]

Rendition and the Self Defense Justification: Time to Face the Music, Michigan State Journal of International Law, Vol. 16 no. 2: 2007, 385–407, p. 388. Based on CIA declassified documents, the ECtHR noted that: "the rationale behind the programme was specifically to remove those persons from any legal protection against torture and enforced disappearance and to strip them of any safeguards afforded by both the US Constitution and international law". ECtHR, *Al Nashiri* v. *Poland*, Appl.No. 28761/11, 24 July 2014, para. 530.

350   AI, USA: Front companies used in secret flights to torture and "disappearance", 5 April 2006, p. 2.

351   Such as, Guantànamo Bay, the Bagram airbase in Afghanistan, CIA secret prisons in Eastern Europe or "floating prisons" on US military ships. EU Council: Parliamentary Assembly, Secret detentions and illegal transfers of detainees involving Council of Europe member states: second report (Marty second report), Doc. 11302 rev, 11 June 2007.

352   Messineo, F., 'Extraordinary Renditions' and State Obligations to Criminalize and Prosecute Torture in the Light of the Abu Omar Case in Italy, Journal of International Criminal Justice, Vol. 7 no. 5: 2009, 1023–1044, p. 1025.

353   The European Parliament's Report on the alleged use of European countries by the CIA for the transportation and illegal detention of prisoners found that at least 1,245 flights operated by the CIA flew into European airspace or stopped at European airports between the end of 2001 and the end of 2005. The report added that an unspecified number of military flights for the same purpose were also operated. The report noted that, while there may were more than the confirmed number of flights, not all these confirmed flights were used for the purposes of extraordinary rendition. Temporary Committee on

Collaborating States include Canada,[354] Sweden,[355] United Arab Emirates,[356] Pakistan,[357] Macedonia,[358] Italy,[359] Poland,[360] Romania,[361] Ireland,[362] the

---

the Alleged Use of European Countries by the CIA for the Transportation and Illegal Detention of Prisoners, European Parliament, Report on the alleged use of European countries by the CIA for the transportation and illegal detention of prisoners, 30 January 2007, para. 42.

354 E.g., it was found that Canadian intelligence officials had provided questionable information to their US counterparts, which led to Arar's rendition to Syria following a routine stopover at John F Kennedy Airport in New York. Commission of inquiry into the actions of Canadian officials in Relation to Maher Arar, Report of the Events Relating to Maher Arar, pp. 13 and 14. See also, Silva, M., Extraordinary Rendition: a Challenge to Canadian and United States Legal Obligations under the Convention Against Torture, California Western International Law Journal, Vol. 39 no. 2: 2009, 313–355, p. 315.

355 E.g., Mohammed Alzery and Ahmed Agiza were picked up by the Swedish Security Police and transferred to Bromma airport, Stockholm, where they were handed over to CIA agents. ComAT, *Agiza* v. *Sweden*, No. 233/2003, 20 May 2005; HRC, *Mohammed Alzery* v. *Sweden*.

356 E.g., Al-Nashiri was arrested in Dubai (United Arab Emirates) by local security forces in October 2002 and handed over into US custody one month later. ECtHR, *Al Nashiri* v. *Poland*, para. 83.

357 E.g., Abu Zubaydah was captured by agents of US and Pakistan in Pakistan in March 2002. ECtHR, *Husayn (Abu Zubaydah)* v. *Poland*, Appl.No. 7511/13, 24 July 2014, para. 82.

358 E.g. Khaled El-Masri was arrested when he was on vacation in Macedonia and interrogated for twenty-three days by Macedonian police before handing him over to a CIA rendition team at Skopje Airport. ECtHR, *El-Masri* v. *The Former Yugoslav Republic of Macedonia* (GC), Appl.No. 39630/09, 13 December 2012.

359 E.g., Osama Mustafa Hassan Nasr (Abu Omar) was abducted by CIA agents with an active role by officials of the Italian military security and intelligence services near his home in Milan (Italy) in February 2003.

360 E.g., Al-Nashiri and Abu Zubaydah were detained in a CIA's secret prison in Poland. ECtHR, *Husayn (Abu Zubaydah)* v. *Poland*; ECtHR, *Al Nashiri* v. *Poland*; HRW, Statement on US Secret Detention Facilities in Europe, 6 November 2005.

361 E.g., Al-Nashiri was detained in a CIA's secret prison in Bucharest, Romania. ECtHR, *Al Nashiri* v. *Poland*, para. 109.

362 With regard to Ireland, the European Parliament expressed its serious concern at the number of suspect flights, with 147 CIA-operated flights stopping in Irish airports. Temporary Committee on the Alleged Use of European Countries by the CIA for the Transportation and Illegal Detention of Prisoners, European Parliament, Report on the alleged use of European countries by the CIA for the transportation and illegal detention of prisoners, para. 123; Londras, F.d., Ireland's Potential Liability for Extraordinary Renditions through Shannon Airport, Irish Law Times, Vol. 25 no. 7: 2007, 106–110.

UK,[363] Germany,[364] and Afghanistan.[365] Other States have assisted in extraordinary rendition operations by accepting holding suspects after they are transferred out of the State from which they were abducted. These States include Egypt,[366] Syria,[367] Jordan, Saudi Arabia, Uzbekistan, Libya and Morocco.[368]

Extraordinary rendition operations violate humanitarian law,[369] aviation law,[370] human rights law,[371] and national laws. They thus raise several issues.

---

363   With regard to the UK, the European Parliament expressed its serious concern at the number of suspect flights, with 170 CIA-operated flights stopping in British airports. Temporary Committee on the Alleged Use of European Countries by the CIA for the Transportation and Illegal Detention of Prisoners, European Parliament, Report on the alleged use of European countries by the CIA for the transportation and illegal detention of prisoners, para. 78.

364   With regard to Germany, the European Parliament expressed its serious concern at the number of suspect flights, with 336 CIA-operated flights stopping in German airports. Ibid., para. 94.

365   E.g., Al-Nashiri, Abu Zubaydah and El-Masri were transferred to CIA-run facility in Afghanistan which is called the "Salt Pit". ECtHR, *El-Masri* v. *The Former Yugoslav Republic of Macedonia* (GC), para. 42; ECtHR, *Al Nashiri* v. *Poland*, para. 84.

366   E.g., Alzery, Agiza and Abu Omar were extraordinarily rendered to Egypt where they allegedly subjected to torture. ECtHR, *Nasr and Ghali* v. *Italy*, Appl.No. 44883/09, communicated 22 November 2011, pending; HRC, *Mohammed Alzery* v. *Sweden*; ComAT, *Agiza* v. *Sweden*; Messineo, F., 2009.

367   E.g. Maher Arar is a dual Canadian-Syrian citizen who had been arrested during a routine stopover in the US, and then deported to Syria where he was detained for 10 months and allegedly abused by police who wanted information on al-Qaeda. Schoenbach, I.A., "No Statutory Exceptions: The Case of Maher Arar and A Call to End Extraordinary Renditions", Southwestern Journal of Law & Trade in the Americas, Vol. 14 no. 1: 2007, 119–142.

368   HRW, Still at Risk: Diplomatic Assurances No Safeguard Against Torture, 14 April 2005; Mayer, J., Outsourcing Torture. The secret history of America's "extraordinary rendition" program, The New Yorker, 14 February 2005; Weissbrodt, D. & Bergquist, A., Extraordinary Rendition: A Human Rights Analysis, Harvard Human Rights Journal, Vol. 19: 2006, 123–160, pp. 128–129.

369   See, Sadat, L.N., Ghost Prisoners and Black Sites: Extraordinary Rendition Under International Law, The Case Western Reserve Journal of International Law, Vol. 37 no. 2 & 3: 2006, 309–342.

370   Venice Commission, opinion on the International Legal Obligations of Council of Europe Member States in Respect of Secret Detention Facilities and Inter-State Transport of Prisoners, CDL-AD(2006)009, 17 March 2006, p. 20.

371   The extraordinary rendition practice violates numerous international human rights instruments, including the UDHR, the ICCPR, the International Covenant on Economic, Social and Cultural Rights, the CSR and its Protocol and the CAT. Weissbrodt, D. & Bergquist, A., 2006.

A victim of such an operation can resort to national courts by filing a criminal claim based on national laws against the personnel who carried out the operation, or against the airlines that facilitated the operation. Claims against personnel and the airlines are hampered by States that claim the State secrets privilege, and by the difficulty of executing judgments.[372] It can be more effective to bring a case before human rights treaty bodies on the grounds that a State violated its human rights obligations, since a State cannot use domestic law to justify non-compliance with its international law obligations.[373] The next subsection addresses the case-law of the ComAT and the ECtHR that applies the principle of Non-Refoulement to extraordinary rendition operations.

II.3.3.2   *The Case-Law of the ComAT and ECtHR Relating to the Extraordinary Rendition*

In *Agiza* v. *Sweden* (2005), the ComAT had the opportunity to address the application of Article 3 CAT to extraordinary rendition. Ahmed Agiza was an Egyptian national who applied for asylum in Sweden, claiming that he had been sentenced in Egypt, *in absentia*, on account of terrorism linked to Islamic fundamentalism and that, if returned to his country, he would be executed. In December 2001, on the same day that his asylum application was rejected by the Swedish government on security grounds, the applicant was picked up by Swedish Security Police and transferred to Bromma airport, Stockholm, where he was handed over to a group of special agents. Those agents conducted a security check on the applicant, during which he was hooded, strip-searched, and his hands and feet were bound. He was transferred to

---

372   The State secrets privilege is a "common law evidentiary rule that protects information from discovery when disclosure would be inimical to the national security". ComAT, *Bakatu-Bia* v. *Sweden*, No. 379/2009, 3 June 2011; Messineo, F., 2009. E.g., the US Supreme Court refused to consider the case of Arar's rendition based on the US government's argument that litigating this case would interfere with foreign relations and affect the government's ability to ensure national security. US Court of Appeals for the Second Circuit, *Arar* v. *Ashcroft*, No, 06-4216- cv, 2 November 2009, p. 34. See also, *Mohamed* v. *Jeppesen Dataplan* which was brought by five victims of the extraordinary rendition program. They argued that Jeppesen Dataplan, a subsidiary of the Boeing Company, had facilitated their extraordinary rendition by the CIA. Their complain was dismissed on the basis of the State secrets privileges. Jensen, M.P., Torture and Public Policy: *Mohamed* v. *Jeppesen Dataplan, Inc.*, Allows "Extraordinary Rendition" Victims to Litigate Around State Secrets Doctrine, Brigham Young University Law Review, 2010, 117–133.

373   UNGA, Resolution adopted by the General Assembly 56/83. Responsibility of States for internationally wrongful acts, Articles 3 and 32.

Egypt on a private aircraft that had just landed, and which was owned by a US company and frequently used by US government. He was allegedly severely tortured in Egypt.[374] Agiza brought his complaint against Sweden before the ComAT. The Committee first considered that the State party's authorities knew or should have known that, at the time of the complainant's removal, there was consistent and widespread use of torture by Egyptian authorities against detainees, particularly those held for political and security reasons. The Committee also noted that the State party knew that its own security intelligence services thought the complainant was involved in terrorist activities, was a threat to its national security, and that he was of interest to the intelligence services of both the US and Egypt. The Committee's natural conclusion from these elements was that the complainant's expulsion would expose him to a real risk of torture in Egypt. In the Committee's view, this conclusion was confirmed by the fact that expulsion was immediately carried out, and the complainant was subjected by foreign agents, with the acquiescence of the State party's police, on the State party's territory, to treatment that violated at least Article 16 CAT. The Committee concluded that the complainant's expulsion to Egypt violated Article 3 CAT and noted that Egypt's DAs did not provide a mechanism for their enforcement, so they did not suffice to protect the applicant from the risk of torture.[375]

The ComAT has found that Article 3 CAT is violated by a State party that co-operates in the extraordinary rendition programme by making the initial arrest of a person, and then extra-judicially handing him over to agents of a foreign State. During the consideration of the periodic reports submitted by States parties to the CAT, the Committee referred to Article 3 CAT when it expressed its concern at the reports of the alleged cooperation of States parties in the rendition program, whether they had served as departure or destination points, or allowed rendition flights to use their airports and airspace. The Committee recommended that the States parties concerned investigate allegations of

---

374   ComAT, *Agiza* v. *Sweden*, paras. 2.1–3.7. Agiza had been removed with another Egyptian national, Mohammed Alzery who brought his case before the HRC. The HRC found that Sweden had violated Article 7 ICCPR by expelling Alzery to Egypt, as his expulsion exposed him to a real risk of torture or ill-treatment. HRC, *Mohammed Alzery* v. *Sweden*; Izumo, A., Diplomatic Assurances against Torture and Ill-treatment: European Court of Human Rights Jurisprudence, Columbia Human Rights Law Review, Vol. 42 no. 1: 2010, 233–277, pp. 238–240.

375   ComAT, *Agiza* v. *Sweden*, para. 13.4. Wouters, K., Reconciling National Security and Non-Refoulement: Exceptions, Exclusion, and Diplomatic Assurances, in: Frías, A.M.S.d., Samuel, K. & White, N., Counter-Terrorism: International Law and Practice, Oxford: Oxford University Press, 2012, 579–595, p. 593.

involvement of its officers in the rendition programme, and prosecute and punish those responsible for such renditions.[376] For example, during its consideration of the second periodic report of the US, the ComAT expressed its concern at the State party's argument that prohibition of refoulement under Article 3 CAT does not apply to a person detained outside his national territory. The Committee was further concerned by the State party's rendition of suspects, without any judicial procedure, to States where they faced a real risk of torture. The Committee recommended the US:

> ...apply the *Non-Refoulement* guarantee to all detainees in its custody, cease the rendition of suspects, in particular by its intelligence agencies, to States where they face a real risk of torture, in order to comply with its obligations under article 3 of the Convention. The State party should always ensure that suspects have the possibility to challenge decisions of *refoulement*.[377]

With regard to the ECtHR's case-law on extraordinary rendition, the Court has defined this practice as:

> ...an extra-judicial transfer of persons from one jurisdiction or State to another, for the purposes of detention and interrogation outside the normal

---

376   ComAT, Consideration of fourth periodic report of Poland, UN. Doc. CAT/C/SR.776, 15 May 2007, para. 11; ComAT, Concluding observations on the third periodic report of Iceland, UN. Doc. CAT/C/ISL/CO/3, 8 July 2008, para. 11; ComAT, Concluding observations on the fifth periodic report of Spain, UN. Doc. CAT/C/ESP/CO/5, 9 December 2009, para. 14; ComAT, Consideration of the initial periodic report of Ireland, UN. Doc. CAT/C/IRL/1, 26 January 2010, para. 9; ComAT, Initial periodic report of Syrian Arab Republic, UN. Doc. CAT/C/SR.951, 4 May 2010, para. 18; ComAT, Consideration of the fifth periodic report of Germany, UN. Doc. CAT/C/DEU/CO/5, 12 December 2011, para. 26; ComAT, Consideration of fourth periodic report of Morocco, UN. Doc. CAT/C/SR.1042, 1043 and 1045, 2 November 2011, para. 11.

377   ComAT, Concluding observations on the second periodic report of the United States of America, para. 20. The ComAT expressed its concerns at reports that, under the pretext of fighting terrorism, Ethiopia had allegedly abducted terrorism suspects from other countries, including Somalia, in breach of Article 3 CAT. The Committee recommended the State party to refrain from abducting terrorism suspects from other States where they may enjoy the protection against refoulement under Article 3 CAT. ComAT, Considered the initial periodic report of Ethiopia, UN. Doc. CAT/C/SR.974 and 975, 3 November 2010, para. 20.

legal system, where there was a real risk of torture or cruel, inhuman or degrading treatment.[378]

The Court has observed that, "extraordinary rendition, by its deliberate circumvention of due process, is anathema to the rule of law and the values protected by the Convention".[379]

In the case of *El-Masri* v. *The Former Yugoslav Republic of Macedonia* (2012), the ECtHR (GC) addressed a situation similar to that of the *Agiza* case. Khaled El-Masri was a German citizen of Lebanese descent who was arrested while on vacation in Macedonia. He was interrogated for 23 days by Macedonian police, and then handed over to a CIA rendition team at Skopje Airport.[380] El-Masri was transferred to Afghanistan, where he was detained in a CIA-run facility outside Kabul known as the "Salt Pit". After nearly five months of secret detention and torture, the CIA concluded that he had no ties to terror organisations and they released him near the Albanian border. El-Masri lodged his application with the ECtHR alleging, *inter alia*, that his transfer into the custody of the US authorities violated Article 3 ECHR.[381] The Court noted the applicant's

---

378 ECtHR, *Babar Ahmad and Others* v. *the United Kingdom* (admissibility decision), Appl. Nos. 24027/07, 11949/08 and 36742/08, 6 July 2010, para. 113; ECtHR, *Al Nashiri* v. *Poland*, para. 454; ECtHR, *Husayn (Abu Zubaydah)* v. *Poland*, para. 451.

379 ECtHR, *Babar Ahmad and Others* v. *the United Kingdom* (admissibility decision), para. 114.

380 The applicant's name was confused with that of Khalid al-Masri, a significant Al-Qaeda member.

381 Before lodging his application with the ECtHR, El-Masri had brought proceedings to seek damages in the US federal courts. However, at the request of the US government, his complaint was dismissed on the basis that the State secrets privilege barred the suit from continuing. He asked Macedonian prosecutors to open a criminal investigation in his case on the ground of the role Macedonia played in his arrest and transfer to US custody. This domestic inquiry was also discontinued. He also brought an action to the Administrative Court of Cologne (Germany) by which he sought to oblige Germany to request the extradition of 13 CIA agents involved in his "extraordinary rendition" from the US. This action was dismissed as not well founded. Barnett, L., Extraordinary Rendition: International Law and the Prohibition of Torture, Library of Parliament, PRB 07-48E, July 2008, p. 18; Wilkitzki, P., German Government Not Obliged to Seek Extradition of CIA Agents for 'Extraordinary Rendition'- Comments on the El-Masri Judgment of the Cologne Administrative Court, Journal of International Criminal Justice, Vol. 9 no. 5: 2011, 1117–1127; Fabbrini, F., The European Court of Human Rights, Extraordinary Renditions and the Right to the Truth: Ensuring Accountability for Gross Human Rights Violations Committed in the Fight Against Terrorism, Human Rights Law Review, Vol. 14 no. 1: 2014, 85–106.

transfer to US custody pursuant to a legitimate extradition request, or any other legal procedure recognised under international law for the transfer of a prisoner to foreign authorities, had not been established. No evidence existed of an arrest warrant that authorised the applicant's delivery into the hands of the CIA agents. The Court further observed that documents issued by the Civil Aviation Administration confirmed that the aircraft by which the applicant was transferred had been allowed to land at Skopje Airport on 23 January 2004 and was given permission to take off for Kabul on the same day. The next day, the authorities authorised the plane's onward route to Baghdad. The Court concluded that the Macedonian authorities had known the destination of the plane.

The Court attached importance to reliable sources who reporting that US authorities tolerated or resorted to practices that were manifestly contrary to the principles of the ECHR.[382] Since this material had been in the public domain before the applicant was transferred into US custody, the Court found that it proved there had been serious reasons to believe that the applicant's transfer under the rendition programme would expose him to a real risk of being subjected to treatment contrary to Article 3. Against this background, the Court held the following: "it must be concluded that the Macedonian authorities knew or ought to have known, at the relevant time, that there was a real risk that the applicant would be subjected to treatment contrary to Article 3 of the Convention".[383] Finally, the Court noted that the respondent government did not dispel doubts that risk of ill-treatment existed, nor did the respondent government seek assurances from the US authorities to avert the risk. The Court concluded that by transferring the applicant into US custody, the respondent State had knowingly exposed him to a real risk of treatment contrary to Article 3. In regard to the manner in which the applicant's transfer took place, the Court considered he was subjected to "extraordinary rendition".[384] The ECtHR has applied the prohibition of refoulement under Article 3 ECHR to a State party that, after arresting a person, extra-judicially transferred him to a foreign

---

382 The Court mentioned that it had previously found some of these reports "worrying" and expressed its grave concerns about the interrogation methods used by the US authorities on persons suspected of involvement in international terrorism and detained in the naval base in Guantànamo Bay and in Bagram (Afghanistan). ECtHR, *AL-Moayad* v. *Germany* (admissibility decision), Appl.No. 35865/03, 20 February 2007, para. 66; ECtHR, *El-Masri* v. *The Former Yugoslav Republic of Macedonia* (GC), para. 218.

383 Ibid., para. 218.

384 Ibid., paras. 216–221.

State, for the purpose of detention and interrogation outside the legal system, where there was a real risk of treatment contrary to this Article.[385]

In *Husayn (Abu Zubaydah) v. Poland* (2014)[386] and *Al Nashiri v. Poland* (2014),[387] the ECtHR addressed the question of whether the principle of Non-Refoulement under Article 3 ECHR is violated by a State party that facilitated the extraordinary rendition of a person by allowing the "rendition flight" to use its national airports, or by hosting a secret CIA detention facility in which the person concerned is detained. *Abu Zubaydah* was captured in Pakistan by agents of the US and Pakistan. He alleged before the ECtHR that, on 22 September 2003, he had been transferred by means of extraordinary rendition from Polish territory to CIA secret detention facilities in locations believed to include Guantànamo Bay in Cuba, Morocco, Lithuania and Afghanistan, from where he was subsequently transferred back to Guantànamo Bay.[388] Abu Zubaydah argued that Poland had violated Article 3 by enabling the CIA to transfer him from its territory to the CIA's other secret prisons.[389] Al Nashiri alleged that he had been captured in Dubai (the United Arab Emirates), and then transferred to the custody of the CIA. The applicant argued that he had been subjected to extraordinary rendition to CIA's secret prisons in Afghanistan, Thailand, Poland, and finally to Guantànamo Bay through Morocco. He submitted that Poland had violated his right under Article 3 by knowingly and intentionally enabling his transfer despite substantial grounds for believing that there was a real risk of further ill-treatment.[390] The ECtHR considered it inconceivable that rendition aircraft could have crossed Polish airspace, landed in and departed from a Polish airport, or that the CIA could have occupied the Stare Kiejkuty detention facility in Poland, and transported detainees there, without

---

385   See also, ECtHR, *Nasr and Ghali v. Italy*, Appl.No. 44883/09, 23 February 2016. In this case, the Court found that Italy had exposed the applicant to a serious and foreseeable risk of ill treatment and of conditions of detention contrary to Article 3 ECHR by actively cooperating with the CIA during the initial phase of the extraordinary rendition of Mr. Nasr.

386   Zayn al-Abidin Muhammad Husayn (known as Abu Zubaydah) a stateless Palestinian, who was captured by agents of US and Pakistan in Pakistan.

387   Abd Al Rahim Hussayn Muhammad (known as Al Nashiri), a Saudi Arabian national of Yemeni descent.

388   ECtHR, *Husayn (Abu Zubaydah) v. Poland*, para. 108.

389   Ibid., para. 458. Abu Zubaydah lodged a similar application against Lithuania. ECtHR, *Abu Zubaydah v. Lithuania*, Appl.No. 46454/11, communicated 14 December 2012, pending, statement of facts, para. 93.

390   ECtHR, *Al Nashiri v. Poland*, para. 460. Al Nashiri lodged similar application against Romania. ECtHR, *Al Nashiri v. Romania*, Appl.No. 33234/12, communicated 18 September 2012, pending, statement of facts, para. 120.

the Polish authorities' knowledge of and involvement in the preparation and execution of such operations on Polish territory. The Court further held it was inconceivable that activities of such nature and level, possibly essential to Poland's military and political interests, could have been undertaken on Polish territory without the government's knowledge, and without the necessary authorisation being issued by the appropriate authority.[391] The Court found:

> Poland knew of the nature and purposes of the CIA's activities on its territory at the material time and that, by enabling the CIA to use its airspace and the airport, by its complicity in disguising the movements of rendition aircraft and by its provision of logistics and services, including the special security arrangements, the special procedure for landings, the transportation of the CIA teams with detainees on land, and the securing of the Stare Kiejkuty base for the CIA's secret detention, Poland cooperated in the preparation and execution of the CIA rendition, secret detention and interrogation operations on its territory.[392]

The Court noted that:

> Where it has been established that the sending State knew, or ought to have known at the relevant time, that a person removed from its territory was subjected to "extraordinary rendition", [...] the possibility of a breach of Article 3 is particularly strong and must be considered intrinsic in the transfer.[393]

The Court concluded that, by enabling the CIA to transfer applicants to its other secret detention facilities, the Polish authorities had exposed those applicants to a foreseeable serious risk of further ill-treatment and conditions of detention in breach of Article 3 ECHR.[394] Accordingly, where a State party to

---

391   ECtHR, *Husayn (Abu Zubaydah)* v. *Poland*, para. 443; ECtHR, *Al Nashiri* v. *Poland*, para. 441.

392   ECtHR, *Husayn (Abu Zubaydah)* v. *Poland*, para. 444; ECtHR, *Al Nashiri* v. *Poland*, para. 442.

393   Ibid., paras. 454 and 518; ECtHR, *Husayn (Abu Zubaydah)* v. *Poland*, paras. 451 and 513.

394   ECtHR, *Al Nashiri* v. *Poland*, para. 518; ECtHR, *Husayn (Abu Zubaydah)* v. *Poland*, para. 513. In both these cases, the Court found that, the treatment to which the applicants had been subjected by the CIA during his detention in Poland at the relevant time amounted to torture within the meaning of Article 3 ECHR. The Court noted that the interrogations and, therefore, torture had inflicted on the applicants at the black site were the exclusive responsibility of the CIA and that it was unlikely that the Polish officials witnessed or knew exactly what happened inside the facility. However, the Polish authorities must have been aware of the serious risk of treatment contrary to Article 3 occurring on Polish territory.

the ECHR knew, or ought to have known at the relevant time, that an airplane crossing its airspace, landing in or departing from its airport, carries a prisoner with the intention of transferring him to a country where he faces a risk of treatment contrary to Article 3, that State party must take all the necessary measures to prevent this action from taking place.[395]

In interaction with the ECtHR's judgments in *Husayn (Abu Zubaydah)* v. *Poland* (2014) and *Al Nashiri* v. *Poland* (2014), the ComAT recommended Poland cooperate fully with the ECtHR on the CIA rendition and secret detention cases against Poland. The Committee further urged Poland to complete the investigation into allegations of its involvement in the CIA extraordinary rendition and secret detention programmes between 2001 and 2008 and to ensure that persons had involved in the alleged crimes of torture and ill-treatment are held accountable.[396]

The Court observed that under Article 1 ECHR, taken together with Article 3, Poland was required to take measures designed to ensure that individuals within its jurisdiction were not subjected to torture or IDTP, including ill-treatment administered by private individuals. Accordingly, the Court concluded that Poland, on account of its "acquiescence and connivance" in the CIA High-Value Detainees Programme must be regarded as responsible for the violation of the applicant's rights under Article 3 committed on its territory. Ibid., paras. 511–512; ECtHR, *Al Nashiri* v. *Poland*, paras. 516–517. The Polish government appeals the ECtHR's judgments in these two cases.

395   Venice Commission, opinion on the International Legal Obligations of Council of Europe Member States in Respect of Secret Detention Facilities and Inter-State Transport of Prisoners, CDL-AD(2006)009. See, Hakimi, M., State Bystander Responsibility, The European Journal of International Law, Vol. 21 no. 2: 2010, pp. 361–362.

396   ComAT, Concluding observations on the fifth and sixth periodic reports of Poland, UN. Doc. CAT/C/SR.1202, 19 November 2013, Report of the ComAT, UN. Doc. A/69/44, 2013–2014, p. 66, para. 10.

CHAPTER 3

The Individual Complaints Procedures in the Context of Non-Refoulement Allegations

This Chapter addresses the main individual complaints procedures before the ECtHR and the ComAT in the Context of Non-Refoulement allegations. Section (I) examines the interim measures as a means to stay the applicant's removal pending the consideration of the merits of the Non-Refoulement application by the ComAT or the ECtHR. Section (II) considers the criteria for admissibility of an individual application before the ECtHR and the ComAT. Section (III) discusses the standard of proof required to apply the principle of Non-Refoulement and burden of proof.

I   Interim Measures

I.1   *ECtHR*
An applicant in Non-Refoulement cases may request the ECtHR to issue an interim measure to stay his forcible removal under Rule 39 of the Rules of the Court.[1] The Court's power to indicate such interim measures is of a paramount importance in Non-Refoulement cases, given the non-suspensive effect of an application lodged with the Court, as well as the serious and irreparable harm that would result if the applicant were removed contrary to Article 3.[2] The vast majority of cases in which the Court has indicated interim measures concern deportation or extradition proceedings.[3] Out of 2,278 requests under Rule 39 received by the Court in 2011, 2,194 requests were in Non-Refoulement cases; of these, the Court accepted the request in 342 cases. Out of 1,972 Rule 39 requests received in 2012, 1,306 requests were in Non-Refoulement cases; of these, the

---

1   According to this Rule "the Chamber or, where appropriate, its President may, at the request of a party or of any other person concerned, or of its own motion, indicate to the parties any interim measure which it considers should be adopted in the interests of the parties or of the proper conduct of the proceedings before it". ECtHR, Rules of Court, entered into force on 1st September 2012, Rule 39.

2   Herrera, C.B. & Haeck, Y., Staying the Return of Aliens from Europe through Interim Measures: The Case-law of the Europe Commission and the European Court of Human Rights, European Journal of Migration and Law, Vol. 11 no. 1: 2011, 31–51, p. 31.

3   ECtHR, *Mamatkulov and Askarov* v. *Turkey* (GC), para. 104.

Court acceded to 103 requests.[4] The Court asserted that these interim measures "permit it not only to carry out an effective examination of the application but also to ensure that the protection afforded to the applicant by the Convention is effective".[5]

The Court makes clear that such measures are indicated "only in limited spheres", namely, in cases where "there is an imminent risk of irreparable damage".[6] For the Court to grant an interim measure in a Non-Refoulement case, the applicant must establish that he is at risk of imminent removal, and that there is a *prima facie* or arguable case of risk of being subjected to treatment proscribed by Article 3 in the proposed receiving State. In *Al Husin* v. BH (2012), the applicant's request for another interim measure was refused on 29 October 2008 because the Court found that he was not subject to expulsion; a deportation order had not yet been issued against him.[7] On 15 March 2011, after a deportation order had been issued for him, and become final, the Court decided to indicate to the government that the applicant should not be expelled to Syria until further notice.[8] However, the existence of a deportation order is not a condition to consider that a person concerned is at imminent risk of being removed, as far as this can be concluded from other facts of the case.

The Court may face a large influx of requests for interim measures about return to a specific State, which strains its time and resources. In such situations, the Court is inclined to indicate that it will impose interim measures for a certain group of applicants for a certain period of time.[9] For example, in 2007, the Court received an increasing number of requests for interim measures by Tamils who were under threat of being returned to Sri Lanka from the UK and other States parties. By October 2007, the Court applied Rule 39 in twenty-two cases that concerned Tamils who sought to block their removal to Sri Lanka from the UK. On 23 October 2007, the Court wrote to the British government:

---

4   All the cases in which the Court acceded to the requests for interim measures under Rule 39 from 2011 till 2015 were Non-Refoulement cases. ECtHR, Interim measures by respondent State and country of destination, 2011; ECtHR, Interim measures by respondent State and country of destination, 2012; ECtHR, Interim measures by respondent State and country of destination, 2013; ECtHR, Rule 39 requests granted and refused in 2012, 2013, 2014 and 2015 by respondent State.

5   ECtHR, *Mamatkulov and Askarov* v. *Turkey* (GC), para. 125.

6   Ibid., para. 104.

7   ECtHR, *Al Husin* v. *Bosnia and Herzegovina*, para. 1.

8   Ibid., paras. 4 and 7.

9   ELENA, Research on ECHR, Rule 39 Interim Measures, April 2012, pp. 40–44.

...pending the adoption of a lead judgment in one or more of the applications already communicated, Rule 39 should continue to be applied in any case brought by a Tamil seeking to prevent his removal.[10]

It further requested the British government to assist the Court by refraining from issuing directions to remove Tamils who claimed that their return to Sri Lanka might expose them to the risk of ill-treatment. The British government refused to refrain from issuing such directions in all cases concerning removal to Sri Lanka, claiming that the situation there did not warrant the suspension of removals for all Tamils who claimed that their return would expose them to a risk of ill-treatment. However, the government asserted that it would comply with any measures indicated by the Court under Rule 39.[11] In July 2008, the Court adopted its judgment in the leading case of *NA.* v. *The UK* (2008), in which the Court found that Tamils as a group were not at risk of serious harm in Sri Lanka. Before this judgment, the Court applied Rule 39 in respect of three hundred and forty-two Tamil applicants who claimed that their removal to Sri Lanka from the UK would be in violation of Article 3 ECHR.[12]

Generally, the majority of interim measures requested by the ECtHR in Non-Refoulement cases are open-ended and issued for the duration of the proceedings before the Court. The Court usually grants them until the case is formally concluded. The Court indicates the respondent State not to remove the applicant to the proposed receiving State "pending the Court's decision".[13] In some situations, the Court grants interim measures "until further notice", without defining a specific time frame.[14] Thus, the Court may decide to discontinue them even before it adopts a decision on the merits of the case.

---

10   ECtHR, *NA.* v. *The United Kingdom*, para. 21.

11   Ibid., para. 21. By contrast, in June 2010, the Dutch government responded with the Court's request to refrain from transferring applicants from South and Central Somalia to Greece pursuant to the Dublin Regulation until further notice from the ECtHR. ELENA, Research on ECHR, Rule 39 Interim Measures, p. 42.

12   ECtHR, *NA.* v. *The United Kingdom*, para. 22.

13   ECtHR, *Soldatenko* v. *Ukraine*, para. 15. In *J.H.* v. *the UK* (2011), the Chamber of the ECtHR found that the applicant's removal to Afghanistan would not give rise to a violation of Article 3. However, it considered that the indication had been made to the British government under Rule 39 on 15 September 2009 must continue in force until this judgment became final or until the Panel of the GC accepts any request by one or both of the parties to refer the case to the GC under Article 43 ECHR. ECtHR, *J.H.* v. *the United Kingdom*, Appl. No. 48839/09, 20 December 2011, paras. 4 and 69.

14   ECtHR, *Abdulazhon Isakov* v. *Russia*, Appl. No. 14049/08, 8 July 2010, para. 4; ECtHR, *Yakubov* v. *Russia*, Appl. No. 7265/10, 8 November 2011, para. 3.

In *Garabayev* v. *Russia* (2007), the Court requested the Russian government not to extradite the applicant to Turkmenistan until further notice.[15] Following assurances by the Russian government that the applicant would not be extradited to Turkmenistan because he was a Russian national, the ECtHR decided to discontinue the interim measures.[16]

Although most of the ECtHR's indications of interim measures in Non-Refoulement cases were complied with, and instances of non-compliance are still relatively rare, there have been a growing number of such instances in recent years,[17] despite the fact that the Court acknowledged the binding nature of interim measures in *Mamatkulov and Askarov* v. *Turkey* (2003), overturning its previous case-law.[18] In the *Mamatkulov and Askarov* case, the applicants were extradited to Uzbekistan a few days after the Court had indicated Turkey should not extradite the applicants to that State, under Rule 39. Since the ECHR is a "living instrument" and taking into account the current trend of other international bodies, including the ComAT, the GC declared that its interim measures were binding. It referred to the Chamber's judgment in this case:

> ...any State Party to the Convention to which interim measures have been indicated in order to avoid irreparable harm being caused to the victim of an alleged violation must comply with those measures and refrain from any act or omission that will undermine the authority and effectiveness of the final judgment.[19]

Accordingly, the GC noted that a failure by a State party to comply with interim measures prevented the Court from effectively examining the applicant's complaint and hindered the effective exercise of his right. Therefore, failure to comply is a violation of Article 34 ECHR, under which States parties undertake

---

15   ECtHR, *Garabayev* v. *Russia*, para. 48.

16   Ibid., para. 54.

17   Harby, C., The changing nature of interim measures before the European Court of Human Rights, European Human Rights Law Review, no. 1: 2010, 73–84, pp. 79–82; Haeck, Y., Herrera, C.B. & Zwaak, L., Strasbourg's Interim Measures under Fire: Does the Rising Number of State Incompliances with Interim Measures Pose a Threat to the European Court of Human Rights?, European Yearbook on Human Rights, Vol. 11 no. 1: 2011, 375–404.

18   In *Cruz Varas and Others* v. *Sweden* (1991), the first applicant was expelled to Chile a few hours after the EComHR had asked the Swedish government not to deport him. Court explicitly acknowledged the non-binding nature of the interim measures. ECtHR, *Cruz Varas and Others* v. *Sweden*, paras. 102–103.

19   ECtHR, *Mamatkulov and Askarov* v. *Turkey*, Appl. Nos 46827/99 and 46951/99, 6 February 2003, para. 110.

not to hinder in any way the effective exercise of the right of individual application.[20]

Even if the Court finds that the respondent State violated Article 34 by removing the applicant contrary to its indication of interim measures, this would not necessarily indicate that the Court would find a violation of the principle of Non-Refoulement under Article 3.[21] The Court's request for interim measures does not in itself indicate that the Non-Refoulement application will be declared admissible, or presage the Court's decision on the merits of the application. In *Abu Salem* v. *Portugal* (2006), the Court had indicated an interim measure, but later found the case inadmissible.[22] Nor does refusal to grant the request for interim measures under Rule 39 preclude the ECtHR from subsequently finding that Article 3 was or would be violated.[23] In several cases, the Court found that the applicant's removal would not expose him to a real risk of ill-treatment in the receiving State, although it had previously indicated that the sending State, under Rule 39, must refrain from removing him.[24]

I.2   *ComAT*

A complaint lodged with the ComAT does not have suspensive effect. However, according to Rule 114 of the ComAT's RoP, the Committee may, at any time after receipt of a complaint, adopt a request for interim measures if it deems necessary to avoid irreparable harm to the victim or victims of the alleged

---

20   ECtHR, *Mamatkulov and Askarov* v. *Turkey* (GC), para. 128. Mowbray, A., A New Strasbourg Approach to the Legal Consequences of Interim Measures, Human Rights Law Review, Vol. 5 no. 2: 2005, 377–386. The binding nature of the interim measures under Rule 39 has been asserted in the Court's subsequent case-law. ECtHR, *Aoulmi* v. *France*, Appl. No. 50278/99, 17 January 2006, para. 111; ECtHR, *Shamayev and 12 others* v. *Georgia and Russia*, paras. 479–480; ECtHR, *Ben Khemais* v. *Italy*, Appl. No. 246/07, 24 February 2009.

21   E.g., *Rrapo* v. *Albania* (2012), the Court held that the applicant's removal contrary to the Court indication of interim measures was a violation of Article 34, although it did not consider his removal was a violation of Article 3. In contrary, while the Court in *Muminov* v. *Russia* held that the applicant's removal was a violation of Article 3, it did not consider that his removal contrary to the Court's indication of interim measures was a violation of Article 34.

22   ECtHR, *Abu Salem* v. *Portugal*, Appl. No. 26844/04, 9 May 2006. See also, ECtHR, *Chentiev and Ibragimov* v. *Slovakia* (admissibility decision).

23   Although the applicant's request for an interim measure in *Auad* v. *Bulgaria* (2011) had been refused, the Court found that his expulsion to Lebanon, if carried out, would be in breach of Article 3. ECtHR, *Auad* v. *Bulgaria*, paras. 4 and 108.

24   ECtHR, *Thampibillai* v. *The Netherlands*, Appl. No. 61350/00, 17 February 2004, paras. 5 and 68; ECtHR, *Al Hanchi* v. *Bosnia and Herzegovina*, paras. 4 and 45.

violation.[25] In light of irreparable harm that may result from returning an individual to torture, complainants in Non-Refoulement cases frequently ask the Committee to request the respondent States, under Rule 114, not remove them to the proposed receiving States until the Committee has taken a final decision on their communications.[26] Between May 2010 and June 2011, the Committee received requests for interim measures in 37 complaints; the Rapporteur for new complaints and interim measures granted 24.[27] Between June 2012 and May 2013, in 30 out of 44 complaints, the Committee acceded to requests for interim measures.[28] Although, there are no statistics on the number of requests for interim measures received by the Committee in Non-Refoulement cases, the vast majority of such requests received by the Committee included an Article 3 situation.

In order for the Rapporteur on new complaints and interim measures to act on the complainant's request for interim measures, the complainant must meet the admissibility criteria set out in Article 22. Domestic remedies need not be exhausted if the only remedies available to the complainant will not automatically stay the execution of the removal order to a State where he might be subjected to torture.[29] The Committee has refused a complainant's request for interim measures when it is not practically possible to implement the removal order against him. In *Chahin v. Sweden* (2011), the complainant's request for interim measures was refused with the indication that this decision could be reviewed, and the applicant could make a new request for interim measures once he emerged from hiding.[30]

In order for the Committee to accede to the complainant's request for interim measures, "a complaint must have a substantial likelihood of success on the merits for it to be concluded that the alleged victim would suffer irreparable harm in the event of his or her deportation".[31] However, the Committee does not apply this condition very strictly. The Committee's request for interim measures does not imply that either the admissibility or the merits of

---

25   ComAT, Rules of procedure, UN. Doc. CAT/C/3/Rev.5, 21 February 2011, Rule. 114 (previously rule 108).

26   Report of the ComAT, UN. Doc. A/67/44, 2011–2012, para. 106.

27   Report of the ComAT, UN. Doc. A/66/44, para. 89.

28   Report of the ComAT, UN. Doc. A/68/44, 2012–2013, para. 107.

29   Report of the ComAT, UN. Doc. A/60/44, 3 October 2005, para. 135.

30   The counsel then informed the ComAT that he could not convince the applicant to emerge from hiding because of the latter's fear of being forcibly removed to Syria. ComAT, *Chahin v. Sweden*, para. 1.2.

31   Report of the ComAT, UN. Doc. A/60/44, para. 135.

the complaint have been determined.[32] For example, in *Nadeem Ahmad Dar v. Norway* (2007), the Committee requested the State party not to expel the complainant to Pakistan, pending the Committee's consideration of his complaint. Subsequently, the Committee declared the complaint inadmissible.[33] In many cases, the Committee found that the removal of complainants was not or would not violate Article 3, although it had requested interim measures under Rule 114.[34]

Generally, the interim measures the ComAT requests in Non-Refoulement cases are open-ended and indicated for the duration of the proceedings. Such interim measures request the State party not to remove the complainant to the proposed receiving State while his case under consideration by the Committee,[35] or pending a final decision on the complaint.[36]

The State party's response to the ComAT's request for interim measures varies from case to case. In the vast majority of Non-Refoulement cases, respondent States respected and acceded to the Committee's request.[37] In some cases, however, the respondent States removed the person concerned, although it had previously accepted the Committee's request for interim measures.[38] In other cases, the respondent States parties did not accede to the Committee's request, or even expressly refused it,[39] and removed the complainant.[40] Since the ComAT's power to request interim measures is not based on a provision of the Convention, but on the Committee's RoP, interim measures are not strictly legally binding in themselves.[41] The Committee, through its case-law,

---

32   Report of the ComAT, UN. Doc. A/67/44, para. 106.

33   ComAT, *K.A.* v. *Sweden* (admissibility decision), No. 308/2006, 16 November 2007.

34   E.g., ComAT, *J.A.G.V.* v. *Sweden*, No. 215/2002, 11 November 2003; ComAT, *Z.T.* v. *Australia*, No. 153/2000, 11 November 2003.

35   ComAT, *Singh* v. *Canada*, No. 319/2007, 30 May 2011, para. 1.2.

36   ComAT, *B.S.S.* v. *Canada*, para. 1.2.

37   E.g., ComAT, *E.T.* v. *Switzerland*, No. 393/2009, 23 May 2012, para. 1.2; ComAT, *M.A.M.A. et al.* v. *Sweden*, No. 391/2009, 23 May 2012, para. 1.2.

38   Although the respondent State party in *Elif Pelit* v. *Azerbaijan* (2007) had accepted the Committee's request, it extradited the complainant to Turkey. ComAT, *Elif Pelit* v. *Azerbaijan*, para. 1.2.

39   ComAT, *Bachan Singh Sogi* v. *Canada*, paras. 1.2–1.5.

40   ComAT, *J.A.G.V.* v. *Sweden*, para. 1.3; ComAT, *Z.T.* v. *Australia*, para. 1.2. In these cases the respondent States maintained that they had not been in a position to comply with the Committee's request for interim measures, since the complainants' deportation was already taking place when the request reached the Government. ComAT, *Mafhoud Brada* v. *France*, No. 195/2002, 17 May 2005, para. 1.3.

41   ComAT, *K.N.* v. *Switzerland*, No. 94/1997, 19 May 1998, paras. 5.1–5.2; ComAT, *Mafhoud Brada* v. *France*, para. 8.2; Nowak, M. & McArthur, E., 2008, p. 740; Raffaelli, R., The UN

considers the failure of the State party to respect the Committee's request for interim measures to violate the provision of the Convention itself. *Cecilia Rosana Nunez Chipana* v. *Venezuela* (1998) was the first refoulement case in which a State party did not comply with the Committee's request for interim measures. The Committee found that the State party violated Article 3 CAT by extraditing the complainant contrary to interim measures requested by the Committee, which, in the Committee's view, represented a failure to "comply with the spirit of the Convention". The Committee considered that:

> ...the State Party, in ratifying the Convention and voluntarily accepting the Committee's competence under Article 22, undertook to cooperate with it in good faith in applying the procedure. Compliance with the provisional measures called for by the Committee in cases it considers reasonable is essential in order to protect the person in question from irreparable harm, which could, moreover, nullify the end result of the proceedings before the Committee.[42]

Thus, the Committee initially qualified the State's non-compliance with a request for interim measures in Non-Refoulement cases as a violation of Article 3. Subsequently, in *Mafhoud Brada* v. *France* (2005),[43] the Committee held that deporting the complainant in the circumstances breached the State party's obligations under Articles 3 and 22 CAT. The Committee reiterated its previous case-law and noted that the request for interim measures is vital to the role entrusted to it under Article 22 CAT. Failure to respect this request through such irreparable action as extraditing an alleged victim undermines the protection of the rights enshrined in the Convention, including the right to be protected from refoulement under Article 3. It also nullifies the effective exercise of the right to individual complaint under Article 22, and renders the Committee's final decision on the merits futile.[44] In subsequent Non-Refoulement cases, the Committee has repeatedly asserted that a State party's failure to respect its

---

Committee against Torture – in Search of Greater Cooperation, in: Cassese, S., Carotti, B., Casini, L., Cavalieri, E. & MacDonald, E., Global Administrative Law: the Casebook, The Institute for Research on Public Administration and the Institute for International Law and Justice, 3rd Ed, 2012, 94–104, p. 103.

42   ComAT, *Cecilia Rosana Nunez Chipana* v. *Venezuela*, para. 8.

43   This case concerned the deportation of an Algerian national from France to Algeria despite the Committee's request for interim measures. ComAT, *Mafhoud Brada* v. *France*.

44   Ibid., paras. 13.4 and 14.

request for interim measures under Rule 114 violates its obligation to cooperate with the Committee under Article 22.[45]

The ComAT may review its request for interim measures based on information and comments received from the State party.[46] Where the Committee finds that interim measures are no longer needed, it may withdraw its previous request.[47] However, even when the Committee withdraws its request for interim measures, it may still find that the complainant's removal was or would violate Article 3 CAT. In *Boily* v. *Canada* (2011), which concerned the extradition of a Mexican national to Mexico, the ComAT decided to withdraw its previous request for interim measures after thoroughly examining the observations submitted by the State party and by the complainant.[48] Four days later, the complainant was extradited to Mexico and transferred to the prison in which he had been accused of having killed a guard.[49] The Committee decided that the State party's extradition of the complainant to Mexico violated Articles 3 and 22 CAT.

1.3   *Conclusion*

An application lodged with the ComAT or the ECtHR is non-suspensive. Irreparable harm could result if an applicant were removed in violation of Article 3 CAT/ECHR. Accordingly, effective protection against refoulement requires that interim measures be respected.

The vast majority of requests for interim measures submitted to both the Court and the Committee have been made in Non-Refoulement cases. Though the Court has received noticeably more requests for interim measures than the Committee, the Committee is more likely to accept them than the Court. For example, between 24 May 2014 and 15 May 2015, the Committee received 62 requests for interim measures, out of which it accepted 48 requests (77,1%).[50] In 2014, the Court received 1,929 requests for interim measures and accepted

---

45   ComAT, *Elif Pelit* v. *Azerbaijan*, para. 10.1–10.2; ComAT, *Bachan Singh Sogi* v. *Canada*, para. 10.11; ComAT, *Kalinichenko* v. *Morocco*, No. 428/2010, 25 November 2011, para. 13.1–13.2; ComAT, *Abdussamatov et al.* v. *Kazakhstan*, No. 444/2010, 1 June 2012, para. 1.3.

46   ComAT, *E.C.B.* v. *Switzerland*, No. 369/2008, 26 May 2011, para. 1.3.

47   ComAT, *E.L.* v. *Canada*, No. 370/2009, 21 May 2012, para. 1.2.

48   ComAT, *Boily* v. *Canada*, paras. 1.2–1.3.

49   The complainant was tortured there by prison guards and he was refused contact with the Canadian Embassy and his lawyer. Ibid., para. 2.4.

50   There are no statistics on whether all of the accepted requests involved Non-Refoulement situations, especially as not all the Committee's decisions in this regard are published. However, the vast majority of these requests were related to claims of removal contrary to Article 3 CAT. Report of the CoAT, UN. Doc. A/70/44, para. 68.

216 requests (11,1%). All the Court's requests involved Non-Refoulement claims under Article 3 ECHR.[51] There may be several reasons for the disparity. Firstly, the number of requests the Court receives is considerably higher than the number received by the Committee. Secondly, the number of requests for interim measures received by the Court has increased significantly in recent years.[52] Thirdly, the vast majority of requests to the Court were refused because they were incomplete; they contained insufficient information and documentation to permit an assessment of the risks that attended the applicant on return. The Court's former President Jean-Paul Costa stated:

> ...the Court is not an appeal tribunal from the asylum and immigration tribunals of Europe, [...] Where national immigration and asylum procedures carry out their own proper assessment of risk and are seen to operate fairly and with respect for human rights, the Court should only be required to intervene in truly exceptional cases.[53]

In accord with this approach, the Court tends to request interim measures only in limited cases, where it finds that an applicant submits an arguable claim that he faces an imminent risk of being removed to a State where he would allegedly be at a real risk of proscribed treatment. Where the Court has previously had the opportunity to address similar cases on the merits, it tends to refuse requests for interim measures. As noted above, in the period between 23 October 2007 and the Court's judgment in *NA. v. The UK* (2008), the Court applied Rule 39 to 342 Tamil applicants who claimed that their removal from the UK to Sri Lanka would be contrary to Article 3 ECHR. Following *NA. v. The UK* (2008), in which the Court found that Tamils as a group were not at risk of serious harm in Sri Lanka, the Court appeared more reluctant to accede to requests under Rule 39 made by Tamils. In 2010, it accepted 13 requests from Tamils who sought to suspend their removal to Sri Lanka (8 from France; 5 from the UK) and refused 94 requests.[54] In 2012, it refused 57 requests.[55]

---

51   ECtHR, Interim measures by respondent State and country of destination, 2014.
52   As noted by the Court's former President Jean-Paul Costa: "Between 2006 and 2010 the Court saw an increase of over 4,000% in the number of requests it received for interim measures under Rule 39 of the Rules of the Court. In 2006 the Court received 112 requests. That figure had increased to 4,786 for 2010". Statement issued by the President of the European Court of Human Rights concerning requests for interim measures, Doc. GT-GDR-C(2012)005, 11 February 2011.
53   ECtHR, Rule 39 requests granted and refused in 2012, 2013, 2014 and 2015 by respondent State.
54   ECtHR, Interim measures by respondent State and country of destination, 2011.
55   ECtHR, Interim measures by respondent State and country of destination, 2012.

In its 2010–2011 report, the Committee noted that it seriously took into account the concerns expressed by a number of States parties that interim measures of protection were requested in too many cases that alleged violations of Article 3 CAT. While the Committee was prepared to discuss those concerns with the States parties concerned,[56] it pointed out that requests for interim measures were, in some cases, lifted by the Rapporteur, pursuant to Rule 114(3), and in the light of pertinent information submitted by the State party.[57] From this reply, it seems that the Committee prefers to accede to the complainant's request for interim measures in Non-Refoulement cases where the request fulfils the admissibility criteria and there is a substantial likelihood of success for the complaint on the merits. It is possible for the respondent State to ask the Committee to withdraw its request for interim measures.

Although the power to request interim measures is not provided for either in the CAT or in the ECHR, both the ComAT and the ECtHR consider the request for interim measures to be legally binding under the CAT and the ECHR. The failure of a State party to comply with requested interim measures constitutes a violation of its obligation to cooperate with the Committee or the Court in good faith, because it prevents these bodies from effectively examining the complainant's Non-Refoulement claim and hinders the effective exercise of his rights.

II   Admissibility Criteria

II.1   *ECtHR*
On ratifying the ECHR, a State automatically accepts the jurisdiction of the ECtHR to review individual applications under Article 34 ECHR.[58] Under this provision, any individual has a right to claim to the Court that his rights under the Convention or its protocols have been violated by one of the States parties. Admissibility criteria for bringing an individual application to the ECtHR are contained in Article 35. According to this provision, the Court may only deal with the matter after all available domestic remedies have been exhausted, and when the application is lodged within six months of the date of the final domestic decision.[59] An application to the Court cannot be anonymous; it

---

56   The Committee did not mention which States expressed those concerns and there are no indication in the report helps to define them.

57   Report of the ComAT, UN. Doc. A/66/44, para. 93.

58   Gomien, D., Short Guide to the European Convention on Human Rights, Strasbourg: Council of Europe, 3rd Ed, 2005, p. 166.

59   ECHR50, Article 35(1).

must set out the name, date of birth, nationality, sex, occupation, and address of the applicant.[60] If the application does not contain identifying elements, it is inadmissible. An application must not be substantially the same as a matter that has been already examined by the Court or other international body. An applicant must therefore choose between bringing his case before the ECtHR or before the ComAT. An individual application is also inadmissible if the Court deems it an abuse of the right of application,[61] it is manifestly ill-founded, or it is incompatible with provisions of the Convention or its Protocols, whether *ratione temporis* (e.g., where the application relates to forcible removal that took place before the Convention entered into force for the respondent State party), *ratione loci* (e.g., where the application relates to forcible removal that took place outside the territorial jurisdiction of the respondent State party), *ratione personae* (e.g., where the respondent State is not a party to the ECHR, or where the applicant cannot show that he is a victim of the alleged violation of Article 3 ECHR), or *ratione materiae* (e.g., where the application relates to alleged violation of the principle of Non-Refoulement under Article 33 CSR, Article 3 CAT or EU Qualification Directive 2004/83/EC).[62] Finally, the Court shall declare an application inadmissible where the applicant has not suffered a significant disadvantage.[63] An action that violates a right must reach a minimum level of

---

60   ECtHR, Rules of CourtRule 47.1 (a). According to para. 3 of the same Rule, the applicant may request to disclose his identity to the public and submit a statement of the reasons justifying such a departure from the normal rule of public access to information in proceedings before the Court. However, even where the Court grants an applicant a request for anonymity, his identity will always be disclosed to the State party concerned in order to be able to response to the complaint. Erdal, U. & Bakirci, H., Article 3 of the European Convention on Human Rights: a practitioner's handbook, Geneva: World Organization Against Torture, OMCT, 2006, p. 139.

61   The Court may find an abuse of the right of application, for example, where it considers that the applicant attempt to mislead the Court in its examination of the application by forging documents or by deliberately concealing relevant facts. Ibid., pp. 137–138.

62   For example, in *NA. v. The United Kingdom* (2008), the Court referred that its sole task under Article 19 ECHR is to ensure the observance of the engagements undertaken by the States parties in the Convention and its Protocols. It added that it is not the Court's task to apply directly the level of protection offered in other international instruments and therefore considered that the applicant's submissions on the basis of Directive 2004/83/EC were outside the scope of its examination of the Non-Refoulement application before it. ECtHR, *NA. v. The United Kingdom*, para. 107.

63   Article 35(3)(b) provides that "the applicant has not suffered a significant disadvantage, unless respect for human rights as defined in the Convention and the Protocols thereto requires an examination of the application on the merits and provided that no case may be rejected on this ground which has not been duly considered by a domestic tribunal".

severity before it warrants consideration by an international Court. The Court interprets this criterion and decides on its application.[64] In view of the severity of the treatment to which the applicant would be subjected in the receiving State, it is unlikely that a Non-Refoulement application will be declared inadmissible on this ground.

Since the Court receives more and more applications, these criteria are very important.[65] The overwhelming majority of applications lodged with the Court are declared inadmissible and rejected; thus, they are not examined on the merits. Most inadmissible applications were rejected for non-exhaustion of domestic remedies, non-compliance with the six-months rule, or both. Many applications were rejected because they were manifestly ill-founded: the applicant failed properly to substantiate his allegations.[66] In the following subsections we examine specific standing and admissibility criteria, as interpreted by the ECtHR in its Non-Refoulement case-law.

II.1.1   Victim Status

According to Article 34 ECHR, the Court may receive an application from any person who claims to be a victim of a violation by a State party to the rights set fourth in the ECHR. The Court asserted, "the word "victim" in the context of Article 34 of the Convention denotes the person directly affected by the act or omission in issue".[67] A person who is not personally and directly affected, or at risk of being directly affected by the act complained of cannot claim to be a

---

This criterion is added to the admissibility criteria laid down in Article 35 ECHR with the coming into force of Protocol No. 14 on 1st June 2010. ECtHR, Practical Guide on Admissibility Criteria, 2011.

64   Ibid., para. 381.

65   For more explanation, see White, R. & Ovey, C., 2010, pp. 30–40; Erdal, U. & Bakirci, H., 2006, pp. 79–80; Leach, P., Taking a Case to the European Court of Human Rights, Oxford, New York: Oxford University Press, 3rd Ed, 2011, pp. 107–158. The number of applications lodged annually with the ECtHR increased from 404 in 1981 to 56,250 in 2014. ECtHR, Annual Report 2001, p. 9, available at: <http://www.echr.coe.int/Documents/Annual_report_2001_ENG.pdf>, last visit 20 April, 2016; ECtHR, Analysis of statistics, 2014, p. 4, <http://www.echr.coe.int/Documents/Stats_analysis_2014_ENG.pdf>, last visit, 30 November 2015.

66   Erdal, U. & Bakirci, H., 2006, p. 79. Out of 86,063 applications that were decided by the Court in 2014, 83,675 applications were declared inadmissible or struck out of the list. ECtHR, General statistics, 2014, available at: <http://www.echr.coe.int/Documents/Stats_annual_2014_ENG.pdf>, last visit, 30 November 2015.

67   ECtHR, *Nasrulloyev v. Russia*, Appl. No. 656/06, 11 October 2007, para. 58; ECtHR, *Budrevich v. the Czech Republic* (admissibility decision), Appl. No. 65303/10, 17 October 2013, para. 66.

victim for the purposes of the Convention.[68] Where the applicant is not a victim of the act complained of, the Court declares the application incompatible *ratione personae*.[69]

Since the act complained of in Non-Refoulement cases is forcible removal carried out by the respondent State, the applicant in such cases must be directly and personally affected by the removal.[70] This does not mean that only the person who has already been removed can be considered a victim. The majority of Non-Refoulement complaints accepted by the ECtHR were submitted by "potential" victims,[71] i.e. persons who face a threat of forcible removal contrary to the principle of Non-Refoulement under Article 3 ECHR. The Court stated in the *Soering* case:

> It is not normally for the Convention institutions to pronounce on the existence or otherwise of potential violations of the Convention. However, where an applicant claims that a decision to extradite him would, if implemented, be contrary to Article 3 [...] by reason of its foreseeable consequences in the requesting country, a departure from this principle is necessary, in view of the serious and irreparable nature of the alleged suffering risked, in order to ensure the effectiveness of the safeguard provided by that Article....[72]

The main factor is that the respondent State has taken measures that led, or would lead, to remove the applicant to a State where he face a real risk of ill-treatment. In *Bonger* v. *The Netherlands* (2005),[73] the Dutch government

---

68   Rogge, K., The "Victim" Requirement in Article 25 of the European Convention on Human Rights, in: Wiarda, G.J., Protecting Human Rights: The European Dimension, Koln: Garl Heymanns, 1990, 539–671, p. 539.

69   Erdal, U. & Bakirci, H., 2006, p. 93.

70   In our opinion, the Court cannot accept a Non-Refoulement application by "indirect victim", such as a family member. The Court should, in certain circumstances, accept Non-Refoulement applications by close relatives on behalf of a removed person such as in a case of forced disappearance. However, a close relative can submit an application under Article 3 ECHR for distress and anguish that the relative personally suffers as a result of the forced disappearance. Ibid., p. 80.

71   Leach, P., Taking a Case to the European Court of Human Rights, Oxford: Oxford University Press, 2nd Ed, 2005, p. 128; ECtHR, Practical Guide on Admissibility Criteria, paras. 26–27.

72   ECtHR, *Soering* v. *the United Kingdom*, para. 90.

73   This case concerned expulsion of a refused asylum seeker to Ethiopia, ECtHR, *Bonger* v. *The Netherlands* (admissibility decision).

indicated that, for the time being, it did not intend to proceed effectively with the applicant's expulsion and, even if it did that, the applicant could challenge his expulsion before the domestic courts on the ground that his expulsion would infringe his rights under Article 3 ECHR. Taking this indication into account, the ECtHR declared the application based on Article 3 inadmissible. The Court stated that:

> …in the absence of any realistic prospects for his expulsion to Ethiopia, the applicant cannot claim to be a victim within the meaning of Article 34 of the Convention as regards his complaint that his expulsion to Ethiopia will be in breach of his rights under Article 3.[74]

In order to be considered a victim in Non-Refoulement cases, the respondent State must have taken factual steps towards returning the person concerned to a State where he allegedly would face a real risk of treatment contrary to Article 3. Subsection (II.1.1.1) discusses whether the existence of a removal order adopted by the State party concerned with respect to the applicant is a ground for granting him victim status. Subsection (II.1.1.2) addresses the loss of victim status.

II.1.1.1   *Removal Order and Victim Status*
If the applicant were removed despite allegations of a risk of ill-treatment in the receiving State, he would be directly and personally affected by the forcible removal and could claim to be a victim within the meaning of Article 34, regardless of whether or not a removal order was issued.[75] Whether the applicant was, or was not, subjected to ill-treatment in the receiving State following his removal is irrelevant.[76]

If the applicant has not yet been removed when the Court considers the admissibility of his application, he can claim victim status when a final and enforceable order mandates his removal to a country where he allegedly would

---

74   Ibid., p. 14. ECtHR, *B.B.* v. *France*, Appl. No. 30930/96, 7 September 1998, paras. 36–37; ECtHR, *N.F.* v. *The Netherlands* (admissibility decision), Appl. No. 21563/08, 14 January 2014, para. 36; ECtHR, *Saleh Mohamed Hussein* v. *Netherlands* (admissibility decision), Appl. No. 7049/13, 1 April 2014, paras. 15–16.

75   ECtHR, *Vilvarajah and Others* v. *the United Kingdom*; ECtHR, *Mamatkulov and Askarov* v. *Turkey* (GC); ECtHR, *Labsi* v. *Slovakia*, Appl. No. 33809/08, 15 May 2012. The Court stated that, "the decision of a Contracting State to remove a person- and, a fortiori, the actual removal itself – may give rise to an issue under Article 3". ECtHR, *Husayn (Abu Zubaydah)* v. *Poland*, para. 451.

76   ECtHR, *Iskandarov* v. *Russia*, para. 132.

face a real risk of treatment contrary to Article 3. In *Auad* v. *Bulgaria* (2011), the government of Bulgaria contested the victim status of the applicant by arguing that he was not at risk of being expelled to Lebanon, where he allegedly faced a risk of ill-treatment or death. The Court noted that the order of his expulsion had been upheld by the Supreme Administrative Court and became final and enforceable. Although this order had been issued more than a year and a half before the ECtHR considered the application, it still had full and legal effect. The Court also found no indication that the Bulgarian authorities had suspended its enforcement, or that there was any possibility of challenging its enforcement. Therefore, it concluded that the applicant could claim to be a victim within the meaning of Article 34 ECHR.[77] In contrast, an applicant in Non-Refoulement cases cannot claim to be a victim when he has merely been notified of a deportation that cannot be executed without a subsequent expulsion order,[78] an extradition or expulsion order that is not enforceable or its enforcement may be challenged,[79] or an order that has been indefinitely stayed or otherwise deprived of the legal effect.[80]

The existence of an extradition or expulsion order is not a condition for holding that the applicant has victim status. In several Non-Refoulement cases,

---

77   ECtHR, *Auad* v. *Bulgaria*, paras. 92–93.

78   In *Vijayanathan and Pusparajah* v. *France*, the Court noted that both applicants had been indicated to leave the French territory and if they failed to comply, they would be liable to expulsion. However, these indications were not enforceable in themselves and no expulsion order was adopted. Even if the order were adopted, it is possible for the applicants to appeal it. The Court concluded that the applicants could not claim to be victims. ECtHR, *Vijayanathan and Pusparajah* v. *France*, Appl. No. 75/1991/327/399-400, 26 June 1992, para. 46.

79   ECtHR, *Svetlorusov* v. *Ukraine*, Appl. No. 2929/05, 12 March 2009, paras. 37–38. Erdal, U. & Bakirci, H., 2006, p. 19.

80   ECtHR, *Budrevich* v. *the Czech Republic* (admissibility decision), para. 66. See e.g., *Nasrulloyev* v. *Russia* (2007), concerned the extradition of a Tajik national to Tajikistan. In light of the fact that the Moscow City Court had overruled the extradition order and that the Supreme Court upheld this decision, the ECtHR found that the applicant might not claim to be a "victim" since the extradition order had no legal effect. ECtHR, *Nasrulloyev* v. *Russia*, paras. 12, 60 and 61. See also, ECtHR, *Andrić* v. *Sweden*, Appl. No 45917/99, 23 February 1999. In *Khodzhamberdiyev* v. *Russia* (2012), the Court based its conclusion that the complaint was inadmissible as manifestly ill-founded on the fact that the applicant would not be removed because his extradition order had been annulled by the national courts therefore he was no longer subject to an extradition order which could be executed. ECtHR, *Khodzhamberdiyev* v. *Russia*, Appl. No. 64809/10, 5 June 2012, para. 77. In our opinion, the Non-Refoulement application in this case should have been declared inadmissible as incompatible *ratione personae*.

the ECtHR acknowledged the victim status of the applicant even though there existed no order to remove him. This approach is most likely to be followed where the State party has placed the applicant in detention pending his removal. The Court has considerd this as an indication that the applicant is at imminent risk of removal, despite the absence of an order; consequently, the applicant can claim to be a victim within the meaning of Article 34. In *Koktysh* v. *Ukraine* (2009),[81] the applicant, who had been charged with murder and robbery in Belarus, was arrested in June 2007 in Ukraine. His arrest was based on an international warrant, and he was placed in detention pending his extradition to Belarus.[82] On 10 October 2007, the ECtHR indicated to the State party that the applicant should not be extradited.[83] The Ukrainian government argued that the applicant was not a victim, since no extradition decision in his respect had been adopted. The government added that no extradition decision would be made until the ECtHR took another decision concerning the implementation of the interim measures, or decided on the merits of the application.[84] The Court observed, at the time the case was under consideration, that the applicant was still being detained pending extradition, nearly two years and five months after detention began, even though no decision on his extradition had been made. The Court concluded that *Koktysh* was still threatened with extradition and had not lost his victim status.[85]

In *Abdolkhani and Karimnia* v. *Turkey* (2009), the Court found another indication that the applicants were at risk of being deported, even though no order had been issued to deport them. The applicants lived in Iraq and were members of an Iranian opposition organisation. On an unspecified date, they illegally entered Turkey, where they were arrested and deported back to Iraq on 17 June 2008. The applicants immediately re-entered Turkey and were re-arrested by the Turkish police. The Turkish government maintained before the ECtHR that the applicants had entered Turkey illegally, so the government deported

---

81   ECtHR, *Koktysh* v. *Ukraine*. In *Shamayev and 12 others* v. *Georgia and Russia* (2005), the Court declared the complaint of certain applicants under Article 3 was inadmissible because of the absence of an extradition order issued against them. None of those applicants were in arrest. ECtHR, *Shamayev and 12 others* v. *Georgia and Russia*, paras. 56, 355–356.

82   On 3 August 2007, the Balaklava Local Court decided that the applicant should be placed in detention pending his extradition without setting a time-limit for that detention. ECtHR, *Koktysh* v. *Ukraine*, paras. 17 and 46.

83   Ibid., para. 18.

84   Ibid., para. 44. Ukraine also used this argument in ECtHR, *Baysakov and Others* v. *Ukraine*, para. 36.

85   ECtHR, *Koktysh* v. *Ukraine*, para. 46; ECtHR, *Z.N.S.* v. *Turkey*, Appl. No. 21896/08, 19 January 2010, paras. 14, 40 and 42.

them directly to Iraq, where they came from. The government also argued that the applicants did not have victim status, since it issued no order to deport them. The ECtHR noted that Turkish authorities had deported the applicants on at least one occasion, to Iraq on 17 June 2008, without a deportation order or without serving them with such an order.[86] The Court found:

> ...the absence of deportation orders cannot lead to a conclusion that the applicants did not risk, and still do not risk, being deported to Iraq or Iran by the Turkish authorities. The Court therefore concludes that the applicants have victim status within the meaning of Article 34 of the Convention and it rejects the Government's objection.[87]

The Court does not restrict the protection against refoulement under Article 3 ECHR to cases in which States parties have decided to remove the applicant. As a result, the Court prevents States from circumventing the principle of Non-Refoulement by forcibly removing an individual without issuing a specific order.

An applicant in Non-Refoulement cases has victim status when he has already been removed, when there is a final and enforceable decision on his removal, or when the respondent State has taken factual steps to return him to a State where he would be at a real risk of being ill-treated.

II.1.1.2   Loss of Victim Status

It is well established in the ECtHR's case-law that the applicant must be able to justify his status as a victim throughout the proceedings before the Court.[88] The applicant may lose his victim status where national authorities have acknowledged the breach of the Convention, either expressly or implicitly, and then afforded redress.[89] The question of whether a State party has acknowledged the breach and appropriately remedied it depends on the circumstances of each case. In *Rrapo v. Albania* (2012), the Albanian Supreme Court acknowledged that the decision of the lower court was illegal, and returned the case for reconsideration. However, the ECtHR noted, the Supreme Court's decision could not reverse the applicant's extradition, which had taken place before the

---

86   ECtHR, *Abdolkhani and Karimnia v. Turkey*, Appl. No. 30471/08, 22 September 2009, paras. 11, 52 and 54; ECtHR, *Keshmiri v. Turkey*, Appl. No. 36370/08, 13 April 2010, para. 25.

87   ECtHR, *Abdolkhani and Karimnia v. Turkey*, para. 55.

88   ECtHR, *Burdov v. Russia*, Appl. No. 59498/00, 7 May 2002, para. 30.

89   ECtHR, *Karimov v. Russia*, Appl. No. 54219/08, 29 July 2010, para. 87; ECtHR, *Abdulazhon Isakov v. Russia*, para. 98; ECtHR, *M.A. v. Cyprus*, Appl. No. 41872/10, 23 July 2013, para. 109. Leach, P., 2005, p. 131.

adoption of this decision. The ECtHR asserted that, in such circumstances, the applicant could continue to claim to be a victim of a violation of Article 3. The Court then rejected the Albanian government's objection that the applicant had lost his victim status.[90]

It has been argued that the applicant would lose his victim status once his removal is suspended in accordance with the ECtHR's indication, under Rule 39 of the Rules of Court, that he not be returned to the proposed receiving State until further notice or pending the Court's decision on the merits. The Russian government made this argument in *Karimov v. Russia* (2010) when it maintained that the applicant could not claim to be the victim of a violation of Article 3 since the ECtHR had suspended his extradition until further notice.[91] The Court observed that the applicant's extradition order was made final subsequent to the Russian government's decision to suspend his extradition, a suspension adopted only because the Court's indication under Rule 39 had been applied. The Court concluded suspending the applicant's extradition to Uzbekistan did not constitute any acknowledgment, whether explicit or implicit, by the Russian authorities that Article 3 had been or would have been violated, or that the applicant's extradition order had been deprived of its legal effect. The Court concluded that the applicant could continue to claim to be a victim within the meaning of Article 34 ECHR.[92] The Court has held that suspending an applicant's removal in compliance with its indication under Rule 39 does not constitute an acknowledgement by the State party of the breach, nor is it an appropriate redress that would deprive the applicant of his victim status.

It is established in the ECtHR's Non-Refoulement case-law that once the applicant no longer risks being expelled from the respondent State, the Court considers the case to have been resolved and strikes it out of its list of cases, whether or not the applicant agrees. In the Court's view, the reason for this approach being that it has consistently considered the refoulement issue as one of a "potential violation" of the ECHR, on the view that the threat of a violation is removed as a result of the decision granting the applicant a residence permit in the respondent State.[93] The ECtHR consideres a respondent

---

90   ECtHR, *Rrapo v. Albania*, para. 64.

91   ECtHR, *Karimov v. Russia*, paras. 10–12, 28 and 51. See also, ECtHR, *Abdulazhon Isakov v. Russia*, para. 96; ECtHR, *Umirov v. Russia*, Appl. No. 17455/11, 18 September 2012, para. 89.

92   ECtHR, *Karimov v. Russia*, paras. 90–91; ECtHR, *Baysakov and Others v. Ukraine*, para. 40; ECtHR, *Mamadaliyev v. Russia*, Appl. No. 5614/13, 24 July 2014, para. 55.

93   ECtHR, *M.E. v. Sweden* (admissibility decision), Appl. No. 71398/12, 8 April 2015, paras. 32–33; ECtHR, *Nasseri v. the United Kingdom* (admissibility decision), Appl. No. 24239/09, 13 October 2015, para. 18.

State to have afforded appropriate redress of the breach in refoulement cases where the State grants the applicant refugee status or any other form of protection that makes him eligible for a residence permit, whether permanent or of limited duration, in its territory.[94] The mere fact of granting the applicant refugee status does not in itself constitute appropriate redress that leads to the loss of victim status if it does not protect him against removal. In *Baysakov and Others* v. *Ukraine* (2010), the Court observed that the prosecutors had challenged the decisions that granted refugee status to the applicants, and that the proceedings concerning the lawfulness of those decisions were pending.[95] In this regard, the Court referred to another Non-Refoulement case of *Kuznetsov* v. *Ukraine*, in which the Ukrainian prosecutors had removed the applicant from Ukraine despite his refugee status. Against this background, the Court concluded that the applicants were still under threat of extradition, despite their refugee status, and therefore did not lose their victim status.[96]

The applicant may voluntarily leave the respondent State party and settle in a third State after he has lodged his application with the ECtHR, and before the Court adopts a decision on the merits. The Court has considerd the question of whether the applicant loses his victim status in such cases to depend on the circumstances of each case. In *A.A.Q.* v. *the Netherlands* (2015), the Court noted that, shortly before his scheduled removal to Afghanistan, the applicant had moved from the respondent State to Germany where he filed an asylum application, and that pending the determination of this application, he was granted a provisional residence permit. Consequently, the Court found that the applicant could not be regarded as a victim because he was not at risk of being removed to Afghanistan.[97] The Court adopted the opposite approach in *S.S. and Others* v. *Denmark* (2011). In this case, the applicants were four Sri

---

94   ECtHR, *Isfahano* v. *The Netherlands* (admissibility decision), Appl. No. 31252/03, 31 January 2008, p. 7; ECtHR, *I.M.* v. *France*, Appl. No. 9152/09, 2 February 2012; ECtHR, *H.* v. *Norway* (admissibility decision), Appl. No. 51666/13, 17 February 2015.

95   The applicants were granted refugee status in Ukraine because there were legitimate grounds to fear that they would risk political persecution in Kazakhstan. ECtHR, *Baysakov and Others* v. *Ukraine*, para. 8.

96   Ibid., paras. 41–42. See also, ECtHR, *Yefimova* v. *Russia* and ECtHR, *K.* v. *Russia*, Appl. No. 69235/11, 23 May 2013, para. 52, in which the applicants were granted temporary asylum in Russia for a year. The Court considered that this measure did not affect the applicants' victim status because the extradition order remained enforceable.

97   ECtHR, *A.A.Q.* v. *the Netherlands* (admissibility decision), Appl. No. 42331/05, 30 June 2015, para. 59. See also, ECtHR, *M.T.* v. *Turkey* (admissibility decision), Appl. No. 46765/99, 30 May 2002; ECtHR, *Ali Ayashi* v. *Turkey* (admissibility decision), Appl. No. 3083/07, 18 November 2008; ECtHR, *A.D. and Others* v. *Turkey*, Appl. No. 22681/09, 22 July 2014, paras. 81–84; Erdal, U. & Bakirci, H., 2006, p. 201.

Lankan nationals: a husband and wife and their two children. After the Danish Refugee Appeals Board had refused their asylum application, the husband departed to Germany, where he obtained a residence permit, while the wife lived with the children in an asylum centre in Denmark.[98] The government of Denmark maintained before the ECtHR that the husband could no longer claim to have victim status because he had departed Denmark and had obtained a residence permit in a third State.[99] The Court observed that the applicants did not have a legal basis for staying in Denmark, and they might forcibly be removed to Sri Lanka if they did not leave voluntarily. Thus, the Court noted that although the husband had left Denmark voluntarily, and obtained a residence permit in Germany, there was no indication that the deportation order could no longer be enforced if he re-entered Denmark for any reason, such as to see his wife and children. Consequently, the Court found that although the imminent danger that the applicant would be forcibly returned to Sri Lanka by the Danish authorities had clearly diminished, it had not been eliminated.[100]

II.1.2   Exhaustion of Domestic Remedies

According to Article 35(1) ECHR, an applicant must exhaust all domestic remedies before he can submit his application to the ECtHR.[101] The rationale behind this rule lies in the subsidiary nature of the Court's role; i.e. the State party ought first to be given the opportunity to prevent or put right the alleged violation through its own legal system before that allegation is submitted to the ECtHR.[102] The subsidiary nature of the Court's role is especially important in light of the increasing number of applications, particularly Non-Refoulement applications,[103] brought before the Court. The sheer number limits the effectiveness of the Court and constitutes a threat to the quality and the consistency of its case-law.[104] An applicant must thus fulfil this rule, even if he invokes the "absolute right" of protection against torture and CIDTP under

---

98   ECtHR, *S.S. and Others* v. *Denmark*, Appl. No. 54703/08, 20 January 2011, para. 5.

99   Ibid., para. 70.

100   Ibid., para. 97.

101   For more explanation see, Shaw, M.N., International Law, Cambridge: Cambridge University Press, 2008, pp. 273–274; Leach, P., 2011, pp. 126–139.

102   ECtHR, *Selmouni* v. *France*, para. 47; Erdal, U. & Bakirci, H., 2006, pp. 95–96.

103   No statistics are available on the number of the Non-Refoulement applications lodged with the ECtHR under Article 3 ECHR particularly that most of these applications were declared inadmissible. The number of Non-Refoulement cases in which the Court delivered a judgment increased from 8 cases during the ten years following the *Soering* case (1989–1999) to 33 cases in 2014.

104   High Level Conference on the Future of the European Court of Human Rights, Interlaken Declaration, 19 February 2010; High Level Conference on the Future of the European

Article 3 ECHR.[105] The domestic remedies required to be exhausted are only those that are effective, available, and could adequately redress the violation and offer a reasonable prospect of success.[106] The Court illustrated this point:

> ...in view of the importance which the Court attaches to Article 3 of the Convention and the irreversible nature of the damage which may result if the risk of ill-treatment materializes, the effectiveness of a remedy for the purposes of Article 35 § 1 imperatively requires that the person concerned should have access to a remedy with automatic suspensive effect.[107]

The Court has repeatedly asserted that where the applicant seeks to prevent his removal by a State party, a domestic remedy will be considered effective and will consequently have to be exhausted only if it has automatic suspensive effect.[108] When the ECtHR considered the application in *Al Hanchi* v. *BH* (2011), the case was pending before the Constitutional Court. The ECtHR observed that an appeal to the Constitutional Court did not have automatic suspensive effect. Though it was possible for the person concerned to request that deportation be suspended as an interim measure, the application for an interim measure was not in itself suspensive. As evidenced in the case under consideration, the Constitutional Court was not required to decide such application before the person was actually deported. While *Al Hanchi* had lodged the application for an interim measure with the Constitutional Court on 3 December 2009, his deportation to Tunisia was scheduled for 10 December 2009 and the Constitutional Court decided that application on 12 January 2010. Against this background, the Court stated in general terms:

> ...where an applicant seeks to prevent his or her removal from Bosnia and Herzegovina to a territory where he or she allegedly faces a risk of ill-treatment contrary to Article 3, an appeal to the Constitutional Court

---

Court of Human Rights, Izmir Declaration, 27 April 2011; High Level Conference on the Future of the European Court of Human Rights, Brighton Declaration, 20 April 2012.

105   ECtHR, *Al Hanchi* v. *Bosnia and Herzegovina*, para. 32.

106   Erdal, U. & Bakirci, H., 2006, p. 99; ECtHR, *Salah Sheekh* v. *The Netherlands*, para. 121.

107   ECtHR, *Al Hanchi* v. *Bosnia and Herzegovina*, para. 32; ECtHR, *M.S.S.* v. *Belgium and Greece* (GC), para. 293.

108   ECtHR, *Jabari* v. *Turkey*; ECtHR, NA. v. *The United Kingdom*, para. 90. Reneman, M., An EU Right to Interim Protection during Appeal Proceedings in Asylum Cases?, European Journal of Migration and Law, Vol. 12 no. 4: 2010, 407–434, p. 408.

cannot be considered to be an effective remedy in preventing removal before a final decision of that court.[109]

By contrast, the Court noted in several cases concerning removal from Norway that it is up to the domestic courts to consider appeals against orders by immigration authorities to expel the applicants. Applicants could seek a judicial injunction to halt the expulsion order, and such a judicial injunction has an immediate and suspensive effect on the applicant's expulsion.[110] The ECtHR decided that judicial review of the decision of the Norwegian immigration authorities to expel the applicant must be regarded as an effective remedy that applicants are required to exhaust before they lodge an application with the ECtHR or request interim measures under Rule 39.

As noted above, the Court has consistently held that, in order to be effective, the domestic remedy must offer a reasonable prospect of success. Mere doubt as to the prospect of success of a particular remedy does not absolve the applicant of the obligation to exhaust that remedy. Where the applicant establishes that an available remedy that he has not exhausted is bound to fail, by providing examples of domestic court decisions that demonstrate the ineffectiveness of that remedy, he cannot be regarded as having failed to exhaust domestic remedies.[111] In *Salah Sheekh* v. *The Netherlands* (2007), although appeal to the Administrative Jurisdiction Division was available to the applicant, the ECtHR held that such appeal had virtually no prospect of success. To reach this conclusion the Court referred to the case-law of the Administrative Jurisdiction Division in cases where the facts were similar to those of the *Sheekh* case. In this regard, the Court noted that in its latest decisions about a Somali national who, like *Sheekh,* belonged to a group subjected to organised, large-scale human right violations, the Administrative Jurisdiction Division required the applicant to establish that specific circumstances existed that related to him

---

109   ECtHR, *Al Hanchi* v. *Bosnia and Herzegovina*, para. 33. The Court took the same approach with regard to the application to the Turkish administrative courts in order to nullify a deportation order. ECtHR, *Abdolkhani and Karimnia* v. *Turkey*, paras. 56 and 59; ECtHR, *Z.N.S.* v. *Turkey*, para. 43; ECtHR, *Dbouba* v. *Turkey*, para. 33. This approach was also followed with regard to the challenging of the extradition orders before the Ukrainian administrative courts under the Code of Administrative Justice. ECtHR, *Kamyshev* v. *Ukraine*, Appl. No. 3990/06, 20 May 2010, para. 42; ECtHR, *A.A.M.* v. *Sweden*, Appl. No. 68519/10, 3 April 2014, paras. 45–46.

110   ECtHR, *Agalar* v. *Norway*, Appl. No. 55120/09, 8 November 2011; ECtHR, *Abdollahpour* v. *Norway* (admissibility decision), Appl. No. 57440/10, 29 May 2012, paras. 47–48.

111   ECtHR, *NA.* v. *The United Kingdom*, para. 89; ECtHR, *Nnyanzi* v. *the United Kingdom*, Appl. No. 21878/06, 8 April 2008, paras. 42–46.

personally before he would be able to benefit from the protection offered by Article 3. Since *Sheekh* did not argue that he would be subjected to treatment different from that which targeted the minority to which he belonged, the ECtHR found it difficult to see how the Administrative Jurisdiction Division could have come to a different conclusion in his case.[112]

In absence of any domestic remedy that offers review of the removal decision and suspends the applicant's removal pending such review, the applicant does not need to wait for the final decision on his removal to be adopted before he lodges an application with ECtHR.[113]

II.1.3   Six-Months Rule

According to Article 35(1) ECHR, a complaint must be lodged with the ECtHR within six months of the final decision taken in the domestic proceedings.[114] This rule is closely connected to the rule of exhaustion of domestic remedies. As a rule, the six-months period begins on the date of the final decision in the process of exhausting domestic remedies.[115] However, in *Varnava and Others* v. *Turkey* (2009), the ECtHR (GC) held that when the alleged violation constitutes a continuing situation, the six-months period begins at the end of the continuing situation. The Court justified this approach by stating that:

> ...if there is a situation of ongoing breach, the time-limit in effect starts afresh each day and it is only once the situation ceases that the final period of six months will run to its end.[116]

---

112   ECtHR, *Salah Sheekh* v. *The Netherlands*, para. 123.

113   ECtHR, *Puzan* v. *Ukraine*, Appl. No. 51243/08, 18 February 2010, para. 29; ECtHR, *Al Hanchi* v. *Bosnia and Herzegovina*.

114   Protocol No. 15 to the ECHR reduces from six to four months the time-limit within which an application may be made to the ECtHR following the date of a final domestic decision. This Protocol will enter into force as soon as all the States parties to the ECHR have signed and ratified it. As of 30 November 2015, out of 47 States parties to the ECHR, 26 States ratified this Protocol and 15 States signed but have not ratified it. Protocol No. 15 to the ECHR, amending the Convention on the Protection of Human Rights and Fundamental Freedoms, adopted on 16 May 2013, Article 4. See, <http://www.conventions.coe.int/Treaty/Commun/ChercheSig.asp?NT=213&CM=8&DF=&CL=ENG>, last visit 11 February 2016.

115   ECtHR, *Paul and Audrey Edwards* v. *the United Kingdom*, Appl. No. 46477/99, 7 June 2001; ECtHR, *Varnava and Others* v. *Turkey* (GC), Appl. Nos. 16064/90, 16065/90, 16066/90, 16068/90, 16069/90, 16070/90, 16071/90, 16072/90 and 16073/90, 18 September 2009, para. 157.

116   Ibid., para. 159. See also, Sanford, D.A., European Human Rights Mechanisms, New York: Transnational Publishers, 2002, p. 352.

In the Non-Refoulement case of *P.Z. and Others* v. *Sweden* (2012), the Swedish government argued that the applicants had not complied with the six-months requirement.[117] The Court noted that in cases in which an applicant alleges that his removal to another country would expose him to a risk of treatment contrary to Article 3, it is the "actual removal" that triggers the responsibility of the State party concerned under the Convention, since the direct consequence of this action is that the sending State exposes the person concerned to the proscribed risk.[118] Accordingly, the Court asserted that, in this type of case, "the potential violation" of Article 3 ECHR is not a result of the final national decision on the applicant's removal but of enforcement of this decision.[119] In the Court's view, this is reflected in its wording when it has found violations in refoulement cases, having concluded that the implementation of a removal order "would involve a violation" of Article 3 ECHR, thus referring to a potential violation occurring at the time of the enforcement of this order.[120] Arguably, the Court has considered that following the final national decision on the applicant's removal and before the implementation of this decision, there is a "potential violation" of the principle of Non-Refoulement under Article 3 ECHR. This potential violation becomes an actual violation only if the applicant is removed. If the removal decision is not implemented (for instance, when a State complies with the Court's request for an interim measure, and the applicant remains in the territory of the State that wishes to remove him) the Court would describe the situation as "an ongoing potential violation" of the Convention, resembling "the continuing situations" described above. In such a situation, the Court would not consider the six-month period to have started for the applicant.[121] Therefore, the "potential victim"[122] could submit his Non-Refoulement complaint to the ECtHR, regardless of the length of time that have passed after the final removal decision was adopted by the national authorities. When the removal decision is implemented, the six-months period begins on date of the applicant's removal and he must submit his complaint to the Court within the next six months. The Court stated:

---

117 ECtHR, *P.Z. and Others* v. *Sweden* (admissibility decision), Appl. No. 68194/10, 29 May 2012, para. 25.

118 Ibid., para. 30.

119 ECtHR, *Soering* v. *the United Kingdom*, para. 90.

120 ECtHR, *P.Z. and Others* v. *Sweden* (admissibility decision), para. 31.

121 Ibid., para. 34.

122 See above, Chapter 3, Section II, the victim status under the ECHR.

...the considerations relevant in determining the date of the sending State's responsibility must be applicable also in the context of the six-month rule. In other words, the date of the State's responsibility under Article 3 corresponds to the date when the six-month period under Article 35 § 1 starts to run for the applicant.[123]

The Court noted that the application in *P.Z. and Others* v. *Sweden* (2012) was submitted more than two years after the final national decision. However, the deportation order had not been enforced when the application was submitted, and the applicants remained in Sweden. Given the circumstances, the Court rejected Sweden's objection because the six-months period had not yet started, and thus the applicants had not failed to comply with the six-months rule.[124]

In the extraordinary rendition case of *El-Masri* v. *the Republic of Macedonia* (2012), the applicant lodged his case with the ECtHR over five and a half years after his secret rendition.[125] The Macedonian government objected that the applicant had failed to comply with the six-months rule. The Court addressed this objection with respect to the applicant's application as whole.[126] It reiterated:

...the Convention is an instrument for the protection of human rights and that it is of crucial importance that it is interpreted and applied in a manner that renders these rights practical and effective, not theoretical and illusory. This concerns not only the interpretation of substantive provisions of the Convention, but also procedural provisions; it impacts on the obligations imposed on respondent Governments, but also has effects on the position of applicants.[127]

---

123   Ibid., para. 34.

124   Ibid., paras. 35–36.

125   While the applicant's rendition took place on 23 January 2004, his application lodged with the Court on 20 July 2009. ECtHR, *El-Masri* v. *The Former Yugoslav Republic of Macedonia* (GC), paras. 20–22.

126   Namely, the applicant's allegations under Article 3 of ill-treatment while being held in the Republic of Macedonia and the responsibility of this State for his transfer into the custody of the US' authorities; his allegations under Article 5 of arbitrary detention in the Republic of Macedonia and the responsibility of this State for his subsequent captivity in Afghanistan, claim under Article 8 that his secret and extrajudicial abduction and arbitrary detention had violated his right to respect for his private and family life, the failure of the respondent State to carry out an effective investigation into the applicant's above mentioned allegations and the lack of effective remedies under Article 13.

127   Ibid., para. 137.

The Court pointed out that, as a rule, the six-months period runs from the date of the final decision in the process of exhaustion of domestic remedies. However, when an applicant avails himself of an existing remedy, and only subsequently becomes aware of circumstances that render this remedy ineffective, the Court considered it appropriate to start the six-months period on the date the applicant first became, or ought to have become, aware of those circumstances. The Court noted that the applicant's criminal complaint was filed in the Republic of Macedonia on 6 October 2008. The delay in bringing this complaint rendered it neither inadmissible nor ineffective, since it was rejected for lack of evidence and not for non-compliance with the admissibility criteria. The Court held that the date when the applicant knew of the final decision on his criminal complaint would mark the starting point of the six-month time-limit. While the applicant's criminal complaint had been rejected on 18 December 2008, this decision was not brought to his attention until 22 November 2010. Since the respondent State did not demonstrate that the applicant received an official notification of the decision or learned about it before 20 January 2009 (the date of the application before the ECtHR), the Court concluded that the applicant had complied with the six-months rule under Article 35(1) ECHR.[128]

Although the above approach was not adopted specifically for the Non-Refoulement claim, it should also be used in Non-Refoulement cases where the argument of non-compliance with the six-months rule is raised under similar circumstances. In such cases, where the applicant, who had not had the opportunity to challenge his removal before it was carried out, seeks a remedy from the sending State, after his removal, by challenging the legality of the removal and trying to obtain effective redress, the six-months time period begins on the date the applicant learns of the final domestic decision on his claim. The sending State can take this opportunity to put right the alleged violation of Non-Refoulement through its legal system before the submission of the allegation to the ECtHR in accordance with the subsidiary nature of the Court's role. This approach also preserves the applicant's right to recourse to the ECtHR in case the State intentionally prolongs the domestic remedy.

II.1.4   The Application is Not Substantially the Same as Another One that Has Been Examined by the Court or Submitted to Another International Body

Under Article 35(2)(b), the Court shall not consider any individual application that is substantially the same as a matter that it has already examined.[129]

---

128   Ibid., paras. 134–148.
129   ECHR50, Article 35(2)(b).

The Court has clarified that applications are considered to be substantially the same where they relate to the same parties, the same facts, and the same complaints.[130] A Non-Refoulement application is considered substantially the same as another application if the same Non-Refoulement complaint, based on Article 3 ECHR, was brought by the same applicant against the same respondent State, and was based on the same facts. In such a case, the Court shall declare the application inadmissible unless it contains relevant new information. For example, if the ECtHR declared the application inadmissible for non-exhaustion of domestic remedies, the applicant may resubmit the same matter to the Court after he has exhausted effective domestic remedies.[131]

The Court may not admit any application that has already been submitted to another procedure of international investigation or settlement, if it does not contain any relevant new information.[132] The ECtHR has not had an opportunity to consider the admissibility of an application that was previously submitted to the ComAT. However, the ComAT is, like the UNHRC which has been regarded by the ECtHR as another international procedure,[133] a treaty body empowered with the individual communications procedure, as it can decide in an individual case whether a State party breached a treaty obligation and achieved remedy.[134] A person, who claims to be a victim of refoulement, should decide in advance whether to bring his claim before the ECtHR or the ComAT.

Since the question has not been raised before the ECtHR, it is not yet clear whether prior examination of the applicant's case by the UNHCR would make the application inadmissible to the ECtHR. Neither the CSR nor the Statute of UNHCR provides for establishing a procedure for international investigation

---

130   EComHR, *Pauger v. Austria* (admissibility decision), Appl. No. 24872/94, 9 January 1995.

131   Leach, P., 2011, p. 147.

132   ECHR50, Article 35(2)(b).

133   EComHR, *Calcerrada Fornieles and Cabeza Mato v. Spain* (admissibility decision), Appl. No. 17512/90, 6 July 1992; EComHR, *Pauger v. Austria* (admissibility decision).

134   Davala, M., Conflict of Interest in Universal Human Rights Bodies, in: Peters, A. & Handschin, L., Conflict of Interest in Global, Public and Corporate Governance, Cambridge: Cambridge University Press, 2012, 125–144 p. 127; Nowak, M. & McArthur, E., 2008, p. 722. In contrary, the Court noted that the UN Human Rights Commission was essentially an inter-governmental organ composed of State representatives, which deals with situations rather than individual complaints and which offers no redress to individual victims. Accordingly, the Court did not consider the UN Human Rights Commission as another international procedure. ECtHR, *Mikolenko v. Estonia* (admissibility decision), Appl. No. 16944/03, 5 January 2006.

or settlement. Therefore, in our view, it should not be considered as another international procedure, within the meaning of Article 35(2)(b).

II.1.5   The Application is Not Manifestly Ill-founded

Under Article 35(3) ECHR, an application may be declared inadmissible for being manifestly ill-founded if the Court is not satisfied, on preliminary investigation, that the applicant has not made a *prima facie* case for a violation of the ECHR.[135] The grounds upon which a Non-Refoulement application under Article 3 ECHR may be declared manifestly ill-founded are various and cannot be identified. The Court defines whether the applicant has submitted a *prima facie* application on the case-by-case basis. For example, the Court has considered an application as manifestly ill-founded if the applicant fails to submit evidence sufficient to substantiate his *prima facie* claims.[136] The applicant may fail to support his allegations with an arrest warrant or any other document that demonstrates the charge against him exists in the country of destination.[137]

In the ECtHR's view, certain facts might indicate that an application is manifestly ill-founded. In *O* v. *the Netherlands* (2009), the Court considered the fact that the Mauritanian authorities had accepted the applicant's request to prolong the validity of his passport as an indication that he had not attracted negative attention from the Mauritanian authorities despite the Dutch authorities suspicions that he was involved in a terrorist organisation.[138] In *Al Hamdani* v. *BH* (2012), in which a suspected terrorist was deported to Iraq, the Court noted that the applicant had visited Iraq twice since the change of regime, in 2003 and 2004. The security situation in Iraq had been much more dangerous at the time of the applicant's visits than the time his case was under consideration by the ECtHR. During his visits in Iraq, the applicant had moved freely, in and out of public buildings and on the streets. Against this background, the Court found the applicant's claim under Article 3 to be manifestly ill-founded and declared

---

135   Leach, P., 2011, p. 157.
136   ECtHR, *Mawajedi Shikpohkt and A. Mahkat Shole* v. *the Netherlands* (admissibility decision), Appl. No. 39349/03, 27 January 2005; ECtHR, *Jeltsujeva* v. *the Netherlands* (admissibility decision), Appl. No. 39858/04, 1 June 2006; ECtHR, *Harutioenyan and others* v. *the Netherlands* (admissibility decision), Appl. No. 43700/07, 1 September 2009.
137   ECtHR, *Karim* v. *Sweden* (admissibility decision), Appl. No. 24171/05, 4 July 2006 and ECtHR, *Gomes v. Sweden*, Appl. No. 34566/04, 7 February 2006.
138   ECtHR, *O* v. *the Netherlands* (admissibility decision), Appl. No. 37755/06, 17 November 2009, para. 38.

it inadmissible.[139] The Court, in these cases, discussed substantive issues in its decisions on admissibility.[140] However, even if an application is declared admissible, it will not necessarily be considered founded on its merits.[141]

II.2   *ComAT*

Under Article 22 CAT, an individual communication can only be lodged with the ComAT against a State party to the CAT that has recognised the Committee's competence to receive and consider communications from individuals who claim to be victims of a violation by this State of the provisions of the CAT. The conditions for admissibility of individual communications before the ComAT are provided for in Article 22 CAT and Rule 113 of the Committee's Rules of Procedure (RoP).[142] The complaint must not have been considered to be an abuse of the right to submit complaints or manifestly unfounded. The complaint must also be compatible with the provisions of the CAT, whether *ratione materiae* (i.e. in refoulement cases, the complaint must relate to an alleged violation of the principle of Non-Refoulement under Article 3 CAT), *ratione personae* (a complainant needs to be a victim of the alleged violation by the respondent State party of Article 3 CAT), *ratione temporis* (the complaint must relate to forcible removal which has taken place after entry into force of the Convention for the respondent State party or after entry into force of Article 22 CAT for this State where it limited the right to individual communications to the situations that have taken place after entry into force of this Article for it),[143] or *ratione loci* (the alleged forcible removal has taken/would take place within the territorial jurisdiction of the respondent State party). The complainant must have exhausted all available domestic remedies before submitting the complaint to the ComAT, and the time elapsed since domestic remedies are exhausted must not be unreasonably prolonged. Another international body must not have examined or currently be examining the matter. In order to reach a decision on the admissibility of a complaint, the ComAT ascertains that all these admissibility conditions have been met; otherwise, the

---

139   ECtHR, *Al Hamdani* v. *Bosnia and Herzegovina*, Appl. No. 31098/10, 7 February 2012, paras. 50–52.

140   ECtHR, *Izevbekhai and others* v. *Ireland*, Appl. No. 43408/08, 17 May 2011.

141   ECtHR, *Harkins and Edwards* v. *the United Kingdom*; ECtHR, *Babar Ahmad and Others* v. *the United Kingdom*; ECtHR, *Yoh-Ekale Mwanje* v. *Belgium*, Appl. No. 10486/10, 20 December 2011.

142   ComAT, Rules of procedure, Rule 113.

143   Nowak, M. & McArthur, E., 2008, p. 750.

complaint shall be declared inadmissible.[144] In the following subsections, we examine certain admissibility conditions, as interpreted by the ComAT in its Non-Refoulement case-law.

II.2.1   Victim Status

According to Article 22(1) CAT, the Committee may receive a complaint from any person who claims to be a victim of a violation of the provisions of this Convention by a State party to the CAT.[145] The complainant can only claim victim status before the ComAT if he is directly and personally affected by the act. If not, his complaint would be declared inadmissible. Where a person was forcibly removed or at risk of being forcibly removed to a State where he allegedly was/would be at risk of being tortured, he could claim before the ComAT to be a victim of a violation of Article 3 CAT by the sending State party. In subsection (II.2.1.1), we examine whether the existence of a removal order for the complainant, which has been adopted by the sending State party, is a condition that is considered in determining victim status. In subsection (II.2.1.2), we address the question of losing victim status.

II.2.1.1   *Removal Order and Victim Status*

If the complainant is removed in spite of allegations of a risk of torture in the State of destination, he can claim to be a victim within the meaning Article 22(1), whether or not a removal order has been issued for him.[146] Whether the complainant was, or was not, subjected to torture in the receiving State following his removal is irrelevant.

If the complainant has not been removed at the time the admissibility of his complaint is considered, he can claim victim status where a final and enforceable removal order has been issued.[147] In *J.A.M.O. et al.* v. *Canada* (2008), which concerned the expulsion of a Mexican national and his wife and daughter, the State party contested the admissibility of the complaint because no expulsion order was issued against the complainant's wife and daughter and that they had visitors' status in Canada. The Committee noted that visitors' status is precarious by nature, and that the wife and daughter also risked being

---

144   For more details on the way of ascertaining whether a complaint is admissible and deciding that, see the Committee's Rules of procedure, Rules 111–113.

145   See also, ComAT, Rules of procedure, Rule 113(a).

146   E.g., ComAT, *Chedli Ben Ahmed Karoui* v. *Sweden*, No. 185/2001, 8 May 2002.

147   E.g. ComAT, *Z.K.* v. *Sweden*, No. 301/2006, 16 May 2008; ComAT, *N.Z.S.* v. *Sweden*, No. 277/2005, 22 November 2006; ComAT, *T.M.* v. *Sweden*, No. 228/2003, 18 November 2003.

deported.[148] Even if there is no order to remove the person concerned, he can still have victim status within the meaning of Article 22(1) if there are indications that he is at risk of removal.

In *Jamal Omer Mohamed* v. *Greece* (1997), the Committee noted that the complainant was not at risk of being removed because the State party did not order his removal to Ethiopia, and he remained in Greece for humanitarian reasons. The Committee added that even if the State party ordered him to be expelled at a later stage, the complainant could appeal such an order. Accordingly, the ComAT found that there was no violation of Article 3.[149] In another case, *J.M.U.M.* v. *Sweden* (1998), the Committee noted in its admissibility decision that the original expulsion order against the complainant was no longer enforceable, and he was not under immediate risk of being expelled to the DRC. Moreover, he presented a new application for a residence permit in Sweden and the decision on this application could be appealed, if necessary. The Committee therefore concluded that his complaint was inadmissible because he had failed to exhaust domestic remedies.[150] In our view, in both these cases the Committee should have concluded that these complaints were inadmissible *ration personae*, since the complainants were not at imminent risk of removal, and thus could not claim victim status within the meaning of Article 22(1) CAT.

The existence of a removal order for a complainant is not a condition for holding that he has victim status. However, the absence of a removal order and any other indication that the complainant is at risk of being removed will lead the Committee to declare his Non-Refoulement application inadmissible.

II.2.1.2   *Loss of Victim Status*

Neither the CAT nor the ComAT's case-law provides clearly for loss of victim status where the respondent State party has acknowledged the breach and appropriately remedied it. However, through its case-law, the Committee has refused to consider the complainant's Non-Refoulement claim where it finds that he is no longer at risk of being removed by the respondent State.

A State party concerned may grant the complainant some form of protection that enables him to stay on its territory. The Committee has held that in such situations the person concerned does not have victim status. In *A.B.A.O.*

---

148   ComAT, *J.A.M.O. et al.* v. *Canada*, para. 9.3.

149   ComAT, *Jamal Omer Mohamed* v. *Greece*, No. 40/1996, 28 April 1997, para. 11.3.

150   ComAT, *J.M.U.M.* v. *Sweden* (admissibility decision), No. 58/1996, 15 May 1998, para. 3.2; ComAT, *B.M.S.* v. *Sweden* (admissibility decision), No. 437/2010, 12 November 2012, paras. 6.2–6.3.

v. *France* (2007), the Committee noted in its admissibility decision that the complainant was granted subsidiary protection in France. Accordingly, a compulsory residence order was issued. The Committee concluded that the complainant did not run any direct risk of being returned to Tunisia.[151] In *A.D.* v. *The Netherlands* (1999), the State party argued before the Committee that the complainant was not at risk of expulsion pending the decision on his request for an extension of his residence permit for medical treatment. The ComAT took into account that the order for the complainant's expulsion was still in force, and decided that the possibility that the complainant would be granted an extended temporary permit for medical treatment was not sufficient to fulfil the State party's obligations under Article 3 CAT.[152] What is decisive in the Committee's view is that the protection granted to the person concerned makes him eligible for a residence permit in the State concerned, and he is no longer at risk of being removed.

The Committee has had the opportunity to deal with the situation where the complainant voluntarily left the respondent State party after lodging the complaint with the Committee, and before it adopted its decision of admissibility. In *H.W.A.* v. *Switzerland* (1996), a few months after the complaint had been lodged with the ComAT, the complainant left Switzerland for Ireland where he applied for asylum and was given a residence permit pending the outcome of his asylum application. Since the complainant was legally present in the territory of another State, the Committee determined that he could not be returned by Switzerland to Syria. The Committee therefore concluded that Article 3 did not apply, and the complaint was held inadmissible.[153] The Committee held that the complainant could not claim to be at immediate risk of being forcibly returned by the State party to his country of origin; therefore, he could not claim to have victim status within the meaning of Article 22(1). In this case, the Committee paid special attention to the fact of the complainant's legal presence in another State. This should not be understood to mean that the Committee's approach in this case applies only where the complainant's

---

151 ComAT, *A.B.A.O.* v. *France* (admissibility decision), No. 264/2005, 8 November 2007, para. 8.3. See also, ComAT, *H.A.S.V.* v. *Canada* (admissibility decision), No. 163/2000, 24 November 2004, in which the complainant was granted asylum status in the State party; and in ComAT, *Nadeem Ahmad Dar* v. *Norway* (admissibility decision), No. 249/2004, 29 March 2007, the complainant withdraw his complaint because he was granted a residence permit in Norway.

152 ComAT, *A.D.* v. *The Netherlands*, para. 7.3.

153 ComAT, *H.W.A.* v. *Switzerland* (admissibility decision), No. 48/1996, 20 May 1996, para. 4.3. See also, ComAT, *I.A.F.B.* v. *Sweden* (admissibility decision), No. 425/2010, 13 November 2012, para. 7.3.

presence in a third State is legal. In *H.S.T.* v. *Norway* (2006), the complainant's exact whereabouts were unknown. In March 2006, he called the Secretariat to enquire about his case and mentioned that he was at that time in Belgium. Subsequently, his counsel informed the Secretariat, in July 2006, that he might be in France at the time.[154] This did not prevent the Committee from reaching the same conclusion as in *H.W.A.* v. *Switzerland*: Article 3 did not apply in this case and the complaint was inadmissible, because the complainant no longer seemed to be within the territorial jurisdiction of the respondent State and, thus, could not be returned to Mauritania by this State.[155]

Finally, the ComAT has made clear that suspending enforcement of the complainant's removal order in compliance with the Committee's request for an interim measure does not affect the complainant's victim status.[156]

II.2.2   Exhaustion of Domestic Remedies

According to Article 22(5)(b), the complainant must exhaust all domestic remedies before he submits his complaint to the ComAT; otherwise, his complaint will be declared inadmissible.[157] The applicant is required to exhaust only those domestic remedies that are available.[158] In the light of the irreparable harm that the complainant might face if returned to a country in violation of Article 3 CAT, the ComAT has held that only domestic remedies that have suspensive effect are considered effective within the meaning of Article 22(5)(b), and only these must be exhausted before the complaint is lodged with the Committee. The requirement that domestic remedies must be exhausted need not be fulfilled if the only remedy available to the complainant does not automatically stay the execution of the removal order to a State where he might be subjected to torture.[159] In *Nadeem Ahmad Dar* v. *Norway* (2007), the Committee noted that the complainant's case was pending in the High Court

---

154   ComAT, *H.S.T.* v. *Norway* (admissibility decision), No. 288/2006, 16 November 2006, para. 5.2.

155   Ibid., para. 6.3.

156   ComAT, *I.A.O.* v. *Sweden*, para. 7; ComAT, *M.R.A.* v. *Sweden*, No. 286/2006, 17 November 2006, para. 4.9.

157   CAT84, Article 22(5)(b). See e.g., ComAT, *K.K.H.* v. *Canada* (admissibility decision), No. 35/1995, 6 November 1995; ComAT, *V.V.* v. *Canada* (admissibility decision), No. 47/1996, 19 May 1998; ComAT, *H.E.-M.* v. *Canada* (admissibility decision), No. 395/2009, 23 May 2011; Nowak, M. & McArthur, E., 2008, pp. 162–163.

158   ComAT, *S.H.* v. *Norway* (admissibility decision), No. 121/1998, 19 November 1999, para. 7.2; ComAT, *Eftekhary* v. *Norway*, No. 312/2007, 25 November 2011, para. 6.3.

159   Report of the ComAT, UN. Doc. A/67/44, para. 108, p. 187. See, Reneman, M., 2010, pp. 425–426.

at the same time it was considering the complaint, and that the High Court's decision could be subsequently appealed. Since neither the appeal before the High Court, nor possible subsequent appeals, would suspend the removal order, the Committee concluded that none of these appeals constituted an effective remedy to the complainant's expulsion. Consequently, the Committee considered that it was not precluded by Article 22(5)(b) CAT from proceeding with the examination of the complaint.[160]

Article 22(5)(b) provides two exceptions to the principle of exhaustion of domestic remedies. Domestic remedies are not required to be exhausted where their application is unreasonably prolonged or is unlikely to bring effective relief to the victim of a violation.[161] Where the application of the domestic remedies is unreasonably prolonged, the person concerned is not required to wait for the result of these remedies before submitting his complaint to the ComAT. In *C.A.R.M. et al. v. Canada* (2007), the Committee noted that the complainants had applied for asylum in Canada on 12 November 2002 and that, more than four years later, their fate was still undecided. Against this background, the Committee considered the proceedings not to have been concluded within a reasonable time; consequently, it declared the complaint admissible.[162]

With regard to the second exception, it is settled in the Committee's jurisprudence that the principle of exhaustion of domestic remedies requires the complainant to use remedies that directly relate to the risk of torture in the proposed receiving State.[163] A remedy that aims to enable the complainant to stay in the State party on humanitarian grounds, or to obtain compensation for ill-treatment allegedly suffered by him following his return, is not a remedy that must be exhausted in order to satisfy the requirement for exhausting domestic remedies.[164] In contrast to the ECtHR, the Committee has made clear that the effectiveness of the domestic remedies does not mean they are capable of offering a prospect of success. In the Committee's view, it lacks the competence to determine if a domestic remedy is capable of offering a prospect of success. In *M.A. v. Canada* (1994), the complainant's case was still pending before the Canadian Court when the Committee considered the admissibility

---

160 ComAT, *Nadeem Ahmad Dar v. Norway* (admissibility decision), paras. 6.2–6.5.

161 CAT84, Article 22(5)(b).

162 ComAT, *C.A.R.M. et al. v. Canada*, No. 298/2006, 18 May 2007, para. 8.4.

163 ComAT, *Boily v. Canada*, para. 13.2; ComAT, *R.A.Y. v. Morocco*, No. 525/2012, 6 May 2014, para. 6.5.

164 ComAT, *A.R. v. Sweden* (admissibility decision), No. 170/2000, 23 November 2001, para 7.2; ComAT, *Enrique Falcon Rios v. Canada*, No. 133/1999, 23 November 2004, para. 7.3; ComAT, *R.S.M. v. Canada*, No. 392/2009, 24 May 2013, para. 4.3.

of his complaint to the ComAT. The complainant argued that there was almost no chance his case would succeed before the Canadian courts, given the prior jurisprudence of those Courts. The Committee declared his complaint inadmissible and clearly observed that:

> ...in principle, it is not within the scope of the Committee's competence to evaluate the prospects of success of domestic remedies, but only whether they are proper remedies for the determination of the author's claims.[165]

Even if the prior jurisprudence of certain domestic courts suggests there is minimal chance of a positive decision, this does not absolve the complainant from the obligation to exhaust these remedies. The Committee has adopted the same approach towards the complainant's lack of success with previous domestic remedies. In the Committee's view, prior failure is not adequate to predict future failure of available domestic remedies.[166]

II.2.3   Time-Limit to Submit the Complaint

Article 22 CAT does not set any time-limit on submitting a complaint to the ComAT. Rule 113(f) of the ComAT's RoP states:

> ...the time elapsed since the exhaustion of domestic remedies is not so unreasonably prolonged as to render consideration of the claims unduly difficult by the Committee or the State party.[167]

The period of time during which complaint must be submitted to the ComAT starts to run for the complainant from the date he has exhausted domestic remedies. The Committee does not define a time-limit during which a complaint must be submitted. However, the elapsed time must not be so unreasonably prolonged that it renders the Committee's consideration of the claim unduly difficult. The Committee determines, on a case-by-case basis, if a complaint is submitted in a reasonable time after the final national decision on the complainant's removal. The Committee has not have the opportunity to discuss this question in Non-Refoulement cases.

---

165   ComAT, *M.A.* v. *Canada* (admissibility decision), para. 3; ComAT, *P.M.P.K.* v. *Sweden* (admissibility decision), No. 30/1995, 14 July 1995, para. 7.

166   ComAT, *Thu AUNG* v. *Canada* (admissibility decision), No. 273/2005, 15 May 2006, para. 6.3.

167   ComAT, Rules of procedure, Rule 113(f).

In our view, if the complainant has not yet been removed, it is hard to imagine a situation in which the time that has elapsed between submission of the complaint to the Committee, and the exhaustion of domestic remedies, is so unreasonably prolonged as to render it unduly difficult to consider a Non-Refoulement claim. In *Amini v. Denmark* (2010), the Committee declared a Non-Refoulement complaint admissible although it had been submitted more than nine months after the final national decision on the complainant's deportation.[168] The Committee should take into account the special nature of Non-Refoulement cases, and that Article 3 CAT is not violated by the final national decision on the complainant's removal, but by enforcement of this decision. Consequently, in such cases, the Committee should view the date of the complainant's removal as the date when the clock starts.

II.2.4 The Matter is Not Being Examined by Another International Body

Under Article 22(5)(a), the Committee shall not consider the complaint if "the same matter" brought before it "has been", or "is being examined" under another procedure of international investigation or settlement.[169] There are two terms for this condition: firstly, the complaint before another procedure related or relates to the same matter; secondly, the complaint was or is being examined by another procedure. The Committee has clarified that "the same matter" must be understood as relating to the same parties, the same facts, and the same substantive rights.[170] The substantive right that should be protected in Non-Refoulement cases is the right to be protected against removal to a State where the complainant would be at risk of being subjected to torture.[171] In the Committee's view, the merits of the complaint must be or have been sufficiently considered by the another international body in order to consider that the complaint has been or is being examined by another procedure.[172] Accordingly, the Committee has refused to consider a Non-Refoulement complaint when the same claim was or has been brought by the same complainant against the same State, and is based on the same facts before the ECtHR, provided that the Court examined or is examining this complaint.[173] The ComAT has refused to consider a Non-Refoulement complaint that was declared inadmissible by

---

168   ComAT, *Amini v. Denmark*, No. 339/2008, 15 November 2010.

169   CAT84, Article 22(5)(a).

170   ComAT, *A.R.A. v. Sweden* (admissibility decision), No. 305/2006, 30 April 2007, para. 6.2. Ingelse, C., 2001, pp. 185–186.

171   ComAT, *A.R.A. v. Sweden* (admissibility decision), para. 6.2.

172   ComAT, *M.T. v. Sweden*, No. 642/2014, 4 September 2015, para. 8.5.

173   ComAT, *A.G. v. Sweden* (admissibility decision), No. 140/1999, 14 April 1999, para. 6.2.

the ECtHR, if the Court's decision was not solely based on mere procedural issues, such as non-compliance with the six-months' time limit, but on reasons that indicate a sufficient consideration of the merits of the case. This is when the Court discussed substantive issues in its decision of admissibility.[174] The fact that the complainant had brought the same matter before the ECtHR, and then withdrawn it before the Court considered it, was not deemed an obstacle to the ComAT's examination of the complaint brought before it.[175]

The examination of the complainant's refoulement claim by the UNHCR to ascertain whether or not his removal would be compatible with the sending State's obligations under Article 33 CSR does not prevent the ComAT from considering the complaint before it. The Committee has observed that neither the CSR nor the Statute of UNHCR establishes a procedure of international investigation or settlement. The Committee has made it clear that:

> ...a written opinion or advice given by a regional or international body on a matter of interpretation of international law in relation to a particular case does not imply that the matter has been subject to international investigation or settlement.[176]

II.2.5   The Complaint is Not Manifestly Ill-founded

A complaint will be declared inadmissible on the grounds of being manifestly ill-founded if the Committee is not satisfied that the complainant has established a *prima facie* or arguable claim for the purpose of admissibility of his complaint.[177] The Committee decides if a complainant has submitted an arguable claim of being at risk of torture in the proposed receiving State on a case-by-case basis. In most Non-Refoulement cases in which the Committee concluded that the complaint was inadmissible, the Committee based its conclusion on the complainant's failure to submit evidence sufficient to substantiate his *prima facie* claims. For example, in its admissibility decision in *R.S. v. Denmark* (2004), the Committee noted that the complainant did not support his claim that he had been politically active in India with any documentary or other pertinent evidence. The Committee found that the complainant failed to establish an arguable claim under the Convention.[178]

---

174   ComAT, *M.T. v. Sweden*, para. 8.5.

175   ComAT, *J.A.G.V. v. Sweden*, para. 6.1.

176   ComAT, *V.X.N. and H.N. v. Sweden*, para. 13.1.

177   ComAT, Rules of procedure, Rule 113(b); ComAT, General Comment No. 1, para. 4.

178   ComAT, *R.S. v. Denmark* (admissibility decision), No. 225/2003, 19 May 2004, para. 6.2.

In some cases, the Committee discussed substantive issues in its admissibility decisions. For example, in its admissibility decision in *S.A.* v. *Sweden* (2004), the Committee observed that the main reason for the complainant's fear of a personal risk of torture if returned to Bangladesh was that he had been previously tortured there because he belonged to what was then the opposition party, the BNP. The Committee noted that, at the time it considered the case, this party was the ruling party in Bangladesh; therefore, the grounds on which the complainant had allegedly been tortured no longer existed. The Committee concluded that the complaint, as formulated, did not give rise to any arguable claim under the Convention.[179]

In other cases, the Committee has held that the argument that the complaint is manifestly ill-founded or incompatible with the provisions of the Convention has raised substantive issues that need to be considered on the merits.[180] The fact that the ComAT made a substantial consideration in the admissibility stage does not mean that, if the complaint were declared admissible, it would necessarily be considered founded on the merits.[181]

11.3 *Conclusion*

To some extent, the admissibility criteria of an individual application before the ECtHR and the ComAT are similar. However, some differences should be highlighted. While the ComAT seems to have taken the view that the applicant would lose his victim status if he voluntary left the respondent State party after he had lodged his Non-Refoulement application with the Committee, the ECtHR has addressed this situation in the light of the circumstances of each case.

Both the ComAT and the ECtHR have found that domestic remedies will only be considered effective if they have an automatic suspensive effect, so that the applicant will not be removed pending the adoption of the final domestic decision on his removal. The ECtHR has also required the domestic remedy to offer reasonable prospects of success in order for it to be considered effective; there is no need to exhaust a remedy that does not offer these prospects. The Court has assessed whether a particular domestic remedy offers reasonable prospects of success in light of the evidence the applicant provides.

---

179   ComAT, *S.A.* v. *Sweden* (admissibility decision), No. 243/2004, 6 May 2004, para. 4.2.
180   ComAT, *M.M.* v. *Canada*, No. 331/2007, 5 November 2009, para. 6.2; ComAT, *M.M.K.* v. *Sweden*, No. 221/2002, 18 May 2005, para. 7.8; ComAT, *S.P.A.* v. *Canada*, No. 282/2005, 7 November 2006, para. 6.3.
181   ComAT, *S.M.R and M.M.R.* v. *Sweden*, No. 103/ 1998, 5 May 1999; ComAT, *X.* v. *Australia*, No. 324/2007, 5 May 2009; ComAT, *R.T-N.* v. *Switzerland*, No. 350/2008, 3 June 2011.

In contrast, the ComAT has assumed that it is not competent to determine if a particular domestic remedy offers a prospect of success. Accordingly, the ComAT might declare an application inadmissible for non-exhaustion of certain domestic remedies, while the ECtHR might consider the same application admissible if the applicant manages to establish that these domestic remedies do not offer a reasonable prospect of success.

A Non-Refoulement application must be submitted to the ECtHR within six months of the date of the applicant's removal, even if the final decision on his removal was adopted by national authorities long before the applicant was actually removed. If the removal decision has not been yet implemented, and the applicant remains on the territory of the State that wishes to remove him, the six-month period has not yet begun for the applicant. According to the ComAT's RoP, the time-period for submitting a complaint to the Committee will begin on the date domestic remedies are exhausted. The RoP do not determine the length of the time-period. It is up to the Committee to decide if the time elapsed between the exhaustion of domestic remedies and the submission of the Non-Refoulement complaint is so unreasonably prolonged as to render consideration of the complaint unduly difficult. The Committee has not had the opportunity to interpret and apply this rule in Non-Refoulement cases. In our opinion, the Committee should follow the approach adopted by the ECtHR in Non-Refoulement cases; the time-period should begin on the date of the complainant's removal. It is hard to imagine a situation where submission of the Non-Refoulement complaint is unreasonably prolonged if the complainant has still not been removed on the date the complaint is filed. If the complainant has been removed, it is up to the Committee to determine if the time elapsed is unreasonably prolonged, based on the circumstances of each case.

It maybe argued that if a Non-Refoulement application was declared inadmissible by the ECtHR for failure to meet the six-month deadline, it could be later declared admissible by the ComAT where the Committee found that the time elapsed since the exhaustion of domestic remedies was not so unreasonably prolonged as to render consideration of the claim unduly difficult.[182]

The ComAT and the ECtHR will both declare an application inadmissible if it has been previously submitted to the other body. The application might have been previously addressed by the Committee on the merits, which may have found that the complainant's removal would not violate Article 3 CAT on the ground that the ill-treatment awaiting him in the proposed receiving State is

---

182   See, ComAT, *Kirsanov* v. *Russia*, No. 478/2011, 14 May 2014, para. 10.2. In this case, which was not a Non-Refoulement cone, the ComAT accepted a communication which had been rejected by the ECtHR for failure to meet the six-month deadline.

not severe enough to amount to torture. If the applicant subsequently submits his Non-Refoulement claim under Article 3 ECHR to the ECtHR against the same respondent State, the Court should not declare this application inadmissible on the ground that it is substantially the same as a matter already examined by the ComAT, because the protection against refoulement under Article 3 ECHR is wider than that under Article 3 CAT. Article 3 ECHR protects the person concerned from removal not only to torture but also to CIDTP. In the same context, if the ComAT found that the complainant's removal would not expose him to a real risk of torture by the authorities in the receiving State, the complainant may subsequently claim before the ECtHR that his removal would expose him to a real risk of ill-treatment resulting from a naturally occurring illness and a lack of sufficient health care resources in this State. In such case, the Court should not declare this application inadmissible on the ground that it is substantially the same as a matter already examined by the ComAT.

III   Standard and Burden of Proof

III.1   *ECtHR*
The existence of a risk of treatment proscribed by Article 3 ECHR in the proposed receiving State has been the key factor that leads the Court to interpret this Article to include an implicit prohibition of refoulement. In the light of the absolute nature of the prohibition under Article 3, the precautionary nature of Non-Refoulement cases, and the serious and irreparable harm that an individual would suffer in case of an incorrect negative decision, the Court does not require the risk of proscribed ill-treatment to be "certain".[183] At the same time, mere possibility of ill-treatment in the proposed receiving State is not in itself sufficient to give rise to a breach of the principle of Non-Refoulement under Article 3.[184] In the landmark case of *Soering* v. *The UK* (1989), the Court adopted a standard of proof that *substantial grounds* have been shown for believing that the person concerned, if removed, would face a *real risk* of being subjected to treatment contrary to Article 3 in the receiving State.[185]

---

183   ECtHR, *Soering* v. *the United Kingdom*, para. 94.

184   ECtHR, *Vilvarajah and Others* v. *the United Kingdom*, para. 111.

185   ECtHR, *Soering* v. *the United Kingdom* para. 91. See also, ECtHR, *Chahal* v. *the United Kingdom*, para. 74; ECtHR, *Saadi* v. *Italy* (GC), para. 125; ECtHR, *Othman (Abu Qatada)* v. *the United Kingdom*, para. 185.

It has been argued that a higher standard of proof must be applied in cases that concern the threat created by international terrorism. As a third-party intervener in the case of *Saadi* v. *Italy* (2008), the UK argued that national security considerations should influence the standard of proof the applicant must satisfy. If the State concerned adduced evidence to demonstrate the existence of a threat to national security, those faced with forcible removal should adduce stronger evidence to prove that they are at risk of ill-treatment in the country of destination. The British government argued that the approach taken by the ECtHR in the *Chahal* case had to be altered and clarified. It further suggested that the individual concerned had to prove that it was "more likely than not" that he would be subjected to treatment proscribed by Article 3.[186] The GC refused this argument and observed that:

> ...such an approach is not compatible with the absolute nature of the protection afforded by Article 3 either. It amounts to asserting that, in the absence of evidence meeting a higher standard, protection of national security justifies accepting more readily a risk of ill-treatment for the individual. The Court therefore sees no reason to modify the relevant standard of proof.[187]

Consequently, the GC reaffirmed that for a planned forcible removal to be in breach of Article 3 ECHR it is necessary and sufficient to establish the existence of substantial grounds for believing that there is a foreseeable, personal and real risk that the person concerned will be subjected to treatment contrary to Article 3 in the proposed receiving State.[188] In *Vilvarajah and Others* v. *The UK* (1991), the Court did not give any weight to the fact that some of the applicants were subjected to ill-treatment following their return to Sri Lanka since, in the Court's view, there were no special distinguishing features in their cases that could or ought to have enabled the respondent State to foresee that they would be ill-treated in the receiving State.[189] In order to establish that the possible future risk is personal, the applicant must show that he, as an individual, risks to be subjected to the treatment proscribed by Article 3 if removed. The applicant does not have to demonstrate that he is being individually

---

186   ECtHR, *Saadi* v. *Italy* (GC), para. 122. See, Moeckli, D., 2008, p. 541.

187   ECtHR, *Saadi* v. *Italy* (GC), para. 140.

188   Ibid., para. 140. See, Hasen, J.V.-, The European Convention on Human Rights, Counter-Terrorism, and Refugee Protection, Refugee Survey Quarterly, Vol. 29 no. 4: 2011, 45–62, pp. 57–58.

189   ECtHR, *Vilvarajah and Others* v. *the United Kingdom*, para. 112.

targeted.[190] The question of which circumstances and facts could constitute substantial grounds sufficient to show that the applicant's removal would expose him to a foreseeable, personal and real risk of being ill-treated in the receiving State will be discussed in Chapter 4.

Turning to the question of burden of proof, it is well settled in the ECtHR's case-law that the initial burden of showing the existence of substantial grounds for believing that the applicant, if removed, would be at risk of ill-treatment is incumbent on the applicant. The Court has repeatedly stated:

> As a rule, it is for applicants to adduce evidence capable of proving that there are substantial grounds for believing that, if the measure complained of were to be implemented, they would be exposed to a real risk of being subjected to treatment contrary to Article 3.[191]

The applicant's claim must be substantiated by evidence that differs according to his allegations. Evidence could include, for example, reports of international bodies or NGOs that describe the general situation in the receiving State, or the situation of a particular group in that State, medical reports that demonstrate the applicant's current health situation, or that he was previously ill-treated, and documents that establish that the applicant is wanted by the authorities of the receiving State.

Taking into account the difficulties the applicant faces in Non-Refoulement cases to prove the existence of a real risk of ill-treatment in the receiving State, the Court has limited the applicant's burden of submitting evidence to "the greatest extent practically possible".[192] It has recognised that direct documentary evidence proving that an applicant himself is wanted for any reason by the authorities of the country of destination may be difficult to obtain.[193] Therefore, in *Mawajedi Shikpohkt and A. Mahkat Shole v. the Netherlands* (2005),[194] the Court noted:

> Neither applicant has submitted any direct documentary evidence proving that they themselves are wanted for any reason by the Iranian

---

190 Frigo, M., 2011, p. 101.

191 ECtHR, *Ryabikin v. Russia*, para. 112; ECtHR, *N. v. Sweden*, para. 53; ECtHR, *Sufi and Elmi v. the United Kingdom*, para. 214.

192 ECtHR, *Bahaddar v. the Netherlands*, Appl. No. 25894/94, 19 February 1998, para. 45; ECtHR, *Said v. The Netherlands*, para 49.

193 ECtHR, *Bahaddar v. the Netherlands*, para. 45; ECtHR, *Said v. The Netherlands*, para 49.

194 This case concerned the expulsion of activists in Rahe Kargar, a Marxist organisation in Iran.

authorities. That, however, cannot be decisive *per se*: the Court has recognised that in cases of this nature such evidence may well be difficult to
obtain [...]. To demand proof to such a high standard may well present even an applicant whose fears are well-founded with a *probatio
diabolica*.[195]

While the ECtHR does not require full proof of all facts and circumstances, a
complete absence of evidence that supports the applicant's allegations, in particular those related to his essential personal circumstances, may undermine
the claim.[196]

As mentioned above, in the case of indirect refoulement, the Court has upheld the presumption that, where the intermediary country is a Contracting
State of the CE, this State will abide by its international law obligations. Accordingly, the applicant must not only provide an arguable claim that his removal to the intermediary country would violate Article 3 ECHR, but he must
also rebut this presumption. The presumption does not exist where general
information contained in reliable resources rebuts it.[197]

It is not just up to the applicant to submit evidence. The Court has made
clear that in determining if the required standard of proof has been established, it will not only assess a case in the light of all the material placed before it, but also, if necessary, material obtained *proprio motu*.[198] The Court has
made clear that it may seek to obtain material on its own initiative, particularly
when the applicant or a third party provides reasoned grounds that cast doubt
on the accuracy of the information relied on by the sending State party.[199] In
N. v. Finland (2005), in order to "carry out its own assessment of the facts", the
Court undertook a fact-finding mission in Finland. The Court appointed two
of its members as Delegates in order to take testimony from the applicant, his
common-law wife E., another asylum seeker originating from the DRC, and a
Finnish civil official.[200] However, only in exceptional circumstances will the
Court appoint a delegation to conduct fact-finding and to assess the credibility

---

195   ECtHR, *Mawajedi Shikpohkt and A. Mahkat Shole* v. *the Netherlands* (admissibility
      decision).

196   Ibid.

197   See above, Chapter 2, prohibition on indirect refoulement.

198   ECtHR, *Cruz Varas and Others* v. *Sweden*, para. 75.

199   ECtHR, *Salah Sheekh* v. *The Netherlands*, para. 136; ECtHR, *Saadi* v. *Italy* (GC), para. 128.

200   ECtHR, *N. v. Finland*, paras. 7, 8 and 152. Spijkerboer, T., Subsidiarity and 'Arguability': the
      European Court of Human Rights' Case Law on Judicial Review in Asylum Cases, Interna-
      tional journal of Refugee Law, Vol. 21 no. 1: 2009, 48–74, p. 60.

of the applicant and witness testimony.[201] Since the proposed receiving State is often a non-State party to the ECHR, the Court has generally relied on fact-finding by secondary sources, such as UN bodies and NGOs, for additional information about the situation in that State.

When the applicant complies with the initial burden of proof and establishes an arguable Non-Refoulement claim, the burden then shifts to the respondent State to put forward any argument or document that casts doubt on the applicant's claim.[202] A respondent State may argue that the applicant has an internal flight alternative; there may be a safe area in the proposed receiving State where he can settle. Respondent States often raise the argument that the risk of ill-treatment has been negated by the fact that national law in the country of destination prohibits ill-treatment and torture, or by pointing out that the proposed receiving State has provided DAs that the applicant would not be subjected to ill-treatment. The effect of these arguments on the Court's assessment of the risk will be discussed in Chapter 4.

III.2   *ComAT*

In order to be granted protection from refoulement under Article 3 CAT substantial grounds must be shown for believing that the complainant's removal would expose him to danger of being subjected to torture.[203] In *E.A.* v. *Switzerland* (1997), the Swiss government argued that the danger to the person concerned must be serious in the sense of being "highly likely" to occur. The Committee rejected this interpretation and held that "substantial grounds"

---

201   Article 38 ECHR provids that: "The Court shall [...], if need be, undertake an investigation, for the effective conduct of which the High Contracting Parties concerned shall furnish all necessary facilities". According to Rule A1(1) of the annex to the Rules of Court (concerning investigation), the Chamber "may adopt any investigative measures which it considers capable of clarifying the facts of the case" and "decide to hear (...) any person whose evidence or statements seem likely to assist it in carrying out its task". Therefore, where there are fundamental factual disputes between the parties of the case, which cannot be resolved by considering documentary evidence only, the ECtHR is able to carry out fact-finding missions in order to establish the facts. The Court carries out its fact-finding role by sending judicial delegations to hear witnesses, or by conducting judicial on-the-spot investigations. For more information about the ECtHR's fact-finding role see, Leach, P., Paraskeva, C. & Uzelac, G., International Human Rights & Fact-Finding. An analysis of the fact-finding mission conducted by the European Commission and Court of Human Rights, London: Report by the Human Rights and Social Justice Research Institute at London Metropolitan University, 2009.

202   ECtHR, *Charahili* v. *Turkey*, para. 60; ECtHR, *Auad* v. *Bulgaria*, para. 104; ECtHR, *Kasymakhunov* v. *Russia*, Appl. No. 29604/12, 14 November 2013, paras. 107 and 110.

203   CAT84, Article 3(1).

in Article 3 require more than a mere possibility of torture but do not need the danger to be highly likely to occur in order to satisfy this Article's conditions.[204] In its General Comment No. 1, the Committee clearly states that the risk of torture in the proposed receiving State must be assessed on grounds that go beyond mere theory or suspicion; however, this risk does not have to meet the test of being highly probable.[205] The question of which circumstances and facts could constitute substantial grounds sufficient to show that the complainant's removal would expose him to danger of being tortured in the proposed receiving State will be addressed in Chapter 4.

According to the ComAT's General Comment No.1, the danger the complainant will be tortured must be personal and present.[206] The Committee has further asserted, through its Non-Refoulement case-law, that "the risk of torture must be foreseeable, real and personal".[207] In *K.N.* v. *Switzerland* (1998), the Committee noted that the complainant's main reason for leaving his country, Sri Lanka, was that he felt caught between the two parties in the internal conflict there. The Committee did not find any indication that the complainant was personally targeted by the Sri Lankan authorities. Therefore, the Committee was of the opinion that no foreseeable, real and personal risk to the complainant was established.[208] In *Chahin* v. *Sweden* (2011), the complainant, a Syrian national, was deported from Sweden to Syria, on 5 January 1997, where he was allegedly tortured. The State party argued that even if it were assumed that he had been tortured on return to Syria, this risk of torture must have been foreseeable at the time the expulsion order was implemented in order to constitute a violation of Article 3 CAT. The ComAT recalled that the complainant had not requested asylum in Sweden prior to his expulsion. Taking into account the contradictory statements made by the complainant before the Swedish authorities with regard to his real nationality, personal circumstances and his travel to Sweden, the Committee noted that such statements made it more

---

204   ComAT, *E.A.* v. *Switzerland*, No. 28/1995, 10 November 1997, paras. 7.1 and 11.3. The US government argued before the ComAT that the danger of torture must be "more likely than not". See, ComAT, Second periodic reports of the United States of America. The wording of Article 3 CAT does not support this interpretation. Droege, C., 2008, pp. 679–680.

205   ComAT, General Comment No. 1, para. 6; ComAT, *M.O.* v. *Denmark*, No. 209/2002, 12 November 2003, para. 6.3; Duffy, A., 2008, p. 380.

206   ComAT, General Comment No. 1, para. 7. See, ComAT, *V.R.* v. *Denmark*, No. 210/2002, 17 November 2003, para. 6.3; ComAT, *Y.G.H. et al.* v. *Australia*, No. 434/2010, 14 November 2013, para. 8.5.

207   ComAT, *Mehdi Zare* v. *Sweden*, No. 256/2004, 17 May 2006, para. 9.4; ComAT, *T.A.* v. *Sweden*, No. 303/2006, 22 November 2007, para 8.3; ComAT, *N.S.* v. *Switzerland*, No. 356/2008, 6 May 2010, para. 7.3.

208   ComAT, *K.N.* v. *Switzerland*, paras. 10.4–10.5.

difficult for the Swedish authorities to assess whether he would be at risk if returned to Syria. The Committee therefore declared that this part of the communication was inadmissible as manifestly unfounded, since his risk of torture upon return to Syria was not foreseeable for the State party at the time of his deportation.[209]

With regard to the burden of proof, the Committee, in its General Comment No.1, states that:

> With respect to the application of article 3 of the Convention to the merits of a case, the burden is upon the author to present an arguable case. This means that there must be a factual basis for the author's position sufficient to require a response from the State party.[210]

The complainant bears the initial burden of showing the existence of substantial grounds for believing that his removal would expose him to a risk of torture.[211] Thus, it is for the complainant to collect and adduce sufficient satisfactory evidence in support of his claims.[212] In the case of *M.M. et al.* v. *Sweden* (2008), the Committee noted that, according to the State party, the complainant was never a member or an employee of the Musavat Party and had not been detained. Moreover, he did not submit any evidence that suggested he was wanted by the authorities in Azerbaijan. Since the burden to present an arguable case is on the complainant, the Committee concluded that the complainant in the present case did not discharge this burden of proof.[213]

While all the facts invoked by the complainant do not need to be established as long as the Committee considers them to be sufficiently substantiated and reliable,[214] a complete absence of evidence that supports the complainant's allegations -in particular those that relate to essential personal circumstances-may undermine his claim.[215] A complainant can support his allegations by any

---

209   ComAT, *Chahin* v. *Sweden*, paras. 4.4, 4.6 and 8.3.

210   ComAT, General Comment No. 1, para. 5.

211   ComAT, *S.P.A.* v. *Canada*, para. 7.5; ComAT, *J.A.M.O. et al.* v. *Canada*, para. 10.4.

212   ComAT, *S.L.* v. *Sweden*, No. 150/1999, 11 May 2001, para. 6.4; ComAT, *A.M.* v. *France*, No. 302/2006, 5 May 2010, para. 13.6.

213   ComAT, *M.M. et al.* v. *Sweden*, No. 332/2007, 1 December 2008, para. 7.6. See also, ComAT, *K.T.* v. *Switzerland*, para. 6.4; ComAT, *N.M* v. *Switzerland*, No. 116/1998, 9 May 2000, paras. 6.5–6.7.

214   ComAT, *Seid Mortesa Aemei* v. *Switzerland*, para. 9.6; ComAT, *E.V.I.* v. *Sweden*, No. 296/2006, 1 May 2007, para. 8.7. Wendland, L., 2002, p. 34.

215   ComAT, *K.T.* v. *Switzerland*, para. 6.4; ComAT, *G.T.* v. *Switzerland*, No. 137/1999, 16 November 1999, para. 6.7; ComAT, *A.A.* v. *The Netherlands*, No. 198/2002, 30 April 2003, para. 7.4.

documentary or other pertinent evidence,[216] such as reports of international bodies or NGOs that describe the general situation of human rights in the country of destination or the situation of a particular group in that country, medical reports that demonstrate that the complainant was previously subjected to torture in the receiving State and is still suffering from the effects of that torture, and documents that establish that the complainant is wanted by the authorities of the receiving State for his previous activities there or his activities in the State party.

When the complainant complies with the initial burden of proof and establishes an arguable claim, the burden then shifts to the respondent State, which must put forward any pertinent information and evidence that casts doubt on the complainant's claim.[217] A respondent State could argue that the complainant has an internal flight alternative in the proposed receiving State, or that the complainant's removal would not violate Article 3 CAT because national law in the receiving State prohibits torture, or that the receiving State has provided DAs that the complainant would not be subjected to torture. These arguments and their effect on the Committee's assessment of risk will be discussed in Chapter 4.

III.3   *Conclusion*

The required standard of proof in Non-Refoulement cases before the ComAT and the ECtHR is that "substantial grounds" must exist for believing that the applicant's removal would expose him to a foreseeable, personal and real risk of being subjected to proscribed ill-treatment. While this standard is explicitly provided for in Article 3 CAT, it was set out by the ECtHR's Non-Refoulement case-law. Whether the ComAT and the ECtHR have interpreted and applied this standard in the same manner, and what circumstances and facts could constitute, in their views, substantial grounds sufficient to show that the applicant's removal would be in violation of the principle of Non-Refoulement, is the topic of the next Chapter.

It is well settled in the case-law of both the Committee and the Court that the applicant bears the burden of proof, and must submit evidence that supports his allegations, whether this evidence relates to his personal circumstances or the general situation in the proposed receiving State. Although neither body requests the applicant to establish all facts and circumstances,

---

216   ComAT, *R.S.* v. *Denmark* (admissibility decision), para. 6.2; ComAT, *Ruben David* v. *Sweden*, No. 220/2002, 17 May 2005, para. 8.3.

217   ComAT, *N.M* v. *Switzerland*, para. 6.5; ComAT, *M.A.K.* v. *Germany*, No. 214/2002, 10 September 2002, para. 13.5.

a complete absence of evidence to support his allegations- in particular those relating to his personal circumstances- may undermine his claim. When an applicant satisfies the initial burden of proof, the burden shifts to the respondent State to put forward any argument or document that casts doubt on the applicant's claim. In addition to materials submitted by the parties, the Court, if necessary, may seek to obtain material on its own initiative, particularly when the applicant provides reasoned grounds that cast doubt on the accuracy of the information relied on by the respondent State. General Comment No. 1, on the implementation of Article 3 CAT in the Context of Article 22, provides that pertinent information may be introduced by either party.[218] Neither in the Committee's General Comment nor in its case-law is there an indication that the Committee has the ability to obtain material on its own initiative. This may be due to the fact that the ComAT has background information on whether and to what extent the practice of torture exists in the receiving State, if it is a State party to the CAT, through the consideration of periodic reports submitted by States parties.[219] If the proposed receiving State is not a party to the CAT, the Committee, as a treaty body, cannot officially and directly request information from this State or appoint a delegation to conduct a fact-finding mission there. Yet, the Committee can gather information from other UN bodies.

---

218   ComAT, General Comment No. 1, para. 7.
219   E.g. ComAT, *Chedli Ben Ahmed Karoui* v. *Sweden*, para 6.4. For information on the States parties' obligation to submit periodic reports to the ComAT under Article 19 CAT see, Nowak, M. & McArthur, E., 2008, p. 624.

CHAPTER 4

Assessment of the Risk of being Subjected to Ill-treatment

This Chapter focuses on the way ECtHR and ComAT has assessed real risk for the applicant of being subjected to proscribed treatment in a receiving State. Section (I) examines the timing of the assessment. Section (II) covers the approach of the Court and the Committee to assessing the evidence before them in Non-Refoulement cases. Section (III) explores the factors taken into consideration by each of these bodies during their assessment. Section (IV) examines the effect of existence of national protection in the receiving State on the risk assessment.

I The Time of the Risk Assessment

I.1 *ECtHR*

For the purpose of determining if the applicant would be at risk of ill-treatment in the receiving State, the ECtHR has repeatedly asserted that risk assessment must focus on the foreseeable consequences of sending the applicant to that State, bearing in mind the general situation there, and his personal circumstances.[1] Since the situation in the country of destination may change over the course of time, the Court makes clear that this assessment must be "full and *ex nunc*".[2] The Court has distinguished between two situations: in the first, the applicant has been removed by the time the Court considers the case; in the second, he has not yet been removed. The following subsections address these different situations.

---

1   ECtHR, *Vilvarajah and Others* v. *the United Kingdom*, para. 180.
2   ECtHR, *Salah Sheekh* v. *The Netherlands*, para. 136; ECtHR, NA. v. *The United Kingdom*, para. 112. The ECtHR's assessment does not address whether the applicant was at risk of proscribed treatment at the time of departure of his country of origin or at the time of considering his Non-Refoulement case by the authorities of the sending State. The Court can therefore take into account information that was not known to the sending State at the time it decided to deport the applicant concerned. Spijkerboer, T., 2009, p. 56.

1.1.1   After the Applicant's Removal

The Court has repeatedly asserted that since the sending State's responsibility under Article 3 ECHR in Non-Refoulement cases is engaged for exposing an individual to the risk of ill-treatment in the receiving State, existence of the risk must be assessed primarily in the light of the facts that were known, or ought to have been known, to the sending State at the time of the removal.[3] If the applicant has already been removed, the material date for assessing whether a real risk exists is the date of his removal.[4] In *Hirsi Jamaa and Others* v. *Italy* (2012), the Court referred to the report of the European Committee for the Prevention of Torture and Inhuman or Degrading Treatment or Punishment (CPT), published on 28 April 2010. The CPT noted, "Italy's policy of intercepting migrants at sea and obliging them to return to Libya or other non-European countries violated the principle of *Non-Refoulement*".[5] The Court also observed that after the UNHCR office in Tripoli closed, in April 2010, and the Libyan revolution of February 2011, the situation in Libya worsened. However, the Court decided that, for the purposes of examining the case before it, it would refer to the situation that prevailed in Libya at the time the applicants were extradited (May 2009).[6] Although the ECtHR considered the case of *Iskandarov* v. *Russia* in 2010, it assessed the existence of the risk of ill-treatment in Tajikistan, the receiving State, in light of circumstances that prevailed there in April 2005, the date of the applicant's removal. The Court made it clear that the question of whether or not the applicant had actually been subjected to ill-treatment after his return to Tajikistan did not bear on the findings of the ECtHR.[7]

The Court may, however, pay attention to information that comes to light after the removal.[8] It could do so to confirm or refuse the appreciation made by the State party concerned, or to consider whether an applicant's fears were well founded.[9] In *Garabayev* v. *Russia* (2007), the Court noted that the applicant returned to Russia three months after he was extradited to Turkmenistan, and provided an account of the events that took place while he was there.

---

3   ECtHR, *Cruz Varas and Others* v. *Sweden*, para. 76; ECtHR, *Chahal* v. *the United Kingdom*, para. 85.

4   ECtHR, *Mamatkulov and Askarov* v. *Turkey* (GC), para. 74; ECtHR, *Muminov* v. *Russia*, para. 92.

5   ECtHR, *Hirsi Jamaa and Others* v. *Italy* (GC), paras. 35–36 and 123.

6   Ibid., para. 124. See also, ECtHR, *Safaii* v. *Austria*.

7   ECtHR, *Iskandarov* v. *Russia*, paras. 129–132. ECtHR, *Vilvarajah and Others* v. *the United Kingdom*, para. 112.

8   ECtHR, *Mamatkulov and Askarov* v. *Turkey* (GC), para. 69; ECtHR, *Abdolkhani and Karimnia* v. *Turkey*, para. 76.

9   ECtHR, *Cruz Varas and Others* v. *Sweden*, para. 76; ECtHR, *Shamayev and 12 others* v. *Georgia and Russia*, para. 338.

The Court was able to assess the situation in light of developments subsequent to the extradition. The Court noted that the applicant had spent most of his three-months detention in a small shared cell, received food twice a day, been forbidden exercise, and was hit by investigators on several occasions. He was denied consular visits from the staff of the Russian Consulate. He was in constant fear for his life and fate and that of his relatives. The Court held that these submissions strengthened its conclusions about the failure of the Russian authorities to properly consider the well-grounded fears of the applicant.[10]

1.1.2   Before the Applicant's Removal

In the second situation, the applicant has not yet been removed at the time the ECtHR considers the case. This situation typically arises when the applicant's removal is delayed by the Court's indication of an interim measure under Rule 39.[11] In such cases, the ECtHR has repeatedly asserted that the risk of ill-treatment must be assessed based on conditions current at the time of the Court's examination.[12] The Court has held the conditions prevailing at the time of its consideration of the case are decisive. Historical facts are not ignored, but are of interest in so far as they shed light on the current situation, and its likely evolution.[13] To assess risk in the receiving State, the ECtHR assesses the situation there in its development, and takes into account the "indications of improvement or worsening of the human rights situation in general or in respect of a particular group or area that might be relevant to the applicant's situation".[14]

---

10   ECtHR, *Garabayev* v. *Russia*, paras. 81–83. See also, ECtHR, *Al-Saadoon and Mufdhi* v. *the United Kingdom*, para. 144.

11   ECtHR, *Mamatkulov and Askarov* v. *Turkey* (GC), para. 69; ECtHR, *Saadi* v. *Italy* (GC), para. 133.

12   See for example the Non-Refoulement case of *A.L.* v. *Austria* (2012), in which the Court concluded "even if the threat uttered by the soldiers in summer 2008 had carried sincere weight as a sign of a real and individual risk of persecution at the time, there is no indication that this is still the case". ECtHR, *A.L.* v. *Austria*, Appl.No. 7788/11, 10 May 2012, paras. 9 and 64–66.

13   ECtHR, *Ahmed* v. *Austria*, para. 43; ECtHR, *Rakhimov* v. *Russia*, Appl.No. 50552/13, 10 July 2014, paras. 98–99.

14   ECtHR, *Dzhaksybergenov* v. *Ukraine*, Appl.No. 12343/10, 10 February 2011, para. 36 and ECtHR, *Sharipov* v. *Russia*, Appl.No. 18414/10, 11 October 2011, para. 34. In *Ahmed* v. *Austria* (1996), the ECtHR gave particular weight to the fact that in 1992 the applicant had been granted refugee status in Austria because he was found to have a fear of persecution in Somalia. The Court noted that there was no indication that the risk to which the applicant would have been exposed in 1992 no longer existed or that the public authorities would be able to protect him if he were to be expelled to Somalia. Consequently, the Court

The Court takes into account information that has come to light after the domestic authorities in the sending State made their final decision.[15] This may be in the interest of the applicant, if the situation in the receiving State has worsened and the current conditions support the applicant's allegation that he would be at risk of ill-treatment there. In *S.F. and others* v. *Sweden* (2012), the last decision of the domestic authorities was on 10 March 2010. The ECtHR noted that at the time it considered the case country information had changed. The situation in Iran appeared to have deteriorated since the Swedish authorities had determined the case. After the date domestic authorities made their last decision, several reports noted that Iranian authorities frequently detained and ill-treated persons who participated in peaceful oppositional or human rights activities in the country.[16] It is also possible that the situation in the receiving State has improved, and the applicant is no longer at risk of being ill-treated there. In *J.H.* v. *The UK* (2011), the applicant argued that his expulsion to Afghanistan would expose him to a real risk of proscribed treatment because his father was a high profile member of the Communist People's Democratic Party of Afghanistan (PDPA).[17] Subsequent to the last decision by British authorities in this case,[18] the December 2010 UNHCR's Eligibility Guidelines for Assessing the International Protection Needs of Asylum-Seekers from Afghanistan were released. In contrast to the July 2009 UNHCR Guidelines,[19] the December 2010 Guidelines did not place former members of the PDPA and their families on the extensive list of potential risk profiles of asylum seekers from Afghanistan. The ECtHR concluded that the omission of PDPA members from the list and, more critically, the change in the UNHCR's position between July 2009 and December 2010, indicated that former PDPA members were no longer to be considered at risk in Afghanistan. According to the Court, this

---

concluded that the applicant could not be expelled to Somalia without being exposed to the risk of treatment contrary to Article 3. ECtHR, *Ahmed* v. *Austria*, paras. 42 and 44–47. The opposite situation occurred in *Mawaka* v. *The Netherlands* (2010), in which the Court refused the applicant's argument that the risk of ill-treatment he could face in the DRC must be assessed in the light of the situation that existed in 1996, when he had been granted refugee status in the Netherlands. In the light of an *ex nunc* assessment, the Court observed that the general situation in the DRC was better than in 1996. ECtHR, *Mawaka* v. *The Netherlands*, Appl.No. 29031/04, 1 June 2010, paras. 41–51.

15   ECtHR, *NA.* v. *The United Kingdom*, para. 112; ECtHR, *J.H.* v. *the United Kingdom*, para. 53.

16   ECtHR, *S.F. and others* v. *Sweden*, Appl.No. 52077/10, 15 May 2012, paras. 36–43 and 63.

17   ECtHR, *J.H.* v. *the United Kingdom*, para. 38.

18   The decision was on 17 September 2009. Ibid., para. 19.

19   Ibid., para. 64. See, ECtHR, *H. and B.* v. *the United Kingdom*, Appl.Nos. 70073/10 and 44539/11, 9 April 2013, para. 107.

conclusion was further corroborated by the absence of any evidence that indicated that the PDPA members continued to be at risk upon their return to Afghanistan. In light of these circumstances, and since the applicant was merely a family member of a former member of the PDPA; the Court was not persuaded that he would be at real risk upon return.[20]

I.2   ComAT
The ComAT's handling of the same two situations is described in the following subsections.

I.2.1   After the Complainant's Removal
In *T.P.S.* v. *Canada* (2000), the complainant was removed from Canada to India in December 1997. In assessing the merits of his communication, the ComAT noted that the complainant had been living in India for more than two years after his removal, and had not been subjected to torture by the authorities. Given the substantial period of time that elapsed after the complainant's removal, the Committee concluded that there was ample time for his fears to be realized. Therefore, the Committee found that the complainant's allegations were unfounded.[21] The Committee, in this case, assessed the existence of the risk in the light of the complainant's current circumstances in the receiving State, and whether he had been subjected to torture following his removal.[22] Committee member Guibril Camara, who offered an individual opinion that the terms of Article 3 made it clear that the existence of risk of torture in the receiving State must be assessed at the time of expulsion, return or extradition, contested the ECtHR's approach.[23]

In the case of *Iratxe Sorzabal Diaz* v. *France* (2005), the Committee clearly stated that the issue before it was whether, on the date the expulsion measure was enforced, the sending State's authorities could have known that the complainant would be exposed to a real risk of torture if she were expelled to Spain.[24] In subsequent cases, the Committee has repeatedly asserted that:

---

20   ECtHR, *J.H.* v. *the United Kingdom*, para. 65. See, ECtHR, *Cruz Varas and Others* v. *Sweden*, para. 80.

21   ComAT, *T.P.S.* v. *Canada*, para. 15.4.

22   The ComAT took the same approach in *G.K.* v. *Switzerland* (2002). The Committee noted that it received no information on torture or ill-treatment suffered by the complainant during incommunicado detention following his removal to Spain. ComAT, *G.K.* v. *Switzerland*, No. 219/2002, 18 October 2002, para. 6.8.

23   ComAT, *T.P.S.* v. *Canada*, para. 16.2.

24   ComAT, *Iratxe Sorzabal Diaz* v. *France*, No. 194/2001, 3 May 2005, para. 9.3. Although the Committee in this case considered the fact that the complainant had been subjected

...in cases where a person has been expelled at the time of its consideration of the complaint, the Committee assesses what the State party knew or should have known at the time of expulsion. Subsequent events are relevant to the assessment of the State party's knowledge, actual or constructive, at the time of removal.[25]

In *Abichou* v. *Germany* (2013), the ComAT noted that, based on information from reliable sources current at the time the applicant was extradited, torture and other cruel and degrading treatment were widespread practices perpetrated by security forces and police in Tunisia.[26] The Committee found that the authorities of the sending State knew, or should have known at the time of Abichou's extradition, that Tunisian authorities routinely resorted to the practice of torture against persons detained for political reasons or charged with ordinary criminal offences.[27]

The ComAT does have some regard to the events that occur subsequent to the time of the complainant's removal. But it can do so only to assess what the sending State had known, or could have deduced, about the risk of torture at that time. In *Bachan Singh Sogi* v. *Canada* (2007), the Committee noted that, at the time of the complainant's removal, the sending State was aware that he was suspected of being a member of an alleged terrorist organization, and that the Indian security and police forces continued to use torture against suspected terrorists in detention centres. Against this background, and taking into account that the complainant was detained and subjected to ill-treatment after his removal, the Committee concluded that the complainant's removal violated Article 3 CAT.[28] Even if the complainant has not actually been subjected to torture after his removal, this fact cannot call into question or minimize the claim he was at real risk of torture at the time he was removed.[29]

---

to torture 17 months after being transferred from the State party, it did so because the complainant's primary focus was this fact. It did not find a casual link between the complainant's removal and the subsequent torture. Ibid., paras. 9.4–9.5.

25 ComAT, *Mafhoud Brada* v. *France*, para. 13.1. See also, ComAT, *Agiza* v. *Sweden*, para. 13.2; ComAT, *Adel Tebourski* v. *France*, para. 8.1; ComAT, *L.J.R.* v. *Australia*, para. 7.5.

26 ComAT, *Abichou* v. *Germany*, No. 430/2010, 21 May 2013, para. 11.6.

27 Ibid., para. 11.7. See also, ComAT, *Agiza* v. *Sweden*, para. 13.4.

28 ComAT, *Bachan Singh Sogi* v. *Canada*, paras. 10.8–10.10. See also, ComAT, *E.L.* v. *Canada*, para. 8.7.

29 ComAT, *Abichou* v. *Germany*, para. 11.7.

I.2.2   Before the Complainant's Removal

The complainant may have not been removed at the time the ComAT considers his complaint, either due to the State party's compliance with the Committee's request for interim measures under Rule 114, or for any other reason. Through its case-law, the Committee has made clear that the material time for assessing of the risk in this situation is at which the ComAT considers the case. In *M.M.K.* v. *Sweden* (2005), the ComAT noted that the complainant had been previously subjected to torture by followers of the Awami League in Bangladesh. But it asserted that the question before it was whether he risked torture upon return to Bangladesh at the current time, when the case was under consideration. In light of this, the Committee gave most importance to the fact that, at the material time, the Awami League was in political opposition, and the complainant was a member of one of the ruling political parties.[30] Although history is taken into account in assessing the risk of torture to the complainant in the receiving State, the conditions that prevail at the time the case is under consideration are decisive for the Committee.[31] Information that has come to light after sending State's domestic authorities have made their final decision is taken into consideration when the Committee assesses the risk. For example, in *Njamba and Balikosa* v. *Sweden* (2010), Swedish authorities made their final domestic decision on 7 June 2007. The Committee considered the report, published on 8 March 2010, from seven UN experts on the situation in the DRC. This report referred to alarming levels of violence against women across the country. The Committee further referred to a report by the UN High Commissioner for Human Rights, dated 28 January 2010, which indicated that cases of sexual violence took place throughout the country and were not limited to areas of armed conflict.[32]

I.3   *Conclusion*

Both the ComAT and the ECtHR have used the same material date to assess if the risk of proscribed treatment exists for the applicant in the receiving State.

---

30   ComAT, *M.M.K.* v. *Sweden*, para. 8.6. See also, ComAT, *M.A.M.* v. *Sweden*, No. 196/2002, 14 May 2004, para. 6.5; ComAT, *M.N.* v. *Switzerland*, No. 259/2004, 17 November 2006, para. 6.6.

31   See, ComAT, *Alp* v. *Denmark*, No. 466/2011, 14 May 2014, para. 8.5, in which the ComAT noted that although refugee status had been granted to the complainant by the Romanian authorities, the question was whether he remained, at present, at risk of torture in Turkey.

32   ComAT, *Njamba and Balikosa* v. *Sweden*, para. 9.5. See also, ComAT, *M.A.F. et al.* v. *Sweden*, No. 385/2009, 23 November 2012, para. 8.6.

When the case is considered after the applicant has been removed, both bodies assess the risk in light of the facts that were known, or ought to have been known, to the sending State at the time of removal, whether or not the applicant has actually been subjected to proscribed treatment after his removal. Neither body is completely precluded from taking subsequent events into account, but can do so only to confirm or refuse the sending State's appreciation of the risk in the light of what the State had known, or could have known, at the time the applicant was removed. If the applicant has not been removed to the proposed receiving State, the material time for assessing the risk is the time at which his application is under consideration by these bodies. Although historical facts and information, including that which comes to light after the final domestic decision, are taken into account by both bodies, the decisive factor being the conditions that prevail at the time the Non-Refoulement case is considered.

II   The Assessment of Evidence

II.1   *ECtHR*

For the purpose of determining if a real risk of ill-treatment exists in the proposed receiving State, the ECtHR, through its case-law, has developed several principles in order to assess the objective information placed before it.[33] As a basis for assessing the conditions in the receiving State, the Court will take all the material placed before it or, if necessary, material obtained *proprio motu*. It will do so particularly when the applicant, or a third party within the meaning of Article 36 ECHR, provides reasoned grounds to doubt the accuracy of the information the respondent State relied upon.[34] The Court has made clear that in cases in which aliens face removal, it cannot rely only on materials submitted by the respondent State. It has considered itself entitled to compare materials made available by this State with those from other reliable and objective sources.[35] In *Khodzhayev* v. *Russia* (2010), the Court referred to recent reports from reliable sources that indicated that torture and ill-treatment, and other human rights violations, were practiced against detainees in Tajikistan

---

33   These principles set out in the Court's decision in *Saadi* v. *Italy* (2008) and have been developed through its subsequent case-law. ECtHR, *Saadi* v. *Italy* (GC), paras. 128–133.

34   Ibid., para. 128.

35   ECtHR, *Chahal* v. *the United Kingdom*, para. 97; ECtHR, *Salah Sheekh* v. *The Netherlands*, para. 136.

to reject the Russian government's argument that Tajikistan respected basic human rights.[36]

As regard the general situation in the country of destination, the Court has often assessed country material before it, particularly in the light of the independence, reliability and objectivity of its source.[37] With regard to the assessment of a report, the Court has considered relevant the authority and reputation of a report's author, the seriousness of the investigations by which it was compiled, and the consistency of its conclusions and their corroboration by other sources.[38] The Court has also recognised that consideration must be given to the presence and reporting capacities of the author of the country material. In this connection, the Court has observed that:

> States (whether the respondent State in a particular case or any other Contracting or non- Contracting State), through their diplomatic missions and their ability to gather information, will often be able to provide material which may be highly relevant to the Court's assessment of the case before it. It finds that same consideration must apply, *a fortiori*, in respect of agencies of the United Nations, particularly given their direct access to the authorities of the country of destination as well as their ability to carry out on-site inspections and assessments in a manner which States and non-governmental organisations may not be able to do.[39]

The Court has relied on evidence by various secondary sources, including independent international human rights protection organisations like the AI,[40] and HRW;[41] UN bodies like the ComAT,[42] and HRC;[43] UN officials like the UN Special Rapporteur on torture,[44] the UN Secretary-General,[45] the UN High

---

36   ECtHR, *Khodzhayev v. Russia*, Appl.No. 52466/08, 12 May 2010, paras. 96–97; ECtHR, *Khaydarov v. Russia*, paras. 103–104.

37   Ovey, C. & White, R., Jacobs and White, the European Convention on Human Rights, Oxford: Oxford University Press, 4th Ed, 2002, p. 105.

38   ECtHR, *Saadi v. Italy* (GC), para. 143; ECtHR, *NA. v. The United Kingdom*, para. 120.

39   Ibid., para. 121; ECtHR, *Sufi and Elmi v. the United Kingdom*, para. 231; ECtHR, *Rustamov v. Russia*, Appl.No. 11209/10, 3 July 2012, para. 123.

40   ECtHR, *Chahal v. the United Kingdom*, paras. 99–100.

41   ECtHR, *Saadi v. Italy* (GC), paras. 131 and 143; ECtHR, *NA. v. The United Kingdom*, para. 119.

42   ECtHR, *Khaydarov v. Russia*, para. 104.

43   ECtHR, *Klein v. Russia*, para. 32.

44   ECtHR, *Chahal v. the United Kingdom*, para. 104.

45   ECtHR, *Soldatenko v. Ukraine*, para. 71; ECtHR, *Muminov v. Russia*, para. 93.

Commissioner for Human Rights;[46] as well as governmental sources, including the us State Department (USSD),[47] and UK Home Office.[48]

Given the difficulties faced by governments and NGOs when they seek to gather information in dangerous situations, the Court has accepted that it is not always possible to conduct investigations in the immediate vicinity of a conflict. In such case, the Court may rely on information provided by a source with first-hand knowledge of the situation in the receiving State. The authority and reputation of the source, and the extent of its presence in the relevant area, will be taken into consideration when the Court gives weight to the evidence. The Court has observed that while sources may wish to remain anonymous where there is legitimate security concern, it is impossible for it to assess their reliability in the absence of any information about the nature of their operations in the relevant area. The weight that the Court has given to the conclusions of anonymous sources depends on how consistent their conclusions are with the remainder of the information before it.[49] In *Sufi and Elmi* v. *The UK* (2011), the Court observed that the description of sources relied on by the fact-finding mission to Nairobi was vague. The majority of those sources were described as "an international NGO", "a diplomatic source", or "a security advisor". According to the Court, these descriptions did not indicate the authority or reputation of sources, or the extent of their presence in southern and central Somalia. The Court found it impossible to assess the reliability of these sources, and consequently was unable to attach substantial importance to them, where their information was contradictory or unsupported.[50]

The Court has often given due weight to the information contained in the most recent reports from independent international sources.[51] In *Nnyanzi* v. *The UK* (2008), which concerned the expulsion of the daughter of a political opponent to Uganda, the Court noted that while the 2006 USSD report on Uganda had referred to accounts claiming that the Ugandan government had punished family members of political opponents, the next USSD report did

---

46   ECtHR, *Klein* v. *Russia*, para. 34.

47   Ibid., para. 35; ECtHR, *N.* v. *Sweden*, para. 35; ECtHR, *Nnyanzi* v. *the United Kingdom*, para. 63.

48   ECtHR, *N.* v. *Sweden*, para. 36; ECtHR, *Nnyanzi* v. *the United Kingdom*, para. 63; ECtHR, *Al Husin* v. *Bosnia and Herzegovina*, para. 42.

49   ECtHR, *Sufi and Elmi* v. *the United Kingdom*, paras. 232–233.

50   Ibid., para. 234.

51   ECtHR, *AL-Moayad* v. *Germany* (admissibility decision), paras. 65–66; ECtHR, *Khodzhayev* v. *Russia*, para. 93; ECtHR, *Klein* v. *Russia*, para. 47; ECtHR, *Kamyshev* v. *Ukraine*, para. 43.

not contain such an indication. The 2007 USSD report noted that, "unlike in the previous year, there were no reports that the government punished family members of suspected criminals and political opposition members".[52]

Taking into account that the goal of the Court's assessment is to determine if there would be a real risk of ill-treatment were the applicant to be returned to the proposed receiving State, the Court has given greater importance to reports that discuss the human rights situation in that State, and directly address the grounds for the alleged risk of ill-treatment in the case before it. Accordingly, the Court has distinguished reports that constitute, by their nature, general assessments of the situation in the receiving State from those that include specific assessment of the applicant's case. While it has been inclined to attach less weight to general assessments, the Court has held that the weight attached to specific assessment must depend on the extent to which such an assessment uses terms similar to those of Article 3 ECHR.[53]

In several Non-Refoulement cases, such as *Jabari* v. *Turkey* (2000), the Court decided that it must give due weight to the UNHCR's conclusions about the applicant's claim with regard to the risk he would face if he were to be removed to the receiving State. The Court observed that the UNHCR had interviewed the applicant and had had the opportunity to determine how credible his fears were, and the veracity of his account of the circumstances in the receiving State.[54] Conversely, where reports are focused on general socio-economic and humanitarian conditions in the receiving State, the Court has been inclined to give them less weight, since such conditions do not necessarily have bearing on the real risk to an individual applicant of treatment proscribed by Article 3.[55] In *F.H.* v. *Sweden* (2009), which concerned the applicant's

---

52   ECtHR, *Nnyanzi* v. *the United Kingdom*, para. 63. See also, ECtHR, *Charahili* v. *Turkey*, para. 56.

53   ECtHR, *NA.* v. *The United Kingdom*, para. 122; ECtHR, *K.* v. *Russia*, para. 61.

54   ECtHR, *Jabari* v. *Turkey*, para. 41. See also, ECtHR, *Abdolkhani and Karimnia* v. *Turkey*, para. 82; ECtHR, *Charahili* v. *Turkey*, para. 59; ECtHR, *Umirov* v. *Russia*, paras. 99–100. In *Auad* v. *Bulgaria* (2011), the Court gave significant weight to the State Refugees Agency's findings that there were substantial grounds for believing that the applicant would face a real risk of ill-treatment in Lebanon. The Court held that those findings carry such weight because that Agency was a specialised body with particular experience in this filed and its officers had conducted a personal interview with the applicant. ECtHR, *Auad* v. *Bulgaria*, para. 102.

55   ECtHR, *Salah Sheekh* v. *The Netherlands*, para. 141; ECtHR, *NA.* v. *The United Kingdom*, para. 122.

expulsion to Iraq, where he would be allegedly exposed to a real risk of ill-treatment and death, the Court was aware that the UNHCR, the UN and IOM had recommended States to refrain from forcibly returning refugees to Iraq. The Court noted that those recommendations were partly based on the general security situation in Iraq, and partly resulted from practical difficulties facing returnees, such as shelter and health care. The Court held that, although the general situation in Iraq was insecure and problematic, it was not serious enough to cause, by itself, a violation of Article 3, if the applicant were to be deported to Iraq.[56] The Court adopted the same approach in *NA*. v. *The UK* (2008), with regard to "the UNHCR Position on the International Protection Needs of Asylum Seekers from Sri Lanka". The Court considered that "substantive weight" should be given to the UNHCR Position Paper. However, the Court made it clear that in contrast to the UNHCR's findings that relied on in the *Jabari* case, the UNHCR Position Paper spoke in broad terms and provided a general survey of the varying risks to each of Sri Lanka's different ethnic groups. The Court did not consider the UNHCR's findings to be decisive in its assessment of the risk to Tamils returning to Sri Lanka.[57]

The Court has tended to accept any evidence that related to an applicant's personal circumstances, as long as it is not forged or fabricated.[58] It has assessed such evidence on a case-by-case basis.[59] For example, the Court has held that when an arrest warrant is issued for the person concerned, he will most likely be detained directly after his removal.[60]

II.2   *ComAT*

According to Article 22(4) CAT, the ComAT shall consider individual communications received under this Article "in the light of all information made available to it by or on behalf of the individual and by the State Party concerned".[61] Thus, the Committee depends on the evidence adduced by the complainant as well as the State party concerned when it assesses the risk of torture. As stated in the ComAT's General Comment No. 1 and repeatedly emphasized in

---

56   ECtHR, *F.H.* v. *Sweden*, paras. 91–93. See also, ECtHR, *D.N.M.* v. *Sweden*, para. 50.

57   ECtHR, *NA*. v. *The United Kingdom*, para. 127. See also, ECtHR, *X.* v. *Norway*, Appl.No. 53351/09, 17 April 2012, para. 82; ECtHR, *T.A.* v. *Sweden*, Appl.No. 48866/10, 19 December 2013, para. 39.

58   Wouters, K., 2009, pp. 270–271; ECtHR, *A.A.M.* v. *Sweden*, para. 65.

59   Caflisch, L., 2002, p. 110.

60   ECtHR, *Sultanov* v. *Russia*, Appl.No. 15303/09, 4 November 2010, para. 72; ECtHR, *Akram Karimov* v. *Russia*, Appl.No. 62892/12, 28 May 2014, para. 131.

61   CAT84, Article 22.4.

its case-law, the Committee is competent to fully examine the facts and evidence before it adopts its decision, even if, by doing so, the Committee has to give considerable weight to the consideration made by the State party's authorities.[62]

To understand the general situation of human rights, or the situation of a particular group in the proposed receiving State, the Committee has often turned to various sources, including independent international human rights protection organisations like the AI,[63] and HRW;[64] bodies of the CE like the CPT,[65] the UN bodies like the UNHCR,[66] the UN Special Rapporteur on torture,[67] the UN Secretary-General,[68] the UN High Commissioner for Human Rights,[69] and the HRC;[70] as well as governmental sources including the USSD.[71] The ComAT has often given weight to reports on the human rights situation in the proposed receiving State from first-hand sources. For example, in *Njamba and Balikosa* v. *Sweden* (2010), the Committee referred to the report of Mr. Titinga Frederic Pacere, an independent expert on the situation of human rights in the DRC, a joint report from the seven UN experts on the situation in the DRC, and the Combined report of seven thematic special procedures on technical assistance to the government of the DRC and urgent examination of the situation in the east of the country.[72]

The Committee has often given due weight to the information contained in the most recent reports from independent sources that describe the human rights situation in the proposed receiving State. For example, in *Jahani* v. *Switzerland* (2011), the Committee referred to several recent reports that indicated that the actual human rights situation in Iran was extremely worrisome, particularly after the presidential elections of June 2009. The Committee noted that many reports described, specifically, the repression and arbitrary

---

62   ComAT, General Comment No. 1, paras. 7 and 9. ComAT, *T.D.* v. *Switzerland*, No. 375/2009, 26 May 2011, para. 7.7.

63   ComAT, *S.N.A.W. et al.* v. *Switzerland*, No. 231/2003, 24 November 2005, para. 7.2.

64   Ibid., para. 7.2; ComAT, *Iya* v. *Switzerland*, No. 299/2006, 16 November 2007, para. 6.7.

65   ComAT, *Josu Arkauz Arana* v. *France*, para. 11.4.

66   ComAT, *Halil Haydin* v. *Sweden*, No. 101/1997, 20 November 1998, para. 6.4.

67   ComAT, *Mutombo* v. *Switzerland*, para. 9.5.

68   ComAT, *Njamba and Balikosa* v. *Sweden*.

69   ComAT, *X, Y and Z* v. *Sweden*, No. 61/1996, 6 May 1998, para. 11.5.

70   ComAT, *Eftekhary* v. *Norway*, paras. 7.5–7.6; ComAT, *A.A.* v. *Switzerland*, No. 268/2005, 1 May 2007, para. 8.5.

71   ComAT, *S.N.A.W. et al.* v. *Switzerland*, para. 7.2.

72   ComAT, *Njamba and Balikosa* v. *Sweden*, see footnote. 12 and para. 9.5.

detention of human rights activists, some of whom were sentenced to death and executed.[73]

The Committee has tended to accept any evidence relating to the complainant's personal circumstances as long as it is not forged.[74] The Committee's assessment of the authenticity and value of such evidence is carried out on a case-by-case basis. The Committee has taken into account first-hand information obtained by the State party's embassy in the proposed receiving State.[75] For example, in the case of *K.M.* v. *Switzerland* (1999), which concerned the expulsion of a Turkish citizen of Kurdish ethnic origin to Turkey, the Committee accepted information provided by the Swiss embassy in Ankara, which claimed that the Turkish police did not establish a file on the complainant and he was not under an order of arrest. Accordingly, the Committee held that he failed to establish that he was under risk of being arrested upon his return.[76]

11.3   *Conclusion*

All information brought before the ECtHR or the ComAT by the applicant and the respondent State must be taken into account in order to assess the risk in a Non-Refoulement case. Both bodies have relied on the most recent reports by a variety of sources to assess the general human rights situation or the situation of a particular group in the proposed receiving State. Documents include these bodies' own Non-Refoulement case-law, governmental sources, independent international human rights organisations, and the UN bodies. The ECtHR, unlike the ComAT, has developed several principles to assess the value of the country material placed before it in Non-Refoulement cases. The ECtHR has given greater weight than the ComAT to the general situation of violence or human rights violations in the receiving State. The Committee is more likely to have information on whether the practice of torture exists in the receiving State if this State is a party to the CAT. This is because of the Committee's competence to receive and consider periodic reports from States parties to the Convention.

---

73 The Committee referred mainly to a report by six human rights experts of the Human Rights Council and a statement by the High Commissioner for Human Rights made on 2 February 2011 which concerned the execution of at least 66 persons in January 2011, including at least 3 political prisoners. See, ComAT, *Jahani* v. *Switzerland*, No. 357/2008, 23 May 2011, para. 9.5. See also, ComAT, *Eftekhary* v. *Norway*, para. 7.4; ComAT, *Bakatu-Bia* v. *Sweden*, para. 10.6.

74 ComAT, *M.B.B.* v. *Sweden*, para. 6.6; ComAT, *K.M.* v. *Switzerland*, No. 107/1998, 16 November 1999, para. 6.6; ComAT, *A.A.M.* v. *Sweden*, No. 413/2010, 23 May 2012, para. 9.7.

75 ComAT, *A.H.* v. *Sweden*, No. 265/2005, 16 November 2006, para. 11.5.

76 ComAT, *K.M.* v. *Switzerland*, para. 6.6.

With regard to the applicant's claims about his personal circumstances, both bodies tend to accept any evidence he provides in support of these claims, as long as the evidence is not forged or fabricated. The value of such evidence is assessed on a case-by-case basis.

III   Factors Used to Assess the Risk

III.1   *ECtHR*
An applicant's removal breaches the principle of Non-Refoulement under Article 3 ECHR where substantial grounds have been shown for believing that the applicant, if removed, would face a real risk of being subjected to treatment proscribed by this Article. This section determines which facts and circumstances can be considered "substantial grounds" sufficient to show that there is a "real risk" of ill-treatment in the receiving State.

Given the absolute nature of the protection afforded by Article 3 and the fact that it enshrines one of the fundamental values of the democratic societies that make up the CE, the ECtHR has repeatedly asserted that assessment of the risk in Non-Refoulement cases must necessarily be rigorous.[77] In *Vilvarajah and Others* v. *The UK* (1991), which concerned the removal of individuals of Tamil ethnic origin to Sri Lanka, the Court noted that the general situation in the country of destination was still unsettled. However, it found that the applicant's removal would not violate Article 3 since no evidence demonstrated that the applicant's personal position was any worse than that of the other members of the general Tamil community.[78] The Court did not give weight to the fact that some applicants were subjected to ill-treatment after they returned. It found no "special distinguishing features" in their cases that could, or ought to have, enabled the respondent State to foresee that they would be ill-treated in Sri Lanka.[79] The Court's decision in this case may suggest that a situation of general instability in the country of destination only gives rise to a breach of Article 3 ECHR if it is established that the applicant's personal situation is worse than the majority of other members of his group.

In *NA.* v. *The UK* (2008), the Court expressly indicated that its earlier decision in the *Vilvarajah* case should not be interpreted as requiring an applicant to show that special distinguishing features exist, if he can otherwise

---

77   ECtHR, *Vilvarajah and Others* v. *the United Kingdom*, para. 108; ECtHR, *Chahal* v. *the United Kingdom*, para. 96; ECtHR, *NA.* v. *The United Kingdom*, para. 111.

78   ECtHR, *Vilvarajah and Others* v. *the United Kingdom*, para. 111.

79   Ibid., para. 112.

show that the general situation of violence in the country of destination is of sufficient level of intensity to make it likely that removal to that country would necessarily violate Article 3.[80] The Court has required an applicant in a Non-Refoulement case to establish the existence of a general situation of violence in the country of destination, or to prove that he has special distinguishing features that put him at a real risk of the proscribed ill-treatment. In *Sufi and Elmi* v. *The UK* (2011), the Court clearly stated that:

> ...the sole question for the Court to consider in an expulsion case is whether, in all the circumstances of the case before it, substantial grounds have been shown for believing that the person concerned, if returned, would face a real risk of being subjected to treatment contrary to Article 3 of the Convention. If the existence of such a risk is established, the applicant's removal would necessarily breach Article 3, regardless of whether the risk emanates from a general situation of violence, a personal characteristic of the applicant, or a combination of the two.[81]

The Court must examine all the facts of the case in order to ascertain if the applicant's removal would expose him to a foreseeable, personal and real risk of ill-treatment in the receiving State. The Court's assessment must focus on foreseeable consequences of the applicant's removal to the proposed receiving State, in the light of the general situation there, as well as the applicant's personal circumstances at the material time.[82] It must consider all relevant factors that may increase the risk of ill-treatment. The Court has given special weight to the applicant's membership in a particular vulnerable group that is systematically exposed to ill-treatment in the proposed receiving State. This fact has been considered sufficient in itself for the Court to conclude that the applicant's removal to that State would violate Article 3.[83] Where this is not the case, the Court has required the applicant to establish that there are further

---

80   ECtHR, *NA.* v. *The United Kingdom*, paras. 115–116.

81   ECtHR, *Sufi and Elmi* v. *the United Kingdom*, para. 218.

82   ECtHR, *Vilvarajah and Others* v. *the United Kingdom*, para. 108; ECtHR, *NA.* v. *The United Kingdom*, para. 113; ECtHR, *Sufi and Elmi* v. *the United Kingdom*, para. 216.

83   In our opinion, the use of vulnerable group concept in the Non-Refoulement cases had positive implications in the ECtHR's case-law. It enhances substantive equality as it ensures that the Non-Refoulement cases of members of a specific group in a certain receiving State are addressed in a same manner. See, Peroni, L. & Timmer, A., Vulnerable groups: The promise of an emerging concept in European Human Rights Convention law, International Journal of Constitutional Law, Vol. 11 no. 4: 2013, 1056–1085.

special distinguishing features in his case that increase his risk. The Court clearly stated that:

> Due regard should also be given to the possibility that a number of individual factors may not, when considered separately, constitute a real risk; but when taken cumulatively and when considered in a situation of general violence and heightened security, the same factors may give rise to a real risk. Both the need to consider all relevant factors cumulatively and the need to give appropriate weight to the general situation in the country of destination derive from the obligation to consider all the relevant circumstances of the case.[84]

Where a State party intends to send an individual to a specific part of the receiving State, the Court's assessment will focus on whether a real risk of ill-treatment exists in that part. In *H. and B.* v. *The UK* (2013), the Court noted that the British government proposed to remove the applicant to Kabul. Since the applicant had not submitted anything to suggest that he would not be able to gain admittance and settle there, the Court did not consider it necessary to examine the risk to the applicant in region of Afghanistan outside Kabul.[85] Establishing the sending State's responsibility for refoulement inevitably requires assessing conditions in the receiving State against the standards of Article 3, however, there is no question of adjudicating on the responsibility of the receiving State.[86]

III.1.1   General Situation in the Receiving State
Through its case-law, the Court has repeatedly decided that the mere possibility of ill-treatment because of the general situation in the receiving State is unsettled is insufficient, in itself, to give rise to a breach of Article 3 ECHR.[87] If sources available to the Court only describe the general situation in the receiving State, the applicant is required to adduce other evidence in support of his allegations.[88] In *Mamatkulov and Askarov* v. *Turkey* (2005), the applicants

---

84   ECtHR, *NA.* v. *The United Kingdom*, para. 130.

85   ECtHR, *H. and B.* v. *the United Kingdom*, paras. 95 and 106; ECtHR, *NA.* v. *The United Kingdom*, para. 123; ECtHR, *Mawaka* v. *The Netherlands* paras. 41–42.

86   ECtHR, *Soering* v. *the United Kingdom*, para. 91; ECtHR, *Salah Sheekh* v. *The Netherlands*, para. 136.

87   ECtHR, *Vilvarajah and Others* v. *the United Kingdom*, para. 111; ECtHR, *H.L.R.* v. *France* (GC), para. 41; ECtHR, *F.H.* v. *Sweden*, para. 90.

88   ECtHR, *Khodzhayev* v. *Russia*, para. 93; ECtHR, *Gaforov* v. *Russia*, paras. 115–116.

were extradited by Turkey to Uzbekistan, where they were suspected of terrorist activities including an attempted attack on the President.[89] They argued before the ECtHR that, at the time they had been extradited, there were substantial grounds to believe that they would be at risk of ill-treatment in the receiving State. The applicants' allegations were based on several reports by international human rights organisations that denounced the administrative practice of torture and ill-treatment of the political dissidents. The Court observed that, although those reports described the general situation in Uzbekistan, they did not support the applicants' specific allegations and required corroboration by other evidence.[90]

In its recent Non-Refoulement case-law under Article 3 ECHR, the ECtHR has distinguished between two situations. The first is where a general situation of violence exists in the proposed receiving State. The second is where a general situation of human rights violations exists there. The Court's case-law on these two situations is explained in the following two subsections.

III.1.1.1   *General Situation of Violence*
In the case of *J.H.* v. *The UK* (2011), the Court stated that:

> ...there are no indications that the general situation of violence in Afghanistan, and in particular Kabul to where the applicant would be returned, is at present of sufficient intensity to create a real risk of ill-treatment simply by virtue of his being exposed to such violence on return.[91]

Thus, while the Court has considerd the mere possibility of ill-treatment on the grounds of the unsettled general situation in the country of destination insufficient to give rise to a breach of Article 3, it has accepted that the general situation of violence there could be serious enough to hold that any removal to that country would necessarily breach Article 3. In this respect, the Court has continuously reiterated that:

> [It] has never ruled out the possibility that a general situation of violence in a country of destination will be of a sufficient level of intensity as to entail that a removal to it would necessarily breach Article 3 of the Convention. Nevertheless, the Court would adopt such an approach only in the most extreme cases of general violence where there is a real risk of

---

89   ECtHR, *Mamatkulov and Askarov* v. *Turkey* (GC), paras. 12 and 18.
90   Ibid., paras. 40–54 and 74.
91   ECtHR, *J.H.* v. *the United Kingdom*, para. 55.

ill-treatment simply by virtue of an individual being exposed to such violence on return.[92]

As mentioned above, where it is proved that the general situation of violence in the country of destination is of sufficient intensity to create a real risk of ill-treatment simply because of the removal to that country, the applicant is not required to establish the existence of any special distinguishing features. The Court has clearly considered that to insist, in such circumstances, the applicant show the existence of special distinguishing features in his case would render illusory the protection offered by Article 3 and would call into question the absolute nature of the protection afforded by it.[93]

Thus, not every situation of general violence will give rise to a real risk of treatment proscribed by Article 3. A general situation of violence in the country of destination is sufficiently intense to pose such a risk only "in the most extreme cases". The Court has not provided further guidance on assessing the intensity of violence that results from conflict. In *Sufi and Elmi* v. *The UK* (2011), the applicants maintained that the indiscriminate violence in Mogadishu, to which they were ordered to return, was of sufficient level of intensity to pose a real risk to the life of any civilian in the city. In order to assess the intensity of the violence in Mogadishu, the ECtHR referred to the following criteria, which had been adopted by the British Asylum and Immigration Tribunal (UKAIT) in the case of *AM & AM (Somalia)*. Firstly, are the parties of the conflict using methods and tactics of war that increase the *risk* of civilian damages or directly target civilians? Secondly, is the use of these methods and/or tactics widespread among the parties of the conflict? Thirdly, is fighting was limited to certain areas or widespread? Fourthly, how many civilians have been killed, injured and displaced as a result of the fighting? The Court made it clear that while these criteria do not comprise an exhaustive list to be applied in all future cases, in the context of this case they formed an appropriate standard to assess the intensity of violence in Mogadishu.[94] The ECtHR took into account the fact that the military offensive and indiscriminate bombardments were carried out by all parties of the conflict in Mogadishu without regard to

---

92   ECtHR, *NA.* v. *The United Kingdom*, para. 115; ECtHR, *Al-Zawatia* v. *Sweden* (admissibility decision), Appl.No. 50068/08, 22 June 2010, para 46; ECtHR, *S.S. and Others* v. *Denmark*, para. 86; ECtHR, *Mohammed* v. *Austria*, para. 93; ECtHR, *A.A.* v. *Switzerland*, Appl.No. 58802/12, 7 January 2014, para. 39.

93   ECtHR, *NA.* v. *The United Kingdom*, para. 116; ECtHR, *Sufi and Elmi* v. *the United Kingdom*, para. 217.

94   Ibid., para. 241.

the civilian population, the number of civilian casualties was unacceptable, a substantial number of people were displaced within and from the capital, and the conflict was widespread, unpredictable and capable of changing from day to day. Against this background, the Court concluded that the level of violence in Mogadishu was sufficiently intense to pose a real risk of treatment contrary to Article 3 ECHR to everyone in the city.[95]

With reference to the UKAIT's decision in *AM & AM (Somalia)*, the Court did not rule out that certain individuals closely connected to "powerful actors" in Mogadishu might be able to obtain protection and live safely in the city. However, the Court asserted that these cases would be rare, because only those with connections at the highest level would be able to obtain such protection. Membership in a majority clan would not be enough. The Court also observed that it was unlikely for an applicant who had not returned to Somalia for some time to have such connections. Therefore, the argument that an applicant had close connections with powerful actors could be successfully raised only against persons who had recently been in Somalia.[96] The Court concluded that:

> ...the violence in Mogadishu is of such level of intensity that anyone in the city, except possibly those who are exceptionally well-connected to "powerful-actors", would be at real risk of treatment prohibited by Article 3 of the Convention.[97]

The Court found that the applicants would be at a real risk of ill-treatment if they were to remain in Mogadishu because of the general violence there. Although the second applicant was a member of a majority clan, the Court did not consider this to be evidence of close connections that could afford him protection in Mogadishu.[98] *Sufi and Elmi* v. *The UK* (2011) was the first case in which the ECtHR applied the principle of Non-Refoulement under Article 3 ECHR to a situation in which the risk of ill-treatment emanated from the

---

95   Ibid., paras, 242–248.

96   Ibid., para. 249.

97   Ibid., para. 250. The ECtHR reviewed this position in *K.A.B.* v. *Sweden* (2013). The Court noted that al-Shabaab was no longer in power in the Mogadishu, there was no front-line fighting or shelling any longer and the number of civilian casualties went down. The Court found that, according to the available country information, the situation in Mogadishu was not, at present, of such a nature as to place everyone in it at a real risk of treatment contrary to Article 3 ECHR. ECtHR, *K.A.B.* v. *Sweden*, Appl.No. 886/11, 5 September 2013, para. 91. See also, ECtHR, *R.H.* v. *Sweden*, Appl.No. 4601/14, 10 September 2015, paras. 65–68.

98   ECtHR, *Sufi and Elmi* v. *the United Kingdom*, paras. 301 and 309.

general situation of violence in the receiving State.[99] In *L.M. and Others* v. *Russia* (2015), the ECtHR had the opportunity to address wether the general situation of violence in Syria is intense enough to conclude that any removal to that country would breach Article 3. The Court noted that it has not yet adopted a judgment to evaluate the allegations of a risk of danger to life or ill-treatment in the context of the ongoing conflict in Syria. This, in the Court's view, was at least in part due to the fact that most European countries have not carried out involuntary returns to Syria. The Court referred to the latest UN reports that described the situation in Syria as a "humanitarian crisis" and spoke of "immeasurable suffering" of the civilians, massive violations of human rights and humanitarian law by all parties of the conflict and the resulting displacement of almost half of the country's population.[100] However, the Court did not clearly stated whether it considered the general situation of violence in Syria is intense enough to create a real risk of ill-treatment simply because of removal to that country. It chose to concentrate on the applicant's personal circumstances as being a member of a vulnerable group.[101]

III.1.1.2 *General Situation of Human Rights Violations*

The Court has expressly applied the principle of Non-Refoulement under Article 3 in a case in which a general situation of violence existed in the receiving State. This gives rise to speculation that the same approach might be followed where there is a general situation of human rights violations in that country. In *Sufi and Elmi* v. *The UK* (2011), the Court seemed prepared to apply this principle to cases where the risk of ill-treatment emanates not from the general situation of violence, but from the general human rights situation in the receiving State. When it considered if there was an internal flight alternative, the Court observed that, according to the country reports, the areas of Somalia where violence was less intense were those under the control of al-Shabaab, an armed Islamic group. But those areas were reported to have the worst human rights situation in Somalia. The Court stated that:

> It is clear that in the areas under their control al-Shabaab is enforcing a particularly draconian version of Sharia law which goes well beyond the

---

99   ECtHR, *H. and B.* v. *the United Kingdom*, paras. 92–93.

100   ECtHR, *L.M. and Others* v. *Russia*, Appl.No. 40081/14, 40088/14 and 40127/14, 15 October 2015, para. 123. With regard the situation in Iraq after June 2014 see ECtHR, *J.K. and others* v. *Sweden*, Appl.No. 59166/12, 19 October 2015, paras. 55–56.

101   ECtHR, *L.M. and Others* v. *Russia*, para. 124.

traditional interpretation of Islam in Somalia [...] and in fact amounts to a repressive form of social control.[102]

Al-Shabaab strictly interpreted Islamic Sharia law and intervened in every detail of individuals' daily life.[103] Since al-Shabaab started controlling parts of southern and central Somalia in late 2006, the Court considered it unlikely that a Somali with no recent experience of living in Somalia would be able to stay in an area under al-Shabaab's control without the risk of attracting its attention. In particular, if a returnee had been out of the country long enough to have Western attributes such as a foreign accent, he would be at greater risk. The Court noted that while it was not possible to foresee with certainty the fate of a returnee who came to the attention of al-Shabaab for not complying with their rules, punishments could attain the minimum level of severity required to fall within the scope of Article 3, including stoning, flogging and corporal punishment, for relatively minor infringements like playing scrabble and wearing the wrong clothing.[104] Consequently, the Court found that a returnee with no recent experience of living in Somalia would be at a real risk of being subjected to treatment proscribed by Article 3 ECHR in an al-Shabaab controlled area.[105] The Court's conclusion did not rely solely on the existence of a general situation of human rights violations in those areas, but also on the fact that the applicant was a member of a group, i.e., returnees with no recent experience of living in Somalia, who are vulnerable to being exposed to these violations.[106]

In *Kaboulov* v. *Ukraine* (2009), which concerned the extradition of a criminal suspect to Kazakhstan, the Court found that the applicant's extradition would violate Article 3 because the human rights violations against criminal suspects in detention centres in Kazakhstan were common.[107] In contrast, in *Dzhaksybergenov* v. *Ukraine* (2011), the ECtHR found that the applicant's extradition to Kazakhstan would not violate Article 3. The Court observed that although international reports still raised serious concerns about the human rights situation in Kazakhstan, and, in particular, about political rights and freedoms, some improvements in the human rights situation and the conditions

---

102   ECtHR, *Sufi and Elmi* v. *the United Kingdom*, para. 273.

103   Ibid., para. 273.

104   Ibid., paras. 275–276.

105   Ibid., para. 277.

106   The same can be said with regard to the dire socio-economic and humanitarian conditions in the receiving State. The ECtHR has held that such conditions did not necessarily have a bearing, and certainly not a decisive bearing, on the question of whether the person concerned would face a real risk of ill-treatment in the receiving State.

107   ECtHR, *Kaboulov* v. *Ukraine*, Appl.No. 41015/04, 19 November 2009, para. 112.

of detention had recently been demonstrated. The Court therefore found no indication that the recent human rights situation in Kazakhstan was serious enough to require a total ban on extradition to that country.[108] The Court might be ready to apply the principle of Non-Refoulement under Article 3 in a situation in which human rights violations were generally serious enough to entail a real risk of ill-treatment to every returnee. However, the Court added:

> Reference to a general problem concerning human rights observance in a particular country cannot alone serve as a basis for refusal of extradition.[109]

The Court has only applied the principle of Non-Refoulement to extradition cases where there is a serious enough human rights situation in the receiving State, i.e. where the person concerned would be handed over to the authorities of the receiving State. Persons who are extradited in such circumstances can be considered a "vulnerable group", such as detainees or criminal suspects. It is doubtful that the Court would follow the same approach in the expulsion cases.[110]

The mere fact that a general situation of human rights violations exists in the proposed receiving State has not been considered as substantial ground to find that the applicant's removal would violate Article 3 ECHR. However, a certain group in a receiving State could be considered as vulnerable to ill-treatment because a general situation of human rights violations in this State exists, and this is the topic of the next section.

III.1.2   Membership in a Vulnerable Group
Where it is not established that the general situation of violence in the country of destination is of sufficient intensity to hold that any removal to that country would necessarily breach Article 3, the applicant is required to adduce other

---

108   ECtHR, *Dzhaksybergenov* v. *Ukraine*, para. 37.

109   Ibid., para. 37. ECtHR, *Kamyshev* v. *Ukraine*, para. 44; ECtHR, *Elmuratov* v. *Russia*, Appl. No. 66317/09, 3 March 2011, para. 82; ECtHR, *Sidikovy* v. *Russia*, Appl.No.73455/11, 20 June 2013, para. 147.

110   In the expulsion case of *N.* v. *Sweden* (2010), the ECtHR was aware of the reports of serious human rights violations in Afghanistan; however, it did not find them to be of such a nature as to show, on their own, that there would be a violation of the ECHR if the applicant were to be returned to that country. The Court, therefore, had to establish whether the applicant's personal circumstances were such that her forcible return to Afghanistan would be contrary to Article 3 ECHR. ECtHR, *N.* v. *Sweden*, para. 52.

evidence to support his Non-Refoulement claim. The claim that the applicant belongs to a group systematically exposed to a practice of ill-treatment in the proposed receiving State has been used before the ECtHR as a ground to prevent the applicant's removal. Through its case-law, the Court has accepted that the risk of being subjected to treatment proscribed by Article 3 can be established on the mere fact of being a member or belonging to a group that is deemed to be vulnerable in the receiving State. The Court has repeatedly asserted that:

> In cases where an applicant alleges that he or she is a member of a group systematically exposed to a practice of ill-treatment, the protection of Article 3 of the Convention enters into play when the applicant establishes, [...], that there are serious reasons to believe in the existence of the practice in question and his or her membership of the group concerned [...]. In those circumstances, the Court will not then insist that the applicant show the existence of further special distinguishing features if to do so would render illusory the protection offered by Article 3.[111]

Where the applicant challenges his removal on the ground that he is a member of a certain vulnerable group in the proposed receiving State, two facts must be established. First, the group must have been systematically exposed to treatment proscribed by Article 3; second, the applicant must be a member of that group. Once these facts are established, the applicant's removal would be in breach of the principle of Non-Refoulement under Article 3 ECHR, regardless of the existence of other special distinguishing features in his case.[112] The determination that a particular group is considered to be vulnerable in the receiving State is determined on a case-by-case basis, taking into account the situation of this group in the State concerned. The number of members the group has is unimportant in determining whether they are at a real risk of ill-treatment in the State concerned. The Court has made clear that members of large groups are no less at risk than individuals where the risk is found to be sufficiently real and probable.[113]

In the following subsections, we will review the related ECtHR's case-law and give some examples of the groups that have been considered as vulnerable in some countries.

---

111   ECtHR, *NA.* v. *The United Kingdom*, para. 116; ECtHR, *Said* v. *The Netherlands*, para. 132.
112   ECtHR, *H. and B.* v. *the United Kingdom*, paras. 95–100.
113   ECtHR, *Hirsi Jamaa and Others* v. *Italy* (GC), para. 136.

III.1.2.1   *Detainees, Criminal Suspects, Deserters and Political Opponents*
The Court has applied the principle of Non-Refoulement under Article 3 to
extradition cases where there is a human rights situation serious enough to
entail a real risk of proscribed ill-treatment in the receiving State. In *Kaboulov* v. *Ukraine* (2009), the Court's conclusion that the applicant's extradition to
Kazakhstan would violate Article 3 was based on the existence of human rights
violations against criminal suspects in detention centres there. The Court
accepted the applicant's argument that the mere fact of being detained as a
criminal suspect in such a situation provided sufficient grounds to fear a serious risk of being subjected to treatment proscribed by Article 3.[114] Arguably,
the ECtHR held that the criminal suspects detained in Kazakhstan in such a
situation constituted a vulnerable group. The Court considered the human
rights situation in Kazakhstan to be serious enough to impose a total ban on
extradition to that country. Since recent international reports have described
improvements in the human rights situation and the conditions of detention
centres in Kazakhstan, the Court in *Dzhaksybergenov* v. *Ukraine* (2011) found
that the human rights situation there was not serious enough to call for a
total ban on extradition to that country.[115] The Court noted that the applicant
had asserted that he did not belong to the political opposition or to any other
vulnerable group. The Court therefore refused the applicant's allegation that
any criminal suspect in Kazakhstan was at a real risk of ill-treatment considering it too general.[116]

Accordingly, where the Court does not hold the human rights situation in
the receiving State to be serious enough to consider that any detainee in that
country is at risk of ill-treatment, the applicant can still benefit from protection of refoulement to that country if he is a member of a particular group
of detainees that is vulnerable to ill-treatment. For example, the applicant
in *Saadi* v. *Italy* (2008) was a Tunisian national who faced a risk of being
removed to Tunisia where he had been sentenced to twenty years' imprisonment for membership in a terrorist organisation operating abroad, and for
incitement to terrorist activities.[117] He argued that enforcement of his deportation would expose him to a risk of ill-treatment because it was "a matter of

---

114   ECtHR, *Kaboulov* v. *Ukraine*, para. 112. See, ECtHR, *Soldatenko* v. *Ukraine*, paras. 71–72.
115   ECtHR, *Dzhaksybergenov* v. *Ukraine*, para. 37. See, ECtHR, *Tershiyev* v. *Azerbaijan*, Appl.
       No. 10226/13, 31 July 2014, para. 55.
116   ECtHR, *Dzhaksybergenov* v. *Ukraine*, para. 37; ECtHR, *Sharipov* v. *Russia*, paras. 35–36;
       ECtHR, *Oshlakov* v. *Russia*, Appl.No. 56662/09, 3 April 2014, para. 86.
117   ECtHR, *Saadi* v. *Italy* (GC), para. 29.

common knowledge" that terrorist suspects, especially those connected with Islamist fundamentalism, were often tortured in Tunisia. The Court referred to recent international reports that described the disturbing situation in Tunisia and mentioned many and regular cases of torture and ill-treatment meted out to persons accused of terrorism.[118] Taking into account the sentence issued against Saadi in Tunisia,[119] the Court concluded that substantial grounds had been established for believing that there was a real risk that the applicant, if deported, would be subjected to treatment proscribed by Article 3.[120] The Court based its decision on the presumption that suspected terrorists and Islamic fundamentalists were, as a group, systematically exposed to torture and ill-treatment in Tunisia; therefore, their removal to that country would violate Article 3.[121] The same approach was followed with regard to the removal of persons suspected of being members of Islamic organisations that were accused of being terrorist, such as *Ennahda* in Tunisia.[122]

Since the general situation has changed in Tunisia, the Court reassessed its previous findings on the situation of Islamic fundamentalists in that country. In *Al Hanchi* v. BH (2011), the applicant argued that, if deported to Tunisia, he would be treated as an Islamist and a suspected terrorist because he had associated with the foreign mujahedin in BH. The Court noted the progress of the democratic transition process in Tunisia. Security forces widely accused of human rights violations during the former regime were dissolved and amnesty was granted to all political prisoners, including those detained under the controversial anti-terrorism law, and a number of officials were dismissed

---

118   The Court referred to reports by the AI, HRW and USSD. Ibid., para. 143.
119   The Court took into account that that AI confirmed the existence of this sentence. Ibid., para. 144.
120   Ibid., para. 146.
121   E.g., *Klein* v. *Russia* (2010), which concerned the extradition of a suspected terrorist to Colombia. ECtHR, *Daoudi* v. *France*, Appl.No. 19576/08, 3 December 2009 paras. 67–73; ECtHR, *H.R.* v. *France*, Appl.No. 64780/09, 22 September 2011, paras. 49–65, which concerned the expulsion of suspected terrorists to Algeria.
122   ECtHR, *Sellem* v. *Italy*, Appl.No. 12584/08, 5 May 2009. In *Dbouba* v. *Turkey*, the applicant's membership to Ennahda was established with reference to a document submitted by him according to which the chairman of Ennahda had stated that the applicant was a member of this organisation in Tunisia and that he would be at risk of imprisonment and torture if returned to Tunisia on account of that affiliation. In *Charahili* v. *Turkey*, the Court found that there was no doubt that the applicant was a member of Ennahda with reference to the fact that he was convicted of membership of a terrorist organisation in Tunisia and sentenced to five years' imprisonment in addition to existence of arrest warrant against him in Tunisia as he was suspected of membership of Ennahda.

and/or prosecuted for past abuses.[123] The Court added that while cases of ill-treatment were still reported, they were separate incidents. There was no indication and no proof that Islamists, as a group, were systematically targeted after the change of regime. On the contrary, Mr. Rachid Ghannouchi, a leader of Ennahda, was able to return to Tunisia after spending twenty-two years in exile and Ennahda was allowed to register as a political party. Against this background, the Court found that the applicant's deportation to Tunisia would not violate Article 3 ECHR.[124] A group that is considered to be vulnerable to ill-treatment in a certain country, can later be considered not to be vulnerable in the same country, or vice versa, in light of recent available information.

Although the Court did not hold the human rights situation in Uzbekistan to be serious enough to consider that all criminal suspects there were at risk of ill-treatment, it found that individuals suspected of politically and/or religiously motivated crimes constitute a vulnerable group susceptible to being ill-treated in that country; consequently, the extradition or expulsion of such individuals to Uzbekistan would be in breach of Article 3.[125] For example see *Muminov* v. *Russia* (2008), which concerned the extradition of an Uzbek national to Uzbekistan where he was accused of participation in the activities of Hizb-ut-Tahrir (HT).[126] In this case, the Court concluded that there were serious reasons to believe that a practice of persecuting members or supporters of HT existed. Accordingly, the Court found that substantial grounds had been shown for believing that the applicant had faced a real risk of being subjected to the proscribed ill-treatment.[127] The fact that the applicant in this case denied his membership of HT did not affect the Court's conclusion that he would be at risk of ill-treatment because of his membership of a vulnerable group. Decisive in the Court's view was the fact that after the applicant had

---

123   The Court referred to the Parliamentary Assembly of the CE and UN Special Rapporteurs. ECtHR, *Al Hanchi* v. *Bosnia and Herzegovina*, para. 43.

124   Ibid., paras. 44–45.

125   ECtHR, *Muminov* v. *Russia*, paras. 96 and 98; ECtHR, *Ismoilov and Others* v. *Russia*; ECtHR, *Rustamov* v. *Russia*, paras. 127–128; ECtHR, *Ergashev* v. *Russia*, Appl.No. 12106/09, 20 December 2011, para. 113; ECtHR, *Zokhidove* v. *Russia*, Appl. No. 67286/10, 5 February 2013; ECtHR, *Khalikov* v. *Russia*, Appl.No. 66373/13, 26 February 2015, paras. 42–43. The same can be said with regard to the removal to Tajikistan on charges relating to politically and/or religiously motivated criminal offence. ECtHR, *Khodzhayev* v. *Russia*; ECtHR, *Azimov* v. *Russia*, Appl.No. 67474/11, 18 April 2013, para. 138; ECtHR, *Savriddin Dzhurayev* v. *Russia*, Appl.No. 71386/10, 25 April 2013, paras. 170–173; ECtHR, *Ismailove* v. *Russia*, Appl. No. 20110/13, 17 April 2014, paras. 86–87.

126   A transnational Islamic organisation with both political and religious aims and which is banned in Russia, Germany and some Central Asian States.

127   ECtHR, *Muminov* v. *Russia*, paras. 93 and 98.

been removed to the requesting State, he was prosecuted and sentenced on the ground of his involvement in the activities of HT. The receiving State considered him to be a member of the organisation, regardless of whether he actually was a member or not.[128] However, the absence of a charge or an arrest warrant against an applicant in the receiving State does not mean that this State does not consider him to be a member in the group concerned. In *A. v. The Netherlands* (2010), the applicant was not charged with or accused of any crime in Libya. He argued that he would be at risk of being detained and ill-treated in Libya because he had been involved with an Islamic extremist network active in the Netherlands. The Court noted that the Libyan authorities opposed militant forms of Islam and they often had good insight into the activities and contacts of Libyans abroad. Accordingly, the Court found it sufficiently plausible for the purposes of Article 3 that the applicant would be identified and detained for questioning upon his arrival in Libya, and would face a real risk of being ill-treated at the hands of the Libyan authorities.[129]

Only the individuals suspected of politically and/or religiously motivated crimes in Uzbekistan were protected against refoulement under Article 3. This protection did not extend to persons who were charged with ordinary criminal offences in this State. The Court made this clear in the case of *Elmuratov v. Russia* (2011), which concerned the extradition of an Uzbek national to Uzbekistan where he was charged with aggravated theft. The Court mentioned that it had found violations of Article 3 in several cases involving extradition and expulsion to Uzbekistan. The applicants in those cases were charged with politically and/or religiously motivated crimes.[130] The Court noted that *Elmuratov* was not at risk of ill-treatment for political reasons, nor did he claim to be a member of any religious movement or any other vulnerable group susceptible of being ill-treated in Uzbekistan.[131] The same decision was adopted in *Shakurov v. Russia* (2012), which concerned the extradition of an Uzbek national to Uzbekistan, where he was charged with an ordinary criminal offence, military desertion.[132]

---

128 The applicants in the *Khodzhayev* and *Gaforov* cases denied their membership of HT. However, the Court gave decisive weight to the fact that the applicants' extradition had been requested because there was a charge or an arrest warrant against the person concerned on account of his membership of HT. ECtHR, *Khodzhayev* v. *Russia*, para. 136; ECtHR, *Gaforov* v. *Russia*, para. 212.

129 ECtHR, *A. v. The Netherlands*, para. 149.

130 ECtHR, *Elmuratov* v. *Russia*, para. 83.

131 Ibid., para. 84. See also, ECtHR, *Bakoyev* v. *Russia*, Appl.No. 30225/11, 5 February 2013, para. 117.

132 ECtHR, *Shakurov* v. *Russia*, Appl.No. 55822/10, 5 June 2012.

In contrast, in *Said* v. *The Netherlands* (2005), the Court found that military deserters constituted a vulnerable group in Eritrea. The applicant in this case was an Eritrean national who claimed protection against refoulement essentially because he had deserted the Eritrean army before demobilisation.[133] The ECtHR observed that the Eritrean army had taken measures, such as roadblocks, street sweeps, and house-to-house searches, in order to find deserters. The Court further noted that general information from public sources described the treatment to which deserters in Eritrea had been subjected. This ranged from "incommunicado detention to prolonged exposure to the sun in high temperatures and the tying of hands and feet in painful positions".[134] The Court had no doubt that such treatment was inhuman. Against this background, the Court considered that substantial grounds had been shown for believing that the applicant would be exposed to a real risk of being subjected to ill-treatment if he were to be expelled to Eritrea.[135] Groups that are considered vulnerable in one State are not necessarily considered vulnerable in another.

The Court has determined that an applicant can benefit from protection against refoulement under Article 3, where it is established that he belongs to a certain minority that is treated differently from other detainees in the receiving State. This approach can be seen in the cases concerning extradition of criminal suspects of non-Turkmen ethnicity to Turkmenistan. The applicant in *Ryabikin* v. *Russia* (2008) was a Turkmen national of Russian ethnic origin. He was under a threat of extradition to Turkmenistan, where he had been charged with embezzlement. He contested his extradition mainly on the grounds that torture and ill-treatment were widespread among detainees in that country and that, as a member of an ethnic minority, he would be in a particularly vulnerable situation. The Court noted that the applicant was charged with a serious crime for which punishment was imprisonment for several years, and that there was an arrest warrant issued against him. If extradited, he would almost certainly be detained and imprisoned for years. In view of the widespread ill-treatment of detainees in Turkmenistan and the vulnerable situation of minorities, the Court found that there were sufficient grounds for believing that the applicant would face a real risk of being subjected to treatment proscribed by Article 3.[136]

---

133   ECtHR, *Said* v. *The Netherlands*, paras. 50–53.
134   Ibid., para. 54.
135   Ibid., para. 54.
136   ECtHR, *Ryabikin* v. *Russia*, para. 121. See, ECtHR, *Makhmudzhan Ergashev* v. *Russia*, Appl. No. 49747/11, 16 October 2012, para. 72; ECtHR, *Khamrakulov* v. *Russia*, Appl.No. 68894/13, 14 September 2015, para. 66; ECtHR, *Nabid Abdullayev* v. *Russia*, Appl.No. 8474/14, 15 October 2015, para. 65.

In some cases, the Court has considered that an applicant's membership in a certain opposition party in the proposed receiving State would expose him to the risk of being detained and consequently subjected to treatment contrary to Article 3.[137] In *Hilal v. The UK* (2001), the Court found that the applicant's deportation to Tanzania would breach Article 3 on the grounds that, *inter alia*, he was an active member of CUF opposition party in Zanzibar and had provided them with financial support, and that the members of this party were suffering serious harassment, arbitrary detention, torture and ill-treatment by the authorities.[138]

The ECtHR has applied the principle of Non-Refoulement to the extradition of criminal suspects where it is established, according to reliable and credible sources, that the human rights situation in the receiving State is serious enough to consider that criminal suspects, as whole, constitute a vulnerable group susceptible to be ill-treated. If this is not the case, the applicant may still benefit from protection against refoulement on this ground where the Court finds that he is a member of or belongs to a particular group of criminal suspects or detainees that is vulnerable to being subjected to ill-treatment in the proposed receiving State. Such a group could consist of suspected terrorists, individuals suspected of politically and/or religiously motivated crimes, minorities, or individuals subjected to treatment contrary to Article 3 in the receiving State because they were suspected of a particular crime.

III.1.2.2   *Ethnic Groups and Minorities*
Where a certain minority or ethnic group is treated differently in detention centres in the receiving State, this particular group of criminal suspects is considered to be vulnerable in that State. In several Non-Refoulement cases, the Court found that the applicants, who were not criminal suspects, would be at a real risk of ill-treatment because they belonged to a certain ethnic or minority group that was subjected to such treatment in the receiving State. In *Salah Sheekh v. The Netherlands* (2007), which concerned the expulsion of a Somali national who belonged to the minority of the Ashraf, the Court noted that human rights abuses of members of minorities, such as the Ashraf, had been

---

137   ECtHR, *Chahal* v. *the United Kingdom*, para. 104; ECtHR, *Baysakov and Others* v. *Ukraine*, paras. 49–50.

138   ECtHR, *Hilal* v. *the United Kingdom*, paras. 64 and 66. In *Puzan* v. *Ukraine* (2010), the Court noted that the applicant, who was convicted in Belarus for drug-related offences, did not claim that he belonged to the political opposition, which was recognised as a particularly vulnerable group in Belarus. ECtHR, *Puzan* v. *Ukraine*, para. 34. See also, ECtHR, *Y.P. and L.P.* v. *France*, Appl.No. 32476/06, 2 September 2010; ECtHR, *Kamyshev* v. *Ukraine*, para. 44.

well-documented, including particular treatment of the kind to which the applicant had been subjected before leaving Somalia.[139] The Court observed that the applicant and his family had been targeted because they were Ashraf, and for that reason it was known that they had no means of protection. The Court found no indication that the situation had changed substantially for the better.[140] Consequently, the Court concluded that the applicant's expulsion to Somalia would violate Article 3.

In *F.H.* v. *Sweden* (2009), the applicant claimed that he would face a real risk of torture or ill-treatment contrary to Article 3 ECHR if forced to return to Iraq, on the basis, *inter alia*, of his membership of the Christian faith. The Court noted that while there had been several attacks directed against Christians in Iraq, those attacks were condemned by the Iraqi government, which intervened with police and the military to ensure the safety of this group. Since those attacks had been also condemned by Islamic groups and no one accepted responsibility for them, the Court held that the reported attacks had been carried out by individuals rather than by organised groups. The Court found that the applicant could seek the protection of the Iraqi authorities if he felt threatened, and that the authorities would be willing and in a position to help him. Thus, the Court decided that if the applicant were to be forcibly returned to Iraq, he would not face a real risk of ill-treatment on the basis of his religious affiliation: Christians did not constitute a vulnerable group in Iraq.[141] This position was reviewed in several cases considered by the ECtHR during 2013. The Court noted that attacks on Christians continued during the subsequent four years and that available evidence suggested that, in comparison with 2008/09, violence had escalated. The Court added that while the great majority of civilians killed in Iraq were Muslims, a higher number of attacks that specifically targeted Christians were recorded in recent years, and these attacks were conducted by organised extremist groups. The Court noted that Christians were considered by the UNHCR to form a vulnerable minority in the southern and central parts of Iraq, either directly due to their faith or due to their perceived wealth, or connections with foreign forces and countries, or to the fact that some of them sell alcohol. The Court agreed with the conclusions drawn by the UK Border Agency in December 2011, that authorities in these parts of Iraq were generally unable to protect Christians and other religious

---

139   ECtHR, *Salah Sheekh* v. *The Netherlands*, para. 146.
140   Ibid., paras. 147–148.
141   ECtHR, *F.H.* v. *Sweden*, para. 97.

minorities.[142] Accordingly, the Court held that Christians constitute a vulnerable group in the southern and central parts of Iraq.[143]

The principle of Non-Refoulement under Article 3 ECHR applies where the Court finds that a minority group is systematically targeted with ill-treatment to a level sufficient to consider that all members of this group are at risk of being subjected to such treatment.

III.1.2.3   *Women*

The human rights situation of women in some countries has been used as a ground to contest the removal of female applicants to such countries. This ground has been used mainly by women who transgress social mores in the proposed receiving State, for example, by requesting divorce, living abroad alone, or having an extramarital relationship. *Jabari* v. *Turkey* (2000) was the first case in which the ECtHR found that the applicant's removal, if implemented, would violate the principle of Non-Refoulement under Article 3 on this ground. The applicant argued that she would be subjected to a real risk of ill-treatment and death by stoning if expelled to Iran, for having committed adultery there. In assessing the risk that the applicant would face if expelled to Iran, the Court gave a due weight to the fact that the UNHCR had granted her refugee status on the ground that:

> ...she had a well-founded fear of persecution as she belonged to a particular social group, namely women who have transgressed social mores according to the UNHCR guidelines on gender-based persecution.[144]

---

142   ECtHR, *M.Y.H. and others* v. *Sweden*, Appl. No. 50859/10, 27 June 2013, para. 60; ECtHR, *M.K.N.* v. *Sweden*, Appl.No. 72413/10, 27 June 2013, para. 33; ECtHR, *N.M.B.* v. *Sweden*, Appl. No. 68335/10, 27 June 2013, para. 35. See, ECtHR, *S.H.* v. *the United Kingdom*, Appl.No. 19956/06, 15 June 2010, paras. 70–71, in which the Court found that the applicant would be at risk of ill-treatment if he were to be returned to Bhutan because he was ethnic Nepalese. The Court considered the ethnic Uzbeks as vulnerable group in Kyrgyzstan. By contrast, see *NA.* v. *the UK* (2008), in which the ECtHR acknowledged that the security situation in Sri Lanka deteriorated with corresponding increase in human rights violations. However, the Court agreed with the British authorities' conclusion that these developments did not create a general risk to all Tamils returning to Sri Lanka. ECtHR, *NA.* v. *The United Kingdom*, paras. 124–125.

143   The same can be said with regard to Mandaeans in the southern and central parts of Iraq. ECtHR, *W.H.* v. *Sweden*, Appl.No. 49341/10, 27 March 2014, para. 65.

144   ECtHR, *Jabari* v. *Turkey*, para. 34.

The Court noted that the State party did not dispute the applicant's reliance on reports of AI, which mentioned several cases of women in Iran who were stoned to death because they were found guilty of adultery. Consequently, the Court held that there was a real risk that the applicant would be subjected to ill-treatment if she were to be deported to Iran.[145] The Court has considered women who face criminal proceedings in Iran for having committed adultery to constitute a vulnerable group, susceptible to being subjected to treatment proscribed by Article 3 in that country.

The same approach was adopted in *N. v. Sweden* (2010), which concerned the deportation of an Afghan woman to Afghanistan. In this case, the Court relied on many factors to determine if the applicant, as a woman, would face a real risk if her deportation were to be implemented. The applicant arrived in Sweden with her husband in 2004 and they directly applied for asylum and a residence permit. After the first decision of the Migration Court to refuse their application, and while considering the appeal against this decision in June 2005, the applicant separated from her husband with the intention of obtaining a divorce. She argued before the Migration Court that by separating from him, she had violated Afghan traditions; therefore, she risked serious persecution if expelled to her home country. In addition, by requesting the divorce in Sweden, she had dishonoured both her own and his husband's family; consequently, her family had disowned her and she would risk reprisals from her husband's family. The Migration Court rejected the appeal and her deportation order became enforceable in September 2007. Later, the applicant requested the Swedish authorities to reconsider her case and to stop her expulsion. She based this request, *inter alia*, on the allegation that she had started a relationship with a Swedish man; she therefore risked the death penalty for adultery in Afghanistan. This request was refused because, according to the Swedish authorities, the applicant had not invoked any new circumstances of importance.[146] In her application to the ECtHR, the applicant maintained that if returned to Afghanistan, she would face a real risk of being persecuted, or even sentenced to death by stoning for adultery.[147] The Court observed that women in Afghanistan are at particular risk of ill-treatment if they do not conform to prescribed gender roles attributed to them by society, tradition and the legal system. In this respect, the Court noted the UNHCR's observance that:

---

145   Ibid., paras. 41–42.

146   ECtHR, *N. v. Sweden*, paras. 10, 14, 19 and 21.

147   Ibid., para. 47.

Afghan women, who have adopted a less culturally conservative lifestyle, such as those returning from exile in Iran or Europe, continue to be perceived as transgressing entrenched social and religious norms and may, as a result, be subjected to domestic violence and other forms of punishment ranging from isolation and stigmatisation to honour crimes for those accused of bringing shame to their families, communities or tribes. Actual or perceived transgressions of the social behavioural code include not only social behaviour in the context of a family or a community, but also sexual orientation, the pursuit of a professional career, and mere disagreements as to the way family life is conducted.[148]

Accordingly, the Court noticed that the applicant had violated the established gender norms by residing in Sweden and, more importantly, by attempting to divorce her husband in Sweden, and expressing a clear intention not to resume the marriage. The Court pointed out that in cases like the one before it, expression of the applicant's intention to divorce could arise from the authority's previous refusal to grant asylum on the grounds originally submitted. Thus, an applicant must demonstrate that the intention to divorce is real and genuine. In the case before it, the Court derived such intention from the fact that the applicant had separated from her husband approximately one year after their entrance into Sweden, while considering the appeal against the first refusal of their asylum application. Thereafter, she saw him only once and she tried in vain to divorce him in Sweden.[149]

Then, the Court turned to address whether the applicant would risk reprisal from her husband because of her attempt to divorce and whether she could have recourse to the Afghan authorities in order to seek protection from him. Since the applicant was still formally married, and her husband had informed the Swedish authorities that he opposed her wish to divorce, the Court considered it likely he might decide to resume their life together against her wish if they were deported to Afghanistan, separately or together. The Court noted that, according to several international reports,[150] up to 80% of Afghan women were subjected to domestic violence. The Afghan authorities saw such violence as legitimate and did not prosecute the perpetrators. In addition, most women

---

148   Ibid., para. 55.

149   Ibid., para. 56.

150   The Court referred to the UNHCR Eligibility Guidelines for Assessing the International Protection Needs of Afghan Asylum-Seekers of July 2009 and reports on Afghanistan issued by the USSD, the UK Home Office and HRW. Ibid., paras. 34–37.

subjected to violence did not seek help because they feared police abuse or corruption as well as reprisal by the perpetrators. The discriminatory treatment of women deterred them from seeking justice against their families. Although the Court acknowledged that the circumstances of the case before it did not substantiate that her husband would subject the applicant to such treatment, it asserted that the general risk indicated by the international report could not be ignored.[151]

With regard to the risk of being persecuted or even sentenced to death for adultery, the Court noted that the applicant failed to submit any detailed information thereon and did not even try to justify her failure. However, the applicant's request for divorce and her other actions should, in the Court's view, lead her husband to conclude that she had an extramarital relationship. In this connection, the Court referred to reports indicating that extramarital relationships were considered a serious crime in Afghanistan and offenders could face a lengthy prison sentence and even the death penalty. The Court also considered if it was possible for the applicant to live separated from her husband in Afghanistan. It quoted the UNHCR's July 2009 Guidelines that explained the situation of women who lived without a male partner, including divorced women. According to these Guidelines, single women face limitations on enjoying a normal social life. They mainly suffer from restrictions on their freedom of movement, since many Afghan women are prevented from leaving their family's compound without a burqa and a male companion who is either a husband or a close relative. Moreover, the few women who do enter domestic violence shelters face years of quasi-detention, and this lead many of them to return to their families where they are often subjected to abuse or honour crimes.[152]

Finally, the Court noted that the applicant no longer had a social network to protect her in Afghanistan since she had no contact with her family for almost five years. Taking into account all the above and the special circumstances of this case, the Court concluded that:

> ...there are substantial grounds for believing that if deported to Afghanistan, the applicant faces various cumulative risks of reprisals which fall under Article 3 of the Convention from her husband X, his family, her own family and from the Afghan society. Accordingly, the Court found that the implementation of the applicant's deportation order to Afghanistan would give rise to a violation of Article 3 ECHR.[153]

---

151   Ibid., paras. 57–58.
152   Ibid., paras. 59–60.
153   Ibid., paras. 61–62. See also, ECtHR, *R.H.* v. *Sweden*, para. 70.

The opposite conclusion was reached in *A.A. and Others* v. *Sweden* (2012), which concerned the deportation of six Yemeni nationals. A.A. and her five children, three daughters and two sons, were ordered to be deported from Sweden to Yemen where they allegedly would face a real risk of being the victims of honour-related crime. The first applicant, the mother, argued that she had left her country to protect her daughters from the risk of being forcibly married off by their father X. The eldest daughter, the second applicant, had been forced to marry an old man when she was 14 years old and X had planned to marry off the middle daughter, the fifth applicant, to a much older man when she was only 13 years old. The first applicant claimed that if she returned to Yemen, she would be at risk of being killed by X because she had dishonoured him when she left the country with their daughters without his permission, and that no one would be able to protect them.[154] When it assessed the risk the applicants would face if deported to Yemen, the Court took into account the same factors that had been noted in *N.* v. *Sweden* (2010). The Court observed that the applicants did not provide any explanation why X waited almost three years after the first and fifth applicant's departure from Yemen before having recourse to the court if her husband had been seriously offended by their departure. Furthermore, the allegation that X had made the sons and youngest daughter leave their home after the departure of the mother and middle daughter would indicate that he had no interest in maintaining any relationship with his family members and did not indicate that he would physically injure them. The Court found that there were no substantial grounds for believing that any of the family members, if they were to be deported to Yemen, would be at risk of being subjected to any honour-related crimes by X.[155]

With regard to the fifth applicant, the Court noted that it was not established that X would still consider marrying her off. Likewise, there was no indication that the man intended by X to marry her was still, after five years, interested in becoming her spouse if she retuned. The Court further observed that there was no evidence that the eldest daughter's husband had tried to know her whereabouts or that he had any interest in getting her back. He had further agreed to divorce her if she paid back her dowry. In the light of these facts, the Court concluded that her husband had a limited interest in her.[156] Accordingly, the Court found that none of the female applicants would be at risk of being a victim of reprisal or honour crime.

---

154   ECtHR, *A.A. and Others* v. *Sweden*, Appl.No. 14499/09, 28 June 2012, para. 11.

155   Ibid., para. 81.

156   Ibid., paras. 89 and 91–92.

The Court further acknowledged that the first applicant had showed independence by recourse to a court in Yemen on several occasions, such as to request a divorce from X and to stop the fifth applicant's marriage. She also showed strength by managing to obtain the necessary financial and practical means to depart Yemen. The Court also observed that by returning as a family unit, the applicants would support each other. The female applicants would be accompanied by two adult sons and, thus, they would have a male network and be able to live apart from X and the eldest daughter's husband. They would also have the support of the first applicant's family, especially her brother, who helped them to leave Yemen and still supporte them by sending them various documents. The Court noted that, according to several international sources, there were NGOs in Yemen's capital that operate shelters and provide help and protection for women in vulnerable situations.[157] Against this background, the Court concluded that substantial grounds for believing that the applicants would be exposed to a real risk of being killed or subjected to treatment contrary to Article 3, if deported to Yemen, had not been shown. Therefore their deportation would not be in violation of Article 3.

From the above case-law, it can be inferred that the ECtHR has developed some criteria for its assessment of whether the applicant, as a woman, would face a risk of ill-treatment in the receiving State on the ground of the poor human rights situation of women in this State. Such criteria include, for example, (i) risk of being a victim of honour crime or of being persecuted and sentenced to death for adultery in the receiving State; (ii) the possibility for her to lead a normal life alone there; (iii) the existence of a social network to protect and support her; (iv) the possibility she could seek protection from the authorities or NGOs working in that State.

III.1.2.4   *Irregular Migrants and Asylum Seekers*

In its case-law, the ECtHR held that the dire socio-economic and humanitarian conditions in the receiving State did not necessarily have a bearing, and certainly not a decisive bearing, on the question of whether the person concerned would face a real risk of ill-treatment in that State.[158] However, the Court has not excluded the possibility that the responsibility of the State party under Article 3 ECHR might be engaged in respect of ill-treatment where

---

157   Ibid., paras. 83, 90 and 95. See also, ECtHR, *Izevbekhai and others* v. *Ireland*, paras. 80–81.
158   ECtHR, *Salah Sheekh* v. *The Netherlands*, para. 141; ECtHR, *S.H.H.* v. *the United Kingdom*, para. 74.

an applicant, who was wholly dependent on State support, found himself faced with official indifference in a situation of serious deprivation or want incompatible with human dignity.[159]

Taking into account the vulnerable situation in which irregular migrants and asylum seekers find themselves in some States, the Court has accepted that they could constitute a vulnerable group for the purpose of applying the principle of Non-Refoulement where their return to such States would expose them to treatment contrary to Article 3.

The ECtHR has followed this approach in cases concerned removals of asylum seekers to another EU State under the Dublin Regulation. The ECtHR has considered that Article 3 cannot be interpreted as obliging a State party to provide everyone within its jurisdiction with a home, and that this Article does not entail any general obligation to give refugees financial assistance to enable them to maintain a certain standard of living.[160] However, in *M.S.S.* v. *Belgium and Greece* (2011), the Court attached great importance to the fact that the applicant was an asylum seeker and, as such, "a member of a particularly underprivileged and vulnerable population group in need of special protection".[161] The Court referred to the broad consensus at the international and European level concerning the asylum seekers' need for special protection, as evidenced by the CRS, the UNHCR's activities and the standards set out in the EU Reception Directive.[162] This, in the Court's view, means that, "the obligation to provide accommodation and decent material conditions to impoverished asylum seekers has now entered into positive law".[163] In *M.S.S.* v. *Belgium and Greece* the Court considered that Greece did not have due regard for the applicant's vulnerability as an asylum seeker, and must be held responsible for the delay in considering the applicant's asylum request that had forced him to live for months in a state of the "most extreme poverty, unable to cater for his most basic needs, food, hygiene and a place to live".[164] The Court observed that the situation in which the applicant had found himself was particularly serious and existed on a large scale.[165] Moreover, the Court questioned how the Greek

---

159 ECtHR, *M.S.S.* v. *Belgium and Greece* (GC), para. 253.

160 ECtHR, *M.S.S.* v. *Belgium and Greece* (GC), para. 249.

161 Ibid., para. 251.

162 Ibid., para. 251. See also, ECtHR, *Tarakhel* v. *Switzerland*, para. 97.

163 ECtHR, *M.S.S.* v. *Belgium and Greece* (GC), para. 250.

164 Ibid., paras. 258 and 263.

165 The Court referred to the observations of UNHCR, the European Commissioner for Human Rights and reports of NGOs. Ibid., para. 255.

authorities could have failed to notice or assume that the applicant was home-
less in Athens, in particular that those authorities themselves acknowledged
that there were fewer than 1,000 places in reception centres to accommodate
tens of thousands of asylum seekers.[166] As these facts were well known before
the applicant's transfer to Greece, the ECtHR found that by transferring the
applicant, the Belgian government had knowingly exposed him to conditions
of detention and living conditions that amounted to degrading treatment and
there was a violation of Article 3 ECHR.[167]

In another Non-Refoulement case of *Tarakhel* v. *Switzerland*, which concerned the removal of a married couple with their six minor children to Italy
under the Dublin Regulation, the applicants claimed that their removal would
be in violation of Article 3 as the overall situation of the reception arrangements for asylum seekers in Italy were beset by systemic deficiencies, relating
to: the slowness of the identification procedure, the inadequate capacity of
the reception facilities and the living conditions in the available facilities.
The ECtHR distinguished this case from *M.S.S.* v. *Belgium and Greece* (2011)
because, in the Court's view, the overall situation of asylum seekers in Italy
cannot be compared to that in Greece at the time of its judgment in the *M.S.S.*
case. With regard to the capacity of the accommodation facilities for asylum
seekers, the Court noted the great discrepancy between the number of asylum
applications made in 2013 (according to the Italian government over 14,000)
and the number of places available in the facilities belonging to the SPRAR
network (9,630 places).[168] Concerning the living conditions in the available
facilities, the Court observed that the UNHCR's Recommendations for 2013 had
described a number of problems, however, they did not refer to situations of
widespread violence or insalubrious conditions, and had welcomed the efforts
undertaken by the Italian authorities to improve reception conditions for asylum seekers. The Human Rights Commissioner, in his 2012 report, had noted
the existence of some problems relating to legal aid, care and psychological
assistance in the emergency reception centres, the time taken to identify vulnerable persons and the preservation of family unity during transfers.[169] The
Court also noted that the specific situation of the applicants in the *Tarakhel*
case was different from that of the applicant in the *M.S.S.* case. Unlike the situation of the applicant in the *M.S.S.* case, the applicants in the *Tarakhel* case

---

166   Ibid., paras. 254, 255 and 258.
167   Ibid., paras. 366–368.
168   Sistema di protezione per richiedenti asilo e rifugiati (Protection System for Asylum
      Seekers and Refugees).
169   ECtHR, *Tarakhel* v. *Switzerland*, paras. 108–114.

were immediately taken charge of by the Italian authorities and it took those authorities only ten days to identify the applicants on their arrival in Italy.[170] Hence, the Court held that the approach in the *Tarakhel* case could not be the same as in the *M.S.S* case.[171]

Against these circumstances, the Court concluded that while "the structure and overall situation of the reception arrangements in Italy cannot in themselves act as a bar to all removals of asylum seekers to that country", "the possibility that a significant number of asylum seekers may be left without accommodation or accommodated in overcrowded facilities without any privacy, or even in insalubrious or violent conditions", was not unfounded.[172] The Court reiterated that as a "particularly underprivileged and vulnerable" population group, asylum seekers require "special protection" under Article 3 ECHR. The Court added that the requirement of special protection of asylum seekers was particularly important when the persons concerned were children, given their "specific needs and their extreme vulnerability", even when they were accompanied by their parents. In view of the above findings concerning the situation of the reception system in Italy, the Court considered that the Swiss authorities were obliged to obtain individual guarantees from the Italian authorities that on their arrival in Italy, the applicants would be received in facilities and in conditions adapted to the age of the children, and that the family would be kept together.[173] The Court held that there would be a violation of Article 3 ECHR by the Swiss government, if the applicants were returned to Italy before the government had obtained the guarantees.[174]

---

170   Ibid., para. 117.

171   Ibid., para. 114.

172   ECtHR, *Tarakhel* v. *Switzerland*, para. 115. See also, the ECtHR's admissibility decision in *Mohammed Hussein* v. *the Netherlands and Italy*, in which the Court considered that: "while the general situation and living conditions in Italy of asylum seekers, accepted refugees and aliens who have been granted a residence permit for international protection or humanitarian purposes may disclose some shortcomings, it has not been shown to disclose a systemic failure to provide support or facilities catering for asylum seekers as members of a particularly vulnerable group of people". ECtHR, *Mohammed Hussein* v. *the Netherlands and Italy* (admissibility decision), para. 78; ECtHR, *Mohammadi* v. *Austria*, paras. 68–70.

173   ECtHR, *Tarakhel* v. *Switzerland*, paras. 118–120.

174   Ibid., para. 122. This reading of the *Tarakel* case is supported by the ECtHR's decision in *A.M.E.* v. *the Netherlands* (2015). The Court noted that unlike the applicants in the *Tarakhel* case, who were a family with six minor children, the applicant in the *A.M.E* case was an able young man with no dependents. Therefore, it found that his removal to Italy would not be a violation of Article 3 ECHR. ECtHR, *A.M.E.* v. *the Netherlands* (admissibility decision), Appl. No. 51428/10, 13 January 2015, para. 34.

Accordingly, when the ECtHR considers a Non-Refoulement allegation in a case concerning transfer under the Dublin Regulation, the Court addresses the applicant's specific situation in the light of the overall situation of the reception arrangements for asylum seekers in the receiving State at the relevant time. The Court first examines the receiving State's asylum reception system, taking into account the speed of the identification process, the capacity of the accommodation facilities for asylum seekers and the living conditions in the available facilities, in order to determine whether the deficiencies in this system are systemic. The Court applies the principle of Non-Refoulement under Article 3 ECHR to all Dublin transfers where there are systemic deficiencies in the receiving State's asylum reception system. In other words, the Court considers that, where the deficiencies in the receiving State's asylum reception system are systemic, the asylum seekers, as whole, constitute a vulnerable group susceptible to being ill-treated in this State. Even if the Court does not consider the deficiencies in the receiving State's asylum reception system to be systemic, the applicant still may benefit from protection against refoulement where he belongs to a category that, in the Court's view, has specific needs and is of extreme vulnerability, such as children or families. However, even in this case, no issue under Article 3 ECHR arises if the transfer is carried out after the sending State has obtained individual assurances from the receiving State that the person concerned would be taken charge of in a manner adapted to his specific situation.

The Court also applies Article 3 ECHR to removal of irregular migrants to a State where they, as a group, are vulnerable to ill-treatment. In *Hirsi Jamaa and Others* v. *Italy* (2012), which concerned the interception of migrants' boats by Italy and their return to Libya, the applicants argued that they had been returned to a country where there were sufficient reasons to believe that, as irregular migrants, they would be subjected to ill-treatment.[175] The Court noted that, according to various international reports,[176] no rule governing the protection of refugees and asylum seekers was complied with by Libya at the material time. Any person entering the country illegally was considered as clandestine and no distinction was made between asylum seekers and irregular migrants. The Court added that:

> ...those persons were systematically arrested and detained in conditions that outside visitors, such as delegations from the UNHCR, Human Rights Watch and Amnesty International, could only describe as inhuman.

---

175   ECtHR, *Hirsi Jamaa and Others* v. *Italy* (GC), para. 88.
176   The Court referred to reports by the CPT, HRW, AI, and HRC. Ibid., paras. 35–41.

Many cases of torture, poor hygiene conditions and lack of appropriate medical care were denounced by all the observers. Clandestine migrants were at risk of being returned to their countries of origin at any time and, if they managed to regain their freedom, were subjected to particularly precarious living conditions as a result of their irregular situation. Irregular immigrants, such as the applicants, were destined to occupy a marginal and isolated position in Libyan society, rendering them extremely vulnerable to xenophobic and racist acts.[177]

The Court noted that the same reports clearly showed that clandestine migrants who disembarked in Libya after they had been intercepted by Italy on the high seas, like the applicants, had been exposed to those risks.[178] The Court found substantial grounds for believing that there had been a real risk that the applicants, as irregular migrants, would be subjected to ill-treatment in Libya. By transferring the applicants to Libya, the Italian authorities had exposed them to treatment contrary to Article 3 ECHR. The Court made it clear that the existence of a large number of irregular migrants in Libya who found themselves in a similar situation did not make the risk any less for an individual, when it is considered to be sufficiently real and probable.[179] Hence, irregular migrants were considered to be vulnerable group in Libya, and their return to this State would be in breach of Article 3 ECHR.

III.1.3   Further Special Distinguishing Features

The protection against refoulement under Article 3 ECHR enters into play where an applicant can establish that there is a situation of general violence in the receiving State that is intense enough to create a real risk of ill-treatment to all returnees to that State, or that the applicant is a member of a vulnerable group that is systematically exposed to ill-treatment in that State. Where none of these factors are established, it is still possible for an applicant to benefit from the protection against refoulement if he demonstrates the existence of further special distinguishing features in his case, which place him at a real risk of ill-treatment contrary to Article 3. In the Court's view, the requirement to demonstrate the existence of further special distinguishing features would not render illusory the protection afforded by Article 3. The Court has repeatedly emphasised that:

---

177   Ibid., para. 125.
178   Ibid., para. 126.
179   Ibid., paras. 136–137.

...the assessment of whether there is a real risk must be made on the basis of all relevant factors which may increase the risk of ill-treatment. [...], due regard should also be given to the possibility that a number of individual factors may not, when considered separately, constitute a real risk; but when taken cumulatively and when considered in a situation of general violence and heightened security, the same factors may give rise to a real risk. Both the need to consider all relevant factors cumulatively and the need to give appropriate weight to the general situation in the country of destination derive from the obligation to consider all the relevant circumstances of the case.[180]

Thus, the assessment of whether the applicant would be at a real risk of ill-treatment in the country of destination must be made on a case-by-case basis and all relevant factors that may increase the risk of ill-treatment must be considered.[181]

While these factors differ from case to case, it seems that the Court has, in principle, agreed to assess individual risk on the basis of a list of risk factors where returnees challenge their removal to a specific country on similar grounds. This approach was adopted in cases that concerned expulsion of ethnic Tamils to Sri Lanka. The applicants argued that they would be at risk of ill-treatment by Sri Lankan authorities that were making an effort to combat the LTTE.[182] The Court found that there was not a general risk of ill-treatment for ethnic Tamils who returned to Sri Lanka. The protection against refoulement under Article 3 ECHR enters into play only when an applicant can establish that there are serious reasons to believe that he would be of sufficient interest to the Sri Lankan authorities to warrant his detention and interrogation upon return.[183] The Court observed that it must assess the risk of ill-treatment for applicants in light of all relevant factors that may increase this risk. According to the Court, those relevant factors include but are not limited to:

---

180   ECtHR, *NA.* v. *The United Kingdom*, para. 130; ECtHR, *S.S. and Others* v. *Denmark*, para 89.

181   Ibid., para. 95.

182   This approach was adopted for the first time in the case of *NA.* v. *The United Kingdom* (2008). The Court considered that: "it is in principle legitimate, when assessing the individual risk to returnees, to carry out the assessment on the basis of the list of 'risk factors', which the domestic authorities, with the benefit of direct access to objective information and expert evidence, had drawn up". The Court observed that the UKAIT had clearly indicated that these risk factors were not intended to be a check list or exhaustive. ECtHR, *NA.* v. *The United Kingdom*, para. 129. See also, ECtHR, *N.S.* v. *Denmark*, para. 77.

183   ECtHR, *NA.* v. *The United Kingdom*, para. 133; ECtHR, *T.N.* v. *Denmark*, Appl. No. 20594/08, 20 January 2011, para. 89.

... a previous record as a suspected or actual LTTE member; a previous criminal record and/or outstanding arrest warrant; bail jumping and/or escaping from custody; having signed a confession or similar document; having been asked by the security forces to become an informer; the presence of scarring; return from London or other centre of LTTE fundraising; illegal departure from Sri Lanka; lack of an ID card or other documentation; having made an asylum claim abroad; and having relatives in the LTTE. The Court would also reiterate that due regard must continue to be given to the possibility that a number of individual factors may not, when considered separately, constitute a real risk, but may do so when taken cumulatively [...] bearing in mind any heightened security measures that may be in place as a result of any increase in the general situation in Sri Lanka.[184]

The Court found, in *NA. v. The UK* (2008), that the applicant's deportation from the UK to Sri Lanka would be contrary to Article 3. It specifically noted that the applicant left Sri Lanka clandestinely after he had been arrested and detained by the army on six occasions because they suspected him of involvement with LTTE. During at least one of those periods of detention he was subjected to ill-treatment and his legs bore scars as a result of beatings with batons. The fact that he had been photographed and his fingerprints had been taken during his most recent detention indicated that there was a record of his detention.[185]

In contrast, the Court found, in several cases concerning deportation of Tamils from Denmark to Sri Lanka, that implementation of the deportation order would not violate Article 3. The Court's decisions were based on various factors, including the age and gender of the applicant,[186] the fact that he left the country lawfully using a passport issued by the Sri Lankan authorities without facing any problem,[187] that he was not a member of LTTE,[188] that there was no indication that the Sri Lankan authorities were informed that he had made an asylum application abroad,[189] that the case disclosed no elements that could suggest that Sri Lankan authorities had any suspicion of his past

---

184   ECtHR, *NA. v. The United Kingdom*, para. 130; ECtHR, *N.S. v. Denmark*, para. 83.

185   ECtHR, *P.K. v. Denmark*, Appl. No. 54705/08, 20 January 2011, para. 96; ECtHR, *T.N. and S.N v. Denmark*, Appl. No. 36517/08, 20 January 2011, para. 114.

186   The applicant in *T.N. v. Denmark* (2011) was a woman and thirty-eight years old ECtHR, *T.N. v. Denmark*, paras. 99 and 107. See also, ECtHR, *T.N. and S. N v. Denmark*, para. 116.

187   ECtHR, *N.S. v. Denmark*, para. 89; ECtHR, *P.K. v. Denmark*, para. 88; ECtHR, *T.N. and S. N v. Denmark*, para. 105; ECtHR, *S.S. and Others v. Denmark*, para. 113.

188   ECtHR, *N.S. v. Denmark*, para. 92.

189   Ibid., para. 95; ECtHR, *P.K. v. Denmark*, para. 97.

as a soldier with the LTTE,[190] that he would not be deported from a location considered to be a centre of LTTE fundraising,[191] that there was no indication he had ever been recorded by Sri Lankan authorities in connection with arrest or detention, that there was no indication that photographs, fingerprints or other means of identification had been stored by the authorities in order to enable them to identify him upon return,[192] and that he was never arrested or detained or had any problems with the Sri Lankan authorities.[193]

The existence of further special distinguishing features in an applicant's case, which would place him at real risk of ill-treatment, must be determined in the light of all relevant factors. It is up to the Court to decide whether the factors in the case before it, taken separately or cumulatively, are sufficient to foresee that the applicant, if removed, would be at real risk in the country of destination. As noted above, the factors that must be taken into account to assess whether there are special distinguishing features in an applicant's case differ from case to case. It is impossible to give an overview of every factor that the Court takes into account in Non-Refoulement cases, so we consider some examples of such factors in the following subsections.

III.1.3.1   *Previous Activities*

The applicant's previous activities in the receiving State could indicate that the applicant would be at risk of ill-treatment if he were to be returned there. The ECtHR has assessed whether or not an applicant still attracts negative attention in the receiving State because of his previous activities there, in the light of the facts of each case. In *Bajsultanov* v. *Austria* (2012), the Court observed that while the applicant had supported the Chechen fighters during the first war in Chechnya, he did not take part in the second war. A considerable time had passed since the first Chechen war, and even active participants in the first war had not been at risk of being persecuted by the present Chechen authorities. Accordingly, the Court did not consider the applicant's past activities as evidence that he would be at risk of ill-treatment if he were to be expelled to Russia.[194]

In *N.* v. *Finland* (2005), the Court took into account the nature and the importance of the applicant's previous activities. The applicant in this case argued

---

190   ECtHR, *T.N.* v. *Denmark*, para. 102.

191   ECtHR, *N.S.* v. *Denmark*, para. 95; ECtHR, *P.K.* v. *Denmark*, para. 97.

192   Ibid., para. 95; ECtHR, *T.N.* v. *Denmark*, para. 105; ECtHR, *T.N. and S.N* v. *Denmark*, para. 113.

193   ECtHR, *T.N.* v. *Denmark*, para. 102.

194   ECtHR, *Bajsultanov* v. *Austria*, Appl.No. 54131/10, 12 June 2012, para. 65; ECtHR, *T.A.* v. *Sweden*, para. 47.

that his expulsion to the DRC would expose him to a risk of ill-treatment because he had worked in the special force that protected former President Mobutu (the DSP), because of his close connections with the former President's family, and because he was of the same ethnic origin as President Mobutu. Since the applicant had left the DSP eight years earlier, the Court could not exclude that the current DRC authorities' interest in detaining and ill-treating him because of his past activities may have diminished with the passage of time. The Court gave some importance to the fact that the applicant had not had a direct connection with President Mobutu and did not have high military rank when he was forced to leave the country. The Court added that, with regards to former members of the Zairian Armed Forces, other factors such as the soldier's ethnicity and his connection to influential persons might also be important when it considered the risk he might face in the DRC. The Court noted that although a number of Mobutu supporters returned voluntarily to the DRC in the recent years, this fact did not have any decisive weight in its assessment of the risk that faced the applicant if he were forcibly returned there. Decisive weight was given to the facts that the applicant had worked as an infiltrator and informant in President Mobutu's special protection force, and that he had been reporting directly to very senior-ranking officers close to the former President. The Court therefore found, on account of those activities, that he would run a substantial risk of ill-treatment, if expelled to the DRC.[195] The Court added that the risk that the applicant would face might not necessarily emanate from the authorities, but from relatives of dissidents who might seek revenge on him because of his past activities in the service of President Mobutu. The Court took into account that the applicant had worked in the DSP and had belonged to the President Mobutu's inner circle, in addition to participating in various events during which dissidents deemed as a threat to the President were singled out for harassment, detention and possibly execution. Against this background, the Court held that the applicant's situation could be worse than that of most other former Mobutu supporters.[196] Though several years had elapsed since the applicant left his country, the Court found that he would still be at risk of ill-treatment because of the importance and nature of his previous activities there.

By contrast, the Court noted in *S.F. and others* v. *Sweden* (2012) that the applicant had been active with the Democratic Party of Iranian Kurdistan only at a very low political level, and that considerable time elapsed since his arrest

---

195   ECtHR, *N.* v. *Finland*, paras. 161–162.

196   Ibid., paras. 163–164. Compare with the Court's assessment of the applicant's previous activities in ECtHR, *F.H.* v. *Sweden*, paras. 96–104.

in 2003. After his release, he had been able to continue his normal work and life and there was no indication that he had attracted any further attention from the Iranian authorities. Consequently, the Court did not find that the applicant would be at a real risk of ill-treatment on the ground of his previous political activities there if he was deported to Iran.[197]

The Court has also noted the fact that the applicant left his country lawfully, holding his authentic passport as an indication that his previous activities do not attract the negative attention of the authorities of that country. In *A.* v. The *Netherlands* (2010), the applicant argued that, since 1988, he had been an active member in a clandestine opposition group. This group held regular meetings, distributed leaflets and informed people about the Libyan regime by, *inter alia,* distributing publications by the Libyan resistance abroad. The Court noted that, as submitted by the applicant, while the group concerned had started having problems with the Libyan regime in late 1992 or early 1993, he had not faced any problems with the Libyan authorities when he left Libya at the end of 1994 via an official border crossing-point, and he had used his own authentic passport. In light of the strict control to which the persons leaving or entering Libya were subjected by border control officials, the Court found that the applicant had not established that he had attracted the negative attention of the Libyan authorities because of his alleged opposition activities before his departure.[198]

III.1.3.2   *Past Ill-treatment*
The fact that the applicant was previously subjected to ill-treatment in the proposed country of destination has been considered in several refoulement cases as a "special distinguishing feature" that would place him at real risk of being ill-treated again if he were to be returned. The applicant must establish that he was personally targeted with the previous ill-treatment, regardless of whether that ill-treatment was inflicted by public officers or non-State actors.[199] In *T.K.H.* v. *Sweden* (2013), the Court refused to take into account the past ill-treatment to which the applicant had subjected as a result of attacks on the military bases where he was working. The Court noted that although those attacks had inflicted serious injuries on the applicant, they must be seen

---

197   ECtHR, *S.F. and others* v. *Sweden*, para. 67. See also, ECtHR, *Venkadjalasarma* v. *The Netherlands*, para. 65; ECtHR, *Thampibillai* v. *The Netherlands*, para. 63.

198   ECtHR, *A.* v. *The Netherlands*, paras. 8 and 147. See, ECtHR, *T.N. and S.N* v. *Denmark*, para. 105.

199   See, ECtHR, *Auad* v. *Bulgaria*.

as events that affected him solely because he was on duty at those places, and not as attacks directed at him personally.[200]

The applicant's allegation of previous experience of ill-treatment must be supported by an examination report from a medical expert. In *Yakubov* v. *Russia* (2011),[201] the Court pointed out that the applicant had repeatedly told the Russian authorities that he had already been subjected to ill-treatment at the hands of the Uzbek authorities in connection with his presumed membership in HT. The applicant presented a detailed description of those alleged past experiences of ill-treatment, claiming that his spine was injured as a result of that experience. He submitted a medical certificate indicating that he suffered from the after-effects of compression fractures of several vertebrae. The Court observed that, although the certificate contained no indication of the date the injuries had been inflicted, it gave further credence to the applicant's otherwise coherent submission concerning his alleged past experience of ill-treatment by the Uzbek authorities, which could not be discarded as completely without foundation.[202]

In *R.C.* v. *Sweden* (2010), the applicant contended that his expulsion to Iran would expose him to a real risk of being arrested, tortured and perhaps even executed because of his previous activities as a critic of the Iranian regime, for which he had been imprisoned and tortured.[203] Upon request by the ECtHR, the applicant had submitted a forensic medical report dated 14 November 2008.[204] The Court accepted the general conclusion of this report, which found that the applicant's injuries, to a large extent, were consistent with having been inflicted on him by other persons and in the manner in which he described, thereby strongly indicating that he was a victim of torture. The Court concluded that the medical evidence corroborated the applicant's story. The Court further observed that, according to the latest information available on Iran, any person who opposed the current Iranian regime in any way was at risk of being detained and ill-treated or tortured. The Court took into account the applicant's submission that he had been arrested with many others when he

---

200   ECtHR, *T.K.H.* v. *Sweden*, para. 50.

201   In this case, the Court found that the applicant, who was accused of politically motivated crime, would be at risk of ill-treatment in Uzbekistan due to his membership of a vulnerable group. The Court noted that although in such circumstances it will normally not insist that the applicant show the existence of further special distinguishing features, it was nonetheless significant to point out that the applicant had repeatedly submitted that he had already been subjected to ill-treatment at the hands of the Uzbek authorities.

202   ECtHR, *Yakubov* v. *Russia*, paras. 89–90. See also, ECtHR, *Rustamov* v. *Russia*, para. 128.

203   ECtHR, *R.C.* v. *Sweden*, Appl.No. 41827/07, 9 March 2010, para. 38.

204   Ibid., para. 23.

had participated in a demonstration against the regime in 2001 and that the torture to which he was subjected occurred in the months following his arrest. The Court considered that the applicant's account to be consistent with the latest information available from independent sources concerning Iran.[205] The Court noted that:

> Having regard to its finding that the applicant has discharged the burden of proving that he has already been tortured, the Court considers that the onus rests with the State to dispel any doubts about the risk of his being subjected again to treatment contrary to Article 3 in the event that his expulsion proceeds.[206]

The ECtHR has established a presumption that, where an applicant in a Non-Refoulement case substantiates his claim that he was previously subjected to treatment proscribed by Article 3 ECHR in the proposed receiving State, it is the responsibility of the State party concerned to demonstrate that the applicant would not be at risk of being subjected to the same treatment if returned there.[207]

The fact that the person concerned was previously ill-treated during detention in the proposed receiving State is not sufficient in itself to conclude that there is a real risk of being ill-treated again. This claim must be supported by evidence about the situation in that State, as well as the applicant's circumstances at the time the case is under consideration. In *Hilal* v. *The UK* (2001), which concerned the expulsion of an active member of an opposition party in Tanzania (the Civic United Front [CUF]) from the UK to Tanzania, the fact that the applicant had been subjected to past ill-treatment was one of the factors that lead the Court to conclude that the applicant's expulsion would violate Article 3. The Court observed that he had been arrested and detained because of his membership in the CUF, and that he had been ill-treated during detention by, *inter alia*, being suspended upside down, which caused him to severely haemorrhage through the nose. The Court noted that the latest reports referred to continuing problems faced by CUF members. Consequently, the Court concluded that the applicant would be at risk of being detained and ill-treated if returned to Zanzibar.[208]

---

205   Ibid., paras. 53–54.
206   Ibid., para. 55. See also, ECtHR, *R.J.* v. *France*, para. 42.
207   ECtHR, *I.* v. *Sweden*, Appl.No. 61204/09, 5 September 2013, para. 62.
208   ECtHR, *Hilal* v. *the United Kingdom*, para. 64–66.

By contrast, in *Venkadjalasarma v. The Netherlands* (2004), the Court noted that although it did not dispute that the applicant had been detained, tortured and ill-treated by the Sri Lankan army on suspicion of being an LTTE supporter, he was released without charge after two days. He was then issued the travel pass he had requested. The Court concluded that the army was not aware of his activities for the LTTE and consequently they would not have an interest in him.[209] In *Nnyanzi v. The UK* (2008), the Court took into account the fact that the applicant, who had fled from Uganda to Kenya after her detention for one day in 1987, voluntarily returned to her home country in January 1997, hoping that the situation had improved. The Court saw this as evidence of the limited negative mental effects of the past detention on the applicant.[210]

III.1.3.3   *Factors Relating to the Applicant's Family Circumstances*
In its assessment of whether the applicant would be at a real risk of ill-treatment in the receiving State, the Court has taken into account allegations that relate to his family circumstances. In *I.K. v. Austria* (2013), the Court noted that the triggering event of the applicant's and his mother's flight from Russia, namely the applicant's father's role in the Chechen security services and his murder in 2001, had already been considered credible and convincing in his mother's asylum proceedings in Austria, and thus she had been awarded the status of a recognised refugee in 2009. The Court observed that there was no indication in the documents before it that the applicant would be at a lesser risk of persecution upon return to Russia than his mother, because of his relationship to his father. The Court also found that the time elapsed since his mother had been awarded refugee status was not long enough to lead it to automatically conclude the contrary. The Court held that there was a strong indication that the applicant would be at a real risk of being subjected to ill-treatment if removed to Russia.[211]

The question that members of the applicant's family were subjected to ill-treatment in the receiving State has been addressed in several Non-Refoulement cases.[212] After finding that the applicant did not belong to any

---

209   ECtHR, *Venkadjalasarma v. The Netherlands*, para. 65.

210   ECtHR, *Nnyanzi v. the United Kingdom*, para. 58.

211   ECtHR, *I.K. v. Austria*, Appl.No. 2964/12, 28 March 2013, paras. 77–79.

212   In *Hilal v. the UK* (2001), the Court grounded its conclusion that the applicant's deportation to Tanzania would breach Article 3 on, *inter alia*, the fact that the applicant's brother, who was like the applicant a CUF supporter, had been detained in the prison and then he was taken from the prison to hospital where he died. The Court found this supported the applicant's allegation that his brother had been ill-treated in prison. ECtHR, *Hilal v. the United Kingdom*, para. 64.

vulnerable group in the receiving State, the Court, in a number of cases, addressed the question of whether there was any evidence that members of the applicant's family were previously persecuted or ill-treated in that State.[213] In *Garayev* v. *Azerbaijan* (2010), which concerned the extradition of a person suspected of non-political crime to Uzbekistan, the Court gave due weight to the fact that the applicant's family members had been previously arrested and subjected to ill-treatment for the same crime. In this case the applicant and his entire family were arrested in Uzbekistan on suspicion of killing six persons and mutilating their corpses. During detention, the applicant and all his family members had been continuously tortured and ill-treated in order to extract confessions from them. Then, they were all released due to lack of evidence, with the exception of the applicant's mother. The applicant was charged with this crime along with his mother, father and elder brother, who were convicted and sentenced to imprisonment. The applicant left Uzbekistan and entered Azerbaijan legally and lived there without a residence permit. On the basis of a search warrant issued by the Uzbek authorities, the Azerbaijani police arrested the applicant and his extradition to Uzbekistan was ordered. The ECtHR did not lose sight of the fact that the applicant's family had been arrested and ill-treated there, and that the applicant himself had been previously ill-treated. Consequently, the Court found that although the applicant was wanted for a non-political crime, there were sufficient reasons to fear that he, as a criminal suspect in such circumstances, would be at serious risk of being subjected to ill-treatment.[214]

In contrast, the fact that an applicant's family lives in the country of destination without problems with the authorities is an indication that the applicant would not be at a real risk of ill-treatment if deported to that country. In *Bajsultanov* v. *Austria* (2012), which concerned the expulsion to Russia of a Russian national of Chechen origin who had supported the Chechen fighters during the first war in Chechnya, the Court noted that the applicant's parents and six siblings continued to live in Chechnya after his departure and the applicant acknowledged that they did not report any harassment or abusive behaviour by local or federal security forces in that region. The Court added that since the applicant had kept in regular telephone contact with his father, he would have known if his relatives in Chechnya suffered acts of retribution. Taking into account the repeatedly reported practice of abuse of relatives of alleged

---

213 ECtHR, *Shakurov* v. *Russia*, para. 137; ECtHR, *Kozhayev* v. *Russia*, para. 91.
214 ECtHR, *Garayev* v. *Azerbaijan*, Appl.No. 53688/08, 10 June 2010, paras. 9–11 and 72.

rebels or supporters and sympathisers, the Court held that the applicant did not seem belong to either of these groups.[215]

The argument that an applicant would be at a real risk of being ill-treated in the receiving State because of the activities of a member of his family has been also raised in several Non-Refoulement cases. In *NA*. v. *The UK* (2008), the Court gave little weight to the fact that the applicant's brother was a member of the LTTE. The Court noted that the applicant provided no details of the involvement of his brother in the LTTE or his current whereabouts.[216] In *J.H.* v. *The UK* (2011), the applicant argued that his expulsion to Afghanistan would expose him to a real risk of proscribed treatment because of his father's high profile in Afghanistan as a member of the PDPA government until its overthrow in 1992. The Court noted that the applicant never claimed to have any personal political involvement or an individual profile in Afghanistan, aside from that based on his relationship with his father, nor had he a role in or knowledge of his father's activities.[217] The Court noted that the applicant failed to adduce any evidence to support his claim that his father was still politically active and/or continued to have a profile in Afghanistan after the applicant's departure from the country to Russia in 1992. The Court deemed it critical that recent evidence did not indicate that family members of PDPA members would be at risk in Afghanistan in the light of the circumstances prevailing there. Accordingly, the Court was not persuaded that the applicant, who was not a PDPA member but merely a family member of a former PDPA member who had left Afghanistan many years ago, demonstrated that he would be at risk upon return.[218]

III.1.4   UNHCR's Assessment of the Case

The Court has distinguished reports that constitute general assessments from those that include specific assessments. It has been inclined to attach less weight to the general assessments than the specific assessment. Accordingly, in several Non-Refoulement cases the ECtHR has taken into account the UNHCR's conclusions on the applicant's claim of the risk he would face if he were to be removed to the proposed receiving State. The Court in *Jabari* v. *Turkey* (2000) gave due weight to the fact that the UNHCR had found that the applicant had a well-founded fear of persecution. Consequently, it granted her refugee status. The Court justified this approach by noting that the UNHCR

---

215   ECtHR, *Bajsultanov* v. *Austria*, para. 66; ECtHR, *F.G.* v. *Sweden*, Appl.No. 43611/11, 16 January 2014, para. 40.

216   ECtHR, *NA*. v. *The United Kingdom*.

217   ECtHR, *J.H.* v. *the United Kingdom*, paras. 38–57.

218   Ibid., para. 61–66. See also, ECtHR, *Nnyanzi* v. *the United Kingdom*, para. 60–64.

had interviewed the applicant and had the opportunity to test the credibility of her fears and the veracity of her account of the circumstances in her home country.[219] The same approach was followed in *Yakubov* v. *Russia* (2012). In this case, the Court found that the applicant would be at risk of ill-treatment in Uzbekistan because he was a member of a vulnerable group. The Court noted that in such circumstances it would not normally insist that the applicant show that further special distinguishing features existed, but it found it to be highly significant that the UNHCR, after having interviewed the applicant and carefully examining his case, concluded that he was eligible for international protection under its mandate.[220]

The Court has often referred to the UNHCR's conclusion on the claim of the person concerned in order to support, in combination with other evidence, its own conclusion in the case before it. However, in some cases, the Court has based its decision mainly on the UNHCR's conclusion on the applicant's claim without conducting its own assessment. For example, in *Z.N.S.* v. *Turkey* (2010), the applicant argued that her expulsion to Iran, if carried out, would expose her to a risk of death or ill-treatment on the grounds that she had been involved in anti-regime activities in Iran, and because she had converted to Christianity, a fact known to the Iranian authorities. The applicant stressed that she was recognised as a refugee by the UNHCR.[221] The Court made no assessment of the applicant's arguments. It merely noted that due weight must be given to the UNHCR's conclusion on the applicant's claim about the risk she would face if she were to be deported to Iran. The Court observed that, after an interview with the applicant, the UNHCR had found that she was at risk of being subjected to persecution in her country of origin.[222] Then, the Court stated that:

> In the light of the UNHCR's assessment, the Court finds that there are substantial grounds for accepting that the applicant risks a violation of her right under Article 3, on account of her religion, if returned to Iran.[223]

Although this approach is reasonable, the ECtHR should keep in mind that the material time for assessing the risk is the time at which the Court considers

---

219   ECtHR, *Jabari* v. *Turkey*, para. 41.

220   ECtHR, *Yakubov* v. *Russia*, paras. 89–91. See, ECtHR, NA. v. *The United Kingdom*, para. 122.

221   ECtHR, *Z.N.S.* v. *Turkey*, para. 46.

222   Ibid., para. 48.

223   Ibid., para. 49. See also, ECtHR, *Dbouba* v. *Turkey*, paras. 42–43; ECtHR, *M.B. and Others* v. *Turkey*, Appl.No. 36009/08, 15 June 2010, paras. 33–34.

the case, or the date of the applicant's removal. Since the UNHCR may have interviewed the applicant and assessed his claim a long time ago and circumstances may have changed since then,[224] the Court should assess the situation at the material time to ensure that no considerable changes have taken place.[225] The UNHCR examines the case in order to determine if the person concerned should be recognised as a refugee under the CSR. The Court should make its own assessment of the case under the ECHR.

III.1.5   Credibility of the Applicant

The credibility of an applicant's statements and documents has to be taken into account in order to assess the existence of a real risk that he will be subjected to ill-treatment in the receiving State. Since the initial burden of proof lies on the applicant to demonstrate the existence of such risk, the respondent State may argue that the applicant's statements and documents lack credibility. The ECtHR has asserted that it must proceed, as far as possible, with an assessment of the general credibility of the statements made by the applicant to the national authorities of the respondent State and during the proceedings before the Court itself.[226] The Court has repeatedly acknowledged that:

> ...owing to the special situation in which asylum seekers often find themselves, it is frequently necessary to give them the benefit of the doubt when it comes to assessing the credibility of their statements and the documents submitted in support thereof. However, when information is presented which gives strong reasons to question the veracity of an asylum seeker's submissions, the individual must provide a satisfactory explanation for the alleged discrepancies.[227]

The Court has recognised that it is often difficult to establish the pertinent facts in the Non-Refoulement cases with precision. As a general principle, national authorities are best placed to assess the facts of the cases and the

---

224   While the applicant in *Z.N.S.* v. *Turkey* was recognised as a refugee by the UNHCR on 29 December 2008, the ECtHR considered her applicant on 15 December 2009. ECtHR, *Z.N.S.* v. *Turkey*.

225   In *Ahmed* v. *Austria* (1996), the Court carried out its own assessment of the case and found that the situation did not change after the Austrian Minister of the Interior had granted the applicant the refugee status in 1992. ECtHR, *Ahmed* v. *Austria*.

226   ECtHR, *Said* v. *The Netherlands*, para. 50; ECtHR, *M.E.* v. *Sweden*, Appl.No. 71398/12, 26 June 2014, para. 83.

227   ECtHR, *N.* v. *Sweden*, para. 53.

general credibility of the applicant's story.[228] In *Samina* v. *Sweden* (2011), which concerned the deportation of a Pakistani national to Pakistan, the ECtHR noted that during the proceedings before the national authorities, the applicant had been interviewed and assisted by an appointed counsel and an adviser. And after a thorough examination of her case by the national authorities, they found she had given a rather vague and unclear account, and that the written evidence submitted was of low evidential value. The ECtHR observed that:

> The national authorities had the benefit of seeing, hearing and questioning the applicant in person, of assessing directly the information and documents submitted by her and of initiating an examination of the veracity of the documents submitted, if that were found necessary.[229]

Consequently, the Court found no reason to conclude that the decision of the national authorities was inadequate or arbitrary. The Court added that there was no indication that the assessment made by national authorities had been insufficiently supported by relevant materials, or that these authorities were wrong in concluding that there were no substantial grounds for believing that the applicant, if deported, would be of interest to the Pakistani authorities or religious fundamentalists.[230]

Where the Court finds that the national authorities' assessment of the general credibility of the applicant is insufficiently supported or wrong, it conducts its own assessment of his credibility. In *R.C.* v. *Sweden* (2010), the Swedish authorities argued that there were serious reasons to question the applicant's credibility since he gave contradictory statements about how he had escaped from prison.[231] The ECtHR did not agree with the government's conclusion that the information provided by the applicant undermined his general credibility. It noted that he consistently maintained that he had participated in demonstrations against the Iranian regime and that, following a demonstration in July 2001, he had been arrested and tortured by the Iranian authorities. The Court found that:

> ...the applicant's basic story was consistent throughout the proceedings and that notwithstanding some uncertain aspects, such as his account as

---

228   ECtHR, *S.F. and others* v. *Sweden*, para. 66.
229   ECtHR, *Samina* v. *Sweden*, Appl.No. *55463/09*, 20 October 2011, para. 54.
230   Ibid., paras. 54–55. See also, ECtHR, *J.H.* v. *the United Kingdom*, paras. 58–59.
231   ECtHR, *R.C.* v. *Sweden*, para. 44.

to how he escaped from prison, such uncertainties do not undermine the overall credibility of his story.[232]

The applicant's credibility may be seriously undermined by various factors. For example, in the admissibility decision in the case of *Eric Nsuwayezu* v. *Sweden* (2009), the Court considered the applicant's general credibility to have been negatively affected because he had lied about his identity and mode of travel to the Swedish authorities upon arrival in Sweden. He gave the authorities a false name and date of birth and submitted a forged identity card. Furthermore, he alleged that he had travelled with a fake passport and without knowing the travel route when, in fact, he had travelled legally to France on his own passport and with a valid entry visa.[233]

Another factor that may negatively affect the applicant's credibility is an unproblematic visit to the proposed receiving State. The Court in *Al Hamdani* v. *BH* (2012) noted that the applicant had visited Iraq twice since the change of regime. During these visits, the applicant moved freely, despite the fact that the security situation in Iraq was much more dangerous during his visits than at the time, the Court considered the case. Against this background, the Court found that the applicant's complaint under Article 3 was manifestly ill-founded.[234]

Moreover, an applicant's delay in submitting statements and documents may cast doubt on its credibility. In the admissibility decision of *A.A.* v. *Sweden* (2018), the Court noted that the applicant did not mention he was threatened by the LLTE until after his asylum application had been refused. More than two years later, he submitted some documents concerning the threats he had allegedly received from the LLTE. The ECtHR agreed with the national authorities' observations that the applicant lacked credibility.[235] In another refoulement case of *H.N.* v. *Sweden* (2012), the Court noted that the applicant's claims

---

232   Ibid., para. 52. See also, ECtHR, *S.F. and others* v. *Sweden*, para. 66. This approach is consistent with the UNHCR's approach that "it is hardly possible for a refugee to 'prove' every part of his case and, indeed, if this were a requirement the majority of refugees would not be recognized. It is therefore frequently necessary to give the applicant the benefit of the doubt". UNHCR, Handbook on Procedures and Criteria for Determining Refugee Status under the 1951 Convention and the 1967 Protocol relating to the Status of Refugees, UN. Doc. HCR/IP/4/Eng/REV.1, 1992, para. 203. By contrast, see, ECtHR, *D.N.W.* v. *Sweden*, Appl. No. 29946/10, 6 December 2012.

233   ECtHR, *Eric Nsuwayezu* v. *Sweden* (admissibility decision), Appl.No. 15009/09, 8 December 2009, para. 30.

234   ECtHR, *Al Hamdani* v. *Bosnia and Herzegovina*, paras. 50–52.

235   ECtHR, *A.A.* v. *Sweden* (admissibility decision), Appl.No. 8594/04, 2 September 2008, para. 67. See, ECtHR, *Cruz Varas and Others* v. *Sweden*, para. 78; ECtHR, *Nasimi* v. *Sweden*

had escalated considerably during the domestic proceedings. It was not until after the original asylum proceedings had been finalised that the applicant stated that he had been the deputy head of the youth section of MIPAREC (*Ministère pour la Paix et la Reconsiliation*).[236] At that point, he also claimed for the first time that the FNL group tried to kill him several times because he refused to join it, and that only two years after his four siblings were abducted had he been informed that they had been found murdered. The Court added if he had experienced the alleged events, it would be reasonable to assume that he could provide specific details rather than vague statements. The Court found it noteworthy that, although the applicant arrived in Sweden about two weeks after he had escaped from prison, where he was allegedly tortured, he did not attempt to draw the Swedish migration authorities' attention to possible injuries, or seek an initial health examination. Consequently, the Court agreed with the Swedish authorities that the applicant had a credibility problem.[237]

III.1.6   Risk *sur Place*

Since the material time for assessing the risk is the time of the Court's consideration of the case, or the applicant's removal, the applicant is not required to have been at a real risk when he left his country of origin in order for the principle of Non-Refoulement to apply under Article 3. Even if the person concerned left his country legally and he was not at risk of ill-treatment at the time of leaving, he can benefit from the protection against refoulement as long as he is at a real risk at the material time. Where reasons give rise to the risk after the person concerned has departed his country of origin, the risk is *sur place*. The concept of a risk *sur place* is well known in the context of the CSR. The UNHCR defines the refugee *sur place* as "a person who was not a refugee when he left his country, but who becomes a refugee at a later date" due to circumstances that arise in his country of origin during his absence, or as a result of his own activities abroad.[238] The same approach has been taken by the ECtHR when it applies Article 3 in Non-Refoulement cases. The Court has applied the concept of a risk *sur place* in cases where the risk emanates from the applicant's own activities in his country of residence as well as where

---

(admissibility decision), Appl.No. 38865/02, 16 March 2004; ECtHR, *I.N.* v. *Sweden* (admissibility decision), Appl. No. 1334/09, 15 September 2009, para. 33.

236   A Christian organisation working for peace and reconciliation in Burundi. ECtHR, *H.N.* v. *Sweden*, Appl.No. 30720/09, 15 May 2012, para. 13.

237   Ibid., para. 40.

238   UNHCR, Handbook on Procedures and Criteria for Determining Refugee Status under the 1951 Convention and the 1967 Protocol relating to the Status of Refugees, paras. 94–96.

it results from sudden changes occurring in the applicant's country of origin after his departure.

The applicant's action abroad could take several forms, including expressing his political views, applying for asylum, or converting to a religion when such activities are not tolerated by the authorities of the country of origin. In *Z.N.S. v. Turkey* (2010), the applicant was an Iranian national who had converted to Christianity more than two years after leaving her own country.[239] Taking into account the UNHCR's assessment of the applicant's claim,[240] the Court found that there were substantial grounds for believing that if she returned to Iran, she would risk a violation of her right under Article 3 on account of her religion.[241]

In *S.F.* v. *Sweden* (2012), the Court explicitly applied the risk *sur place* concept by assessing the risk of ill-treatment in light of the applicants' *sur place* activities and incidents that occurred after they had arrived in Sweden in September 2007. The applicants were an Iranian married couple and their son. They argued that their removal to Iran would expose them to a real risk of treatment contrary to Article 3 based, *inter alia*, on their *sur place* activities. They referred to several interviews and articles they had written, which could be found on several sites on the Internet.[242] The Court noted that since 2008, the applicants continuously participated in political activities of intensifying importance. They appeared with photographs and names on several Internet sites and TV interviews where they expressed, *inter alia*, their personal views on the human rights situation in Iran and criticised the Iranian regime. They took leading roles and the husband was the international spokesperson for the support of Kurdish prisoners and human rights in Iran on a European committee. They expressed their opinions in several articles published on well-known Kurdish Internet sites. Against this background, the Court found that the applicants had been involved in extensive and genuine political and human rights activities, which must be taken into account in determining their risk on return to Iran.[243] The Court then addressed whether these activities would expose the applicants to the proscribed treatment if they were to be returned to Iran. The Court observed that, according to country information on Iran, there was a specific intelligence unit whose task was to monitor internet communications

---

239   ECtHR, *Z.N.S.* v. *Turkey*, para. 11. See also, ECtHR, *N.* v. *Sweden*, para. 56.
240   After interviewing the applicant, the UNHCR recognised her and her son as refugees on religious grounds. ECtHR, *Z.N.S.* v. *Turkey*, paras. 22 and 48.
241   Ibid., para. 49.
242   ECtHR, *S.F. and others* v. *Sweden*, para. 54.
243   Ibid., para. 68.

and criticisms of the Iranian regime, whether within or outside the country. The Court added that since Iranians returning to Iran were screened on arrival, the Iranian authorities could use the above-mentioned resources to identify the applicants.[244] Consequently, the Court considered the applicants' *sur place* activities to be one of the factors that led it to conclude that there were substantial grounds for believing that the applicants would be at a real risk of being subjected to treatment contrary to Article 3 ECHR if deported to Iran.[245]

The concept of a risk *sur place* has been also applied in the case where the risk emanates from the fact that the applicant was subjected to trial in the State party. In the case of *A. v. The Netherlands* (2010), the applicant alleged that he would be at risk of being detained and ill-treated in Libya because, *inter alia*, he had been prosecuted in the Netherlands on suspicion of involvement in an Islamic extremist organisation active in the Netherlands. The Court noted that although the applicant had been acquitted, these proceedings had received considerable media attention and the applicant's identity and nationality were revealed in several printed media reports. Furthermore, the Libyan mission in the Netherlands was informed that the applicant had been placed in aliens' detention pending his removal.[246] The Court in this case also took into account the information that Libyan authorities often had good knowledge of the activities and contacts of Libyans abroad and that they exercised strict control over persons arriving in Libya. In light of these facts, the Court considered it sufficiently plausible for the purposes of Article 3 ECHR that the applicant would be identified and detained for questioning after his arrival in Libya entailing a real risk of being ill-treated at the hands of the Libyan authorities.[247]

Noticeably, the publicity around the applicant's proceedings was the main factor in the Court's assessment of whether these proceedings gave rise to a risk *sur place*. The publicity that surrounded the applicant's asylum claim has been also given special importance. In *N. v. Finland* (2005), the Court made clear that:

> Neither can it be excluded that the publicity surrounding the applicant's asylum claim and appeals in Finland might engender feelings of revenge

---

244   Ibid., para. 69.
245   Ibid., paras. 70–71.
246   ECtHR, *A. v. The Netherlands*, para. 148. See also, ECtHR, *Al Husin* v. *Bosnia and Herzegovina*, para. 53.
247   ECtHR, *A. v. The Netherlands*, para. 149.

in relatives of dissidents possibly affected by the applicant's actions in the service of President Mobutu. It is relevant in this connection that the applicant himself does not appear to have played any active role in making his asylum case known to the public and, in particular, to other DRC nationals currently in Finland.[248]

The second sentence of this quotation indicates that the Court gave some weight to the fact that the applicant had not played any active role in creating publicity around his case. In *Kolesnik* v. *Russia* (2010), the Moscow City Court requested the authorities in Turkmenistan to comment on the applicant's complaints about the risk of ill-treatment and the situation in that country. The ECtHR did not rule out that this request could endanger the applicant' situation even further. The Court added:

> It should be noted that the first applicant herself did not take any steps to make her claims about ill-treatment known to the authorities of Turkmenistan and thus create an "unwanted" publicity around her case.[249]

The ECtHR has also applied the concept of risk *sur place* where the proscribed risk emanates from the changes that have taken place in the applicant's country of origin after his departure. In *Muminov* v. *Russia* (2008), the applicant was an Uzbek national who had left his country voluntarily and arrived in Russia in July 2000, seeking employment. In 2005, he was accused in Uzbekistan of membership of HT and participation in serious criminal offences.[250] In light of this situation, the ECtHR held that it would be appropriate to address whether the applicant fell within the definition of a refugee *sur place*. The Court noted that Russian authorities had not considered this question.[251] Therefore, in its assessment of the risk, the ECtHR considered the risk *sur place* to be one of the factors that led it to conclude that there were substantial grounds for believing that the applicant had faced a real risk of treatment contrary to Article 3.[252]

III.1.7   Medical Situation

Throughout its case-law, the ECtHR has repeatedly emphasised that, in principle, it is not possible for an alien who is subject to removal to claim any

248 ECtHR, *N.* v. *Finland*, para. 165; ECtHR, *Hilal* v. *the United Kingdom*, para. 65.

249 ECtHR, *Kolesnik* v. *Russia*, para. 70.

250 ECtHR, *Muminov* v. *Russia*, para. 10.

251 Ibid., para. 88.

252 Ibid., paras. 94 and 96.

entitlement to remain on the territory of the State party so that he can continue to benefit from the medical and social assistance and service provided by this State. The person concerned cannot claim a breach of Article 3 based on the mere fact that his circumstances would be significantly reduced as a result of the removal from the State party. As mentioned previously, the ECtHR has applied the principle of Non-Refoulement under Article 3 in the case of removing an alien who suffers from a serious mental or physical illness if the facilities for treating that illness in the receiving State are inferior to those available in the sending State.[253] The Court has made clear that this approach is followed "only in very exceptional cases where the humanitarian grounds against the removal are compelling".[254]

Such a very exceptional situation was first found in *D* v. *The UK* (1997), which concerned the expulsion of an HIV-infected applicant to St. Kitts after he had served a sentence of imprisonment in the UK. The Court noted that the applicant was in the advanced stages of a fatal and incurable illness at the time the case was considered.[255] His immune system was severely and irreparably damaged and he appeared to be close to death. He was therefore counselled on how to approach death and had formed bonds with his carers. There was a serious risk that the conditions of adversity awaiting him in St. Kitts would subject him to severe mental and physical suffering, because the medical facilities there did not have the capacity to provide him with the treatment he needed and his already limited life expectancy would be reduced. He had no family home or even a close relative ready to look after him in St. Kitts. While the Court emphasised that the conditions awaiting him in the receiving State did not in themselves violate the standards of Article 3, his expulsion would expose him to a real risk of dying under most distressing circumstances and would therefore amount to inhuman treatment. In view of these "exceptional circumstances", and taking into consideration the critical stage reached in the applicant's terminal illness, the Court found that implementing the decision of expulsion to St. Kitts would amount to inhuman treatment contrary to Article 3 ECHR.[256]

---

253   See above, Chapter 2, the treatment from which the person is protected under Article 3 ECHR. The Court has made clear that Article 3 does not place an obligation on the State party to provide free and unlimited health care to all aliens without a right to stay within its jurisdiction. ECtHR, *N.* v. *the United Kingdom* (GC), para. 44.

254   ECtHR, *D.* v. *the United Kingdom*, para. 54; ECtHR, *H. and B.* v. *the United Kingdom*, para. 114.

255   ECtHR, *D.* v. *the United Kingdom*, para. 50; ECtHR, *N.* v. *the United Kingdom* (GC), para. 35.

256   ECtHR, *D.* v. *the United Kingdom*, paras. 51–53. See, Palmer, S., AIDS, Expulsion and Article 3 of the European Convention on Human Rights, European Human Rights Law Review, no. 5: 2005, 533–540.

The Court has reasserted its approach in the *D.* case in its subsequent Non-Refoulement case-law under Article 3 where the expected ill-treatment resulting from a naturally occurring illness and the lack of sufficient resources to deal with it in the receiving State. Three main factors must exist in order to conclude that there are "very exceptional circumstances". First, the applicant's fatal illness has reached an advanced stage. Second, no adequate medical treatment for the applicant's illness is available in his country of origin. Third, the applicant does not have family members there willing or able to look after him or provide him with a basic level of food, shelter or social support.[257] This approach was taken in *Amegnigan v. the Netherlands* (2004), towards the expulsion of a Togolese HIV-positive national to his country of origin. The ECtHR noted that, according to the most recent medical report, the applicant's clinical situation was stable and there was no direct danger to his health. However, the report added, if the anti-HIV treatment were to cease, the applicant would fall back to an advanced stage of his incurable illness, which would entail a direct risk to his life. The Court found that the applicant had not reached the stage of full-blown AIDS, nor was he suffering from any HIV-related illness. Adequate medical treatment was in principle available in Togo, albeit at considerable expense, and his mother and a younger brother resided there. Though the applicant's circumstances in Togo would be less favourable than those he enjoyed in the sending State party, the Court did not consider this fact decisive from the point of view of Article 3. Although the Court acknowledged the seriousness of Mr. *Amegnigan's* medical situation, it did not find that the circumstances of his situation were of a very exceptional nature. The Court accordingly held that the application was manifestly ill-founded and declared it inadmissible.[258] The GC reached the same decision in *N. v. The UK* (2008). The applicant in this case, who was HIV positive, challenged her expulsion to Uganda on the grounds that she had a serious medical situation and sufficient treatment was not available for her disease in her country of origin, particularly in the rural area from which she came.[259] The Court observed that, while the applicant's life conditions as well as her life expectancy would be

---

257   ECtHR, *N. v. the United Kingdom* (GC), para. 42; ECtHR, *M.T.* v. *Sweden*, Appl.No. 1412/12, 26 February 2015.

258   ECtHR, *Amegnigan* v. *the Netherlands* (admissibility decision), Appl.No. 25629/04, 15 November 2004. See also, ECtHR, *Karara* v. *Finland* (admissibility decision), Appl. No. 40900/98, 29 May 1998; ECtHR, *Arcila Henao* v. *the Netherlands*, Appl. No. 12699/03, 24 June 2003; ECtHR, *M.* v. *the United Kingdom* (admissibility decision), Appl.No. 25087/06, 24 June 2008.

259   ECtHR, *N.* v. *the United Kingdom* (GC), para. 46.

diminished if she were removed to Uganda, she was not critically ill at the time the case was considered. The Court added that:

> The rapidity of the deterioration which she would suffer and the extent to which she would be able to obtain access to medical treatment, support and care, including help from relatives, must involve a certain degree of speculation, particularly in view of the constantly evolving situation as regards the treatment of HIV and AIDS worldwide.[260]

Although all the above-mentioned cases concerned the expulsion of persons with an HIV and AIDS-related condition, the Court has made it clear that:

> ...the same principles must apply in relation to the expulsion of any person afflicted with any serious, naturally occurring physical or mental illness which may cause suffering, pain and reduced life expectancy and require specialised medical treatment which may not be so readily available in the applicant's country of origin or which may be available only at substantial cost.[261]

An application for protection against refoulement may be lodged with the ECtHR on the ground that there is a real risk of ill-treatment resulting from a naturally occurring mental illness. Several Non-Refoulement cases were brought before the Court on this ground.[262] The Court found a violation of Article 3 in *Aswat* v. *The UK* (2013), which concerned the extradition of the applicant who was suffering from paranoid schizophrenia to the US where he was indicted as a co-conspirator in a conspiracy to establish a *jihad* training camp. The Court noted that the question in this case was whether the applicant could be extradited to the US, where he would face an uncertain future in an, as yet, undetermined detention institution. The Court observed that there was no guarantee that the applicant, if convicted, would not be detained in ADX Florence, where he would be exposed to a "highly restrictive" regime with long periods of social isolation. Taking into account the severity of the applicant's mental condition, the Court distinguished this case from that of *Babar Ahmad and Others* v. *The UK* (2012), where it had not accepted the

---

260   Ibid., para. 50.
261   Ibid., para. 45.
262   E.g., ECtHR, *Paramsothy* v. *the Netherlands* (admissibility decision), Appl.No. 14492/03, 10 November 2005; ECtHR, *Husseini* v. *Sweden*, Appl.No. 10611/09, 13 October 2011, paras. 90–94.

possibility that conditions in ADX Florence would reach the Article 3 threshold for persons in good health, or with less serious mental health problems. The Court also distinguished the *Aswat* case from *Bensaid* v. *The UK* (2001), which concerned the expulsion of the applicant who suffered from schizophrenia to his home country, Algeria. The Court observed that the present case concerned extradition to a county where he had no ties, where he would not have the support of family and friends and where he would be detained. Accordingly, in light of the applicant's current medical situation, the Court found that there was a real risk that his extradition to "a different country and to a different, and potentially more hostile, prison environment would result in a significant deterioration in his mental and physical health and that such a deterioration would be capable of reaching the Article 3 threshold".[263]

It was argued before the Court that the applicant's deportation would cause him irreparable damage, due to his very poor mental health, and entail a serious risk for his life because he has suicidal tendencies or even has a record of previous suicide attempts. In *Goncharova and Alekseytsev* v. *the Netherlands* (2007), which concerned the expulsion of two Russian nationals to Russia, the second applicant was diagnosed as suffering from depression caused by his uncertain situation as a rejected asylum seeker. He had been hospitalised twice after suicide attempts. While the Court accepted that the applicant's uncertain situation caused him mental distress, it noted that there was no reason to believe that he would not benefit from health care in Russia, should this be necessary. The Court reasserted that even if the second applicant's circumstances in his home country would be less favourable than those he had enjoyed in Sweden, it could not be regarded as decisive from the perspective of Article 3. The Court reiterated that:

> ...the fact that a person, whose deportation has been ordered, threatens to commit suicide does not require the Contracting State to refrain from enforcing the deportation, provided that concrete measures are taken to prevent the threat from being realised.[264]

The Court observed that after the second applicant's first suicide attempt in August 2004, he had been deported to Russia along with his parents in November 2004 without any incidents. After his second attempt to commit suicide in July 2006, he was not in contact with the Swedish health care system except

---

263 ECtHR, *Aswat* v. *the United Kingdom*, paras. 56–57. See, ECtHR, *Bensaid* v. *the United Kingdom*, paras. 37–38.

264 ECtHR, *A.A.* v. *Sweden* (admissibility decision), para. 71.

for occasional visits to his counsellor. The Court further took note of the Swedish government's submission that a deportation order would be carried out in such a way as to minimise the suffering of the second applicant, with regard to his medical condition. Moreover, the Court did not find any reason to doubt that the second applicant would receive help from his father who was living in Russia. Against this background, and taking into account the high threshold set by Article 3, particularly where the case does not concern the direct responsibility of the State party for the possible harm, the Court concluded that the second applicant's deportation to Russia would not be in breach of this Article. Thus, the Court considered that the present case did not disclose the exceptional circumstances established in the *D.* case and followed this reasoning in its subsequent related case-law.[265]

III.2   *ComAT*

In order to be protected against refoulement under Article 3 CAT, the complainant must establish that "substantial grounds" exist for believing that his removal would expose him to a foreseeable, current, real and personal risk of being subjected to torture. The ComAT has made it clear that in assessing this risk, it must take into account all relevant considerations.[266] Since the treatment to which a person may not be removed is torture, as defined under Article 1 CAT, the aim of the assessment is to determine if the complainant is of interest to the authorities in the receiving State.[267]

This section determines the facts and circumstances that could be considered as substantial grounds sufficient to show that there is a foreseeable, real and personal risk of torture in the proposed receiving State. Where a State party intends to send an individual to a specific part of the receiving State, the ComAT, like the ECtHR, has focused its assessment on whether there is a real

---

265   ECtHR, *Goncharova and Alekseytsev* v. *the Netherlands* (admissibility decision), Appl.No. 31246/06, 3 May 2007. The Court adopted the same approach in all other Non-Refoulement cases concerned suffering mental illness associated with the risk of suicide. E.g., ECtHR, *Paramsothy* v. *the Netherlands* (admissibility decision); ECtHR, *Kaldik* v. *Germany* (admissibility decision), Appl.No. 28526/05, 22 September 2005; ECtHR, *A.A.* v. *Sweden* (admissibility decision), para. 71; Ibid., para. 16; ECtHR, *Al-Zawatia* v. *Sweden* (admissibility decision), paras. 56–63.

266   ComAT, *T.I.* v. *Canada*, No. 333/2007, 15 November 2010, para. 7.3; ComAT, *Josu Arkauz Arana* v. *France*, para. 11.3.

267   ComAT, *X* v. *The Netherlands*, No. 36/1995, 8 May 1996, para. 8; ComAT, *Ktiti* v. *Morocco*, No. 419/2010, 26 May 2011, para. 8.7; ComAT, *Sivagnanaratnam* v. *Denmark*, No. 429/2010, 11 November 2013, para. 10.5.

risk of torture to him in that part of the State.[268] Paragraph 8 of the ComAT's General Comment No.1 provides a non-exhaustive list of information that would be pertinent to assessing the risk the complainant may be tortured in the proposed receiving State.[269] In the following subsections, we discuss these factors as they are interpreted in the ComAT's Non-Refoulement case-law.

III.2.1   General Situation in the Receiving State

The general situation of human rights in the proposed receiving State is one of the main factors that the ComAT has taken into account when it assesses if there are substantial grounds for believing that the complainant would be in danger of being subjected to torture there. The second paragraph of Article 3 CAT provides that:

> For the purpose of determining whether there are such grounds, the competent authorities shall take into account all relevant considerations including, where applicable, the existence in the State concerned of a consistent pattern of gross, flagrant or mass violations of human rights.[270]

The Committee has repeatedly asserted that the aim of its assessment is to determine if the person concerned would be personally at risk of being subjected to torture. Consequently, the Committee has considered a general situation of human rights violations in a country to be insufficient, in itself, to conclude that a particular person would be at risk of torture upon his return to that country, when there is no evidence that demonstrates that he would personally be at risk of such treatment. In several cases, the Committee has expressed its concern at the many reports of human rights violations, including the use of torture, in the proposed receiving State. However, it has found that the complainant's removal would not violate Article 3 CAT because no other ground for personal risk was established.[271] In *T.I.* v. *Canada* (2010), the

---

268   E.g. In *N.B-M.* v. *Switzerland* (2011), the Committee noted that the State party intended to return the complainant to Kinshasa; accordingly it considered whether she would be at risk if returned there. ComAT, *N.B-M.* v. *Switzerland*, No. 347/2008, 14 November 2011, para. 9.5.

269   ComAT, General Comment No. 1, para. 8.

270   CAT84, Article 3(2).

271   E.g., with regard to the expulsion to the DRC see, ComAT, *M.D.T.* v. *Switzerland*, No. 382/2009, 14 May 2012 para, 7.8; ComAT, *Mutombo* v. *Switzerland*, para. 9.5; expulsion to Burundi see, ComAT, *A.A.M.* v. *Sweden*, para. 9.5. ComAT, *H.M.H.I.* v. *Australia*, para. 6.5; expulsion to Turkey see, ComAT, *E.A.* v. *Switzerland*, para. 11.5; expulsion to Sri Lanka see, ComAT, *S.N.A.W. et al.* v. *Switzerland*, paras. 7.2–7.3; ComAT, *K.N.* v. *Switzerland*, para. 10.4;

ComAT was aware of the poor human rights situation in Uzbekistan. In its concluding observations on the third periodic report of Uzbekistan, the Committee cited numerous, on-going and consistent allegations that the Uzbek authorities had used, instigated, or consented to torture and CIDTP, often to extract confessions or information to be used in criminal proceedings. It also cited Uzbekistan's failure to conduct sufficient investigations into claims of torture. In spite of this, the Committee noted that the complainant did not provide other grounds to support his claim that he would be at a personal risk of torture if deported to Uzbekistan.[272] Thus, the existence of a general situation of human rights violations in the proposed receiving State is not considered as a substantial ground sufficient in itself to show that the complainant's removal would expose him to a risk of torture.

The Committee has adopted the same approach in cases where a general situation of violence exists in the receiving State. In *Kalonzo* v. *Canada* (2012), which concerned the expulsion of a Congolese national to the DRC, the Committee noted the difficult human rights situation in the receiving State, and that Canada had declared a moratorium on the removal of rejected asylum seekers to that country. The Committee observed that the moratorium had been put in place because of the widespread violence that existed in the DRC, and that the moratorium would not apply in the complainant's case because of his criminal record. Accordingly, the Committee concluded that this moratorium procedure discretionary, whereas, in the spirit of Article 3 CAT, "it is to be understood that a moratorium on the removal of persons who would be at risk in their country because of widespread violence should apply to everyone without distinction".[273] This quotation might indicate that the ComAT was ready to accept that a general situation of violence in the DRC could be of a sufficient level of intensity as to entail that any removal to that country would necessarily violate Article 3 CAT. The Committee did find that the complainant's expulsion in this case would violate Article 3, but this conclusion was also based on other grounds.[274] On the same day the Committee adopted its decision in another case, *J.L.L.* v. *Switzerland* (2012), concerning expulsion to

---

expulsion to Togo, ComAT, *R.S.M.* v. *Canada*, para. 7.4; and expulsion to Salvador see, ComAT, *M.C.M.V.F.* v. *Sweden*, No. 237/2003, 14 November 2005, para. 6.4.

272   ComAT, *T.I.* v. *Canada*.

273   ComAT, *Kalonzo* v. *Canada*, No. 343/2008, 18 May 2012, para. 9.5.

274   The Committee's conclusion was also based on the grounds that the complainant was a son of an opposition party leader, and he had already been the victim of violence during his previous detention in the DRC as a result of which he was suffering from post-traumatic stress disorder. Ibid., paras. 9.6–9.7.

the DRC. In this case, the Committee found that the complainant's expulsion to the DRC would not constitute a breach of Article 3 CAT.[275] Consequently, the Committee's approach in the *Kalonzo* case is more related to the way Canada implemented its moratorium than to the principle of Non-Refoulement under Article 3.[276] Although the Committee in the *Kalonzo* case observed widespread violence existed in the DRC, in *J.L.L.* v. *Switzerland* this was not sufficient to conclude that the complaint's removal to the DRC would violate Article 3.

In conclusion, the existence of a general situation of violence or human rights violations in the receiving State does not constitute in itself a sufficient ground to apply the principle of Non-Refoulement under Article 3 CAT.

Similarly, the Committee has held that absence of a consistent pattern of gross violations of human rights in the proposed receiving State does not necessarily indicate that an applicant is not in danger of being subjected to torture because of his specific circumstances.[277] Although the Committee in *A.I.* v. *Switzerland* (2004) noted that the practice of torture was not systematic in Sri Lanka and that a large number of Tamil refugees returned to that country in recent years, it did not rule out the possibility that the complainant could be at personal risk of being tortured if returned there.[278]

III.2.2   Previous Activities

According to General Comment No.1, when the ComAT assesses of whether a complainant's removal would violate Article 3 CAT, it should take into account any previous engagement in political or other activities in the receiving State that would appear to make him particularly vulnerable to the risk of being subjected to torture if returned.[279] The Committee has sought to find out if a complainant's previous activities still attract negative attention in the proposed receiving State, and based its determination on the facts of each case. For example, the Committee found his previous activities put the complainant at no real risk of torture in the receiving State because he had been acquitted

---

275   ComAT, *J.L.L.* v. *Switzerland*, No. 364/2008, 18 May 2012, para. 9.

276   This conclusion is supported by the Committee's decision in *E.L.* v. *Canada* (2012), which concerned the expulsion from Canada to Haiti. In this case the Committee recalled that the Canadian's moratorium on the removal of persons to a country in crisis should apply to everyone, without any distinction. ComAT, *E.L.* v. *Canada*, para. 8.3.

277   ComAT, *T.I.* v. *Canada*, para. 7.3.

278   ComAT, *A.I.* v. *Switzerland*, No. 182/2001, 12 May 2004, paras. 6.3–6.5. See also, ComAT, *K.K.* v. *Switzerland*, No. 186/2001, 11 November 2003, paras. 6.3–6.5; ComAT, *F.A.B.* v. *Switzerland*, No. 348/2008, 17 November 2009, para. 7.4.

279   ComAT, General Comment No. 1, para. 8(e).

of responsibility for those activities,[280] he did not submit any evidence suggesting that the authorities in the receiving State have been looking for him,[281] or because individuals carried out the same activities as the complainant had not been arrested or tortured.[282] In other cases, the Committee found that the complainant's previous activities attracted no negative attention from the authorities in the receiving State because that State issued him a passport,[283] or he was able to visit the State on several occasions without experiencing any difficulties with national authorities.[284] In *M.Z.A.* v. *Sweden* (2012), the Committee noted that the complainant failed to adduce any evidence that suggested he was wanted for his previous political activities in Azerbaijan. He did not present a copy of an arrest warrant or proof that he, personally, was the subject of an on-going investigation.[285]

The Committee has also given special weight to the nature and the importance of the complainant's previous activities. It has rejected a claim that the complainant would be at risk of torture if returned to the proposed receiving State since his previous political activities there were not significant enough to attract interest of the authorities.[286] In *E.J. et al.* v. *Sweden* (2008), the ComAT noted that the main complainant had been an active member of the Azerbaijan Democratic Party, an opposition political party in Azerbaijan, but he did not appear to have taken a leading position in this Party. The political activities in which he was allegedly involved were very low level and took place over four years prior. A number of political prisoners had been released

---

280   E.g., ComAT, *V.N.I.M.* v. *Canada*, No. 119/1998, 12 November 2002, para. 8.5; ComAT, *G.B.M.* v. *Sweden*, No. 435/2010, 14 November 2012, para. 7.8; ComAT, *R.A.* v. *Switzerland*, No. 389/2009, 20 November 2012, para. 9.5.

281   ComAT, *M.A.H. and F.H.* v. *Switzerland*, No. 438/2010, 7 November 2013, para. 7.6.

282   ComAT, *J.U.A* v. *Switzerland*, No. 100/1997, 10 November 1998, para. 6.4. By contrast, the Committee in *Singh Khalsa et al.* v. *Switzerland* (2011) observed cases where individuals who had participated in airplanes' hijackings, as the complainants, had been arrested, detained in inhuman conditions, tortured and/or killed. ComAT, *Singh Khalsa et al.* v. *Switzerland*, No. 336/2008, 26 May 2011, para. 11.4.

283   ComAT, *E.A.* v. *Switzerland*, para. 11.4.

284   In *S.V. et al.* v. *Canada* (2001), the ComAT noted that although the complainant had been tortured by the Sri Lankan army in 1990, he was able to leave Sri Lanka legally and returned several times without being subjected to torture. ComAT, *S.V. et al.* v. *Canada*, para. 9.6. See also, ComAT, *U.S.* v. *Finland*, No. 197/2002, 15 May 2003, para. 7.7; *S.U.A.* v. *Sweden*, No. 223/2002, 22 November 2004.

285   ComAT, *M.Z.A.* v. *Sweden*, No. 424/2010, 22 May 2012, paras. 8.4–8.5.

286   E.g., ComAT, *F.F.Z.* v. *Denmark*, No. 180/2001, 30 April 2002, para. 11; ComAT, *R.K. et al.* v. *Sweden*, No. 309/2006, 16 May 2008; ComAT, *H.O.* v. *Sweden*, No. 178/2001, 13 November 2001, para. 14; ComAT, *E.T.* v. *Switzerland*, para. 7.5.

after presidential pardons, including the Azerbaijan Democratic Party's leader himself. Therefore, the Committee concluded that the complainant failed to present evidence that demonstrated that he would attract the particular interest of the authorities in Azerbaijan if returned there.[287] On the contrary, in *Singh* v. *Canada* (2011), the Indian courts had formally acquitted the complainant of the charge of being a militant. The ComAT took into account the fact that the complainant was well known to the Indian authorities because he was active as a Sikh priest, his political activities in an opposition party, and his leadership role in the local structures of this party, which had continually exposed him to harassment by the police. The Committee therefore considered that the complainant's profile was sufficiently high to put him at risk of torture.[288]

III.2.3   Past Ill-treatment

According to the ComAT's General Comment No.1 para. 8(b), the fact that the complainant was previously subjected to torture or maltreated in the proposed receiving State is one of the pertinent factors that would be considered in the ComAT's assessment of his risk of torture in that State.[289] The Committee's interest in taking past experience of ill-treatment into account is not to right an earlier wrong, but to prevent the complainant from being tortured again in the future.[290] The Committee has also held that absence of past ill-treatment does not indicate, *per se*, that the risk of torture does not exist:[291] it has found that a complainant's removal may violate Article 3 even if he has not been ill-treated previously.[292] Under the Committee's General Comment No.1, several conditions must be met for the complainant's previous experience of torture in the receiving State to be considered an indication that his removal would place him at risk of being tortured again.

---

287   ComAT, *E.J. et al.* v. *Sweden*, No. 306/2006, 14 November 2008, paras. 8.6–8.7. See also, ComAT, *A.H.* v. *Sweden*, para. 11.6; ComAT, *Asim Elmansoub* v. *Switzerland*, No. 278/2005, 8 May 2006, para. 6.5; ComAT, *Z.K.* v. *Sweden*, para. 8.5.

288   ComAT, *Singh* v. *Canada*, para. 8.5. See also, ComAT, *Tahir Hussain Khan* v. *Canada*, para. 12.4.

289   ComAT, General Comment No. 1, para. 8 (b). See also, ComAT, *X, Y and Z* v. *Sweden*, para. 11.3.

290   Miller, D.J., 2003, p. 303; Sorensen, B., CAT and articles 20 and 22, in: Alfredsson, G., International Human Rights Monitoring Mechanisms: Essays in Honour of Jakob Th. Moller, The Hague: Martinus Nijhoff Publishers, 2001, 167–183, p. 180.

291   ComAT, *M.Z.A.* v. *Sweden*, paras. 8.4–8.5.

292   ComAT, *A.L.N.* v. *Switzerland*, No. 90/1997, 19 May 1998, para. 8.3.

First, the past experience of torture or maltreatment must have been inflicted "by or at the instigation of or with the consent or acquiescence of a public official or other person acting in an official capacity".[293] In *M.C.M.V.F. v. Sweden* (2005), the complainant alleged that she and her daughter were abducted by gunmen who, according to the complainant, treated them in the same way the police did when they were captured earlier. The complainant and her daughter were released 30 minutes later, with a warning not to complain about the incident to the police.[294] The ComAT decided the applicant failed to provide sufficient proof that the incident was "attributable to state agents or to groups acting on behalf of or under the effective control of state agents".[295] In a number of cases, the ComAT did not take the complainant's allegation of previous experience of torture in the receiving State into account because he was not personally targeted by this treatment, or it was of a general nature. In *Y.H.A. v. Australia* (2003), the Committee rejected the complainant's claim specifically on the ground that the attacks against him were more likely to have resulted from the general climate of violence in Mogadishu than from a deliberate attempt to target him.[296]

Second, a medical report or other independent evidence must support the complainant's allegation of having been previously subjected to torture.[297] The complainant is responsible for adducing a recent medical report that supports his claim that he was a victim of torture.[298] The Committee has held that the medical report is still important, even if the examination took place several years after the alleged incidents of torture and ill-treatment.[299] The weight that the Committee has given to a medical report depends on the extent to which the report confirms that the applicant was tortured.[300] The medical report must confirm that the complainant suffers from post-traumatic

---

293   ComAT, General Comment No. 1, para. 8(b). This condition is derived from the fact that Article 3 protects a person only from torture in the receiving State.

294   ComAT, *M.C.M.V.F. v. Sweden*, para. 2.6.

295   Ibid., para. 6.4. See, ComAT, *B.M. v. Sweden*, No. 179/2001, 30 April 2002, para. 5.3; ComAT, *M.A.K. v. Germany*, para. 13.7.

296   ComAT, *Y.H.A. v. Australia*, No. 162/2000, 23 November 2003, para. 7.3.

297   ComAT, General Comment No. 1, para. 8(c).

298   ComAT, *S.N.A.W. et al. v. Switzerland*, para. 7.5; ComAT, *M.X. v. Switzerland*, No. 311/2007, 7 May 2008, para. 9.4; ComAT, *Dewage v. Australia*, No. 387/2009, 14 November 2013, para. 10.7.

299   ComAT, *M.M.K. v. Sweden*, para. 8.5.

300   ComAT, *Enrique Falcon Rios v. Canada*, para. 8.4.

stress disorder, or that there are scars on his body consistent with torture.[301] There must be a causal link between the complainant's current state of health and the alleged past ill-treatment.[302] In *K.Y.Tala* v. *Sweden* (1996), the complainant was previously detained and tortured in Iran for his political affiliation with the People's Mujahedin Organization and activities. As a result, he suffered from post-traumatic stress disorder. The Committed noted, based on the medical evidence, that the burn scars on his body could only have been inflicted intentionally by another person.[303] Consequently, the complainant's past experience of torture was one of the factors that led the Committee to conclude that deporting him to Iran would violate Article 3.

Third, the Committee is only interested in torture suffered by the complainant in the recent past.[304] In several cases, the Committee has refused the complainant's argument that his past experience of torture in the receiving State indicated that his removal would violate Article 3 because he was tortured too long ago.[305] The Committee has repeatedly asserted that even if the complainant was tortured in the proposed receiving State in the past, it does not automatically follow that he would still be at risk of being tortured if he returned there in the near future, particularly if a long time had elapsed since the previous torture occurred. The current risk of torture is what matters.[306] To determine if the complainant's past experience of torture in the proposed receiving State constitutes an indication that he would be at risk of torture if returned to this State the Committee would assess both the current human rights situation in the State, and the complainant's personal circumstances at

---

301 In *Z.K.* v. *Sweden* (2008), the Committee noted that the medical certificates submitted by the complainant did not conclusively state that he had been tortured. Hence, the Committee found that it could not be definitely concluded from these certificates that the complainant had been tortured. However, the Committee did not completely disregard these certificates because they stated that the scars on the complainant's body could have occurred as a result of past torture. ComAT, *Z.K.* v. *Sweden*, para. 8.4.

302 ComAT, *T.A.* v. *Sweden*, para. 8.5; ComAT, *Gbadjavi* v. *Switzerland*, No. 396/2009, 1 June 2012, para. 7.8.

303 ComAT, *K.Y.Tala* v. *Sweden*, No. 43/1996, 15 November 1996, para. 10.3.

304 ComAT, General Comment No. 1, para. 8(b).

305 ComAT, *A.R.* v. *The Netherlands*, No. 203/2002, 14 November 2003, (20 years ago) para. 7.4. ComAT, *H.A.D.* v. *Switzerland*, No. 126/1999, 10 May 2000 (15 years), para. 8.6; ComAT, *S.N.A.W. et al.* v. *Switzerland*, (10 years), para. 7.5; ComAT, *K.K.* v. *Switzerland*, (7 years), para. 6.6; ComAT, *S.S.* v. *The Netherlands*, (7 years).

306 ComAT, *M.M. et al.* v. *Sweden*, para. 7.5; ComAT, *H.B.H., T.N.T., H.J.H., H.O.H., H.R.H. and H.G.H.* v. *Switzerland*, No. 192/2001, 29 April 2003, para. 6.6.

the material time.[307] In the Committee's view, if the circumstances remained the same as they had been when the complainant was tortured earlier, that would be decisive. In the case of *S.S.S.* v. *Canada* (2005), the ComAT noted that the complainant had submitted evidence, including medical reports, to support his allegation that he had been tortured during his detention in India in 1999. However, the Committee pointed out that even if it assumed that the Punjabi police had tortured the complainant previously, it did not automatically follow that, six years later, he would still be at risk of torture if he were returned to India.[308]

The Committee has required the applicant to establish that previous torture occurred in circumstances that are relevant to the current political situation in the proposed receiving State. In *A.A.C.* v. *Sweden* (2006), the complainant argued that, by expelling him to Bangladesh, Sweden would violate Article 3 CAT on the grounds, *inter alia*, that he had been previously tortured for his membership in the Bangladesh Freedom Party.[309] The Committee noted that this torture took place in 1997 and in 1999, and thus could not be deemed recent. Furthermore, the political circumstances had changed a great deal, because the Bangladesh Freedom Party was no longer the opposition party.[310]

The Committee has given due weight to the complainant's previous experience of torture where it is established that the circumstances in the proposed receiving State have not changed since the occurrence of this experience, or they have become worse.[311] The Committee has taken the same approach with regard to changes in the personal circumstances of the complainant. In *Mostafa Dadar* v. *Canada* (2005), the Committee found that, although the complainant's past experience of torture was not in the recent past, he was still involved with the Iranian opposition forces, which would expose him to questioning if returned to Iran. Thus, the Committee found that the possibility the applicant might be questioned upon return increased his risk of torture.[312]

---

307   ComAT, *A.D.* v. *The Netherlands*, para. 7.4.

308   ComAT, *S.S.S.* v. *Canada*, No. 245/2004, 16 November 2005, para. 8.4.

309   ComAT, *A.A.C.* v. *Sweden*, No. 227/2003, 16 November 2006, para. 3.1.

310   Ibid., para. 8.3; ComAT, *M.S.H.* v. *Sweden*, No. 235/2003, 14 November 2005, paras. 6.5–6.6.

311   ComAT, *Amini* v. *Denmark*, paras. 9.7–9.9; ComAT, *E.T.B.* v. *Denmark*, No. 146/1999, 30 April 2002, para. 10.

312   ComAT, *Mostafa Dadar* v. *Canada*, paras. 8.6–8.7. See also, ComAT, *C.T. and K.M.* v. *Sweden*, No. 279/2005, 17 November 2006. On the contrary, see, *A.K.* v. *Australia*, in which the complainant was not still involved in the political activities for which he had been previously tortured. ComAT, *A.K.* v. *Australia*, No. 148/1999, 5 May 2004; ComAT, *K.H.* v. *Denmark*, No. 464/2011, 23 November 2012, para. 8.7.

III.2.4   Membership in a Vulnerable Group

While the ComAT's General Comment No.1 does not expressly provide for membership in a vulnerable group as one of the factors that should be taken into account when risk is assessed, it clearly states that its list is not exhaustive. Through its Non-Refoulement case-law, the Committee has taken into account the complainant's membership of political, professional or social groups targeted for repression and torture by the authorities in the receiving State.[313] In some cases, the complainant's membership of particular group was understood to be a ground for the complainant's previous experience of ill-treatment. In other cases, the Committee found that the complainant would be at risk of torture because of his previous activities in support of a particular political group. The Committee has considered simple membership of group vulnerable to torture in the receiving State to be a ground for believing that the complainant's removal would violate Article 3 CAT. On this ground, the Committee developed two conditions to consider if a complainant's removal would expose him to a risk of torture. First, the complainant must establish that he belongs to a particular group in the proposed receiving State. Second, he must establish that this group is vulnerable to torture in the receiving State. In the following subsections, we review the ComAT's case-law on this subject, and give some examples of groups that have been considered vulnerable in some countries.

III.2.4.1   *Detainees, Criminal Suspects and Political Opponents*

The Committee has refused to apply the principle of Non-Refoulement where the complainant's removal is challenged solely on the ground of the existence of torture in detention centres in the proposed receiving State. In *M.M.K. v. Sweden* (2005), the complainant argued that since charges were still pending against him in Bangladesh, he risked detention upon his arrival there and thus risked being tortured by the police. The Committee clearly stated that:

> ...the existence of torture in detention as such does not justify a finding of a violation of article 3, given that the complainant has not demonstrated how he personally would be at risk of being tortured.[314]

---

313   ComAT, *X. v. Switzerland*, No. 38/1995, 9 May 1997, para. 10.5; ComAT, *P.Q.L. v. Canada*, No. 57/1996, 17 November 1997, para. 10.4; ComAT, *X.Y. v. Switzerland*, No. 128/1999, 15 May 2001, para. 10.5.

314   ComAT, *M.M.K. v. Sweden*, para. 8.7. See also, ComAT, *L.M.T.D. v. Sweden*, No. 164/2000, 15 May 2002, para. 9.

Arguably, in the Committee's view, the fact that a certain State uses torture during detention does not imply that criminal suspects detained in that State constitute a vulnerable group, and does not warrant a total ban on extradition to that State. Other grounds have to be established, such as his previous experience of torture in the proposed receiving State or the applicant's political activities. However, the Committee has sometimes designated certain groups of criminal suspects or detainees as vulnerable to torture in certain States. When a complainant belongs to this group, his removal to this State would violate Article 3. For example, in *Guclu* v. *Sweden* (2010), which concerned the deportation of a Turkish citizen who was a member of the PKK, the Committee noted that, according to various sources, Turkish security and police forces still tortured criminals, including those suspected of terrorism, during investigations and in detention centres. Since the complainant was wanted in Turkey for prosecution under anti-terrorist laws, the Committee considered her to be at risk of arrest and torture upon her return.[315] The Court adopted the same approach in a removal to Tunisia of persons who were accused of political opposition activities, including having links with the Islamic *Ennahda* party.[316] In *A.* v. *The Netherlands* (1998), the complainant repeatedly denied that he supported the *Ennahda*, and this led the State party to conclude that he would be of no interest to the Tunisian authorities. The Committee noted, however, that the complainant had been previously tortured in Tunisia, while held in police custody, because he had helped an *Ennahda* member to flee to Algeria, and emphasized that the torture resulted from the *Ennahda* association. The Committee thus held that if the complainant had been previously tortured,

---

315   ComAT, *Guclu* v. *Sweden*, No. 349/2008, 11 November 2010, paras. 6.6–6.7. See also, ComAT, *Orhan Ayas* v. *Sweden*; ComAT, *Halil Haydin* v. *Sweden*. See also, ComAT, *Cecilia Rosana Nunez Chipana* v. *Venezuela*, para. 6.4. An author addressed the treatment to which a suspected terrorist had been subjected under the US's custody and concluded that a risk of torture may create a mandate for all States parties to the CAT to consider suspected terrorists personally at risk of being subjected to torture if extradited to the US's custody. Mueller, D., Unsafe Haven: Could Article 3 of the UN Convention Against Torture Prevent the Extradition of Terrorist Suspects to U.S. Custody?, Penn State International Law Review, Vol. 28 no. 3: 2010, 549–580, p. 580.

316   ComAT, *A.* v. *The Netherlands*, No. 91/1997, 13 November 1998; ComAT, *Chedli Ben Ahmed Karoui* v. *Sweden*; ComAT, *Adel Tebourski* v. *France*. The Committee observed that individuals who had participated in airplanes' hijackings of the Indian Airlines had been arrested, detained in inhuman conditions, tortured and/or killed. ComAT, *Singh Khalsa et al.* v. *Switzerland*, para. 11.4. The same approach was followed with regard to removal of persons accused of terrorist activities to Spain, ComAT, *Josu Arkauz Arana* v. *France*; and with regard to removal of suspected terrorist to Egypt, ComAT, *Agiza* v. *Sweden*, para. 13.2.

despite not being an *Ennahda* supporter, he could also be tortured again, due to his previous detention and his assistance of an *Ennahda* member to flee.[317] In another Non-Refoulement case, *B.M. v Sweden* (2002), the complainant was accused in Tunisia, *inter alia*, of providing financial support to families of imprisoned members of the *Ennahda* party. Although the chairman of this party and the AI claimed that a risk of torture existed for the complainant, and that there was evidence that supporters and sympathisers of the *Ennahda* party were persecuted, the Committee held that the complainant was not at risk of torture. The Committee based its conclusion mainly on the grounds that the complainant did not belong to the *Ennahda* party and was not involved in any political activity, but only in humanitarian work, and that he had not been subjected to torture in the past.[318] In these two cases, the Committee gave due weight to the fact the complainant had not been tortured in the past, and to the nature of the complainant's activities for the *Ennahda* party. We disagree on the ground that, since the ComAT found that the members, supporters and sympathisers of the *Ennahda* party were at risk of being tortured in Tunisia, the Committee should have held that all persons seen by the Tunisian authorities as members, supporters and sympathisers of this party would be at risk of torture, regardless of the nature of their activities and whether they had been subjected to torture in the past.

The Committee has observed that certain groups are more vulnerable to arrest, detention and torture in some States. For example, the Committee noted that the human rights situation in Iran was very worrisome after the 2009 Iranian presidential elections. It also referred to many recent reports that specifically described the repression and arbitrary detention of many reformers, students, journalists and human rights defenders, some of them were detained in secret; others were sentenced to death and executed.[319] Given this background, the Committee, in *Eftekhary v. Norway* (2011), found that the complainant's removal to Iran would violate Article 3 CAT, putting him at risk because he was a journalist.[320] A group designated as vulnerable in a certain country is not necessarily vulnerable in another country. While the Committee considered that journalists, as a group, were vulnerable to detention and torture in Iran, it held that journalists in Djibouti were not targeted for repression.[321]

---

317   ComAT, *A. v. The Netherlands*, para. 6.7.

318   ComAT, *B.M. v. Sweden*, para. 5.3.

319   ComAT, *Jahani v. Switzerland*, para. 9.5; ComAT, *Faragollah et al. v. Switzerland*, No. 381/2009, 21 November 2011, para. 9.4.

320   ComAT, *Eftekhary v. Norway*, para. 7.7.

321   ComAT, *I.A.O. v. Sweden*, para. 14.5.

In some cases, the Committee has considered that a complainant's membership in a certain opposition party in the receiving State would expose him to
the risk of being detained and consequently subjected to torture. In *Gbadjavi* v.
Switzerland (2012), the Committee found that the complainant's expulsion to
Togo would violate Article 3 CAT on the grounds that he belonged to the main
opposition party in Togo and that the members of this party were at risk of
detention and torture, regardless of whether they were well-known or not.[322]

III.2.4.2   *Ethnic Groups and Minorities*

Membership of certain ethnic or minority group was one of the factors the
Committee took into account in several Non-Refoulement cases where it found
the complainant's removal would violate Article 3 CAT.[323] The complainant in
Elmi v. *Australia* (1999) claimed that his removal to Somalia would be contrary
to Article 3 because he belonged to a minority clan, the Shikal, which was,
according to information by reliable sources, vulnerable to severe human rights
violations, particularly by the Hawiye clan that had effective control over the
area where most of the Shikal lived. The Committee took these circumstances
into account. It further noted that the complainant was particularly vulnerable to torture because his family had been targeted in the past by the Hawiye
clan. His father and brother had been killed, his sister was raped, and the rest
of the family was forced to flee. Against this background and in the light of the
publicity that surrounded the complainant's case, which could expose him to
reprisal by the Hawiye, the Committee found that the complainant's removal
would constitute a breach of Article 3.[324]

In another case, *S.M. et al.* v. *Sweden* (2011), the complainants argued deporting them to Azerbaijan would expose them to a risk of ethnically motivated
persecution. The Committee noted that the complainants had been previously
subjected to torture in Azerbaijan because they were Armenian. According to
general information available to the Committee, the general public was hostile towards ethnic Armenians who lived in Azerbaijan. Persons of Armenian
origin suffered the risk of discrimination in their daily life; they were harassed
or they had to pay bribes when they applied for passports, and they often hid
their identity by legally changing the ethnic description in their passports. The

---

322   ComAT, *Gbadjavi* v. *Switzerland*, para. 7.7.
323   ComAT, *Mutombo* v. *Switzerland*, para. 9.4; ComAT, *Mondal* v. *Sweden*, No. 338/2008,
        23 May 2011, para. 7.7; ComAT, *S.M. et al.* v. *Sweden*, No. 374/2009, 21 November 2011, para.
        9.7.
324   ComAT, *Elmi* v. *Australia*, paras. 6.7–6.8.

Committee found that, in these circumstances, removing the complainants would violate Article 3 CAT.[325]

Noticeably, in these two cases the Committee gave due weight to the fact that the complainants and/or their families had previously suffered ethnically motivated torture in the proposed receiving State. Could the same approach be followed where neither the complainant nor his family had been subjected to torture because of their ethnic origin? This question was addressed by the Committee in *Z.Z. v. Canada* (2001), in which the complainant argued that as a member of the Tajik ethnic group, he would face a risk of torture upon return to Afghanistan. The Committee noted that the complainant had not been subjected to torture in Afghanistan. It found that, in spite of the difficulties encountered by some ethnic groups in that country, mere membership of Tajik ethnic group did not sufficiently substantiate the risk that the complainant would be subjected to torture upon return.[326] In the Committee's view, mere membership in a certain ethnic or minority group vulnerable to torture in the receiving State is not sufficient in itself to conclude that the complainant will be at a real and personal risk of torture in this State.

III.2.4.3   *Women*

The poor human rights situation of women in a receiving State may also be sufficient ground for the Committee to believe that women constitute a vulnerable group in that country. In the case of *A.S. v. Sweden* (2000), which concerned the expulsion to Iran of a married woman sentenced to death by stoning for adultery, the Committee held that the complainant's removal would violate Article 3. The Committee based its conclusion on several reports that confirmed that married women had recently been sentenced to death by stoning for adultery.[327] Arguably, the Committee decided that women sentenced to death by stoning for adultery constituted a vulnerable group in Iran.

In *Njamba and Balikosa v. Sweden* (2010), the Committee found that the complainants, a Congolese mother and daughter,[328] would face a risk to their

---

325   ComAT, *S.M. et al. v. Sweden*, paras. 9.6–9.7.

326   ComAT, *Z.Z. v. Canada*, No. 123/1998, 15 May 2001, paras. 8.4–8.5. See also, ComAT, *M.B. v. Switzerland*, No. 439/2010, 31 May 2013, para. 7.7.

327   The Committee mainly referred to the report of the Special Representative of the Commission on Human Rights on the situation of human rights in Iran (E/CN.4/2000/35) of 18 January 2000. ComAT, *A.S. v. Sweden*, para. 8.7.

328   Ms. Njamba's husband was implicated in activities of treason and espionage on behalf of rebels, including purchasing of arms for rebels in Equateur. Since Ms. Njamba knew about her husband's activities, many families considered her as his accomplice, which

security upon return to the DRC. It based this conclusion mostly on several recent UN reports that indicated that men with guns, and civilians throughout the country, were committing alarming levels of sexual violence against women, in and outside areas of armed conflict.[329] The Committee referred to its General Comment No. 2 on Article 2, which states that:

> ...the failure of the State to exercise due diligence to intervene to stop, sanction and provide remedies to victims of torture facilitates and enables non-State actors to commit acts impermissible under the Convention with impunity.[330]

Accordingly, the Committee decided that the conflict in the DRC, which UN reports attested to, made it impossible for the Committee to identify areas of the country in which the applicants would be safe in their current and evolving situation.[331] The Committee found substantial grounds for believing that the applicants would be in danger of being tortured if returned to the DRC.[332] Noticeably, the Committee did not consider whether a female applicant had a social network to protect and support her in that receiving State. Women were held to constitute a vulnerable group because women were widely deprived of their human rights in this State and, in particular, because sexual violence against women was widespread and the authorities failed to protect them.

---

put her at risk. The police would not protect her. While the husband and three of their children were killed allegedly by Congolese militia in a fight, the mother and the daughter survived because they were hiding. Around three months later, the two applicants fled the DRC and arrived in Sweden in March 2005. ComAT, *Njamba and Balikosa* v. *Sweden*, paras. 2.2–2.3.

329 Ibid., see footnote 12 and para. 9.5. The Swedish government argued that the applicants would be returned to their home province where there had been no armed conflict contrary to the eastern parts of the DRC. Ibid., para. 8.5.

330 ComAT, General Comment No. 2, para. 18.

331 ComAT, *Njamba and Balikosa* v. *Sweden*, para. 9.5.

332 Ibid., para. 9.6. See also, ComAT, *Bakatu-Bia* v. *Sweden*, paras. 10.6–10.8; ComAT, *N.B-M.* v. *Switzerland*, para. 9.4; ComAT, *E.K.W.* v. *Finland*, No. 490/2012, 25 June 2015. The complainant's removal to the DRC in these cases were challenged, *inter alia*, on the ground that there was sexual violence against women there, by contrast, the complainant in *E.L.* v. *Switzerland* (2011) challenged her removal to the DRC on the ground of her previous political activities there. Therefore, the Committee did not take into account the women's human rights situation there. ComAT, *E.L.* v. *Switzerland*, No. 351/2008, 15 November 2011.

III.2.5   Credibility of the Complainant

According to the Committee's General Comment No.1, the credibility of the complainant is a factor that is taken into account when it assesses the existence of a risk of torture in the proposed receiving State. Through its case-law, the Committee has found that the complainant's credibility may be seriously undermined by various factors, such as submission of forged documents,[333] using different names and identity documents in his protection visa application,[334] and factual inconsistency or the unconvincing nature of a claim.[335] For example, in *M.B.B.* v. *Sweden* (1999), the Committee doubted the complainant's credibility because the account of his activities in Iran that he provided to the Committee differed in important aspects from the account he had provided to the Swedish authorities.[336]

The Committee has repeatedly asserted that complete accuracy is rarely expected of a victim of torture, and that inconsistencies in the complainant's presentation of the facts do not raise doubts about the general veracity of his claims.[337] Hence, the contradictions and inconsistencies in the complainant's story in *K.Y.Tala* v. *Sweden* (1996) were explained, in the Committee's view, by the fact that he suffered from post-traumatic stress disorder because he had been subjected to torture in Iran.[338]

A delay in the submission of statements and documents by an applicant may cast doubt on his credibility. In *Zubair Elahi* v. *Switzerland* (2005), the ComAT noted that the complainant's claims had escalated considerably during the domestic proceedings. The Committee observed that only after the Swiss authorities had refused the complainant's application for asylum, did he

---

333   ComAT, *A.M.* v. *France*, para. 13.5; ComAT, *S.G. et al.* v. *Switzerland*, No. 352/2008, 30 May 2011, para. 11.5.

334   ComAT, *X.Q.L.* v. *Australia*, No. 455/2011, 2 May 2014, para. 9.4.

335   ComAT, *V.X.N. and H.N.* v. *Sweden*, para. 13.6; ComAT, *A.K.* v. *Australia*, para. 6.2.

336   ComAT, *M.B.B.* v. *Sweden*, para. 6.6. See also, ComAT, *S.U.A.* v. *Sweden*, No. 223/2002, 22 November 2004, para. 6.5 and footnote 1; ComAT, *R.D.* v. *Switzerland*, No. 426/2010, 8 November 2013, paras. 9.5 and 9.7.

337   ComAT, *C.T. and K.M.* v. *Sweden*, paras. 7.5–7.6; ComAT, *Ismail Alan* v. *Switzerland*, No. 21/1995, 8 May 1996, para. 11.3; ComAT, *Ke* v. *Australia*, No. 416/2010, 5 November 2012, para. 7.5.

338   ComAT, *K.Y.Tala* v. *Sweden*, para. 10.3; ComAT, *A.F.* v. *Sweden*, para. 6.5. By contrast, the Committee has refused to justify the inconsistent in the complainant's statement where he cannot establish that he suffers from a post-traumatic stress disorder resulting from the past experience of ill-treatment. See e.g., ComAT, *X. Y.* v. *Switzerland* para. 10.4; ComAT, *N.P.* v. *Australia*, No. 106/1998, 6 May 1999; ComAT, *A.M.A.* v. *Switzerland*, No. 344/2008, 12 November 2010, para. 7.7.

put forward the claim he risked being arrested, if returned to Pakistan, because of his apostasy from Islam.[339] In the Committee's view, this adversely affected his credibility. However, in the case of *V.L.* v. *Switzerland* (2006), the Committee considered it well-known that:

> ...the loss of privacy and prospect of humiliation based on revelation alone of the acts concerned may cause both women and men to withhold the fact that they have been subject to rape and/or other forms of sexual abuse until it appears absolutely necessary. Particularly for women, there is the additional fear of shaming and rejection by their partner or family members.[340]

In this case, the Committee accepted the complainant's explanation that when she had admitted being raped to her husband, he reacted by humiliating her, and forbidden her to mention it in their asylum proceedings. The Committee further noted that, as soon as her husband left her, the complainant immediately disclosed the rapes to the Swiss authorities. Accordingly, the Committee rejected the State party's argument that the complainant's allegations of sexual abuse and the medical report that supported these allegations lacked credibility because they were submitted late in the domestic proceedings.[341]

III.2.6   Factors Relating to the Complainant's Family Circumstances

In assessing if a complainant would be at a real risk of torture in the proposed receiving State, the ComAT has taken into account allegations that relate to the applicant's family circumstances, such as the fact that members of the complainant's family were subjected to torture in the receiving State.[342] In *Tapia Paez* v. *Sweden* (1996), the Committee found no ground to distinguish between the complainant and his mother and sister, who were granted asylum in Sweden because they feared being persecuted due to their membership in a family connected to Sendero Luminoso. The Committee concluded that the State party had an obligation to refrain from forcibly returning the complainant to Peru.[343]

---

339   ComAT, *Zubair Elahi* v. *Switzerland*, No. 222/2002, 3 May 2005, para. 6.4.

340   ComAT, *V.L.* v. *Switzerland*, No. 262/2005, 20 November 2006, para. 8.8.

341   Ibid., para. 8.8.

342   ComAT, *Elmi* v. *Australia*, para. 6.8; ComAT, *Orhan Ayas* v. *Sweden*, para. 6.5.

343   ComAT, *Tapia Paez* v. *Sweden*, paras. 14.4–15. See also, *Faragollah et al.* v. *Switzerland* (2011), in which the fact that the applicant's son was granted refugee status in Switzerland was

The fact that a complainant's family has lived in the receiving State without any problems with the authorities may indicate that the complainant would not be at risk of ill-treatment if returned. In *X.* v. *Switzerland* (1997), the Committee noted that the complainant's wife had returned to Sudan without facing any problem with the authorities there.[344]

The argument that a complainant would be at risk of being tortured in the proposed receiving State because of the activities of a member of his family has been also raised before the ComAT in several Non-Refoulement cases. In *Kalonzo* v. *Canada* (2012), the fact that the complainant's father was a leader of the main opposition party in the DRC was one of the factors taken into account by the Committee when it found that the complainant's return to the DRC would violate Article 3.[345]

The Committee has given importance to the distance of the family tie. In the case of *M.V.* v. *The Netherlands* (2003), the complainants founded their Non-Refoulement claim on their family relationship to the leadership of the PKK, an allegedly terrorist organization. The Committee rejected this argument because the complainant's family ties of some distance with the PKK leadership were insufficient to ground a Non-Refoulement claim.[346] The Committee has required that the activities of the complainant's family members must be important enough to continue to attract the interest of the authorities in the receiving State.[347] In *Avedes Hamayak Korban* v. *Sweden* (1998), the Committee found that the complainant would be in danger of being tortured if returned to Iraq because, *inter alia*, he might be held responsible for his son's desertion from the Iraqi army.[348]

---

one of the factors that were taken into account by the ComAT. ComAT, *Faragollah et al.* v. *Switzerland*, paras. 9.5–9.6.

344 ComAT, *X.* v. *Switzerland*, No. 27/1995, 28 April 1997, para. 11.3. See also, ComAT, *Y.S.* v. *Switzerland*, No. 147/1999, 15 May 2001, para. 6.6; ComAT, *H.D.* v. *Switzerland*, No. 112/1998, 30 April 1999, para. 6.5.

345 ComAT, *Kalonzo* v. *Canada*, para. 9.7. See also, ComAT, *M.A.M.A. et al.* v. *Sweden*, para. 9.7; ComAT, *X and Z* v. *Finland*, Nos. 483/2011 and 485/2011, 12 May 2014, para. 7.6. By contrast see *Hanan Attia* v. *Sweden* (2003), which concerned the expulsion of a wife of a suspected terrorist to Egypt where she would allegedly be at risk of torture in order to obtain information concerning her husband. In this case, the Committee depended on the DAS to conclude that Mrs. Attia would not be at risk in Egypt, consequently, it found that his wife's expulsion would not be in violation of Article 3 CAT. ComAT, *Hanan Attia* v. *Sweden*, No. 199/2002, 17 November 2003, para. 12.3.

346 ComAT, *M.V.* v. *The Netherlands*, No. 201/2002, 2 May 2003, para. 7.

347 ComAT, *A.A.* v. *Switzerland*, No. 251/2004, 17 November 2006, para. 7.6.

348 ComAT, *Avedes Hamayak Korban* v. *Sweden*, para. 6.4. See also, ComAT, *T.A.* v. *Sweden*, No. 226/2003, 27 May 2005, para. 7.3. By contrast, the Committee found that there was no

The complainant's previous activities or experience of torture are not relevant to his Non-Refoulement claim if they are not in the recent past. A ortiori, this also applies to the previous experience of torture or political activities of a member of the complainant's family. In *S.N.A.W. et al.* v. *Switzerland* (2005), the ComAT noted that the political activities and execution of the complainant's brother had not occurred in the recent past, and it did not take them into account.[349]

III.2.7   Medical Situation

Most of the claims that a complainant's removal to his country of origin would result in aggravating the condition of his physical or mental health have not been raised under Article 3 CAT. Some have argued that removal in these circumstances would amount to degrading treatment that violates Article 16,[350] which is outside the scope of this study. However, the claim has been raised under Article 3 CAT in some Non-Refoulement cases.

In *N.B-M.* v. *Switzerland* (2011), the complainant argued that her state of health was an important factor the ComAT should take into account in assessing the risk she would face if deported to the DRC, including the risk of suicide.[351] The Committee noted that, in spite of the uncertainties and high cost of health care in the DRC, there were facilities to treat depression. The Committee suggested that the complainant could consult a doctor in the DRC and added that, even if the complainant's state of health were to deteriorate as a result of her deportation, this would not, in itself, amount to torture that could be attributed to the sending State within the meaning of Article 3, read in conjunction with Article 1 CAT.[352]

Consequently, the Committee has repeatedly affirmed that even if a complainant's removal to the proposed receiving State could aggravate his state of health, this is not sufficient ground to impose an obligation on the sending

---

reason for the complainant to fear persecution on the basis of family co-responsibility because of the desertion from the Sri Lankan army of her ex-husband, as her marriage was dissolved by divorce judgment. ComAT, *S.N.A.W. et al.* v. *Switzerland*, para. 7.7.

349   Ibid., para. 7.5. See also, ComAT, *Z.T.* v. *Australia*, para. 6.3. ComAT, *A.I.* v. *Switzerland*, para. 6.7.

350   The ComAT has repeatedly asserted that such claim is generally insufficient, in the absence of additional factors, to amount to degrading treatment in violation of Article 16. ComAT, *G.R.B.* v. *Sweden*, para. 6.7; ComAT, *T.M.* v. *Sweden*, para. 6.2; ComAT, *M.F.* v. *Sweden*, No. 326/2007, 26 November 2008, para. 6.4.

351   ComAT, *N.B-M.* v. *Switzerland*, para. 5.2.

352   Ibid., para. 9.8. ComAT, *K.K.* v. *Switzerland*, para. 6.8; ComAT, *A.I.* v. *Switzerland*, para. 6.8; ComAT, *Bachan Singh Sogi* v. *Canada*, para. 9.3; ComAT, *E.L.* v. *Canada*, para. 8.6.

State to refrain from proceeding with removal to the receiving State under Article 3, if adequate medical care is available.[353] The Committee's reference to adequate medical care in the proposed receiving State may indicate that its decision would have been different if there were no adequate medical care; in such a case, Article 3 might be violated if it resulted in aggravating the applicant's medical condition. The Committee has not had the opportunity to consider such an application. Since Article 3 CAT applies only to torture, we argue that the prohibition against refoulement under this Article is not applicable when the proposed receiving State generally lacks medical resources. However, the Committee should apply Article 3 where the complainant who may be detained in the receiving State can establish that the authorities of this State intentionally fail to provide medical care to detainees.

III.2.8   Risk *sur Place*

According to the ComAT's General Comment No.1,[354] substantial grounds for believing that an complainant's removal would expose him to the risk of being tortured may be based both on his previous activities in his country of origin and also on activities carried out in the sending State party. The Committee clearly mentioned that the wording of Article 3 CAT does not distinguish between acts the complainant has committed in his country of origin, before his departure, or in the sending State, after his deportation. Even if the activities the complainant is accused of committing in the proposed receiving State are insufficient for Article 3 to apply, his activities subsequent to the departure from this State could prove sufficient to apply that Article.[355]

The Committee has held that the *sur place* action must be sufficiently important to draw the attention of the proposed receiving State.[356] The complainant must establish that the authorities of his country of origin are aware of the activities abroad that would place him at particular risk of torture upon return.[357] He might be at risk resulting from expressing his political views,[358] involvement in activities of an organization considered illegal in

---

353   ComAT, *S.G. et al.* v. *Switzerland*, para. 11.6.

354   ComAT, General Comment No. 1, para. 8(e).

355   ComAT, *Seid Mortesa Aemei* v. *Switzerland*, para. 9.5.

356   ComAT, *X, Y and Z* v. *Sweden*, para. 11.4; ComAT, *M.K.O.* v. *The Netherlands*, No. 134/1999, 9 May 2001, para. 7.4; ComAT, *Gamal El Rgeig* v. *Switzerland*, No. 280/2005, 15 November 2006, para. 7.4.

357   ComAT, *S.G.* v. *The Netherlands*, No. 135/1999, 12 May 2004, para. 6.5.

358   Such as by publishing several articles or participating in demonstrations or in radio broadcasts where he expressed his political opinions against the regime rolling in the receiving State. ComAT, *Jahani* v. *Switzerland*, paras. 9.6–9.7. The Committee held that

the receiving State,[359] applying for asylum,[360] or converting to a religion when that is forbidden by the authorities in his country of origin.[361] In *Faragollah et al.* v. *Switzerland* (2011), the applicant was an Iranian national who arrived in Switzerland in 2000. From 2005, he was a senior active member in the Democratic Association for Refugees and held a position as the Association's representative for the Canton of Obwald. In addition to writing articles criticizing the Iranian regime, distributing the association's publications and participating in several events, the applicant claimed that he was a strategic planner of the association's activities, and his name and address were published in its monthly magazine. In light of the applicant's *sur place* activities, the Committee was of the opinion that he would attract the attention of the Iranian authorities if he returned.[362] The same conclusion was reached in another case concerned removal from Switzerland to Iran of another member of the same Association, who held a position as a cantonal representative.[363] In *Elmi* v. *Australia* (1999), the Committee gave due weight to the wide national and international publicity that surrounded the complainant's case.[364]

---

the mere participation on one occasion in a mass demonstration, in the absence of other elements, did not make it possible to believe that the complainant would run the risk of being subjected to torture in the event of his return to Iran. ComAT, *M.B.* v. *Switzerland*, para. 7.8.

359   ComAT, *Seid Mortesa Aemei* v. *Switzerland*, para. 9.7.

360   ComAT, *P.M. Kisoki* v. *Sweden*, No. 41/1996, 8 May 1996, para. 9.5; ComAT, *Tursunov* v. *Kazakhstan*, No. 538/2013, 3 July 2015, para. 9.6.

361   ComAT, *M.B.B.* v. *Sweden*, para. 6.7. In this case, the Committee considered that the complainant failed to substantiate his claim that he would be at risk of torture if returned to Iran because of his conversion to Christianity after he had left Iran. In the Committee's opinion, he failed to establish that converts to Christianity were, in general, at risk of being subjected to torture, especially if they were not prominent members of the Christian community.

362   ComAT, *Faragollah et al.* v. *Switzerland*, paras. 9.5–9.6.

363   ComAT, *Jahani* v. *Switzerland*, paras. 9.6–9.7. By contrast see, ComAT, *T.D.* v. *Switzerland*, para. 7.7–7.8. Which concerned the deportation of an Ethiopian national from Switzerland where he was a cantonal representative of an Ethiopian opposition party. The Committee noted that merely being a supporter or member of an Ethiopian opposition party did not in itself entail a risk of persecution, with the exception of two specific parties. The Committee observed that the complainant was not a member of any of these two parties and that merely being a cantonal representative was not sufficient in itself to hold that he constituted a threat to the Ethiopian government. Consequently, the Committee concluded that the complainant's deportation would not expose him to a risk of being tortured in Ethiopian.

364   ComAT, *Elmi* v. *Australia*, para. 5.11.

Accordingly, the Committee found that the complainant's removal to Somalia would expose him to a risk of torture because, *inter alia*, he could be accused of damaging the reputation of the Hawiye clan.[365]

III.2.9   UNHCR's Assessment of the Case

The ComAT has rarely referred to the UNHCR's assessment of a complainant's claim regarding the risk he would face if removed to the proposed receiving State. Although the UNHCR had already examined the cases of the complainants in *V.X.N. and H.N.* v. *Sweden*, the ComAT, when it considered the merits of the case, did not mention the UNHCR's conclusion.[366] In some cases, the Committee has referred to the UNHCR's general assessment of the risk of torture or CIDTP in the receiving State. In *U.S.* v. *Finland* (2003), the ComAT pointed to the UNHCR's opinion of March 1999 as evidence of the improving human rights situation in Sri Lanka. The UNHCR had ruled that asylum seekers who did not fulfil refugee criteria, including those of Tamil origin like the complainant, may be returned to Sri Lanka, and that a large number of Tamil refugees had returned to Sri Lanka in 2001 and 2002. Also, the complainant had not been politically active since the mid-1980s, so the Committee considered that the complainant had not established the existence of a personal and real risk of torture.[367]

In *Elif Pelit* v. *Azerbaijan* (2007), the ComAT referred to a conclusion adopted by the UNHCR's Executive Committee. One of the factors the ComAT took into account was that the complainant had been recognised as a refugee by Germany, where it was determined that she would be at risk of persecution if returned to Turkey. The Committee noted that the complainant's refugee status was valid at the time Azerbaijan deported her to Turkey. It recalled the conclusion of the UNHCR's Executive Committee which referred to the extra-territorial effect of determining refugee status: when a person is given refugee status by one State party to the CSR, that status will be recognized by the other States parties to this Convention. The Committee observed that Azerbaijan did not show why it had not respected this in the *Elif Pelit* case, in circumstances

---

365   Ibid. para. 6.8.

366   ComAT, *V.X.N. and H.N.* v. *Sweden*.

367   ComAT, *U.S.* v. *Finland*, paras. 7.7–7.8. See also *X, Y and Z* v. *Sweden*, which concerned the deportation of refused asylum seekers to the DRC. ComAT, *X, Y and Z* v. *Sweden*, para. 11.5. In another case of *P.M. Kisoki* v. *Sweden* (1996), the Committee noted the UNHCR's position that deportees to Zaire who were discovered to have sought asylum abroad undergo interrogation upon their arrival at the airport, and they would be at risk of detention and ill-treatment if they were believed to have a political profile. ComAT, *P.M. Kisoki* v. *Sweden*, para. 9.5.

where the general situation of persons like the complainant, and the complainant's own past experiences raised real issues under Article 3 CAT.[368]

III.3   *Conclusion*

When it comes to protecting persons from ill-treatment under the principle of Non-Refoulement, the difference between Article 3 ECHR and Article 3 CAT is reflected in the way each body interprets the factors it uses to assess risk in the proposed receiving State. While Article 3 ECHR protects the person concerned against removal to torture and CIDTP, Article 3 CAT protects the person only against refoulement to torture as defined under Article 1 CAT. Consequently, the ComAT's assessment of the risk focuses on determining if the complainant is personally of interest to the authorities in the receiving State. This leads the ComAT to apply a more restrictive interpretation of the "personal nature" of the risk than that adopted by the ECtHR. We derive this conclusion from the following findings:

The ECtHR's Non-Refoulement case-law under Article 3 ECHR has firmly established that the mere possibility of ill-treatment because of an unsettled general situation in the receiving State is, in principle, not sufficient, in itself, to give rise to a violation of this Article. The Court has recently distinguished between two situations in the receiving State. The first is a general situation of human rights violations. In the Court's view, this situation does not constitute, in itself, a substantial ground to apply the principle of Non-Refoulement. The applicant has to establish the existence of special distinguishing features in his case that put him at a real risk of the proscribed ill-treatment. The second is a general situation of violence. The Court has considerd the applicant's removal to constitute a violation of Article 3 if this situation is intense enough to create a real risk of ill-treatment simply because the applicant is removed to this country. The applicant does not need to establish the existence of any special distinguishing features in his case. The Court has considered that any individual who finds himself in such a general situation of violence is at personal risk of being subjected to treatment contrary to Article 3 ECHR. In the Court's view, this does not change the personal nature of the risk that the applicant faces, as an individual, in the receiving State because this personal nature of the risk does not mean the applicant is individually targeted by the risk. The ComAT has not distinguished between these situations. It does not consider the existence of a general situation of violence or of human rights violations in the receiving State to constitute, in itself, sufficient grounds to apply Article 3 CAT. The Committee has always requested the complainant

---

368   ComAT, *Elif Pelit* v. *Azerbaijan*, para. 11.

to demonstrate that there are personal distinguishing features in his case that demonstrate that the authorities in the receiving State are likely to personally target him. However, the Committee does not interpret the personal nature of the risk to mean that the complainant is individually targeted; it means that he, personally, is of interest to the authorities because there are distinguishing features in this case.

The Court has considered the existence of a general situation of serious human rights violations in the detention centres of the receiving State to be a substantial ground for applying the principle of Non-Refoulement under Article 3 ECHR to all extradition cases. To be protected under Article 3 ECHR, the Court has considered it is sufficient for the applicant to establish the existence of a general situation of serious human rights violations in the detention centres of the State that requested his extradition. Arguably, this is a special distinguishing feature in case of the applicant who faces a risk of extradition that may expose him to ill-treatment. Where the Court is not satisfied that all detainees in the receiving State constitute a vulnerable group, the applicant can still benefit from the protection against refoulement if he demonstrates that he is a member of a particular group of detainees that is vulnerable to ill-treatment. The Committee has goen further in restricting the interpretation of the "personal nature" of the risk by refusing to consider the existence of a general situation of serious human rights violations in detention centres of the receiving State as a substantial ground for the decision to apply Article 3 CAT to extradition cases, and has always required a complainant to demonstrate distinguishing features that relate to him personally, such as being a member of a particular group of detainees targeted by torture in detention centres.

The ComAT has followed the restrictive interpretation of the personal nature of the risk also to assessing the removal of a person belonging to a certain ethnic group or minority. The ECtHR seems ready to apply Article 3 ECHR where the person to be removed demonstrates that he belongs to a certain ethnic group or minority that is systematically subjected to ill-treatment. But the ComAT has expressly refused to apply Article 3 CAT only on this ground if the complainant does not demonstrate that he or/and his family have already suffered ethnically motivated torture in the proposed receiving State.

The Committee does not seem to follow this restrictive interpretation of the "personal nature" of the risk in cases that concern the removal of a woman to a State where a general situation of violence against women exists, carried out by non-State actors, and where the authorities of this State fail to protect them and provide remedies. In this situation, the Committee has held that women constitute a vulnerable group in the receiving State and applies Article 3 without requesting the complainant to give evidence relating to her personal circumstances. But the ECtHR does request the applicant to establish that she has no social network to protect and support her in that country.

Both the ComAT and the ECtHR have given special weight and applied almost the same principles when they assess the factors that determine the credibility of the applicant, the facts that establish that he, or a member of his family, has already been ill-treated in the receiving State, or that he may attract negative attention in the receiving State because of his previous activities there, or the activities of a member of his family. While the Committee has taken into account the complainant's previous activities only where they attract the negative attention of the receiving State's authorities, the Court has not distinguished between activities that attract the negative attention of the authorities and those that attract negative attention of non-State actors in the receiving State. The Committee, unlike the Court, has taken the applicant's past experience of ill-treatment into account only when this treatment was "inflicted by or at the instigation of or with the consent or acquiescence of a public official or other person acting in an official capacity".

The Court has considered that the principle of Non-Refoulement under Article 3 ECHR applies to the removal of a person who is afflicted with any serious, naturally occurring physical or mental illness that may cause suffering, pain and reduced life expectancy and require specialised medical treatment that may not be as readily available in the receiving State, or that may be available only at substantial cost. In contrast, the Committee has held that Article 3 CAT does not apply to the complainant's removal solely on the ground that it could aggravate his illness, if adequate medical care is available. We argue that the Committee's reference to the existence of adequate medical care in the receiving State could indicate that it might apply Article 3 CAT if the complainant, who faces a risk of being detained in the receiving State, can establish that the authorities of this State intentionally and systematically fail to provide medical care to detainees for a purpose, such as, extracting information or a confession, and that this practice would cause him severe pain or suffering given his poor health.

Finally, both the ComAT and the ECtHR have taken into account the related assessment by the UNHCR. However, the Court has tended to give less weight to the UNHCR's general assessment of the risk in the receiving State than it has given to the specific assessment of the applicant's claim about the risk he would personally face if returned. In contrast, while in no case the Committee has given weight to the UNHCR's specific assessment of the complainant's case, in some cases it has referred to the most recent UNHCR general assessment of the risk of torture or CIDTP in the proposed receiving State. The ComAT's approach may be justified because the UNHCR's assessment of the complainant's case was done long before the material time of the Committee's assessment. The UNHCR assessments under Article 33 CSR determine if the complainant faces a risk to his life or freedom on account of his race, religion, nationality, membership of particular social group, or political opinion. However, this assessment should not be ignored since it might help the body concerned to conduct its own assessment.

IV   The National Protection Arguments and Their Effects on the Risk Assessment

When the applicant establishes an arguable Non-Refoulement claim, the burden of proof then shifts to the respondent State, which must submit arguments that cast doubt on the applicant's claim. Among the arguments most commonly put forward are the following: there is an internal flight alternative in the proposed receiving State, national laws in this State prohibit ill-treatment and torture, and the receiving State has provided DAs that the applicant will not be subjected to the prescribed treatment upon his removal. We discuss these arguments and their effect on ECtHR and ComAT assessments of the risk in the following subsections.

IV.1   *Internal Flight Alternative*
IV.1.1   ECtHR
In several Non-Refoulement cases, sending States have argued that there is an internal flight alternative in the proposed receiving State, so that even if there were a real risk the applicant would be ill-treated in one part of the country of destination, he could be safely resettled in another part. Thus, the applicant's removal would not violate Article 3 ECHR. Through its case-law, the ECtHR has repeatedly asserted that:

> Article 3 does not, as such, preclude Contracting States from placing reliance on the existence of an internal flight alternative in their assessment of an individual's claim that a return to his country of origin would expose him to a real risk of being subjected to treatment proscribed by that provision.[369]

The Court has, however, held that reliance on an internal flight alternative does not reduce the responsibility of the sending State to ensure that the

---

369   ECtHR, *Chahal v. the United Kingdom*, para. 98; ECtHR, *Hilal v. the United Kingdom*, para. 67–68.

applicant is not, as a result of its decision to remove him, exposed to treatment proscribed by Article 3. Therefore, the Court has required that:

> ...as a precondition of relying on an internal flight alternative, certain guarantees have to be in place: the person to be expelled must be able to travel to the area concerned, gain admittance and settle there, failing which an issue under Article 3 may arise, the more so if in the absence of such guarantees there is a possibility of his ending up in a part of the country of origin where he may be subjected to ill-treatment.[370]

In *Chahal* v. *The UK* (1996), the applicant was a well-known supporter of Sikh separatism. The British government contended that deporting the applicant would not expose him to a real risk of ill-treatment, and emphasised that he was to be returned to any part of India he chose, and not necessarily to Punjab. The Court noted that, although the applicant would be most at risk within the State of Punjab, he could not be considered to be safe elsewhere in India because the Punjab police were fully capable of pursuing suspected Sikh militants into other areas of India far away from Punjab; the police in other areas were also reported to be involved in serious human rights violations.[371]

Where a State party intends to return the applicant to a specific part of the country of destination, the ECtHR has focused its assessment on whether there is a real risk of the proscribed ill-treatment in this part. If the sending State argues that the applicant has an internal flight alternative, the Court has noted that it cannot limit its assessment to the particular internal destination to which the State intends to send the applicant. Although, in the case of *Sufi and Elmi,* the British government intended to return both applicants to Mogadishu, the Court did not limit its consideration of the risk to assessing conditions in Mogadishu. The UKAIT had found that even if there were a real risk in the capital, it would be possible for the applicants to relocate to a safer region in southern or central Somalia.[372] The ECtHR addressed question of internal flight alternative in detail in this case. The Court first noted that given the humanitarian crisis in Somalia and the strain it placed both on individuals and the traditional clan structure, a returnee could not find refuge or

---

370   ECtHR, *Salah Sheekh* v. *The Netherlands*, para. 141; ECtHR, *Sufi and Elmi* v. *the United Kingdom*, para. 266; ECtHR, *B.K.A.* v. *Sweden*, Appl.No. 11161/11, 19 December 2013, para. 44; ECtHR, *A.A.M.* v. *Sweden*, para. 68.

371   ECtHR, *Chahal* v. *the United Kingdom*, para. 104. See also, ECtHR, *Hilal* v. *the United Kingdom*, paras. 67–68.

372   ECtHR, *Sufi and Elmi* v. *the United Kingdom*, para. 265.

support in an area where he had no close family connections. If he had no such connections, or if he could not safely travel to an area where he had such connections, the Court considered it reasonably likely that he would seek refuge in an internally displaced person (IDP) settlement or refugee camp. Hence, in considering the internal flight alternative, the Court first asked if a returnee would face a risk of ill-treatment either in transit, or upon settling in another part of southern or central Somalia, before it considered if he would be at a real risk of ill-treatment in an IDP settlement or refugee camp because of poor humanitarian conditions there.[373]

The Court noted that although there were some airports in southern and central Somalia, all applicants who faced removal from the UK had been issued removal directions to Mogadishu International Airport. Since this airport was regularly used and under the Transitional Federal government's control, the Court noted that a person who was removed to southern and central Somalia would not be at real risk of being subjected to proscribed ill-treatment at the airport.[374] Though the Court found that Mogadishu was not a safe place for the majority of Somalis, it was possible for a returnee to travel from the Mogadishu International Airport to another region of southern and central Somalia without entering the city. Since the fighting outside the capital was described as sporadic and localised around strategic towns, the Court was ready to believe that it might be possible for a returnee to travel from Mogadishu International Airport to another part of southern and central Somalis without facing a risk of ill-treatment in the context of general violence. However, the safety of a particular returnee would depend on where their home area was. If the applicant's home area were affected by the fighting, the Court would have to assess the general situation of violence there against the requirements of Article 3 at the time of removal.[375]

The Court noted that the areas of southern and central Somalia with the lowest levels of general violence were those under al-Shabaab's control. Al-Shabaab imposed strictly interpreted Sharia law and meted out severe punishments for infringements. Consequently, the Court found that a returnee with no recent experience of living in Somalia would be at a real risk of ill-treatment because of the human rights situation in areas under al-Shabaab's control. The Court further noted that al-Shabaab imposed its rules on persons living in these areas, and also on those travelling through them. Al-Shabaab established checkpoints at the entrances and exits of towns under its control,

---

373   Ibid., para. 267.
374   Ibid., para. 268.
375   Ibid., paras. 270–271.

and searched people and goods to ensure they complied with Al-Shabaab's strict Islamic rules. Persons who did not obey these rules could face difficulties at these checkpoints, including flogging for a woman who sat next to a man in a vehicle, and forcible recruitment of young men and children.[376] The Court concluded that:

> ...if a returnee's home area is in an al-Shabaab controlled area, or if it could not be reached without travelling through an al-Shabaab controlled area, the Court does not consider that he could relocate within Somalia without being exposed to a real risk of Article 3 ill-treatment.[377]

Against this background, the Court noted that the first applicant's hometown was under the control of Al-Shabaab. Since he had no experience of living under Al-Shabaab's repressive regime, it would expose him to a real risk of ill-treatment by Al-Shabaab if he attempted to relocate there.[378] The Court considered the second applicant unable to relocate safely within southern and central Somalia because he had no close family connections there, and he had no experience of living under the Al-Shabaab regime. The Court observed that country information indicated that persons like the applicant, who came from Somaliland and/or had strong clan connections to this region, would be admitted. But the assertion of the British authorities that the returnee would be admitted to Somaliland contradicted their claim that they had chosen to return him to Mogadishu, rather than the airport in Somaliland. The Court found that the second applicant would not be able to travel to his hometown, gain admittance and settle there.[379]

The Court turned to address whether the IDP or refugee camps could constitute an internal flight alternative for a returnee who had no close family connections or could not safely travel to an area where he had such connections. While the Court considered it reasonably likely that such a returnee would have to seek refuge in an IDP or refugee camp, it held that the humanitarian conditions in these camps were sufficiently dire to amount to treatment that reached the threshold of Article 3 ECHR. Consequently, the Court found that any returnee forced to seek refuge in any of these camps would be at a real risk of treatment contrary to Article 3, since humanitarian conditions were so

---

376   Ibid., para. 274.
377   Ibid., para. 277.
378   Ibid., para. 302.
379   Ibid., paras. 310–312.

dire.[380] The Court concluded that such camps did not constitute an internal flight alternative for the applicants.

According to the ECtHR's case-law, even if the applicant's removal to a specific part of the proposed receiving State would expose him to a real risk of ill-treatment, the principle of Non-Refoulement under Article 3 would not be violated if there is an internal flight alternative for him.[381] Relocation in a safe area in the receiving State constitutes an internal flight alternative for the applicant if he can safely travel, gain admittance and settle there.

IV.1.2   ComAT

The internal flight alternative argument was used in the case of *B.S.S.* v. *Canada* (2004), which concerned the expulsion of an Indian national of Sikh origin to India. The ComAT noted that evidence adduced by the complainant merely indicated the risk he would be tortured in Punjab. The Committee found that he failed to substantiate his claim that he would face a risk of torture in another part of India. The Committee stated that the mere fact that the complainant may not be able to return to his home village and his family did not, as such, constitute torture for the purpose of applying Article 3.[382] In *S.S.S.* v. *Canada* (2005), the Committee added that high-profile Sikhs might be at risk in parts of India other than Punjab.[383]

While the ComAT has, in principle, accepted the notion of an internal flight alternative, or as it has called the notion of "local danger", ComAT has admitted that this notion is not sufficient to completely dispel the personal risk of being tortured in all cases. The Committee has made it clear that "the notion of "local danger" does not provide for measurable criteria and is not sufficient to entirely dispel the personal danger of being tortured".[384]

---

380   Ibid., para. 292.

381   See e.g., *Husseini* v. *Sweden* (2011), in which the Court found that the applicant had an internal flight alternative in Afghanistan. The Court considered that although Christians constitute a vulnerable minority and could face a real risk of being ill-treated in the southern and central parts of Iraq, they might reasonably relocate to the Kurdistan Region where they would not face such a risk. ECtHR, *M.K.N.* v. *Sweden*, paras. 35–40; ECtHR, *A.G.A.M.* v. *Sweden*, Appl.No. 71680/10, 27 June 2013, paras. 39–44; ECtHR, *N.M.B.* v. *Sweden*, paras. 37–42; ECtHR, *N.A.N.S.* v. *Sweden*, paras. 34–39; ECtHR, *M.Y.H. and others* v. *Sweden*, paras. 62–67. The Kurdistan Region was also considered as an internal relocation alternative for an Arab Sunni Muslim fearing persecution or ill-treatment in other parts of Iraq. See, ECtHR, *A.A.M.* v. *Sweden*.

382   ComAT, *B.S.S.* v. *Canada*, para. 11.5.

383   ComAT, *S.S.S.* v. *Canada*, para. 8.5. See also, ComAT, *Ismail Alan* v. *Switzerland*, para. 11.4.

384   ComAT, *Mondal* v. *Sweden*, para. 7.4; ComAT, *Kalonzo* v. *Canada*, para. 97.

Even if a part of the receiving State is considered safe for the group to which the complainant belongs, his personal circumstances must be taken into account to determine if he would be in a personal danger of being tortured in that part. In *Singh Khalsa et al.* v. *Switzerland* (2011), which concerned the expulsion to India of Indian nationals of Sikh origin who had hijacked airplanes from Indian Airlines, the Committee noted the respondent State party's submission that numerous Sikh militants returned to India, that Sikhs live in great numbers in different parts of India and that, therefore, the complainants could relocate to a part of Indian other than Punjab, their state of origin. The Committee, however, observed that some Sikhs who were alleged to be involved in terrorist activities had been arrested by the authorities when they arrived at the airport, taken to prisons, and charged with various offences. Since the Indian police continued to look for the complainants, the Committee concluded that they would not be able to lead a life free of torture in other parts of India.[385] In another case, *Kalonzo* v. *Canada* (2012), the Committee noted that although the Luba, an ethnic group to which the complainant belonged, did not seem to be threatened by violence in Kinshasa, his resettlement there would not entirely remove him from personal danger. This conclusion was based, *inter alia*, on the fact that the complainant had already been the victim of violence when he was detained in Kinshasa in 2002.[386]

IV.2 *Prohibition of Torture and CIDTP in the Receiving State's National Laws and the Relevant International Treaties*

IV.2.1 ECtHR

In several Non-Refoulement cases, the respondent State has argued that the risk of ill-treatment for the applicant does not exist in the receiving State because the receiving State's national laws and the international treaties to which it is a party prohibit the practice of torture and ill-treatment. The Azerbaijani government raised this argument in the case of *Garayev*, which concerned an expulsion to Uzbekistan, by maintaining that torture and ill-treatment were prohibited by Uzbekistan's domestic law.[387] In *Khaydarov* v. *Russia* (2010), the Russian government argued that there had been no reason not to extradite the applicant to Tajikistan, since the requesting State was a member of the UN, had undertaken to comply with the UDHR and had ratified the ICCPR, the CSR,

---

385   ComAT, *Singh Khalsa et al.* v. *Switzerland*, para. 11.6. See, ComAT, *Njamba and Balikosa* v. *Sweden*, para. 9.5; ComAT, *Bakatu-Bia* v. *Sweden*, para. 10.7.

386   ComAT, *Kalonzo* v. *Canada*, para. 9.7.

387   ECtHR, *Garayev* v. *Azerbaijan*, para. 73. See also, ECtHR, *Muminov* v. *Russia*, para. 96; ECtHR, *Umirov* v. *Russia*, para. 120.

the CAT and other treaties.[388] The ECtHR is not persuaded that, just because a State has ratified the major legal human rights instruments, an applicant runs no risk of being subjected to the proscribed ill-treatment in the receiving State. The Court observed that the Russian government failed to convincingly establish that the general human rights situation in Tajikistan had substantially improved, and compared its claims to the situation described in the latest reports by reliable and objective organisations.[389] In this connection, the Court has repeatedly asserted that:

> ...the existence of domestic laws and accession to international treaties guaranteeing respect for fundamental rights in principle are not in themselves sufficient to ensure adequate protection against the risk of ill-treatment where, [...], reliable sources have reported practices resorted to or tolerated by the authorities which are manifestly contrary to the principles of the Convention.[390]

This approach has been applied even when the receiving State is a member to the ECHR itself. In *Shamayev and 12 others* v. *Georgia and Russia* (2005), the Georgian government contended that when the extradition decision was taken, Russia's membership of the CE had been taken into account.[391] The Court found, in light of the situation of persons of Chechen origin in Russia, described by the latest reports from reliable sources,[392] that enforcing the extradition decision would violate Article 3.[393] In *Bajsultanov* v. *Austria* (2012), which concerned the expulsion of a Russian national of Chechen origin to

---

388   ECtHR, *Khaydarov* v. *Russia*, para. 92. In *Yakubov* v. *Russia* (2011), the Russian government argued that in assessment of the applicant's asylum application the national authorities had taken into account that Uzbekistan ratified the CAT. ECtHR, *Yakubov* v. *Russia*, para. 52. In *Klein* v. *Russia* (2010), the Russian government also claimed that Colombia, the receiving State, was a party to the majority of international human rights instruments, including the ICCPR and the CAT. ECtHR, *Klein* v. *Russia*, para. 37.

389   ECtHR, *Khaydarov* v. *Russia*, para. 105. See also, ECtHR, *Khodzhayev* v. *Russia*, para. 98.

390   ECtHR, *Saadi* v. *Italy* (GC), para. 147; ECtHR, *Muminov* v. *Russia*, para. 96; ECtHR, *Yakubov* v. *Russia*, para. 93; ECtHR, *Zokhidove* v. *Russia*, para. 140; ECtHR, *Egamberdiyev* v. *Russia*, Appl.No. 34742/13, 26 June 2014, para. 49.

391   ECtHR, *Shamayev and 12 others* v. *Georgia and Russia*, para. 325.

392   Ibid., paras. 365–367.

393   In his dissenting opinion Judge Kovler stated that: "the Court lacks valid grounds for stating that it is 'established' that there would be a violation of Article 3 of the Convention in the event of the applicant's extradition to a country which is a signatory to the Convention", Ibid.

Russia, the Court noted that, in spite of certain improvements in Chechnya, the general security situation there could not be considered safe. However, the Court found that the applicant's personal circumstances did not show substantial grounds for believing that he would be at a real risk of ill-treatment if he were to be returned to Russia.[394] The Court attached importance to the fact that the case concerned an expulsion to a State party to the ECHR, which has undertaken to secure the fundamental right guaranteed under Article 3 of this Convention.[395]

From the case-law mentioned above, it is clear that, where reports by reliable sources indicate improvements in the general situation in the receiving State, the Court could accept the argument that an applicant's risk of ill-treatment is negated by the existence of domestic laws and/or accession to international treaties that guarantee respect for fundamental rights. In *Al Hanchi* v. *BH* (2011), after referring to recent reports that described the improvements in the general situation in Tunisia since the change of regime, the Court indicated to the facts that on 29 June 2011, Tunisia acceded to the Optional Protocol to the CAT, and set up a preventive system of regular visits to places of detention, as well as to the Optional Protocol to the ICCPR, recognising the competence of the HRC to consider individual cases. The Court held this showed "the determination of the Tunisian authorities to once and for all eradicate the culture of violence and impunity which prevailed during the former regime".[396]

IV.2.2   ComAT

It has been repeatedly argued before the ComAT that the risk of torture for the complainant in the proposed receiving State is not exist because the receiving State's national laws and the international treaties to which it is a party prohibit torture. In *Njamba and Balikosa* v. *Sweden* (2010), the Swedish government maintained that the DRC had ratified the main human rights treaties. However, the factual situation in the DRC, as described in the latest UN reports that asserted the existence of factual human rights abuses there, was

---

394   ECtHR, *Bajsultanov* v. *Austria*, para. 67.

395   Ibid., para. 70. See also, ECtHR, *Tomic* v. *the United Kingdom* (admissibility decision), Appl. No. 17837/03, 14 October 2003, which concerned the expulsion to Croatia; ECtHR, *Jeltsujeva* v. *the Netherlands* (admissibility decision); ECtHR, *Hukic* v. *Sweden* (admissibility decision), Appl.No. 17416/05, 27 September 2005 which concerned the deportation to BH; and ECtHR, *Harutioenyan and others* v. *the Netherlands* (admissibility decision), para. 29, which concerned the expulsion to Armenia.

396   ECtHR, *Al Hanchi* v. *Bosnia and Herzegovina*, para. 44.

decisive for the Committee.[397] In *Ismail Alan* v. *Switzerland* (1996), the State party argued that the proposed receiving State, Turkey, was a party to the CAT and had recognized the ComAT's competence under Article 22 CAT to receive and examine individual communications. Referring to the ComAT's findings in its inquiry under Article 20 CAT, the Committee noted that the practice of torture was still systematic in Turkey. It observed that:

> ...the main aim and purpose of the Convention is to *prevent* torture, not to redress torture once it has occurred, and finds that the fact that Turkey is a party to the Convention and has recognized the Committee's competence under article 22, does not, in the circumstances of the instant case, constitute a sufficient guarantee for the author's security.[398]

The mere fact that a receiving State is a party to international human rights treaties, including the CAT, is not sufficient, in itself, to conclude that the returnee would not be at a real risk of torture when there is a practice of torture and human rights abuses in that State. In several Non-Refoulement cases where the Committee found that a complainant's removal would violate Article 3 CAT, the fact that the receiving State was not a party to the CAT was one of the factors taken into account, since such a State may not have made any internationally binding undertaking to prohibit torture in its territory.[399] In *Singh Khalsa et al.* v. *Switzerland* (2011), the Committee decided that, as India was not a party to the CAT, if the complainants were expelled to this country, they would be in danger of being tortured and would not have the legal possibility of applying to the ComAT for protection.[400] In *Gbadjavi* v. *Switzerland*

---

397 ComAT, *Njamba and Balikosa* v. *Sweden*, paras. 4.3 and 9.5.

398 ComAT, *Ismail Alan* v. *Switzerland*, para. 11.5. See also, the case of *S.C.* v. *Denmark* (2000), which concerned the expulsion to Ecuador. Although the Committee did not dispute that the complainant might encounter difficulties with the Ecuadorian authorities because of her political activities, it found that her expulsion would not be in violation of Article 3 as she had carried out her activities as a member of a lawful political party of a country which had ratified not only the CAT, but had also accepted the ComAT's competence under Article 22 CAT. ComAT, *S.C.* v. *Denmark*, No. 143/1999, 10 May 2000, para. 6.5. This conclusion could be understood in the light of the fact that the complainant had not adduced any evidence supported her allegations that she was previously subjected to torture in Ecuador because of her political activities or that there was a systematic practice of torture there.

399 Burgers, H. & Danelius, H., 1988, p. 127.

400 ComAT, *Singh Khalsa et al.* v. *Switzerland*, para. 11.7. See also, ComAT, *Mutombo* v. *Switzerland*, para. 9.6; ComAT, *Tahir Hussain Khan* v. *Canada*, para. 12.5.

(2012), the Committee took into account that the national law in the receiving State, Togo, did not prohibit torture.[401]

However, where there are factual indications that the general situation in the receiving State is improving, the Committee seems to accept the argument that the complainant's risk of being tortured is negated by the existence of domestic laws and/or accession to international treaties that guarantee respect for fundamental rights. In *A.H.* v. *Sweden* (2006), one of the factors the ComAT took into account was that the receiving State, Azerbaijan, had joined the CE and, since then, this country had made some progress in improving the human rights situation and had been making efforts towards releasing political prisoners. The Committee thus found that the complainant's deportation to Azerbaijan would not violate Article 3 CAT.[402]

IV.3   *Diplomatic Assurances (DAS)*

IV.3.1   General Comments

Since the absolute nature of the principle of Non-Refoulement contradicts the State's interest in ejecting unwanted foreigners or those who pose a threat to national security, many States seek diplomatic assurances from the proposed receiving State to ensure that the returnee would not be subjected to proscribed ill-treatment upon return.

According to the UNHCR,

> ...the term diplomatic assurances, as used in the context of the transfer of a person from one State to another, refers to an undertaking by the receiving State to the effect that the person concerned will be treated in accordance with conditions set by the sending State or, more generally, in keeping with its human rights obligations under international law.[403]

The practice of seeking diplomatic assurances against torture and CIDTP (DAS) in the context of removals, especially in the extradition cases, is not new.[404] After the attacks of 11 September 2001 and in the scope of the so-called "War on Terror", States have increasingly resorted to this practice in order to facilitate the extradition of non-citizens they consider a threat to national security to countries that are known to practice systematic or routine

---

401   ComAT, *Gbadjavi* v. *Switzerland*, para. 7.7.

402   ComAT, *A.H.* v. *Sweden*, para. 11.7.

403   UNHCR, UNHCR Note on Diplomatic Assurances and International Refugee Protection, 2006, para. 1.

404   Ibid., para. 2.

torture.[405] The receiving State assures the sending State it will not subject the returnee to torture or CIDTP. Sometimes the receiving State provides further guarantees, like a fair trial, medical care, and visits from his family and the representatives of the sending State, or claims an independent organization will supervise his conditions. The main motive for sending States to seek DAS is that by asking for and receiving DAS, they comply with their absolute obligation of Non-Refoulement.[406] The function of DAS is to mitigate an existing risk that the person concerned will be ill-treated in the receiving State. By doing so, the DAS confer legitimacy on the refoulement that is otherwise illegal under international law.[407]

The form of DAS varies from case to case. They are usually contained in formal written instruments from one State to another, such as exchange of letters,[408] diplomatic notes,[409] and *notes verbales*.[410] They may also be merely oral assurances.[411] However, the practice of States is to confirm in writing the oral assurances obtained previously.[412] DAS have been generally sought

---

405   The increase in the use of DAS is pointed out in many reports such as the series of reports prepared by HRW which detailed this practice: HRW, 'Empty Promises' Diplomatic Assurances No Safeguard against Torture, 14 April 2004; HRW, Still at Risk: Diplomatic Assurances No Safeguard Against Torture; HRW, Cases Involving Diplomatic Assurances against Torture, Developments since May 2005, 23 January 2007; Johnston, J.G., The Risk of Torture as a Basis for Refusing Extradition and the Use of Diplomatic Assurances to Protect against Torture after 9/11, International Criminal Law Review, Vol. 11 no. 1: 2011, 1–48, pp. 7–8.

406   Jones, K., I. Deportations with Assurances: Addressing Key Criticisms, International and Comparative Law Quarterly, Vol. 57 no. 1: 2008, 183–192, p. 185.

407   Skoglund, L., Diplomatic Assurances Against Torture – An Effective Strategy? A Review of Jurisprudence and Examination of the Arguments, Nordic Journal of International Law, Vol. 77 no. 4: 2008, 319–364, p. 320.

408   E.g. the exchange of letters between Algeria and the UK. Shah, N., Promises to Keep, Diplomatic Assurances Against Torture in US Terrorism Transfers, Columbia Law School Human Rights Institute, December 2010, p. 141 and Appendix I.

409   E.g. the American assurances contained in diplomatic notes in *Harkins and Edwards* v. the *UK*.

410   E.g. the assurances issued by India in the Chahal case and the Turkish assurances in *Mamatkulov and Askarov v. Turkey*.

411   E.g. the assurances regarding post-return monitoring in the *Agiza* case.

412   Jones, M., Lies, Damned Lies and Diplomatic Assurances: The Misuse of Diplomatic Assurances in Removal Proceedings, European Journal of Migration and Law, Vol. 8 no. 1: 2006, 9–39. This practice maybe reflected in the MOU between the United Kingdom and Jordan (2005), which provides that "a response to a request under the terms of this arrangement maybe given verbally, but must be confirmed in writing within 14 days [...] before any return can take place".

and given on individual basis, for a particular person who the sending State is intending to remove.[413] A new form of DAS has recently emerged: memorandums of understanding (MOUs). These memorandums are framework agreements in which individual assurances will be made.[414] They thus reflect a general pattern of cooperation where two States use DAS in deportation cases,[415] leaving the details of the assurances to be defined in each individual case.[416]

While DAS are traditionally used to transfer persons between the territories of two States, they have also been used to transfer persons within the territory of the same State, under MOUs between the national government and the States that contribute to peacekeeping operations in that State. Examples

---

413   UNHCR, 2006, para. 4.

414   Great Britain: Parliament: Joint Committee on Human Rights, The UN Convention Against Torture (UNCAT), Nineteenth Report of Session 2005–06, 2006, para. 106. According to this report the MOUs "form the basis for individual diplomatic assurances as to the safety of individual detainees. Many details which would be crucial in establishing the independence and efficacy of the monitoring mechanisms for the assurances remain to be resolved".

415   Schimmel, C.A., Returning Terrorist Suspects against Diplomatic Assurances: Effective Safeguard or Undermining the Absolute Ban on Torture and Other Cruel, Inhuman and Degrading Treatment? Human Rights Law Commentary, Vol. 3: 2007, p. 9.

416   In reaction to the bomb attacks on the London transport network on 7 July 2005, the British government concluded MOUs with each of Jordan, Libya, and Lebanon. In addition to the general assurances that they "will comply with their human rights obligations under international law" and the deported person "will be treated in a human and proper manner on accordance with internationally accepted standards", the MOUs provide for a post-return monitoring mechanism, according to which the person will have unimpeded access, for three years after his return, to a monitoring body nominated by both governments to monitor the implementation of the assurances. If the person is arrested, detained or imprisoned, he will be entitled to contact and have regular visits from a representative of the monitoring body, these visits will include the opportunity of private interviews with the returned person. The monitoring body will report both governments. Each of these memorandums provides clearly that "requests under this Memorandum may include requests to receiving State for further specific assurances". See, e.g., the assurances in the *Abu Qatada* case, ECtHR, *Othman (Abu Qatada) v. the United Kingdom*. The provisions of those MOUs are available at: <www.fco.gov.uk/en>. Moreover, the British government relied upon an exchange of letters and notes verbales between the former British Prime Minister, Tony Blair, and the Algerian President as assurances against ill-treatment of any suspected returned person. Metcalfe, E., The False Promise of Assurances against Torture, Justice Journal, Vol. 6 no. 1: 2009, 63–92, p.77. In December 2008, the UK concluded another MOU with Ethiopia, see HRW, UK: Ethiopian 'Assurances' No Guarantee Against Torture, 17 September 2009.

include the MOUs concluded between ISAF and the Afghan government,[417] and MOUs concluded to transfer detainees from the US contingent of MNF-I to the Iraqi government.[418] Under MOUs, the national authorities undertake to treat detainees handed over by the peacekeeping troops in accordance with international standards.[419]

It is hard to determine how often DAs are used, since States are often keen to keep secret those removals where there is a risk of ill-treatment, especially since most of the removal cases relate to the national security of the sending State.[420] The use of DAs has been strongly criticised by human rights experts and NGOs. They accuse States of using DAs as a tool to circumvent the absolute prohibition of refoulement.[421] The former Special Rapporteur on torture, Manfred Nowak, stated, "diplomatic assurances are nothing but an attempt by European and other States to circumvent their obligation to respect the principle of Non-Refoulement".[422] Opponents have argued that the DAs are "unenforceable promises"; it is unlikely that the receiving State will face any serious consequences if it violates them.[423] The Commissioner for Human

---

417   Canadian, Danish, Dutch, Norwegian, and British MOUs concluded with the Afghan Ministry of Defence. This practice has been criticized strongly by NGOs. See, AI, Afghanistan detainees transferred to torture: ISAF complicity?; HRW, Special Committee on the Canadian Mission in Afghanistan, Parliament of Canada.

418   Deeks, A., Promises Not to Torture: Diplomatic Assurances in U.S. Courts, The American Society of International Law, Discussion Paper Series, December 2008, pp. 18 and 69.

419   Skoglund, L., 2008, pp. 321 and 326.

420   Jones, M., 2006, p. 12. While most States, including European countries and Canada, have made public the assurances they receive, the US has kept them secret. In contrast to the US practice in the extradition context, the American government has publicly stated that it obtained assurances for certain Guantanamo transfers. Although as in extradition cases the US has not revealed the content of those assurances. See, Deeks, A., December 2008, pp. 9 and 28.

421   Joint statement by AI, Association for the Prevention of Torture, HRW, International Commission of Jurists, International Federation of Action by Christians for the Abolition of Torture, International Federation for Human Rights, International Helsinki Federation for Human Rights, and World Organisation Against Torture, Torture/Terrorism, Call for action against the use of diplomatic assurances in transfers to risk of torture and ill-treatment, 12 May 2005, p. 3; Schutter, O.D., 2010, pp. 278–279.

422   Nowak, M., Challenges to the Absolute Nature of the Prohibition of Torture and Ill-treatment, Netherlands Quarterly of Human Rights, Vol. 23 no. 4: 2005, 674–688, 687. For more information about the approach of the UN bodies and experts on DAs see, Shah, N., December 2010, p. 65.

423   HRW, Not the Way Forward, The UK's Dangerous Reliance on Diplomatic Assurances, 22 October 2008.

Rights of the CE described the problematic nature of DAS, saying, "the weakness inherent in the practice of diplomatic assurances lies in the fact that where there is a need for such assurances, there is clearly an acknowledged risk of torture and ill-treatment".[424] The legality of DAS has also been questioned in academic debate.[425] Despite wide disagreement about the legality of DAS when used in Non-Refoulement cases, they have been extended to cover various types of transfers, including deportation of rejected asylum seekers, rendition of terrorist suspects, and transfers of detainees from Guantànamo Bay.[426] The question of whether the DAS are binding is not particularly useful in determining if these assurances eliminate in practice the risk of ill-treatment faced by the person concerned. For the purpose of assessing whether the person's removal would violate the principle of Non-Refoulement, the relevant question is whether compliance with the DAS that cover his removal is likely, and whether such compliance would be sufficient to remove any real risk of ill-treatment he faces in the receiving State.[427] Neither the ECtHR nor the ComAT has concentrated its analysis on determining the legal nature and value of specific assurances. Instead they have focused on the criteria that enable them to assess the practical value of these assurances and their adequacy to remove any risk of ill-treatment of the person concerned. In the following subsections, we refer to the case-law of both the ECtHR and the ComAT where those

---

424   Report by Alvaro Gil-Robes, Commissioner for Human Rights, on his visit to Sweden (21–23 April 2004), CommDH (2004) 13, para. 19.

425   See e.g., Bruin, R. & Wouters, K., 2003; Joseph, S., Rendering Terrorists and the Convention Against Torture, Human Rights Law Review, Vol. 5 no. 2: 2005, 339–346; Skoglund, L., 2008; Parsad, K.C., Illegal Renditions and Improper Treatment: an Obligation to Provide Refugee Remedies Pursuant to the Convention against Torture, Denver Journal of International Law and Policy, Vol. 37 no. 4: 2009, 681–702; Pergantis, V., Soft Law, Diplomatic Assurances and the Instrument Alisation of Normativity: Wither a Liberal Promise? Netherlands International Law Review, Vol. 56 no. 2: 2009, 137–166; Schmid, E., The End of the Road on Diplomatic Assurances: The Removal of Suspected Terrorists under International Law, Essex Human Rights Review, Vol. 1 no. 11: 2011, 298–320, p. 228; Wouters, K., 2012; Worster, W.T., Between a Treaty and Not: A Case Study of the Legal Value of Diplomatic Assurances in Expulsion Cases, Minnesota Journal of International Law, Vol. 21 no. 2: 2012, 253–346.

426   It must be mentioned here that the US has consistently maintained that Article 3 CAT does not apply as a legal matter to its activities outside its territory. Since Guantanamo Bay is not part of American territory, the US takes the position that its activities in Guantanamo are not subjected to the obligation of Non-Refoulement under Article 3 CAT. Deeks, A., December 2008, pp. 3, 10, and 28.

427   Schmid, E., 2011, p. 228.

bodies consider DAs in cases of Non-Refoulement to torture and other forms of ill-treatment.

IV.3.2   ECtHR
IV.3.2.1   *Introduction*
In its Non-Refoulement case-law under Article 3 ECHR, the ECtHR has had many opportunities to deal with allegations by respondent States that the risk of ill-treatment of the applicant is mitigated because DAs were obtained from the proposed receiving State. The Court has noted the widespread concern within the international community, with regard to the practice of seeking DAs to allow States to remove those considered a threat to national security. However, the Court has clearly stated:

> ...it is not for this Court to rule upon the propriety of seeking assurances, or to assess the long term consequences of doing so; its only task is to examine whether the assurances obtained in a particular case are sufficient to remove any real risk of ill-treatment.[428]

While the Court has wanted to avoid debate on the propriety of using DAs in refoulement cases and the impact of this practice on the absolute nature of the principle of Non-Refoulement, it has accepted that such assurances could be sufficient to remove any real risk of ill-treatment of the applicant. The Court has held that in cases where DAs have been provided by the receiving State to protect the applicant, the Court must take those assurances into account, along with its consideration of the general situation of human rights in that State, and the applicant's personal circumstances. This does not mean that the assurances constitute, in themselves, a sufficient guarantee to ensure adequate protection for the applicant against the risk of ill-treatment. The sending State is obligated to examine whether the assurances provide this guarantee in their practical application. The Court has given weight to the DAs on a case-by-case basis, and has considerd the circumstances that prevail at the material time.[429] Through its case-law, the Court has developed criteria to determine the weight given to assurances, and judges whether they provide adequate protection for an applicant who demonstrates substantial grounds for believing that he would face a real risk of ill-treatment if removed.[430] These criteria were

---

428   ECtHR, *Othman (Abu Qatada)* v. *the United Kingdom*, para. 186.

429   Ibid., para. 187; ECtHR, *Savriddin Dzhurayev* v. *Russia*, para. 153.

430   Where the applicant cannot demonstrate the existence of substantial grounds for a real risk of ill-treatment in the receiving State, the Court does not deem it necessary to assess the DAs. ECtHR, *Oshlakov* v. *Russia*, para. 90.

outlined in *Abu Qatada* v. *The UK* (2012).[431] Below, we examine these criteria in the context of the Court's case-law on the use of DAs in Non-Refoulement cases under Article 3 ECHR.

To assess the practical application of DAs and determining the weight they should be given, the Court has held that the preliminary question is if the general situation of human rights in the receiving State excludes accepting any assurances whatsoever. Although the Court made clear in the *Abu Qatada* case that "it will only be in rare cases that the general situation in a country will mean that no weight at all can be given to assurances",[432] it did not describe the situations in which this will occur. As examples of such situations, the Court referred to four extradition cases, *Gaforov* v. *Russia* (2010) (an extradition to Tajikistan) and *Sultanov* v. *Russia* (2010), *Yuldashev* v. *Russia* (2010) and *Ismoilov and Others* v. *Russia* (2008) (extraditions to Uzbekistan).[433] All these cases considered the extradition of individuals who were suspected of politically and/or religiously motivated crimes in the receiving State, where reputable international sources described the practice of torture as systematic. The Court was not persuaded that assurances from the authorities of the receiving States offered a reliable guarantee against the risk of ill-treatment.[434] In these cases, the Court concluded that no weight could be given to assurances from those countries.

However, the Court excluded this understanding in *Abu Qatada* v. *The UK* (2012), which concerned the extradition to Jordan of a terrorist suspect convicted in absentia on the sole basis of evidence obtained by torture. In this case, the Court observed that, according to reports of UN bodies and NGOs, the practice of torture, was used systematically in Jordan, particularly against Islamist detainees. The Court noted that the applicant had argued that if Jordan did not reliably comply with its legally binding, multinational international obligation not to torture, it could not be trusted to respect non-binding

---

431   ECtHR, *Othman (Abu Qatada)* v. *the United Kingdom*, paras. 188–189. For the *Abu Qatada* case before the English Courts in relation to Article 3 ECHR see, Michaelsen, C., The renaissance of Non-Refoulement? The Othman (Abu Qatada) decision of the European Court of Human Rights, International and Comparative Law Quarterly, Vol. 61 no. 3: 2012, 750–765, pp. 757–759.

432   ECtHR, *Othman (Abu Qatada)* v. *the United Kingdom*, para. 188.

433   See also, ECtHR, *Kozhayev* v. *Russia*, para. 84; ECtHR, *Sidikovy* v. *Russia*, para. 150.

434   ECtHR, *Ismoilov and Others* v. *Russia*, para. 127; ECtHR, *Yuldashev* v. *Russia*, Appl.No. 1248/09, 8 July 2010, para. 85; ECtHR, *Sultanov* v. *Russia*, para. 73; ECtHR, *Gaforov* v. *Russia*, para. 138.

bilateral assurances not to do so. The Court decided that this argument was not supported by its case-law on DAS. It stated:

> ...the Court has never laid down an absolute rule that a State which does not comply with multilateral obligations cannot be relied on to comply with bilateral assurances; the extent to which a State has failed to comply with its multilateral obligations is, at most, a factor in determining whether its bilateral assurances are sufficient. Equally, there is no prohibition on seeking assurances when there is a systematic problem of torture and ill-treatment in the receiving State.[435]

The Court added that it did not consider that the general situation of human rights in Jordan exclude the validity of all assurances from the Jordanian government. Instead, the Court noted that the British and Jordanian governments had made genuine efforts to reach transparent and detailed assurances that ensured that the applicant would not be ill-treated upon return to Jordan. In the Court's view, the MOU that resulted from those efforts was superior in both detail and formality to any assurances that the Court had previously examined.[436] After it compared the Jordanian assurances to the criteria outlined by the Court, it considered those assurances sufficient to allow the applicant's removal to Jordan, which otherwise would have been prohibited under Article 3 ECHR. The fact that human rights are systematically violated in the receiving State does not ensure its consideration as a rare case in which assurances will carry no weight. Taking into account that the Court assessed the value of DAS in cases concerned removal to Uzbekistan and Tajikistan other than those it considered as examples of the rare cases, what the Court has really meant by the rare cases is questionable.[437]

The Court has considered the existence of a systematic practice of torture in the receiving State as one of the factors, which are taken into account when assessing the value of DAS. As concluded above, a general situation of violence in the receiving State has been considered sufficient to apply the principle of

---

435   ECtHR, *Othman (Abu Qatada)* v. *the United Kingdom*, para. 193. On the contrary, see ECtHR, *Karimov* v. *Russia*, para. 101; ECtHR, *Abdulazhon Isakov* v. *Russia*, para. 111; ECtHR, *Yuldashev* v. *Russia*, para. 85. In these cases, the Court noted that the practice of torture in Uzbekistan was described by reputable international sources as systematic, accordingly, it was not persuaded that the assurances from the Uzbek authorities offered a reliable guarantee against the risk of ill-treatment.

436   ECtHR, *Othman (Abu Qatada)* v. *the United Kingdom*, para. 194.

437   ECtHR, *Muminov* v. *Russia*, para. 97; ECtHR, *Garayev* v. *Azerbaijan*, para. 74.

Non-Refoulement under Article 3 ECHR. In our opinion, this is the kind of situation that the Court should consider a "rare case", in which no weight at all can be given to assurances given by the proposed receiving State. The Court should also refuse to give weight to DAs where the practice of torture and ill-treatment in that State is documented as systemic by reputable international human rights sources.

The Court has stated that, more usually, it will first assess the quality of the assurances given in the case under consideration and, second, decide if they can be relied upon, given the receiving State's practice. The Court has outlined a non-exclusive list of factors that it will take into account when it does its assessment. We discuss these factors in the following subsections, in light of the Court's case-law on DAs in Non-Refoulement cases under Article 3, both before and after the Court's decision in *Abu Qatada* v. *The UK* (2012).

IV.3.2.2   *Criteria to Assess DAS*

IV.3.2.2.a   Disclosure of the Terms of the Assurances to the ECtHR

The ECtHR has refused to give weight to DAs if the respondent State does not submit to the Court any copy of them.[438] The sending State cannot argue that it has discharged its obligation of Non-Refoulement under Article 3 by simply claiming to have received DAs. The Court must assess the effectiveness of the receiving State's assurances to determine if they will protect the applicant against torture and CIDTP.

IV.3.2.2.b   Content

In *Mamatkulov and Askarov* v. *Turkey* (2005), the Uzbek government pointed out that Uzbekistan was a party to the CAT, and accepted and reaffirmed its obligations under this Convention.[439] The ECtHR relied on those assurances, in addition to other evidence, in its conclusion that the applicant's removal would not breach Article 3 ECHR. A minority of the Court criticized this position, and referred specifically to AI's finding that Uzbekistan failed to implement its treaty obligations under the CAT and that the country widely had been accused of torture and ill-treatment.[440] The Court changed this approach in the *Saadi* case:

---

438   ECtHR, *Ryabikin* v. *Russia*, para. 119; ECtHR, *Muminov* v. *Russia*, para. 97; ECtHR, *Sultanov* v. *Russia*, para. 73; ECtHR, *Abdulazhon Isakov* v. *Russia*, para. 111.

439   ECtHR, *Mamatkulov and Askarov* v. *Turkey* (GC), para. 28.

440   Ibid., joint partly dissenting opinion of judges Bratza, Bonello and Hedigan, para. 11. Furthermore, the Russian authorities' failure to comply with its assurances to the Court in *Shamayev and 12 others* v. *Russia and Georgia* was considered as an illustration of the fact that mere accession to international human rights agreements does not constitutes

...the existence of domestic laws and accession to international treaties guaranteeing respect for fundamental rights in principle are not in
themselves sufficient to ensure adequate protection against the risk of
ill-treatment where, as in the present case, reliable sources have reported
practices resorted to or tolerated by the authorities which are manifestly
contrary to the principles of the Convention.[441]

Accordingly, when a receiving State only repeats its obligations under the
domestic laws or international treaties that prohibit torture, the ECtHR has
not accepted these statements as sufficient assurances it will prohibit torture.
In *Azimov* v. *Russia* (2013), the Court noted that there is no State in the modern
world that would not claim that its adherence to basic international human
rights norms like the prohibition of torture, and no State that does not have at
least some form of protective mechanism at the domestic level. Though these
elements are important, they should not be taken literally. A somewhat critical approach should be taken to assurances when reliable sources report that
authorities in a receiving State practise or tolerate treatment manifestly contrary to the principles of the ECHR.[442]

The ECtHR has considered itself bound to question the value of assurances
that are couched in general terms,[443] are vague or lack precision,[444] or which

---

guarantee that a State will comply with its obligations under these agreements. See HRW,
'Empty Promises' Diplomatic Assurances No Safeguard against Torture, p. 8.

441   ECtHR, *Saadi* v. *Italy* (GC), paras. 147–148. The Tunisian assurances were provided by
the Minister of Foreign Affairs in two notes verbales. In the first one, the Tunisian government merely stated that they were prepared "to accept the transfer to Tunisia of Tuni-
sians imprisoned abroad once their identity has been confirmed, in strict conformity with
the national legislation in force and under the sole safeguard of the relevant Tunisian
statutes". The second note pointed out that Tunisian laws guarantee prisoners' rights and
that Tunisia had voluntarily acceded to "the relevant international treaties and conventions". Ibid., paras. 54–55. Gentili, G., European Court of Human Rights: An absolute ban
on deportation of foreign citizens to countries where torture or ill-treatment is a genuine
risk, International Journal of Constitutional Law, Vol. 8 no. 2: 2010, 311–322, p. 313. See also,
ECtHR, *Trabelsi* v. *Italy*, Appl. No. 50163/2008, 13 April 2010, paras. 43–48. Arguably, the
Court, in the *Saadi* case, made clear that the sending State party must look beyond the
wording of the receiving State's assurances and examine its actions and human rights
record.

442   ECtHR, *Azimov* v. *Russia*, para. 133.

443   ECtHR, *Kaboulov* v. *Ukraine*, para. 113; ECtHR, *Abdulkhakov* v. *Russia*, para. 150; ECtHR,
Savriddin Dzhurayev v. *Russia*, paras. 21 and 174; ECtHR, *Yefimova* v. *Russia*, para. 203;
ECtHR, *Ermakov* v. *Russia*, Appl.No. 43165/10, 7 November 2013, para. 205.

444   ECtHR, *Klein* v. *Russia*, para. 55; ECtHR, *Khodzhayev* v. *Russia*, paras. 84 and 103.

contain no guarantee that they will be applied in practice.[445] In *Khaydarov v. Russia* (2010), the Court gave no weight to assurances provided by Tajikistan because they "contained no reference whatsoever to the protection of the applicant from treatment proscribed by Article 3 of the Convention".[446] In *Klein* v. *Russia* (2010), the Court questioned the value of the assurances because they were vague and imprecise, although they specifically guaranteed that the applicant "shall not be subjected to capital punishment or tortures, inhuman or degrading treatment or punishment".[447] The Court has required specific assurances and is not satisfied with even explicit reference to torture or Article 3 ECHR, if the details are not specific.[448] For example, in *Makhmudzhan Ergashev* v. *Russia* (2012), the Court held that the assurances of the Kyrgyz Republic were specific. According to those assurances the Kyrgyz Republic Prosecutor General had guaranteed, *inter alia*, that the applicant would not be extradited to a third State without the Russian Prosecutor General's consent, that he would not be prosecuted or sentenced for any crime other than that for which his extradition was requested, that the original crime was not of a political nature, that he would not be subjected to torture, violence, CIDTP or discrimination on any ground, including ethnic origin, that he would not be sentenced to death, and that he would be provided with every opportunity to defend himself, including legal aid.[449]

Abu Qatada v. The UK (2012) was the first case in which the Court assessed the assurances contained in a MOU. The Court noted that the MOU concluded between the UK and Jordanian government in 2005, was "specific and comprehensive". The Court observed that when a returnee was accepted under the terms of the MOU, paragraphs 1- 8 of the MOU, which address directly the protection of the applicant's Convention rights in Jordan, would apply together with any further specific assurances provided by the receiving State.[450]

---

445   ECtHR, *Savriddin Dzhurayev* v. *Russia*, para. 174.

446   ECtHR, *Khaydarov* v. *Russia*, para. 111; ECtHR, *Kaboulov* v. *Ukraine*, paras. 113 and 143; Izumo, A., 2010, p. 264.

447   ECtHR, *Klein* v. *Russia*, paras. 55 and 16. See also, ECtHR, *K.* v. *Russia*, para. 65.

448   Shah, N., December 2010, p. 70.

449   ECtHR, *Makhmudzhan Ergashev* v. *Russia*, paras. 15, 17 and 75. See also *Rrapo* v. *Albania* (2012), in which the Court considered the assurances were "specific, clear and unequivocal". ECtHR, *Rrapo* v. *Albania*, para. 19.

450   ECtHR, *Othman (Abu Qatada)* v. *the United Kingdom*, para. 194, and for the provisions of paragraphs 1–8 of the MOU see, Ibid., paras. 77–78.

IV.3.2.2.c   Source

The ECtHR has given considerable importance to the credibility of the person who offers assurances. He should be able to ensure the guarantees are applied, and must be willing to implement them in good faith. In the *Abu Qatada* case, the Court noted that assurances had been approved at the highest levels of the Jordanian government, and had the express approval and support of the King of Jordan. Accordingly, the Court found that, whatever the legal status of the MOU in Jordanian law, assurances had been provided by officials capable of binding the receiving State. Senior officials of the Jordanian General Intelligence Directorate had also approved and supported these assurances. The Court held that these factors made it more likely Jordan would strictly comply with the letter and spirit of the MOU.[451]

In *Shamayev and 12 others* v. *Georgia and Russia* (2005), the Court gave special importance to the assurances given by the Russian Procurator General, who supervises the activities of all prosecutors in the Russian Federation and argues the prosecution case before the courts. He also monitors the implementation of prisoners' rights in the Russian Federation through unlimited visits to the places of detention.[452] In contrast, in *Soldatenko* v. *Ukraine* (2008), which concerned the extradition of the applicant to Turkmenistan, the Court noted that Deputy Prosecutor General of Turkmenistan promised in writing to fulfil requirements of Article 3, and that the applicant would not be subjected to torture or CIDTP after he was extradited. The Court observed that it was not clear if the Deputy Prosecutor General or the institution that he represented had the power to provide such assurances on behalf of the sending State.[453] In its decisions, the Court determines if the person who gives assurances on behalf of the applicant has the power to make binding agreements for the receiving State.

The Court has repeatedly recognised that, in extradition matters, Diplomatic Notes are a standard means for providing DAs and that in international relations such Diplomatic Notes carry a presumption of good faith. The Court has presumed the good faith of a requesting State that has a long history of respect for democracy and human rights.[454] In *Harkins and Edwards* v. *The UK* (2012), the assurances given by the US government, the Florida prosecutors,

---

451   Ibid., para. 195.

452   ECtHR, *Shamayev and 12 others* v. *Georgia and Russia*, paras. 344–345.

453   ECtHR, *Soldatenko* v. *Ukraine*, para. 73. See, ECtHR, *Baysakov and Others* v. *Ukraine*, para. 51; ECtHR, *Garayev* v. *Azerbaijan*, para. 74.

454   ECtHR, *Babar Ahmad and Others* v. *the United Kingdom* (admissibility decision), para. 105; ECtHR, *Nivette* v. *France* (admissibility decision), Appl. No. 44190/98, 3 July 2001.

and the trial judge in the applicant's case were clear and unequivocal, since they were issued in Diplomatic Notes issued by the US Embassy in the UK.[455] However, the existence of good faith is insufficient in itself to persuade the Court to accept the assurances. The Court has closely examined the circumstances in the receiving State, including the ability of the government to control its forces and adjust the general situation there. Although the Court, in *Chahal* v. *The UK* (1996), confirmed its confidence that the Indian government had provided its assurances in good faith, it pointed to the security situation in Punjab and the government's inability to effectively control certain members of the security force in Punjab and elsewhere in India.[456]

In *Chahal* v. *The UK* (1996), the Court noted that although it did not doubt the good faith of the Indian government in giving DAs against ill-treatment of the applicant, despite the government's efforts to bring about reform, certain members of the security forces in Punjab and elsewhere in India continued to violate human rights; this was an enduring problem. Thus, the Court was not persuaded that the government's assurances would adequately guarantee Chahal's safety against ill-treatment.[457] Thus, where DAs are provided by the central government of the receiving State, the Court has not given any weight to these assurances if local authorities in the part of this State, to which the applicant is expected to be removed, cannot be expected to abide by these DAs in practice. In *Makhmudzhan Ergashev* v. *Russia* (2012), which concerned the extradition of a Kyrgyzstani national of Uzbek origin to Kyrgyzstan, the Court noted that the situation in the south of the receiving State, where the applicant would be extradited, was characterised by torture and ill-treatment of ethnic Uzbeks by law-enforcement officers. Against these circumstances, the Court

---

455   ECtHR, *Harkins and Edwards* v. *the United Kingdom*, para. 85.

456   ECtHR, *Chahal* v. *the United Kingdom*, para. 104. *Ben Khemais* v. *Italy* (2009), in which the Court referred to the AI's report 2008 on Tunisia that indicated the failure of the government to carry out investigations on allegations of torture in police custody or bring the alleged perpetrators to justice. Accordingly, the Court decided to refuse the Tunisian assurances in this case. ECtHR, *Ben Khemais* v. *Italy*, para. 59.

457   ECtHR, *Chahal* v. *the United Kingdom*, paras. 104–105. ECtHR, *Soering* v. *the United Kingdom*, paras. 97–98. See also *Nivette* v. *France* (2001), in which the Court considered that the question might legitimately be raised whether and to what extent the declarations by the US federal government were binding on the State of California. In the Court's view the US government's declarations were not necessarily inadequate or ineffective on that account, in as much as they complemented the undertakings made by the Californian prosecuting authorities. The Court clearly stated that it was the view of the Californian prosecuting authorities that was the decisive factor in this instance. ECtHR, *Nivette* v. *France* (admissibility decision).

held that while the assurances given by the Kyrgyz authorities appeared to be formally binding on the local authorities, local authorities in the south of the country might not abide by them in practice.[458]

IV.3.2.2.d   Legal Nature of the Treatment Proscribed by the DAs in
              the Receiving State

To determine if assurances will be applied in practice, the Court has attended to the legality of treatment proscribed by assurances under the national laws of the receiving State. In *Nivette* v. *France* (2001), the applicant claimed that his extradition to the US would violate Article 3 ECHR if he were sentenced to life imprisonment with no possibility of early release. When it decided the admissibility of the case, the Court attached particular importance to the fact that, according to the California Penal Code, a sentence of life imprisonment without any possibility of early release could not be imposed if the District Attorney did not file a special circumstance, and that the District Attorney had undertaken not to make such a filing.[459]

Even when a receiving State assures the Court that proscribed treatment is illegal there, the Court may consider these assurances insufficient if the State has failed to uphold these laws in practice. For example, in the *Ergashev* case, the Court noted that the assurances given by the Kyrgyz authorities that torture and CIDTP were absolutely prohibited in Kyrgyz law. The Court had serious doubts, in light of the poor human rights record in the south of that country, that local authorities could be expected to abide by the assurances in practice.[460]

IV.3.2.2.e   Assurances Given by a State Party to the ECHR

The Court has given weight to the fact that DAs were given by a State party to the ECHR. In its admissibility decision in *Chentiev and Ibragimov* v. *Slovakia* (2010), the Court found it relevant that the assurances protecting the applicants of treatment proscribed by Article 3 had been issued by authorities of a member State of the CE and a State party to the ECHR, and noted that a possible failure to abide by such assurances would seriously undermine the State's credibility.[461] However, the Court did not consider those assurances

---

458   ECtHR, *Makhmudzhan Ergashev* v. *Russia*, para. 75.

459   ECtHR, *Nivette* v. *France* (admissibility decision). See also, ECtHR, *Cipriani* v. *Italy* (admissibility decision), Appl. No. 22142/07, 30 March 2010; ECtHR, *Saoudi* v. *Spain* (admissibility decision), Appl. No. 22871/06, 18 September 2006.

460   ECtHR, *Makhmudzhan Ergashev* v. *Russia*, paras. 41, 46 and 75.

461   ECtHR, *Chentiev and Ibragimov* v. *Slovakia* (admissibility decision), p. 15.

were sufficient to protect the applicant of the risk of ill-treatment. The mere statement that the receiving State ratified the ECHR is not enough when reliable sources report that the authorities in this State resort to or tolerate practices that are manifestly contrary to the principles of the Convention.[462] The Court has negatively weighted the fact that the receiving State is not a State party to the ECHR.[463]

IV.3.2.2.f   The Bilateral Relations between the Sending and Receiving States
Among of the factors that the Court has taken into account when it assesses the practical application of DAs is the length and strength of bilateral relations between the sending and receiving States, the history of these relations in refoulement cases, and the receiving State's record in complying with similar assurances.[464] In assessing the Jordanian assurances contained in MOU in the *Abu Qatada* case, the Court gave weight to the fact that these assurances were provided by a government that historically has had strong bilateral relations with the UK. The Court gave weight also to the importance of the MOU to these relations.[465]

The strength of bilateral relations is not sufficient in itself to support assurances that do not adequately protect the applicant against the risk of ill-treatment. In the *Soering* case, the Court found that even diplomatic relations as strong as those between the US and the UK did not result in sufficient assurances.[466] In *Babar Ahmad* v. *The UK* (2010) (admissibility decision), the Court observed that, in extradition cases, "Diplomatic Notes are a standard means for the requesting State to provide any assurances which the requested State considers necessary for its consent to extradition". The Court recognised that, "in international relations, Diplomatic Notes carry a presumption of good faith".[467]

> ...in extradition cases, it is appropriate that that presumption [of good faith] be applied to a requesting State which has a long history of respect for democracy, human rights and the rule of law, and which has long-standing extradition arrangements with Contracting States.[468]

---

462   ECtHR, *Khaydarov* v. *Russia*, para. 111.
463   ECtHR, *Rustamov* v. *Russia*, para. 131.
464   ECtHR, *Othman (Abu Qatada)* v. *the United Kingdom*, para. 189.
465   Ibid., para. 195.
466   ECtHR, *Soering* v. *the United Kingdom*, para. 98. See Larsaeus, N., The Use of Diplomatic Assurances in the Prevention of Prohibited Treatment, Refugee Studies Centre, 2006, University of Oxford Working Paper No. 32, p. 14.
467   ECtHR, *Babar Ahmad and Others* v. *the United Kingdom* (admissibility decision), para. 105.
468   Ibid., para. 105.

The Court then asserted that it would assess the reliability of the assurances in light of their quality and the requesting State's practices in similar cases.[469] In refoulement cases, the Court has considered longstanding positive relations between the sending and the receiving States to support the claim that assurances from the receiving State provide, in their practical application, a sufficient guarantee that the applicant will be protected against the risk of ill-treatment. In the *Babar Ahmad* case, the Court felt it had to weigh heavily the fact that the applicants were unable to point to any instance in which the American government had breached its agreements with the British government or any other State party to the ECHR for an extradition request, either before or after the events of 11 September 2001.[470] In contrast, in *Azimov v. Russia* (2013), the Court was concerned about reported cases of ill-treatment of persons who had been extradited or forcibly returned to Tajikistan, in breach of DAs given by the Tajikistani government. It referred to a report by AI that described a series of recent cases in which the Tajikistani authorities made extradition requests (many of them from Russia) based on unreliable information, for people it thought were members of banned Islamic groups; these persons were alleged to have been tortured on their return.[471]

IV.3.2.2.g   Monitoring Mechanisms
Since the assessment of DAs focuses on their practical application, the Court has given special importance to the post-return monitoring mechanism. The Court has determined "whether compliance with the assurances can be objectively verified through diplomatic or other monitoring mechanisms, including providing unfettered access to the applicant's lawyers".[472]

In its early case-law on DAs in Non-Refoulement cases, the ECtHR did not appear to think adequacy of the follow-up mechanism was very important. It sometimes ignored aspects of this question, which could raise serious doubts

---

469   ECtHR, *Harkins and Edwards* v. *the United Kingdom*, paras. 85–86.

470   ECtHR, *Babar Ahmad and Others* v. *the United Kingdom* (admissibility decision), para. 107. See also *Rrapo* v. *Albania* (2012), in which the Court stated that "The United States long-term interest in honouring its extradition commitments alone would be sufficient to give rise to a presumption of good faith against any risk of a breach of those assurances". ECtHR, *Rrapo* v. *Albania*, para. 73.

471   ECtHR, *Azimov* v. *Russia*, para. 92.

472   ECtHR, *Othman (Abu Qatada)* v. *the United Kingdom*, para. 189(viii). The follow-up mechanism has two functions: the first one aims to prevent ill-treatment from happening i.e. the deterrence. Given that the receiving State knows that it is under monitoring, it would do its best to secure that the removed person is treated in accordance with the provisions of the assurances. The second function is to detect any breach of the assurances. Larsaeus, N., 2006, pp. 18–19.

about the effectiveness of assurances. Despite the repeated postponement by the Russian government of the Court delegates' visit to Shamayev and other removed applicants, the Court decided to cancel its fact-finding visit to Russia and considered its assurances sufficient in the light of the evidence before it.[473] In *Mamatkulov and Askarov* v. *Turkey* (2005), the Court based its judgment on medical certificates issued by prison military doctors employed by the receiving State.[474] The Court relied on these assurances even though the representatives of the applicants pointed out that they had not been able to contact their clients, by either letter or telephone, the trial was not fair or public, that conditions in Uzbek prisons were bad, and that prisoners were subjected to torture.[475]

The Court has started to give greater weight to the effectiveness of the follow-up mechanism in its judgment in *Ben Khemais* v. *Italy* (2009).[476] In this case, the Court took into account the Tunisian prisoners' lack of access to independent foreign lawyers, even when they were parties to a case before an international court. Once an applicant was removed to Tunisia, his lawyer might not be able to communicate with him to verify his conditions. The Court

---

473 ECtHR, *Shamayev and 12 others* v. *Georgia and Russia*, para. 49.

474 The Turkish government submitted that two officials from the Turkish Embassy had visited the applicants more than two years after the men were returned. ECtHR, *Mamatkulov and Askarov* v. *Turkey* (GC), para. 63. However, it must be borne in mind that these visits from foreign diplomats will hardly ever reveal evidence of torture. Wouters, K., 2009, p. 229.

475 ECtHR, *Mamatkulov and Askarov* v. *Turkey* (GC), para. 31. See also, ECtHR, *Ismoilov and Others* v. *Russia*, para. 106. Although the Court in this case did not consider the assurances adequate to offer a reliable guarantee against the risk of ill-treatment, this conclusion was not based on the impossibility of monitoring the compliance with the assurances because of the Uzbek government's refusal to give the representatives of the international community any access to the extradited individuals.

476 See also, ECtHR, *Sellem* v. *Italy*, paras. 43–44; ECtHR, *Abdelhedi* v. *Italy*, Appl.No. 2638/07, 24 March 2009, paras. 50–51; ECtHR, *Ben Salah* v. *Italy*, Appl.No. 38128/06, 24 March 2009, paras. 39–40; ECtHR, *Bouyahia* v. *Italy*, Appl.No. 46792/06, 24 March 2009, paras. 42–43; ECtHR, *Darraji* v. *Italy*, Appl.No. 11549/05, 24 March 2009, paras. 66–67; ECtHR, *O.* v. *Italy*, Appl.No. 37257/06, 24 March 2009, paras. 44–45; ECtHR, *Soltana* v. *Italy*, Appl.No. 37336/06, 24 March 2009, paras. 46–47; ECtHR, *C.B.Z.* v. *Italy*, Appl.No. 44006/06, 24 March 2009, paras. 43–44. In all these cases, which concerned the extradition of suspected terrorists from Italy to Tunisia, the Court referred to the existence of reliable reports of individuals suspected of terrorism being subjected to torture and ill-treatment, that those allegations of ill-treatment were not investigated, that there was no effective system of protection against torture and that the Tunisian authorities were reluctant to cooperate with independent human rights organizations.

noted that the Italian government also could not verify their conditions, since their ambassador was forbidden to visit Ben Khemais in custody.[477] The Court also took into account statements made by the applicant's Tunisian lawyer; the lawyer claimed, after visiting his client, that the applicant had not alleged any ill-treatment and that his safety was confirmed by a medical report annexed to the assurances. The Court noted that, while the applicant had not suffered of ill-treatment in the weeks after he was deported, this did not in any way predict his future fate.[478] This conclusion can be read two ways. On the one hand, it can be seen as the Court's confirmation of the importance of continued monitoring over a reasonable period of time.[479] On the other hand, the Court's reliance on medical reports prepared by doctors appointed by the Tunisian government is problematic, particularly if we take into consideration the Tunisian government's refusal to allow the applicant to be examined by another doctor.

The MOU between the governments of the UK and Jordan provided that persons returned to Jordan were allowed contact and prompt and regular visits from a representative of an independent body nominated jointly by both governments.[480] The British government signed a monitoring agreement with the Adaleh Centre for Human Rights Studies.[481] In the *Abu Qatada* case, the Court noted that the Adaleh Centre did not have the same expertise or resources as international NGOs, such as AI, HRW or ICRC. This Centre did not have the same good reputation in Jordan as, for instance, the National Centre of Human Rights. However, the Court found that it was the fact of monitoring

---

477 ECtHR, *Ben Khemais* v. *Italy*, para. 60.

478 Ibid., paras. 63–64.

479 In the same line the HRC stated, in *Alzery* v. *Sweden*, that: "The visits by the State party's ambassador and staff commenced five weeks after the return, neglecting altogether a period of maximum exposure to risk of harm". HRC, *Mohammed Alzery* v. *Sweden*, para. 11.5. Reading those conclusions together shows the need for continued monitoring from the date of return onward.

480 For more information about the monitoring mechanisms under MOUs between the UK government, on the one side, and each of the Libyan, Jordanian, Lebanese and Ethiopian governments, on the other side, see, Shah, N., December 2010, pp. 77–79.

481 ECtHR, *Othman (Abu Qatada)* v. *the United Kingdom*, para. 24. See, by contrast, ECtHR, *Yefimova* v. *Russia*, para. 203. In this case, the Court noted that although the assurances provided by the Kazakhstani authorities contained a statement to the effect that the competent Russian authorities would be allowed access to the applicant during the criminal proceedings, the State party failed to elaborate on this point and did not indicate if there was any specific mechanism by which compliance with those assurances could be objectively checked.

visits that was important. The Court was further persuaded that the capacity of this Centre to monitor the assurances had significantly increased though funding provided by the British government and that this funding provided the Centre a measure of independence from the Jordanian government. Given the British government's interest in seeing that the assurances were respected, the Court assumed this funding would continue.[482] The Court also noted that the applicant would receive private visits from a delegation that included medical and psychiatric specialists capable of detecting physical or psychological ill-treatment. The Court added that it would clearly be in the applicant's interest to meet the delegation on a pre-arranged timetable, and that it was unlikely the Jordanian General Intelligence Directorate would escape monitoring by telling the delegation that the applicant did not wish to see them. The Court noted, that if the delegation were to receive such a response, this would "rapidly escalat[e] diplomatic and Ministerial contacts and reactions". For these reasons, the Court was satisfied that, despite its limitations, the Adaleh Centre could verify that the assurances were respected.[483]

The Court emphasized that a detainee's risk of ill-treatment is greatest during the first hours or days of his detention. The Court noted that it was unusual, under Jordanian law, for lawyers to accompany detainees when they appeared before the Public Prosecutor. Since the applicant would be brought before the Public Prosecutor within twenty-four hours of his return, this would be the first public opportunity for the Jordanian authorities to demonstrate their intention to comply with the assurances. The Court thus found that it was unlikely that the Public Prosecutor would refuse to allow the applicant's lawyer to be present. Moreover, the Court noted that the monitors who would travel with the applicant from the UK to Jordan would remain with him for at least part of the first day he was detained in Jordan. In the Court's view, this significantly diminished any risk of ill-treatment might arise from a lack of clarity in the MOU.[484] The Court accepted Jordanian assurances as sufficient to remove any real risk of ill-treatment of the applicant upon extradition to Jordan.

The Court's decision to accept DAS in the *Abu Qatada* case has opened them to criticism on the grounds that it undermines the absolute nature of the principle of Non-Refoulement under both Article 3 CAT and Article 3 ECHR. Even if we accept the Court's approach that DAS, if they meet certain criteria,

---

482 ECtHR, *Othman (Abu Qatada) v. the United Kingdom*, para. 203. Middleton, B., European Court of Human Rights: Assuring Deportation of Terrorist Suspects, The Journal of Criminal Law, Vol. 76 no. 3: 2012, 213–219, p. 217; Michaelsen, C., 2012, pp. 759–760.

483 ECtHR, *Othman (Abu Qatada) v. the United Kingdom*, para. 204.

484 Ibid., para. 198.

can remove the risk of ill-treatment to an applicant who, without assurances, would be at a real risk of such treatment in the receiving State, the Court's decision in the *Abu Qatada* case is cause for concern. Although the assurances provided in this case were more comprehensive than those provided in other similar cases, such as the *Saadi* case, they were still very weak, particularly with regard to the post-return monitoring mechanism. There was no guarantee that the monitoring body would always be granted access to the applicant. The body nominated to monitor the applicant's condition had little experience in this field. The Court did not consider these weaknesses substantial enough to make the State's assurances of protection inadequate.[485] The Court gave particular importance to its assumption that the monitoring body was independent of the receiving State's authorities, but the Court ignored the fact that the monitoring body also received funding from the sending State. In fact, it was not independent from the sending State, and may thus have also had an interest in reassuring the British government that Jordan's assurances were complied with, and that the applicant was not subjected to ill-treatment there. We argue that the body that monitors the applicant after his return must be independent both from the receiving State and from the sending State.

To assess whether DAs provide, in practical application, sufficient guarantees against the risk of ill-treatment for the applicant, the Court has considered developments subsequent to the applicant's removal. The Court has clearly stated that: "the reliability of the assurances [...] must also be assessed in the light of the information and evidence obtained subsequent to the applicants' extradition".[486]

In *Labsi v. Slovakia* (2012), the applicant was detained for trial in Algeria after the Algerian authorities provided DAs that justified his expulsion. The Slovakian Ministry of the Interior asked the Algerian Embassy in Vienna to arrange an official visit to discuss the applicant's situation in Algeria. There seemed to have been no follow-up to this request. The Court noted that the Slovakian Ministry of the Interior refused to inform Mr. Hrbáň, a lawyer who took over the defense of the applicant's rights before the ECtHR, about the applicant's address. The Court concluded that these Algerian assurances could not be objectively verified through diplomatic or other monitoring mechanisms. In this case, the Court found that developments subsequent to the applicant's expulsion insufficient to ensure he would be adequately protected against the risk of ill-treatment. The Court concluded that these assurances could not affect its conclusion that, at the time of the applicant's expulsion,

---

485   Michaelsen, C., 2012, p. 764.
486   ECtHR, *Shamayev and 12 others v. Georgia and Russia*, para. 346.

there were substantial grounds to believe that the applicant faced a real risk of being subjected to ill-treatment in Algeria.[487]

IV.3.2.2.h   The Protection against Torture in the Receiving State
One factor that the Court has given particular importance in its assessment of the practical application of assurances a receiving State provides is if there is an effective system of protection against torture in this State. It has asked if the authorities of the receiving State are willing to cooperate with international human rights monitoring mechanisms and if they are willing to investigate allegations of torture, and to punish those responsible for torture if it takes place.[488] The Court has repeatedly asserted that:

> ...diplomatic assurances were not in themselves sufficient to ensure adequate protection against the risk of ill-treatment where reliable sources have reported practices resorted to or tolerated by the authorities which were manifestly contrary to the principles of the Convention.[489]

In *Soldatenko v. Ukraine* (2008), which concerned the applicant's extradition to Turkmenistan, the Court noted that because there was no effective system of protection against torture in the receiving State, it was difficult to accept Turkmen assurances that human rights would be respected. The international human rights reports available to the Court indicated that the Turkmen authorities had serious problems cooperating in the human rights field and categorically denied violations despite consistent information to the contrary from reliable governmental and non-governmental sources. The Court disagreed with the Ukrainian government that these assurances would suffice to guarantee the applicant would not be ill-treated if he were extradited.[490] In another refoulement case, *Rustamov v. Russia* (2012), after noting that the receiving State, Uzbekistan, was not a party to the ECHR, the Court observed that the Uzbek authorities had not demonstrated that an effective system of legal protection against torture existed, or that it had a system equivalent to that required of the States parties. According to numerous reports available to the Court, the Uzbek authorities were reluctant to investigate allegations

---

487   ECtHR, *Labsi v. Slovakia*, paras. 44, 64, 93, 130 and 131.

488   ECtHR, *Othman (Abu Qatada) v. the United Kingdom*, para. 189.

489   ECtHR, *Saadi v. Italy* (GC), paras. 147–148; ECtHR, *Kolesnik v. Russia*, para. 73.

490   ECtHR, *Soldatenko v. Ukraine*, paras. 73–74. See also, ECtHR, *Ben Khemais v. Italy*, paras. 59–60; ECtHR, *Koktysh v. Ukraine*, para. 63; ECtHR, *Ryabikin v. Russia*, para. 119; ECtHR, *Kolesnik v. Russia*, para. 73.

of torture or to punish those responsible, and did not quickly cooperate with international human rights monitoring mechanisms. The Court was not persuaded by assurances from the Uzbek authorities, and found these assurances insufficient to ensure adequate protection against the risk the applicant would be ill-treated.[491]

The ECtHR has noted that the sending State is still allowed to seek assurances, even if the receiving State seems to systematically torture and ill-treatment returnees.[492] In the *Abu Qatada* case, although reports by UN bodies and NGOs demonstrated that torture was perpetrated systematically, particularly against Islamist detainees, the Court decided that the general human rights situation in Jordan did not prevent it from accepting all assurances from the Jordanian government. While the Court found that the applicant's extradition to Jordan would expose him, as a high profile Islamist, to a real risk of ill-treatment, it also found the assurances contained in the MOU, and monitored by Adaleh Centre, removed any risk of ill-treatment of the applicant.[493]

IV.3.2.2.i   The Applicant's Previous Ill-treatment in the Receiving State

If the applicant was previously subjected to ill-treatment in the proposed receiving State, the Court has held that no assurances could be considered sufficient to protect him against the risk of ill-treatment unless the sending State establishes that the situation has changed to the extent that excludes any possibility of ill-treatment. In *Koktysh* v. *Ukraine* (2009), the Court noted that the applicant had been previously ill-treated by the Belarusian authorities. Furthermore, the Ukrainian government did not establish that the applicant's situation had changed to the extent that excluded any possibility of ill-treatment in the future. The Court concluded that it could not agree with the Ukrainian government that the assurances given in respect to the applicant would suffice to protect him against the risk of ill-treatment if extradited to Belarus.[494]

---

491   ECtHR, *Rustamov v. Russia*, para. 131. See also, ECtHR, *Gaforov v. Russia*, para. 138; ECtHR, *Yuldashev* v. *Russia*, para. 85; ECtHR, *Nizomkhon Dzhurayev v. Russia*, Appl.No. 31890/11, 3 October 2013, para. 132; ECtHR, *Gayratbek Saliyev v. Russia*, Appl.No. 39093/13, 17 April 2014, para. 66.

492   ECtHR, *Muminov v. Russia*, para. 97; ECtHR, *Garayev v. Azerbaijan*, para. 74; ECtHR, *Khaydarov* v. *Russia*, para. 111.

493   ECtHR, *Othman (Abu Qatada) v. the United Kingdom*, paras. 191–194 and 205.

494   ECtHR, *Koktysh* v. *Ukraine*, para. 64.

IV.3.2.2.j   The Examination of the DAs by the Courts of the Sending State
The mere fact that a receiving State provides DAs is insufficient, in itself, to
ensure adequate protection against the risk of ill-treatment. The State party
has an obligation to determine if these assurances constitute, in their practical
application, a sufficient guarantee that the applicant will be protected against
such risk.[495] In *Kolesnik* v. *Russia* (2010), the Court was not convinced that Russian authorities could rely, without any assessment, on Turkmen assurances
that they would exclude the risk of ill-treatment.[496] Where the domestic courts
of the sending State have carefully examined the reliability of assurances based
on reliable evidence, the ECtHR has given weight to this examination. In its
admissibility decision in *Babar Ahmad and Others* v. *The UK* (2010), the Court
attached importance to the fact that the meaning and the likely effect of DAs
the US government provided had been carefully considered by British domestic courts in the light of a substantial body of evidence about the current situation in the US. The Court noted that the domestic courts had been able to do
so because the US government was a party to the proceedings before them and
was able to adduce evidence to assist those Courts in assessing the weight that
should be given to the assurances.[497] In another refoulement case, *Zokhidove* v.
Russia (2013), the Court took into account the doubts of the Russian Supreme
Court about the reliability of assurances given by the Uzbek authorities in this
case, basing those doubts on conclusions drawn by the ECtHR in a number
of similar cases where it was determined that the ill-treatment of detainees
in Uzbekistan was a serious problem, and that the guarantees of the Uzbek
authorities were not sufficient to dispel the risk of such treatment.[498]

IV.3.3   ComAT
IV.3.3.1   *Introduction*
The Committee has considered the use of DAs in refoulement cases when it
considered the periodic reports submitted to it by the States parties and in
its case-law on Article 3 CAT. The Committee has repeatedly recommended
States parties to refrain from seeking and accepting DAs as a safeguard against
torture or ill-treatment where there are substantial grounds for believing that
an applicant would be in danger of being subjected to torture or ill-treatment

---

495   ECtHR, *Othman (Abu Qatada)* v. *the United Kingdom*, para. 187.
496   ECtHR, *Kolesnik* v. *Russia*, para. 121. See, ECtHR, *Abdulkhakov* v. *Russia*, para. 150.
497   ECtHR, *Babar Ahmad and Others* v. *the United Kingdom*, para. 106. See also, ECtHR,
        AL-Moayad v. *Germany* (admissibility decision), paras. 66–69.
498   ECtHR, *Zokhidove* v. *Russia*, paras. 44 and 141.

upon return.[499] In its case-law, the Committee has recalled that DAs cannot be used as an instrument to avoid the application of the principle of Non-Refoulement under Article 3 CAT.[500] However, the Committee has not refused to take DAs into consideration in Non-Refoulement cases. The Committee states that:

> Article 3 of the Convention obliges the State that decides whether or not to extradite a person under its jurisdiction to another State to take all necessary steps to prevent torture from occurring. This obligation means that it has the duty to examine carefully and take into account all existing circumstances that may reasonably be considered to indicate a risk of torture [...]. The standards that must be met to ensure prevention are still more stringent when the State decides to request diplomatic assurances before proceeding with extradition (or any other type of handover), given that such a request demonstrates that the extraditing State harbours concerns about the treatment that may be reserved for the extradited person in the destination country.[501]

It seems that, in its case-law, the ComAT has followed an approach similar to that of the ECtHR, i.e., it considers that its task is not to rule upon the propriety of using DAs in refoulement cases, but to examine if the DAs provided in a specific case are sufficient to remove any real risk of torture to the applicant. The Committee has not developed clear criteria to assess if assurances obtained in a particular case are sufficient to ensure adequate protection for the complainant against torture. The weight that is given to assurances is determined on a case-by-case basis. The Committee's case-law in this regard does demonstrate that it has given particular importance to certain factors, including whether the assurances have been disclosed to the Committee, whether they are specific or vague, whether the complainant was previously ill-treated, whether there are any post-return monitoring mechanism to ensure the receiving State will comply with the assurances, and whether there is an effective system of protection against torture in this State. We will discuss

---

499   See, e.g. Report of the ComAT, UN. Doc. A/61/44, 1 November 2006, the third periodic report of Georgia, para. 11; Report of the ComAT, UN. Doc. A/63/44, 2007–2008, the Committee's consideration of the third periodic report of Australia; ComAT, Consideration of the fifth periodic report of Germany.

500   ComAT, *Abdussamatov et al.* v. *Kazakhstan*, para. 13.10; ComAT, *X.* v. *Kazakhstan*, No. 554/2013, 9 October 2015, para. 12.8.

501   ComAT, *Boily* v. *Canada*, para. 14.4.

these criteria in the following subsections, but it is appropriate to note here that the Committee has never addressed the question of whether the person who gives the assurances can bind the receiving State.

In *Agiza* v. *Sweden* (2005), the Swedish government noted, "if assurances are to have effect, they must be issued by someone who can be expected to be able to ensure their effectiveness". The government argued that the assurances it obtained must be given weight since they were issued by the person in charge of the Egyptian security service, and it was difficult to imagine anyone better placed in Egypt to ensure adherence to these assurances.[502] The Committee failed to examine this question in the case of *Agiza* and in following Non-Refoulement cases. However, as we will find, the Committee has believed that the main criterion for assessing the effectiveness of assurances is the existence of follow-up mechanism.

IV.3.3.2   *Criteria to Assess DAS*

IV.3.3.2.a   Disclosure of the Terms of the Assurances to the ComAT

To assess the effectiveness of DAS in a specific case, the ComAT has required the respondent State to provide it with a copy of those assurances. In *Elif Pelit* v. *Azerbaijan* (2007), the State party argued that it had received clear and convincing DAS from the Turkish authorities, and that these assurances ruled out torture and CIDTP against the complainant after she was extradited. The ComAT noted that the State party did not supply the assurances to the Committee and thus the Committee could not perform its own independent assessment of their effectiveness in protecting the complainant against torture.[503]

IV.3.3.2.b   Content

When Sweden accepted a DA for the extradition of Agiza and Alzery to Egypt, the assurances took the form of an exchange of aide-memoires. The Swedish government asked the Egyptian government to ensure that the two men "will not be subjected to inhuman treatment or punishment of any kind by any authority of the Arab Republic of Egypt".[504] In its response, the Egyptian government stated it understood the terms of the assurances in the Swedish aide-memoire, but it added, "this will be done according to what Egyptian

---

502 ComAT, *Agiza* v. *Sweden*, paras. 4.24 and 12.24.

503 ComAT, *Elif Pelit* v. *Azerbaijan*, paras. 7.12.

504 Kingdom of Sweden, aide-méoire to the Arab Republic of Egypt, (12 December 2001), as cited by Noll, G., Diplomatic Assurances and the Silence of Human Rights Law, Melbourne Journal of International Law, Vol. 7 no. 1: 2006, 104–124, p. 109.

constitution, and law stipulates".[505] Since Sweden and other western countries object to domestic law reservations, the complainant argued that Egypt must interpret the fact Sweden did not object to this added sentence as implicit acceptance that reference to the domestic law constituted a limitation to Egypt's international obligations to honour these assurances. The Egyptian aide-memoire decreased the scope of the commitments the Swedish aide-memoire suggested that Egypt make, and this added sentence "would reduce the assurances to whatever the Egyptian Constitution and Egyptian law stipulates".[506] The Committee did not address the effect of this referral on Egypt's obligations under the CAT, but it confirmed that Egypt is a State party to the CAT and is thus bound to treat prisoners in accordance with its rules; otherwise it would be in breach of the Convention's provisions.[507]

In *Kalinichenko* v. *Morocco* (2011), the request of the Russian government for the complainant's extradition was accompanied by DAs that promised he would not be subjected to torture or ill-treatment after he was extradited. The complainant argued, with reference to the Committee's jurisprudence,[508] that the DA would be insufficient to ensure compliance with the absolute prohibition of refoulement provided for in Article 3. He maintained that the general pledge by the Russian authorities to comply with international human rights standards could not overturn reliable evidence that indicated a pattern of gross, flagrant and mass violations of human rights in Russia, and also claimed a well-founded fear of being exposed to a risk of torture.[509] After concluding that the complainant had sufficiently demonstrated his foreseeable, personal, and real risk of torture upon return to Russia, the ComAT noted that obtaining such DAs was insufficient to protect him against this risk, in the light of their general and non-specific nature.[510] The Committee has not given weight to assurances that only reiterate the receiving State's obligations under its national law and/or international human rights treaties.

IV.3.3.2.c   The Complainant's Previous Ill-treatment in the Receiving State
In *Boily* v. *Canada* (2011), the Committee took the fact that the complainant had been previously subjected to torture in the requesting State, Mexico, into

---

505   Arab Republic of Egypt, aide-méoire to the Kingdom of Sweden, (12 December 2001), as cited by Ibid., p. 109.
506   Ibid., pp. 111–112.
507   ComAT, *Hanan Attia* v. *Sweden*, para. 12.3.
508   He mainly referred to the ComAT's decision in the *Agiza* case, paras. 13.4–13.5 and the HRC's decision in *Alzery* case, HRC, *Mohammed Alzery* v. *Sweden*, para. 11.5.
509   ComAT, *Kalinichenko* v. *Morocco*, para. 5.10.
510   Ibid., paras. 6.3 and 15.6.

account when it assessed the DAs. The Committee needed to determine if the assurances Mexico provided were of a nature to eliminate all reasonable doubt that the complainant would be subjected to torture after he was extradited. The Committee held that it had to determine if the assurances included a post-return monitoring mechanism that would guarantee their effectiveness.[511] The complainant's previously ill-treatment in Mexico arguably prompted the Committee to place more importance on the existence of a follow-up mechanism.

IV.3.3.2.d   Monitoring Mechanisms

In order to increase the effectiveness of DAs, States concerned are sometimes keen on providing a mechanism for post-return monitoring to supervise the treatment of the person concerned following his removal. Such a mechanism is included either in the DAs themselves, or in a later separate agreement, such as the agreement for post-return monitoring in the *Agiza* case. The ComAT has refused to give weight to DAs that do not establish a follow-up mechanism,[512] or those in which the sending State fails to provide sufficiently specific details as to whether it has engaged in an objective, impartial and trustworthy mechanism.[513] The Committee has held that such monitoring would have to be "in fact and in the complainant's perception, objective, impartial and sufficiently trustworthy".[514]

In *Attia* v. *Sweden* (2003), the ComAT gave particular significance to the lack of an effective follow-up mechanism when it assessed the adequacy of the DA. In this case, the Committee relied on the effectiveness of the monitoring mechanism in a related case. Since Attia challenged her removal to Egypt mainly on the ground of her family relationship with her husband, Agiza, who had been extradited two years before, the Committee noted that the conditions under which the complainant's husband had been detained were monitored by regular visits from the Swedish authorities, which had not found that the assurances were breached. Consequently, the Committee found that the DAs were effective and Attia was not at a substantial personal risk of torture.[515] For the purpose of assessing the credibility of the assurances in the case before it, the ComAT has noted the effectiveness of a similar monitoring mechanism

---

511   ComAT, *Boily* v. *Canada*, para. 14.4.

512   ComAT, *Kalinichenko* v. *Morocco*, para. 15.6.

513   ComAT, *Abdussamatov et al.* v. *Kazakhstan*, para. 13.10; ComAT, *Elif Pelit* v. *Azerbaijan*, para. 11.

514   Ibid., para. 11. See, Frigo, M., 2011, p. 107.

515   ComAT, *Hanan Attia* v. *Sweden*, para. 12.3.

in related or similar cases over a certain period of time.[516] NGOs considered this decision troubling because the Committee had ignored a great deal of information about the way the monitoring was actually carried out. The Swedish officials' visits started five weeks after Agiza was removed. None of the visits were conducted in private; Egyptian prison personnel were present and took notes. There was also a contradiction between the statements of the Swedish representatives about Agiza's treatment, and the way his relatives and a journalist who visited him described it. The Committee did not consider that Attia was not suspected of a criminal act by the Egyptian authorities, which meant she would not be handed directly to Egyptian authorities. This made monitoring her condition more problematic.[517] However, in *Agiza* v. *Sweden* (2005), the Committee reconsidered the effectiveness of this monitoring mechanism and after new facts emerged, it changed its assessment of the assurances.[518]

The Committee has also taken into account the fact that a detainee's risk of torture is highest in the first days of his detention. In *Boily* v. *Canada* (2011), the ComAT noted that the diplomatic and consular authorities of the sending State had not been given notice of the complainant's extradition and were not informed of the need to keep close and continuous contact with him from the time he was extradited. The Court found:

> In this case the diplomatic assurances and the foreseen consular visits failed to anticipate the likelihood that the complainant had the highest risk of being tortured during the initial days of his detention.[519]

Since the complainant was subjected to torture during the first four days after he was extradited to Mexico, and since the State party waited a week after his extradition before it tried to check on his safety, the Court concluded that the Canadian system of DAs was not designed carefully enough to effectively prevent torture; therefore, the Court requested the State party to review its system of DAs so it could avoid similar violations in the future.[520] The ComAT has

---

516 Schimmel, C.A., 2007, p. 20.

517 HRC, *Mohammed Alzery* v. *Sweden*, paras. 11.5; AI, Sweden The case of Mohammed El Zari and Ahmed Agiza: violations of fundamental human rights by Sweden confirmed, AI Index: EUR 42/001/2006, 2006, p. 5; HRW, 'Empty Promises' Diplomatic Assurances No Safeguard against Torture, p. 5.

518 ComAT, *Agiza* v. *Sweden*, para. 13.5.

519 ComAT, *Boily* v. *Canada*, para. 14.5.

520 Ibid., paras. 14.5 and 15. See also, ECtHR, *Othman (Abu Qatada)* v. *the United Kingdom*, para. 198; HRC, *Mohammed Alzery* v. *Sweden*, para. 11.5.

taken developments subsequent to the complainant's removal into account in its assessment of whether DAs provide sufficient guarantees for the complainant against the risk of torture.

IV.3.3.2.e   Protection against Torture in the Receiving State
According to the ComAT:

> ...torture is practiced systematically when it is apparent that the torture cases reported have not occurred fortuitously in a particular place or at a particular time, but are seen to be habitual, widespread and deliberate in at least a considerable part of the territory of the country in question. Torture may in fact be of a systematic character without resulting from the direct intention of a Government. It may be the consequence of factors that the Government has difficulty in controlling, and its existence may indicate a discrepancy between policy as determined by the central Government and its implementation by the local administration. Inadequate legislation, which in practice allows room for the use of torture, may also add to the systematic nature of this practice.[521]

The former Special Rapporteur on torture, Theo van Boven, believed that wherever systematic torture took place, "the principle of Non-Refoulement must be strictly observed and diplomatic assurances should not be resorted to".[522] He believed the use of DAs was precluded in all circumstances envisaged in this definition. When the ComAT considered the second periodic report of the US, it expressed its concerns about the State party's use of DAs in refoulement cases:

> When determining the applicability of its Non-Refoulement obligations under article 3 of the Convention, the State party should only rely on "diplomatic assurances" in regard to States which do not systematically violate the Convention's provisions, and after a thorough examination of the merits of each individual case.[523]

---

521   UNGA, Report of the ComAT, UN. Doc. A/48/44/Add.1, 15 November 1993, para. 39.
522   Report of the Special Rapporteur on Torture and other Cruel, Inhuman or Degrading Treatment or Punishment, Theo van Boven, UN. Doc. A/59/324, para. 37.
523   Report of the ComAT, UN. Doc. A/61/44, second report of the United States of America, para. 21.

Through its Non-Refoulement case-law under Article 3 CAT, the Committee has not strictly excluded the use of DAS in cases of systematic torture.[524] The receiving State in the *Attia* case and the *Agiza* case was Egypt; in both cases the applicants claimed that widespread use of torture existed there, but the conclusions of the Committee were different in each case.

The Committee did not consider Attia to be at a substantial personal risk of torture if she were returned to Egypt because, according to the Committee's jurisprudence, family ties are not accepted as a sufficient ground for an allegation of a risk of torture under Article 3.[525] Thus, her removal would not breach the principle of Non-Refoulement, even if no assurances were sought. Though this conclusion suggests that the DAS had no role in the outcome of the case, the Committee expressed its satisfaction with those assurances and noted that the sending State's authorities regularly monitored their application.

The same assurances were rejected in the *Agiza* case. He was found in a real risk of torture in Egypt because, "Egypt resorted to consistent and widespread use of torture against detainees, and [...] the risk of such treatment was particularly high in the case of detainees held for political and security reasons".[526] The Committee justified its different conclusions in the two similar cases, and the fact that its position on the same assurances had changed, with facts that had not been available to it when it had considered the Attia case.[527] These new facts related to the circumstances of Agiza's removal and his subsequent treatment.

The *Agiza* decision might lead us to conclude that the pattern of systematic torture in Egypt played no role in the Committee's assessment of the sufficiency of those assurances. And we might think similarly about *Kalinichenko*

---

524   In this regard, the HRC held that "the more systematic the practice of torture or cruel, inhuman or degrading treatment or punishment, the less likely it will be that a real risk of such treatment can be avoided by such assurances, however stringent any agreed follow-up procedures may be". HRC, Concluding observations on the second and third periodic reports of the United States of America, UN. Doc. CCPR/C/USA/CO/3/Rev.1, 18 December 2006, para. 16.

525   Attia founded her allegation of a risk of torture only on the ground of her relationship with her husband. ComAT, *Hanan Attia* v. *Sweden*, para. 12.3.

526   ComAT, *Agiza* v. *Sweden*, para. 13.4. To illustrate the existence and widespread use of torture in Egypt, the Committee cited particularly its report to the UNGA (A/51/44), paras. 180 to 222 and its Conclusions and Recommendations on the fourth periodic report of Egypt (CAT/C/CR/29/4, 23 December 2002).

527   Ibid.

v. *Morocco* (2011), where the Committee took into account its concluding
observations on the receiving State's fourth periodic report. According to this
report acts of torture and CIDTP continued to be committed in Russia by law-
enforcement officers, often with the goal of obtaining a confession. The report
also documented the lack of independence of the Procurator's Office, and its
failure to conduct prompt, impartial and effective investigations into allegations of torture and ill-treatment. The Committee asserted that additional
grounds must be adduced to show that the complainant would be personally at risk and found the following facts relevant: his business partners had
been either found dead or disappeared; two of his partners had died while in
the custody of the Russian authorities; after he reported a criminal plot, the
complainant had received death threats from organized crime groups, after
which he decided to leave the country. The Committee concluded that the
complainant had sufficiently established the existence of a foreseeable, real
and personal risk of torture upon his extradition to Russia. The Committee
considered the DAs in this case to be insufficient to protect the complainant against this risk, given the circumstances of the case, the general and
non-specific nature of the assurances, and the fact no follow-up mechanism
was established. The Committee found that the sending State had breached
Article 3 CAT.[528]

In conclusion, according to the ComAT's Non-Refoulement case-law, the
existence of a systematic practice of torture in the receiving State is not sufficient, in itself, to lead the Committee to conclude that the complainant's
removal would violate Article 3 CAT, nor does it exclude the use of specific and
clear assurances that would establish an objective, impartial and sufficiently
trustworthy follow-up mechanism.

IV.3.4   Concluding Observations
It is clear from the case-law of both the ComAT and the ECtHR that almost
all countries asked to provide DAs have poor human rights records with
regard to the universal prohibition against torture. Arguably, by seeking DAs
from such States, the sending State acknowledges the existence of a real risk
that the applicant will be ill-treated in the receiving State,[529] and tries to
circumvent its obligation under the principle of Non-Refoulement. In itself,

---

528   ComAT, *Kalinichenko* v. *Morocco*, para. 15.6. See also, ComAT, *Abichou* v. *Germany*, para.
       11.7.
529   Report of the Special Rapporteur on torture and other cruel, inhuman or degrading treat-
       ment or punishment, M. Nowak, UN. Doc. E/CN.4/2006/6, 23 December 2005, para. 31.b.

this constitutes a violation of its obligation to perform its treaty obligations in good faith.[530]

Neither body has considered the existence of a systematic practice of torture and ill-treatment in the proposed receiving State, in itself, to prohibit the sending State from seeking assurances. This situation is one of the factors these bodies take into account when they assess the adequacy of DAs to protect applicants against torture and ill-treatment. Although the ECtHR has held that, in "rare cases", the general situation of human rights in the receiving State excludes accepting any assurances whatsoever, it has not defined the situations in which this will occur. The ECtHR's case-law is inconsistent in this regard. While the Court acknowledged such rare cases exist in, for example, *Ismoilov and Others* v. *Russia* (2008), *Sultanov* v. *Russia* (2010) and *Yuldashev* v. *Russia* (2010), which concerned the extradition to Uzbekistan,[531] it considered the value of DAs in other cases, such as *Muminov* v. Russia (2008), *Garayev* v. *Azerbaijan* (2010) and *Khaydarov* v. *Russia* (2010), that concerned removal to the same receiving State. This leads us to conclude that what the ECtHR has meant by "rare cases" is a case in which there is a general situation of violence in the receiving State.[532] However, we argue that no weight at all should be given to DAs that are provided by a State where there is, according to reliable sources, a systematic practice of torture and ill-treatment.

Unlike the ComAT, the ECtHR has focused on the question of whether the person who issued the assurances has the power to bind the receiving State. It is uncommon for the sending State to obtain commitments from a low-level officer in the receiving State, who clearly does not have authority over the police and security services.[533] An assurance is credible only if a competent official issues it. The good faith of the receiving State that supplies the DAs is always in question, especially in cases where neither the receiving State nor the sending State has any interest in discovering that the removed person has been tortured. Sometimes the sending and receiving States have a common

---

530   VCLT69, Article 26. See, Schoenbach, I.A., 2007, p. 141. In the view of HRW, a sending State, which relies on assurances from such countries, "are either engaging in wishful thinking or using the assurances as a fig leaf to cover their complicity in torture and their role in the erosion of the international norm against torture". HRW, Still at Risk: Diplomatic Assurances No Safeguard Against Torture, pp. 8–10.

531   See also, ECtHR, *Kozhayev* v. *Russia*, para. 84; ECtHR, *Sidikovy* v. *Russia*, para. 150.

532   ECtHR, *Muminov* v. *Russia*, para. 97; ECtHR, *Garayev* v. *Azerbaijan*, para. 74.

533   Deeks, A.S., Avoiding Transfers to Torture, Council on Foreign Relations CSR no. 35, June 2008, p. 10.

interest in extracting information from the person that has been removed.[534] We cannot assume that assurances that a returnee will not be subject to torture are given in good faith when they are offered by a State that has adopted torture as a State policy and persistently denies the practice.[535] Since such a State fails to respect its legal obligations under international multilateral treaties, there is no reason to expect it would adhere to its bilateral obligations?[536]

Some argue that the *de facto* function of DAs is to elevate an individual case to a level of diplomatic significance, and that the effectiveness of and compliance with assurances depends less on their legal status, and more on the bilateral diplomatic relationship and the incentives the receiving and sending States have to comply with them.[537] The receiving State's failure to respect its obligations under such assurances can seriously affect its relations with the sending State.[538] Diplomacy is a sensitive matter, and it is possible that making this connection between the effectiveness of DAs and diplomatic relationships between the sending and receiving States might weaken protection DAs offer. Diplomacy is intended to promote the common interests of States. The Human rights may be one of those interests, but the maintenance of friendly relations usually remains the State's priority, even at the expense of protecting human rights.[539]

In contrast to the general rule in international law, human rights, as *erga omnes* obligations, are exempt from the principle of reciprocity,[540] for

---

534   HRW, Still at Risk: Diplomatic Assurances No Safeguard Against Torture, para. 27. See also, Giuffre, M., An Appraisal of Diplomatic Assurances One Year after Othman (Abu Qatada) v United Kingdom (2012), International Human Rights Law Review, Vol. 2 no. 1: 2013, 266–293, p. 288.

535   HRW, 'Empty Promises' Diplomatic Assurances No Safeguard against Torture, p. 4.

536   Joint statement by AI, Association for the Prevention of Torture, HRW, International Commission of Jurists, International Federation of Action by Christians for the Abolition of Torture, International Federation for Human Rights, International Helsinki Federation for Human Rights, and World Organisation Against Torture, Torture/Terrorism, Call for action against the use of diplomatic assurances in transfers to risk of torture and ill-treatment, p. 2.

537   Larsaeus, N., 2006, pp. 8 and 28. See also Jones, K., 2008, p. 188; Hasen, J.V.-, 2011, p. 60.

538   In this context, Nowak considered that it was unclear why States that already breached their binding obligations under international human rights law, without any concern about the consequences of that, should comply with non-legally binding assurances. Nowak, M., 2005, para. 31.d.

539   HRW, Still at Risk: Diplomatic Assurances No Safeguard Against Torture, pp. 24–26; Schmid, E., 2011, p. 229.

540   According to this principle a State is only obliged to comply with an obligation created by an international norm towards other States that have also accepted this norm. Djik, P.V.,

example, when the former Swedish ambassador was asked why he waited five weeks after Agiza was deported to visit him in prison, he answered that asking immediately for a meeting with Agiza would have signalled Sweden's lack of trust in the Egyptian authorities.[541] The Swedish government justified withholding some information from the embassy's report of the first visit on the ground, with the rationalization that if the disclosed information were incorrect, it would have negatively affected relations between Sweden and Egypt.[542] In the *Soering* case, the Court found that even diplomatic relations as strong as those between the US and the UK could not promote sufficient assurances.[543]

Both the ComAT and the ECtHR have given particular importance to the existence of a post-return monitoring mechanism, but neither of these bodies has developed clear criteria as to what constitutes a sufficient monitoring process.[544] Assessments of the adequacy of this mechanism should be done on a case-by-case basis, and should take into account all the relevant circumstances, including the existence of widespread practice of torture in the receiving State. Many NGOs and human rights experts have questioned the effectiveness of the post-return monitoring mechanism in securing compliance with DAs and in detecting a breach.[545] Neither the sending or receiving States may have

---

General Course. The Law of Human Rights in Europe. Instruments and Procedures for a Uniform Implementation, in: Law, A.o.E., Collected Courses of the Academy of European Law, The Hague: Kluwer Law International, 1997, 22–50, pp. 25–26.

541   In an interview with the former Swedish ambassador to Egypt Sven Linder, 17 May 2004, available at:<http://www.hrw.org/legacy/english/docs/2004/05/17/sweden8620.htm>, last visit 26 October 2009.

542   ComAT, *Agiza* v. *Sweden*, paras. 12.15 and 13.10. The ComAT found that Sweden had committed a breach of its obligation to make available to it all relevant information under Article 22.4.

543   ECtHR, *Soering* v. *the United Kingdom*, para. 98.

544   It was suggested to seek practical guidelines from a number of existing standards for effective prison monitoring, such as the UN Standard Minimum Rules for the Treatment of Prisoners, and the OPCAT, which provides for independent scrutiny of places of detention by independent national monitoring bodies designated by the State, as well as by a sub-committee of the ComAT. Larsaeus, N., 2006, p. 18.

545   Report of the Special Rapporteur on torture and other cruel, inhuman or degrading treatment or punishment, M. Nowak, UN. Doc. A/60/316, 30 August 2005, para. 46; Report of the Special Rapporteur on torture and other cruel, inhuman or degrading treatment or punishment, M. Nowak, UN. Doc. E/CN.4/2006/6, para. 31(e); AI, Reject Rather than Regulate: Call on Council of Europe Member States not to Establish Minimum Standards for the Use of Diplomatic Assurances in Transfers to Risk of Torture and Other Ill-treatment, 2005, p. 12.

an interest in detecting the existence of torture.[546] Even if the sending State monitors in good faith, its capacity is limited by the fact that torture is often practiced in secret, and by persons who are generally experts in keeping it from being detected.[547] Monitoring visits usually lack privacy, and even if they are private, many detainees will still refuse to speak of abusive treatment because they fear reprisals, against themselves or their families.[548]

Sometimes it is hard to identify the person or the body who does the monitoring. Since many respected organisations, including the ICRC, AI and HRW, have already refused to serve in this capacity. Monitors are usually diplomats, and they are caught between acting as human rights agents and as representatives of their States. In some cases, the task of post-return monitoring has been entrusted to local or national organisations that were contracted by governments. Organisations like Adaleh Centre, which was nominated by the British and Jordanian governments to monitor the treatment of Jordanian nationals returned from the UK to Jordan, often make monitoring visits to ensure adherence to the MOU.[549] And like Adaleh Centre, they may have little experience in monitoring and little independence from the authorities of the sending and receiving States. Most have no ability to demand unrestricted access to all places of detention in their countries, they may lack the influence and authority to ensure that if they detect torture or CIDTP, an impartial and independent investigation of those allegations will be conducted so that those responsible can be punished. But even the most rigorous post-return monitoring mechanism cannot possibly change the irreparable nature of the harm

---

546   In his report on the situation in Uzbekistan, the Special Rapporteur on Torture expressed his conviction that torture was connived, if not encouraged, by the heads of the places of detention. And even if those leaderships did not know of the existence of the practice of torture, which the Special Rapporteur's delegation had been able to discover in few days, it could only be because they did not want to know that. Report of the Special Rapporteur on the question of torture, Theo van Boven, submitted in accordance with Commission resolution 2002/38, mission to Uzbekistan, UN. Doc. E/CN.4/2003/68/Add.2, 3 February 2003, para. 69.

547   Alzery alleged that his torture was monitored by doctors who made sure that it would not leave him with visible scars. AI, Sweden The case of Mohammed El Zari and Ahmed Agiza: violations of fundamental human rights by Sweden confirmed, p. 5.

548   As it was cited by HRW building on the statements of Agiza's family members, he was threatened with more abuse after he disclosed to the Swedish embassy officials that he had been tortured in Egypt custody. HRW, Still at Risk: Diplomatic Assurances No Safeguard Against Torture, p. 32.

549   The Ethiopian National Human Rights Commission agreed to make visits to Ethiopians returned from the UK to Ethiopia. AI, Dangerous Deals, Europe's Reliance on 'Diplomatic Assurances' against Torture, EUR 01/012/2010, 2010, p. 11.

caused by torture.[550] No system of post-return monitoring will render DAS an acceptable alternative to rigorous respect for the absolute nature of the principle of Non-Refoulement under Article 3 CAT and Article 3 ECHR.

Whether we approve of them or not, DAS have been increasingly used in refoulement cases. Given the damaging effects of this practice on the absolute nature of the principle of Non-Refoulement under the CAT and the ECHR, it would be better if monitoring were carried out by international NGOs that specialise in human rights. The post-return monitoring mechanism might be adequate to protect returnees against ill-treatment, if monitoring is carried out by reliable, independent and international NGOs with the necessary expertise to detect signs of torture and ill-treatment. Monitoring should start from the moment a person is handed over to the receiving State onward, and meetings between the returnee and monitors must be private and hold to a pre-arranged timetable.

---

550   Ibid., pp. 11–12.

CHAPTER 5

Summary of the Conclusions

I   General Findings

I.1   *Dimensions of the Principle of Non-Refoulement*

This study set out to explore the principle of Non-Refoulement under Article 3 CAT and Article 3 ECHR. The purpose of this principle is to prevent the removal of a person in order to protect him from the risk of ill-treatment awaiting him in the receiving State. The rationale behind the principle of Non-Refoulement under both Conventions is that: a State's obligation to protect a person from ill-treatment requires it not only to refrain from subjecting him to ill-treatment, but it must also protect him from such treatment at the hands of another State. Consequently, the State is under an obligation to refrain from removing a person to another State where he faces the risk of such ill-treatment. While Article 3 CAT provides expressly for this principle, the ECHR contains no express provision on this matter. The Strasbourg bodies have developed this principle under the absolute prohibition of torture and CIDTP under Article 3 ECHR.

Both the ComAT and the ECtHR conduct an assessment of the human rights situation in the receiving State in order to determine whether the applicant's removal would expose him to a risk of ill-treatment in the receiving State. However, both bodies have made it clear that the responsibility in Non-Refoulement cases is not that of the receiving State but of the sending State. The responsibility of the sending State is based on its own act of removal, which leads, or would lead to, the ill-treatment of the removed person in the receiving State.

I.1.1   Absolute Nature

The prohibition against refoulement is absolute and no derogation or limitation is permissible either under Article 3 CAT, or under Article 3 ECHR. The protection against refoulement under both Articles is afforded to any person who is under threat of being removed to another State where he faces a risk of ill-treatment, regardless of the seriousness and the nature of his conduct. This prohibition applies even in the case of expulsion of terrorist suspects or criminal offenders for reasons of national security. Both the ECtHR and the ComAT have not accepted any balancing test between the risk of ill-treatment

© KONINKLIJKE BRILL NV, LEIDEN, 2016 | DOI 10.1163/9789004319394_007 to a person if removed and the threat he represents to national security if he remains.

I.1.2   Treatment from Which a Person is Protected in the Receiving State

While Article 3 CAT protects a person only from removal to torture as defined under Article 1 CAT, Article 3 ECHR prohibits removal to torture and other CIDTP. Several differences follow from this distinction with regard to the intention and purpose of the conduct and the required minimum level of severity of the pain resulting from the conduct. These differences, in themselves, are generally not fundamental in Non-Refoulement cases because of the prospective nature of the assessment of the future ill-treatment. However, the most important difference stems from the fact that Article 1 CAT restricts the definition of torture to cases where there is involvement of a public official. This condition affects the ComAT's freedom of interpretation of the principle of Non-Refoulement under Article 3 CAT. In this regard two points should be noted:

I.1.2.a   *Source of the Risk*

I.1.2.a.i   Public Officials or Non-state Actors

Both the ECtHR and the ComAT have applied the principle of Non-Refoulement where the ill-treatment in the receiving State emanates from acts of public officials or of non-State actors where the authorities of this State do not want to afford the applicant appropriate protection. The divergence between the Committee's and the Court's case-law, in this context, appears where the authorities of the receiving State are not able to obviate the risk of ill-treatment by non-State actors by providing appropriate protection.

The Court has applied Article 3 ECHR even if it is established that the receiving State has fulfilled its positive obligation to prevent ill-treatment within its national territory by taking reasonable measures to control the non-State actors but it does not manage to guarantee sufficient level of safety. In contrast, the Committee has given importance to the fact that the receiving State has fulfilled its positive obligation to prevent torture by non-State actors by exercising due diligence to intervene to stop this torture and punish the perpetrator. The Committee has held that in this case it cannot be argued that the receiving State acquiesced in torture by non-State actors. This divergence is due to the fact that while Article 3 CAT applies only where there is a risk of torture inflicted, directly or indirectly, by the State authorities, Article 3 ECHR applies regardless of the source of the alleged risk.

However, this divergence between the Committee's and the Court's case-law may in reality not make a big difference for the following reasons:

a.   The Committee has applied Article 3 CAT where the risk of torture would
     be inflicted by a non-governmental entity that occupies and exercises
     quasi-governmental authority over the territory to which the complain-
     ant would be returned.
b.   To avoid protection gaps when the risk stems from private actors, it seems
     that the Committee has interpreted the State's positive obligations to pre-
     vent torture within its territory very broadly, rather as obligation of result
     instead of obligation of means.

I.1.2.a.ii   Other Sources

The ECtHR has applied the principle of Non-Refoulement under Article 3
ECHR, in very exceptional cases, where the risk of ill-treatment in the receiving
State results from factors that cannot engage, either directly or indirectly, the
responsibility of State authorities or non-State actors. The Court has taken this
approach in cases where the risk in the receiving State results from a naturally
occurring illness and a lack of sufficient health care resources in this State.
The ComAT has affirmed that even if a complainant's removal could aggravate
his state of health, this is not sufficient ground to impose an obligation under
Article 3 CAT on the sending State to refrain from proceeding with removal, if
adequate medical care is available in the receiving State. The Committee's reference to adequate medical care might implicitly indicate that the Committee
could apply Article 3 CAT to the complainant's removal where this removal resulted in aggravation of his medical condition if there was no adequate medical care in the receiving State. The Committee has not had the opportunity
to consider such a case. Since Article 3 CAT applies only to torture, we argue
that the ComAT might apply Article 3 CAT where the applicant, who may be
detained in the receiving State, can establish that the authorities of this State
intentionally fail to provide medical care to detainees.

    The Court seems ready to extend the protection of Article 3 to situations
where the risk in the receiving State results neither from an act of a State or non-
State actors nor from naturally occurring illness. The ECtHR has considered
that Article 3 ECHR applies in very exceptional cases, in which humanitarian
grounds against removal are compelling where dire humanitarian conditions
in the receiving State are solely, or even predominantly, caused by poverty, or
by the State's lack of resources to deal with a naturally occurring phenomenon, such as drought. However, the ECtHR has not applied this approach in a
Non-Refoulement case. In our opinion, the principle of Non-Refoulement
under Article 3 CAT cannot apply to such situations as it only protects an individual from ill-treatment at the hands of public officials.

I.1.2.b   *Exception of Lawful Sanctions*

Article 1 CAT makes an exception to the definition of torture: it allows intentional infliction of pain or suffering that arises from, or is inherent in, or incidental to lawful sanction. The ComAT seems to rely on national and international laws to define the legality of the sanction. A State party to the CAT cannot remove a person to a State where he faces a risk of a punishment that is illegal under international law, even if the punishment is legal under the receiving State's national law. The ComAT has accepted that the manner in which sanctions are implemented may constitute a means of torture even if these sanctions are not considered as torture, such as detention and the death penalty.

Article 3 ECHR does not include any exception that justifies infliction of torture or IDTP for any reason. Through its case-law, the ECtHR has held that suffering or humiliation must exceed the inevitable suffering or humiliation caused by a given form of legitimate punishment before a punishment is considered inhuman or degrading. The Court has considered that the nature of the punishment and the manner of its execution should be taken into account when it determines if a certain punishment violates Article 3 ECHR. Accordingly, even if the detention is not considered as inhuman or degrading punishment, the conditions of detention may reach Article 3 ECHR threshold.

While the mere possibility of being subjected to a life imprisonment sentence, in the receiving State, is not sufficient in itself to give rise to an issue under Article 3 ECHR, this Article prohibits the removal of a person who faces, in the receiving State, a risk of being subjected to a discretionary or mandatory life imprisonment sentence, without the possibility of parole: (i) if this sentence is grossly disproportionate with the offence the removed person allegedly committed; or (ii) if a life imprisonment sentence the applicant would face in the receiving State were irreducible *de facto* and *de jure*, even if such sentence were not grossly disproportionate with the offence. The ECtHR has held that the applicant has a "hope of release" at the time of imposition of the life imprisonment where there is an adequate review mechanism requiring the authorities in the receiving State to determine, on the basis of objective, pre-established criteria of which the prisoner had precise knowledge at the time of imposition of this sentence, whether, while serving his sentence, he has progressed to such an extent that continued detention can no longer be justified on legitimate penological grounds.

Protocol No. 13 abolishes the death penalty in all circumstances, so this punishment is *per se* incompatible with the ECHR, whether or not it is imposed after unfair trial, and whether or not its execution is inhuman. Accordingly, the

ECtHR has concluded that a State party to the ECHR cannot return a person to another State if there are substantial grounds for believing that he would be in danger of being subjected to the death penalty.

1.1.3   Prohibited Conducts

The principle of Non-Refoulement under both Conventions does not only prohibit the formal measures of removal (such as expulsion, return, deportation and extradition), but it also applies to all measures by which a person is physically transferred to another State including the informal transfer or rendition, non-admission at the border, indirect refoulement as well as *de facto* refoulement. Accordingly, we argue that the prohibition against refoulement under both the ECHR and the CAT applies to any measure taken by a State that directly and immediately forces a person to go to another State where he faces a risk of ill-treatment.

1.1.4   Receiving State

Neither the ECtHR nor the ComAT have imposed any limit on States to which refoulement is prohibited. The principle of Non-Refoulement applies without regard to the State of destination, whether or not it is a person's country of origin. Both bodies have even applied this principle to the transfer of a person within the territory of the same State, when he is transferred from effective control of one State to the effective control of another State.

1.1.5   Personal Scope

The protection against refoulement under both Conventions is afforded to every person within the State's jurisdiction, regardless of whether he is a foreigner (a national of another State or stateless person) or a national of the sending State.

1.1.6   Territorial Scope
1.1.6.a   *Jurisdiction Inside the State Territory*

Given that a State has jurisdiction over its own territory, a State party to the ECHR or the CAT must respect its obligation of Non-Refoulement towards every person physically present within its national territory, regardless of his legal status within this territory and whether he entered the State legally or illegally (refused asylum seekers, those deprived of the protection of CSR under its Article 1(F), recognized refugees or asylum-seekers registered with UNHCR, trafficking victims, persons without a residence permit, and those who have visitor's status or a residence permit pending the decision of the Court or the Committee).

1.1.6.b   *Jurisdiction Outside the State Territory*

A State party to the CAT or the ECHR is obligated to respect its conventional obligation of Non-Refoulement extraterritorially where it has jurisdiction outside its national territory. This study found that the principle of Non-Refoulement applies extraterritorially where a State exercises effective control over a foreign territory whether lawfully (such as aboard ships flying its flag, embassies and consulates, military bases or detention facilities established by the consent of the host State), or unlawfully (such as the case of military occupation of other State's territory). The principle of Non-Refoulement also applies extraterritorially where a State's agents exercise control or authority over a person in a territory of another State, regardless of whether the State's agents act lawfully (such as diplomatic and consular officers, border officials in customs-free zones, immigration control officers or airline liaison officers working at foreign airports, international peace-keeping or peace-enforcement troops) or unlawfully (such as security agents who kidnap a person abroad, or military forces that illegally occupy foreign territory) on the territory of another State.

1.2   *Selected Policies and Measures*

Against these findings, the book examined the application of the principle of Non-Refoulement under Article 3 ECHR and Article 3 CAT to some of the policies adopted by States to counter the increasing threat of international terrorism, combat irregular migration and regulate migration flows.

1.2.1   Selected Immigration Control Measures

1.2.1.a   *Creation of International or Transit Zones*

Neither the ECtHR nor the ComAT has had the opportunity to address the application of the principle of Non-Refoulement in such zones. However, the ECtHR has held that international zones remain part of the State's national territory and do not have extraterritorial status. Accordingly, the obligation of Non-Refoulement under Article 3 ECHR applies in transit zones. It is likely that the ComAT would follow the ECtHR's approach because under international public law a State exercises jurisdiction over the whole of its territory and should not, by adopting legal or administrative obstacles, hinder the right of persons who are physically within its territories to be effectively protected from refoulement.

1.2.1.b   *Visa Entry Measures*

A State's responsibility for refoulement may be engaged because of a conduct of its diplomatic or consular officials regarding protection seeker's application for an entry visa, if there is causal connection between rejection of this application by the State's officials, and a foreseeable risk the applicant will be ill-treated. We argue that the diplomatic or consular officials of the State party must grant an applicant entry when rejection of an entry visa application will result, as a foreseeable, immediate, and direct consequence, in exposing the applicant to a real risk of ill-treatment, if no other protection alternative is available to him. A State party to the CAT or the ECHR is obligated to grant the entry visa to the protection seeker who resorts to its embassy in his country of origin if rejecting his application may foreseeably, directly and immediately expose him to a risk of ill-treatment. This does not apply to the protection seeker who applies by electronic mail for an entry visa to a State because the application State, when it refuses his request, has not exposed him to ill-treatment as a direct and immediate consequence of its actions. Moreover, an applicant in this situation is not subject to the control of the State he has applied to, and therefore this State does not have extraterritorial jurisdiction over him.

It should be stressed here that granting an entry visa in such a situation is neither equivalent to granting protection under Article 3 CAT/ECHR, nor to obliging the State party to admit that such a person deserves its protection. The decision to grant this protection depends on the assessment of the circumstances of each case. The State may decide to remove him if it is later found that the applicant does not deserve the protection from refoulement. We do not argue here that it is generally illegal to apply visa requirements under Article 3 CAT/ECHR. What we do argue is that imposition of an entry visa application on all foreigners, including protection seekers, is contrary to the essence of the principle of Non-Refoulement. While it seems that the ECtHR has followed this approach, the ComAT has not have the opportunity to consider a Non-Refoulement case in this context.

I.2.1.c   *Carrier Sanctions*

It may be argued that the responsibility of a State party for refoulement under both Conventions might be engaged because of the acts of carriers who take responsibility for checking travel documents before allowing passengers to board in order to avoid sanctions imposed by the State party. Carrier officials act as *de facto* officials of the State party, where they prevent a passenger from boarding the flight because he is found to be improperly documented. Even if a State exempts carriers from fines where the undocumented passenger is later found to be eligible to international protection, this does not change the situation that the carrier officials, who lack training or experience in international protection issues, cannot conduct an adequate assessment of individual protection needs. In case of doubt, carrier officials will, due to economic considerations, tend to refuse to carry the passenger and to risk sanctions. The principle of Non-Refoulement also applies to the acts of a State's immigration control officers and airline liaison officers who assist carrier officials in checking travel documents at airports of countries of origin or important transit countries. In any case, allowing a passenger to board is not decided based on protection need but on possession of proper documentation. As a result, the policy of carrier sanctions undermines the protection against refoulement provided for in both the CAT and the ECHR. Neither the ECtHR nor the ComAT has considered the compatibility of imposing carrier sanctions with the conventional obligation of Non-Refoulement. Therefore, it is likely to be a case of refoulement if a State's immigration control officers who work in a foreign airport notify local authorities without investigating the claim for protection, when an improperly documented passenger tries to board a flight. To avoid allegations of refoulement, a passenger who claims to be at real risk of ill-treatment in his home country should be given a chance to make his claim credible before he is handed over to the local authorities who might be the source of the risk.

I.2.1.d   *Interception Measures*

The study addressed the application of the principle of Non-Refoulement to the interception measures a State carries out to prevent vessels suspected of carrying irregular migrants or protection seekers from entering its territorial water and return them back to their country of origin. The interception measures are often carried out without individual assessment of the passengers' status to determine if they are at risk of ill-treatment upon their return to the receiving States. These measures therefore constitute a threat to the principle of Non-Refoulement. The description of the interception measures as rescue of persons in distress at sea does not absolve the intercepting State from its obligation of Non-Refoulement. The study has found that there are two scenarios for interception measures at sea. First, a coastal State may intercept the protections seekers' vessel inside its territorial waters or a contiguous zone. As a State exercises jurisdiction over the whole of its territory, including territorial waters and the contiguous zone, when a State party to the ECHR and/or the CAT carries out such measures, it is obligated to respect its obligation of Non-Refoulement under Article 3 CAT and/or Article 3 ECHR. Although, theoretically, a ship that has been denied entry into territorial water may travel to any other coastal State in the World, a coastal State breaches its obligation of Non-Refoulement if there is sufficient proof that the passengers have no alternative than to return, directly or indirectly, to a State where they face a risk of ill-treatment. Second, the interception measures may be carried out on the high seas or inside the territorial waters of another State. In this scenario, we distinguished between two situations. First, where an intercepted vessel flies the flag of the intercepting State, or intercepted persons are transferred onto a vessel that flies the flag of the intercepting State, this State exercises jurisdiction over those intercepted persons and is therefore obligated to respect their right of Non-Refoulement. Second, where the intercepting State has effective control over the intercepted vessel that flies a foreign flag and/or its crew, the intercepted persons fall within the jurisdiction of the intercepting State and it is obligated to protect them against refoulement. The decision as to whether the intercepting State exercises effective control will depend on the circumstances of each case. If the interception measures are carried out within the territorial waters of another State, the responsibility of the intercepting State does not exclude the host State's responsibility for violating the principle of Non-Refoulement if it participates in the interception measures, or if it declines to intervene to prevent the act of refoulement.

In exercising its right to control the flow of migrants to its territory, a State party to the ECHR and/or the CAT must respect the principle of Non-Refoulement under Article 3 ECHR and/or Article 3 CAT. A State cannot avoid its Non-Refoulement obligation by intervening before arrival to its national territory or by outsourcing control tasks to a private party or to a third State. Persons who face extraterritorial immigration control measures cannot be returned to a State where there is a real risk of being subjected to ill-treatment, otherwise a State will have escaped its conventional obligation of Non-Refoulement simply by changing the location of decision-making. To ensure that the right of Non-Refoulement is not only legally but practically protected and to prevent the arbitrary application of extraterritorial immigration control measures, such measures should be accompanied with certain safeguards such as the right of effective judicial review for persons who were refused visas or permission to travel and those who are prevented from embarking and special consideration for persons entitled to international protection. A State should also, with the assistance of NGOs working in this field, train its consular staff, immigration control officials, and carrier officials on asylum and international protection issues.

1.2.2   Extraordinary Rendition

The study also examined the applicability of the principle of Non-Refoulement on the extraordinary rendition practice by which terrorist suspects are extrajudicially transferred to foreign countries where they face a risk of extended detention without trial, and a high possibility of torture. Although the practice of extraordinary rendition is mostly carried out by the US, it cannot be accomplished without the collaboration, complicity or acquiescence of other governments by initially seizing a victim, turning a blind eye to his abduction by foreign agents on their national territories, allowing "rendition flights" to use their national airports, and hosting secret CIA detention facilities. The victim of this practice cannot bring an application against the US before neither the ECtHR nor the ComAT because the US is not a party to the ECHR nor has it accepted the ComAT's competence to receive and examine individual complaints. Both the ECtHR and the ComAT have applied the prohibition of refoulement to a State party that cooperated in the extraordinary rendition programme by making the initial arrest of a person and extra-judicially transferring him to a foreign State, for the purpose of detention and interrogation outside the legal system, where there was a real risk of ill-treatment. The ECtHR has further considered that the principle of Non-Refoulement under Article 3 ECHR is violated by a State party that facilitates the extraordinary rendition of a person by allowing the "rendition flight" to use its national airports, or by hosting a secret CIA detention facility in which the person concerned is detained. Where a State party to the ECHR knew, or ought to have known at the relevant time, that an airplane crossing its airspace, landing in or departing from its airport, carries a prisoner with the intention of transferring him to a country where he faces a risk of treatment contrary to Article 3 ECHR, that State party must take all the necessary measures to prevent this action from taking place. The ComAT has not had the opportunity to address this question. However, during the consideration of the periodic reports submitted by States parties to the CAT, the ComAT referred to Article 3 CAT when it expressed its concern at the reports of the alleged cooperation of States parties in the rendition program, whether they served as departure or destination points, or allowed rendition flights to use their airports and airspace.

1.2.3   Multinational Operations

Participation of States' military forces in multinational operations overseas raises the question of applicability of the principle of Non-Refoulement on the transfer of detainees in the course of multinational military operations, whether between different contingents of the multinational forces or from the multinational forces to the local authorities. The study found that a State party to the ECHR or/and the CAT remains bound by its conventional obligation of Non-Refoulement, when its military forces participate in multinational operations overseas, or where they work under authorisation of the UN, or where they are placed at the disposal of the UN, a regional organisation, such as NATO or even another State. The criterion for attributing a removal act either to the participating State or to the international organization is the factual control over the act by the forces placed at the organization's disposal. Where a State exercises factual control over transfer measures, the removal act is attributed to that State. A State party to the CAT that participates in multinational forces must assess whether the transfer of a person to the US forces would expose him to a risk of torture. In this context, the sending State must take into account the fact that the US refuses extraterritorial application of the CAT; thus, the CAT does not protect persons transferred to US forces.

II   Procedural Issues

II.1   *Interim Measures*

As the individual applications to both the ECtHR and the ComAT do not have suspensive effect and irreparable harm could result if applicants were removed in violation of the principle of Non-Refoulement, the effective protection against refoulement, whether under Article 3 ECHR or Article 3 CAT, requires that interim measures be respected.

Both the ComAT and the ECtHR consider the request for interim measures to be legally binding under the CAT and the ECHR. The failure of a State to comply with requested interim measures constitutes a violation of its obligation to cooperate with the ComAT or the ECtHR in good faith, because it prevents these bodies from effectively examining the complainant's Non-Refoulement claim and hinders the effective exercise of his rights. However, the finding that the respondent State, by removing the applicant, violated its obligation to respect the interim measures does not necessarily indicate that there would be a violation of the principle of Non-Refoulement. The request for interim measures does not in itself indicate that the Non-Refoulement application will be declared admissible, or presage the Court's decision on the merits of the application. Nor does refusal to grant the request for interim measures preclude subsequently finding that the principle of Non-Refoulement was violated.

II.2   *Admissibility Criteria*

Both the ECtHR and the ComAT may receive a Non-Refoulement application from a person who was allegedly forcibly removed or who faces a threat of being forcibly removed to a State where there is a real risk of being subjected to the proscribed ill-treatment. To some extent, the admissibility criteria of an individual application before the ECtHR and the ComAT are similar. However, some points should be highlighted.

II.2.1   Victim Status

An applicant in Non-Refoulement cases has victim status when he has already been removed, when there is a final and enforceable decision on his removal, or when the respondent State has taken factual steps to return him to a State where he would be at a real risk of being ill-treated. Both bodies do not restrict the protection against refoulement to cases in which States parties decided to remove the applicant. Otherwise, a State may circumvent the principle of Non-Refoulement by forcibly removing an individual without issuing a specific order. While the ComAT seems to take the view that the applicant would lose his victim status if, after he had lodged his Non-Refoulement application with the Committee, he voluntary left the respondent State party, the ECtHR has considered this situation in the light of the circumstances of each case.

II.2.2   Exhaustion of Domestic Remedies
Before lodging his Non-Refoulement application with the ECtHR or the ComAT, the applicant must exhaust all available and effective domestic remedies. In contrast to the ComAT, the ECtHR requires exhaustion of the domestic remedy to offer reasonable prospects of success in order to be effective. Accordingly, the ComAT might declare an application inadmissible for non-exhaustion of specific domestic remedies, while the ECtHR might consider the same application admissible if the applicant manages to establish that the domestic remedy that he did not exhaust does not offer a reasonable prospect of success.

II.2.3   Time-Limit to Submit the Complaint
If the applicant's removal is carried out, the Non-Refoulement application must be submitted to the ECtHR within six-months of the date of removal. If the removal is not yet carried out, the six-month period has not yet begun for the applicant. An applicant might not have the opportunity to challenge his removal before it was carried out, and after his removal, he sought a remedy from the sending State by challenging the legality of the removal and trying to obtain effective redress. In this case, we argue that the six-months time period begins on the date the applicant learns of the final domestic decision on his claim. This approach enables the sending State to put right the alleged violation of Non-Refoulement through its legal system before the submission of the claim to the ECtHR in accordance with the subsidiary nature of the Court's role. This approach also preserves the applicant's right to recourse to the ECtHR in case the sending State intentionally prolongs the domestic remedy or where he was a victim of extraordinary rendition and subjected to more than six months secret detention after rendition. The time-period for submitting an individual complaint to the ComAT will begin on the date domestic remedies are exhausted. With regard to the length of the time-period, it is up to the Committee to decide if the time elapsed between the exhaustion of domestic remedies and the submission of the Non-Refoulement complaint is so unreasonably prolonged as to render consideration of the complaint unduly

difficult. The Committee has not had the opportunity to apply this rule in Non-Refoulement cases. In our view, the Committee should follow the approach adopted by the ECtHR in Non-Refoulement cases; time period should begin on the date of the complainant's removal. It is hard to imagine a situation where submission of the Non-Refoulement complaint was unreasonably prolonged if the complainant has not been removed on the date the complaint was filed. If the complainant has been removed, it is up to the Committee to determine if the time elapsed is unreasonably prolonged, based on the circumstances of each case.

In our view, if a Non-Refoulement application was declared inadmissible by the ECtHR for failure to meet the six-month deadline, it could be later declared admissible by the ComAT where the Committee finds that the time elapsed since the exhaustion of domestic remedies was not so unreasonably prolonged as to render consideration of the claim unduly difficult.

11.2.4   The Matter is Not Being Examined by Another International Body

Both the ComAT and the ECtHR will declare an application inadmissible if it has been previously submitted to the other body. Therefore, there is no potential for conflicting jurisdiction between these two bodies. Accordingly, no conflicting jurisprudence, in a formal sense, may occur between the ECtHR and the ComAT. However, in our view, if the ComAT found that the complainant's removal would not expose him to a risk of torture by the authorities in the receiving State, the complainant may subsequently claim before the ECtHR that his removal would expose him to a real risk of ill-treatment resulting from a naturally occurring illness and a lack of sufficient health care resources in this State. In such case, the ECtHR should not declare this application inadmissible on the ground that it is substantially the same as a matter already examined by the ComAT, because the protection against refoulement under Article 3 ECHR is wider than that under Article 3 CAT.

11.3   Standard and Burden of Proof

The required standard of proof in Non-Refoulement cases, whether before the ComAT or the ECtHR, is that there are "substantial grounds" for believing that the applicant's removal would expose him to a foreseeable, personal and real risk of being subjected to the proscribed ill-treatment.

It is for the applicant, whether before the ComAT or the ECtHR, to submit evidence that supports his allegations. When the applicant satisfies the initial burden of proof, the burden shifts to the respondent State to put forward any argument or document capable of casting doubt on the applicant's claim.

The ECtHR may seek to obtain material on its own initiative particularly when the applicant provides reasoned grounds that cast doubt on the accuracy of the information relied on by the respondent State. The ECtHR may carry out its fact-finding role by sending judicial delegations to hear witnesses or by conducting judicial on the spot investigations. However, since the proposed receiving States are often non-States parties to the ECHR, the Court has generally relied on fact-finding by secondary sources for additional information about the situation in the receiving State. In the course of considering Non-Refoulement applications, the ComAT has not obtained material on its own initiative or conduct fact-finding missions. This may be due to the fact that the ComAT has background information on whether and to what extent the practice of torture exists in the proposed receiving State, if it is a State party to the CAT, through the consideration of periodic reports which Article 19 CAT obliges States parties to submit every four years. If the proposed receiving State is not a party to the CAT, the Committee, as a treaty body, cannot officially and directly request information from this State or appoint a delegation to conduct fact-finding there.

III   Substantive Issues

III.1   *Risk Assessment*
III.1.1   Time of the Risk Assessment
Both the ECtHR and the ComAT have distinguished whether or not the applicant's removal was carried out before they consider his application. If the applicant *has not been removed* at the time the ECtHR or the ComAT considers his Non-Refoulement application, the material time of risk assessment is the time at which his application is under consideration by these bodies. If the applicant *was removed before* the ECtHR or the ComAT considers the case, the risk is assessed in light of the facts which were known or ought to have been known to the sending State at the time of removal, regardless of whether or not he was actually subjected to proscribed treatment following his removal. The subsequent events are taken into account only for the purpose of confirming or refusing the sending State's appreciation of the risk.

III.1.2   Assessment of Evidence
Both the ECtHR or the ComAT have taken into account all information brought before them in order to assess the risk in a Non-Refoulement case. Regardless of whether or not the applicant is removed at the time of consideration of his

case, the ComAT and the ECtHR assess the possibility of a future risk. This prospective nature of the assessment of the future ill-treatment leads both bodies to rely on the most recent reports by a variety of sources to assess the general human rights or the situation of a particular group in the receiving State. Documents include these bodies' own Non-Refoulement case-law and the reports of governmental sources, NGOs, and the UN bodies. Both bodies tend to accept any evidence adduced by the applicant in support of his claims about his personal circumstances, as long as this evidence is not forged.

III.1.3   Factors Used to Assess the Risk

A thorough examination of the ECtHR's and ComAT's Non-Refoulement case-law indicates that, in doing their risk assessment, both bodies give weight to certain facts and circumstances.

III.1.3.a   *General Findings*

The study shows that the ECtHR's risk assessment is carried out in three steps:

1.   The Court has examined if there is a *general situation of violence* in the receiving State of sufficient level of intensity to create a real risk of ill-treatment to any person simply because of the removal to this State. In this case, the Court has considered the applicant's removal is/would be a violation of Article 3 ECHR with no need to establish the existence of any further features in his case.

2.   If there is not a general situation of violence in the receiving State, the Court has examined if the applicant belongs to a *particular vulnerable group* that is systematically exposed to ill-treatment in the receiving State. Such a group could be, for example, a gender group, ethnic group, religious group, professional group, social group such as asylum seekers, migrants, detainees or persons suspected or charged with a particular crime. In this context, the Court has applied Article 3 ECHR on the applicant's removal where he establishes that: (i) the group must have been subjected to treatment proscribed by this Article; (ii) he must be a member of this group.

3.   Where this is not the case, the Court has required the applicant to establish that there are further *special distinguishing features* in his case that increase his risk, such as that he attracts negative attention of the authorities or non-State actors in the receiving State because of his past experience of ill-treatment in this State, his previous or *sur place* activities, the activities of a member of his family.

Other factors could affect the Court's risk assessment such as the applicant's credibility. Through its Non-Refoulement case-law, the ECtHR has accepted as a ground for believing that the applicant's removal would be in violation of Article 3 ECHR if the applicant is in an advanced stage of naturally occurring illness and there are not sufficient health care resources in the receiving State. It is up to the Court to decide whether the factors in the case before it, taken separately or cumulatively, are sufficient to foresee that the applicant would be at risk in the receiving State.

As Article 3 CAT protects the person concerned only from refoulement to torture as defined under Article 1 CAT, the ComAT's risk assessment has focused on determining whether the complainant is personally of interest for the authorities in the receiving State. In the ComAT's view, the existence of a general situation of violence or human rights violations in the receiving State does not constitute in itself a sufficient ground to apply the principle of Non-Refoulement under Article 3 CAT. The Committee has considered this situation to be one of the factors that must be taken into account when assessing the risk. Other factors include, for example, the applicant's past experience of ill-treatment that was inflicted by or at the instigation of or with the consent or acquiescence of a public official or other person acting in an official capacity', the *sur place* or previous activities of the complainant or a member of his family, the credibility of the complainant and the factual inconsistencies in his claim. Through its Non-Refoulement case-law, the ComAT has also accepted as a ground for believing that the complainant's removal would expose him to a risk of torture in the receiving State the fact that he was a member in a political, professional or social group vulnerable to torture in this State. In this context, the Committee has developed two conditions similar to those of the ECtHR.

III.1.3.b   *Personal Nature of the Risk*

To some extent, the ComAT and the ECtHR have taken into account the same factors when assessing the existence of the risk of proscribed ill-treatment in the receiving State. However, we argue that the ComAT has applied a more restrictive interpretation of the "personal nature" of the risk than that adopted by the ECtHR, as the Committee has required the complainant to establish that he, as an individual, risks to be subjected to torture in the receiving State. The ComAT's restrictive interpretation of the personal nature of the risk results in a divergence between the two bodies' case-law on the principle of Non-Refoulement. This conclusion is derived from the following findings:

1. The ECtHR has accepted applying Article 3 ECHR where the risk in the receiving State emanates only from a *general situation of violence* with no need to establish the existence of any special distinguishing features in the applicant's case. By contrast, in the ComAT's view, even if there is a general situation of violence in the receiving State, the complainant must also demonstrate that there is a personal distinguishing features in his case that make him personally targeted by the authorities in this State. In our view, the ComAT should apply Article 3 CAT where there are general situation of violence in the receiving State if: (i) this situation was of a sufficient level of intensity to create a real risk of torture simply because of the removal to that State; (ii) the authorities in that State were unable or unwilling to intervene to stop this violence and provide remedies to the victims.

2. In the ECtHR's view, the existence of a general situation of *serious human rights violations in the detention centres* of the receiving State constitutes in itself substantial ground for applying Article 3 ECHR on all extradition cases. Where the Court is not satisfied that the detainees, as a whole, constitute a vulnerable group in the receiving State, the applicant can still benefit from the protection against refoulement if he demonstrates that he belongs to a particular group of detainees which is vulnerable to ill-treatment in this State. The ComAT has refused to consider the existence of a general situation of serious human rights violations in the detention centres of the receiving State as a substantial ground for applying Article 3 CAT on the extradition cases. The complainant is always required to demonstrate how he personally would be at risk of torture by establishing distinguishing features relating to him personally as being a member of a particular group of detainees who is targeted by torture in the detention centres. We also believe that the ComAT should apply Article 3 CAT on the extradition cases where, according to recent reports from reliable sources, there is widespread and systematic practice of torture in the receiving State.

3. The ECtHR has accepted applying Article 3 ECHR where the person to be removed demonstrates that he belongs to a *certain ethnic group or minority* which is systematically subjected to ill-treatment. The ComAT has refuseed to apply Article 3 CAT merely on this ground where the complainant cannot demonstrate that he or/and his family was previously subjected to ethnically motivated torture in the receiving State. In our opinion, the ComAT should apply Article 3 CAT where the removed person establishes that he belongs to a certain ethnic group or

minority that is systematically subjected to torture in the receiving State, regardless of whether or not he was previously subjected to torture on this ground in that State.

However, the ComAT should be credited for not following this restrictive interpretation of the "personal nature" of the risk in cases that concern the removal of a woman to a State where there is a general situation of violence against women, carried out by non-State actors and where the authorities of this State fail to protect them and provide remedies to the victims. In such a situation, the ComAT has accepted that women could constitute a vulnerable group in the receiving State and has applied Article 3 without requesting the complainant to submit evidence relating to her personal circumstances. By contrast, the ECtHR does request the applicant to establish factors relating to her personal situation such as that she does not have a social network to protect and support her in the receiving State.

III.1.3.c *UNHCR's Assessment*

Both the ComAT and the ECtHR have given weight to the UNHCR's related assessment. The ECtHR tends to give less weight to the UNHCR's general assessment of the risk in the receiving State than that given to the specific assessment of the applicant's claim regarding the risk he would personally face if removed. By contrast, while in no case the ComAT has given weight to the UNHCR's specific assessment of the complainant's case, in some cases, it referred to the most recent UNHCR's general assessment of the risk of torture or CIDTP in the receiving State. In our view, the UNHCR's assessment of the complainant's case should be one of the factors taken into account when considering his Non-Refoulement case by the ECtHR or the ComAT. But this assessment must not be a decisive factor in the Court's or the Committee's risk assessment because the UNHCR's assessment of the complainant's case might have been conducted a long time before the material time for these bodies' assessment. The UNHCR's assessment under Article 33 CSR focuses on whether the complainant faces a risk to his life or freedom on account of his race, religion, nationality, membership of a particular social group, or political opinion. Furthermore, the prohibition against refoulement under Article 33 CSR is not absolute, contrary to that under Article 3 CAT and Article 3 ECHR.

III.2 *National Protection Arguments*

In order to refute the arguable Non-Refoulement claim established by the applicant, States submit several arguments which aim to demonstrate that the applicant has a national protection in the receiving State. The study examined three of the most commonly used arguments and their impact on the risk assessment by the ComAT and the ECtHR.

III.2.1   Internal Flight Alternative

The ECtHR has accepted that even if the applicant's removal to a specific part of the receiving State would expose him to a real risk of ill-treatment, Article 3 ECHR would not be violated if there were an internal flight alternative for the applicant. The Court has required certain guarantees to be in place: the applicant must be able to travel to the safe area in the receiving State and gain admittance and settle there. The ComAT seems more reluctant to rely on the internal flight alternative as, in its view, the internal alternative does not provide for measurable criteria and is not sufficient to entirely dispel the personal danger of being tortured. The Committee has focused its assessment on the personal circumstances of the person to be expelled in the allegedly safe area of the receiving State. In our view, the ComAT's approach is consistent with the fact that Article 3 CAT protects a person from being subjected to torture at the hands of the authorities in the receiving State.

III.2.2   Prohibition of Ill-treatment in the Receiving State's National Laws and the Relevant International Treaties

Both the ComAT and the ECtHR have considered the fact that ill-treatment is prohibited in the receiving State's national laws or in the relevant international treaties is not sufficient to ensure adequate protection against ill-treatment where reliable sources have reported practices of ill-treatment. This approach is taken even when the receiving State is a party to the ECHR or the CAT. However, where there are factual indications that the general situation in the receiving State is improving, both bodies could accept the argument that an applicant's risk of ill-treatment is negated by the existence of domestic laws and/or accession to international treaties that guarantee respect for fundamental rights.

III.2.3   Diplomatic Assurances

Both the ECtHR and the ComAT have avoided debate on the propriety of using DAs in refoulement cases and the impact of this practice on the absolute nature of the principle of Non-Refoulement. These bodies have focused their assessment on the question of whether the DAs provided in a given case are sufficient in practice to remove any real risk of ill-treatment of the applicant. In order to assess if assurances obtained in a given case are sufficient to ensure adequate protection for the applicant against torture and ill-treatment, both bodies, to some extent, give particular importance to the same factors, such as, whether the assurances have been disclosed to the ECtHR or the ComAT, whether they are specific or vague, whether the complainant was previously ill-treated, whether there are any post-return monitoring mechanisms to ensure the receiving State will comply with the assurances, and whether there is an effective system of protection against torture in this State. Neither body has considerd the existence of a systematic practice of torture and ill-treatment in the receiving State to prohibit, in itself, the sending State from seeking assurances. This situation is one of the factors they take into account when assessing the adequacy of DAs to protect applicants against torture and ill-treatment. Although the ECtHR has held that, in "rare cases", the general situation of human rights in the receiving State excludes accepting any assurances whatsoever, it does not define the situations in which this will occur. The ECtHR's case-law is inconsistent in this regard. In our view, what the ECtHR means by "rare cases" is a case in which there is a general situation of violence in the receiving State. However, we argue that neither the ComAT nor the ECtHR should give weight to DAs that are provided by a State where there is, according to reliable sources, a systematic practice of torture and ill-treatment. Regardless of the doubt whether the DAs could, in practice, eliminate any real risk of ill-treatment of the applicant, and taking into account the increasing use of DAs in refoulement cases and the damaging effects of this practice on the absolute nature of the principle of Non-Refoulement under the CAT and the ECHR, we argue that international NGOs that specialise in human rights should take the role of monitoring the implementation of the assurances. The post-return monitoring mechanism might be adequate to protect returnees against ill-treatment, if monitoring is carried out by reliable, independent and international NGOs with the necessary expertise to detect signs of torture and ill-treatment. Monitoring should start from the moment a person is handed over to the receiving State, and meetings between the returnee and monitors must be private and held according to a pre-arranged timetable.

IV   Interaction between the ECtHR and the ComAT

The study established that there are several aspects of convergence between the ECtHR's and the ComAT's Non-Refoulement case-law

- the absolute nature of the principle under both Article 3 CAT and Article 3 ECHR.
- both Articles prohibit all forms of physical transfer to another State.

- both bodies apply the prohibition of refoulement regardless of whether or not the receiving State is a person's country of origin.
- both bodies consider that a State is obligated to respect its obligation of Non-Refoulement where it has jurisdiction, whether within or outside its national territory.
- the prohibition of refoulement under both Articles applies to the transfer of a person within the territory of the same State.
- both Articles protect every person within the State's jurisdiction.
- both bodies apply the principle of Non-Refoulement where the risk of ill-treatment in the receiving State emanates from acts of public officials or of non-State actors where the authorities of this State do not want to afford the applicant appropriate protection.
- the interim measures indicated by the ECtHR and the ComAT are of a binding nature.
- both the ECtHR and the ComAT refuse to accept an application which has been considered on the merits by another body.
- before both bodies, the applicant must establish that his removal would expose him to a foreseeable, present, personal and real risk of ill-treatment. It is for the respondent State to put forward any evidence capable of casting doubt on the applicant's claim.
- the time of the risk assessment is the same for both the ECtHR and the ComAT.
- both bodies consider the fact that the applicant is a member of a particular vulnerable group in the receiving State is sufficient to apply the principle of Non-Refoulement.
- both bodies give special importance to the applicant's past experience of ill-treatment and his past or *sur place* activities.
- both bodies consider that the prohibition of ill-treatment under national law of the receiving State or under relevant international treaties is not sufficient to remove the risk where reliable sources have reported practices of ill-treatment in this State.
- to some extent, both bodies take into account the same factors in order to assess DAS.

There are also aspects of divergence between the two bodies' Non-Refoulement case-law

- while Article 3 CAT applies only where there is a risk of torture, Article 3 ECHR applies where there is a risk of torture and CIDTP. Accordingly, in contrast to ECtHR, the ComAT does not apply Article 3 CAT where the risk

emanates only from non-State actors without the acquiescence of the public authorities or from a naturally occurring illness.

- in the ComAT's view, even if a lawful sanction is not considered as torture,
  such as detention and death penalty, the manner of its execution may constitute torture. The ECtHR applies the principle of Non-Refoulement under
  Article 3 ECHR where there is a risk of the death penalty and life imprisonment with no hope of release at the time of its imposition.
- if the applicant leaves the respondent State after he has submited his Non-
  Refoulement application, he loses victim status before the ComAT. The
  ECtHR decides whether or not he loses victim status based on the circumstances of each case.
- the Non-Refoulement application must be submitted to the ECtHR during
  six months after the applicant's removal. There is no such time limit to submit the communication to the ComAT. It is up to the Committee to decide
  if the time elapsed between the exhaustion of domestic remedies and the
  submission of the Non-Refoulement complaint makes the consideration of
  the complaint unduly difficult.
- in contrast to the ECtHR, the ComAT has not applied Article 3 CAT where
  the risk emanates only from a general situation of violence or from serious
  human rights violations in detention centres in the receiving State.
- while the ComAT has been reluctant to accept the internal flight alternative
  argument, the ECtHR has accepted this argument under certain conditions.
- while the existence of a systematic practice of torture in the receiving State
  is one of the factors taken into account by both bodies in order to assess
  the DAs, the ECtHR has considered that, in rare cases, the general situation of human rights in the receiving State excludes the acceptance of DAs
  whatsoever.

The study showed that there is a great level of interaction between the ECtHR and
the ComAT in the field of Non-Refoulement. The ComAT's Non-Refoulement
case-law and concluding observations on the periodic reports of States parties to the CAT are often referred to before the ECtHR by any of the parties
to the case or even by third-party interveners.[1] The ECtHR has regularly cited
the ComAT's concluding observations on the periodic reports of the receiving
State in order to determine the human rights situation in this State.[2] In no case
the ECtHR has referred to the ComAT's first General Comment concerning the

---

1   ECtHR, *Kadirzhanov and Mamashev* v. *Russia*, para. 85; ECtHR, *Ramzy* v. *the Netherlands* (ad-
    missibility decision), para. 135.
2   ECtHR, *Klein* v. *Russia*, para. 53; ECtHR, *Gaforov* v. *Russia*, para. 130.

implementation of Article 3 CAT in the context of the individual communications process. The ECtHR has explicitly cited the ComAT's Non-Refoulement case-law in two cases. In *Mamatkulov and Askarov v. Turkey* (2005), the ECtHR referred, *inter alia*, to the ComAT's findings in *Chipana v. Venezuela* (1998) and *T.P.S. v. Canada* (2000) in order to show that the current trend of other international bodies is to acknowledge the legally binding nature of the interim measures. Accordingly, the Court acknowledged the binding nature of the interim measures, overturning its previous case-law. In *Abu Qatada v. The UK* (2012), the ECtHR compared the MOU between the UK and Jordan with the Egyptian DAs the ComAT examined in the *Agiza* case. The Court found that the MOU were superior to the assurances examined by the ComAT as the MOU was specific and comprehensive. Thus, the ECtHR's explicit reference to the ComAT's Non-Refoulement case-law has been made in very rare cases and only for the purpose of supporting the Court's own findings. This could be due to the leading and creative role which has been played by the Strasbourg bodies in the context of interpreting and developing the principle of Non-Refoulement.

The ECtHR tends to implicitly borrow from the ComAT's case-law without making an explicit reference. For example, in May 2008, the third-party interveners in *Ramzy v. the Netherlands*, referred to the ComAT's case-law, according to which, in the assessment of the question of whether an individual was personally at risk, particular weight was given to any evidence that he belonged, or was perceived to belong, to a specific group which in the receiving State had been targeted for torture or ill-treatment. The ComAT's assessment focused on the treatment of the group by the receiving State and whether sufficient evidence had been provided that this State would believe the complainant to be associated with the targeted group. In such cases, the principle of Non-Refoulement could come into play even if there was no evidence that the person concerned had previously been ill-treated or had been personally sought by the receiving State's authorities, or when the general human rights situation in that State had improved.[3] In *NA. v. The UK* (July 2008), without making an explicit reference to the ComAT, the ECtHR stated that where an applicant alleges that he is a member of a group systematically exposed to a practice of ill-treatment in the receiving State, the protection of Article 3 ECHR enters into play when he establishes that there are serious reasons to believe in the existence of the practice in question and his membership of the group concerned. In such case, the Court will not then insist that the applicant shows the existence of further special distinguishing features.[4]

---

3 ECtHR, *Ramzy v. the Netherlands* (admissibility decision), para. 135.
4 ECtHR, *NA. v. The United Kingdom*, para. 116.

Both complainants and respondent States regularly refer to the ECtHR's Non-Refoulement case-law in their submissions to the ComAT,[5] but it is not clear to what extent this plays a role in the ComAT's view as the Committee has not explicitly cited the ECtHR's Non-Refoulement case-law. This could be due to the Committee members' will to avoid the criticisms of States parties that they go beyond their mandate, which is the interpretation and application of the CAT and that they relied on a regional European court's jurisprudence which reflects the European understanding of human rights. However, the ComAT tends to implicitly borrow from the ECtHR's case-law, without making an explicit reference to it. For example, in *B.s.s.* v. *Canada* (2004), the complainant before the ComAT referred to the ECtHR's judgment in *Chahal* v. *The UK* (1996), in which the Court had found that although the applicant, a well-known supporter of Sikh separatism, would be most at risk within the State of Punjab, he could not be considered to be safe elsewhere in India because the Punjab police were fully capable of pursuing suspected Sikh militants into other areas of India far away from Punjab; the police in other areas were also reported to be involved in serious human rights violations. Without making any reference to the ECtHR's judgment, the ComAT found that the complainant had an internal flight alternative in parts of India other than Punjab. Although the ComAT did not explain in this case the reason that led it to reach a conclusion other than that of the ECtHR in the *Chahal* case, in *s.s.s.* v. *Canada* (2005), the Committee added that high-profile Sikhs might be at risk in parts of India other than Punjab. Accordingly, the ComAT implicitly borrowed from the ECtHR's judgment in the *Chahal* case. The Committee took the same approach in *Elmi v. Australia* (1999). In this case also, the ComAT did not make any explicit reference to the ECtHR's judgment in *Ahmed* v. *Austria* (1996), in which the Court had found that deportation to Somalia would breach Article 3 ECHR because it would expose the applicant to ill-treatment by fighting clans. However, the Committee implicitly borrowed the Court's approach by refusing the respondent State's view that the acts of torture the complainant feared he would be subjected to in Somalia would not fall within the definition of torture as the perpetrator of the acts was a non-State actor.

Accordingly, there is a judicial dialogue going on between the ECtHR and the ComAT in the field of the principle of Non-Refoulement. Both bodies tend to implicitly borrow from each other's Non-Refoulement case-law, through considering what the other body has concluded in adjudicating similar cases.

---

5   ComAT, *Agiza* v. *Sweden.*

v   **Overall Concluding Remarks**

The principle of Non-Refoulement is a concept that has been and still is being developed under both the ECHR and the CAT. The prohibition of refoulement as contained and developed under these two Conventions has common features but there are also remarkable differences. Providing a comparison and comprehensive analysis of the prohibitions of refoulement will contribute to a better understanding of the right to be protected from refoulement under both Conventions. We end this study with perhaps the first question to be asked: Whether Article 3 CAT or Article 3 ECHR provides greater protection from refoulement? Or which of the ComAT or the ECtHR is more favorable for a person's specific Non-Refoulement case?

Undoubtedly, this question cannot be answered in a general and definitive way. The answer will be on the basis of the circumstances of the individual case. However, the protection of refoulement afforded by Article 3 CAT remains limited in comparison with that included in Article 3 ECHR. On the one hand, the fact that Article 3 CAT applies only where there is a risk of torture as defined under Article 1 CAT has restricted the ComAT's freedom of interpretation of the principle of Non-Refoulement, as the ComAT's risk assessment focuses on determining whether the complainant is personally of interest for the authorities in the receiving State. Accordingly, the ComAT does not apply Article 3 CAT where the risk in the receiving State emanates only from a general situation of violence, a general situation of serious human rights violations in detention centers, non-State actors in the absence of consent or acquiescence of the public authorities, or a naturally occurring illness and a lack of sufficient health care resources in this State. On the other hand, because of the ECtHR's concern to interpret and apply the ECHR so as to make its safeguards practical and effective, the protection from refoulement under Article 3 ECHR has been and is being interpreted in a way that widens the scope of application of this protection.

Bibliography

I   **Books**

Bassiouni, M.C., International Extradition United States Law and Practice, Oxford: Oxford University Press, 5th Ed, 2007.

Boon, K.E., Huq, A. & Lovelace, D.C., Terrorism, Commentary on Security Documents, Extraordinary Rendition, Oxford: Oxford University Press, 2010.

Boulesbaa, A., The U.N. Convention on Torture and the Prospects for Enforcement, The Hague: Martinus Nijhoff Publishers, 1999.

Burgers, H. & Danelius, H., The United Nations Convention against Torture. A Handbook on the Convention against Torture and Other Cruel, Inhuman or Degrading Treatment or Punishment, Dordrecht: Martinus Nijhoff Publishers, 1988.

Coleman, N., European Readmission Policy: Third Country Interests and Refugee Rights, Leiden: Martinus Nijhoff Publishers, 2009.

Correard, M.H. & Grundy, V., The Concise Oxford-Hachette French Dictionary, Oxford: Oxford University Press, 4th Ed, 2007.

Costa, K.D., The Extraterritorial Application of Selected Human Rights Treaties, Leiden: Martinus Nijhoff Publishers, 2012.

Cruz, A., Shifting Responsibility, Carriers' Liability in the Member States of the European Union and North America, Oakhill: Trentham Books, 1995.

Dijk, P.v. & Hoof, G.J.H.v., Theory and Practice of the European Convention on Human Rights, The Hague: Kluwer Law International, 3rd Ed, 1998.

Erdal, U. & Bakirci, H., Article 3 of the European Convention on Human Rights: a practitioner's handbook, Geneva: World Organization against Torture, OMCT, 2006.

Frias, A.S.d., Counter-terrorism and human rights in the case law of the European Court of Human Rights, Strasbourg: Council of Europe, 2012.

Frigo, M., Migration and International Human Rights Law, Geneva: International Commission of Jurists, 2011.

Gomien, D., Short Guide to the European Convention on Human Rights, Strasbourg: Council of Europe, 3rd Ed, 2005.

Gondek, M., The Reach of Human Rights in a Globalising World: Extraterritorial Application of Human Rights Treaties, Antwerp: Intersentia, 2009.

Goodwin-Gill, G.S. & McAdam, J., The Refugee in International Law, Oxford: Oxford University Press, 2007.

Guilfoyle, D., Shipping Interdiction and the Law of the Sea, Cambridge: Cambridge University Press, 2009.

Hansen, T., Access to Asylum, International Refugee Law and the Globalisation of Migration Control, Cambridge: Cambridge University Press, 2011.

Hirsch, M., The Responsibility of International Organizations toward Third Parties, Dordrecht: Martinus Nijhoff Publishers, 1995.

Ingelse, C., The UN Committee against Torture, An Assessment, The Hague: Kluwer Law International, 2001.

Katayanagi, M., Human Rights Functions of United Nations Peacekeeping Operations, The Hague: Martinus Nijhoff Publishers, 2002.

Lauterpacht, S.E. & Bethlehem, D., The Scope and Content of the Principle of Non-Refoulement, Geneva: UNHCR, 20 June 2001.

Lawson, R. & Schermers, H.G., Leading cases of the European Court of Human Rights, Nijmegen: Ars Aequi Libri, 2nd Ed, 1999.

Leach, P., Taking a Case to the European Court of Human Rights, Oxford: Oxford University Press, 2nd Ed, 2005.

Leach, P., Taking a Case to the European Court of Human Rights, Oxford, New York: Oxford University Press, 3rd Ed, 2011.

Lomba, S.D., The Right to Seek Refugee Status in the European Union, Antwerp: Intersentia, 2004.

Milanovic, M., Extraterritorial Application of Human Rights Treaties, Law, Principles, and Policy, Oxford: Oxford University Press, 2011.

Mole, N. & Meredith, C., Asylum and the European Convention on Human Rights, Strasbourg: Council of Europe, 2010.

Noll, G., Negotiating Asylum – The EU Acquis, Extraterritorial Protection and the Common Market of Deflection, The Hague: Martinus Nijhoff Publishers, 2000.

Nowak, M. & McArthur, E., The United Nations Convention against Torture. A Commentary, Oxford, New York: Oxford University Press, 2008.

Nykanen, E., Fragmented State Power and Forced Migration: A Study on Non-State Actors in Refugee Law, Leiden, Boston: Martinus Nijhoff Publishers, 2nd Ed, 2012.

Ovey, C. & White, R., Jacobs and White, the European Convention on Human Rights, Oxford: Oxford University Press, 4th Ed, 2002.

Parry, J., Understanding Torture: Law, Violence, and Political Identity, Ann Arbor: The University of Michigan Press, 2010.

Sanford, D.A., European Human Rights Mechanisms, New York: Transnational Publishers, 2002.

Scholten, S., The Privatisation of Immigration Control through Carrier Sanctions, The Role of Private Transport Companies in Dutch and British Immigration Control, Boston, Leiden: Brill, Nijhoff, 2015.

Schutter, O.D., International Human Rights Law. Cases, Materials, Commentary, Cambridge: Cambridge University Press, 2010.

Shah, N., Promises to Keep, Diplomatic Assurances against Torture in US Terrorism Transfers, Columbia Law School Human Rights Institute, December 2010.

Shaw, M.N., International Law, Cambridge: Cambridge University Press, 2008.

Sinha, S.P., Asylum and International Law, The Hague: Martinus Nijhoff Publishers, 1971.

Sitaropoulos, N., Refugees and the Principle of Non-Refoulement, United Kingdom: Dissertation, University of Essex, 1990.

Truscan, I., Geneva Academy, The Independence Of UN Human Rights Treaty Body Members, Geneva Academy of International Humanitarian Law and Human Rights, December 2012.

Wendland, L., A Handbook on State Obligations under the UN Convention against Torture, Geneva: Association for the Prevention of Torture, 2002.

White, R. & Ovey, C., Jacobs, White & Overy: The European Convention on Human Rights, Oxford: Oxford University Press, 5th Ed, 2010.

Wouters, K., International Legal Standards for the Protection from Refoulement, Leiden: Intersentia, 2009.

II   Book Chapters

Barnes, R., The International Law of the Sea and Migration Control, in: Ryan, B. & Mitsilegas, V., Extraterritorial Immigration Control, Legal Challenges, Leiden: Martinus Nijhoff Publishers, 2010, 103–150.

Blake, N., Developments in the Case Law of the European Court of Human Rights, in: Bogusz, B., Cholewinski, R., Cygan, A. & Szyszczak, E., Irregular Migration and Human Rights: Theoretical, European and International Perspectives, Leiden: Martinus Nijhoff Publishers, 2004, 431–451.

Brouwer, E., Extraterritorial Migration Control and Human Rights: Preserving the responsibility of the EU and its Member States, in: Ryan, B. & Mitsilegas, V., Extraterritorial Immigration Control, Legal Challenges, Leiden: Martinus Nijhoff Publishers, 2010, 199–229.

Caflisch, L., The Contribution of the European Court of Human Rights to the Development of the International Law on Asylum, in: Chetail, V. & Debbas, V.G., Switzerland and the International Protection of Refugee, Geneva: The Graduate Institute of International Studies, 2002, 207–217.

Cassese, A., Prohibition of Torture and Inhuman or Degrading Treatment or Punishment, in: MacDonald, R.St.J., Matscher, F. & Petzold, H., The European System for the Protection of Human Rights, Dordrecht: Martinus Nijhoff Publishers, 1993, 248–249.

Clapham, A., Non-State Actors, in: Moeckli, D., Shah, S. & Sivakumaran, S., International Human Rights Law, Oxford: Oxford University Press, 2010, 531–550.

Davala, M., Conflict of Interest in Universal Human Rights Bodies, in: Peters, A. & Handschin, L., Conflict of Interest in Global, Public and Corporate Governance, Cambridge: Cambridge University Press, 2012, 125–144.

Djik, P.V., General Course. The Law of Human Rights in Europe. Instruments and Procedures for a Uniform Implementation, in: Law, A.o.E., Collected Courses of the Academy of European Law, The Hague: Kluwer Law International, 1997, 22–50.

Etzwiler, N.G., The Treatment of Asylum Seekers at Ports of Entry and the Concept of "International Zones", in: Kjaerum, M., Hughes, J., Hansen, J. & Bodtcher, A., The Effects of Carrier Sanctions on the Asylum System, Copenhagen: Danish Refugee Council, 1991, 14–22.

Flinterman, C., Chapter 38. Reservations (Article 57), in: Dijk, P.V., Hoof, F.V., Rijn, A.V. & Zwaak, L., Theory and Practice of the European Convention on Human Rights, Antwerp, Oxford: Intersentia, 4th Ed, 2006, 1101–1114.

Guiraudon, V., Chapter 5: Enlisting Third Parties in Border Control: a Comparative Study of its Causes and Consequences, in: Caparini, M. & Marenin, O., Borders and Security Governance: Managing Borders in a Globalised World, Geneva: Geneva Centre for the Democratic Control of Armed Forces, 2006, 79–98.

Hansen, T., The Refugee, the Sovereign and the Sea: European Union Interdiction Policies, in: Nissen, R. & Hansen, T., Sovereignty Games, Instrumentalizing State Sovereignty in Europe and Beyond, New York: Palgrave Macmillan, 2008, 171–195.

Heijer, M.D., European beyond its Borders: Refugee and Human Rights Protection in Extraterritorial Immigration Control, in: Ryan, B. & Mitsilegas, V., Extraterritorial Immigration Control, Legal Challenges, London. Boston: Martinus Nijhoff Publishers, 2010, 169–198.

Kellberg, L., The Case-Law of the European Commission on Human Rights on Art. 3 of the ECHR, in: Cassese, A., The International Fight against Torture: La Lutte Internationale Contre La Torture, Baden-Baden: Nomos Verlagsgesellschaft, 1991, 97–129.

Kjaerum, M., Human Rights for Immigrants and Immigrants for Human Rights, in: Guild, E., International Migration and Security: Opportunities and Challenges, London, New York: Taylor and Francis, 2006, 51–63.

Klug, A. & Howe, T., The Concept of State Jurisdiction and the Applicability of the Non-Refoulement Principle to Extraterritorial Interception Measures, in: Ryan, B. & Mitsilegas, V., Extraterritorial Immigration Control: Legal Challenges, Leiden: Martinus Nijhoff Publishers, 2010, 69–101.

Lawson, R., Life After Bankovic: on the Extraterritorial Application of the European Convention on Human Rights, in: Coomans, F. & Kamminga, M., Extraterritorial Application of Human Rights Treaties, Antwerp, Oxford: Intersentia, 2004, 83–124.

Loucaides, L., The Rules of Interpretation of the European Convention on Human Rights, in: The European Convention on Human Rights, Collected Essays, Leiden: Martinus Nijhoff Publishers, 2007, 1–16.

Miltner, B., Human Security and Protection from *Refoulement* in the Maritime Context, in: Edwards, A. & Ferstman, C., Human Security and Non-Citizens, Law, Policy and International Affairs, Cambridge: Cambridge University Press, 2010, 195–224.

Mole, N., Problems Raised by Certain Aspects of the Present Situation of Refugees from the Standpoint of the European Convention on Human Rights, in: UNHCR, The European Convention on Human Rights and the Protection of Refugees, Asylum-Seekers and Displaced Persons, Geneva: UNHCR, 1996, Part 3.

Noll, G., Return of Persons to States of Origin and Third States, in: Aleinikoff, T.A. & Chetail, V., Migration and International Legal Norms, The Hague: T.M.C. ASSER PRESS, 2003, 61–74.

Nowak, M., Obligations of States to Prevent and Prohibit Torture in an Extraterritorial Perspective, in: Gibney, M. & Skogly, S., Universal Human Rights and Extraterritorial Obligations, Philadelphia: University of Pennsylvania Press, 2010, 12–29.

O'Boyle, M., The European Convention on Human Rights and Extraterritorial Jurisdiction: A Comment on 'Life After Bankovic', in: Coomans, F. & Kamminga, M., Extraterritorial Application of Human Rights Treaties, Antwerp, Oxford: Intersentia, 2004, 125–139.

Pascale, A.d., Migration Control at Sea; The Italian Case, in: Ryan, B. & Mitsilegas, V., Extraterritorial Immigration Control: Legal Challenges, Leiden: Martinus Nijhoff Publishers, 2010, 281–310.

Raffaelli, R., The UN Committee against Torture – in Search of Greater Cooperation, in: Cassese, S., Carotti, B., Casini, L., Cavalieri, E. & MacDonald, E., Global Administrative Law: the Casebook, The Institute for Research on Public Administration and the Institute for International Law and Justice, 3rd Ed, 2012, 94–104.

Randall, M.H., Le dialogue entre le juge suisse et le juge européen, in: Bellanger, F. & Werra, J.d., Genève au confluent du droit interne et du droit international, ZÜrich: Schulthess: Mélanges offerts par la Faculté de droit de l'Université de Genève à la Société suisse des juristes à l'occasion du congrès 2012, 2012, 19–59.

Rogge, K., The "Victim" requirement in Article 25 of the European Convention on Human Rights, in: Wiarda, G.J., Protecting Human Rights: The European Dimension, Koln: Garl Heymanns, 1990, 539–671.

Rozakis, C.L., The Territorial Scope of Human Rights Obligations: the Case of the European Convention on Human Rights, in: Commission, V., The Status of International Treaties on Human Rights, Strasbourg: Council of Europe, 2006, 55–73.

Ryan, B., Extraterritorial Immigration Control: What Role for Legal Guarantees? in: Ryan, B. & Mitsilegas, V., Extraterritorial Immigration Control: Legal Challenges, Leiden: Martinus Nijhoff Publishers, 2010, 3–38.

Sari, A., Autonomy, Attribution and Accountability: Reflections on the Behrami Case, in: Collins, R. & White, N.D., International Organisations and the Idea of Autonomy, London: Routledge, 2010, 257–277.

Sorensen, B., CAT and articles 20 and 22, in: Alfredsson, G., International Human Rights Monitoring Mechanisms: Essays in Honour of Jakob Th. Moller, The Hague: Martinus Nijhoff Publishers, 2001, 167–183.

Vandova, V., Protection of Non-citizens against Removal under International Human Rights Law, in: Edwards, A. & Ferstman, C., Human Security and Non-Citizens, Law, Policy and International Affairs, Cambridge: Cambridge University Press, 2010, 495–523.

Vermeulen, B.P., Chapter 7. Freedom from Torture and Other Inhuman or Degrading Treatment or Punishment (Article 3), in: Dijk, P.V., Hoof, F.V., Rijn, A.V. & Zwaak, L., Theory and Practice of the European Convention on Human Rights, Antwerp, Oxford: Intersentia, 4th Ed, 2006, 405–441.

Wilde, R., Compliance with Human Rights Norms Extraterritorially: 'Human Rights Imperialism?' in: Chazournes, L. & Kohen, M., International Law and the Quest for its Implementation/ Le droit international et la quête de sa mise en oeuvre, Liber Amicorum Vera Gowlland-Debbas, Boston, Leiden: Brill, Martinus Nijhoff Publishers, 2010, 319–350.

Wouters, K., Reconciling National Security and Non-Refoulement: Exceptions, Exclusion, and Diplomatic Assurances, in: Frías, A.M.S.d., Samuel, K. & White, N., Counter-Terrorism: International Law and Practice, Oxford: Oxford University Press, 2012, 579–595.

III   Journal Articles

Allan, R., The European Court of Justice in Context: Forms and Patterns of Judicial Dialogue, European Journal of Legal Studies, Vol. 1 no. 2: 2007, 5–14.

Barnett, L., Extraordinary Rendition: International Law and the Prohibition of Torture, Library of Parliament, PRB 07–48E, July 2008.

Basaran, E., Evaluation of the "Carriers' Liability" Regime as a Part of the EU Asylum Policy under Public International Law, USAK Yearbook of International Politics and Law, Vol. 2: 2009, 101–115.

Battjes, H., Landmarks: Soering's Legacy, Amsterdam Law Forum, Vol. 11 no. 1: 2008, 139–150.

Battjes, H., In Search of a Fair Balance: The Absolute Character of the Prohibition of *Refoulement* under Article 3 ECHR Reassessed, Leiden Journal of International Law, Vol. 22 no. 3: 2009, 583–621.

Bello, J.H. & Kokott, J., Amuur v. France, American Journal of International Law, Vol. 91 no. 1: 1997, 147–152.

Bhuta, N.C., Conflicting International Obligations and the Risk of Torture and Unfair Trial, Journal of International Criminal Justice, Vol. 7 no. 5: 2009, 1133–1147.

Borelli, S., Casting Light on the Legal Black Hole: International Law and Detentions Abroad in the "War on Terror", International Review of the Red Cross, Vol. 87 no. 857: 2005, 39–68.

Boulesbaa, A., Analysis and Proposals for the Rectification of the Ambiguities Inherent in Article 1 of the U.N. Convention on Torture, Florida International Law Journal, Vol. 5 no. 3: 1990, 293–326.

Bourgon, S., The Impact of Terrorism on the Principle of 'Non-Refoulement' of Refugees: the Suresh Case before the Supreme Court of Canada, Journal of International Criminal Justice, Vol. 1 no. 1: 2003, 169–185.

Brouwer, A. & Kumin, J., Interception and Asylum: When Migration Control and Human Rights Collide, Refuge, Vol. 21 no. 4: 2003, 6–24.

Bruin, R. & Wouters, K., Terrorism and the Non-derogability of Non-Refoulement, International Journal of Refugee Law, Vol. 15 no. 1: 2003, 5–29.

Cassese, A., Are International Human Rights Treaties and Customary Rules on Torture Binding upon US Troops in Iraq? Journal of International Criminal Justice, Vol. 2: 2004, 872–878.

Coley, W.J.G., The Evolution of International Zones: British Case Studies, International Human Rights and Refugee Law, 1996, 1–14.

Cruz, A., Carrier Sanctions in four European Community States: Incompatibilities Between International Civil Aviation and Human Rights Obligations, Journal of Refugee Studies, Vol. 4 no. 1: 1991, 63–81.

Deeks, A., Promises Not to Torture: Diplomatic Assurances in U.S. Courts, The American Society of International Law, Discussion Paper Series, December 2008.

Deeks, A.S., Avoiding Transfers to Torture, Council on Foreign Relations CSR no. 35, June 2008.

Droege, C., Transfers of Detainees: Legal Framework, Non-Refoulement and Contemporary Challenges, International Review of the Red Cross, Vol. 90 no. 871: 2008, 669–701.

Duffy, A., Expulsion to Face Torture? Non-Refoulement in International Law, International Journal of Refugee Law, Vol. 20 no. 3: 2008, 373–390.

Fabbrini, F., The European Court of Human Rights, Extraordinary Renditions and the Right to the Truth: Ensuring Accountability for Gross Human Rights Violations Committed in the Fight against Terrorism, Human Rights Law Review, Vol. 14 no. 1: 2014, 85–106.

Feller, E., Carrier Sanctions and International Law, International Journal of Refugee Law, Vol. 1 no. 1: 1989, 48–66.

Fitzpatrick, J., Speaking Law to Power: the War against Terrorism and Human Rights, European Journal of International Law, Vol. 14 no. 2: 2003, 241–264.

Fox, P.D., International Asylum and Boat People: The Tampa Affair and Australia's "Pacific Solution", Maryland Journal of International Law, Vol. 25 no. 1: 2010, 356–373.

Gentili, G., European Court of Human Rights: An absolute ban on deportation of foreign citizens to countries where torture or ill-treatment is a genuine risk, International Journal of Constitutional Law, Vol. 8 no. 2: 2010, 311–322.

Gibney, M.J., Beyond the Bounds of Responsibility: Western States and Measures to Prevent the Arrival of Refugees, No. 22: January 2005.

Gillard, E.C., There's no Place Like Home: States' Obligations in Relation to Transfers of Persons, International Review of the Red Cross, Vol. 90 no. 871: 2008, 703–750.

Giuffre, M., An Appraisal of Diplomatic Assurances One Year after Othman (Abu Qatada) v United Kingdom (2012), International Human Rights Law Review, Vol. 2 no. 1: 2013, 266–293.

Gondek, M., Extraterritorial Application of the European Convention on Human Rights: Territorial Focus in the Age of Globalization? Netherlands International Law Review, Vol. 52 no. 3: 2005, 349–387.

Haeck, Y., Herrera, C.B. & Zwaak, L., Strasbourg's Interim Measures under Fire: Does the Rising Number of State Incompliances with Interim Measures Pose a Threat to the European Court of Human Rights? European Yearbook on Human Rights, Vol. 11 no. 1: 2011, 375–404.

Hakimi, M., State Bystander Responsibility, The European Journal of International Law, Vol. 21 no. 2: 2010.

Harby, C., The changing nature of interim measures before the European Court of Human Rights, European Human Rights Law Review, no. 1: 2010, 73–84.

Hasen, J.V., The European Convention on Human Rights, Counter-Terrorism, and Refugee Protection, Refugee Survey Quarterly, Vol. 29 no. 4: 2011, 45–62.

Heijer, M.D., Whose Rights and Which Rights? The Continuing Story of *Non-Refoulement* under the European Convention on Human Rights, European Journal of Migration and Law, Vol. 10 no. 3: 2008, 277–314.

Heijer, M.D., Reflections on Refoulement and Collective Expulsion in the Hirsi Case, International Journal of Refugee Law, Vol. 25 no. 2: 2013, 265–290.

Herrera, C.B. & Hacck, Y., Staying the Return of Aliens from Europe through Interim Measures: The Case-law of the Europe Commission and the European Court of Human Rights, European Journal of Migration and Law, Vol. 11 no. 1: 2011, 31–51.

Izumo, A., Diplomatic Assurances against Torture and Ill-treatment: European Court of Human Rights Jurisprudence, Columbia Human Rights Law Review, Vol. 42 no. 1: 2010, 233–277.

Jensen, M.P., Torture and Public Policy: *Mohamed v. Jeppesen Dataplan, Inc.*, Allows "Extraordinary Rendition" Victims to Litigate Around State Secrets Doctrine, Brigham Young University Law Review, 2010, 117–133.

Johnston, D., At a Secret Interrogation, Dispute Flared Over Tactics, The New York Times, 10 September 2006.

Johnston, J.G., The Risk of Torture as a Basis for Refusing Extradition and the Use of Diplomatic Assurances to Protect against Torture after 9/11, International Criminal Law Review, Vol. 11 no. 1: 2011, 1–48.

Jones, K., I. Deportations with Assurances: Addressing Key Criticisms, International and Comparative Law Quarterly, Vol. 57 no. 1: 2008, 183–192.

Jones, M., Lies, Damned Lies and Diplomatic Assurances: The Misuse of Diplomatic Assurances in Removal Proceedings, European Journal of Migration and Law, Vol. 8 no. 1: 2006, 9–39.

Joseph, S., Rendering Terrorists and the Convention against Torture, Human Rights Law Review, Vol. 5 no. 2: 2005, 339–346.

King, H., The Extraterritorial Human Rights Obligations of States, Human Rights Law Review, Vol. 9 no. 4: 2009, 521–556.

Klepp, S., A Contested Asylum System: the European Union between Refugee Protection and Border Control in the Mediterranean Sea, European Journal of Migration and Law, Vol. 12 no. 1: 2010, 1–12.

Kneebone, S., The Pacific Plan: The Provision of 'Effective Protection?' International Journal of Refugee Law, Vol. 18 nos. 3–4: 2006, 696–721.

Kunzli, A., Ocalan v. Turkey: Some Comments, Leiden Journal of International Law, Vol. 17 no. 1: 2004, 141–154.

Lambert, H., Protection against Refoulement from Europe, Human Rights Law Comes to the Rescue, International and Comparative Quarterly, Vol. 48 no. 3: 1999, 515–544.

Larsaeus, N., The Use of Diplomatic Assurances in the Prevention of Prohibited Treatment, Refugee Studies Centre, 2006, University of Oxford Working Paper No. 32.

Lavers, T., Extraordinary Rendition and the Self Defense Justification: Time to Face the Music, Michigan State Journal of International Law, Vol. 16 no. 2: 2007, 385–407.

Law, D.S. & Chang, W.-C., The Limits of Global Judicial Dialogue, Washington Law Review, Vol. 86 no. 3: 2011, 523–577.

Legomsky, S.H., The USA and the Caribbean Interdiction Program, International Journal of Refugee Law, Vol. 18 nos. 3–4: 2006, 677–695.

Léonard, S., EU border security and migration into the European Union: FRONTEX and securitisation through practices, European Security, Vol. 19 no. 2: 2010, 231–254.

Lillich, R.B., The Soering Case, The American Journal of International Law, Vol. 85 no. 1: 1991, 128–149.

Londras, F.d., Ireland's Potential Liability for Extraordinary Renditions through Shannon Airport, Irish Law Times, Vol. 25 no. 7: 2007, 106–110.

Lowes, S., The Legality of Extraterritorial Processing of Asylum Claims: The Judgment of the High Court of Australia in the 'Malaysian Solution' Case, Human Rights Law Review, Vol. 12 no. 1: 2012, 168–182.

Lutterbeck, D., Policing Migration in the Mediterranean, Mediterranean Politics, Vol. 11 no. 1: 2006, 59–82.

Magner, T., A less than 'Pacific' Solution for asylum seekers in Australia, International Journal of Refugee Law, Vol. 16 no. 1: 2004, 53–90.

Mallia, P., Case of M.S.S. v. Belgium and Greece: A Catalyst in the Re-thinking of the Dublin II Regulation, Refugee Survey Quarterly, Vol. 30 no. 3: 2011, 107–128.

Mayer, J., Outsourcing Torture. The secret history of America's "extraordinary rendition" program, The New Yorker, 14 February 2005.

Messineo, N.M.F., Relatively Absolute? The Undermining of Article 3 ECHR in Ahmad v UK, The Modern Law Review, Vol. 76 no. 3: 2013, 589–619.

Messineo, F., 'Extraordinary Renditions' and State Obligations to Criminalize and Prosecute Torture in the Light of the Abu Omar Case in Italy, Journal of International Criminal Justice, Vol. 7 no. 5: 2009, 1023–1044.

Metcalfe, E., The False Promise of Assurances against Torture, Justice Journal, Vol. 6 no. 1: 2009, 63–92.

Michaelsen, C., The renaissance of Non-Refoulement? The Othman (Abu Qatada) decision of the European Court of Human Rights, International and Comparative Law Quarterly, Vol. 61 no. 3: 2012, 750–765.

Middleton, B., European Court of Human Rights: Assuring Deportation of Terrorist Suspects, The Journal of Criminal Law, Vol. 76 no. 3: 2012, 213–219.

Milanovic, M., From Compromise to Principle: Clarifying the Concept of State Jurisdiction in Human Rights Treaties, Human Rights Law Review, Vol. 8 no. 3: 2008, 411–448.

Miller, D.J., Holding States to their Convention Obligations: the United Nations Convention against Torture and the Need for Broad Interpretation of State Action, Georgetown Immigration Law Journal, no. 17: 2003, 299–323.

Moeckli, D., Saadi v. Italy: The Rules of the Game Have Not Changed, Human Rights Law Review, Vol. 8 no. 3: 2008, 534–548.

Moreno-Lax, V., Seeking Asylum in the Mediterranean: Against a Fragmentary Reading of EU Member States' Obligations Accruing at Sea, International Journal of Refugee Law, Vol. 23 no. 2: 2011, 174–220.

Moreno-Lax, V., Dismantling the Dublin System: *M.S.S. v. Belgium and Greece*, European Journal of Migration and Law, Vol. 14 no. 1: 2012, 1–31.

Moreno-Lax, V., Hirsi Jamaa and Others v. Italy or the Strasbourg Court versus Extraterritorial Migration Control? Human Rights Law Review, Vol. 12 no. 3: 2012, 574–598.

Mowbray, A., A New Strasbourg Approach to the Legal Consequences of Interim Measures, Human Rights Law Review, Vol. 5 no. 2: 2005, 377–386.

Mueller, D., Unsafe Haven: Could Article 3 of the UN Convention against Torture Prevent the Extradition of Terrorist Suspects to U.S. Custody? Penn State International Law Review, Vol. 28 no. 3: 2010, 549–580.

Nadelmann, E.A., The Evolution of United States Involvement in the International Rendition of Fugitive Criminals, New York University Journal of International Law and Politics, Vol. 25 no. 4: 1993, 813–886.

Nance, D.S., The Individual Right to Asylum under Article 3 of the European Convention on Human Rights, Michigan Yearbook of International Legal Studies, Vol. 3: 1982, 477–495.

Nascimbene, B. & Pascale, A.D., The 'Arab Spring' and the Extraordinary Influx of People who Arrived in Italy from North Africa, European Journal of Migration and Law, Vol. 13 no. 4: 2011, 341–360.

Neuman, G.L., Extraterritorial Violations of Human Rights by the United States, American University Journal of International Law and Policy, Vol. 9 no. 4: 1994, 213–242.

Nicholson, F., Implementation of the Immigration (Carriers' Liability) Act 1987: Privatising Immigration Functions at the Expense of International Obligations? International and Comparative Law Quarterly, Vol. 46 no. 3: 1997, 586–634.

Nino, M., The Abu Omar case in Italy and the effects of CIA extraordinary renditions in Europe on law enforcement and intelligence activities, Revue internationale de droit pénal, Vol. 78 no. 1: 2007, 113–141.

Noll, G., Seeking Asylum at Embassies: A Right to Entry under International Law? International Journal of Refugee Law, Vol. 17 no. 3: 2005, 542–573.

Noll, G., Diplomatic Assurances and the Silence of Human Rights Law, Melbourne Journal of International Law, Vol. 7 no. 1: 2006, 104–124.

Nowak, M., Challenges to the Absolute Nature of the Prohibition of Torture and Ill-treatment, Netherlands Quarterly of Human Rights, Vol. 23 no. 4: 2005, 674–688.

Nowak, M., What Practices Constitute Torture? US and UN Standards, Human Rights Quarterly, Vol. 28 no. 4: 2006, 809–841.

Palmer, S., AIDS, Expulsion and Article 3 of the European Convention on Human Rights, European Human Rights Law Review, no. 5: 2005, 533–540.

Papastavridis, E., 'Fortress Europe' and FRONTEX: Within or Without International Law? Nordic Journal of International Law, Vol. 79 no. 1: 2010, 75–111.

Parsad, K.C., Illegal Renditions and Improper Treatment: an Obligation to Provide Refugee Remedies Pursuant to the Convention against Torture, Denver Journal of International Law and Policy, Vol. 37 no. 4: 2009, 681–702.

Pedersen, M.P., Territorial Jurisdiction in Article 1 of the European Convention on Human Rights, Nordic Journal of International Law, Vol. 73 no. 3: 2004, 279–305.

Peers, S., Legislative Update, EC Immigration and Asylum Law: The New Visa Code, European Journal of Migration and Law, Vol. 12 no. 1: 2010, 105–131.

Pergantis, V., Soft Law, Diplomatic Assurances and the Instrument Alisation of Normativity: Wither a Liberal Promise? Netherlands International Law Review, Vol. 56 no. 2: 2009, 137–166.

Peroni, L. & Timmer, A., Vulnerable groups: The promise of an emerging concept in European Human Rights Convention law, International Journal of Constitutional Law, Vol. 11 no. 4: 2013, 1056–1085.

Reneman, M., An EU Right to Interim Protection during Appeal Proceedings in Asylum Cases? European Journal of Migration and Law, Vol. 12 no. 4: 2010, 407–434.

Rodenhauser, T., Another Brick in the Wall: Carrier Sanctions and the Privatization of Immigration Control, International Journal of Refugee Law, Vol. 26 no. 2: 2014, 1–25.

Rosati, K., The United Nations Convention against Torture: A self-Executing Treaty that Prevents the Removal of Persons Ineligible for Asylum and Withholding of Removal, Denver Journal of International Law and Policy, Vol. 26 no. 4: 1998, 533–590.

Sadat, L.N., Ghost Prisoners and Black Sites: Extraordinary Rendition under International Law, The Case Western Reserve Journal of International Law, Vol. 37 nos. 2 & 3: 2006, 309–342.

Sari, A., Jurisdiction and International Responsibility in Peace Support Operations: the Behrami and Saramati cases, Human Rights Law Review, Vol. 8 no. 1: 2008, 151–170.

Schimmel, C.A., Returning Terrorist Suspects against Diplomatic Assurances: Effective Safeguard or Undermining the Absolute Ban on Torture and Other Cruel, Inhuman and Degrading Treatment? Human Rights Law Commentary, Vol. 3: 2007.

Schmid, E., The End of the Road on Diplomatic Assurances: The Removal of Suspected Terrorists under International Law, Essex Human Rights Review, Vol. 1 no. 11: 2011, 298–320.

Schoenbach, I.A., No Statutory Exceptions: The Case of Maher Arar and A Call to End Extraordinary Renditions, Southwestern Journal of Law & Trade in the Americas, Vol. 14 no. 1: 2007, 119–142.

Scott, C., Saadi v Italy: Preventing Deportation under Article 3 and National Security Concerns: The European Court of Human Rights Struggles To Find a Balance, Tulane Journal of International and Comparative Law, Vol. 17 no. 2: 2009, 601–616.

Seaman, A., Permanent Residency for Human Trafficking Victims in Europe: The Potential Use of Article 3 of the European Convention as a Means of Protection, Columbia Journal of Transnational Law, Vol. 48 no. 2: 2010, 287–320.

Silva, M., Extraordinary Rendition: a Challenge to Canadian and United States Legal Obligations under the Convention against Torture, California Western International Law Journal, Vol. 39 no. 2: 2009, 313–355.

Skoglund, L., Diplomatic Assurances against Torture – An Effective Strategy? A Review of Jurisprudence and Examination of the Arguments, Nordic Journal of International Law, Vol. 77 no. 4: 2008, 319–364.

Smith, R., The Margin of Appreciation and Human Rights Protection in the 'War on Terror': Have the Rules Changed before the European Court of Human Rights? Essex Human Rights Review, Vol. 8 no. 1: 2011, 124–153.

Spijkerboer, T., Subsidiarity and 'Arguability': the European Court of Human Rights' Case Law on Judicial Review in Asylum Cases, International journal of Refugee Law, Vol. 21 no. 1: 2009, 48–74.

Tondini, M., Fishers of Men? The Interception of Migrants in the Mediterranean Sea and Their Forced Return to Libya, INEX Paper, Converging and conflicting ethical values in the internal/external security continuum in Europe, European Commission, 7th Framework Programme, 2010.

Vining, J.A., Providing Protection from Torture by "Unofficial" Actros, Brooklyn Law Review, Vol. 70 no. 1: 2004, 331–360.

Weissbrodt, D. & Hortreiter, I., The Principle of Non-Refoulement: Article 3 of the Convention against Torture and Other Cruel, Inhuman or Degrading Treatment or Punishment in Comparison with the Non-Refoulement Provisions of other International Human Rights Treaties, Buffalo Human Rights Law Review, Vol. 5 no. 1: 1999, 1–74.

Weissbrodt, D. & Bergquist, A., Extraordinary Rendition: A Human Rights Analysis, Harvard Human Rights Journal, Vol. 19: 2006, 123–160.

Whitney, K.M., Does the European Convention on Human Rights Protects Refugees from "Safe" Countries? Georgia Journal of International and Comparative Law, Vol. 26: 1997, 375–408.

Wilkitzki, P., German Government Not Obliged to Seek Extradition of CIA Agents for 'Extraordinary Rendition' – Comments on the El-Masri Judgment of the Cologne Administrative Court, Journal of International Criminal Justice, Vol. 9 no. 5: 2011, 1117–1127.

Worster, W.T., Between a Treaty and Not: A Case Study of the Legal Value of Diplomatic Assurances in Expulsion Cases, Minnesota Journal of International Law, Vol. 21 no. 2: 2012, 253–346.

Wouters, K. & Heijer, M.D., The Marine I Case: a Comment, International Journal of Refugee Law, Vol. 22 no. 1: 2010, 1–19.

IV   Case-Law

A   *EComHR*

EComHR, *Austria* v. *Italy*, Appl. No. 788/60, Y.B. ECHR. 4, 1961.

EComHR, *Calcerrada Fornieles and Cabeza Mato* v. *Spain* (admissibility decision), Appl. No. 17512/90, 6 July 1992.

EComHR, *Cyprus* v. *Turkey*, Appl. Nos. 6780/74 and 6950/75, EComHR Dec & Rep. 12, 26 May 1975.

EComHR, *Pauger* v. *Austria* (admissibility decision), Appl. No. 24872/94, 9 January 1995.

EComHR, *Stocké* v. *The Federal Republic of Germany*, Appl. No. 11755/85, Series. A Vol. 199, 12 October 1989.

EComHR, *Temeltasch* v. *Switzerland*, Appl. No. 9116/80, EComHR Dec & Rep. 31, 5 May 1982.

EComHR, *W.M.* v. *Denmark*, Appl. No. 17392/90, 14 October 1992.

EComHR, *X* v. *Austria and Yugoslavia*, Appl. No. 2143/64, Y.B.ECHR. 7, 1964.

EComHR, *X* v. *The Federal Republic of Germany*, Appl. No. 1611/62, Y.B. ECHR. 8, 25 September 1965.

Report the Commission of 5 November 1969, *The Greek Case*, Yearbook XXI, 1969.

B   *ECtHR*

i   Non-Refoulement Cases

a   *Decisions*

ECtHR, *A.A.* v. *Sweden* (admissibility decision), Appl. No. 8594/04, 2 September 2008.

ECtHR, *A.A.Q.* v. *the Netherlands* (admissibility decision), Appl. No. 42331/05, 30 June 2015.

ECtHR, *Abdollahpour* v. *Norway* (admissibility decision), Appl. No. 57440/10, 29 May 2012.

ECtHR, *Al Ahmad* v. *Greece and Sweden* (admissibility decision), Appl. No. 73398/14, 22 September 2015.

ECtHR, *Ali Ayashi* v. *Turkey* (admissibility decision), Appl. No. 3083/07, 18 November 2008.

ECtHR, *AL-Moayad* v. *Germany* (admissibility decision), Appl. No. 35865/03, 20 February 2007.

ECtHR, *Al-Saadoon and Mufdhi* v. *The United Kingdom* (admissibility decision), Appl. No. 61498/08, 30 June 2009.

ECtHR, *Al-Zawatia* v. *Sweden* (admissibility decision), Appl. No. 50068/08, 22 June 2010.

ECtHR, *A.M.E.* v. *the Netherlands* (admissibility decision), Appl. No. 51428/10, 13 January 2015.

ECtHR, *Amegnigan* v. *the Netherlands* (admissibility decision), Appl. No. 25629/04, 15 November 2004.

ECtHR, *Babar Ahmad and Others* v. *The United Kingdom* (admissibility decision), Appl. Nos. 24027/07, 11949/08 and 36742/08, 6 July 2010.

ECtHR, *Bonger* v. *The Netherlands* (admissibility decision), Appl. No. 10154/04, 15 September 2005.

ECtHR, *Budrevich* v. *the Czech Republic* (admissibility decision), Appl. No. 65303/10, 17 October 2013.

ECtHR, *Chentiev and Ibragimov* v. *Slovakia* (admissibility decision), Appl. Nos. 21022/08 and 51946/08, 14 September 2010.

ECtHR, *Cipriani* v. *Italy* (admissibility decision), Appl. No. 22142/07, 30 March 2010.

ECtHR, *Eric Nsuwayezu* v. *Sweden* (admissibility decision), Appl. No. 15009/09, 8 December 2009.

ECtHR, *Gomes* v. *Sweden* (admissibility decision), Appl. No. 34566/04, 7 February 2006.

ECtHR, *Goncharova and Alekseytsev* v. *the Netherlands* (admissibility decision), Appl. No. 31246/06, 3 May 2007.

ECtHR, *H.* v. *Norway* (admissibility decision), Appl. No. 51666/13, 17 February 2015.

ECtHR, *Harutioenyan and others* v. *the Netherlands* (admissibility decision), Appl. No. 43700/07, 1 September 2009.

ECtHR, *Hukic* v. *Sweden* (admissibility decision), Appl. No. 17416/05, 27 September 2005.

ECtHR, *Ignaoua and others* v. *The United Kingdom* (admissibility decision), Appl. No. 46706/08, 18 March 2014.

ECtHR, *I.N.* v. *Sweden* (admissibility decision), Appl. No. 1334/09, 15 September 2009.

ECtHR, *Isfahano* v. *The Netherlands* (admissibility decision), Appl. No. 31252/03, 31 January 2008.

ECtHR, *Jeltsujeva* v. *the Netherlands* (admissibility decision), Appl. No. 39858/04, 1 June 2006.

ECtHR, *Kaldik* v. *Germany* (admissibility decision), Appl. No. 28526/05, 22 September 2005.

ECtHR, *Karara* v. *Finland* (admissibility decision), Appl. No. 40900/98, 29 May 1998.

ECtHR, *Karim* v. *Sweden* (admissibility decision), Appl. No. 24171/05, 4 July 2006.

ECtHR, *Kochieva and others* v. *Sweden* (admissibility decision), Appl. No. 75203/12, 30 April 2013.

ECtHR, *K.R.S.* v. *The United Kingdom* (admissibility decision), Appl. No. 32733/08, 2 December 2008.

ECtHR, *M.* v. *The United Kingdom* (admissibility decision), Appl. No. 25087/06, 24 June 2008.

ECtHR, *Mawajedi Shikpohkt and A. Mahkat Shole* v. *the Netherlands* (admissibility decision), Appl. No. 39349/03, 27 January 2005.

ECtHR, *M.E.* v. *Sweden* (admissibility decision), Appl. No. 71398/12, 8 April 2015.

ECtHR, *Mohammed Hussein* v. *the Netherlands and Italy* (admissibility decision), Appl. No. 27725/10, 2 April 2013.

ECtHR, *M.T.* v. *Turkey* (admissibility decision), Appl. No. 46765/99, 30 May 2002.

ECtHR, *Nasimi* v. *Sweden* (admissibility decision), Appl. No. 38865/02, 16 March 2004.

ECtHR, *Nasseri* v. *the United Kingdom* (admissibility decision), Appl. No. 24239/09, 13 October 2015.

ECtHR, *N.F.* v. *The Netherlands* (admissibility decision), Appl. No. 21563/08, 14 January 2014.

ECtHR, *Nivette* v. *France* (admissibility decision), Appl. No. 44190/98, 3 July 2001.

ECtHR, *O* v. *the Netherlands* (admissibility decision), Appl. No. 37755/06, 17 November 2009.

ECtHR, *Paez* v. *Sweden* (admissibility decision), Appl. No. 29482/95, 30 October 1997.

ECtHR, *Paramsothy* v. *the Netherlands* (admissibility decision), Appl. No. 14492/03, 10 November 2005.

ECtHR, *P.Z. and Others* v. *Sweden* (admissibility decision), Appl. No. 68194/10, 29 May 2012.

ECtHR, *Ramzy* v. *the Netherlands* (admissibility decision), Appl. No. 25424/05, 27 May 2008.

ECtHR, *Saleh Mohamed Hussein* v. *Netherlands* (admissibility decision), Appl. No. 7049/13, 1 April 2014.

ECtHR, *Saoudi* v. *Spain* (admissibility decision), Appl. No. 22871/06, 18 September 2006.

ECtHR, *T.I.* v. *The United Kingdom* (admissibility decision), Appl. No. 43844/98, 7 March 2000.

ECtHR, *Tomic* v. *The United Kingdom* (admissibility decision), Appl. No. 17837/03, 14 October 2003.

b   *Judgments*

ECtHR, *A.* v. *The Netherlands*, Appl. No. 4900/06, 20 July 2010.

ECtHR, *A.A.* v. *Switzerland*, Appl. No. 58802/12, 7 January 2014.

ECtHR, *A.A. and Others* v. *Sweden*, Appl. No. 14499/09, 28 June 2012.

ECtHR, *A.A.M.* v. *Sweden*, Appl. No. 68519/10, 3 April 2014.

ECtHR, *Abdelhedi* v. *Italy*, Appl. No. 2638/07, 24 March 2009.

ECtHR, *Abdolkhani and Karimnia* v. *Turkey*, Appl. No. 30471/08, 22 September 2009.

ECtHR, *Abdulazhon Isakov* v. *Russia*, Appl. No. 14049/08, 8 July 2010.

ECtHR, *Abdulkhakov* v. *Russia*, Appl. No. 14743/11, 2 October 2012.

ECtHR, *Abu Salem* v. *Portugal*, Appl. No. 26844/04, 9 May 2006 (the Non-Refoulement application was rejected).

ECtHR, *Abu Zubaydah* v. *Lithuania*, Appl. No. 46454/11, communicated 14 December 2012 (pending).

ECtHR, *Agalar* v. *Norway*, Appl. No. 55120/09, 8 November 2011 (the Non-Refoulement application was rejected).

ECtHR, *A.G.A.M.* v. *Sweden*, Appl. No. 71680/10, 27 June 2013.

ECtHR, *Al Hamdani* v. *Bosnia and Herzegovina*, Appl. No. 31098/10, 7 February 2012 (the Non-Refoulement application was rejected).

ECtHR, *Al Hanchi* v. *Bosnia and Herzegovina*, Appl. No. 48205/09, 15 November 2011.

ECtHR, *Al-Saadoon and Mufdhi* v. *The United Kingdom*, Appl. No. 61498/08, 2 March 2010.

ECtHR, *Ahmed* v. *Austria*, Appl. No. 25964/94, 17 December 1996.

ECtHR, *Akram Karimov* v. *Russia*, Appl. No. 62892/12, 28 May 2014.

ECtHR, *A.L.* v. *Austria*, Appl. No. 7788/11, 10 May 2012.

ECtHR, *Al Husin* v. *Bosnia and Herzegovina*, Appl. No. 3727/08, 7 February 2012.

ECtHR, *Al Nashiri* v. *Poland*, Appl. No. 28761/11, 24 July 2014.

ECtHR, *Al Nashiri* v. *Romania*, Appl. No. 33234/12, communicated 18 September 2012 (pending).

ECtHR, *Andrić* v. *Sweden*, Appl. No. 45917/99, 23 February 1999 (the Non-Refoulement application was rejected).

ECtHR, *Arcila Henao* v. *the Netherlands*, Appl. No. 12699/03, 24 June 2003 (the Non-Refoulement application was rejected).

ECtHR, *Aswat* v. *The United Kingdom*, Appl. No. 17299/12, 16 April 2013.

ECtHR, *Auad* v. *Bulgaria*, Appl. No. 46390/10, 11 October 2011.

ECtHR, *Azimov* v. *Russia*, Appl. No. 67474/11, 18 April 2013.

ECtHR, *Babar Ahmad and Others* v. *The United Kingdom*, Appl. Nos. 24027/07, 11949/08, 36742/08, 66911/09 and 67354/09, 10 April 2012.

ECtHR, *Bader and Others* v. *Sweden*, Appl. No. 13284/04, 8 November 2005.

ECtHR, *Bajsultanov* v. *Austria*, Appl. No. 54131/10, 12 June 2012.

ECtHR, *Bakoyev* v. *Russia*, Appl. No. 30225/11, 5 February 2013.

ECtHR, *Baysakov and Others* v. *Ukraine*, Appl. No. 54131/08, 18 February 2010.

ECtHR, *B.B* v. *France*, Appl. No. 30930/96, 7 September 1998 (strike out of the list).

ECtHR, *Ben Khemais* v. *Italy*, Appl. No. 246/07, 24 February 2009.

ECtHR, *Ben Salah* v. *Italy*, Appl. No. 38128/06, 24 March 2009.

ECtHR, *Bensaid* v. *The United Kingdom*, Appl. No. 44599/98, 6 February 2001.

ECtHR, *B.K.A.* v. *Sweden*, Appl. No. 11161/11, 19 December 2013.

ECtHR, *Bouyahia* v. *Italy*, Appl. No. 46792/06, 24 March 2009.

ECtHR, *Čalovskis* v. *Latvia*, Appl. No. 22205/13, 24 July 2014.

ECtHR, *C.B.Z.* v. *Italy*, Appl. No. 44006/06, 24 March 2009.

ECtHR, *Chahal* v. *The United Kingdom*, Appl. No. 22414/93, 15 November 1996.

ECtHR, *Charahili* v. *Turkey*, Appl. No. 46605/07, 13 April 2010.

ECtHR, *Cruz Varas and Others* v. *Sweden*, Appl. No. 15576/89, 20 March 1991.

ECtHR, *D.* v. *The United Kingdom*, Appl. No. 30240/96, 2 May 1997.

ECtHR, *D. and Others* v. *Turkey*, Appl. No. 24245/03, 22 June 2006.

ECtHR, *Daoudi* v. *France*, Appl. No. 19576/08, 3 December 2009.

ECtHR, *Darraji* v. *Italy*, Appl. No. 11549/05, 24 March 2009.

ECtHR, *Dbouba* v. *Turkey*, Appl. No. 15916/09, 13 July 2010.

ECtHR, *D.N.M.* v. *Sweden*, Appl. No. 28379/11, 27 June 2013.

ECtHR, *D.N.W.* v. *Sweden*, Appl. No. 29946/10, 6 December 2012.

ECtHR, *Dzhaksybergenov* v. *Ukraine*, Appl. No. 12343/10, 10 February 2011.

ECtHR, *Egamberdiyev* v. *Russia*, Appl. No. 34742/13, 26 June 2014.

ECtHR, *El-Masri* v. *The Former Yugoslav Republic of Macedonia* (GC), Appl. No. 39630/09, 13 December 2012.

ECtHR, *Elmuratov* v. *Russia*, Appl. No. 66317/09, 3 March 2011.

ECtHR, *Ergashev* v. *Russia*, Appl. No. 12106/09, 20 December 2011.

ECtHR, *Ermakov* v. *Russia*, Appl. No. 43165/10, 7 November 2013.

ECtHR, *F.G.* v. *Sweden*, Appl. No. 43611/11, 16 January 2014.

ECtHR, *F.H.* v. *Sweden*, Appl. No. 32621/06, 20 January 2009.

ECtHR, *F.N. and others* v. *Sweden*, Appl. No. 28774/09, 18 December 2012.

ECtHR, *Gaforov* v. *Russia*, Appl. No. 25404/09, 21 October 2010.

ECtHR, *Garayev* v. *Azerbaijan*, Appl. No. 53688/08, 10 June 2010.

ECtHR, *Garabayev* v. *Russia*, Appl. No. 38411/02, 7 June 2007.

ECtHR, *Gayratbek Saliyev* v. *Russia*, Appl. No. 39093/13, 17 April 2014.

ECtHR, *Hamraoui* v. *Italy*, Appl. No. 16201/07, 24 Marsh 2009.

ECtHR, *H. and B.* v. *The United Kingdom*, Appl. Nos. 70073/10 and 44539/11, 9 April 2013.

ECtHR, *Harkins and Edwards* v. *The United Kingdom*, Appl. No. 9146/07 and 32650/07, 17 January 2012.

ECtHR, *Hilal* v. *The United Kingdom*, Appl. No. 145276/99, 6 March 2001.

ECtHR, *Hirsi Jamaa and Others* v. *Italy* (GC), Appl. No. 27765/09, 23 February 2012.

ECtHR, *H.L.R.* v. *France* (GC), Appl. No. 24573/94, 29 April 1997.

ECtHR, *H.N.* v. *Sweden*, Appl. No. 30720/09, 15 May 2012.

ECtHR, *H.R.* v. *France*, Appl. No. 64780/09, 22 September 2011.

ECtHR, *Husayn (Abu Zubaydah)* v. *Poland*, Appl. No. 7511/13, 24 July 2014.

ECtHR, *Husseini* v. *Sweden*, Appl. No. 10611/09, 13 October 2011.

ECtHR, *I.* v. *Sweden*, Appl. No. 61204/09, 5 September 2013.

ECtHR, *I.K.* v. *Austria*, Appl. No. 2964/12, 28 March 2013.

ECtHR, *I.M.* v. *France*, Appl. No. 9152/09, 2 February 2012 (the Non-Refoulement application was rejected).

ECtHR, *Iskandarov* v. *Russia*, Appl. No. 17185/05, 23 September 2010.

ECtHR, *Ismailove* v. *Russia*, Appl. No. 20110/13, 17 April 2014.

ECtHR, *Ismoilov and Others* v. *Russia*, Appl. No. 2947/06, 24 April 2008.

ECtHR, *Izevbekhai and others* v. *Ireland*, Appl. No. 43408/08, 17 May 2011 (the Non-Refoulement application was rejected).

ECtHR, *Jabari* v. *Turkey*, Appl. No. 40035/98, 11 July 2000.

ECtHR, *J.H.* v. *The United Kingdom*, Appl. No. 48839/09, 20 December 2011.

ECtHR, *J.K. and others* v. *Sweden*, Appl. No. 59166/12, 19 October 2015.

ECtHR, *K.* v. *Russia*, Appl. No. 69235/11, 23 May 2013.

ECtHR, *K.A.B.* v. *Sweden*, Appl. No. 886/11, 5 September 2013.

ECtHR, *Kaboulov* v. *Ukraine*, Appl. No. 41015/04, 19 November 2009.

ECtHR, *Kamyshev* v. *Ukraine*, Appl. No. 3990/06, 20 May 2010 (the Non-Refoulement application was rejected).

ECtHR, *Karimov* v. *Russia*, Appl. No. 54219/08, 29 July 2010.

ECtHR, *Kasymakhunov* v. *Russia*, Appl. No. 29604/12, 14 November 2013.

ECtHR, *Keshmiri* v. *Turkey*, Appl. No. 36370/08, 13 April 2010.

ECtHR, *Khalikov* v. *Russia*, Appl. No. 66373/13, 26 February 2015.

ECtHR, *Khamrakulov* v. *Russia*, Appl. No. 68894/13, 14 September 2015.

ECtHR, *Khaydarov* v. *Russia*, Appl. No. 21055/09, 20 May 2010.

ECtHR, *Khodzhayev* v. *Russia*, Appl. No. 52466/08, 12 May 2010.

ECtHR, *Khodzhamberdiyev* v. *Russia*, Appl. No. 64809/10, 5 June 2012 (the Non-Refoulement application was rejected).

ECtHR, *Klein* v. *Russia*, Appl. No. 24268/08, 1 April 2010.

ECtHR, *Koktysh* v. *Ukraine*, Appl. No. 43707/07, 10 December 2009.

ECtHR, *Kolesnik v. Russia*, Appl. No. 26876/08, 17 June 2010.

ECtHR, *Kozhayev v. Russia*, Appl. No. 60045/10, 5 June 2012.

ECtHR, *Labsi v. Slovakia*, Appl. No. 33809/08, 15 May 2012.

ECtHR, *L.M. and Others v. Russia*, Appl. No. 40081/14, 40088/14 and 40127/14, 15 October 2015.

ECtHR, *M.A.* v. *Cyprus*, Appl. No. 41872/10, 23 July 2013 (the Non-Refoulement application was rejected).

ECtHR, *Makhmudzhan Ergashev v. Russia*, Appl. No. 49747/11, 16 October 2012.

ECtHR, *Mamadaliyev v. Russia*, Appl. No. 5614/13, 24 July 2014.

ECtHR, *Mamatkulov and Askarov v. Turkey*, Appl. Nos. 46827/99 and 46951/99, 6 February 2003.

ECtHR, *Mamatkulov and Askarov v. Turkey* (GC), Appl. Nos. 46827/99 and 46951/99, 4 February 2005.

ECtHR, *Mawaka v. The Netherlands*, Appl. No. 29031/04, 1 June 2010.

ECtHR, *M.B. and Others v. Turkey*, Appl. No. 36009/08, 15 June 2010.

ECtHR, *M.E.* v. *France*, Appl. No. 50094/10, 6 June 2013.

ECtHR, *M.E.* v. *Sweden*, Appl. No. 71398/12, 26 June 2014.

ECtHR, *M.K.N.* v. *Sweden*, Appl. No. 72413/10, 27 June 2013.

ECtHR, *Mohammed v. Austria*, Appl. No. 2283/12, 6 June 2013.

ECtHR, *Mohammadi v. Austria*, Appl. No. 71932/12, 3 July 2014.

ECtHR, *MO.M.* v. *France*, Appl. No. 18372/10, 18 April 2013.

ECtHR, *M.S.S.* v. *Belgium and Greece* (GC), Appl. No. 30696/09, 21 January 2011.

ECtHR, *M.T.* v. *Sweden*, Appl. No. 1412/12, 26 February 2015.

ECtHR, *Muminov v. Russia*, Appl. No. 42502/06, 11 December 2008.

ECtHR, *M.Y.H. and others* v. *Sweden*, Appl. No. 50859/10, 27 June 2013.

ECtHR, *N.* v. *Finland*, Appl. No. 38885/02, 26 July 2005.

ECtHR, *N.* v. *Sweden*, Appl. No. 23505/09, 20 July 2010.

ECtHR, *N.* v. *The United Kingdom* (GC), Appl. No. 26565/05, 27 May 2008.

ECtHR, *NA.* v. *The United Kingdom*, Appl. No. 25904/07, 17 July 2008.

ECtHR, *Nabid Abdullayev v. Russia*, Appl. No. 8474/14, 15 October 2015.

ECtHR, *N.A.N.S.* v. *Sweden*, Appl. No. 68411/10, 27 June 2013.

ECtHR, *Nasr and Ghali v. Italy*, Appl. No. 44883/09, communicated 22 November 2011 (pending).

ECtHR, *Nizomkhon Dzhurayev v. Russia*, Appl. No. 31890/11, 3 October 2013.

ECtHR, *Nizamov and others v. Russia*, Appl. Nos. 22636/13, 24034/13, 24334/13 and 24528/13, 7 May 2014.

ECtHR, *N.M.B.* v. *Sweden*, Appl. No. 68335/10, 27 June 2013.

ECtHR, *Nnyanzi v. The United Kingdom*, Appl. No. 21878/06, 8 April 2008.

ECtHR, *N.S.* v. *Denmark*, Appl. No. 58359/08, 20 January 2011.

ECtHR, *Nsona v. The Netherlands*, Appl. No. 23366/94, 28 November 1996.

ECtHR, *O.* v. *Italy*, Appl. No. 37257/06, 24 March 2009.

ECtHR, *Oshlakov* v. *Russia*, Appl. No. 56662/09, 3 April 2014.

ECtHR, *Othman (Abu Qatada)* v. *The United Kingdom*, Appl. No. 8139/09, 17 January 2012.

ECtHR, *P.K.* v. *Denmark*, Appl. No. 54705/08, 20 January 2011.

ECtHR, *Puzan* v. *Ukraine*, Appl. No. 51243/08, 18 February 2010 (the Non-Refoulement application was rejected).

ECtHR, *Rakhimov* v. *Russia*, Appl. No. 50552/13, 10 July 2014.

ECtHR, *Ramzy* v. *The Netherlands*, Appl. No. 25424/05, 29 July 2010 (strike out of the list).

ECtHR, *R.C.* v. *Sweden*, Appl. No. 41827/07, 9 March 2010.

ECtHR, *R.H.* v. *Sweden*, Appl. No. 4601/14, 10 September 2015.

ECtHR, *R.J.* v. *France*, Appl. No. 10466/11, 19 September 2013.

ECtHR, *Rrapo* v. *Albania*, Appl. No. 58555/10, 25 September 2012.

ECtHR, *Rustamov* v. *Russia*, Appl. No. 11209/10, 3 July 2012.

ECtHR, *Ryabikin* v. *Russia*, Appl. No. 8320/04, 19 June 2008.

ECtHR, *S.A.* v. *Sweden*, Appl. No. 66523/10, 27 June 2013.

ECtHR, *Saadi* v. *Italy* (GC), Appl. No. 37201/06, 28 February 2008.

ECtHR, *Safaii* v. *Austria*, Appl. No. 44689/09, 7 May 2014.

ECtHR, *Said* v. *The Netherlands*, Appl. No. 2345/02, 5 July 2005.

ECtHR, *Salah Sheekh* v. *The Netherlands*, Appl. No. 1948/04, 11 January 2007.

ECtHR, *Samina* v. *Sweden*, Appl. No. 55463/09, 20 October 2011.

ECtHR, *Savriddin Dzhurayev* v. *Russia*, Appl. No. 71386/10, 25 April 2013.

ECtHR, *Sellem* v. *Italy*, Appl. No. 12584/08, 5 May 2009.

ECtHR, *S.F. and others* v. *Sweden*, Appl. No. 52077/10, 15 May 2012.

ECtHR, *S.H.* v. *The United Kingdom*, Appl. No. 19956/06, 15 June 2010.

ECtHR, *Shakurov* v. *Russia*, Appl. No. 55822/10, 5 June 2012.

ECtHR, *Shamayev and 12 others* v. *Georgia and Russia*, Appl. No. 36378/02, 12 October 2005.

ECtHR, *Sharifi* v. *Austria*, Appl. No. 60104/08, 5 December 2013.

ECtHR, *Sharifi and Others* v. *Italy and Greece*, Appl. No. 16643/09, 21 October 2014.

ECtHR, *Sharipov* v. *Russia*, Appl. No. 18414/10, 11 October 2011.

ECtHR, *S.H.H.* v. *The United Kingdom*, Appl. No. 60367/10, 29 January 2013.

ECtHR, *Sidikovy* v. *Russia*, Appl. No. 73455/11, 20 June 2013.

ECtHR, *Soering* v. *The United Kingdom*, Appl. No. 14038/88, 7 July 1989.

ECtHR, *Soldatenko* v. *Ukraine*, Appl. No. 2440/07, 23 October 2008.

ECtHR, *Soltana* v. *Italy*, Appl. No. 37336/06, 24 March 2009.

ECtHR, *S.S. and Others* v. *Denmark*, Appl. No. 54703/08, 20 January 2011.

ECtHR, *Sufi and Elmi* v. *The United Kingdom*, Appl. Nos. 8319/07 and 11449/07, 28 June 2011.

ECtHR, *Sultanov* v. *Russia*, Appl. No. 15303/09, 4 November 2010.

ECtHR, *Svetlorusov* v. *Ukraine*, Appl. No. 2929/05, 12 March 2009 (the Non-Refoulement application was rejected).

ECtHR, *T.A.* v. *Sweden*, Appl. No. 48866/10, 19 December 2013.

ECtHR, *Tarakhel* v. *Switzerland*, Appl. No. 29217/12, 4 November 2014.

ECtHR, *Tershiyev* v. *Azerbaijan*, Appl. No. 10226/13, 31 July 2014.

ECtHR, *Thampibillai* v. *The Netherlands*, Appl. No. 61350/00, 17 February 2004.

ECtHR, *T.K.H.* v. *Sweden*, Appl. No. 1231/11, 19 December 2013.

ECtHR, *T.N. and S. N* v. *Denmark*, Appl. No. 36517/08, 20 January 2011.

ECtHR, *T.N.* v. *Denmark*, Appl. No. 20594/08, 20 January 2011.

ECtHR, *Trabelsi* v. *Italy*, Appl. No. 50163/2008, 13 April 2010.

ECtHR, *Trabelsi* v. *Belgium*, Appl. No. 140/10, 4 September 2014.

ECtHR, *Umirov* v. *Russia*, Appl. No. 17455/11, 18 September 2012.

ECtHR, *Venkadjalasarma* v. *The Netherlands*, Appl. No. 58510/00, 17 February 2004.

ECtHR, *Vilvarajah and Others* v. *The United Kingdom*, Appl. Nos. 13163/87, 13164/87, 13165/87, 13447/87 and 3448/87, 30 October 1991.

ECtHR, *W.H.* v. *Sweden*, Appl. No. 49341/10, 27 March 2014.

ECtHR, *X.* v. *Norway*, Appl. No. 53351/09, 17 April 2012.

ECtHR, *Yakubov* v. *Russia*, Appl. No. 7265/10, 8 November 2011.

ECtHR, *Yefimova* v. *Russia*, Appl. No. 39786/09, 19 February 2013.

ECtHR, *Yoh-Ekale Mwanje* v. *Belgium*, Appl. No. 10486/10, 20 December 2011.

ECtHR, *Y.P. and L.P.* v. *France*, Appl. No. 32476/06, 2 September 2010.

ECtHR, *Yuldashev* v. *Russia*, Appl. No. 1248/09, 8 July 2010.

ECtHR, *Z.N.S.* v. *Turkey*, Appl. No. 21896/08, 19 January 2010.

ECtHR, *Zokhidove* v. *Russia*, Appl. No. 67286/10, 5 February 2013.

ii   Other Cases

ECtHR, *A. and Others* v. *The United Kingdom*, Appl. No. 3455/05, 19 February 2009.

ECtHR, *A.D. and Others* v. *Turkey*, Appl. No. 22681/09, 22 July 2014.

ECtHR, *Aksoy* v. *Turkey* (admissibility decision), Appl. No. 21987/93, 18 December 1996.

ECtHR, *Al-Skeini and Others* v. *The United Kingdom*, Appl. No. 55721/07, 7 July 2011.

ECtHR, *Amuur* v. *France*, Appl. No. 19776/92, 25 June 1996.

ECtHR, *Aoulmi* v. *France*, Appl. No. 50278/99, 17 January 2006.

ECtHR, *Assanidze* v. *Georgia*, Appl. No. 71503/01, 8 April 2004.

ECtHR, *Bahaddar* v. *the Netherlands*, Appl. No. 25894/94, 19 February 1998.

ECtHR, *Bankovic et al* v. *Belgium and 16 other Contracting States* (admissibility decision), Appl. No. 52207/99, 12 December 2001.

ECtHR, *Behrami and Behrami* v. *France and Saramati* v. *France, Germany and Norway* (Admissibility decision), Appl. Nos. 71412/01 and 78166/01, 2 May 2007.

ECtHR, *Bosphorus* v. *Ireland*, Appl. No. 45036/98, 30 June 2005.

ECtHR, *Burdov* v. *Russia*, Appl. No. 59498/00, 7 May 2002.

ECtHR, *Chember* v. *Russia*, Appl. No. 7188/03, 3 July 2008.

ECtHR, *Cyprus* v. *Turkey* (GC), Appl. No. 25781/94, 10 May 2001.

ECtHR, *Djavit An* v. *Turkey*, Appl. No. 20652/92, 20 February 2003.

ECtHR, *Drozd and Janousek* v. *France and Spain*, Appl. No. 12747/87, 26 June 1992.

ECtHR, *E.S. and Others* v. *Slovakia*, Appl. No. 8227/04, 15 September 2009.

ECtHR, *Golder* v. *The United Kingdom*, Appl. No. 4451/70, 1975.

ECtHR, *Hussun and Others* v. *Italy*, Appl. Nos. 10171/05, 10601/05, 11593/05 and 17165/05, 19 January 2010.

ECtHR, *Ilascu and Others* v. *Moldova and Russian* (admissibility decision), Appl. No. 48787/99, 4 July 2001.

ECtHR, *Ilascu and Others* v. *Moldova and Russia*, Appl. No. 48787/99, 8 July 2004.

ECtHR, *Ireland* v. *The United Kingdom*, Appl. No. 5310/71, 18 January 1978.

ECtHR, *Issa and others* v. *Turkey*, Appl. No. 31821/96, 16 November 2004.

ECtHR, *Ivanţoc and Others* v. *Moldova and Russia*, Appl. No. 23687/05, 15 November 2011.

ECtHR, *Khashiyev and Akayeva* v. *Russia*, Appl. Nos. 57942/00 and 57945/00, 24 February 2005.

ECtHR, *Loizidou* v. *Turkey*, Appl. No. 15318/89 (Preliminary Objections), 23 March 1995.

ECtHR, *Loizidou* v. *Turkey*, Appl. No. 15318/89, 18 December 1996.

ECtHR, *Mahmut Kaya* v. *Turkey*, Appl. No. 22535/93, 18 March 2000.

ECtHR, *Mangouras* v. *Spain*, Appl. No. 12050/04, 28 September 2010.

ECtHR, *M.C.* v. *Bulgaria*, Appl. No. 39272/98, 4 December 2003.

ECtHR, *Medvedyev and Others* v. *France* (GC), Appl. No. 3394/03, 29 March 2010.

ECtHR, *Mikolenko* v. *Estonia* (admissibility decision), Appl. No. 16944/03, 5 January 2006.

ECtHR, *Mubilanzila Mayeka and Kaniki Mitunga* v. *Belgium*, Appl. No. 13178/03, 12 October 2006.

ECtHR, *Nasr and Ghali* v. *Italy*, Appl. No. 44883/09, 23 February 2016.

ECtHR, *Nasrulloyev* v. *Russia*, Appl. No. 656/06, 11 October 2007.

ECtHR, *Nolan and K.* v. *Russia*, Appl. No. 2512/04, 12 February 2009.

ECHR, *Ocalan* v. *Turkey* (GC), Appl. No. 6221/99, 12 May 2005.

ECtHR, *Opuz* v. *Turkey*, Appl. No. 33401/02, 9 June 2009.

ECtHR, *Paul and Audrey Edwards* v. *The United Kingdom*, Appl. No. 46477/99, 7 June 2001.

ECtHR, *Ramirez Sanchez* v. *France*, Appl. No. 59450/00, 4 July 2006.

ECtHR, *Selmouni* v. *France*, Appl. No. 25803/94, 28 July 1999.

ECtHR, *Shamsa* v. *Poland*, Appl. Nos. 45355/99 and 45357/99, 27 November 2003.

ECtHR, *Tyrer* v. *The United Kingdom*, Appl. No. 5856/72, 25 April 1978.

ECtHR, *Umalatov and Others* v. *Russia*, Appl. No. 8345/05, 8 April 2010.

ECtHR, *Van der Mussele* v. *Belgium*, Appl. No. 8919/80 (Series A, n. 70), 23 November 1983.

ECtHR, *Varnava and Others* v. *Turkey* (GC), Appl. Nos. 16064/90, 16065/90, 16066/90, 16068/90, 16069/90, 16070/90, 16071/90, 16072/90 and 16073/90, 18 September 2009.

ECtHR, *Vijayanathan and Pusparajah* v. *France*, Appl. No. 75/1991/327/399-400, 26 June 1992.

ECtHR, *Vinter and others v. the United Kingdom*, Appl. Nos. 66069/09, 130/10 and 3896/10, 9 July 2013.

ECtHR, *Wemhoff* v. *Germany*, Appl. No. 2122/64, 25 April 1968.

ECtHR, *Women on Waves and others* v. *Portugal*, Appl. No. 31276/05, 3 February 2009.

ECtHR, *Yonghong* v. *Portugal*, Appl. No. 50887/99 Reports of Jud. & Dec. IX, 25 November 1999.

C ComAT
i Non-Refoulement Cases
a Admissibility Decisions

ComAT, *A.B.A.O.* v. *France* (admissibility decision), No. 264/2005, 8 November 2007.

ComAT, *A.G.* v. *Sweden* (admissibility decision), No. 140/1999, 14 April 1999.

ComAT, *A.R.* v. *Sweden* (admissibility decision), No. 170/2000, 23 November 2001.

ComAT, *A.R.A.* v. *Sweden* (admissibility decision), No. 305/2006, 30 April 2007.

ComAT, *B.M.S.* v. *Sweden* (admissibility decision), No. 437/2010, 12 November 2012.

ComAT, *H.A.S.V.* v. *Canada* (admissibility decision), No. 163/2000, 24 November 2004.

ComAT, *H.E.-M.* v. *Canada* (admissibility decision), No. 395/2009, 23 May 2011.

ComAT, *H.S.T.* v. *Norway* (admissibility decision), No. 288/2006, 16 November 2006.

ComAT, *H.W.A.* v. *Switzerland* (admissibility decision), No. 48/1996, 20 May 1996.

ComAT, *I.A.F.B.* v. *Sweden* (admissibility decision), No. 425/2010, 13 November 2012.

ComAT, *J.H.A.* v. *Spain* (admissibility decision), No. 323/2007, 21 November 2008.

ComAT, *J.M.U.M.* v. *Sweden* (admissibility decision), No. 58/1996, 15 May 1998.

ComAT, *K.A.* v. *Sweden* (admissibility decision), No. 308/2006, 16 November 2007.

ComAT, *K.K.H.* v. *Canada* (admissibility decision), No. 35/1995, 6 November 1995.

ComAT, *K.N.* v. *France* (admissibility decision), No. 93/1997, 18 November 1999.

ComAT, *L.J.R.C.* v. *Sweden* (admissibility decision), No. 218/2002, 23 November 2004.

ComAT, *M.A.* v. *Canada* (admissibility decision), No. 22/1995, 14 December 1994.

ComAT, *Nadeem Ahmad Dar* v. *Norway* (admissibility decision), No. 249/2004, 29 March 2007.

ComAT, *P.M.P.K.* v. *Sweden* (admissibility decision), No. 30/1995, 14 July 1995.

ComAT, *Prashanthan Chelliah* v. *Australia* (admissibility decision), Application no. 211/2002, 3 May 2005.

ComAT, *R.S.* v. *Denmark* (admissibility decision), No. 225/2003, 19 May 2004.

ComAT, *S.A.* v. *Sweden* (admissibility decision), No. 243/2004, 6 May 2004.

ComAT, *S.H.* v. *Norway* (admissibility decision), No. 121/1998, 19 November 1999.

ComAT, *Thu AUNG* v. *Canada* (admissibility decision), No. 273/2005, 15 May 2006.

ComAT, *V.V.* v. *Canada* (admissibility decision), No. 47/1996, 19 May 1998.

b   *Decisions on the Merits*

ComAT, *A.* v. *The Netherlands*, No. 91/1997, 13 November 1998.

ComAT, *A.A.* v. *The Netherlands*, No. 198/2002, 30 April 2003.

ComAT, *A.A.* v. *Switzerland*, No. 251/2004, 17 November 2006.

ComAT, *A.A.* v. *Switzerland*, No. 268/2005, 1 May 2007.

ComAT, *A.A.C.* v. *Sweden*, No. 227/2003, 16 November 2006.

ComAT, *A.A. et al.* v. *Switzerland*, No. 285/2006, 10 November 2008.

ComAT, *A.A.M.* v. *Sweden*, No. 413/2010, 23 May 2012.

ComAT, *A.A.R.* v. *Denmark*, No. 412/2010, 13 November 2012.

ComAT, *Abdussamatov et al.* v. *Kazakhstan*, No. 444/2010, 1 June 2012.

ComAT, *Abichou* v. *Germany*, No. 430/2010, 21 May 2013.

ComAT, *A.D.* v. *The Netherlands*, No. 96/1997, 12 November 1999.

ComAT, *Adel Tebourski* v. *France*, No. 300/2006, 1 May 2007.

ComAT, *A.F.* v. *Sweden*, No. 89/1997, 8 May 1998.

ComAT, *Agiza* v. *Sweden*, No. 233/2003, 20 May 2005.

ComAT, *A.H.* v. *Sweden*, No. 265/2005, 16 November 2006.

ComAT, *A.I.* v. *Switzerland*, No. 182/2001, 12 May 2004.

ComAT, *A.K.* v. *Australia*, No. 148/1999, 5 May 2004.

ComAT, *A.L.N.* v. *Switzerland*, No. 90/1997, 19 May 1998.

ComAT, *Alp* v. *Denmark*, No. 466/2011, 14 May 2014.

ComAT, *A.M.* v. *France*, No. 302/2006, 5 May 2010.

ComAT, *A.M.A.* v. *Switzerland*, No. 344/2008, 12 November 2010.

ComAT, *Amini* v. *Denmark*, No. 339/2008, 15 November 2010.

ComAT, *A.R.* v. *The Netherlands*, No. 203/2002, 14 November 2003.

ComAT, *A.S.* v. *Sweden*, No. 149/1999, 24 November 2000.

ComAT, *Asim Elmansoub* v. *Switzerland*, No. 278/2005, 8 May 2006.

ComAT, *Avedes Hamayak Korban* v. *Sweden*, No. 88/1997, 16 November 1998.

ComAT, *Bachan Singh Sogi* v. *Canada*, No. 297/2006, 16 November 2007.

ComAT, *Bakatu-Bia* v. *Sweden*, No. 379/2009, 3 June 2011.

ComAT, *B.M.* v. *Sweden*, No. 179/2001, 30 April 2002.

ComAT, *B.S.S.* v. *Canada*, No. 183/2001, 12 May 2004.

ComAT, *Boily* v. *Canada*, No. 327/2007, 14 November 2011.

ComAT, *C.A.R.M. et al.* v. *Canada*, No. 298/2006, 18 May 2007.

ComAT, *Cecilia Rosana Nunez Chipana* v. *Venezuela*, No. 110/1998, 10 November 1998.

ComAT, *Chahin* v. *Sweden*, No. 310/2007, 30 May 2011.

ComAT, *Chedli Ben Ahmed Karoui* v. *Sweden*, No. 185/2001, 8 May 2002.

ComAT, *C.T. and K.M.* v. *Sweden*, No. 279/2005, 17 November 2006.

ComAT, *Dewage* v. *Australia*, No. 387/2009, 14 November 2013.

ComAT, *E.A.* v. *Switzerland*, No. 28/1995, 10 November 1997.

ComAT, *E.C.B.* v. *Switzerland*, No. 369/2008, 26 May 2011.

ComAT, *Eftekhary* v. *Norway*, No. 312/2007, 25 November 2011.

ComAT, *E.J. et al.* v. *Sweden*, No. 306/2006, 14 November 2008.

ComAT, *E.K.W.* v. *Finland*, No. 490/2012, 25 June 2015.

ComAT, *E.L.* v. *Switzerland*, No. 351/2008, 15 November 2011.

ComAT, *E.L.* v. *Canada*, No. 370/2009, 21 May 2012.

ComAT, *Elif Pelit* v. *Azerbaijan*, No. 281/2005, 1 May 2007.

ComAT, *Elmi* v. *Australia*, No. 120/1998, 14 May 1999.

ComAT, *Enrique Falcon Rios* v. *Canada*, No. 133/1999, 23 November 2004.

ComAT, *E.R.K. and Y.K.* v. *Sweden*, Nos. 270 & 271/2005, 2 May 2007.

ComAT, *E.T.* v. *Switzerland*, No. 393/2009, 23 May 2012.

ComAT, *E.T.B.* v. *Denmark*, No. 146/1999, 30 April 2002.

ComAT, *E.V.I.* v. *Sweden*, No. 296/2006, 1 May 2007.

ComAT, *F.A.B.* v. *Switzerland*, No. 348/2008, 17 November 2009.

ComAT, *Faragollah et al.* v. *Switzerland*, No. 381/2009, 21 November 2011.

ComAT, *F.F.Z.* v. *Denmark*, No. 180/2001, 30 April 2002.

ComAT, *Gamal El Rgeig* v. *Switzerland*, No. 280/2005, 15 November 2006.

ComAT, *Gbadjavi* v. *Switzerland*, No. 396/2009, 1 June 2012.

ComAT, *G.B.M.* v. *Sweden*, No. 435/2010, 14 November 2012.

ComAT, *G.K.* v. *Switzerland*, No. 219/2002, 18 October 2002.

ComAT, *G.R.B.* v. *Sweden*, No. 83/1997, 15 May 1998.

ComAT, *G.T.* v. *Switzerland*, No. 137/1999, 16 November 1999.

ComAT, *Guclu* v. *Sweden*, No. 349/2008, 11 November 2010.

ComAT, *H.A.D.* v. *Switzerland*, No. 126/1999, 10 May 2000.

ComAT, *Halil Haydin* v. *Sweden*, No. 101/ 1997, 20 November 1998.

ComAT, *Hanan Attia* v. *Sweden*, No. 199/2002, 17 November 2003.

ComAT, *H.B.H., T.N.T., H.J.H., H.O.H., H.R.H. and H.G.H.* v. *Switzerland*, No. 192/2001, 29 April 2003.

ComAT, *H.D.* v. *Switzerland*, No. 112/1998, 30 April 1999.

ComAT, *H.M.H.I.* v. *Australia*, No. 177/2001, 1 May 2002.

ComAT, *H.O.* v. *Sweden*, No. 178/2001, 13 November 2001.

ComAT, *I.A.O.* v. *Sweden*, No. 65/1997, 6 May 1996.

ComAT, *Iratxe Sorzabal Diaz* v. *France*, No. 194/2001, 3 May 2005.

ComAT, *Ismail Alan* v. *Switzerland*, No. 21/1995, 8 May 1996.

ComAT, Iya v. Switzerland, No. 299/2006, 16 November 2007.

ComAT, *J.A.G.V.* v. *Sweden*, No. 215/2002, 11 November 2003.

ComAT, *Jahani* v. *Switzerland*, No. 357/2008, 23 May 2011.

ComAT, *Jamal Omer Mohamed* v. *Greece*, No. 40/1996, 28 April 1997.

ComAT, *J.A.M.O. et al.* v. *Canada*, No. 293/2006, 9 May 2008.

ComAT, *J.L.L.* v. *Switzerland*, No. 364/2008, 18 May 2012.

ComAT, *Josu Arkauz Arana* v. *France*, No. 63/1997, 9 November 1999.

ComAT, *J.U.A* v. *Switzerland*, No. 100/1997, 10 November 1998.

ComAT, *Kalinichenko* v. *Morocco*, No. 428/2010, 25 November 2011.

ComAT, *Kalonzo* v. *Canada*, No. 343/2008, 18 May 2012.

ComAT, *Ke* v. *Australia*, No. 416/2010, 5 November 2012.

ComAT, *K.H.* v. *Denmark*, No. 464/2011, 23 November 2012.

ComAT, *Ktiti* v. *Morocco*, No. 419/2010, 26 May 2011.

ComAT, *K.K.* v. *Switzerland*, No. 186/2001, 11 November 2003.

ComAT, *K.M.* v. *Switzerland*, No. 107/1998, 16 November 1999.

ComAT, *K.N.* v. *Switzerland*, No. 94/1997, 19 May 1998.

ComAT, *K.T.* v. *Switzerland*, No. 118/1998, 19 November 1999.

ComAT, *K.Y.Tala* v. *Sweden*, No. 43/1996, 15 November 1996.

ComAT, *L.J.R.* v. *Australia*, No. 316/2007, 26 November 2008.

ComAT, *L.M.T.D.* v. *Sweden*, No. 164/2000, 15 May 2002.

ComAT, *M.A.F. et al.* v. *Sweden*, No. 385/2009, 23 November 2012.

ComAT, *Mafhoud Brada* v. *France*, No. 195/2002, 17 May 2005.

ComAT, *M.A.H. and F.H.* v. *Switzerland*, No. 438/2010, 7 November 2013.

ComAT, *M.A.K.* v. *Germany*, No. 214/2002, 10 September 2002.

ComAT, *M.A.M.* v. *Sweden*, No. 196/2002, 14 May 2004.

ComAT, *M.A.M.A. et al.* v. *Sweden*, No. 391/2009, 23 May 2012.

ComAT, *M.B.* v. *Switzerland*, No. 439/2010, 31 May 2013.

ComAT, *M.B.B.* v. *Sweden*, No. 104/1998, 5 May 1999.

ComAT, *M.C.M.V.F.* v. *Sweden*, No. 237/2003, 14 November 2005.

ComAT, *M.D.T.* v. *Switzerland*, No. 382/2009, 14 May 2012.

ComAT, *Mehdi Zare* v. *Sweden*, No. 256/2004, 17 May 2006.

ComAT, *M.F.* v. *Sweden*, No. 326/2007, 26 November 2008.

ComAT, *M.K.O.* v. *The Netherlands*, No. 134/1999, 9 May 2001.

ComAT, *M.M.* v. *Canada*, No. 331/2007, 5 November 2009.

ComAT, *M.M. et al.* v. *Sweden*, No. 332/2007, 1 December 2008.

ComAT, *M.M.K.* v. *Sweden*, No. 221/2002, 18 May 2005.

ComAT, *M.N.* v. *Switzerland*, No. 259/2004, 17 November 2006.

ComAT, *M.O.* v. *Denmark*, No. 209/2002, 12 November 2003.

ComAT, *Mondal* v. *Sweden*, No. 338/2008, 23 May 2011.

ComAT, *Mostafa Dadar* v. *Canada*, No. 258/2004, 23 November 2005.

ComAT, *M.P.S.* v. *Australia*, No. 138/1999, 30 April 2002.

ComAT, *M.R.A.* v. *Sweden*, No. 286/2006, 17 November 2006.

ComAT, *M.S.H.* v. *Sweden*, No. 235/2003, 14 November 2005.

ComAT, *M.T.* v. *Sweden*, No. 642/2014, 4 September 2015.

ComAT, *Mutombo* v. *Switzerland*, No. 13/1994, 27 April 1994.

ComAT, *M.V.* v. *The Netherlands*, No. 201/2002, 2 May 2003.

ComAT, *M.X.* v. *Switzerland*, No. 311/2007, 7 May 2008.

ComAT, *M.Z.A.* v. *Sweden*, No. 424/2010, 22 May 2012.

ComAT, *Nasirov* v. *Kazakhstan*, No. 475/2011, 14 May 2014.

ComAT, *N.B-M.* v. *Switzerland*, No. 347/2008, 14 November 2011.

ComAT, *Njamba and Balikosa* v. *Sweden*, No. 322/2007, 14 May 2010.

ComAT, *N.M* v. *Switzerland*, No. 116/1998, 9 May 2000.

ComAT, *N.P.* v. *Australia*, No. 106/1998, 6 May 1999.

ComAT, *N.S.* v. *Switzerland*, No. 356/2008, 6 May 2010.

ComAT, *N.Z.S.* v. *Sweden*, No. 277/2005, 22 November 2006.

ComAT, *Orhan Ayas* v. *Sweden*, No. 97/1997, 12 November 1998.

ComAT, *P.M. Kisoki* v. *Sweden*, No. 41/1996, 8 May 1996.

ComAT, *P.Q.L.* v. *Canada*, No. 57/1996, 17 November 1997.

ComAT, *R.A.* v. *Switzerland*, No. 389/2009, 20 November 2012.

ComAT, *R.A.Y.* v. *Morocco*, No. 525/2012, 6 May 2014.

ComAT, *R.D.* v. *Switzerland*, No. 426/2010, 8 November 2013.

ComAT, *R.K. et al.* v. *Sweden*, No. 309/2006, 16 May 2008.

ComAT, *R.S.M.* v. *Canada*, No. 392/2009, 24 May 2013.

ComAT, *R.T-N.* v. *Switzerland*, No. 350/2008, 3 June 2011.

ComAT, *Ruben David* v. *Sweden*, No. 220/2002, 17 May 2005.

ComAT, *S.C.* v. *Denmark*, No. 143/1999, 10 May 2000.

ComAT, *Seid Mortesa Aemei* v. *Switzerland*, No. 34/1995, 9 May 1997.

ComAT, *S.G. et al.* v. *Switzerland*, No. 352/2008, 30 May 2011.

ComAT, *S.G.* v. *The Netherlands*, No. 135/1999, 12 May 2004.

ComAT, *Singh Khalsa et al.* v. *Switzerland*, No. 336/2008, 26 May 2011.

ComAT, *Singh* v. *Canada*, No. 319/2007, 30 May 2011.

ComAT, *Sivagnanaratnam* v. *Denmark*, No. 429/2010, 11 November 2013.

ComAT, *S.L.* v. *Sweden*, No. 150/1999, 11 May 2001.

ComAT, *S.M. et al.* v. *Sweden*, No. 374/2009, 21 November 2011.

ComAT, *S.M.R and M.M.R.* v. *Sweden*, No. 103/ 1998, 5 May 1999.

ComAT, *S.N.A.W. et al.* v. *Switzerland*, No. 231/2003, 24 November 2005.

ComAT, *S.P.A.* v. *Canada*, No. 282/2005, 7 November 2006.

ComAT, *S.S.H.* v. *Switzerland*, No. 254/2004, 15 November 2005.

ComAT, *S.S.* v. *The Netherlands*, No. 191/2001, 5 May 2003.

ComAT, *S.S.S.* v. *Canada*, No. 245/2004, 16 November 2005.

ComAT, *S.U.A.* v. *Sweden*, No. 223/2002, 22 November 2004.

ComAT, *S.V. et al.* v. *Canada*, No. 49/1996, 15 May 2001.

ComAT, *T.A.* v. *Sweden*, No. 226/2003, 27 May 2005.

ComAT, *T.A.* v. *Sweden*, No. 303/2006, 22 November 2007.
ComAT, *Tahir Hussain Khan* v. *Canada*, No. 15/1994, 15 November 1994.
ComAT, *Tapia Paez* v. *Sweden*, No. 39/1996, 28 April 1996.
ComAT, *T.D.* v. *Switzerland*, No. 375/2009, 26 May 2011.
ComAT, *T.I.* v. *Canada*, No. 333/2007, 15 November 2010.
ComAT, *T.M.* v. *Sweden*, No. 228/2003, 18 November 2003.
ComAT, *T.P.S.* v. *Canada*, No. 99/1997, 16 May 2000.
ComAT, *Tursunov* v. *Kazakhstan*, No. 538/2013, 3 July 2015.
ComAT, *U.S.* v. *Finland*, No. 197/2002, 15 May 2003.
ComAT, *V.L.* v. *Switzerland*, No. 262/2005, 20 November 2006.
ComAT, *V.N.I.M.* v. *Canada*, No. 119/1998, 12 November 2002.
ComAT, *V.R.* v. *Denmark*, No. 210/2002, 17 November 2003.
ComAT, *V.X.N. and H.N.* v. *Sweden*, Nos. 130/1999 and 131/1999, 15 May 2000.
ComAT, *X* v. *The Netherlands*, No. 36/1995, 8 May 1996.
ComAT, *X.* v. *Switzerland*, No. 27/1995, 28 April 1997.
ComAT, *X.* v. *Switzerland*, No. 38/1995, 9 May 1997.
ComAT, *X.* v. *Australia*, No. 324/2007, 5 May 2009.
ComAT, *X.* v. *Kazakhstan*, No. 554/2013, 9 October 2015.
ComAT, *X and Z* v. *Finland*, Nos. 483/2011 and 485/2011, 12 May 2014.
ComAT, *X.Q.L.* v. *Australia*, No. 455/2011, 2 May 2014.
ComAT, *X.Y.* v. *Switzerland*, No. 128/1999, 15 May 2001.
ComAT, *X, Y and Z* v. *Sweden*, No. 61/1996, 6 May 1998.
ComAT, *Y.* v. *Switzerland*, No. 431/2010, 21 May 2013.
ComAT, *Y.G.H. et al.* v. *Australia*, No. 434/2010, 14 November 2013.
ComAT, *Y.H.A.* v. *Australia*, No. 162/2000, 23 November 2003.
ComAT, *Y.S.* v. *Switzerland*, No. 147/1999, 15 May 2001.
ComAT, *Z.K.* v. *Sweden*, No. 301/2006, 16 May 2008.
ComAT, *Z.T.* v. *Australia*, No. 153/2000, 11 November 2003.
ComAT, *Zubair Elahi* v. *Switzerland*, No. 222/2002, 3 May 2005.
ComAT, *Z.Z.* v. *Canada*, No. 123/1998, 15 May 2001.

ii   Other Cases
ComAT, *Kirsanov* v. *Russia*, No. 478/2011, 14 May 2014.
ComAT, *Sonko* v. *Spain*, No. 368/2008, 25 November 2011.

D   *Other Case-Law*
HRC, *Mohammed Alzery* v. *Sweden*, Communication No. 1416/2005, 10 November 2006.
ICJ, *Advisory opinion on the legal consequences of the construction of a wall in the occupied Palestinian territory*, 9 July 2004.

ICJ, *Democratic Republic of the Congo* v. *Uganda*, 19 December 2005.

ICTFY, *Prosecutor* v. *Furundzija*, case No. IT-95-17/1-T, 10 December 1998.

ICTFY, *Prosecutor* v. *Kunarac, Kovac and Vukovic*, IT-96-23 & IT-96-23/I-A, 12 June 2002.

Federal Court of Canada, *Amnesty International Canada* v. *Canada* (National Defence), 2007 FC 1147, 12 March 2008.

The Supreme Court of Canada, *Suresh* v. *Canada* (Minister of Citizenship and Immigration), SCC 1, [2002] 1 S.C.R. 3, 2002.

The US Supreme Court, *Sale* v. *Haitian Centers Council*, 509 U.S. 155, 1993.

US Court of Appeals for the Second Circuit, *Arar* v. *Ashcroft*, No. 06-4216-cv, 2 November 2009.

V   Documents

A   *International and Regional Conventions and Protocols*

American Convention on Human Rights, 1969.

Convention against Torture and Other Cruel, Inhuman or Degrading Treatment or Punishment, CAT, 1984.

Convention Implementing the Schengen Agreement of 14 June 1985, 19 June 1990.

European Convention on Human Rights, ECHR, 1950.

Geneva Convention Relative to the Protection of Civilian Persons in Time of War, 1949.

Geneva Convention Relating to the Status of Refugees, CSR, 1951.

Inter-American Convention to Prevent and Punish Torture, 1985.

International Convention for the Safety of Life at Sea, SOLAS, 1974.

International Covenant on Civil and Political Rights, ICCPR, 1966.

International Convention on Maritime Search and Rescue, SAR, 1079.

Optional Protocol to the CAT, OPCAT, 2002.

Protocol No. 4 to the ECHR, entered into force on 2nd May 1968.

Protocol No. 6 to the ECHR, concerning the Abolition of the Death Penalty, entered into force on 1st March 1985.

Protocol No. 11 to the ECHR, restructuring the control machinery established thereby, entered into force on 1st November 1998.

Protocol No. 13 to the ECHR, concerning the abolition of the death penalty in all circumstances, entered into force on 1st July 2003.

Protocol No. 15 to the ECHR, amending the Convention on the Protection of Human Rights and Fundamental Freedoms, adopted on 16 May 2013.

United Nations Convention on the Law of the Sea, 1982.

Universal Declaration of Human Rights, UDHR, 1948.

Vienna Convention on the Law of Treaties, VCLT, 1969.

B   *General Comments*

ComAT, General Comment No. 1, UN. Doc. A/53/44, Annex IX, On the Implementation of Article 3 of the Convention in the Context of Article 22, 21 November
1997.

ComAT, General Comment No. 2, UN. Doc. CAT/C/GC/2/CRP.1/Rev.4, On the Implementation of Article 2 by States parties, 23 November 2007.

HRC, General Comment No. 20, Replaces general comment 7 concerning prohibition
of torture and cruel treatment or punishment (Article. 7), 3 October 1992.

HRC, General Comment No. 7, Torture or cruel, inhuman or degrading treatment or
punishment (Article. 7), 30 May 1982.

HRC, General Comment No. 27, Freedom of movement (Article 12), U.N. Doc
CCPR/C/21/Rev.1/Add.9 (1999), 2 November 1999.

HRC, General Comment No. 31, The Nature of the General Legal Obligation Imposed
on States Parties to the Covenant, Adopted on 29 March 2004, UN. Doc. CCPR/C/21/
Rev.1/Add.13, 26 May 2004.

C   *ECtHR*

High Level Conference on the Future of the European Court of Human Rights,
Interlaken Declaration, 19 February 2010.

High Level Conference on the Future of the European Court of Human Rights, Izmir
Declaration, 27 April 2011.

High Level Conference on the Future of the European Court of Human Rights, Brighton
Declaration, 20 April 2012.

ECtHR, Analysis of statistics, 2014.

ECtHR, Annual Report 2001.

ECtHR, General statistics, 2014.

ECtHR, Interim measures by respondent State and country of destination, 2011.

ECtHR, Interim measures by respondent State and country of destination, 2012.

ECtHR, Interim measures by respondent State and country of destination, 2013.

ECtHR, Interim measures by respondent State and country of destination, 2014.

ECtHR, Practical Guide on Admissibility Criteria, 2011.

ECtHR, Rule 39 requests granted and refused in 2012, 2013, 2014 and 2015 by responding
State.

ECtHR, Rules of Court, entered into force on 1st September 2012.

ECtHR, Survey of Activities, 1998.

D   *ComAT*

i   Annual Reports

Report of the ComAT, UN. Doc. A/47/44, 26 June 1992.

UNGA, Report of the ComAT, UN. Doc. A/48/44/Add.1, 15 November 1993.

Report of the ComAT, UN. Doc. A/55/44, 2 January 2000.

Report of the ComAT, UN. Doc. A/56/44, 12 October 2001.

Report of the ComAT, UN. Doc. A/60/44, 3 October 2005.

Report of the ComAT, UN. Doc. A/61/44, 1 November 2006.

Report of the ComAT, UN. Doc. A/63/44, 2007–2008.

Report of the ComAT, UN. Doc. A/64/44, 2008–2009.

Report of the ComAT, UN. Doc. A/65/44, 2009–2010.

Report of the ComAT, UN. Doc. A/66/44, 2010–2011.

Report of the ComAT, UN. Doc. A/67/44, 2011–2012.

Report of the ComAT, UN. Doc. A/68/44, 2012–2013.

Report of the ComAT, UN. Doc. A/69/44, 2013–2014.

Report of the CoAT, UN. Doc. A/70/44, 2014–2015.

ii   Periodic Reports of States Parties to the CAT

Comments by the Government of the United Kingdom of Great Britain and Northern Ireland to the conclusions and recommendations of the Committee against Torture (CAT/C/CR/33/3), UN. Doc. CAT/C/GBR/CO/4/Add.1, 8 June 2006.

ComAT, Conclusions and recommendations on the initial periodic report of Guyana, UN. Doc. A/62/44, para. 33, 22 November 2006.

ComAT, Conclusions and recommendations on the initial periodic report of Saudi Arabia, UN. Doc. CAT/C/CR/28/5, 12 June 2002.

ComAT, Conclusions and recommendations on the initial periodic report of Yemen, UN. Doc. CAT/C/CR/31/4, 5 February 2004.

ComAT, Conclusions and recommendations on the fourth periodic report of Italy, UN. Doc. A/62/44, para. 40, 7 May 2007.

ComAT, Conclusions and recommendations on the fourth periodic report of the United Kingdom of Great Britain and Northern Ireland, UN. Doc. CAT/C/CR/33/3, 10 December 2004.

ComAT, Conclusions and recommendations on the fourth and fifth periodic reports of Canada, UN. Doc. CAT/C/CR/34/CAN, 7 July 2005.

ComAT, Conclusions and recommendations on the fifth periodic report of Denmark, UN. Doc. CAT/C/DNK/CO/5, 16 July 2007.

ComAT, Conclusions and recommendations on the fifth periodic report of Norway, UN. Doc. CAT/C/NOR/CO/5, 5 February 2008.

ComAT, Consideration of the initial report of Ethiopia, UN. Doc. CAT/C/SR.974 and 975, 3 November 2010.

ComAT, Consideration of the initial periodic report of Ireland, UN. Doc. CAT/C/IRL/1, 26 January 2010.

ComAT, Concluding observations on the initial periodic report of Syria, UN. Doc. CAT/C/SYR/CO/, 25 May 2010.

ComAT, Consideration of the initial periodic report of El Salvador, UN. Doc. CAT/C/SR.422, 15 December 2000.

ComAT, Consideration of first supplementary report of Canada, UN. Doc. CAT/C/ SR.139, 20 July 1993.

ComAT, Consideration of the second periodic report of Benin, UN. Doc. CAT/C/BEN/2, 16 November 2007.

ComAT, Concluding observations on the second periodic report of Indonesia, UN. Doc. CAT/C/IDN/CO/2, 2 July 2008.

ComAT, Consideration of second periodic report of Jordan, UN. Doc. CAT/C/JOR/ CO/2, 25 May 2010.

ComAT, Consideration of second periodic report of Senegal, UN. Doc. CAT/C/SR.247, 29 May 1996.

ComAT, Consideration of the second periodic report of the United Kingdom of Great Britain and Northern Ireland and dependent territories, UN. Doc. CAT/C/SR.234, 22 November 1995.

ComAT, Concluding observations on the second periodic report of the United States of America, UN. Doc. CAT/C/USA/CO/2, 25 July 2006.

ComAT, Consideration of the second periodic report of Venezuela, UN. Doc. CAT/C/ SR.538, 21 November 2002.

ComAT, Concluding observations on the second periodic report of Yemen, UN. Doc. CAT/C/SR.952, 14 May 2010.

ComAT, Concluding observations on the second periodic report of Zambia, UN. Doc. CAT/C/ZMB/CO/2, 26 May 2008.

ComAT, Concluding observations on the third periodic report of Iceland, UN. Doc. CAT/C/ISL/CO/3, 8 July 2008.

ComAT, Concluding observations on the third periodic report of Liechtenstein, UN. Doc. A/65/44, para. 61, 5 May 2010.

ComAT, Consideration of fourth periodic report of Morocco, UN. Doc. CAT/C/SR.1042, 1043 and 1045, 2 November 2011.

ComAT, Consideration of fourth periodic report of Poland, UN. Doc. CAT/C/SR.776, 15 May 2007.

ComAT, Consideration of fifth periodic report of Denmark, UN. Doc. CAT/C/SR.757, 2 May 2007.

ComAT, Consideration of the fifth periodic report of Germany, UN. Doc. CAT/C/DEU/ CO/5, 12 December 2011.

ComAT, Consideration of the fifth periodic report of Norway, UN. Doc. CAT/C/SR.791, 12 November 2007.

ComAT, Consideration of the fifth periodic report of Norway, UN. Doc. CAT/C/SR.794, 13 November 2007.

ComAT, Concluding observations on the fifth periodic report of Spain, UN. Doc. CAT/C/ESP/CO/5, 9 December 2009.

ComAT, Concluding observations on the fifth periodic report of Sweden, UN. Doc. CAT/C/SWE/CO/5, 4 June 2008.

ComAT, Concluding observations on the fifth periodic report of the United Kingdom of Great Britain and Northern Ireland, UN. Doc. CAT/C/SR.1160 and 1161, 27 May 2013.

ComAT, Concluding observations on the fifth and sixth periodic reports of Poland, UN. Doc. CAT/C/SR.1202, 19 November 2013.

ComAT, Initial report of Syrian Arab Republic, UN. Doc. CAT/C/SR.951, 4 May 2010.

ComAT, Second periodic reports of the United States of America, UN. Doc. CAT/C/48/Add.3/Rev.1, 13 January 2006.

ComAT, Thirty-third session, list of Issues, the United Kingdom, UN. Doc. CAT/C/33/L/GBR, 15–26 November 2004.

E   UN

ComAT, Rules of procedure, UN. Doc. CAT/C/3/Rev.5, 21 February 2011.

Declarations and reservations on the CAT.

HRC, Report of the Human Rights Committee to the General Assembly / Fifty-third Session, UN. Doc. A/53/40, 15 September 1998.

HRC, Concluding observations on the report of Israel, UN. Doc. CCPR/CO/78/ISR, 21 August 2003.

HRC, Concluding observations on the second and third periodic reports of the United States of America, UN. Doc. CCPR/C/USA/CO/3/Rev.1, 18 December 2006.

ILC, Report of the International Law Commission, Sixty-first session (4 May–5 June and 6 July–7 August 2009), General Assembly, Official Records, Sixty-fourth session, Supplement No. 10 (A/64/10).

Report by Alvaro Gil-Robes, Commissioner for Human Rights, on his visit to Sweden (21–23 April 2004), CommDH (2004) 13.

Report of the Special Rapporteur on torture and other cruel, inhuman or degrading treatment or punishment, P. Kooijmans, UN. Doc. E/CN.4/1986/15, 16 February 1986.

Report of the Special Rapporteur on the question of torture, Theo van Boven, submitted in accordance with Commission resolution 2002/38, mission to Uzbekistan, UN. Doc. E/CN.4/2003/68/Add.2, 3 February 2003.

Report of the Special Rapporteur on Torture and other Cruel, Inhuman or Degrading Treatment or Punishment, Theo van Boven, UN. Doc. A/59/324, 1 September 2004.

Report of the Special Rapporteur on torture and other cruel, inhuman or degrading treatment or punishment, M. Nowak, UN. Doc. A/60/316, 30 August 2005.

Report of the Special Rapporteur on torture and other cruel, inhuman or degrading treatment or punishment, M. Nowak, UN. Doc. E/CN.4/2006/6, 23 December 2005.

Report of the Special Rapporteur on torture and other cruel, inhuman or degrading treatment or punishment, M. Nowak, UN. Doc. A/HRC/10/44, 14 January 2009.

Report of the Special Rapporteur on torture and other cruel, inhuman or degrading treatment or punishment, M. Nowak, UN. Doc. A/HRC/13/39/Add.5, 5 February 2010.

The US' reservations, declarations and understandings to the CAT.

UNGA, Fragmentation of International Law: Difficulties Arising from the Diversification and Expansion of International Law, Report of the Study Group of the International Law Commission, UN. Doc. A/CN.4/L.682, 13 April 2006.

UNGA, Resolution adopted by the General Assembly 56/83. Responsibility of States for internationally wrongful acts, UN. Doc. A/RES/56/83, 28 January 2002.

UNHCR, Asylum Trends 2013, Levels and Trends in Industrialized Countries, 21 March 2014.

UNHCR, Advisory Opinion on the Extraterritorial Application of Non-Refoulement Obligations under the 1951 Convention relating to the Status of Refugees and its 1967 Protocol, 2007.

UNHCR, Conclusion adopted by the Executive Committee on International Protection, Conclusion on Protection Safeguards in Interception Measures, 21 November 2008.

UNHCR, Global Trends 2013: War's Human Cost, 20 June 2014.

UNHCR, Handbook on Procedures and Criteria for Determining Refugee Status under the 1951 Convention and the 1967 Protocol relating to the Status of Refugees, UN. Doc. HCR/IP/4/Eng/REV.1, 1992.

UNHCR, Human Rights and Refugee Protection Self-study, Module. 5 Vol. II, 15 December 2006.

UNHCR, Interception of Asylum-Seekers and Refugee: The International Framework and Recommendations for a Comprehensive Approach, UN. Doc. EC/50/SC/CRP.17, 9 June 2000.

UNHCR, Submission by the UNHCR in the Case of *Hirsi and Others v. Italy* (Application no. 27765/09), available at: <http://www.unhcr.org/refworld/pdfid/4b97778d2.pdf>, March 2010.

UNHCR, UNHCR Note on Diplomatic Assurances and International Refugee Protection, 2006.

United Nations Economic and Social Council, Report on the Situation of Detainees at Guantanamo Bay, UN. Doc. E/CN.4/2006/120, 27 February 2006.

UNSC, Resolution 1386, UN. Doc. S/RES/1386, 20 December 2001.

UNSC, Resolution 1510, UN. Doc. S/RES/1510 (2003), 13 October 2003.

UNSC, Resolution 1546, UN. Doc. S/RES/1546, 8 June 2004.

F   NGOs

i   HRW

HRW, 'Empty Promises' Diplomatic Assurances No Safeguard against Torture, 14 April 2004.

HRW, Cases Involving Diplomatic Assurances against Torture, Developments since May 2005, 23 January 2007.

HRW, Lost in Transit, Insufficient Protection for Unaccompanied Migrant Children at Roissy Charles de Gaulle Airport, 2009.

HRW, Not the Way Forward, The UK's Dangerous Reliance on Diplomatic Assurances, 22 October 2008.

HRW, Pushed Back, Pushed Around Italy's Forced Return of Boat Migrants and Asylum Seekers, Libya's Mistreatment of Migrants and Asylum Seekers, 2009.

HRW, Special Committee on the Canadian Mission in Afghanistan, Parliament of Canada, 5 May 2010.

HRW, Statement on US Secret Detention Facilities in Europe, 6 November 2005.

HRW, Still at Risk: Diplomatic Assurances No Safeguard against Torture, 14 April 2005.

HRW, UK: Ethiopian 'Assurances' No Guarantee against Torture, 17 September 2009.

ii   *AI*

AI, Afghanistan detainees transferred to torture: ISAF complicity? ASA 11/011/2007, 13 November 2007.

AI, Dangerous Deals, Europe's Reliance on 'Diplomatic Assurances' against Torture, EUR 01/012/2010, 2010.

AI, Denmark: A Briefing for the Committee against Torture, EUR 18/001/2007, April 2007.

AI, Reject Rather than Regulate: Call on Council of Europe Member States not to Establish Minimum Standards for the Use of Diplomatic Assurances in Transfers to Risk of Torture and Other Ill-treatment, 2005.

AI, Seeking safety, finding fear, refugees, asylum-seekers and migrants in Libya and Malta, December 2010.

AI, Sweden The case of Mohammed El Zari and Ahmed Agiza: violations of fundamental human rights by Sweden confirmed, AI Index: EUR 42/001/2006, 2006.

AI, USA: Front companies used in secret flights to torture and "disappearance", 5 April 2006.

Joint statement by AI, Association for the Prevention of Torture, HRW, International Commission of Jurists, International Federation of Action by Christians for the Abolition of Torture, International Federation for Human Rights, International Helsinki Federation for Human Rights, and World Organisation against Torture, Torture / Terrorism, Call for action against the use of diplomatic assurances in transfers to risk of torture and ill-treatment, 12 May 2005.

G   *Other Documents*

AFP, Italy returns new wave of boat people to Libya.

Commission of inquiry into the actions of Canadian officials in Relation to Maher Arar, Report of the Events Relating to Maher Arar.

Council Regulation (EC), No. 539/2001, listing the third countries whose nationals must be in possession of visas when crossing the external borders and those whose nationals are exempt from that requirement, 15 March 2001.

EC Directive 2001/51/EC of 28 June 2001 supplementing the provisions of Article 26 of the Convention implementing the Schengen Agreement of 14 June 1985.

EC, Recommendation 1163 (1991) on the Arrival of Asylum-Seekers at European Airports, available at: <http://www.unhcr.org/refworld/docid/3ae6b37f3c.html> [accessed 30 November 2010], 23 September 1991.

ELENA, Research on ECHR, Rule 39 Interim Measures, April 2012.

EU Council: Parliamentary Assembly, Secret detentions and illegal transfers of detainees involving Council of Europe member states: second report (Marty second report), Doc. 11302 rev, 11 June 2007.

EU Council: New rules for the surveillance of the EU external sea borders, 6463/14, Presse 68, 20 February 2014.

EU Council: no. 2007/2004 (26 October 2004).

EU Council: Parliamentary Assembly, Alleged secret detentions and unlawful interstate transfers of detainees involving Council of Europe member states (Marty first report), Doc. 10957, 12 June 2006.

EU Council: Proposal for a Regulation of the European Parliament and of the Council establishing rules for the surveillance of the external sea borders in the context of operational cooperation coordinated by the FRONTEX (12 February 2014) 6269/14, Interinstitutional File: 2013/0106 (COD), Available at: <http://www.statewatch.org/ news/2014/feb/eu-council-frontex-search-and-rescue-final-compromise-6269-14 .pdf>.

EU Council: Regulation no. 810/2009 of the European Parliament and of the Council of 13 July 2009 establishing a Community Code on Visas.

FRONTEX, Annual Risk Analysis 2014.

FRONTEX Fundamental Rights Strategy, adopted on 31 March 2011.

Great Britain: Parliament: Joint Committee on Human Rights, The UN Convention against Torture (UNCAT), Nineteenth Report of Session 2005–06, 2006.

Leach, P., Paraskeva, C. & Uzelac, G., International Human Rights & Fact-Finding. An analysis of the fact-finding mission conducted by the European Commission and Court of Human Rights, London: Report by the Human Rights and Social Justice Research Institute at London Metropolitan University, 2009.

Moreno-Lax, V., Europe in Crisis: Facilitating Access to Protection (Discarding) Offshore Processing and Mapping Alternatives for the Way Forward, Red Cross EU Office, December 2015.

Rehabilitation and Research Centre for Torture Victims, Alternative report to the list of issues (CAT/C/DNK/Q/5/rev.1) dated 19 February 2007 to be considered by the UNCAT during the examination of the 5th periodic report of Denmark, April 2007.

Statement issued by the President of the European Court of Human Rights concerning requests for interim measures, Doc. GT-GDR-C(2012)005, 11 February 2011.

Temporary Committee on the Alleged Use of European Countries by the CIA for the Transportation and Illegal Detention of Prisoners, European Parliament, Report on the alleged use of European countries by the CIA for the transportation and illegal detention of prisoners, 30 January 2007.

Venice Commission, opinion on the International Legal Obligations of Council of Europe Member States in Respect of Secret Detention Facilities and Inter-State Transport of Prisoners, CDL-AD(2006)009, 17 March 2006.

Working Group Report on Detainee Interrogations in the Global War on Terrorism; Assessment of Legal, Historical, Policy, and Operational Considerations, Final Report, 4 April 2003.

H   *Internet*

Merriam-Webster Online Dictionary, 2011, available at: <www.merriam-webster.com>.
Oxford Dictionary, available at <http://oxforddictionaries.com>.

Index